USMC

A COMPLETE HISTORY

TOM LOVELL
AFTER AP

USMC

A COMPLETE HISTORY

Colonel Jon T. Hoffman, USMCR
Beth L. Crumley, Illustration Editor

MARINE CORPS ASSOCIATION
BEAUX ARTS EDITIONS

MARINE CORPS ASSOCIATION

Page 2: *Marines raising the flag on Mt. Suribachi, 23 February 1945. (Tom Lovell, Marine Corps Art Collection)*

At Guantanamo Bay, Cuba, on 25 April 1913, Marines of the Second Provisional Brigade formed the Marine Corps Association. John A. Lejeune, then a lieutenant colonel, headed its first executive committee. The purpose of the MCA was defined then and continues to drive the Association into the 21st century, to: "disseminate knowledge of military art and science to its members; to provide for professional advancement; to foster the spirit and preserve the traditions of the United States Marine Corps."

For all who have earned and worn the Eagle, Globe, and Anchor, the Marine Corps Association is the professional organization for all Marines—active duty, reserve, retired and Marine veterans. The MCA understands and identifies with the sacrifices made and the services rendered as a Marine to this great country. Once a Marine, always a Marine!

A member of the Marine Corps Association is part of a brotherhood rich with history, traditions, and accomplishments. Membership is the lifeblood of the MCA. Regardless of status—active duty, reserve, retired, or veteran—we urge eligible individuals to become members of the professional association of the Marines.

Individuals may learn more about the Marine Corps Association and become an MCA member at http://www.mca-marines.org.

Marine Corps Association
Box 1775
Quantico, Virginia 22134
Tel: (703) 640-6161
http://www.mca-marines.org

Beaux Arts Editions
Published by Hugh Lauter Levin Associates, Inc.

Design: Charles J. Ziga
Project Editor: James O. Muschètt
Illustration Editor: Beth L. Crumley
Technical Editor: Colonel John Greenwood, USMC (Ret)

ISBN 0-88363-617-4
Printed in China
http://www.HLLA.com

TABLE OF CONTENTS

I.	1775–1844	Marines in the Fighting Tops	6
II.	1845–1882	By Sea and by Land	62
III.	1883–1913	Steam, Steel, and Stamina	110
IV.	1914–1918	First to Fight	158
V.	1919–1938	Thinkers and Fighters	194
VI.	1939–1943	Holding the Line	244
VII.	1943–1945	On the Offensive	304
VIII.	1945–1953	Hot Opening to a Cold War	406
IX.	1954–1975	The Long War	500
X.	1976–2003	A Force in Readiness	616
		Index	660

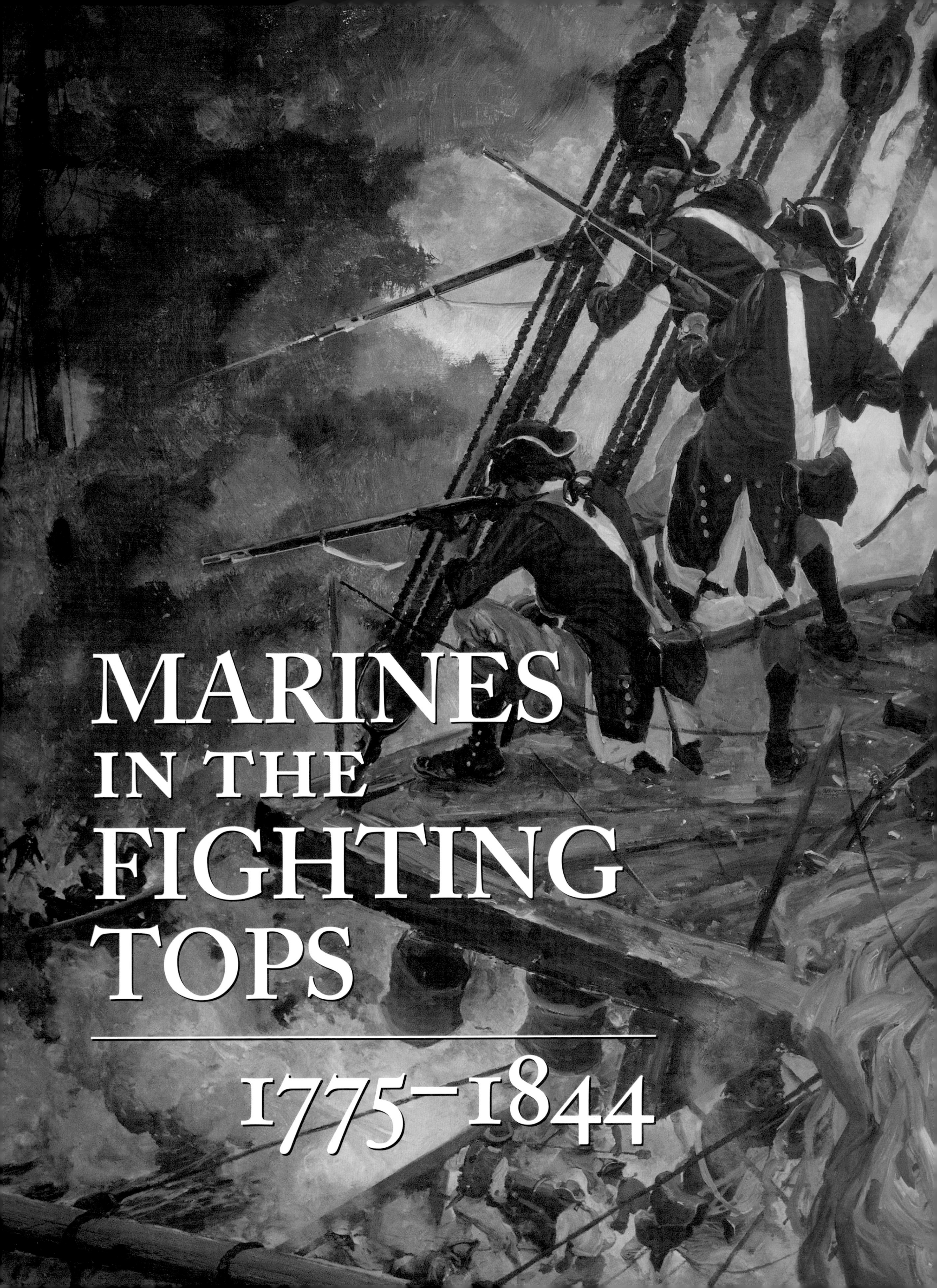
MARINES
IN THE
FIGHTING
TOPS
1775–1844

MARINES IN THE FIGHTING TOPS

1775–1844

The concept of a corps of Marines was well established when the colonies in America rebelled against Great Britain in 1775. Since the seventeenth century, the Royal Navy had used army regiments, and then its own dedicated force of sea soldiers, for a variety of specific missions. During battles at sea, Marines employed muskets against exposed enemy personnel, repelled attempts to board, and provided assistance in manning the great guns if required. For combat ashore, their skill with small arms made them the core of the landing force (with sailors often fleshing out the expedition). Marines and their muskets also enforced regulations among the crew and served as the bulwark against mutiny.

It was natural, then, that when the American revolutionaries decided to form their own navy, they made an immediate provision for Marines to help man the fleet. Thus the Continental Congress decreed on 10 November that "two Battalions of Marines be raised." Continental Navy warships subsequently recruited detachments of Marines for each cruise. State navies, privateers, and other forces such as General Benedict Arnold's flotilla on Lake Champlain, likewise provided for this necessary component of warfare on the water.

The American Marines made an immediate impact, sailing with the first Continental Navy squadron in early 1776 and leading the first amphibious landing at New Providence in the Bahamas. The auspicious beginning in the Caribbean heralded what would become the primary mission of the Corps—landings on hostile shores. It was not a natural outcome, since the Royal Marines never focused on this task to any great degree. And New Providence might have remained a rare exception, given the thorough defeat American landing forces suffered in the Penobscot Bay expedition in 1779. Nevertheless, the association of American Marines with operations across the beach was firmly ingrained.

The Continental Marines served in another role that later would prove important, even if their employment in this capacity during the Revolutionary War was inconsequential. Major Samuel Nicholas's battalion of Marines fought as part of General George Washington's army at Princeton and Trenton in the desperate period around Christmas 1776 and suffered the same hardships in winter quarters near Morristown, New Jersey. This campaign set a lasting precedent—Marines would not limit themselves to service in naval operations, but would lend a hand even in extended land operations as an adjunct of the Army.

The Continental Marines and their counterparts in the state navies ceased to exist following the end of the Revolutionary War. This had nothing to do with their utility, often demonstrated during the conflict, but came about solely because the navies which they served also went out of existence. When the Congress of the

Left: *Continental Marines on* Alfred *suffer casualties as they engage HMS* Glasgow *on 6 April 1776. ("A Marine Lieutenant Dies," Col Charles Waterhouse, USMCR (Ret), Marine Corps Art Collection)*

Pages 6–7: *Marines fight with muskets and grenades from their perch high above the deck. ("Fighting Tops," Col Charles Waterhouse, USMCR (Ret), Marine Corps Art Collection)*

newly established United States decided to build a navy in 1794, the lawmakers provided again for Marines. In its first few years, the new U.S. Marine Corps saw frequent action on ship as part of the Quasi War with France and the Barbary Wars. In a rare exception to this traditional role during this period, Lieutenant Presley O'Bannon and seven enlisted Marines made an epic overland march and led an attack on the fortress of Derna that helped bring a successful conclusion to the war with Tripoli. Marines also began guarding the Navy's first shore installations, and established their own first permanent facility, Marine Barracks 8th and I, in Washington, D.C.

The War of 1812 brought more of the same; frequent participation in ship-to-ship duels, punctuated by an occasional operation as a purely land force. Ships' detachments were in the thick of many famous sea battles that established the reputation of the fledgling U.S. Navy. Marines also were there with General Andrew Jackson's Army during the famous victory at New Orleans in 1815, but they played a much more prominent part in the 1814 Battle of Bladensburg. Although the latter was a crushing defeat, Marines and reinforcing sailors fought well and briefly stemmed the relentless British advance on Washington, D.C. In the long period of relative peace following the War of 1812, the Marine Corps fought on ship and shore with the Navy in suppressing piracy and the slave trade, and alongside the Army in the Seminole Wars. The opening of the latter campaign showcased what would become another hallmark of the Corps. In a relatively short period of time, Commandant Archibald Henderson put together a regiment from ships detachments and Marine barracks and deployed it into battle.

Throughout these first six decades of the existence of American Marines, their numbers seldom rose much above 1,000 men and frequently were considerably lower. This minuscule body of Marines also had established a combat reputation, afloat and ashore, that at least matched that of their soldier and sailor compatriots. The Corps was quick to find other ways to endear itself to government leaders and the public. The Marine Band became an early fixture at social events and celebrations around the national capital, while budget-conscious commandants looked for every opportunity to trim expenditures.

The record of the Corps was not perfect, but it was largely positive and it contained nearly all the elements that would distinguish subsequent generations of Marines—courage and resourcefulness in battle, readiness for war at a moment's notice, a miserly regard for the public's tax dollars, a sense of pomp and pageantry, and a determination to perform whatever service was most needed without regard for formal roles and missions. The Corps was small, but it occupied an important niche in the armed forces of the United States.

MARINES IN THE FIGHTING TOPS

1775–1844

1775

19 April
American Revolution
The American Revolution opens with the battles of Lexington and Concord.

9 May
Lake Champlain
Soldiers from Brigadier General Benedict Arnold's Massachusetts force capture a British sloop at Skenesborough on Lake Champlain and rename her *Liberty*. Massachusetts soldiers, turned sailors and Marines, man her.

10 May
Lake Champlain
Liberty participates in the capture of Fort Ticonderoga from the British.

18 May
Lake Champlain
At St. John's on Lake Champlain, Marines from *Liberty* assist Arnold's force in capturing another British sloop. Arnold mans her with more improvised sailors and Marines and renames her *Enterprise*. The crew of the sloop was reinforced with 18 Marines in all. The first known Marine officer, listed on the payroll, was Lt James Watson.

25 May
Manpower
The first recorded mention of American Marines appears in an account describing eight Connecticut Marines escorting pay for troops to Albany, New York, for further shipment to Ticonderoga. These Marines often are referred to as the "Original Eight."

10 June
Manpower
The Continental Congress passes a resolution bringing all American forces (including Marines) operating on and around Lake Champlain under the control of the Congress and providing that they be paid from 3 May.

15 June
Atlantic
Marines participate in the action between *Katy* and *Washington* (Rhode Island Navy) and an armed tender supporting the British frigate *Rose*.

July
Atlantic
Marines in *Spy* (Connecticut Navy) participate in the capture of the Tory brig *Nancy*.

24 August
Massachusetts
Hannah, the first ship in the fleet fitted out by General Washington, goes into Continental service. Soldiers from Washington's army serve as the crew and Marines of the ship.

7 September
Massachusetts
Hannah and her Marines recapture the unarmed *Unity* off Massachusetts.

October
Atlantic
Connecticut Marines in *Spy* assist in the capture of a large British ship.

5 October
Massachusetts
The Continental Congress mentions Marines for the first time when it directs Washington to give "Proper encouragement to the Marines and seamen" serving on the two armed vessels under "Continental risque and pay."

10 October
Massachusetts
Marines participate in the action between *Hannah* and the British sloop *Nautilus* off the Massachusetts coast.

13 October
Manpower
Congress directs the acquisition, fitting out, and manning of two vessels for the Continental Navy. Since Marines are a normal part of a warship's complement, this is the first (albeit indirect) authorization for the enlistment of Continental Marines.

5 November
Massachusetts
Marines in *Harrison* (Washington's fleet) participate in the capture of the British supply vessels *Polly* and *Industry* off Boston.

7 November
Massachusetts
Lee (Washington's fleet) and her Marines recapture the sloop *Ranger* in Massachusetts Bay.

10 November
Force Structure
The Continental Congress formally establishes an organization of Marines with the following resolution:

> "Resolved, That two battalions of Marines be raised consisting of one colonel, two lieutenant-colonels, two majors, and other officers, as usual in other regiments; that they consist of an equal number of privates with other battalions; that particular care be taken that no persons be appointed to office, or enlisted into said battalions, but such as are good seamen, or so acquainted with maritime affairs as to be able to serve

Opposite: *A Marine reaches into his cartridge box to reload. ("Continental Marine, 1775," Donald Dickson,* Leatherneck *magazine)*

Above: *"Continental Marine Officer, 1775," Col Donna Neary, Marine Corps Art Collection*

Left: *Commodore Esek Hopkins greets General George Washington when he visits Hopkins's flagship,* Alfred. *Captain Samuel Nicholas and his Marines provide the honor guard. ("Aboard the* Alfred,*" H. Charles McBarron, Marine Corps Art Collection)*

to advantage by sea when required; that they be enlisted and commissioned to serve for and during the present war with great Britain and the colonies, unless dismissed by order of Congress; that they be distinguished by names of First and Second Battalions of American Marines, and that they be considered as part of the number which the Continental Army before Boston is ordered to consist of."

11 November
South Carolina
Marines in *Defence* (South Carolina Navy) participate in the action against the British ships *Tamar* and *Cherokee* at Charleston, South Carolina.

17 November
Canada
Marines from *Hancock* and *Franklin* (Washington's fleet) make an unopposed landing at Charlottetown, Prince Edward Island.

19 November
Manpower
The first discord between the Army and the Marines occurs when General Washington takes issue with orders from Congress to supply personnel from his force for the Marine battalions authorized on 10 November. The general noted that since the men "must be acquainted with maritime affairs," he would have to select from and therefore disrupt many of his units.

20 November
Canada
Marines join in the raid by *Hancock* and *Franklin* on Canso Harbor, Nova Scotia.

24 November
Massachusetts
Marines in *Harrison* participate in her fight with three British warships in Boston Bay.

27 November
Atlantic
Lee's Marines play their part in capturing the sloop *Polly* off the New England coast.

28 November
Commandants
Samuel Nicholas of Philadelphia is commissioned a captain of Marines by the Continental Congress. The senior Marine officer throughout the Revolutionary War, he is regarded as the first Commandant of the Marine Corps.

Right: *The Continental Marines of Commodore Esek Hopkins's squadron capture Fort Montagu on 3 March 1776. Contrary to the depiction here, there was no assault, as the local militiamen had abandoned the fortress. ("Marine Raid on Fort Montagu," H. Charles McBarron, Marine Corps Art Collection)*

28 November
Massachusetts
Over the next several weeks, Marines aboard ships of Washington's fleet help capture numerous British ships in the waters off Boston.

December
Force Structure
The Continental Marines form their first unit, for service on board the brig *Cabot*.

4 December
Massachusetts
Marines are among those taken prisoner when *Washington* is captured in Massachusetts Bay by two British frigates.

1776

3 March
Bahamas
At New Providence Island in the Bahamas, Captain Samuel Nicholas and a battalion of Marines and sailors land from Commodore Hopkins's squadron, seize the fort, and capture stores for Washington's army. This was the first amphibious landing by Continental Marines.

16 March
Bahamas
Hopkins's squadron and Marines withdraw from New Providence.

April
Manpower
John Martin enlists to serve on the Continental brig *Reprisal* and becomes the first black Marine.

5 April
New York
Marines participate in the capture of the British brig *Bolton* by Hopkins's squadron in the waters off New York City.

6 April
New York
Several Marines are killed or wounded during the battle between Hopkins's *Alfred* and *Cabot* and the British frigate *Glasgow* off Long Island, New York. The casualties include the first Continental Marine officer to die in battle.

7 April
Virginia
The Continental brig *Lexington* and her Marines defeat the British armed tender *Edward* off the Virginia Capes.

THE RAID ON NEW PROVIDENCE

The Continental Navy was only a few weeks old when Congress dispatched it on a mission overseas. Commodore Esek Hopkins was to take his eight ships and their Marines to New Providence Island in the Bahamas and capture a large supply of gunpowder rumored to be there. The fleet had hardly gotten into the Atlantic from Chesapeake Bay in mid-February 1776 when two of the ships collided in bad weather and had to turn back. Two weeks later, the Americans were in sight of their objective. Nassau was the main town on the island, with Hog Island offshore providing a protected anchorage for the port city. The entrances to the harbor around either end of Hog Island were guarded by Fort Nassau in the west and Fort Montagu in the east. Both were in disrepair, and the defenders consisted of a few hundred militiamen subject to call up.

The fleet put Captain Samuel Nicholas and his 234 Marines ashore two miles east of Fort Montagu at noon on 3 March. Since it was clear the townspeople had observed the approach of the ships and there would be no surprise, 50 sailors were provided as reinforcements. But in response to the drum roll to muster, only about a hundred militiamen had appeared at the rallying point at Fort Nassau. These were soon dispatched to Montagu. A militia lieutenant directed to reconnoiter the enemy marched his detail of 30 men toward the landing site and then ordered one to go forward with a flag of truce and inquire who the invaders were and what they wanted. After a brief parlay he reported back to the fort.

As the Americans approached the bastion, the British governor (also acting as commander) fired three cannon at nothing in

Left: *Continental Marines storm the beach of New Providence Island. ("Landing at New Providence," Col Charles Waterhouse, USMCR (Ret), Marine Corps Art Collection)*

Opposite: *Fifty seamen reinforce the Marines in the New Providence raid. The initial objective, Fort Montagu, is in the left background. ("New Providence Invasion," V. Zveg, Navy Art Collection)*

particular and ordered a retreat to Fort Nassau. Some of his men deserted as they passed their homes in the town. Captain Nicholas was not inclined to be aggressive either. After taking the just-abandoned eastern fort, he decided to rest his force until the next day. That evening, Hopkins issued a manifesto to the town promising not to harm people or private property, if they turned powder and arms over to him. He also kept his ships well away from the port.

The British governor, in a rare fit of boldness and energy, used the delay to load most of the 200 barrels of gunpowder at Fort Nassau on two merchant ships, which conveyed it to safety that night. With the work done and little left to defend at the fort, the remainder of the militia melted away. After ascertaining that Fort Nassau was deserted the next morning, Nicholas and his force marched to the western fortification, occupied it, and raised the Continental flag over foreign soil for the first time. Two weeks later, the flotilla sailed for home.

Although Hopkins and Nicholas had not achieved their primary aim of capturing gunpowder badly needed by Washington's army, they had acquired 46 cannon, thousands of round shot, and a considerable quantity of other military stores. It was the first landing against a hostile shore mounted by American Marines and sailors, and would presage bigger, more elaborate, and much fiercer amphibious assaults in the many decades to come.

Just two years later, in 1778, a lone Continental ship and its 28 Marines reprised the attack on New Providence, but in a much more daring fashion. Landing at night, the small detachment of Marines silently reached Fort Nassau and captured its surprised sentinels. Pretending to have a force of several hundred, Captain John Trevett bluffed Fort Montagu into surrendering the next day. The Americans then seized five merchantmen in the harbor and made off with another supply of British arms.

Left: *Captain Nicholas's Marines depart as men haul away the guns captured at Fort Montagu, New Providence. Although the main goal of the raid against the Bahamas was to acquire gunpowder for Washington's army, most of it was spirited away before the forts fell. ("Marines Leave Fort Montagu," Donald Dickson, Marine Corps Art Collection)*

8 May
Pennsylvania
Marines of the Pennsylvania Navy employ row galleys to drive off two British warships in the Delaware River.

17 May
Atlantic
Marines assist *Franklin* of Washington's fleet in capturing the transport *Hope*, laden with 1,000 carbines and 75 tons of gunpowder.

29 May
Atlantic
Andrew Doria and her Marine contingent capture two British transports bearing two companies of infantry.

16 June
Massachusetts
Washington's fleet and its Marines capture two British troopships trying to reinforce Boston (already abandoned by the British army).

25 June
Manpower
Samuel Nicholas is promoted to the rank of major. Innkeeper Robert Mullan is commissioned as a captain in Philadelphia and begins recruiting enlisted men from his establishment, Tun Tavern.

29 June
New Jersey
Marines assist in the unloading of arms and gunpowder from the grounded *Nancy* under fire from the British frigate *Orpheus*.

4 July
American Revolution
The Declaration of Independence is signed.

27 July
Martinique
Marines and sailors of the brig *Reprisal* drive off the British sloop *Shark* and deliver an agent to Martinique to acquire intelligence and arms.

5 September
Uniforms
The Marine Committee of the Continental Congress decrees the first uniform for Marines—green coats faced with white, white trousers, and a single silver epaulette for officers.

20 September
Atlantic
Marines participate in the action between the sloop *Providence* and the British frigate *Milford*. Although surprised while the crew is fishing, the smaller American ship is able to escape in a day of expert sailing.

Right: *"The First Recruits, Col Charles Waterhouse, USMCR (Ret), Marine Corps Art Collection*

22 September
Canada
Providence and her Marines raid Canso Harbor, Nova Scotia, then strike at Isle Madame the next day, destroying fishing boats.

October
Manpower
Sergeants William Hamilton and Alexander Neilson are promoted to lieutenant. These are the first recorded "mustangs," enlisted Marines who become officers. Many Marines in the future will follow the same path.

11–13 October
Lake Champlain
Marines participate with Arnold's fleet in the Battle of Valcour Island on Lake Champlain. Although defeated, the Americans delay a British invasion until the following year.

December
Atlantic
Lexington is captured by the British frigate *Pearl*. Soon after, Marine Captain Abraham Boyce leads his men and *Lexington*'s sailors in overwhelming the small British prize crew and escaping to the harbor at Baltimore.

Right: *Continental Marines go into battle. ("Don't Tread on Me," H. Charles McBarron, Marine Corps Art Collection)*

2 December
New Jersey
Major Samuel Nicholas and three companies of Marines are dispatched from Philadelphia to reinforce Washington's army as it retreats from New York through New Jersey.

9 December
Atlantic
Marines participate in the action between the *Alfred* and the British frigate *Milford*. The American ship outsails its better-armed opponent and escapes unharmed.

26 December
New Jersey
A portion of Washington's army crosses the Delaware River at night and defeats the Hessian forces at Princeton, New Jersey. Brigadier General John Cadwalader's division, which includes Samuel Nicholas's Marine battalion, gets across the river too late and misses the battle. The victory temporarily ends the British threat to Philadelphia, the seat of the Continental Congress.

1777

2 January
New Jersey
Major Samuel Nicholas and his battalion participate in Washington's defense of Trenton against Lord Cornwallis' British army. The Marines help hold the important Assunpink Bridge against a Hessian attack.

3 January
New Jersey
During the night, Washington's force silently departs the battlefield and marches toward Princeton. Marines assist in defeating the British garrison and capturing the town.

4 January
New Jersey
Samuel Nicholas's battalion goes into camp at Sweets Town, not far from Washington's bivouac at Jockey Hollow, Morristown, New Jersey. The American forces begin a long winter of hardship due to inadequate clothing and food.

Opposite: *"Defeat on Lake Champlain," Col Charles Waterhouse, USMCR (Ret), Marine Corps Art Collection*

Right: *"Marines With Washington at Princeton," Col Charles Waterhouse, USMCR (Ret), Marine Corps Art Collection*

Below: *"The March to Jockey Hollow," Col Charles Waterhouse, USMCR (Ret), Marine Corps Art Collection*

1 February
New Jersey
The Marines transfer to Morristown and assume the role of artillerymen for the remainder of the winter.

5 February
France
Marines of *Reprisal* lead a boarding party that storms and captures the British *Swallow* in the Bay of Biscay off France.

8 March
Atlantic
The British frigate *Levant* defeats the Pennsylvania Navy ship *Montgomery* and her Marines.

20 March
Atlantic
The Connecticut Navy ship *Defence* and her Marines capture the British ship *Grog*.

7 June
Atlantic
Frigates *Hancock* and *Boston* and their Marine detachments capture the British frigate *Fox*.

14 June
Heritage
Congress adopts the Stars and Stripes as the national flag.

7 July
Atlantic
Hancock defeated by the British frigate *Rainbow*.

4 September
Atlantic
Marines on board the frigate *Raleigh* assist in a bold attack on the British sloop *Druid* escorting a large convoy, but are unable to sink or capture any ships.

19 September
France
Lexington and her Marine detachment are defeated by the British cutter *Alert* near France. Captain Henry Johnson and Sergeant John Barry eventually would escape from an English prison.

27 September
Pennsylvania
Frigate *Delaware* and her Marines are driven onto a shoal in the Delaware River as they fight with British batteries guarding the approaches to Philadelphia (now occupied by the British). The ship is captured, but many of the Marines are able to escape.

1778

10 January
Mississippi River
A company of Marines under Navy Captain James Willing depart Fort Pitt (Pittsburgh) in the armed boat *Rattletrap* for an expedition to New Orleans.

15 January
Civil Support
Marines from the frigate *Randolph* help fight a blaze that destroys hundreds of buildings in Charleston, South Carolina.

Above: *There is too little to eat and too little to wear during the hard winter at Morristown, New Jersey, in 1777. ("Marine Sentry, 1777," Col Charles Waterhouse, USMCR (Ret), Marine Corps Art Collection)*

Left: *Marines go back to the Bahamas in 1778 and raise the Stars and Stripes over foreign soil for the first time. ("Flag Raising at New Providence," Col Charles Waterhouse, USMCR (Ret), Marine Corps Art Collection)*

Right: *Naval Captain James Willing leads an expedition down the Mississippi River in 1778 in an effort to weaken Britain's hold on the waterway. He and his Marines raid Loyalist plantations along the way. ("Willing's Marine Expedition," Col Charles Waterhouse, USMCR (Ret), Marine Corps Art Collection)*

28 January
Bahamas
In a surprise night attack, Marines of the sloop *Providence* again seize the forts at New Providence Island in the Bahamas and raise the Stars and Stripes over a foreign shore for the first time. They also capture five ships in the harbor.

23 February
Mississippi River
Marines from *Rattletrap* capture the British sloop *Rebecca* on the Mississippi River and temporarily free that waterway from enemy domination.

7 March
Caribbean
Randolph and her Marines (reinforced by Continental soldiers) take on the 64-gun ship-of-the-line *Yarmouth* near Barbados. In the midst of the battle, *Randolph*'s powder magazine explodes, and she sinks with the loss of 301 sailors, Marines, and soldiers.

7 March
Pennsylvania
Marines join the crewmen of two armed barges in capturing two British supply ships in the Delaware River. The barges also support General Anthony Wayne's brigade as it forages in New Jersey for food for Washington's army at Valley Forge.

9 March
Atlantic
Alfred is defeated by the British ships *Ariadne* and *Ceres* in the Atlantic, and her sailors and Marines are taken prisoner.

28 March
Rhode Island
Marines hold off an attack by Royal Marines while crewmen unload valuable equipment from the grounded *Columbus* near Newport, Rhode Island.

15 April
Atlantic
Marines participate in the actions in which the Connecticut Navy ships *Oliver Cromwell* and *Defence* capture the British letters-of-marque *Admiral Keppel* and *Cyrus*.

23 April
Great Britain
John Paul Jones and sailors and Marines of the sloop *Ranger* make a dawn raid on the British port of Whitehaven, setting fire to ships and spiking the cannon of the fort. Later that day they land at St. Mary's Isle to capture a British earl, but find him away from home and instead take the family silver.

24 April
Great Britain
Ranger and her Marines defeat the British sloop *Drake* in the Irish Sea.

1 May
Rhode Island
Marines assist in a night battle with the British frigate *Lark* in Narragansett Bay as *Providence* escapes the blockade and makes it to the open sea.

August
Atlantic
The brigantine *General Gates* and her Marines defeat the British letter-of-marque brig *Montague* in the Atlantic.

7 August
Canada
Marines participate in *Providence*'s attack on a 30-ship convoy off Nova Scotia. They inflict damage on an armed transport carrying Highland troops.

27 September
Maine
The British ships *Experiment* and *Unicorn* engage *Raleigh* off the Penobscot River, Maine, and force her aground. Some of the Marines and sailors escape to shore, but most are captured.

1779

April
Marksmanship
First recorded marksmanship practice by Marines takes place at Nantasket Beach, Massachusetts, and on board Commodore Hopkins's fleet composed of *Ranger*, *Warren*, and *Queen of France*.

6–7 April
Virginia
Off Cape Henry, Virginia, Marines assist Commodore Hopkins's fleet in capturing the armed British schooner *Hibernia*, the escort ship *Jason*, and six merchantmen carrying supplies for the British Army.

Above: *John Paul Jones inspects the Marine detachment aboard the frigate* Ranger *in 1778. ("Marines Aboard the* Ranger,*" H. Charles McBarron, Marine Corps Art Collection)*

Right: *The original of this painting depicting the 1779 battle was destroyed by the terrorist attack on the Pentagon on 11 September 2001. ("Assault on Penobscot," Col Charles Waterhouse, USMCR (Ret), Marine Corps Art Collection)*

7 May
New Jersey
The sloop *Providence* and her Marines defeat the British brig *Diligent* off Sandy Hook, New Jersey.

18 July
Atlantic
Ranger, *Queen of France*, and the frigate *Providence* use the cover of heavy fog to cut out and capture 10 ships of a large convoy near the Newfoundland Banks.

24 July
Maine
An expedition sails from Massachusetts with the goal of destroying the British base under construction in Penobscot Bay, Maine. The fleet is composed of Continental ships *Warren*, sloop *Providence*, and brig *Diligence*, reinforced with four ships of the Massachusetts and New Hampshire state navies, a dozen privateers, and 20 merchantmen carrying supplies and troops (Continentals and state militiamen).

24 July
Maine
Marines from the Massachusetts Navy ship *Tyrannicide* land on Fox Island in Penobscot Bay to reconnoiter the area.

26 July
Maine
Marines land on Banks Island, Maine, and install batteries to fire on British ships and positions around Penobscot Bay.

28 July
Maine
Marines land as the right flank of the American force, which successfully attacks up a steep slope and establishes a lodgment ashore near the British fort at Penobscot. The Americans settle down to build a fortified line instead of continuing the assault, which likely would have succeeded. A lack of coordination between land and sea forces contributes to the ultimate failure of the campaign.

Above: Bonhomme Richard, *under John Paul Jones, defeated HMS* Serapis *off the coast of England in September 1776. ("The* Serapis *and the* Bonhomme Richard," *William Elliott, U.S. Naval Academy Museum)*

Right: "Bonhomme Richard *and* Serapis," *J. O. Davidson, Marine Corps Art Collection*

13–15 August
Maine
After a British fleet arrives off Penobscot Bay, the American landing force re-embarks in an attempt to withdraw. The American fleet tries to evade the British, but all American ships are subsequently captured or scuttled. Escaping Marines, sailors, and soldiers start an overland trek back to Massachusetts.

10 September
Louisiana
Marines aboard an armed schooner assist in defeating and taking possession of the British sloop *West Florida* on Lake Pontchartrain near New Orleans.

23 September
Great Britain
Captain John Paul Jones's flagship *Bonhomme Richard* engages the British frigate *Serapis* off Flamborough Head. In bitter fighting, both ships are badly damaged and more than 250 men are killed and wounded. *Serapis* strikes her colors after Marines and sailors in the tops of Jones's ship use grenades and musket fire to sweep the tops and weather decks of the British ship. (*Bonhomme Richard*'s Marines were mainly Irishmen serving in the French Army.)

1780

15–17 March
Florida
West Florida and her Marines participate in the successful Spanish attack on the British fort at Mobile.

21 March
South Carolina
Marines of the Continental fleet at Charleston are sent ashore to bolster artillery batteries defending the city against a pending British attack by land and sea.

10 May
South Carolina
Charleston surrenders after the British fleet and army completely surround the city.

2 June
Atlantic
Frigate *Trumbull* and her Marines battle the 36-gun British letter-of-marque *Watt* to a bloody draw. Three Marine lieutenants and a sergeant are among the American dead.

December
Atlantic
Marines participate in the engagement between John Paul Jones's *Ariel* and the British privateer *Triumph*.

1781

5 January
Atlantic
Sloop *Saratoga* and her Marines defeat the 16-gun British privateer *Resolution* and the letter-of-marque *Tonyn*.

2 April
France
Marines of the *Alliance* assist in defeating British privateer brigs *Mars* and *Minerva* off the coast of France.

28 May
Atlantic
British sloops *Atlanta* and *Trepassey* surrender to

Opposite: *"John Adams and John Paul Jones With Marines of the* Bonhomme Richard,*" Col Charles Waterhouse, USMCR (Ret), Marine Corps Art Collection*

Right: Alliance *is the last ship of the Continental Navy to release her Marines following the end of the Revolutionary War. ("Mustering Out Marines of the* Alliance,*" Col Charles Waterhouse, USMCR (Ret), Marine Corps Art Collection)*

Alliance after a long fight in the Atlantic Ocean.

9 August
Atlantic
Partially dismasted by a storm, *Trumbull* and her Marines are defeated by the British frigate *Iris* off the Delaware Capes.

6 September
South Carolina
Marines on board the Pennsylvania privateer *Congress* help defeat the British sloop *Savage*, which recently had plundered General Washington's estate at Mount Vernon.

Fall
Civil Support
Major Samuel Nicholas is in charge of safeguarding the delivery from Boston to Philadelphia of a million silver coins, a loan from France to the Continental government.

1782

8 April
Atlantic
The Continental privateer *Hyder Ally* and her Marines defeat the British sloop *General Monk* off Delaware Bay.

8 May
Bahamas
Marines from the South Carolina Navy ship *South Carolina* participate in another landing at New Providence, Bahamas, that helps secure those islands for Spain.

1783

10 March
Caribbean
Alliance and her Marines engage the British frigate *Sybil* in the West Indies and inflict heavy damage on her. This is the last naval battle of the Revolutionary War.

11 April
American Revolution
The Treaty of Paris is signed to end hostilities in the Revolutionary War.

1784

26 April
Manpower
The last recorded mention of a Continental Marine is of Private Robert Stout serving in *Alliance*. With the end of the war, the Continental Navy and Marines are disbanded.

1785

3 June
Force Structure
Congress authorizes the sale of *Alliance*, the last vessel of the Continental Navy.

1790

27 August
Commandants
Major Samuel Nicholas, the senior Marine to serve during the Revolutionary War and considered the first Commandant of the Corps, dies in Philadelphia.

1794

27 March
Manpower
By the Navy Act of 1794, Congress authorizes Marines, totaling six officers and 310 enlisted men, to serve aboard the six frigates that will constitute the United States Navy, once the ships are built. This marks the rebirth of the Corps, this time designated the U.S. Marine Corps (as distinguished from the Continental Marines).

1796

20 April
Manpower
Due to lessening of tensions with the Barbary states, Congress continues construction of only three of the six planned frigates and cuts authorized Marine strength in half.

1797

4 January
Manpower
The first recorded mention is made of U.S. Marines serving on a U.S. Navy ship, the frigate *United States*. The detachment provides sharpshooters, boarders, and guards.

1 July
Manpower
President John Adams signs legislation detailing the size of Marine detachments on ships, pay scales, enlistment terms, and retirement regulations.

24 August
Uniforms
The Secretary of War prescribes the uniform for Marines: blue coats with red lapels.

1798

9 April
Force Structure
The Secretary of War recommends to Congress the raising of an additional "regiment of infantry . . . to act in the double capacity of Marines and Infantry."

30 April
Department of the Navy
Congress establishes a separate Department of the Navy to handle naval affairs.

28 May
Quasi War
The Quasi War with France officially begins when President John Adams instructs commanders of armed ships of the United States to make reprisals upon the commerce of France.

30 June
Manpower
At the end of the government's fiscal year, Marine strength stands at 25 officers and 58 enlisted.

11 July
Force Structure
President John Adams signs an act "Establishing and Organizing a Marine Corps," giving the Corps an institutional footing.

12 July
Commandants
The President commissions William Ward Burrows as a major and second Commandant of the Marine Corps.

20 November
Guadeloupe
The French frigates *L'Insurgente* and *Volontaire* force the outgunned Navy schooner *Retaliation* and her Marines to surrender. She is the only ship lost by the United States in the Quasi War.

1799

3 February
Martinique
Marines on board frigate *United States* assist in sinking the French privateer *L'Amour de la Patrie* off the island of Martinique.

9 February
Caribbean
Frigate *Constellation* and her Marines defeat the French frigate *L'Insurgente* off the island of Nevis.

2 March
Manpower
President John Adams approves legislation raising the strength of the Marine Corps to one major, 40 other officers, and 1,044 enlisted.

30 June
Manpower
The actual size of the Marine Corps is 25 officers and 343 enlisted.

18 October
Guadeloupe
Marines participate in the action between the revenue cutter *Pickering* and the French privateer *L'Egypt Conquise* off Guadeloupe.

30 December
Guadeloupe
Frigate *Connecticut* and her Marines engage the French privateer *L'Italie Conquise* off the island of Guadeloupe.

Opposite: *The artist executed this 1988 portrait of the first Commandant based on a known likeness. It replaced an earlier one done without research. ("Samuel Nicholas," Col Donna Neary, USMCR, Marine Corps Art Collection)*

Right: *"American Merchant Ship* Planter *vs French Privateer," Marine Corps Art Collection*

MAJOR DANIEL CARMICK

Daniel Carmick was born in Philadelphia in 1772 and appointed a lieutenant in the recently revived Marine Corps on 5 May 1798. He commanded the Marine detachment of *Ganges*, the first ship of the new United States Navy to go to sea, and won a quick promotion to captain in August as the fledgling Corps expanded to man the burgeoning fleet. In May 1799 he took command of the 50 Marines of USS *Constitution*.

A year later, during the Quasi War with France, Carmick led half his detachment in a foray under command of Navy Lieutenant Isaac Hull. Their objective was to seize the French corvette *Sandwich* hiding in a harbor in Santo Domingo. *Constitution* drew too much water to enter, so her captain commandeered a merchant ship. Hull and Carmick secreted their men below decks, sailed into the harbor, and drew alongside the unwary enemy. The Marines "went on board like devils" and took control of the ship in minutes. Surprise was so complete that Carmick and his men immediately rowed ashore, seized the over-watching Spanish fort, and spiked the guns, all without a shot. Then the sailors and Marines had to wait the rest of the day and night, prepared to repel boarders, until the wind and tide allowed them to sail the prize out to sea.

Carmick's reputation for audacity took him on a far different mission at home later that year. The Commandant, Major William Ward Burrows, was dismayed that a Marine lieutenant had been struck by a Navy officer. Burrows wrote the young officer and told him to challenge the

Opposite: *The Marine detachment of* Constitution *awaits its new commander in Boston. ("Captain Carmick Arrives for Inspection," Col Charles Waterhouse, USMCR (Ret), Marine Corps Art Collection)*

Right: *Marines and sailors seize a French privateer. ("Cutting Out of the* Sandwich,*" Col Charles Waterhouse, USMCR (Ret), Marine Corps Art Collection)*

offending party to a duel to uphold the honor of the Corps, citing the experience of another Marine lieutenant who had shot an insolent Navy officer—"afterwards Politeness was restored." The Commandant also added that he had assigned Carmick "to call on you and be your Friend. He is a Man of Spirit, and will take care of you." The ensuing challenge and Carmick's backing brought forth an apology without a duel.

During the Barbary Wars, Carmick headed the detachment in the flagship *Chesapeake* in 1802, but saw no action. His lasting memory of the campaign was the aftermath of yet another pistol duel between Marine and Navy officers. This time a Leatherneck captain upheld his honor and that of the Corps at the cost of his life, and Carmick was "obliged to see a Brother Officer's heart cut out, that I might certify that the Ball had passed through the center of it."

In 1804 Carmick and 100 Marines helped establish U.S. authority over the just-acquired Louisiana Purchase. He remained there in command of all Marines around New Orleans, rising to the rank of major in 1809 when his force grew to 300 men. There were occasional clashes with Spanish troops from Texas and Florida, with Indians, and with pirates. In September 1814, while most American servicemen were preoccupied with the war against Britain, Carmick led his Marines and some Army reinforcements against the pirate stronghold of Barataria. They cleaned it out and burned it to the ground.

The War of 1812 came to Louisiana that December in the form of a British fleet and 9,000 soldiers. Carmick and his men participated in a spoiling attack on the night of 23 December by General Andrew Jackson's small army; it caught the British advance guard by surprise and mauled it. The invaders probed Jackson's formidable defensive line five days later and were repulsed with significant losses. The Americans suffered just 17 casualties, but one of them was Carmick, who must have exposed himself above the defensive works. He lay in a New Orleans hospital when Jackson's force resoundingly defeated the main British assault in January. The Marine major never fully recovered from his wounds and died in 1816. His New Orleans tomb bears the inscription: "Where shall we find such another?"

Left: *One of the original frigates of the U.S. Navy,* Constitution *made history with her victories during the War of 1812. Perhaps the most storied warship ever to fly the Stars and Stripes, she is still in commission in Boston Harbor. ("USS* Constitution,*" Carlton T. Chapman, Marine Corps Art Collection)*

1800

1 February
Guadeloupe
Marines on board *Constellation* assist in defeating the French frigate *La Vengeance* off Guadeloupe. The French ship escapes in the night, but is run aground to avoid sinking.

31 March
Washington, D.C.
Marines arrive in Washington, D.C., to establish a Marine Barracks and guard the Navy Yard there.

22 April
Commandants
Congress authorizes the rank of Lieutenant Colonel Commandant for the head of the Marine Corps.

1 May
Commandants
Commandant William Ward Burrows becomes the first Marine promoted to lieutenant colonel.

11 May
Santo Domingo
At Puerto Plata, Santo Domingo, Captain Daniel Carmick and Marines and sailors from the frigate *Constitution* use the sloop *Sally* to capture *Sandwich* from the French. The Marines then land and spike the guns of a shore battery to permit a clean escape.

17 June
Guadeloupe
Marines participate in the action between the schooner *Enterprise* and the French privateer *La Cygne* off Guadeloupe.

30 June
Manpower
The Marine Corps has 38 officers and 487 enlisted on duty.

4 July
Marine Band
The Marine Band makes its first appearance in public at Tun Tavern in Philadelphia.

9 July
Guadeloupe
Enterprise and her Marines capture the French privateer *L'Aigle* off Guadeloupe.

15 July
HQMC
Lieutenant Colonel Commandant Burrows and his staff arrive in Washington, D.C., and establish a temporary headquarters in Georgetown.

23 July
Caribbean
Marine musket fire helps decide the battle between *Enterprise* and the French privateer *Le Flambeau* off Nevis Island.

Right: *"First Headquarters of the U.S. Marines," Arman T. Manookian, National Archives*

Below: *Marine musicians often helped drum up recruits, as pictured here in a scene set in front of Philadelphia's Independence Hall. ("Marine Band, 1798," Col Donna Neary, USMCR, Marine Corps Art Collection)*

1 September
Caribbean
The schooner *Experiment* and her Marines engage the French privateer *Le Deux Amis* off St. Bartholomew, West Indies.

13 September
Caribbean
Marines participate in the fighting between *Experiment* and the French privateer *La Diana* north of St. Bartholomew.

23–24 September
Caribbean
The sloop *Patapsco* bombards protective forts (recently captured by French troops) in the harbor of Willemstad, Curacao, then her Marines land and assist Dutch forces defending the town against the French invasion.

12 October
Atlantic
Marines on board the frigate *Boston* assist in defeating the French corvette *Le Berceau* in the Atlantic Ocean. Neither ship was aware that a peace agreement recently had been signed between the two nations.

1801

1 January
Marine Band
The Marine Band plays for the first New Year's reception held at the White House in Washington.

3 February
Quasi War
The treaty ending the Quasi War with France is ratified by the U.S. Senate.

3 March
Marine Barracks 8th and I
Congress appropriates $20,000 to build a Marine Barracks in Washington. The site is chosen within the month and purchased by June.

MARINE BARRACKS 8TH AND I

The history of the Marine Barracks in Washington, D.C., is entwined with that of the national capital itself. When the federal government first moved to Washington from Philadelphia in 1800, Lieutenant Colonel Commandant Burrows and his small headquarters soon followed on 15 July. Since the city itself was being built largely from scratch, accommodations were hard to come by. Burrows and his few staff officers initially worked and lived together in a private residence in Georgetown, but he made it clear: "I care not for myself where my house is, so I can get my men comfortably provided for."

The enlisted Marines and their officers arrived soon after and first set up camp on a hill in Georgetown. After a period in another bivouac site in Washington itself, they moved into winter quarters in a rented building. Newly sworn-in President Thomas Jefferson took a keen interest in permanently settling his Marines. On 31 March 1801, Burrows recorded: "I have been all this morning engaged riding with the President looking for a proper place to fix the Marine Barracks on." The two men had focused their attention in the southeast quadrant of the city, between Capitol Hill and the new Navy Yard along what would later be named the Anacostia River. They settled on a plot bounded by 8th, 9th, G, and I Streets. It had to be purchased from a private owner at a cost of $6,247.18.

Congress already had approved $20,000 and plans for the new facility, so work quickly got underway. The contemplated barracks for 500 men and officers, plus a residence for the Commandant, was projected to cost $50,000.

The Secretary of the Navy assumed the difference would be made up by the labor of the Marines themselves, and so it was. Spurred on by an extra ration of rum per day, the men toiled at construction instead of drill. They were assisted by contractors, but the efforts of the latter did not satisfy the new Commandant, Lieutenant Colonel Wharton. He accepted the southern wing of the barracks and the Center House officers' quarters in early 1804, but the northern half of the barracks had to be taken down and rebuilt. Congress appropriated an additional $11,000 to complete the complex. The northern wing and the Commandant's house were finished around the end of 1805. The layout at that time consisted of the two-story Center House flanked by one-story barracks buildings on the 8th Street side of the lot, with the Commandant's house along G Street. Ancillary buildings housing Headquarters Marine Corps and other functions completed the perimeter of the square.

While the Commandant's residence was built with especially thick walls that have stood the test of time, the remainder of the buildings fell into poor condition by the end of the century. The offices of Headquarters Marine Corps moved out in 1901 to a building on New York Avenue. A band hall and other support facilities were completed about this time and temporarily pressed into service as barracks space while the old living quarters were demolished. New barracks went up soon after along 9th Street. The last of the current buildings around the parade deck were the quarters for senior officers built along 8th Street and completed in 1908. A new Center House in that location still serves as a gathering place for the officers of the post.

The Marine Barracks has performed a number of functions in its long history. In addition to being the home of Headquarters Marine Corps for almost a century, it early on served as the primary training ground for new officers and men. It also frequently has provided expeditionary forces in wartime. Captain Miller, the Adjutant of the Marine Corps, led the men of the Barracks into the Battle of Bladensburg in 1814. Commandant Henderson went off to Florida for the Seminole Wars, leaving behind just 16 men and the Marine Band. Subsequent organized detachments from the Barracks fought in the Mexican War, the Civil War, the Spanish-American War, and even Desert Storm.

Today, the Marines of 8th and I perform three major roles. Since 1920 they have operated the Marine Corps Institute, which educates Marines in a wide range of professional subjects via correspondence courses. The Silent Drill Platoon and the other Marines of the Barracks also perform ceremonial functions from the Evening Parades to funerals at Arlington National Cemetery. And all stand ready to play their part in providing a provisional infantry battalion if the need arises in war, just as their predecessors have done throughout the 200-year history of the "Oldest Post of the Corps."

Opposite: *"Placing the Barracks," Col Charles Waterhouse, USMCR (Ret), Marine Corps Art Collection*

Above: *The Commandant's house as it appears today. (Eric Long)*

Left: *Navy Lieutenant Stephen Decatur, 52 sailors, and eight Marines enter Tripoli Harbor on the night of 16 February, 1804 and burn the captured* Philadelphia. *("Burning of the* Philadelphia,*" Marine Corps Art Collection)*

31 March
Marine Barracks 8th and I
Lieutenant Colonel Commandant Burrows records, "I have been all this morning engaged in riding with the President [Thomas Jefferson] looking for a proper place to fix the Marine Barracks on."

14 May
Barbary Wars
Tripoli declares war on the United States, marking the formal beginning of the Barbary Wars.

21 June
Marine Barracks 8th and I
The government purchases land at the corner of 8th and I Streets in Washington, D.C., for $6,247.18 for a site for the Marine Barracks.

30 June
Manpower
The strength of the Marine Corps on active duty is 38 officers and 319 enlisted.

1 August
Tripoli
Enterprise forces the Tripolitan ship *Tripoli* to surrender after a three-hour cannonade. Marines play an important role by sweeping the enemy decks with musket fire whenever the corsair approached to board.

4 August
Marine Band
The Marine Band plays at the first inaugural parade in Washington, D.C.

29 September
Tripoli
Frigates *Philadelphia* and *Essex* and their Marines battle two gunboats near Tripoli.

1802

30 January
Budget
The Secretary of the Navy reports that the annual expense of the Marine Corps is $99,109.23.

30 June
Manpower
The strength of the Marine Corps on active duty is 29 officers and 330 enlisted.

22 July
Tripoli
Constellation and her Marines engage nine gunboats off the coast of Tripoli.

1803

9 May
Tripoli
Marines participate in the action between frigate *John Adams* and seven gunboats off Tripoli.

2 June
Tripoli
Marines and sailors from the U.S. blockading squadron land on shore in a bay near Tripoli to drive off defending soldiers while other Americans burn 10 small enemy cargo ships.

30 June
Manpower
The strength of the Marine Corps on active duty is 25 officers and 317 enlisted.

31 October
Tripoli
Frigate *Philadelphia* runs aground while pursuing a small cargo ship and surrenders when surrounded by Tripolitan gunboats. Her crew and Marines are imprisoned and the ship brought into the harbor after a storm floats her off the sandbar.

23 December
Tripoli
Enterprise and her Marines capture the ketch *Mastico*, renamed *Intrepid*, off the coast of Tripoli.

1804

16 February
Tripoli
Navy Lieutenant Stephen Decatur, 52 sailors, and eight Marines (led by Sergeant Solomon Wren) use *Intrepid* to enter Tripoli Harbor during the night and burn the captured *Philadelphia*.

7 March
Commandants
Lieutenant Colonel Burrows resigns as Commandant for health reasons.

1 April
Commandants
Captain Franklin Wharton is named the Lieutenant Colonel Commandant. He is the third Commandant of the Marine Corps.

30 June
Manpower
The strength of the Marine Corps on active duty is 25 officers and 364 enlisted.

3 August
Tripoli
As the U.S. squadron bombards the forts at Tripoli Harbor, four gunboats under command of Captain Stephen Decatur attack 11 Tripolitan boats. In close quarters fighting with muskets and cutlasses, the Americans capture three of the boats and inflict nearly 100 casualties among the enemy at a cost of one dead (Decatur's brother) and three wounded.

Right: *Marines help man 24-pounder long guns during the August 1804 sea bombardment of forts guarding Tripoli Harbor. ("Marines at the Great Guns," Col Charles Waterhouse, USMCR (Ret), Marine Corps Art Collection)*

LIEUTENANT PRESLEY N. O'BANNON

Presley O'Bannon was born on the large family homestead in Fauquier County, Virginia, sometime between 1776 and 1784. His father, William, had served as an army captain in the Revolutionary War and a maternal uncle had been a general. In 1801 the young man took a commission as a second lieutenant in the Marine Corps and also married Matilda Heard, a granddaughter of Revolutionary War hero General Daniel Morgan. O'Bannon would more than live up to his ancestral heritage.

The new lieutenant deployed to the Mediterranean Sea in 1802 on the frigate *Adams*. He and his ship spent most of the first months overseas blockading a Tripolitan warship at Gibraltar. His fellow officers found him a pleasant companion; when time dragged heavy, he would entertain them with his fiddle, playing songs such as "Hogs in the Cornfield." Even after they rejoined the squadron, there was little action under a relatively unaggressive commodore. O'Bannon's only brush with battle came in June 1803 when his ship and others sent forces inshore to burn Tripolitan merchant ships. He ended the cruise in late 1803 as a first lieutenant.

Transferred to frigate *President* the following year, he sailed again to the Mediterranean. One of the passengers was William Eaton, a former diplomat now on a mission to open a new front in the war with Tripoli. The young Marine officer was impressed by Eaton's boldness, and the respect was apparently mutual. When the ship arrived in North African waters, Eaton shifted to the brig *Argus*, and O'Bannon transferred as well to take command of the Marine detachment on that ship. Soon after, they went ashore in Egypt and launched their audacious expedition to overthrow the bashaw of Tripoli.

The close bond between the two Americans, and O'Bannon's own sense of duty and daring, came through at Bomba. Eaton's shaky army had endured considerable hardship and turmoil up to that point, and the teetering coalition hardly seemed capable of attacking and defeating an entrenched, superior force. The commodore of the U.S. squadron clearly expressed his own lack of confidence when he refused to provide any American reinforcements and in fact claimed that he needed the handful of Marines with Eaton back on the ships. O'Bannon stayed ashore and sent out a note to the captain of *Argus*: "Unwilling to abandon an expedition this far conducted, I have to request your permission to continue." The brig's commanding officer did not enforce the commodore's will. That decision was important, because the determination and discipline of O'Bannon and his seven Marines made all the difference a few days later at Derna.

Following the campaign against Tripoli, *Argus* and O'Bannon sailed back to the United States in 1806. The Virginia legislature had voted a richly designed ceremonial sword for its courageous native son in December 1805, but it was not presented to him until 1811. In the meantime, he had resigned his commission in 1807. Although there has been speculation that O'Bannon was upset at the lack of a brevet promotion or other recognition for his efforts, no one really knows why he left the Marine Corps. Soon after, he moved to Kentucky where members of his family ran a successful distillery business. O'Bannon eventually entered politics, served in the Kentucky legislature for a number of years, and died at the age of 74 in 1850.

This portrait of Lieutenant Presley O'Bannon, painted by a former editor of the Marine Corps Gazette, *was presented to the Basic School by the Warrant Officer Class of 1960. ("Lieutenant Presley O'Bannon," Donald L. Dickson, Marine Corps Art Collection)*

Legend has it that the Mameluke sword carried by Marine officers today was patterned after one given to O'Bannon by Hamet, the former Bashaw of Tripoli. In reality, the Mameluke-style sword first came into the Corps when the Marine quartermaster ordered a batch from England in 1825. Except for a brief period during and immediately following the Civil War, it has remained the sword of Marine officers ever since.

29 November
Derna
Lt Presley N. O'Bannon, former consul William Eaton, and seven Marines land at Alexandria, Egypt, with the objective of leading an assault against Tripoli in conjunction with the bashaw's brother.

1805

8 March
Derna
Presley O'Bannon and his landing party, reinforced by several hundred Greek and Arab mercenaries, start the 600-mile trek to Tripoli.

27 April
Derna
Supported by American warships, O'Bannon and his force storm and capture the fortress town of Derna, in western Tripoli. Two Marines are killed, and Eaton and one Marine are wounded.

13 May
Derna
O'Bannon and his Marines help repel an assault against Derna by 1,200 Tripolitan soldiers.

28 May
Derna
O'Bannon leads a small force in a spoiling attack against Tripolitan forces camped outside Derna.

4 June
Barbary Wars
Tripoli signs a peace treaty with the United States.

12 June
Derna
Marines cover the seaborne withdrawal of Eaton's force from Derna.

30 June
Manpower
Marines on active duty are 22 officers and 556 enlisted.

1806

30 June
Manpower
Marines on active duty are 11 officers and 307 enlisted.

15 August
Gibraltar
Marines participate in an action between *Enterprise* and Spanish gunboats in the Straits of Gibraltar.

27 October
New Orleans
The Secretary of the Navy directs the Commandant to send four officers and 74 enlisted Marines to New Orleans to replace a sickly force and defend against possible Spanish operations.

1807

22 June
Virginia
Marines are on board the frigate *Chesapeake* off Chesapeake Bay when she is attacked by the British frigate *Leopard* searching for Royal Navy deserters.

30 June
Manpower
Marines on active duty are 11 officers and 392 enlisted.

1808

8 May
South Carolina
A Marine Barracks is established at Charleston, South Carolina.

Opposite: *Marines leap to another ship to finish the battle in hand-to-hand fighting. ("Boarders Away," Jack Gray, Marine Corps Art Collection)*

Right: *In one of the first sea battles of the War of 1812, frigate* Constitution *defeats HMS* Guerriere. *The successes of the fledgling U.S. Navy shook the Royal Navy and the British public. ("USS* Constitution *and HMS* Guerriere,*" Michael F. Corne, U.S. Naval Academy Museum)*

30 June
Manpower
The strength of the Marine Corps on active duty is 11 officers and 861 enlisted.

1809

3 March
Manpower
Congress authorizes an increase in the Marine Corps to 46 officers and 1,823 enlisted. The period of enlistment is changed from three years to five.

4 March
Marine Band
The Marine Band plays for the first Inaugural Ball held in Washington, D.C., for President Jefferson.

30 June
Manpower
The strength of the Marine Corps on active duty is 10 officers and 513 enlisted.

1810

24 June
Bahamas
Brig *Vixen* and her Marines are fired upon in the night by the British sloop *Moselle*. The British captain claims he thought the American warship was a French privateer, and he apologizes.

30 June
Manpower
The strength of the Marine Corps on active duty is nine officers and 440 enlisted.

7 October
Civil Support
Marines from the sloop *Wasp* assist in fighting fires in Charleston, South Carolina.

1811

4 May
Florida
Marines establish a post at Cumberland Island, off the southeast coast of Georgia, to deal with smuggling from Spanish Florida.

16 May
Atlantic
In search of an impressed American seaman, frigate *President* and her Marines engage the British sloop *Little Belt* off the east coast of the United States. The smaller British ship loses nine killed and 23 wounded in the night action, which further heightens tensions between the two nations.

THE DERNA CAMPAIGN

Early in 1805, *Argus* sailed to Egypt with William Eaton, the former consul to nearby Tunis. His mission was to find Hamet, the previous bashaw of Tripoli, who had been deposed by his brother. Eaton took along Lieutenant O'Bannon, seven enlisted Marines, and a midshipman. The party tracked down their quarry in chaotic Egypt and enlisted him in a bold scheme to overthrow the current bashaw and end the war with Tripoli. The Marine lieutenant then recruited a force of several dozen western mercenaries (from a number of countries) to reinforce 100 Arab soldiers under Hamet. Along with Eaton and a retinue of camel drivers, the tiny army set out across the North African desert on 8 March 1805. Once on the march, Eaton's outfit was swelled by another few hundred Arabs willing to fight for a fee.

Water was scarce, food ran low, the sun broiled, rumors of growing enemy opposition repeatedly surfaced, and tensions flared between the disparate groups. The polyglot expedition nearly fell apart almost every day, with camel drivers, Arab horsemen, or the mercenaries taking turns demanding additional pay or threatening to desert when the going seemed to get the roughest. O'Bannon and his Marines provided the backbone that repeatedly held the force together.

Possibly the worst moment came on 15 April when the army straggled into the Bay of Bomba, where Eaton had promised that the U.S. Navy would provide fresh supplies and reinforcements. There were no ships. The next morning, as the various contingents prepared to abandon the enterprise, *Argus* came over the horizon with food and preserved the shaky alliance one more time. But the commodore refused to lend any of his other Marines.

The army departed Bomba on 23 April and reached the hills above Derna on the evening of the 25th. The 600-mile march was finally at an end. The 800 defenders and their nine artillery pieces outnumbered and outgunned Eaton's force, which would have to attack across an open plain against a fort and a line of breastworks on the eastern edge of the city. The former consul made one last attempt at diplomacy, sending in a note that offered the city's governor the chance to continue in office under Hamet if he did not fight. The governor's bold reply presaged a tough battle: "My head or yours."

Three U.S. Navy ships arrived off Derna over the next two days. They put ashore two heavy guns, but Eaton could get only one to the front in time for the attack on the afternoon of 27 April. Hamet took most of the Arabs around to the southern flank of the city, O'Bannon led a force of about 60 men against the eastern defenses, and the ships bombarded the fort. Heavy fire initially checked O'Bannon's wing, but Eaton called for a charge. The Marines led the way, the western mercenaries followed, and the defenders cracked at the sight of bayonet-tipped muskets rushing toward them. Eaton was hit in the arm, and three Marines went down, but O'Bannon kept the remainder moving right through the breastworks and into the fort itself. There he raised the U.S. flag over foreign soil for the first time (as opposed to the first raising of the Stars and Stripes of the Continental government at New Providence, Bahamas, in 1778). Meanwhile, Hamet's force captured the governor's palace on the opposite side of town. The formerly bold governor sought refuge in a harem. At a cost of two dead Marines (Privates

John Witten and Edward Steward), Eaton had placed the bashaw's rule in jeopardy. A larger Tripolitan army tried to retake the town during the next few weeks, but failed.

On 3 June, the bashaw held on to his throne by signing a peace treaty with the United States and freeing the crew of *Philadelphia*. The news arrived by sea at Derna on 11 June. In a well-planned operation, Eaton, O'Bannon, Hamet, and the reliable elements of the force withdrew with the fleet, and the Barbary Wars came to an end.

Reinforced by a handful of mercenaries and Arab soldiers, William Eaton, Lt Presley O'Bannon, and seven enlisted Marines storm the fortress at Derna. Their victory forces an end to the war with Tripoli on U.S. terms. ("Attack on Derna," Col Charles Waterhouse, USMCR (Ret), Marine Corps Art Collection)

1812

17 March
Marine Barracks 8th and I
The Marine Corps establishes its reputation for frugality by completing the Marine Barracks complex in Washington, D.C., for $5,571.16 less than the amount appropriated by Congress.

18 March
Florida
In order to prevent the British from taking over Florida, U.S. Marines and soldiers support an advance by "patriots" (unofficial militiamen) across the St. Mary's River into Spanish-controlled Florida.

18 June
War of 1812
The War of 1812 begins when Congress passes and President James Madison signs a declaration of war against Great Britain.

30 June
Manpower
Despite having an authorized strength of 1,869, the number of Marines on active duty consists of just 10 officers and 483 enlisted.

13 August
Atlantic
Marines participate in frigate *Essex*'s defeat of the British sloop *Alert*.

19 August
Atlantic
In the Atlantic Ocean east of Boston, *Constitution* and her Marines defeat British frigate *Guerriere*, which is so badly damaged the Americans scuttle it the next day.

12 September
Florida
While escorting a wagon convoy in Florida, Marines drive off an ambushing Indian force at a cost of two dead and six wounded.

18 October
Atlantic
The 17 Marines on sloop *Wasp* help defeat the British sloop *Frolic* southwest of Bermuda. Later that same day the American warship, as it tends to the battered *Frolic*, is captured by British ship of the line *Poictiers*.

25 October
Atlantic
Near Africa, *United States* defeats British frigate *Macedonian*, but entirely by long-range firepower, thus leaving little role for the Marines to play.

28 November
Canada
Marines and sailors join Army troops in capturing the British fort at Red House, Canada.

Opposite, top: *"Capture of* Frolic *by* Wasp,*" J. J. Barralett, Marine Corps Art Collection*

Opposite, bottom: *"Lt William Bush of the* Constitution,*" J. Eichholtz, Marine Corps Art Collection*

Right: *"Capture of* Macedonian *by Frigate* United States,*" J. J. Barralett, Marine Corps Art Collection*

Below: *"Taking a Blow," Col Charles Waterhouse, USMCR (Ret), Marine Corps Art Collection*

29 December
Atlantic
Constitution and her Marines defeat the British frigate *Java* off Brazil.

1813

9 February
Florida
Marines and soldiers destroy two Indian towns in east Florida that were home to those who had ambushed the wagon convoy in September 1812.

24 February
Atlantic
Marines assist the sloop *Hornet* in defeating and sinking the British brig *Peacock* off the coast of British Guiana.

16 April
Florida
Marines participate in the Army-Navy expedition to Mobile, but the Spanish defenders surrender without a fight in the face of superior strength.

27 May
Canada
Marines from the Lake Ontario squadron participate with an Army regiment in a landing on the Canadian shore and the subsequent seizure of Fort George.

1 June
Massachusetts
Chesapeake is defeated by British frigate *Shannon* off Boston. The American Marine force of 44 officers and men suffers losses of 14 killed and 20 wounded in close combat with British boarders.

22 June
Virginia
Fifty Marines from *Constellation* reinforce the fort on Craney Island, Virginia, guarding Norfolk Navy Yard and assist in repelling a British amphibious assault.

LIEUTENANT COLONEL JOHN GAMBLE

John Marshall Gamble came from a thoroughly military family. His father had served as a major in the Revolutionary War and his three brothers would all die while on active service with the U.S. Navy. He was born in New Jersey around 1790 and received his commission in the Marine Corps in July 1809. Two years later he took charge of the Marine detachment on frigate *Essex* under the command of Captain David Porter. Gamble and his 31 Marines were the first Leathernecks to see action in the War of 1812, participating in *Essex*'s defeat of a British ship two months after the conflict began. The fame of Porter, Gamble, and *Essex* was yet to come, but the Marine officer almost missed it. On a subsequent combat cruise, following orders to return "that night" with a boatload of provisions from the Brazilian coast, Gamble and a Navy lieutenant braved a severe storm and were tossed into the sea. The two men kept afloat for hours and swam to the ship before daylight.

Porter sailed *Essex* around Cape Horn and into the South Pacific in February 1813. He devastated the British whaling fleet there and turned two prizes into warships. In an unprecedented mark of confidence, Gamble received command of *Greenwich*. He upheld Porter's judgment on 14 July by defeating the 14-gun *Seringapatam* with astute tactical handling of his own small ship. In October, Porter took his little fleet of warships and prizes to Nukuhiva in the Marquesas Islands (far southeast of Hawaii) to refit them. The Navy officer took an interest in tribal politics, helping one group defeat another, and then subjugating a third unfriendly faction. In December Porter sailed with his two largest warships and the richest prize, leaving

Gamble with *Greenwich* and three smaller whalers. The Marine lieutenant had a force of 18 men and six prisoners. His orders were to guard the base for five months, then depart for the States with the two largest ships if Porter had not returned.

Trouble began almost immediately with the much more numerous natives. Gamble had to forcibly recover supplies stolen from his encampment, then maintain a continuous guard with his tiny force. The Marine officer was "amiable, gentle, yet firm," but nevertheless discipline was difficult to maintain as many of the men routinely gave the local women some of the limited food supplies. His force dwindled after one man drowned and four others who had been punished deserted in a small boat. As time came to depart the island, disaffection grew among the prisoners and a few of their captors.

The Englishmen incited a mutiny on *Seringapatam* and subdued Gamble and two midshipmen, shooting the Marine in the heel in the melee. At sea that night, the three were placed in a leaky boat, but they managed to make it back to Nukuhiva and rejoin the few loyal men still there. A battle with the islanders, who tried to take advantage of the weakened force, resulted in a loss of four more men. At one point in the fight, Gamble hobbled from cannon to cannon firing them alone to cover the rescue of a wounded man.

With only three of the eight men fit for duty, no charts, and a damaged ship, Gamble's force nevertheless sailed to the Hawaiian Islands over the next three weeks. Having secured food and needed equipment from friendly natives there, his plans for the next leg of the journey were dashed when the British warship *Cherub* captured him and his band. He was detained until the war was over and did not make it back to the United States until August 1815. He spent his first day in America writing a lengthy report to the Secretary of the Navy that closed: "I arrived here last evening, and have the honour to wait either the orders of the Navy Department or of the Commandant of the Marine Corps." Gamble served the rest of his career uneventfully as a barracks commander and died on active duty as a lieutenant colonel in 1836.

Opposite: *"John Gamble, Equestrian," Anthony Lewis DeRose, Marine Corps Art Collection*

Below: *"Gamble at Nukuhiva," Col Charles Waterhouse, USMCR (Ret), Marine Corps Art Collection*

Opposite: *On board* Lawrence *at Lake Erie. ("Marines to the Rigging," Col Charles Waterhouse, USMCR (Ret), Marine Corps Art Collection)*

Left: *"Battle of Plattsburgh, Lake Champlain, 1814," Edward Tufnell, Navy Art Collection*

Below: *"Battle of Lake Erie," William H. Powell, Courtesy of the U.S. Capitol*

30 June
Manpower
The strength of the Marine Corps on active duty is 12 officers and 579 enlisted.

14 July
Pacific
Marine Lieutenant John Gamble, captain of the prize *Greenwich*, defeats the British armed whaler *Seringapatam* near the Galapagos Islands.

31 July
Canada
Marines and soldiers land at York and burn British barracks, naval stores, and public buildings.

14 August
Ireland
Argus and her Marines are defeated and captured by the British ship *Pelican* off the coast of Ireland.

4 September
Maine
The Marines of *Enterprise* assist in her victory over the British brig *Boxer* in the waters near Maine.

10 September
Lake Erie
Marines participate in Commodore Oliver Hazard Perry's complete victory over the British fleet on Lake Erie, thus gaining permanent control of the western Great Lakes.

24 October
Marine Barracks, Portsmouth
The Marine Barracks is established at Portsmouth Navy Yard, New Hampshire.

24 December
Marquesas
Lieutenant John Gamble leads a handful of Marines and sailors in a show of force to restore order on the Island of Nukuhiva in the Marquesas, which was serving as the base for Captain David Porter's small Pacific squadron.

1814

28 March
Chile
Essex and her Marines are defeated and captured by the British frigate *Phoebe* and the sloop *Cherub* in Chilean coastal waters.

BATTLE OF BLADENSBURG

With the end of the Napoleonic Wars in the spring of 1814, the British suddenly had substantial additional forces to throw into the fray in North America. While their primary interest remained Canada and New England, they sent major forces to attack the mid-Atlantic coast and New Orleans. General Robert Ross landed about 4,000 men on the banks of the Patuxent River off Chesapeake Bay in August. His initial target was Washington, D.C. Brigadier General Henry Winder mustered almost 6,500 soldiers (mainly militia) to defend the national capital. Winder himself was not a professional officer, and most of his units came together for the first time on the battlefield, many of them after days of hard marching in hot, humid weather.

The two forces came to grips on 26 August near Bladensburg, Maryland, where a bridge crossed over what is now the Anacostia River at a point northeast of Washington. Winder's men were arrayed more or less in three lines near the road ascending up the slope from the river. The three formations did not mutually support each other, there were almost no defensive works, and Winder gave them no plan of action.

Commodore Joshua Barney was ordered at the last minute to support Winder with roughly 400 sailors, 114 Marines under command of Captain Samuel Miller, and five artillery pieces. The naval contingent arrived as the battle was underway, and the men ran to join the middle of the third line, occupying a small hillock near the road. The Marines were on the left of Barney's position, the guns in the center, and sailors acting as infantry were on the right. Militiamen were off to the left of Barney and a body of regular soldiers to the right.

The British attacked across the shallow river and suffered some casualties from two artillery pieces in the first American line, but the militia soon pulled back in the face of the enemy's determined charge. Winder's second line momentarily checked the British thrust with musket fire, then an American regiment counterattacked and temporarily drove back the invaders. As a second British brigade crossed the river and began to envelop the second line, and frightening (but not particularly dangerous) Congreve rockets soared overhead, most of these American units broke and fled. Winder ordered his counterattacking force to withdraw, but too late for them to do so in good order.

Flushed with relatively easy success, Ross's soldiers moved boldly up the road. Barney held his fire until they were close, then unleashed grape shot from a heavy cannon. In the words of his subsequent report, that "completely cleared the road." The British recoiled, then charged twice, each time being turned back by artillery and musket fire from the naval contingent. The fourth time the enemy worked to the flanks, at which point the American forces there, which had not yet been engaged, withdrew hastily after a few volleys. With his ammunition almost exhausted, on the verge of being surrounded, and men now falling steadily to British sharpshooters, the commodore ordered his tiny force to retire from the field. Barney himself had already had his horse shot from under him and then been hit in the thigh; he was forced to remain behind. Captain Miller also had received a severe wound in the arm. Twelve other Marines were wounded, one killed, and two captured.

Afterward the British swept into Washington and burned all the public buildings, to include

"Final Stand at Bladensburg," Col Charles Waterhouse, USMCR (Ret), Marine Corps Art Collection

the Capitol and the White House. The Commandant's House and the Marine Barracks were spared, and legend has credited Ross's respect for the fighting spirit of the Marines at Bladensburg. While probably apocryphal—British forces never approached that part of the city—Ross did say later that Barney's Marines and sailors "have given us our only real fighting."

29 April
Atlantic
Marines participate in sloop *Peacock*'s defeat of the British warship *Epervier* in the Atlantic.

12 June
Maryland
Captain Samuel Miller leads a small battalion of Marines from Washington, D.C., to reinforce American units guarding the approaches to the capital along the Patuxent River.

26 June
Maryland
Marines assist Captain Joshua Barney's gunboat fleet in driving off a British attack in the Patuxent River.

28 June
Atlantic
Marines play a conspicuous role in sloop *Wasp*'s victory over the British warship *Reindeer*, repelling an attempt to board and then sweeping the enemy decks with musket fire as American sailors counterattacked onto the British ship.

30 June
Manpower
The strength of the Marine Corps on active duty is 11 officers and 637 enlisted.

11 July
Atlantic
Brig *Rattlesnake* and her Marines are defeated and captured by the British frigate *Leander* in the Atlantic Ocean.

4 August
Lake Huron
Marines assist Lieutenant Colonel George Croghan's Army force in a landing against the British and Indians holding Fort Mackinac on Lake Huron. The Americans are forced to withdraw after significant losses.

24 August
Bladensburg
Captain Samuel Miller's force of 103 Marines and Barney's sailors beat back three British assaults during the closing stages of the Battle of Bladensburg in Maryland. The British subsequently occupy and burn Washington, D.C.

1 September
Virginia
Marines and sailors at White House, Virginia, fire artillery at British warships withdrawing down the Potomac River.

Top: *"Shipbuilding at Sackett's Harbor," Col Charles Waterhouse, USMCR (Ret), Marine Corps Art Collection*

Right: *"USS* Essex *vs HMS* Cherub *and HMS* Phoebe,*" Marine Corps Art Collection*

Opposite, top: "Wasp *vs* Reindeer,*" John Clymer, Marine Corps Art Collection*

Opposite, bottom: *"Christmas Day, 1814," Col Charles Waterhouse, USMCR (Ret), Marine Corps Art Collection*

1 September
Atlantic
Wasp and her Marines sink the British sloop *Avon* in the Atlantic Ocean.

16 September
New Orleans
Marines and soldiers form the landing party that wipes out the pirate stronghold on Grand Terre Island at the mouth of the Mississippi River.

15 December
New Orleans
Marines serve aboard Navy Lieutenant Thomas Catesby Jones's small squadron of gunboats, which battle a larger British fleet of small craft and delay the enemy's advance on New Orleans.

22 December
Civil Support
Marines from the Portsmouth Barracks and *Congress* fight fires in Portsmouth, New Hampshire.

23 December
New Orleans
Marines aboard the schooner *Carolina* assist in the bombardment of the British camp a few miles below New Orleans, while a company of Marines participate in a night attack on the British force by elements of General Andrew Jackson's army.

24 December
War of 1812
The Treaty of Ghent is signed in Europe to bring the War of 1812 to an end. News of the peace is not received in the U.S. until much later.

27 December
New Orleans
Carolina duels with British shore batteries and is eventually sunk.

28 December
New Orleans
Marines with Andrew Jackson help repel a British probing attack against the defensive works along the Rodriguez Canal below New Orleans.

1815

8 January
New Orleans
Marines participate in Andrew Jackson's repulse of the British assault on his lines. The enemy lose more than 2,000 soldiers, while American forces suffer only 13 casualties.

15 January
New York
In a battle against a British squadron off Long Island, *President* and her Marines cripple the frigate *Endymion*, but suffer enough damage that they are forced to surrender to three other enemy frigates.

Opposite: *A re-created painting of the fifth Commandant, whose official portrait shows him as a much older man. Archibald Henderson took over leadership of the Marine Corps at 37 and served in that billet for 38 years. ("Archibald Henderson," Col Avery Chenoweth, USMCR (Ret), Marine Corps Art Collection)*

20 February
Atlantic
Marines on *Constitution* participate in her victory over the British sloops *Cyane* and *Levant* near Madeira Island.

3 March
Barbary Wars
President Madison signs legislation authorizing force against Algiers.

23 March
Atlantic
Sloop *Hornet* and her Marines defeat the British brig *Penguin* off Tristan d'Acunha.

17 June
Barbary Wars
Marines in Commodore Stephen Decatur's squadron assist in the defeat of the Algerian frigate *Mashuda*.

30 June
Barbary Wars
A treaty of peace is concluded with Algiers.

Manpower
The strength of the Marine Corps on active duty is eight officers and 680 enlisted.

1816

30 June
Manpower
The strength of the Marine Corps on active duty is 21 officers and 451 enlisted.

Top: *"Repulse of the Highlanders, New Orleans," Col Charles Waterhouse, USMCR (Ret), Marine Corps Art Collection*

Right: *"Defeat of the British Army at New Orleans," Heathe Laclotte, Marine Corps Art Collection*

27 July
Florida
Marines assist the crews of two gunboats in capturing and destroying a fort on the Apalachicola River in Florida, built by Indians and runaway slaves who had turned to piracy.

1817

3 March
Manpower
Congress passes the Peace Establishment Act, which sets the authorized strength of the Marine Corps at 50 officers and 942 enlisted.

30 June
Manpower
The strength of the Marine Corps on active duty is 14 officers and 652 enlisted.

23 December
Florida
Marine detachments from six Navy ships participate in a joint operation with the Army to seize Amelia Island, Florida, from pirates.

1818

30 June
Manpower
The strength of the Marine Corps on active duty is 24 officers and 536 enlisted.

19 August
Oregon
Sergeant McFadian and his Marines from the sloop *Ontario* help raise the flag along the Columbia River to strengthen the U.S. claim to the Oregon Territory.

1 September
Commandants
Lieutenant Colonel Commandant Franklin Wharton dies in office. Brevet Major Samuel Miller takes over as acting Commandant.

16 September
Commandants
Brevet Major Archibald Henderson takes over as acting Commandant.

1819

3 March
Commandants
Brevet Major Anthony Gale is appointed Lieutenant Colonel Commandant. He is the fourth Commandant of the Marine Corps.

30 June
Manpower
The strength of the Marine Corps on active duty is 21 officers and 664 enlisted.

1820

5–12 April
Slavery Suppression
Marines participate in the capture of seven slave-trading ships by the corvette *Cyane* off the coast of Africa.

30 June
Manpower
The strength of the Marine Corps on active duty is 19 officers and 552 enlisted.

Left: *On 14 November 1824, 15 Marines attack a Spanish fort in Puerto Rico. Its garrison abandons it, leaving behind two loaded 18-pound cannon. ("Foray Into Fajardo Bay," Col Charles Waterhouse, USMCR (Ret), Marine Corps Art Collection)*

Opposite: *"U.S. Marine, 1825," C. Floyd, Marine Corps Art Collection*

30 August
Commandants
Lieutenant Colonel Commandant Gale is arrested for trial by court-martial, and Brevet Major Samuel Miller becomes acting Commandant.

16 October
Commandants
A general court-martial convicts Gale of conduct unbecoming an officer for his public drunkenness, and he is dismissed from the Corps on this date.

1821

2 January
Commandants
President Monroe appoints Brevet Major Archibald Henderson to be the Lieutenant Colonel Commandant. He is the fifth Commandant of the Marine Corps.

30 June
Manpower
The strength of the Marine Corps on active duty is 35 officers and 844 enlisted.

16 October
Cuba
Marines participate in the capture of five pirate ships by the brig *Enterprise* off Cuba.

21 December
Cuba
Enterprise and her Marines seize a pirate schooner off Cuba.

1822

8 March
Cuba
Marines and sailors from *Enterprise* land at Cape Antonio, Cuba, to pursue pirates.

June
Caribbean
Marines assist in the capture of two pirate schooners, *Shark* and *Grampus*, in the West Indies.

30 June
Manpower
The strength of the Marine Corps on active duty is 23 officers and 708 enlisted.

16 August
Caribbean
Grampus and her Marines engage the pirate brig *Palmyra* in the West Indies.

9 November
Cuba
Marines participate in the fight between schooner *Alligator* and several pirate schooners in the harbor of Matanzas, Cuba.

1823

1 February
Florida
The Secretary of the Navy orders the establishment of a naval station and a Marine barracks at Key West, Florida, to serve as a base for operations against Caribbean pirates.

8 April
Cuba
Marines and sailors from *Peacock* land near Havana, Cuba, to deal with pirates.

30 June
Manpower
The strength of the Marine Corps on active duty is 2c officers and 681 enlisted.

22 July
Cuba
Marines and sailors go ashore from the schooners *Greyhound* and *Beagle* near Cape Cruz, Cuba, and engage pirates.

1824

12 March
Civil Support
Marines from the Boston Navy Yard subdue a riot at the state prison in Boston, Massachusetts.

30 June
Manpower
The strength of the Marine Corps on active duty is 50 officers and 890 enlisted.

14 November
Puerto Rico
Following the detention of a Navy officer in Puerto Rico, Commodore David Porter sends Marines ashore. They capture the local fort without a shot, spike the guns, and force an apology from the local officials.

1825

12 February
Virgin Islands
Grampus sends Marines and sailors ashore to fight a fire in St. Thomas, Virgin Islands.

4 March
Puerto Rico
Marines participate in the action between *Grampus* and a pirate sloop off Puerto Rico.

30 June
Manpower
The strength of the Marine Corps on active duty is 35 officers and 746 enlisted.

1826

1 May
Uniforms
The Mameluke hilt is prescribed for Marine officers' swords.

30 June
Manpower
The strength of the Marine Corps on active duty is 39 officers and 796 enlisted.

Left: *In 1823, Archibald Henderson, the fifth commandant, married Anne Maria Casenove, with a reception on the lawn of the Commandant's House. ("LtCol Commandant Henderson Takes a Wife," Col Charles Waterhouse, USMCR (Ret), Marine Corps Art Collection)*

Opposite: *Mameluke sword, 1826. (Eric Long)*

1827

30 June
Manpower
The strength of the Marine Corps on active duty is 43 officers and 903 enlisted.

15–16 October
Mediterranean
Schooner *Porpoise* and her Marines fight Greek pirates in the Aegean Sea.

1 November
Mediterranean
Marines and sailors from sloop *Warren* land and burn the pirate town of Miconi in the Cyclades Islands near Greece.

7 November
Mediterranean
Warren's Marines and sailors go ashore at Andros, Greece, to capture pirate ships.

1828

30 June
Manpower
The strength of the Marine Corps on active duty is 40 officers and 892 enlisted.

1829

20 February
Marine Barracks 8th and I
Center House, the location of Headquarters Marine Corps, burns, resulting in the destruction of many official records.

30 June
Manpower
The strength of the Marine Corps on active duty is 43 officers and 852 enlisted.

1830

5 June
Slavery Suppression
Marines participate in the capture of the slave-trader *Fenix* by the *Grampus* off Haiti.

30 June
Manpower
The strength of the Marine Corps on active duty is 37 officers and 854 enlisted.

1831

30 June
Manpower
The strength of the Marine Corps on active duty is 35 officers and 780 enlisted.

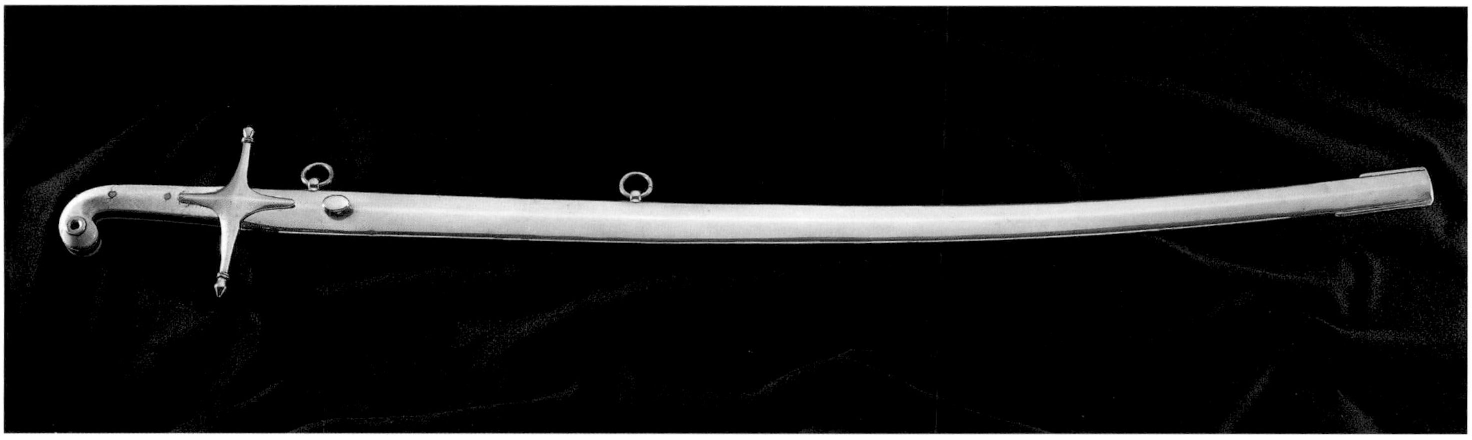

1832

1 January
Falklands
Marines and sailors from sloop *Lexington* go ashore in the Falklands to rescue three American commercial ships detained by the Argentinians in a dispute over ownership of the islands.

7 February
Sumatra
Frigate *Potomac* lands 250 Marines and sailors at Quallah Battoo, Sumatra. In retaliation for pirate attacks on American shipping, the force captures pirate forts and burns the town.

30 June
Manpower
The strength of the Marine Corps on active duty is 38 officers and 860 enlisted.

1833

31 March
Civil Support
Marines guard the Treasury Building in Washington, D.C., after it is partially destroyed by fire.

10 April
Uniforms
President Andrew Jackson orders that green and buff replace blue and scarlet as the colors of the Marine Corps uniform.

30 June
Manpower
The strength of the Marine Corps on active duty is 43 officers and 853 enlisted.

31 October
Argentina
Marines and sailors from a U.S. Navy squadron go ashore to protect American lives and property in Buenos Aires, Argentina.

1834

30 June
Department of the Navy
Congress passes "An Act for the Better Organization of the United States Marine Corps." The key provision states that Marines were under naval jurisdiction unless detached by the President for service with the Army.

30 June
Manpower
The strength of the Marine Corps on active duty is 46 officers and 869 enlisted.

1835

30 June
Manpower
The strength of the Marine Corps on active duty is 68 officers and 1,349 enlisted.

19 July
Civil Support
During a large fire in New York City, Marines from the Brooklyn Navy Yard deploy to prevent looting.

10 December
Peru
Four Marines from the frigate *Brandywine* go ashore in Peru and proceed to Lima to protect the American consulate. The remainder of the Marine

Left: *Marines and sailors destroy a pirate stronghold in Sumatra in 1832. ("Storming of Quallah Battoo," Col Charles Waterhouse, USMCR (Ret), Marine Corps Art Collection)*

Opposite: *The U.S. Marines replace their traditional blue uniforms with Continental Marine green in April 1833. ("Return to Green," Col Charles Waterhouse, USMCR (Ret), Marine Corps Art Collection)*

detachment would join them on 17 December. The force would return to its ship on 24 January.

24 December
Seminole War
Indians resisting relocation west of the Mississippi massacre an Army column departing Fort Brooke, Tampa Bay, Florida. This marks the start of the Second Seminole War.

1836

22 January
Seminole War
Marines from *Constellation* and sloop *St. Louis* reinforce Fort Brooke, Florida, against expected Seminole attack.

17 March
Seminole War
Marines and sailors from sloop *Vandalia* start a boat expedition up the Manatee River, Florida, and return on 28 March.

22 March
Seminole War
Marines and soldiers from Fort Brooke launch an operation that results in several skirmishes with the Seminoles. They return to Fort Brooke on 4 April.

31 March
Seminole War
Marines and sailors from *Vandalia* join Army troops in an expedition up the Myacca River, returning to Tampa Bay on 27 April.

21 May
Seminole War
President Jackson accepts Colonel Commandant Henderson's offer of a Marine regiment to assist in the fighting in Florida.

24 May
Seminole War
Commandant Henderson reports to the War Department in compliance with a General Order directing "all the disposable force on shore . . . to proceed to Alabama."

2 June
Seminole War
Commandant Henderson and the 1st Battalion of Marines depart Fort Monroe, Virginia, by steamer for the Georgia coast.

23 June
Seminole War
After a march of 224 miles in 14 days, Henderson's outfit arrives at Columbus, Georgia. The Creek Indians in that region also now are resisting relocation to the western United States.

30 June
Manpower
The strength of the Marine Corps on active duty is 43 officers and 1,298 enlisted.

1 July
Seminole War
The 2d Battalion of Marines under Lieutenant Colonel William H. Freeman joins Henderson's command near Columbus, Georgia. The combined force has been mobilized from Navy yard guards and constitutes more than half the total strength of the Corps.

August
Seminole War
The Creek Indians end their resistance and join with the Marines. Henderson shifts his force to Fort Brooke, Florida.

13 October
Seminole War
Marines and sailors from *Vandalia* launch a boat expedition from Key West to Cape Florida and then up the Miami River, returning to the ship on 9 December.

21 November
Seminole War
Allied Creek Indians and Marines defeat a group of Seminoles at Wahoo Swamp, Florida.

1837

3 January
Seminole War
Henderson and his Marines depart Fort Brooke with an Army expedition that remains in the field until 18 May.

8 January
Seminole War
The Army of the South reorganizes itself into two brigades, with Colonel Henderson commanding the Second Brigade (composed of his Marine regiment, the Army's Fourth Infantry Regiment, a regiment of Georgia volunteers, a battalion of Creek Indians, and an artillery regiment).

27 January
Seminole War
Henderson's Brigade meets a large Seminole force in position on the opposite bank of the Hatchee-Lustee River. The Americans cross over single-log bridges and swim the river to launch an attack, and the enemy disperses into a swamp.

6 March
Seminole War
The Seminole chiefs sign an agreement to end the war. They will eventually breach the truce and resume fighting.

23 May
Seminole War
Commandant Henderson and part of his staff depart for Washington, leaving Lieutenant Colonel Samuel Miller as the senior Marine in the field in Florida.

30 June
Manpower
The strength of the Marine Corps on active duty is 37 officers and 1,524 enlisted.

1838

23 July
Seminole War
The remaining Marines serving with the Army in Florida return to Washington, D.C. Marines still serve with the Navy in Florida, primarily with the "Mosquito Fleet" composed of small boats and canoes for patrolling the interior waterways. This force conducts active operations against the Seminoles for the next four years.

Left: *The Seminoles and the swampy lands of Florida prove to be tough adversaries for the Marines in the mid-1830s. ("Marines Battle Seminoles," John Clymer, Marine Corps Art Collection)*

Opposite: *The mission of suppressing the slave trade took the Navy and Marine Corps to Africa on many occasions before the U.S. Civil War. ("Marines and Liberians," Tom Lovell, Marine Corps Art Collection)*

19 August
Wilkes Expedition
Marines sail from New York on board sloops *Vincennes* and *Peacock* and brig *Porpoise* with the Wilkes Expedition. The primary objective is exploration of Antarctica's coastline, but the squadron also conducts many scientific studies and charts the coasts and waters of south Pacific islands and the Pacific rim of North America.

1839

2 January
Sumatra
Marines land from frigate *Columbia* and sloop *John Adams* to seize forts and burn a town in Sumatra in retribution for harassment of American commercial shipping.

30 June
Manpower
The strength of the Marine Corps on active duty is 34 officers and 916 enlisted.

1840

16 April
Seminole War
Marines and sailors from schooner *Otsego* land on the east coast of Florida and fight a three-hour battle with Seminoles.

30 June
Manpower
The strength of the Marine Corps on active duty is 46 officers and 1,223 enlisted.

4 July
Uniforms
Commandant Henderson orders a change in the colors of the Marine uniform from green to blue with scarlet facings.

12 July
Wilkes Expedition
Marines and sailors of the Wilkes Expedition seize and burn a village in the Fiji Islands in retaliation for an attack on a small party making scientific observations.

26 July
Wilkes Expedition
Following the murder of two Navy officers, the Wilkes Expedition destroys two more Fijian towns.

1841

25 February
Wilkes Expedition
Marines and sailors of the Wilkes Expedition land on Upolu, Samoa, and burn three villages in response to the murder of an American seaman.

6 April
Wilkes Expedition
Marines searching for a sailor missing from the Wilkes Expedition meet opposition from the islanders and destroy two towns in the Gilberts.

30 June
Manpower
The strength of the Marine Corps on active duty is 44 officers and 1,156 enlisted.

1842

20 June
Seminole War
The Secretary of the Navy disbands the Florida Squadron and orders its Marines and sailors to Norfolk, Virginia.

30 June
Manpower
The strength of the Marine Corps on active duty is 46 officers and 1,243 enlisted.

9 August
Slavery Suppression
The United States and Great Britain sign a treaty requiring both nations to maintain warships off the coast of Africa to suppress the slave trade.

14 August
Seminole War
The Second Seminole War is terminated officially.

21 October
California
Under the mistaken belief that war has begun with Mexico, Marines and sailors from *United States* and *Cyane* seize Monterey, California. They withdraw when they find out there is no war.

1843

6 March
Commandants
Commandant Henderson is awarded the brevet rank of brigadier general as of 27 January 1837 for his service against the Seminoles.

30 June
Manpower
The strength of the Marine Corps on active duty is 43 officers and 1,041 enlisted.

29 November
Slavery Suppression
Commodore Matthew Perry lands with 75 Marines and sailors in Liberia, to root out the slave trade and piracy in the area.

14 December
Slavery Suppression
Following a dispute with slave traders, Perry's Marines burn a town in the Ivory Coast.

1844

18 June
China
Marines go ashore from *St. Louis* to protect Americans following a riot in Canton, China. The force remains there until 20 July.

30 June
Manpower
The strength of the Marine Corps on active duty is 40 officers and 1,046 enlisted.

BY SEA AND BY LAND

1845–1882

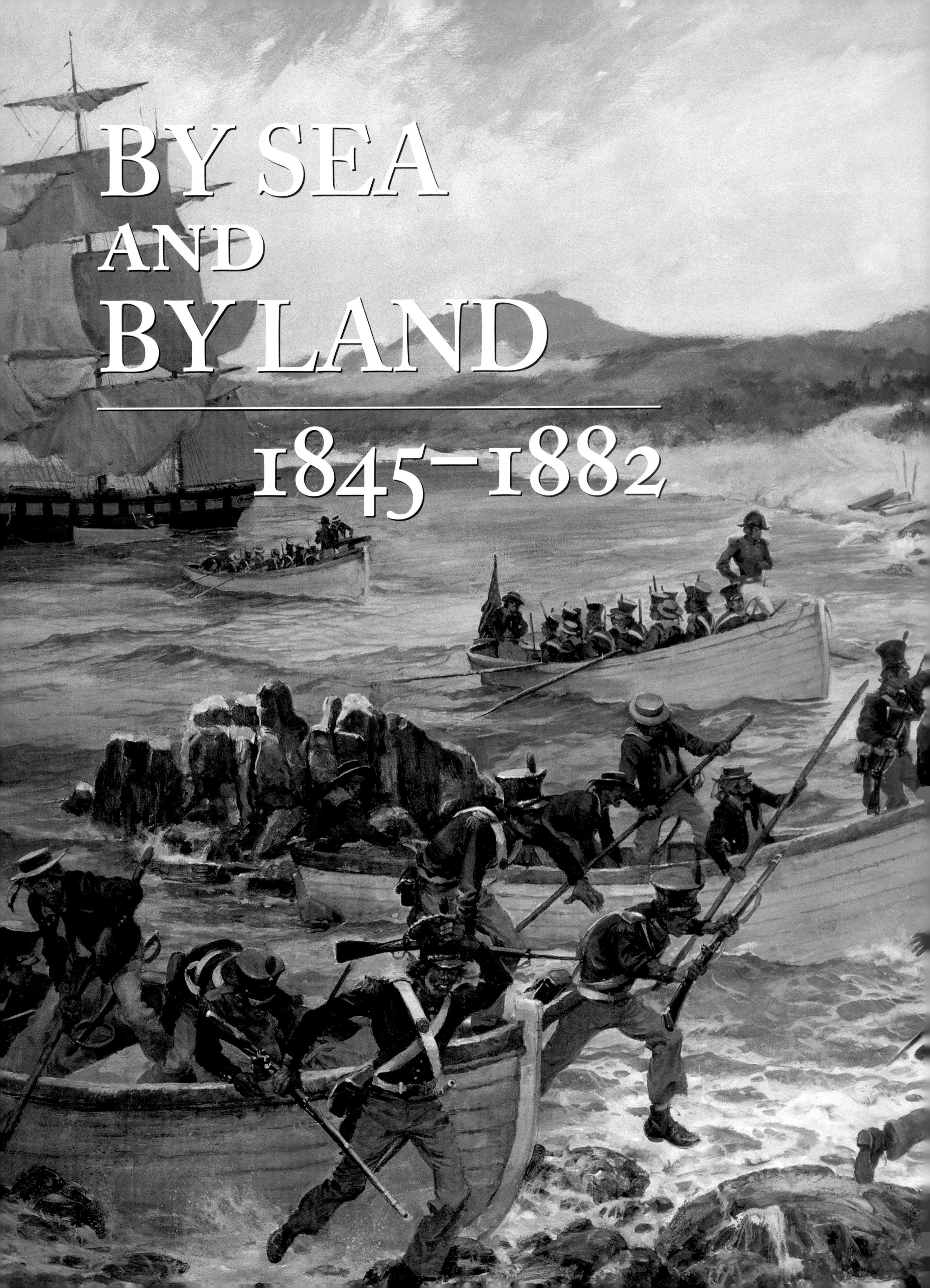

BY SEA AND BY LAND

1845–1882

The middle of the nineteenth century began well enough for the Marine Corps. In a classic campaign that would meet the late-twentieth-century definition of operational maneuver from the sea, a handful of ships' detachments, reinforced by sailors and transported by sea, secured the vast reaches of California for the United States during the opening days of the War with Mexico. The feat was all the more remarkable because it took place on the opposite side of the continent from the locus of U.S. strength east of the Mississippi River. Mexico, with no similar naval forces, was powerless to reinforce or defend its California territory. Elements of the U.S. Navy and Marine Corps performed equally valuable service striking both coasts of Mexico itself. Commandant Henderson also managed to scrape together a battalion of Marines for deployment with the American Army moving on Mexico City. The small unit received a potentially important role in the assault on the outer defenses of the enemy capital, but its performance was mixed. Nevertheless, the Corps could justifiably add the "halls of Montezuma" to its battle honors.

A few bold individuals seemed to play a large part in success on the battlefield. Lieutenant Archibald Gillespie carried out a secret mission for the president of the United States early in the California campaign, then took command of local volunteers on horseback to help seal the victory. Following the confused seizure of Chapultepec Castle, Captain George Terrett led a part of his company in an aggressive pursuit that captured one of the portals into Mexico City itself.

Just over a decade later, the United States careened into the Civil War. In many respects, this massive conflict brought the U.S. Army to maturity. After four years of campaigning, the nation's ground force was adept at training, maneuvering, supplying, and fighting armies of hundreds of thousands of men. It was a far cry from the earlier amateurish, problem-plagued efforts against Great Britain. The U.S. Navy also grew exponentially and evolved from its single-ship success of previous wars to master the art of complex fleet operations. The Marine Corps, by contrast, played by far its most limited role in any of the nation's major conflicts. It also experienced almost no expansion, barely doubling its size to just over 3,000 men.

Like the opening operations in the War with Mexico, the lead up to the Civil War seemed to presage good things for the Corps. When an anti-slavery guerrilla fighter and terrorist named John Brown captured a government arsenal and attempted to foment rebellion in 1859, it was a body of Marines that beat the U.S. Army to the scene and brought the crisis to a swift end. But when a third of the Corps' officers (20 of 63), including many of the best, went south to join the Confederacy, the service never quite recovered, perhaps because it was simply too small to handle such a severe loss. The Corps underwent a small

Pages 62–63: *Most Marines fought the Mexican War as small detachments on Navy warships, executing a series of successful amphibious landings on both coasts of Mexico and along the coast of California. ("Landing at Monterrey," Col Charles Waterhouse, USMCR (Ret), Marine Corps Art Collection)*

Right: *A Civil War Marine detachment drills aboard USS* Kearsarge. *(National Archives)*

and rapid expansion at the beginning of the war, which allowed it to field a battalion for the First Battle of Bull Run in 1861. But almost the entire force had only a few weeks of military service under its belt when it went into battle. The number of veterans was too few and the time too short to provide enough training. Although the Marine battalion performed no worse than the rest of the hastily raised Union Army, the debacle brought an end to Marine participation in the extended land campaigns that would play the most prominent part in defeating the Confederacy.

There would be plenty of opportunity for amphibious operations in support of the Navy's vital campaign to blockade the South. But here the Corps seemed to lack the imagination and drive to build a force capable of filling this role. Instead, U.S. Army units worked with the Navy to capture coastal forts and ports. In the rare instances when Marines participated in amphibious landings, the outcome was often failure. An attempted night assault on Fort Sumter in 1863 met defeat, while an attack against Fort Fisher in 1865 turned into a fiasco.

There were some bright spots for the Corps, but in an unusual mission. Most Marines deployed on ship, but not primarily in their traditional role as marksmen in the fighting tops. Instead, they more often manned guns in the main batteries. In this capacity, they participated in some of the Navy's greatest victories, such as the assault on Mobile Bay in 1864 and *Kearsarge*'s sinking of Confederate raider *Alabama*. In this type of action, the heroism and leadership of Marine enlisted men came to the fore for the first time in the history of the Corps. It was Marine NCOs, such as Corporal John Mackie and Sergeant Miles Oviatt, who affected the course of battles and earned lasting fame.

In the peaceful years before and after the Civil War, Marine detachments kept busy with the fleet. As U.S. economic power grew and fostered increasing trade around the globe, so did the role of naval forces in protecting commerce, aiding diplomacy, and maintaining respect for the U.S. flag and American citizens abroad. During the mid-1800s, Marines went ashore in a host of countries they would come to know much more intimately in the next century. Small-scale interventions in China, Japan, Korea, Nicaragua, Okinawa, Panama, and elsewhere demonstrated the ability of small groups of Marines to handle brush-fire contingencies far from the United States and any hope of reinforcement. The Corps still lacked many attributes of professionalism, such as written doctrine, advanced schooling, and formal training programs, but reliance on the initiative and daring of the lieutenants and sergeants commanding ships' detachments perhaps emphasized small-unit leadership to a degree not present in the other services. This would become another of the hallmarks of the Corps.

BY SEA AND BY LAND

1845–1882

1845

30 June
Manpower
The strength of the Marine Corps on active duty is 42 officers and 986 enlisted.

18 October
California
Lieutenant Archibald H. Gillespie receives orders from the President to prepare for a mission to California.

30 November
Slavery Suppression
Marines on sloop *Yorktown* help capture a slave ship off Africa.

1846

17 April
California
Lieutenant Gillespie arrives in Monterey, California, and delivers secret instructions to the American consul.

7 May
California
Gillespie completes a hazardous journey through dangerous country and contacts army Captain John C. Fremont and his expedition near Klamath Lake, Oregon.

8 May
Texas
Marines and sailors from the Home Squadron occupy Port Isabel, Texas, to defend it against a possible Mexican invasion.

12 May
Mexican War
The United States formally declares war on Mexico.

18 May
Mexico
Marines and sailors from frigates *Cumberland* and *Potomac* boat up the Rio Grande and assist Army troops in establishing a position on the south side of the river. These are the first U.S. forces to invade Mexico.

24 May
Mexico
Marines on board sloop *St. Mary's* participate in the shelling of Tampico, Mexico.

30 June
Manpower
The strength of the Marine Corps on active duty is 41 officers and 1,126 enlisted.

Opposite: *"Marine of 1846," Col Charles Waterhouse, USMCR (Ret) Marine Corps Art Collection)*

Right: *"Horse Marines," Col Charles Waterhouse, USMCR (Ret), Marine Corps Art Collection*

Below: *Savannah's* *Marines served on horse for part of the California campaign. ("Fauntleroy's Dragoons," Col Charles Waterhouse, USMCR (Ret), Marine Corps Art Collection)*

7 July
California
Marines and sailors under Commodore Sloat land at Monterey, California, and occupy the town. California is proclaimed a part of the United States.

9 July
California
Marines and sailors from sloop *Portsmouth* land and occupy Yerba Buena (San Francisco) and Sonoma, California.

29 July
California
Sloop *Cyane* puts Marines and sailors ashore to seize San Diego, California.

4 August
California
Marines and sailors from frigate *Congress* take possession of Santa Barbara, California.

MAJOR ARCHIBALD GILLESPIE

Archibald H. Gillespie earned his commission in the Marine Corps from the ranks. Born in New York in 1812, he enlisted in June 1830. The tall, dark-haired young man evidently proved to be a capable and resourceful Marine, since he was promoted to sergeant less than two years later and became a lieutenant just a few months after that. His early tours were relatively uneventful. He commanded Marine detachments on sloops in the Pacific, ran a barracks for a time, and went to sea again on board the ship of the line *North Carolina* in the Pacific. Promoted to first lieutenant in 1838, he went to Headquarters Marine Corps for a time, then to barracks duty in Pensacola, Florida, and later in Virginia. Perhaps his most interesting assignment came in 1843, when he took over the Marine detachment on the frigate *Brandywine*. As part of her two-year voyage around the Orient, she delivered the first American commissioner to China.

Shortly after his return to the States, despite having requested a quiet tour at a barracks for health reasons, he was directed to report to the Secretary of the Navy. Within days, on 30 October 1845, he was ushered into a meeting with President James Polk. The President explained that the Marine lieutenant was to carry out an important mission in California. Polk gave Gillespie a letter to Thomas Larkin, the American consul in California, in which Polk expressed "entire confidence" in the Marine officer and appointed him a "confidential agent" of the President. Larkin's mission was to convince California to seek annexation from the United Sates. Gillespie's qualifications for this special duty appear to have stemmed from his long experience in the Pacific and his knowledge

Left: *During Gillespie's brief stay with Fremont, the American force had to fight off a local Indian tribe. ("Gillespie and Fremont at Klamath Lake," Col Charles Waterhouse, USMCR (Ret), Marine Corps Art Collection)*

Opposite: *"Archibald Gillespie: Messenger of Destiny," Col Charles Waterhouse, USMCR (Ret), Marine Corps Art Collection*

of the Spanish language acquired during his time in Pensacola. The Secretary of State also provided a letter of introduction to explorer John C. Fremont, who then was operating along the west coast of the continent. Fremont's father-in-law, Senator Thomas Hart Benton, entrusted a packet of family letters to the Marine.

Given the lack of cross-continental transport, Gillespie would have to go via Mexico, even though the United States was on the verge of war with that nation. He assumed the guise of a civilian merchant, sailed for Vera Cruz, and memorized and then destroyed the dispatch to Larkin. He made it by wagon to Mexico City and was waylaid there by a military coup. After more than a month's delay, he made his way overland to the Pacific coast, where he hitched a ride on a Navy sloop sailing for Hawaii (apparently to allay any Mexican suspicions). He finally arrived in Monterey, California, on 17 April 1846, and delivered his verbal message to Larkin. It was much tougher to make contact with Fremont, but Gillespie finally tracked him down near the Klamath River in the dangerous wilderness of northern California on 9 May.

By June, Fremont had recruited local Californians into a mounted battalion and made Gillespie his adjutant. Although Fremont was a brevet captain in the army engineers, Gillespie believed that the explorer had no experience as a line officer and that his own tactical knowledge would make all the difference in the subsequent campaign. His finest hour came in the battle at San Pascual in December, where he was wounded by lance thrusts, but managed to fire an artillery piece and thus help drive off the enemy.

Already a brevet captain for his early efforts in California, the Marine Corps made him a brevet major in July 1848 for his actions at San Pascual. He subsequently commanded various barracks detachments, but his service was interrupted by continuing poor health. Shortly

after Gillespie was assigned to a shipboard detachment in 1854, the ship's captain charged him with swindling money. The major resigned rather than go through the ordeal of a court-martial. He retired to California and held various small government jobs until his death in 1873.

Left: *"Fremont Enters Monterey," Col Charles Waterhouse, USMCR (Ret), Marine Corps Art Collection*

7 August
Mexico
A landing force of Marines and sailors in boats fails in an assault against Alvarado, Mexico, due to strong river currents and heavy enemy fire.

13 August
California
Marines and sailors, reinforced by volunteers, march into Los Angeles, California.

7 October
California
Frigate *Savannah*'s Marines reinforce sailors and a volunteer outfit under Gillespie. The combined force captures San Pedro, California.

8–9 October
California
Marines participate in the overland movement from San Pedro to retake Los Angeles, but the small expedition retires to San Pedro and its ships after small skirmishes.

23–26 October
Mexico
Commodore Matthew C. Perry uses Marines and sailors from his squadron to seize Frontera, Mexico, and then conduct a raid 70 miles up the Tabasco River to briefly capture the town of San Juan Bautista.

27 October
California
Marines from Commodore Stockton's squadron assist in retaking San Pedro. The town had been lost to Californians revolting against the small U.S. forces trying to hold the vast territory.

14 November
Mexico
Perry's Marines and sailors capture Tampico, Mexico.

19 November
Mexico
Marine Captain Alvin Edson leads 20 Marines and 12 sailors 80 miles upriver from Tampico to destroy enemy supplies.

6 December
California
Gillespie is wounded in the battle of San Pascual, California, in which a body of Californians engage Kearney's force of soldiers and volunteers.

11 December
California
Lieutenant Jacob Zeilin and Marines and sailors of Stockton's squadron march to the relief of Kearney.

21 December
Mexico
Perry sends ashore his ships detachments and sailors to raid the port of Carmen, Mexico.

29 December
California
Stockton leads a force of 600 men overland against Los Angeles, with the Marines of his squadron organized as a separate company under Zeilin.

1847

2 January
California
Captain Ward Marston and the Marines of sloop *Dale* defeat a force of Californians at Santa Clara.

8 January
California
Stockton's force defeats Californians in the Battle of San Gabriel.

Top: *Gillespie fights with Kearney's force against mounted Californians, resulting in a draw. ("San Pascual," Col Charles Waterhouse, USMCR (Ret), Marine Corps Art Collection)*

Right: *"Marston at Santa Clara," Col Charles Waterhouse, USMCR (Ret), Marine Corps Art Collection*

Left: *Marines on the way to La Mesa in January 1847. ("Rest Stop at Las Flores," Col Charles Waterhouse, USMCR (Ret), Marine Corps Art Collection)*

Below: *Marines participate in Stockton's victory on 8 January 1847. ("Bayonets at San Gabriel," Col Charles Waterhouse, USMCR (Ret), Marine Corps Art Collection)*

9 January
California
Marines participate in Stockton's victory over the Californians in the Battle of La Mesa.

10 January
California
Stockton retakes Los Angeles without fighting.

9 March
Mexico
The ships detachments of Connor's squadron form a battalion that lands at Vera Cruz, Mexico, as part of Brigadier General William Worth's division of General Winfield Scott's army. The Marines participate in the siege of the city, which surrenders on 29 March.

Right: *Lt Jacob Zeilin, a future Commandant, leads Marines against the Californians. ("Final Skirmish at La Mesa," Jaroslav Gebr, Marine Corps Art Collection)*

Below: *Marines and sailors go ashore in longboats. ("Landing at Veracruz," Marine Corps Art Collection)*

30 March
Mexico
Marines and sailors from sloop *Portsmouth* land and occupy San Jose, Mexico.

30 March
Manpower
Congress authorizes an increase in the Corps of 12 officers and 1,000 enlisted.

3 April
Mexico
Portsmouth's ships detachments and sailors go ashore and take San Lycas, Mexico.

13 April
Mexico
Marines from *Portsmouth* help capture La Paz, Mexico.

18 April
Mexico
Commodore Perry forms his squadron Marines into a battalion under Captain Edson, and they participate in the seizure of three forts and the town of Tuxpan, Mexico.

15 May
Mexico
Steamer *Mississippi*'s Marines take part in the landing at, and capture of, Carmen, Mexico.

21 May
Force Structure
The Secretary of the Navy directs the Corps to form a regiment for service with Scott's army in Mexico.

14 June
Mexico
Captain Edson's battalion assists Perry's landing brigade in moving up the Tabasco River and seizing San Juan Bautista, Mexico.

24 June
Mexico
Marines garrisoning Tabasco, Mexico, repel attacks on the town.

30 June
Mexico
Marines and sailors from Tabasco launch a spoiling attack against Mexican forces at nearby Tamultay and drive off the enemy.
Manpower
The strength of the Marine Corps on active duty is 75 officers and 1,757 enlisted.

6 August
Mexico
Lieutenant Colonel Samuel Watson's Marine battalion joins Scott's army at Puebla, Mexico.

13 September
Mexico
Watson's Marines participate in the battle at Chapultepec on the edge of Mexico City.

1 October
Mexico
Dale's Marines and sailors drive Mexican forces out of Muleje, Mexico.

20 October
Mexico
Marines and sailors from *Portsmouth* and *Congress* land and temporarily seize Guaymas, Mexico.

Left: *This engraving depicts the American expeditionary force after coming ashore for the battle at Veracruz in March 1847. More than 200 Marines land in the initial waves with the soldiers. ("The Battle of Veracruz," H. Bilings, Marine Corps Art Collection)*

Right: *This contemporary painting of one of Commodore Perry's ships was destroyed in the 11 September 2001 attack on the Pentagon. ("U.S. Steam Frigate* Mississippi,*" Lt H. Walke, USN, Marine Corps Art Collection)*

Below: *"Naval Expedition Ascending the Tabasco River at the Devil's Bend," Lt H. Walke, USN, Marine Corps Art Collection*

11 November
Mexico
A show of force by 600 Marines and sailors from *Congress*, *Cyane*, and razee *Independence* causes Mexican army to abandon Mazatlan.

17 November
Mexico
A Marine and Navy landing force of 65 men from *Dale* drives 300 Mexican soldiers out of Guaymas.

19–21 November
Mexico
The Marine detachments of *Congress*, *Cyane*, and *Independence* occupy San Jose in Lower California and hold the mission complex against two night assaults by a superior force.

13 December
Mexico
A Marine night patrol surprises and defeats a Mexican force at Palos Prietos, outside Mazatlan.

1848

22 January
Mexico
The Marines in the San Jose mission are besieged by Mexican soldiers, but hold on until relieved by naval forces on 15 February.

30 January
Mexico
Marines and sailors from *Dale* make a night landing and overland approach followed by a dawn attack to defeat a Mexican force at Cochori, near Guaymas.

2 February
Mexican War
The Treaty of Guadalupe Hidalgo ends the Mexican War, though some forces in the field will not learn of it for several weeks.

13 February
Mexico
Dale's Marine detachment, reinforced by sailors, marches inland from Guaymas and captures Bocachicacampa after a small skirmish.

THE EAGLE, GLOBE, AND ANCHOR

Marines have worn a distinguishing emblem on their uniforms from the very beginning. Continental Marines wore a silver or pewter "foul anchor" (one in which a chain is twisted around the anchor). The first recorded mention of an official device for U.S. Marines came in 1804, when it consisted of a brass eagle on a square plate. By the War of 1812, this had become a more elaborate octagonal brass plate bearing an eagle, foul anchor, drums, and a flag. Thus, two of the three critical elements of the final Marine emblem were joined together in the early years of the Corps.

During the middle of the 19th century, the symbol changed several times, but it usually centered around the letter "M." One new feature eventually would be incorporated in the designs of ornaments for the dress uniform—the use of a combination of white metal and yellow metal. In 1859, the Corps adopted a device with a white metal or silver "M" inside a yellow metal or gold hunting horn. This looked too much like the emblem of the U.S. Army infantry, however, which featured a bugle. But it remained in use until after the end of the Civil War.

On 2 May 1867, a Marine Corps order directed that the ornament of the officer uniform consist of a silver eagle surmounting a silver globe showing the continents of the Western Hemisphere in gold. The adoption of the globe in the device paralleled the longstanding use of a similar feature in the emblem of the British Royal Marines. Barely a month later, this directive was inexplicably revoked, perhaps because there was considerable discussion over the proper symbol for U.S. Marines. The following year, on 12 November 1868, Brigadier General Commandant Jacob Zeilin appointed three of his officers to a board "for the purpose of deciding, and reporting upon the various devices of cap ornaments proposed for the Marine Corps." Things moved rapidly after that. The board met the very next day to evaluate designs submitted by several officers and completed the work before the sun went down that evening. The Commandant agreed with their conclusions and forwarded them on the 17th to the Secretary of the Navy. Two days later, the Secretary formally approved the change. On 30 November Headquarters directed its far-flung detachments to convert to the new device by 1 July 1869.

The 1868 emblem for officers consisted of the continents of North and South America in gold superimposed on a silver globe and surmounted by a spread eagle in silver. In addition, the eagle held a ribbon in its mouth emblazoned with the motto of the Corps—Semper Fidelis—although

Opposite: *"Eagle, Globe and Anchor, 1868," George Schultz, Marine Corps Art Collection*

Right: *This stylized version of the Marine Corps emblem was embroidered on silk around 1860. ("Semper Fidelis," Marine Corps Art Collection)*

the ribbon was omitted in the actual uniform ornaments. Enlisted men would use the same device, except that it would be struck entirely from solid brass. Initially, this ornament was for use only on fatigue uniforms (those for everyday wear). The old bugle and "M" device continued for dress uniforms until November 1869, when it was also replaced by the 1868 version.

The new eagle, globe, and anchor emblem has endured since then with only minor changes. The 1904 regulations established a variation in dull bronze for use with field uniforms. World War II saw the first use of plastic devices, in a brown color similar to the dull bronze they were supplementing. Black emblems came into use in 1964 for all except the dress uniform. The adoption of an official seal for the Marine Corps in 1954 brought a barely noticeable but significant change to the emblem. For both the seal and the uniform device, the 1868 crested eagle (a type of bird prevalent around the world) was supplanted by the bald eagle, a peculiarly American breed.

Left: *"Capture of the City of Tabasco," Lt H. Walke, USN, Marine Corps Art Collection*

Opposite: *On 11 July 1853, Lt S. Bent in the first cutter from USS* Mississppi *forces its way into the Bay of Tokyo, Japan, impressing upon the Japanese Commodore Matthew Perry's intent to negotiate a treaty. ("Passing the Rubicon," W. Heine Brown, Navy Art Collection)*

15 February
Mexico
A force of Marines and sailors from *Cyane* goes ashore and fights its way through enemy opposition to relieve the garrison at San Jose.

15 March
Mexico
A Marine and Navy landing force from *Dale* again drives the enemy out of Cochori.

9 April
Mexico
Dale's Marines and sailors make a foray near Guaymas to spike abandoned heavy guns and skirmish briefly with Mexicans on their return march.

1849

17 April
Okinawa
Marines were on board the sloop *Preble* when she became the first U.S. warship to visit Okinawa.

30 June
Manpower
The strength of the Marine Corps on active duty is 46 officers and 1,030 enlisted.

1850

6 June
Slavery Suppression
Brig *Perry* and her Marines capture a ship supporting the slave trade off Africa.

30 June
Manpower
The strength of the Marine Corps on active duty is 46 officers and 1,055 enlisted.

1851

30 June
Manpower
The strength of the Marine Corps on active duty is 43 officers and 1,150 enlisted.

9 August
Madagascar
Marines from *Dale*, in a harbor in the Comora Islands near Madagascar, put down a mutiny by civilian sailors on the American bark *Paulina.*

September
Civil Support
Marines from Philadelphia assist authorities in Christiana, Pennsylvania, in apprehending persons charged with murder following a riot.

1852

3 February
Argentina
Marines from the Brazil Squadron join British and French forces ashore to protect international lives and property in Buenos Aires, Argentina, during a revolution. In a skirmish with looters, the Marines kill four of them, and order soon returns.

5 February
Nicaragua
Sailors and Marines land from sloop *Albany* to help fight a fire in San Juan del Norte, Nicaragua.

30 June
Manpower
The strength of the Marine Corps on active duty is 47 officers and 1,121 enlisted.

17 September
Argentina
Sloop *Jamestown* sends her Marines ashore to protect the American consulate in Buenos Aires.

1853

11 March
Nicaragua
Marines from *Cyane* land at San Juan del Norte to stabilize unsettled conditions as American prospectors pass through on their way to the California gold fields.

6 June
Okinawa
Marines and seamen escort Commodore Perry into Naha, Okinawa, where he is entertained by local dignitaries.

30 June
Manpower
The strength of the Marine Corps on active duty is 49 officers and 1,205 enlisted.

14 July
Japan
Commodore Perry goes ashore at Uraga, Japan, to deliver President Fillmore's letter and open negotiations with the closed nation. One hundred Marines under Major Jacob Zeilin land first and provide the honor guard for the admiral's arrival.

11 September
China
At the request of a Siamese captain, Marines from steamer *Mississippi* board his commercial ship in the Canton River near Hong Kong and put down a mutiny.

3 December
Slavery Suppression
Constitution and her Marines capture a slave ship off the Congo River in Africa.

1854

8 March
Japan
All Marines in Perry's squadron escort him ashore at Yokohama to negotiate a treaty with Japan.

10 March
Slavery Suppression
Marines on *Perry* assist in seizing a slave ship off the west coast of Africa.

13 March
Japan
A company of Marines escorts presents for delivery to the emperor of Japan.

4 April
China
Sloop *Plymouth*'s Marines and sailors go ashore at Shanghai, China, to protect American lives during a Taiping rebellion.

5 April
China
In conjunction with British troops, U.S. naval forces drive back Chinese troops encroaching on the foreign settlement in Shanghai. The Marines remain at the American consulate until 15 June.

30 June
Manpower
The strength of the Marine Corps on active duty is 49 officers and 1,312 enlisted.

6 July
Okinawa
Marines from steamer *Powhatan* land on Okinawa to demand punishment of the murderers of an American.

11 July
Okinawa
Perry lands at Okinawa with an escort of Marines to begin treaty negotiations.

12–13 July
Nicaragua
A landing party of Marines and sailors off *Cyane* seizes weapons and gunpowder at San Juan del Norte following an attack on American consular officials in Nicaragua.

Left: *Gifts from the United States to the emperor of Japan are presented at Yokohama on 13 March, 1854. ("American Presents at Yokohama," Sarony Lithograph, Navy Art Collection)*

Right: *Commodore Perry's East India Squadron included a detachment of 200 Marines. The Marines' uniforms, bayoneted muskets, and precision drill made a lasting impression on the Japanese. ("Landing of Commodore Perry at Yokohama," W. Heine Brown, Navy Art Collection)*

17 November
Okinawa
Sloop *Vincennes* sends Marines and seamen ashore on Okinawa to enforce treaty provisions.

1855

19 May
China
Powhatan puts her Marines ashore in Shanghai for two days due to unsettled conditions there.

30 June
Manpower
The strength of the Marine Corps on active duty is 52 officers and 1,552 enlisted.

4 August
China
British forces assist *Powhatan*'s Marines and sailors in a punitive expedition against pirates near Hong Kong.

28 August
Uruguay
Sloop *Germantown* sends her Marines into Montevideo, Uruguay, to protect American lives and property when a revolution appears imminent.

12 September
Fiji Islands
Marines from sloop *John Adams* make a show of force ashore, to prevent depredations against American trading ships.

22 September
Fiji Islands
A landing party of Marines and sailors from *John Adams* seizes the king on Viti Levu Island and convinces him to guarantee protection to American property.

3 October
Fiji Islands
After the king of Viti Levu fails to abide by the agreement, *John Adams*'sMarines and sailors defeat a native force and burn a village on the island.

28 October
Fiji Islands
Continuing the Viti Levu punitive campaign, an American force burns two more villages.

25 November
Uruguay
Germantown's Marine detachment goes ashore to guard the U.S. consulate during a revolution. The Marines spend a week there and prevent a massacre of insurgents who surrender to the Uruguayan army.

Left: *Marines from the East India Squadron helped the British win a lopsided victory in 1856 over the four "Barrier Forts" protecting the port of Canton, China. ("The Attack on the Barrier Forts," A. Poinsett, Marine Corps Art Collection)*

Opposite: *Marines participate in the capture of key Confederate posts in August 1861. ("Forts at Hatteras Inlet," Currier & Ives, Marine Corps Art Collection)*

1856

26 January
Seattle
Sloop *Decatur* lands her Marines, some sailors, and a howitzer to protect American settlers in Seattle from hostile Indians. In a night-long battle, the naval force drives away the threatening marauders.

30 June
Manpower
The strength of the Marine Corps on active duty is 57 officers and 1,414 enlisted.

20 September
Panama
Marines and seamen from *St. Mary's* and *Independence* guard the railroad station on the Panama Isthmus to protect American travelers from rioters.

23 October
China
Portsmouth commits her 19 Marines and 64 sailors to safeguard Americans in Canton, China, during a civil war there. They are reinforced by men from *Levant* and steam frigate *San Jacinto* on 27 October and 12 November respectively.

16 November
China
The landing force in Canton begins to return to its ships. Upriver from the city, a ship's boat is fired on from one of the Barrier Forts. *Portsmouth* engages the forts with cannon fire, and a Marine is wounded.

20 November
China
A landing party of 287 Marines and sailors attacks and captures the first of the Barrier Forts, then repels three assaults by thousands of Chinese.

21 November
China
The American force storms two more Barrier Forts and seizes both in heavy fighting. In both cases, Marine Corporal William McDougal reached the walls under severe fire and planted the American colors in the midst of the assault.

22 November
China
The Marines and sailors attack the final Barrier Fort and take it, then turn back a counterattack. The naval force destroys all four stone forts and their large number of cannon. The cost is 29 killed and wounded.

1857

1 June
Civil Support
During a rancorous election in Washington, D.C., Baltimore thugs (known as "Plug-Uglies") come to the city and begin to take over the polling places. A company of Marines from the 8th and I barracks restores order as Commandant Henderson personally confronts a mob armed with a small cannon.

30 June
Manpower
The strength of the Marine Corps on active duty is 57 officers and 1,694 enlisted.

1858

2 January
Uruguay
The Marine detachment of frigate *St. Lawrence* lands alongside a British force to protect foreign lives and property during civil disorder in Montevideo. The Americans remain there until 27 January.

16 June
Civil Support
Twenty Marines help restore order at the jail in Washington, D.C.

30 June
Manpower
The strength of the Marine Corps on active duty is 52 officers and 1,555 enlisted.

2 September
Civil Support
Sixty-five Marines from the New York Navy Yard and the steamer *Sabine* protect government buildings housing yellow fever patients on Staten Island from mobs intent on burning them.

8 September
Slavery Suppression
Marines on board sloop *Marion* participate in the capture of a ship supporting the slave trade off Africa.

6 October
Fiji Islands
Marines and sailors from *Vandalia* defeat a native force on Waya Island in the Fijis, to avenge the earlier murder of two Americans.

Left: *A parade formation in front of the old Center House at Marine Barracks 8th and I during the Civil War. (National Archives)*

17 October
Paraguay
A force of 300 Marines participates in a large demonstration of naval power in Paraguayan waters after troops fire on an American ship doing survey work.

1859

6 January
Commandants
Brevet Brigadier General Henderson dies in office at the age of 76. He had served as the fifth Commandant for almost 39 years.

7 January
Commandants
Lieutenant Colonel John Harris is appointed to serve as the Colonel Commandant of the Corps. He already had served 45 years as a Marine officer before becoming the sixth Commandant.

21 April
Slavery Suppression
Marion and her Marines capture a ship supporting the slave trade near the Congo River in Africa.

27 April
Slavery Suppression
Marion seizes another slave ship off the African coast.

30 June
Manpower
The strength of the Marine Corps on active duty is 47 officers and 1,804 enlisted.

31 July
China
Marines and sailors from *Mississippi* go ashore at Shanghai to protect American interests during unrest related to combat between British and Chinese forces. The naval contingent remains there three days.

18 October
Harper's Ferry
Marine Barracks 8th and I dispatches a company to put down an insurrection launched by John Brown at Harper's Ferry, West Virginia, in what was then Virginia. The force is led by Army Colonel Robert E. Lee, then home on leave in Arlington.

October
Uniforms
Among other new uniform regulations, the Mameluke sword for officers is replaced by the same sword used by U.S. Army infantry officers. It also becomes the sword for Marine NCOs.

Right: *Civil War U.S. Marines in dress uniform. (Marine Corps Research Center)*

Below: *"Bombardment of Port Royal, South Carolina," Currier & Ives, Marine Corps Art Collection*

1860

1 March
Africa
A landing force from *Marion* goes ashore at Kissembo, Angola, in Portuguese West Africa, to protect American lives and property from local unrest.

14 May
Civil Support
Marines from the Washington Navy Yard participate in the ceremony welcoming the first Japanese embassy personnel to the U.S. capital.

30 June
Manpower
The strength of the Marine Corps on active duty is 46 officers and 1,755 enlisted.

27 September
Panama
The Marine detachment of *St. Mary's* lands at Bay of Panama in Columbia to protect Americans and the railroad from revolutionaries.

1861

5 January
Fort Sumter
In New York City, four officers and 250 enlisted Marines board the steamer *Star of the West*, bound for the relief of Fort Sumter, South Carolina. The ship later is not allowed to land them at the fort.

5 January
Maryland
Forty Marines from the Washington Navy Yard garrison Fort Washington, Maryland, on the Potomac River.

9 January
Maryland
The Washington Navy Yard guard dispatches 30 Marines to garrison Fort McHenry in Baltimore.

THE HALLS OF MONTEZUMA

Commandant Henderson was not one to let a war pass by the Marine Corps. As the conflict with Mexico progressed into 1847, it was clear that the small regular army was woefully short of manpower. In May, the Marine general met with the Secretary of the Navy and President Polk and offered a regiment of 600 sea soldiers to the War Department under the provisions of the Act of 1834. The civilian leaders readily agreed. But even the resourceful Henderson found difficulty cobbling together enough Marines from his far-flung barracks and ships detachments. By 1 June he had mustered only about 300 officers and men. They formed a battalion under command of Brevet Lieutenant Colonel Samuel E. Watson, with Major Levi Twiggs as his executive officer. Later reinforced by an additional 60 or so Marines from Pensacola and the ships on blockading duty off Mexico, the unit landed at Veracruz on 29 June.

During the move overland to catch up with General Winfield Scott's army, the Marine battalion served as the rear guard of the reinforcing echelon. On 21 July, Watson's men fought their first battle of the war in driving off an enemy assault on the column. Upon joining Scott for the final approach to Mexico City, the Marines were brigaded with the 2d Pennsylvania Regiment, with Watson as the commander of the combined force. The division commander was Major General John A. Quitman. There was plenty of hard marching in hot, dry, ascending terrain to reach the vicinity of the enemy capital. There was hard fighting, too, but again the Marines were part of the rear guard, and this time saw no action. The brigade was in position south of Mexico City on 11 September.

Scott's plan of attack required the capture of Chapultepec Castle, a large fortified complex of walls and buildings sitting on a hill that dominated the few causeways crossing the often swampy ground southwest of the capital. A force of 800 Mexicans and several artillery pieces held the formidable position. Quitman would strike from the south, while another division attacked the western slope. The Marines received their first taste of the enemy's strength when Major Twiggs led a detachment escorting their division

Left: *("Storming of Chapultepec," C. Nebel, Marine Corps Art Collection)*

Opposite: *This drawing of Marines and soldiers in the assault was made by an observer at the battle. ("Castle of Chapultepec," J. Allison, Marine Corps Art Collection)*

commander during a 12 September reconnaissance of the objective. They drew considerable fire from the defenders, and seven men were wounded.

In a complex setup for the 13 September assault on the castle, Quitman created two storming parties and a pioneer unit, each composed of Marines and soldiers from several other division units. Twiggs commanded one party, and Marine Captain John G. Reynolds led the pioneers, while Watson resumed command of the remainder of the Marine force. The rump battalion would provide covering fire for the other three lead elements as they attempted to open a hole in the enemy defenses for the rest of the division.

The attack began badly. As the Americans moved up the causeway, they came under heavy fire that drove all four elements to cover in a ditch beside the elevated road. In the process, the soldiers and Marines from the different groups became intermingled. Twiggs was trying to sort out the confusion when he was killed by a bullet in the chest. (In a strange twist of fate, Twiggs's son, an Army lieutenant, had been killed during the march from Veracruz. The father and grandfather of the two men, Army Brigadier General David E. Twiggs, also served in the campaign, but survived.) Watson's force was accomplishing its mission of taking the castle under fire, so he was content to remain where he was. The other parties never resumed their assault as planned. When the other division broke through the western defenses, the follow-up echelon's of Quitman's division then attacked and breached the southern walls. With enemy fire reduced, the storming parties finally moved out and took an artillery position near the eastern end of the redoubt. Watson's men joined in the general attack at this point and helped secure a portion of the sprawling fortification.

During the confusion, Captain George Terrett and a portion of his Marine company became separated from the division. (Among the group was the Commandant's son, Lieutenant Charles

Henderson.) Terrett led his men in pursuit of Mexicans retreating up a causeway running northeast toward the San Cosme Gate into the capital. They joined forces with some soldiers and an artillery battery and drove off a regiment of Mexican lancers, then seized enemy outworks near the important entryway into Mexico City. Further strengthened by another pursuing detachment under Army Lieutenant U. S. Grant, they took the San Cosme Gate itself. The bold actions of these small, aggressive units gave the American army an important foothold in the enemy capital.

Simultaneous with Terrett's audacious advance, Quitman got his division moving along another causeway toward the Belen Gate. This attack also was successful in breaching the perimeter of Mexico City. Watson and his battalion reached the scene soon enough to participate in driving off several desperate Mexican counterattacks before darkness fell.

The Mexican Army withdrew from the remainder of the city during the night rather than engage in a bloody urban battle the next day. That morning, the Americans occupied the rest of Mexico City, with the Marines receiving the mission of clearing looters from the National Palace. Watson had lost a total of 7 dead and 24 wounded in the battle for the capital. Although the Marine performance was mixed, the Corps could rightfully claim a part of conquering the "Halls of Montezuma."

10 January
Florida
The Pensacola Navy Yard surrenders to armed Floridians, and 38 Marines are taken prisoner.

12 April
Florida
The Navy delivers 110 Marines and other forces to reinforce Fort Pickens, on an island off Pensacola, Florida.

12 April
Fort Sumter
Confederate forces fire on Fort Sumter, the first shots of the Civil War.

20 April
Virginia
Fifty Marines sail from the Washington Navy Yard on sloop *Pawnee* to reinforce the Gosport Navy Yard at Norfolk, Virginia. The yard commander soon surrenders it to Virginia forces, but the Marine detachments of Gosport and Washington escape by sea.

30 June
Manpower
The strength of the Marine Corps on active duty is 48 officers and 2,388 enlisted.

21 July
First Bull Run
A Marine battalion of 12 officers and 353 enlisted participates in the First Battle of Bull Run in northern Virginia.

25 July
Manpower
Congress increases the authorized size of the Marine Corps to 93 officers and 3,074 enlisted.

28 August
North Carolina
Marines from frigates *Minnesota* and *Wabash* and sloops *Cumberland* and *Susquehanna* assist soldiers in capturing Fort Clark off Hatteras Inlet, North Carolina, after a landing and four-hour battle.

14 September
Florida
Marines and sailors from frigate *Colorado* row into the harbor of Pensacola and board and burn the Confederate privateer *Judah.*

2–3 November
Atlantic
The transport *Governor* begins sinking in a gale, and the Marine battalion aboard it transfers to frigate *Sabine.* Only seven of 300 men are lost in the perilous operation.

Left: *The capture of Confederate officials on board a British mail steamer causes a diplomatic furor. ("*San Jacinto *Seizes the* Trent,*" Marine Corps Art Collection)*

Opposite: *The battle of the ironclads USS* Monitor *and CSS* Virginia *at Hampton Roads on 9 March 1862 revolutionizes naval warfare. ("USS* Monitor *vs. CSS* Virginia, *John Schmidt, Naval Historical Center)*

8 November
South Carolina
The Marines rescued by *Sabine* form the backbone of a landing force that occupies Fort Walker on Hilton Head, after Confederate troops abandoned the outpost guarding Port Royal, South Carolina.

8 November
Atlantic
Steam frigate *San Jacinto*'s Marines and sailors board the British ship *Trent* and capture Confederate diplomats John Slidell and James Mason.

8 December
Georgia
Marines and sailors from sloop *Savannah* occupy Tybee Island off Savannah, Georgia.

12 December
South Carolina
Dale's Marine detachment takes a small steamer up the Ashepoo River in South Carolina. The force defeats a small group of Confederates and burns their post.

26 December
South Carolina
Marines from *Dale* skirmish with Confederate troops at the mouth of the Edisto River in South Carolina.

1862

13 January
Florida
Steamer *Hatteras* lands her Marines to burn Confederate military supplies at Cedar Keys, Florida.

4 March
Florida
Marines from *Wabash* and *Susquehanna* go ashore and occupy the town of Fernandina, Florida. A detachment of Marines and sailors from sloop *Mohican* take over the recently abandoned fort on nearby Cumberland Island.

8–9 March
Virginia
Marines on board *Congress*, *Minnesota*, and *Cumberland* participate in the battle with the Confederate ironclad *Virginia* in Hampton Roads, Virginia.

11 March
Florida
Wabash's Marines assist in accepting the surrender of St. Augustine, Florida.

HARPER'S FERRY

On the night of 16 October 1859, anti-slavery guerrilla John Brown of Kansas led a small group of followers in a raid on Harper's Ferry, Virginia. His goal was to capture the federal arsenal there and provide the arms to a slave revolt inspired by his action. He and his 18 men had no difficulty seizing their objective from the lone night watchman. They then took several hostages. Over the course of the following morning, fire from armed citizens drove the revolutionaries into the arsenal's fire-engine house, while militia units from Virginia and Maryland converged on the scene. Casualties and desertions reduced Brown's force to just a few men, though rumors placed it in the hundreds.

The federal government learned of the insurrection late in the morning on the 17th. President Buchanan assigned the Secretary of War to handle the situation. He in turn assigned command of the operation to Colonel Robert E. Lee, who happened to be on leave at home in Arlington, Virginia. Lee picked Lieutenant J. E. B. Stuart as his aide. The nearest army troops were at Fort Monroe, two days away, so the Secretary of War asked the Navy Department for assistance. The Secretary of the Navy sent a messenger to Colonel Commandant John Harris at the Marine Barracks. The officer of the day, Lieutenant Israel Greene, mustered all men fit for duty. Six sergeants and 80 other men were armed and at the railroad station in time for the next train at 1520 that day. Harris dispatched the only other officer available, a paymaster major, but the senior staff officer could provide only advice and not command.

The Marines reached a Maryland station across from Harper's Ferry that evening and waited for Lee and Stuart, who did not make it there until midnight. The Army colonel led his small, unfamiliar force across a railroad bridge

Left: *Marine bayonets ends John Brown's attempted insurrection. ("At All Times Ready," Don Stivers, Marine Corps University Foundation)*

Opposite: *"U.S. Armory at Harper's Ferry," Edward Beyer, Marine Corps Art Collection*

into the town, and they quickly took over the perimeter of the arsenal from the militiamen. Not wanting to injure the hostages, Lee waited for daylight. He offered the mission of attacking the firehouse to both state militias, but their leaders declined. One of them remarked: "You are paid for doing this kind of work." Lieutenant Greene eagerly accepted the job.

After a night of light rain, Lee sent Stuart to deliver a note to Brown demanding his surrender. If the rebel refused, Stuart was to wave his hat, and the Marines would launch an immediate assault. The storming party consisted of Greene and 12 men, with an additional two Marines armed with sledgehammers and another 12 in reserve. Lee's orders were to rely solely on the bayonet, again to protect the hostages.

Around 0700, Stuart made his attempt to obtain a peaceful end to the affair. Brown rejected the offer, the cavalry officer made his signal, and the Marines rushed forward. When the sledgehammers proved incapable of doing the job, Greene ordered his men to grab a heavy ladder. Two blows from this makeshift battering ram broke a hole in the door. The lieutenant was the first man through, and his men "came rushing in like tigers." He struck down Brown with his sword, and the Marines bayoneted two other insurrectionists, but not before two of their own were shot. Private Luke Quinn died soon after. The Marines then safeguarded their prisoners from a lynch mob and made it back to Washington by 20 October. Brown was hanged a few weeks later after he was convicted of murder and treason.

Lee officially praised "the conduct of the detachment of Marines, who were at all times ready and prompt in the execution of any duty." Stuart agreed that Greene "did his duty handsomely." Lee subsequently sent a personal note to Commandant Harris: "Your Corps has captivated so many hearts in Virginia."

24 April
Louisiana
Marine detachments man ship's guns in Admiral David G. Farragut's fleet as it fights past two Confederate forts and several enemy warships below New Orleans. Marine losses total six killed and 22 wounded in the fierce battle.

25 April
Louisiana
Sloop *Pensacola*'s Marines land near New Orleans, seize the quarantine station, and run up the U.S. flag.
North Carolina
Marines on board the steamer *State of Georgia* participate in the bombardment and occupation of Fort Macon near Beaufort, North Carolina.

29 April
Louisiana
Captain John L. Broome and 200 Marines land and occupy New Orleans pending the arrival of Army forces.

8 May
Virginia
Marines man some of the heavy guns in the fleet that duels for four hours with the Confederate fort at Sewell's Point near Norfolk.

9 May
Louisiana
Orderly Sergeant Aaron Gilbert and the Marines of steamer *Iroquois* raise the flag over Baton Rouge, Louisiana.

15 May
Virginia
A Navy squadron battles the Confederate fort at Drewry's Bluff on the James River below Richmond, Virginia. Union Marines on ship return the musket fire of Confederate Marines on shore. When a gun crew on *Galena* is wiped out by a shell, the Marine detachment takes over and keeps it in action. For his leadership in this battle, Corporal John Mackie later will become the first Marine ever awarded the Medal of Honor.

Top: *("The* Merrimac *Sinking the* Cumberland,*" Alexander C. Stewart, Marine Corps Art Collection)*

Left: *An April 1862 photo of the pivot gun and crew on USS* Wissahickon, *with Marines in background. (National Archives)*

Opposite, top: *"Capture of New Orleans," J. O. Davidson, Marine Corps Art Collection*

Opposite, bottom: *"Corporal John Mackie," Col Charles Waterhouse, USMCR (Ret), Marine Corps Art Collection*

26 June
South Carolina
Marines from several ships participate in a gunboat raid up the Santee River in South Carolina and skirmish with Confederate troops on shore.

26–28 June
Mississippi
Marines man some of the heavy guns of Farragut's fleet as it battles past the forts at Vicksburg, Mississippi.

30 June
Manpower
The strength of the Marine Corps on active duty is 51 officers and 2,355 enlisted.

15 July
Mississippi
Marine gun crews participate in the fleet's battle with Confederate ram *Arkansas* and in a second duel with the Vicksburg forts.

17 July
Mississippi
Marines and sailors from *Potomac* land at Pascagoula, Mississippi, and destroy the telegraph. Back aboard a launch, they skirmish with Confederate troops ashore.

23 August
New York
Brooklyn Navy Yard Marines quell a drunken riot among Army recruits in the city.

25 September
Florida
Marines reoccupy the Pensacola Navy Yard.

7 December
Caribbean
Confederate raider *Alabama* captures the mail steamer *Ariel* and the 136 Marines on board her on their way to Mare Island, California. They are forced to give up their arms, but are paroled and continue on to their destination.

1863

10 January
Mexico
The Marine detachment of *Wachusett* ejects a Mexican force from the Confederate steamer *Virginia* and takes control of the ship as it lays at anchor in the harbor of Mugeres, Mexico.

14 March
Louisiana
Marines man heavy guns in Farragut's fleet as it tries to fight its way past the Confederate fort at Port Hudson, Louisiana, in the Mississippi River. *Mississippi* is destroyed and other ships are severely damaged. Orderly Sergeant Pinkerton Vaughn later becomes the second Marine to receive the Medal of Honor.

SERGEANT MILES OVIATT

The small town of Olean in southwestern New York gave four of its sons to the Marine Corps in 1862. One of them, Miles M. Oviatt, was a 21-year-old apprentice tinsmith. Along with Willard M. Smith, George W. Kelsey, and George H. Bandfield, he traveled to Brooklyn to enlist. They were sworn in on 19 August by Captain Charles Heywood (a future Commandant). The ex-tinsmith volunteered for duty in the newly converted sidewheel steamer *Vanderbilt*, but soon regretted his hasty decision to enlist. Monotony, guard duty in foul weather, the rough seas, and even rougher discipline made him homesick his first few weeks afloat. In 14 months of fruitless searching for the CSS *Alabama*, the only fighting came when the *Vanderbilt* crossed the equator. The sailors tried to force the Marines to go through the ancient rite of passage for first-timers, but the Marines settled the discussion with their fists.

In April 1864, Oviatt transferred to the crew placing the wooden screw sloop USS *Brooklyn* back into commission. Now a corporal, he was second-in-command of the Marines manning the ships two 60-pound Parrot rifles. The steam sloop boasted 24 guns all told, but accommodations for the crew were spartan, with only 14 inches allowed for each man's hammock. *Brooklyn* was destined to see plenty of action, though. By the end of May she joined the fleet gathering off Mobile Bay, one of the best ports still in Southern hands. The defenses were formidable, with three forts and numerous sea mines (then called torpedoes) guarding the entrance to the bay, and the ironclad CSS *Tennessee* and three gunboats waiting inside to pounce on any Federal ship that ran the gauntlet. There was a narrow, clear channel through the torpedoes, but it passed right under the guns of Fort Morgan, the largest of the fortifications. The Union commander, Admiral David G. Farragut, planned to enter the bay with his 14 wooden ships lashed together in pairs, so that if one sustained a loss of power, its sister could bring it through. The seven couplets would steam in column, with the four available monitors forming their own column between the rest of the fleet and Fort Morgan. *Brooklyn*, with the best forward-firing armament and a special device on the bow to sweep mines away from the hull, drew the critical mission of leading the procession.

Corporal Oviatt and his shipmates arose at 0300 on Friday, 5 August 1864, ate a quick breakfast, and pulled up anchor at 0500. The rebel fort fired first at 0650, as the Union fleet steamed into range, then the *Tennessee* hove into view at the far end of the channel. The monitor *Tecumseh* sped forward and crossed in front of *Brooklyn* to deal with the enemy ironclad, but promptly struck a torpedo and sank in less than 30 seconds. *Brooklyn*'s captain ordered his ship to stop and back away to avoid the mines; in moments he was turned sideways, and nearly blocking the channel right under the guns of Fort Morgan. In a command that would ring down into history, Farragut shouted: "Damn the torpedoes! Full speed ahead!" His flagship, USS *Hartford*, and her consort steamed into the minefield, past *Brooklyn*, and into the bay. The fuses of the mines, apparently corroded by long immersion in the salt water, failed to detonate. *Brooklyn* got underway again and the remainder of the fleet followed on Farragut's heels.

From the first shot at 0650, the deafening roar of heavy cannonade reverberated across the bay. The Federal ships traded broadsides with the forts and with the rebel fleet. The battle became a melee as vessels from each side tried to ram an opponent or gain better firing position. At mid-morning, *Brooklyn* made a run at *Tennessee*, but missed and received a rebel broadside for her troubles. The enemy shells swept much of the gun deck, killing and wounding nearly 30 sailors and Marines. In the midst of the chaos, Oviatt and a compatriot from Olean, Willard Smith, kept their Marine gun crews at work. The Marine corporal was said to have encouraged his compatriots with the shout: "Stand fast, men. Steady!" One of the sailor-manned pieces got off a shell that tore away the ironclad's funnel. Then the Marine 60-pound Parrot rifles spoke. One round severed the exposed rudder chains of *Tennessee*, while shots from the monitors finally began to damage her armor. With all control lost and the battle clearly going against him, the captain of the rebel ironclad surrendered at 1000. It took 18 more days to force the surrender of the last of the forts, but the issue was essentially settled at this point.

Brooklyn had sustained 59 hits from Confederate guns and lost 14 killed and more than 30 wounded. She had almost lost the battle with her unexpected hesitation in the channel, then reclaimed her honor with her stalwart attack on the ironclad. Oviatt's part in the fight was not insignificant and did not go unnoticed. On 4 September he was promoted to sergeant. Nearly a year after the battle, on 17 June 1865, he would receive the Medal of Honor (as would Smith). His citation read in part: "Despite severe damage to his ship and the loss of several men on board as enemy fire raked the deck, Corporal Oviatt fought his gun with skill and courage throughout the furious two-hour battle."

There was still more action left in his career as a Marine. Just days after the last fort surrendered, four of his shipmates died from an explosion as they swept mines from the channel. In December 1864 and January 1865, he and *Brooklyn* participated in the seizure of Fort Fisher off Wilmington, North Carolina. Oviatt left the Marine Corps in 1866 and returned to Olean. He died in 1880 from illness contracted as a captain in command of a volunteer cavalry unit preparing to participate in the Indian Wars.

A Marine works as part of a gun crew on the deck of a Navy gun boat on the Mississppi in 1864. (National Archives)

Left: *"The Splendid Naval Triumph on the Mississippi," Currier & Ives, Navy Art Collection*

Opposite: *In the final moments of the battle of Mobile Bay, USS* Hartford *closely engages CSS* Tennessee. *Admiral Farragut oversees the action from the rigging. ("An August Morning with Farragut," William H. Overend, Wadsworth Atheneum)*

19 March
Mississippi
Farragut's flagship *Hartford* and her Marines engage a fort at Grand Gulf, Mississippi.

22 March
Mississippi
Hartford Marines participate in a fight with Confederate batteries at Warrenton, Mississippi.

30 June
Manpower
The strength of the Marine Corps on active duty is 69 officers and 2,931 enlisted.

13 July
Civil Support
A battalion of Marines forms part of the naval brigade that helps restore order during antidraft riots in New York City.

16 July
Japan
The Marine detachment of sloop *Wyoming* participates in her battle with Japanese shore batteries and ships in the Straits of Shimonoseki.

10 August
South Carolina
A Marine battalion under Major Jacob Zeilin goes ashore on Morris Island, near Charleston, to reinforce Army troops for a planned assault on Battery Wagner. Zeilin proves unaggressive and is eventually relieved of command when he falls ill.

6 September
South Carolina
The Marines assist in the occupation of Battery Wagner after Confederate troops abandon it.

8 September
South Carolina
A force of seven officers and 127 enlisted Marines joins about 400 sailors in launching a night attack in boats on Fort Sumter in Charleston harbor. The assault is repulsed with significant losses, including 44 Marines killed, wounded, or captured.

26 September
South Carolina
The battalion on Morris Island moves to Folly Island to guard the anchorage for the squadron blockading Charleston.

1864

1 January
South Carolina
One officer and 30 enlisted Marines, reinforced by sailors, land at Murrell's Inlet, South Carolina, and destroy a Confederate schooner.

19 April
North Carolina
Marines on board the gunboat *Miami* exchange musket fire with sailors aboard the Confederate ironclad *Albermarle* during a battle at the mouth of the Roanoke River in North Carolina.

6 May
North Carolina
Marines aboard the Union gunboats in Albermarle Sound, North Carolina, participate in the battle with CSS *Albermarle*.

12 May
Commandants
Colonel John Harris, the sixth Commandant of the Marine Corps, dies in office.

9 June
Commandants
Major Jacob Zeilin is appointed the seventh Commandant of the Marine Corps.

19 June
France
Marines under Orderly Sergeant Charles Young serve one of the main guns on steamer *Kearsarge*, which sinks Confederate raider *Alabama* off Cherbourg, France.

30 June
Manpower
The strength of the Marine Corps on active duty is 64 officers and 3,075 enlisted.

3 July
South Carolina
Sixty Marines manning two light howitzers support army troops in a skirmish with Confederate forces during an unsuccessful Union raid near White Point, South Carolina.

10 July
Maryland
The Philadelphia Navy Yard provides sailors and 124 Marines to defend the railroad line at Havre de Gras, Maryland, following a Confederate cavalry raid in the area.

5 August
Alabama
Marines serve heavy guns and provide musket fire in support of Farragut's battle with forts and the Confederate ironclad *Tennessee* in Mobile Bay,

Left: *Nearly 60 naval warships participate in the assault on Fort Fisher in January 1865. The fall of Fort Fisher closes the last port connecting the Confederacy with the outside world. ("Bombardment of Fort Fisher," J. O. Davidson, Navy Art Collection)*

Below: *Marines in formation at Washington Navy Yard in 1864. (Naval Historical Center)*

Alabama. Eight Marine NCOs were subsequently awarded the Medal of Honor.

6 August
Alabama
Captain Charles Heywood and 25 Marines from *Hartford* and *Richmond* occupy Fort Powell at the entrance to Mobile Bay.

10 November
South Carolina
Marines from steamer *Lancaster* assist in the capture of agents attempting to seize a Union cargo ship off the coast of Columbia, South Carolina.

30 November
South Carolina
The blockading squadron furnishes a naval brigade, including a battalion of 182 Marines, for a joint expedition with army troops to link up with General Sherman's army during its march to the sea. The combined force is defeated at Honey Hill, South Carolina.

6–9 December
South Carolina
In a fresh advance, the Marine battalion and accompanying soldiers and sailors drive back a Confederate force at Tullifinney Crossroads, South Carolina, and occupy a position threatening the Charleston-Savannah rail line.

24–25 December
North Carolina
Marines man guns of rear Admiral David D. Porter's fleet as it bombards Fort Fisher, North Carolina. A number of Marines are killed or wounded, mainly from five Parrott guns that burst during the heavy cannonade.

1865

13–15 January
North Carolina
Admiral Porter's fleet and its Marines again bombard Fort Fisher.

15 January
North Carolina
Four hundred Marines and 1,600 sailors of the fleet participate in the ground assault on Fort Fisher. Although the naval brigade is beaten back, it diverts the attention of Confederate defenders and allows the Union army to penetrate the defenses and capture the bastion.

26 February
South Carolina
A Marine battalion occupies Georgetown, South Carolina.

9 April
Civil War
General Robert E. Lee surrenders the main Confederate army at Appomattox Courthouse, Virginia, effectively bringing the Civil War to an end.

15 April
Civil Support
Washington Navy Yard Marines take over the guard of those accused of conspiring in the assassination of President Abraham Lincoln.

30 June
Manpower
The strength of the Marine Corps on active duty is 87 officers and 3,773 enlisted.

1866

30 April
Civil Support
The Marine detachment of *St. Mary's* boards the mail steamer *Golden City* in the Caribbean at the request of her captain to quell a riot.

20–25 June
China
Marines and sailors from *Wachusett* land at Newchwang, China, to capture those responsible for an assault on the American consul.

Above: *Photo of Marine officers in 1865 (left to right): Brevet Captain William Wallace, Captain McLane Tilton, and Second Lieutenant George C. Reid. (National Archives)*

Right: *"Fort Fisher," Col Charles Waterhouse, USMCR (Ret), Marine Corps Art Collection*

CONFEDERATE STATES MARINE CORPS

The very first Marine officer to leave the service of the United States following the start of the Civil War was Second Lieutenant Calvin L. Sayre. He hailed from Alabama and tendered his resignation, after two and a half years of service, on 14 February 1861. A month later, he received a commission as a first lieutenant in the Confederate States Marines. Nineteen more Marine officers (of a total of 63) followed him south. At first, senior U.S. Marines were sympathetic to this natural pull to one's home state; Commandant Harris and others wrote recommendations for some of the initial officers who resigned. After the fighting at Fort Sumter in April, officers tendering resignations were dismissed instead and sometimes even imprisoned for a brief period. All but one of the officers who left the Marine Corps ended up joining its southern counterpart.

The Confederate States Marine Corps officially came into being on 16 March 1861, when the Southern Congress passed legislation authorizing such an outfit. Subsequent action established its strength at 46 officers and 944 men, organized into a headquarters and 10 companies. A former Army officer, Colonel Lloyd J. Beall, was appointed commandant, while former U.S. Marine Major Henry B. Tyler received the only lieutenant colonel's commission in the CSMC. Recruiting for the ranks never kept up with the demand, in part due to shorter enlistment periods and higher pay for the army and, later, the workings of the conscription law. One arm of the corps, consisting almost entirely of roughly a hundred enlisted men who had left the U.S. Marines, gathered at Richmond in the summer of 1861. Fresh recruits initially went primarily to the naval station at Pensacola for training. (A "conscript camp" eventually was established near Raleigh, North Carolina.) By October 1864, there were only 539 Southern Marines, officer and enlisted (and 67 of them were Northern prisoners of war).

The Confederate Marines served in much the same capacity as their opposites above the Mason-Dixon Line. They provided detachments on many (but not all) of the Confederate navy warships and commerce raiders, guarded naval stations, and on a few occasions operated in the field alongside the army. They participated in some of the most famous engagements of the war. Fifty-four Marines were aboard CSS *Virginia* when the ironclad battled the Union blockading fleet in March 1862. The ship's captain later noted that the "tranquil mien" of the Marine detachment commander "gave evidence that the hottest fire was no novelty to him." A contingent in CSS *Tennessee* served some of her guns when she sallied forth to take on Farragut's fleet at Mobile Bay. During the December 1864 and January 1865 assaults on Fort Fisher, a substantial number of Confederate Marines manned a battery of heavy artillery pieces. They fought from gun position to gun position as the Union army battered its way through the fortification and finally took it on the second attempt. A provisional battalion defended Drewry's Bluff below Richmond in 1862 and again in 1864.

One of the most spectacular actions of the CSMC came in February 1864, when a company of Marines participated in a raid to capture the Federal gunboat *Underwriter*, which was anchored under the Union shore batteries at New Bern, North Carolina (near the site of

A Confederate States Marine Corps officer, two enlisted Marines, and two sailors prepare for action during the Civil War. ("Confederate States Marine Corps," Don Troiani, www.historicalartprints.com)

present day Camp Lejeune). The Southern Marines and sailors achieved surprise and took control of the ship, but could not sail it away and ended up having to destroy it. The last battle of the CSMC took place in early April 1865 during the Appomattox campaign. Although the Marines under Major George Terrett fought well, their war came to an end when General Ewell surrendered his Confederate army, to which they were attached.

30 June
Manpower
The strength of the Marine Corps on active duty is 79 officers and 3,258 enlisted.

7 July
Civil Support
Two companies of Marines from the navy yard in Portsmouth, New Hampshire, arrive in Portland, Maine, to restore order after a fire.

14 July
China
Wachusett sends 100 Marines and sailors ashore to escort the American consul at Tung Chow Foo, China.

9 August
China
Marines from *Wachusett* land at Shanghai, China, to assist in fighting a fire.

1867

2 March
Commandants
Jacob Zeilin assumes the rank of Brigadier General Commandant.

April
Civil Support
Four companies of Marines from the Brooklyn Navy Yard assist civil authorities in raids on illegal distilleries in the city.

1 May
Japan
Marines from steamers *Wyoming* and *Shenandoah* escort the American minister to Japan during a civil war in that country.

13 June
China
A landing force of Marines and sailors from *Hartford* and *Wyoming* attempts to punish natives in southern Formosa following the murder of a shipwrecked American crew. The naval force is unable to close with the elusive enemy.

30 June
Manpower
The strength of the Marine Corps on active duty is 73 officers and 3,438 enlisted.

18 October
Alaska
Marines officially raise the U.S. flag over newly purchased Alaska at Sitka.

Left: *"Attack on Formosan Pirates," Marine Corps Art Collection*

1868

19 January
Japan
A Marine guard is posted at the residence of the American minister to Japan in Yokohama during a period of civil strife.

1 February
Japan
Steamer *Oneida* lands Marines and sailors to protect American lives during a period of hostility to foreigners at Hiogo, Japan.

7 February
Uruguay
Marines from the South Atlantic Squadron join forces from other powers in landing at Montevideo, Uruguay, during a military revolt there. Uruguayan forces lay down their arms.

8 February
Japan
Shenandoah sends Marines and sailors ashore at Nagasaki, Japan, to protect the American consul during a period of unrest.

19 February
Uruguay
Naval forces again land at Montevideo to guard the American consulate during renewed rebel activity.

March
Civil Support
Marines from the Brooklyn Navy Yard again assist local authorities in closing down illegal distilleries.

4 April
Japan
Steamers *Monocacy* and *Iroquois* land Marines and seamen at Yokohama, Japan, to safeguard American lives and property during a period of hostility to foreigners.

30 June
Manpower
The strength of the Marine Corps on active duty is 81 officers and 2,979 enlisted.

November
Civil Support
Brooklyn Navy Yard Marines make another foray into the city to enforce the distillery laws.

1869

30 June
Manpower
The strength of the Marine Corps on active duty is 70 officers and 2,314 enlisted.

Right: *The punitive assaults upon the forts along the Salee River in Korea were a small but bloody action. This scene of Marine casualties would presage even heavier combat in the region eight decades later. (Marine Corps Historical Center)*

THE FIRST BATTLE OF BULL RUN

The Marine Corps entered the Civil War hobbled by the loss of officers to the South, including such stalwarts as George Terrett of Mexican War fame and Israel Greene of Harper's Ferry, who also happened to be the only trained artillery officer. Fully one-third of its leaders departed for the Confederacy, but primarily those in the company grades who would bear the burden of frontline fighting. The rapid expansion of the Navy also drained officers and NCOs into numerous new ships detachments. An increase in authorized strength in 1861 brought a substantial number of recruits to the barracks, but there was hardly anyone to train them. At the Marine Barracks in Washington in mid-July, one officer noted that the 377 junior enlisted men "are not fit to go into the field, for every man of them is as raw as you please, not more than a hundred of them have been here over three weeks." Many of the lieutenants were equally new to the service and being trained themselves. Nevertheless, on 15 July the Secretary of the Navy ordered Commandant Harris to form a battalion of 12 officers and 336 enlisted for service with the Army in the first offensive against the Confederacy. Of that number, only six officers, nine NCOs, and seven privates had been in the Corps before the war.

There was little time to mull over the future, as the battalion received orders to depart the next day for the field. Major John G. Reynolds, the commanding officer, recognized the shortcomings of his force and used each halt in the march on 16 July to run his men through the manual of arms. Along the way, the Marines learned they were to be part of the 1st Brigade of the 2d Division and took their assigned place behind the brigade's battery of horse-drawn artillery. The rest of the Army, largely composed of short-service volunteers, was hardly better prepared for a campaign. After a bivouac in the field that night, there was only a short advance on the 17th. Reynolds spent the balance of the day again drilling his force and kept the men at it

Left: *The first battle of Bull Run, 21 July 1861, was the only extended service of the Marine Corps in joint land operations with the Union Army during the Civil War. (National Archives)*

after the sun went down. The 18th brought another brief march, to Centerville, Virginia, where the division camped the next two days. Drill continued for the Marines.

The Union commander elected to attack on 21 July. The 2d Division drew the mission of flanking the Confederate line after a march starting at 0200. Surprise was lost after delays stretched the movement into daylight. The rebel forces responded to the threat, but the Union soldiers initially pushed them back in heavy fighting. The Marine battalion followed the artillery battery, which inflicted severe casualties on the enemy flank. The raw Marines kept good order when they could, but were physically drained after running to catch up with two quick moves by the heavy guns. As yet they had not played any significant role in the battle.

On Henry Hill late in the morning, the battery came under unexpected fire from a Virginia infantry regiment at close range. With gunners falling in large numbers, the artillery commander called for infantry support from the Marines and a New York regiment. At the same time, Confederate artillery fire began to strike the Marines. The inexperienced battalion wavered, with officers and NCOs forcing the weaker spirits back into line. Just then a cavalry force under Colonel J. E. B. Stuart (the same lieutenant who had served with Greene at Harper's Ferry) attacked the New Yorkers and put them to flight. Almost simultaneously, the Virginia infantry regiment advanced and directed its volley fire at the Marines. Under this determined attack, with other units around them dissolving, the battalion also broke and ran.

Marine leaders rallied the force at a nearby crossroads, and they soon advanced with another New York regiment tasked with recapturing the guns lost on Henry Hill. At first they had some success driving Confederates off the high ground, only to encounter Brigadier General Thomas Jackson's Virginia Brigade firing from a pine woods. The first volleys nearly sent them reeling, but the Marines and New Yorkers made one more push into the forest. Continuous heavy fire from the Virginians routed the Federals a second time. A surgeon with the Virginians gave the 8th and I battalion a compliment nonetheless, noting that the woods in front of his position were filled with Northern casualties, "but the only men that were killed and wounded twenty or thirty yards behind and in the rear of our lines were the United States Marines."

Reynolds corralled most of his men once more at the crossroads, and they participated in one last attack to regain Henry Hill. This time a South Carolina brigade came up and fired on the Union forces from the flank. Nearby, a fresh Federal brigade was put to flight. This time there was no stopping the disorganized Northern troops. Even that part of the Union Army that initially retreated in good order was soon put to the rout by pursuing Confederate fire. It would take days for the last stragglers to make it back to Washington for a final accounting.

Losses to the Marine battalion totaled 44 dead, wounded, and taken prisoner. Moreover, they had lost most of their equipment and arms. The Commandant lamented the embarrassment to the Corps, for "it was the first instance in recorded history where any portion of its members turned their backs to the enemy." There was one bright spot—the battalion had not lost its colors to the rebels. Harris was not about to suffer a repeat of raw troops being thrown into battle, and he asked the Secretary of the Navy to obtain the release of the Marine battalion from the War Department. The request was granted on 24 July. For the remainder of the momentous Civil War, the Corps would avoid extended service on land with the U.S. Army, a role it had successfully carried out in the Mexican War and which it would reprise with glory in World War I and subsequent conflicts.

16 July
Civil Support
Fifty Marines from Brooklyn Navy Yard take a revenue cutter to Gardiner's Island off Long Island and capture 125 men preparing to invade Cuba.

1870

January
Colombia
A detachment of 63 Marines assists an expedition surveying a possible route for an interoceanic canal through Colombia.

28 March
Civil Support
Brooklyn Navy Yard Marines, reinforced by the detachment of the *Vermont*, work with revenue agents in seizing illegal distilleries.

17 June
Mexico
Steamer *Mohican* sends Marines and sailors to Boca Teacapan, Mexico, to destroy a pirate ship.

30 June
Manpower
The strength of the Marine Corps on active duty is 77 officers and 2,469 enlisted.

11 October
Civil Support
Marines from the Philadelphia Navy Yard help quell a disturbance in the city during the first vote by black Americans following passage of the 15th Amendment to the U.S. Constitution.

2 November
Civil Support
The Brooklyn Navy Yard dispatches 245 Marines to aid local law enforcement officials in rooting out illegal distilleries in the city.

1871

14 January
Civil Support
Marines from the Navy Yard guard 14 legal distilleries in Brooklyn against attacks by workers from the illegal operations.

10–11 June
Korea
In response to Koreans firing on a survey party, four Marine officers and 105 enlisted men lead the landing of a naval brigade on the banks of the Salee River near Inchon. In two days of fighting, the force assaults and destroys four large forts and captures hundreds of cannon. Six Marines earn the Medal of Honor. Later renamed the Han River, this would be the scene of more Marine battles roughly 80 years in the future.

30 June
Manpower
The strength of the Marine Corps on active duty is 74 officers and 2,439 enlisted.

14 July
Civil Support
Brooklyn Navy Yard Marines quell disturbances in the city following raids on illegal distilleries.

September
Civil Support
Marines from the Brooklyn Navy Yard assist revenue agents in seizing ships with cargoes of contraband whiskey in New York harbor.

17 October
Civil Support
Brooklyn Marines guard seized illegal distilleries.

1872

30 June
Manpower
The strength of the Marine Corps on active duty is 77 officers and 2,126 enlisted.

10 November
Civil Support
Marines from the Boston Navy Yard help restore order following a destructive fire in Boston, Massachusetts.

1873

7 May
Colombia
Marines and sailors from the steamers *Pensacola* and *Tuscarora* land at the Bay of Panama in Colombia, to protect American lives and property during a period of political unrest.

30 May
Civil Support
Marines from the Boston Navy Yard, *Ohio,* and *Powhatan* help maintain order after a fire in Boston.

25 June
Peru
Marines from *St. Mary's* assist in putting out a fire aboard an Italian merchant ship in the harbor of Callao, Peru.

30 June
Manpower
The strength of the Marine Corps on active duty is 87 officers and 2,675 enlisted.

24 September
Panama
Steamers *Pensacola* and *Benicia* deploy Marines and sailors ashore to protect American lives and the railroad during a revolt in the Panamanian Isthmus of Colombia. The isthmus and its railroad are critical to the United States since it constitutes a key link in the quickest transportation route from the east coast to the west coast of North America.

1874

24 January
Training
The Marine detachments of the ships of the

Opposite: *"Korea, 1871," John Joseph Capolino, Marine Corps Art Collection*

Right: *Capt McLane Tilton poses with a captured Korean flag and Medal of Honor recipients Cpl Charles Brown and Pvt Hugh Purvis of the Marine detachment USS* Colorado, *after 1871 landings in Korea. (Marine Corps Historical Center)*

Atlantic Squadron participate in a battalion field exercise under command of Lieutenant Colonel Charles Heywood, as the fleet awaits possible orders to intervene in disorder in Cuba.

12 February
Hawaii
To assist in preserving order during the inauguration of a new king, Marines from *Portsmouth* and *Tuscarora* go ashore at Honolulu, Hawaii.

6 June
Commandants
Commandant Jacob Zeilin is reverted to the rank of colonel due to the dwindling strength of the Marine Corps.

30 June
Manpower
The strength of the Marine Corps on active duty is 85 officers and 2,184 enlisted.

1875

30 June
Manpower
The strength of the Marine Corps on active duty is 76 officers and 2,037 enlisted.

1876

16 May
Mexico
Marines land at Matamoros, Mexico, at the request of the American consul after civil control in the city dissolves during a revolution.

30 June
Manpower
The strength of the Marine Corps on active duty is 76 officers and 1,904 enlisted.

25 October
Heritage
In commemoration of Marine service with the U.S. Army in the Mexican War, the Navy Department authorizes the Corps to adopt the motto, "*Per Mare, Per Terram*" ("By Sea, By Land").

1 November
Commandants
Commandant Jacob Zeilin retires. Colonel Charles G. McCawley assumes duties as the eighth Commandant of the Marine Corps.

1877

30 June
Manpower
The strength of the Marine Corps on active duty is 73 officers and 1,824 enlisted.

21 July
Civil Support
A battalion of Washington Navy Yard Marines under Lieutenant Colonel Heywood moves to Baltimore to protect railroad property during a major strike by rail workers. After securing the situation there, the unit moves on to Philadelphia.

26 July
Civil Support
Lieutenant Colonel James Forney forms a battalion from the Marines of the Norfolk Navy Yard and ships of the Atlantic Squadron. His force guards the arsenal in Washington and railroad property in Baltimore.

1878

3 April
Expositions
A detachment of Marines arrives at Le Havre, France, on board *Constitution* to serve as the honor guard for the American exhibit at the Universal Exposition in Paris.

30 June
Manpower
The strength of the Marine Corps on active duty is 77 officers and 2,257 enlisted.

1879

30 June
Manpower
The strength of the Marine Corps on active duty is 62 officers and 1,906 enlisted.

1880

8 June
Department of the Navy
Congress establishes the office of Judge Advocate General of the Navy. Marine Captain William B. Remey is the first officer appointed to fill the billet.

30 June
Manpower
The strength of the Marine Corps on active duty is 69 officers and 1,870 enlisted.

1881

March
Arctic
The Marines of *Alliance* participate in an attempt to locate Arctic explorers lost north of Norway.

30 June
Manpower
The strength of the Marine Corps on active duty is 70 officers and 1,832 enlisted.

1882

30 June
Manpower
The strength of the Marine Corps on active duty is 63 officers and 1,806 enlisted.

14 July
Egypt
Marines and sailors from the Mediterranean Squadron land at Alexandria, Egypt, to protect American lives and the U.S. consulate during a rebellion against the government.

Opposite: *Marines plunge into the mud flats on the banks of the Salee River and struggle to pull a landing gun through the muck. ("The Storming of Fort Ch'ojijin," John Clymer, Marine Corps Art Collection)*

Right: *Fort Monocacy, named for one of the ships that supported Marines in its capture in Korea in 1871. (National Archives)*

STEAM, STEEL, AND STAMINA

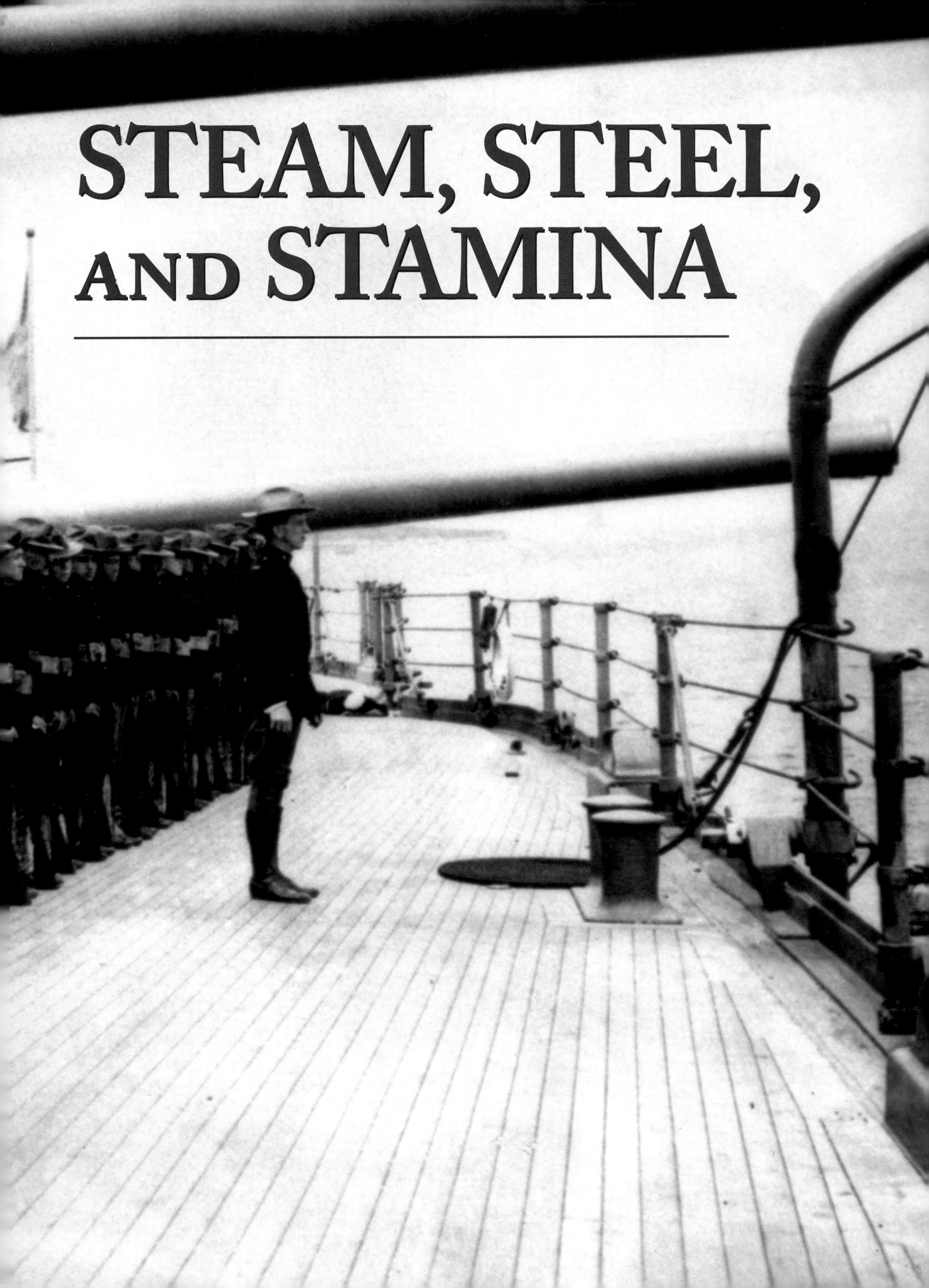

STEAM, STEEL, AND STAMINA

1883–1913

The three decades spanning the end of the 1800s and the beginning of the 1900s proved to be among the most important in the history of the Corps. Nearly irrelevant during the Civil War—the nation's largest conflict to date—Marines found new and vital missions and became a professional force as the new century dawned. Strangely, their existence also came under significant attack for the first time, thus giving rise to an institutional paranoia that would keep Marines looking over their shoulders from this point forward.

The transformation of the Corps during this period sometimes paralleled changes in the Navy. The Navy began acquiring its first steel ships, converting fully to steam power, and adopting Mahanian doctrine as a rationale for its growth and employment. Some influential Navy officers saw the Corps as an anachronism, since there would be no more need for men with muskets in fighting tops. In fact, the first major attempt to abolish the Marines came from within the Navy in 1890. Another, spurred by President Teddy Roosevelt, occurred in 1908. The Corps survived, but its officers saw the need to build their professionalism and to focus on a mission that made them a valuable contribution to national defense.

One of the first reforms was an improvement in officer selection and training, which took a dramatic leap forward when Naval Academy graduates began providing most new lieutenants from 1882 onward. Although this source would decline in relative numbers and importance within two decades, it set a standard that all other officer candidates would have to meet or exceed. In 1891 the Corps instituted the School of Application to train newly commissioned officers. Enlisted men benefitted from more formalized and centralized recruit training. Participation in shooting competitions and more emphasis on marksmanship began in 1901, further refining combat skills. The Corps' first advanced professional training program, the Advance Base School, opened in 1910. The following year officers formed the Marine Corps Association to enhance professional knowledge.

The search for a mission received an enormous boost from the Spanish-American War in 1898. A Marine battalion made an amphibious landing at Guantanamo Bay, Cuba, to seize and secure an anchorage for coaling the warships blockading the Spanish fleet at nearby Santiago. In the new steam and steel navy, such expeditionary bases were a prerequisite for projecting naval power around the globe and fulfilling the strategic and doctrinal dictates of Admiral Alfred Thayer Mahan. The Marines brought two advantages over the Army in this emerging role. They had proven over the years (from Bladensburg to Harper's Ferry to the Spanish-American War) that they were able to form units and mount out ready for action on a moment's notice. Most important, the Corps was an integral part of the Navy Department and subject to naval command, which made it simple for fleet commanders to field a force that would

Pages 110–111: *The Marine detachment of an early battleship musters under the big guns in October 1913. (National Archives)*

Right: *"The Fight at Guantanamo," F. C. Yohn, National Archives*

work ashore on their behalf. Before long, the Marine Corps adopted the advance base mission as its own, and began training and equipping a standing force dedicated to fulfilling the requirement. Since most expeditionary bases would have to be captured or occupied in a process involving some sort of amphibious landing, the Corps also renewed its interest in this type of operation. Many leading naval officers strongly supported the new Marine focus. Admiral George Dewey, the hero of Manila Bay, proclaimed that a landing force of Marines operating with his fleet would have prevented the Philippine Insurrection.

The acquisition of overseas territory as a result of the war, and America's expanding international trade, created another mission for the Corps. Suddenly there was a need for something much larger than a ship's detachment to handle crises in far-flung corners of the world. The United States had hardly driven the Spanish from the Philippines when elements of the population rose up to declare independence. The expanding Corps contributed several battalions to the fight. Trouble flared in China in 1900 and more Marines went there to help safeguard U.S. citizens and commercial interests from the Boxer Rebellion. Major interventions in Panama, Cuba, and Nicaragua followed. Although the Army contributed large forces to some of these operations, the Corps often proved adept at getting there first with units composited from ships' detachments and overseas barracks. Marines also learned how to deal with these brush fire wars (ultimately dubbed "small wars"), which were considerably different from the major conflicts that now drew the primary attention of the Army. Simultaneously the Corps began to develop closer relations with the diplomats of the State Department, and even began guarding the U.S. Embassy in Peking, China.

These new missions had a large impact on the Corps. The service that had barely reached 3,000 men during the Civil War ended this period, when the nation was largely at peace, with almost 10,000. Marines were also becoming a professional force, improving training, education, doctrine, and manpower policies to better prepare for expanded roles. The Corps was now capable of operating in brigade strength with combined arms, to include an infant aviation element beginning in 1912. It was a far cry from the mid-nineteenth century, though one thing had not changed. Marines still had to exhibit courage and determination to carry out their missions. If anything, the requirements in that regard had increased, since the demands of chasing down opponents in the trackless jungles or rough terrain typical of small wars called for the utmost in stamina, resolve, and bravery.

STEAM, STEEL, AND STAMINA

1883–1913

1883

12 February
Hawaii
Marines from screw sloops *Lackawanna* and *Wachusett* land at Honolulu, Hawaii, to take part in the inauguration ceremonies for King Kalakaua.

3 March
Technology
Congress authorizes construction of three new protected cruisers (*Atlanta*, *Boston*, and *Chicago*) and the unprotected cruiser *Dolphin*, the first steel ships of the U.S. Navy.

30 June
Manpower
The strength of the Marine Corps on active duty is 60 officers and 1,724 enlisted.

1884

April
Greenland
Gunboat *Alert* and her Marine detachment participate in the ultimately successful attempt to rescue the Greeley Expedition west of Greenland.

30 June
Manpower
The strength of the Marine Corps on active duty is 66 officers and 1,822 enlisted.

1885

18 January
Panama
In response to revolutionary activity in Colombia and the Isthmus of Panama, Marines from gunboat *Alliance* land at Colon, Panama, to

Left: *A depiction of Heywood's battalion moving by train in 1885. ("Marines in Panama," Col Charles Waterhouse, USMCR (Ret), Marine Corps Art Collection)*

Opposite: *The Marine detachment of USS* Portsmouth *forms on her deck about 1885. (National Archives)*

protect the Caribbean end of the railroad. They remain only a few days.

16 March
Panama
Continuing political unrest brings steam bark *Galena* to Colon. Marines go ashore to protect the U.S. consulate. The revolutionaries seize the railroad and set fires in the city.

31 March
Panama
Screw sloop *Shenandoah* lands a company of Marines and reinforcing sailors at Panama City, the Pacific terminus of the rail line. Screw frigate *Tennessee* and screw sloop *Swatara* put a landing force ashore at Colon.

3 April
Panama
One day after receiving orders to form a battalion from East Coast detachments and barracks, Lieutenant Colonel Charles Heywood sails from New York with 10 officers and 212 enlisted.

7 April
Panama
A second battalion of 15 officers and 250 men departs New York along with a battalion of sailors and some artillery.

12 April
Panama
Heywood's battalion lands at Colon, takes the train to Panama City, and establishes control of the rail line.

15 April
Panama
The second battalion of Marines arrives at Colon. All Marine forces ashore are grouped into a brigade under command of Heywood. This is the first brigade-size force established by the Marine Corps in its history.

25 May
Panama
The last Marines forces depart Panama following the arrival of Colombian troops to restore government control.

Left: *The Marine detachment of USS* Galena *in formation alongside Navy officers in 1888. (National Archives)*

30 June
Manpower
The strength of the Marine Corps on active duty is 65 officers and 1,819 enlisted.

1886

30 June
Manpower
The strength of the Marine Corps on active duty is 66 officers and 1,934 enlisted.

1887

30 June
Manpower
The strength of the Marine Corps on active duty is 61 officers and 1,870 enlisted.

1888

19 June
Korea
Marines and sailors from steam bark *Essex* land at Chemulpo, Korea, and march to Seoul to protect the U.S. consulate during a period of political turmoil.

30 June
Manpower
The strength of the Marine Corps on active duty is 72 officers and 1,829 enlisted.

14 November
Samoa
Steam bark *Nipsic*'s Marines go ashore at Apia, Samoa, to protect American lives and property during a time of unrest.

20 December
Haiti
Marines participate in the show of force by steam barks *Galena* and *Yantic* at Port-au-Prince to secure the release of an American commercial ship wrongfully seized by the Haitian government.

1889

15 March
Samoa
Marines are among those lost when the screw steamer *Trenton* and screw sloop *Vandalia* sink in Apia Harbor during a typhoon. Naval Academy cadet John A. Lejeune is one of the survivors.

21 April
Expositions
Thirty Marines arrive in Le Havre, France, to provide security for U.S. exhibits during the Universal Exposition in Paris (which features the opening of the Eiffel Tower).

30 June
Manpower
The strength of the Marine Corps on active duty is 54 officers and 1,718 enlisted.

30 July
Hawaii
Steam bark *Adams* sends her Marine detachment ashore at Honolulu, Hawaii, to protect American lives during election disturbances.

1890

8 February
Japan
Marines and seamen from steam bark *Omaha* land at Nodogaya, Japan, to assist local authorities in fighting a fire at Kanagawa.

30 June
Manpower
The strength of the Marine Corps on active duty is 61 officers and 1,986 enlisted.

30 July
Argentina
Schooner *Tallapoosa*'s Marines deploy to Buenos Aires, Argentina, to guard the U.S. consulate during a revolution.

November
Roles and Missions
U.S. Naval Institute Proceedings publishes an article by Navy Lieutenant William Fullam that argues that Marines are no longer needed on warships.

1891

29 January
Commandants
Commandant Charles McCawley retires at 64.

30 January
Commandants
Lieutenant Colonel Charles Heywood is appointed to serve as the ninth Commandant of the Marine Corps.

1 May
Training
The School of Application, the first formal post-commissioning training program for brand-new Marine second lieutenants, opens at Marine Barracks 8th and I.

Right: *Based on a newspaper drawing of the time, this painting depicts the Marines shortly after their arrival at Guantanamo Bay, Cuba, in 1898. ("First Hoisting of the Stars and Stripes," Marine Corps Art Collection)*

2 June
Caribbean
Marines land from steam bark *Kearsarge* on Navassa Island, between Jamaica and Haiti, to maintain order among contract laborers.

26 June
Bases
A small Marine guard is established to protect the new Navy base at Port Royal, South Carolina. This base will eventually become known as Parris Island.

30 June
Manpower
The strength of the Marine Corps on active duty is 66 officers and 2,092 enlisted.

2 July
Alaska
To enforce prohibitions against hunting seals, a Navy squadron and a special force of five officers and 113 enlisted Marines arrive in Alaskan waters. They remain on station until 5 October.

28 August
Chile
Marines and sailors from cruisers *San Francisco* (C-5) and *Baltimore* (C-3) land at Valparaiso, Chile, to protect the U.S. legation during a revolution.

1892

30 June
Manpower
The strength of the Marine Corps on active duty is 66 officers and 1,973 enlisted.

1 September
Training
The School of Application inaugurates its first class for NCOs.

14 September
Civil Support
During an outbreak of cholera among immigrants, a Marine battalion formed from navy yards and ships detachments guards a quarantine camp at Sandy Hook, New York.

7 October
Venezuela
Cruiser *Chicago* sends her Marines ashore at La Guaira, Venezuela, to guard the U.S. consulate during a revolution.

1893

16 January
Hawaii
Marines from cruiser *Boston* land at Honolulu after the Hawaiian queen revoked the constitution, and American sugar planters deposed her and formed a provisional government.

6 May
Expositions
A Marine detachment assumes guard duties for the World's Columbian Exposition in Chicago.

30 June
Manpower
The strength of the Marine Corps on active duty is 63 officers and 2,070 enlisted.

27 August
Civil Support
Personnel of the Marine Barracks, Port Royal, South Carolina, assist in rescue operations following a tidal wave.

1894

25 March
China
The Marine detachment of sidewheel gunboat *Monocacy* provides the honor guard for the first visit of the Chinese Viceroy to the U.S. consulate in Tientsin.

30 June
Manpower
The strength of the Marine Corps on active duty is 67 officers and 2,309 enlisted.

July
Civil Support
During a railroad strike in California, Marines from the Mare Island Navy Yard and ships guard the mails.

6 July
Nicaragua
Cruiser *Marblehead's* (C-11) Marines and sailors go ashore at Bluefields to safeguard American lives and property during a period of political unrest.

24 July
Korea
Baltimore's Marines land at Chemulpo and march overland to Seoul to protect American lives following the outbreak of war between China and Japan.

31 July
Nicaragua
Marines from cruiser *Columbia* (C-12) go ashore to reinforce their compatriots in Bluefields. The combined force returns to its ships a week later.

6 December
China
Sixty Marines land at Taku and move to Tientsin to protect U.S. interests in China during a time of political turmoil.

Opposite, top: *The national ensign and Marine Corps colors fly in Cuba during the Spanish-American War. (Marine Corps Research Center)*

Opposite, bottom: *LtCol Robert W. Huntington (center) with two staff officers at Guantanamo. (National Archives)*

Right: *Marines stand guard around the camp at Guantanamo. (Marine Corps Research Center)*

1895

1 March
Korea
The Marine detachment of *Yorktown* (Gunboat No. 1) assumes guard of the U.S. legation at Seoul.

4 March
Trinidad
A U.S. squadron sends its Marines ashore at Port au Spain, Trinidad, to help fight a fire.

8 March
Colombia
Atlanta's Marines land at Boca del Toro, Colombia, to protect American lives during political disturbances.

30 June
Manpower
The strength of the Marine Corps on active duty is 71 officers and 2,814 enlisted.

1896

2 May
Nicaragua
In response to continuing troubles in Nicaragua, Marines from *Alert* move ashore at Corinto.

6 June
Manpower
Congress authorizes an increase in Marine strength to 93 officers and 3,574 enlisted.

30 June
Manpower
The strength of the Marine Corps on active duty is 72 officers and 2,145 enlisted.

Top: *"Captain Elliott's Reconnaissance Ride," Col Charles Waterhouse, USMCR (Ret), Marine Corps Art Collection*

Left: *The sunken USS* Maine *in Havana Harbor. (Naval Historical Center)*

Opposite, top: *Detachment of USS* Brooklyn *in 1898. (National Archives)*

Opposite, bottom: *Marines form up in their camp in Cuba, 1898. (Marine Corps Research Center)*

1897

27 April
Heritage
The Marine Band and two battalions of Marines take part in the dedication ceremonies for Grant's Tomb in New York City.

30 June
Manpower
The strength of the Marine Corps on active duty is 71 officers and 3,735 enlisted.

18 August
Manpower
The first Marine Corps post exchange is established at Marine Barracks, Newport, Rhode Island.

28 December
Force Structure
A Marine barracks is established at Pensacola Navy Yard, Florida.

1898

1–12 January
Cuba
The North Atlantic Squadron and its Marine detachments assemble in the Gulf of Mexico due to political turmoil in Cuba.

7 February
Nicaragua
Marines and sailors from *Alert* land at San Juan del Sur, Nicaragua, in response to political unrest.

15 February
Spanish-American War
The battleship *Maine* explodes and sinks in the harbor of Havana, Cuba. Twenty-eight Marines and 232 sailors die. Private William Anthony, orderly to the ship's captain, wins acclaim for calmly reporting to his superior below decks and aiding the captain's movement to the quarterdeck of the sinking ship.

17 April
Force Structure
Commandant Heywood directs Lieutenant Colonel Robert W. Huntington to form a unit for overseas service from East Coast barracks establishments.

21 April
Spanish-American War
The U.S. declares war on Spain.

22 April
Force Structure
The 1st Marine Expeditionary Battalion of 14 officers and 623 enlisted sails from New York on board the transport *Panther*.

1 May
Philippines
Marines man some secondary batteries of Admiral George Dewey's fleet during its lopsided victory over the Spanish in the Battle of Manila Bay.

3 May
Philippines
Baltimore's Marines land at Cavite Navy Yard and raise the U.S. flag over the Philippine Islands.

4 May
Manpower
Congress increases the permanent strength of the Marine Corps by 473 men and provides for an additional 43 officers and 1,580 men for temporary service during the war. The Commandant is elevated again to the rank of brigadier general.

11 May
Cuba
Marines and sailors of *Marblehead* cut the transoceanic telegraph cable off Cienfuegos, Cuba.

12 May
Puerto Rico
Marines man some of the secondary batteries of the North Atlantic Squadron when it bombards San Juan de Puerto Rico.

24 May
Force Structure
Lieutenant Colonel Robert Huntington's 1st Marine Battalion goes ashore at Key West, Florida.

31 May
Cuba
Admiral William P. Sampson's fleet and its assigned Marines shell the Spanish fortress at Santiago, Cuba.

6 June
Cuba
Marines participate in the North Atlantic Squadron's bombardment of Santiago, Cuba.

Left: *Marines attack during the Philippine Insurrection in 1898. ("Red Pants at Novaleta," Col Charles Waterhouse, USMCR (Ret), Marine Corps Art Collection)*

Opposite: *Marines pause for a unit portrait during the Spanish-American War. (Marine Corps Research Center)*

7 June
Cuba
The Marine battalion re-embarks on *Panther* at Key West for transport to Cuba. Eighty Marines from cruiser *New York* (ACR-2), battleship *Oregon* (BB-3), and *Marblehead* conduct an amphibious reconnaissance at Guantanamo Bay.

10 June
Guantanamo Bay
Lieutenant Colonel Robert Huntington's battalion lands at Guantanamo Bay and occupies a hill nearby.

11–12 June
Guantanamo Bay
Spanish soldiers fire on the Marine camp both nights. The Marine detachment of battleship *Texas* comes ashore to reinforce the battalion.

13–14 June
Guantanamo Bay
The Spanish attack the Marines at first light both days.

14 June
Guantanamo Bay
Two companies of Marines advance two miles and defeat a larger enemy force at Cuzco Wells. After destroying the well, the only water supply in the vicinity of the Marine base, the companies return to their camp. Sergeant John H. Quick later receives the Medal of Honor for signaling the fire support ship while under fire.

16 June
Cuba
Marine detachments participate in the North Atlantic Squadron's bombardment of Santiago.

22 June
Guam
Cruiser *Charleston* (C-2) sends her Marines and some sailors ashore to occupy the town of Apra and claim the island of Guam for the U.S.

30 June
Manpower
The strength of the Marine Corps on active duty is 98 officers and 3,481 enlisted.

3 July
Cuba
Marines man some of the secondary batteries of the Atlantic fleet when it sinks the Spanish fleet off Santiago.

7 July
Spanish-American War
A company of Marines takes charge of the newly established camp for Spanish prisoners at Portsmouth, New Hampshire.

GUANTANAMO BAY

The U.S. Navy succeeded in blockading the Atlantic fleet of the Spanish in the harbor of Santiago in southeastern Cuba on 28 May 1898. But the narrow entrance to the cove, defended by sea mines and shore batteries, prevented Admiral William T. Sampson from getting at his opponent and destroying him. And as long as the Spanish ships remained in existence, they were a threat to any seaborne invasion of Cuba. The Americans needed a nearby refuge to coal their warships, however, if they wanted to maintain a strong blockade. The perfect place for this was Guantanamo Bay, roughly 40 miles to the east. The U.S. Army still was trying to build a force of volunteers in the States, but Huntington's Marine battalion was waiting impatiently at Key West for action. On 7 June, the Marines embarked on transport *Panther*.

While the Marine expeditionary force sailed for Cuba, part of Sampson's fleet went to work. After bombarding Spanish shore positions, the warships sent a reconnaissance party of 60 seagoing Marines ashore. They found a suitable landing place on the eastern shore of the bay. On 10 June, *Panther* arrived and deposited her Marines at the assigned location. Moving inland to a hill, Huntington's men established a fortified camp. That night Spanish forces harassed the Marine base with heavy rifle fire. Using signal lanterns, the defenders called in naval gunfire around their perimeter. The Marines moved to more defensible ground on the 12th, but the Spanish hit them that evening, as well as at dawn on the 13th and the 14th.

Huntington determined that the key to the area was Cuzco Well, about two miles distant. It was the only source of fresh water

Left: *LtCol Robert W. Huntington astride his horse following the victory of his Marines at Guantanamo Bay. (National Archives)*

Opposite: *This staged photo probably accurately depicts Marines adapting their uniforms to the tropic battlefield in Cuba. (Marine Corps Historical Center)*

in the vicinity, so if he neutralized it, the Spaniards would have to pull back about nine miles to Guantanamo City itself. (The Marines received their water from the ships.) He dispatched two companies on the mission at midmorning on 14 June. The commander of the operation was George F. Elliott (a 52-year-old captain, which was not unusual in a Corps saddled with promotion by seniority). Dispatch boat *Dolphin* sailed along the coast to provide fire support. Fifty Cuban rebels joined the force.

The Marines and Cubans achieved surprise and gained the crest of a horseshoe-shaped ridge overlooking the well. From the thick brush below, the Spanish forces returned a heavy fire. A signalman wig-wagged a request to *Dolphin,* and its shelling sent the enemy scurrying for new cover in the valley. Next Elliott wanted fire on a blockhouse dominating the well. A Marine (probably Private John Fitzgerald) had to expose himself to enemy fire on the top of the ridge to send the message. The ship's guns opened up again, but long shots began to fall on part of Elliott's position. Sergeant John Quick answered the call for a signalman. Tying a large blue polka dot scarf to his bayonet, he went to the crest, turned his back on the enemy rifle fire, and calmly informed *Dolphin* of the situation. Reporter Stephen Crane crouched below and noted that the only trace of emotion on the sergeant's face came when his improvised signal flag caught on a thorn bush for a moment: "He looked annoyed."

The naval shells and Marine rifles took the fight out of the Spanish by midafternoon. As they melted away, Elliott and his men occupied the site and destroyed the well. They determined that enemy losses were 60 killed and 18 captured. Friendly casualties were two Cubans killed and one Marine wounded. Another 23 men had to be evacuated to the ship with heat prostration. The battle had the desired effect, and no more attacks came against the Marine base in the bay. More importantly, Guantanamo Bay was rendered safe for use by the fleet. And Marines were now firmly established in their role of seizing and defending advance bases for the Navy.

11 July
Heritage
The Secretary of the Navy observes the 100th birthday of Congress's creation of the U.S. Marine Corps (as distinguished from its predecessor, the Continental Marines).

27 July
Puerto Rico
Marines from auxiliary cruiser *Dixie* land at Playa del Ponce, Puerto Rico, and raise the U.S. flag over the island for the first time.

5 August
Guantanamo Bay
Huntington's battalion embarks on transport *Resolute* for future landing operations.

12 August
Hawaii
Marines from steamship *Mohican* and cruiser *Philadelphia* (C-4) participate in ceremonies at Honolulu marking the annexation of the Hawaiian Islands by treaty on 7 July.

13 August
Spanish-American War
Huntington's battalion was preparing to go ashore to assault Manzanillo, Cuba, when word arrived of the armistice ending the Spanish-American War. Spain eventually gave the Philippines, Guam, and Puerto Rico to the United States.

26 August
Force Structure
The 1st Marine Expeditionary Battalion arrives in Portsmouth, New Hampshire.

22 September
Force Structure
Elements of the disbanded 1st Marine Expeditionary Battalion march through the capital and are reviewed by President McKinley.

2 October
South Carolina
The Marine barracks at Port Royal recovers from a severe tropical storm.

26 October
Puerto Rico
Marines establish a barracks at the naval station at San Juan, Puerto Rico.

4 November
China
Marines from *Baltimore*, *Boston*, and cruiser *Raleigh* (C-8) land at Taku, China, and proceed to Peking to establish a guard at the U.S. legation.

12 November
China
Additional Marines from the same ships go ashore at Taku and move overland to Tientsin to guard the U.S. consulate. Both outfits remain until 15 March 1899.

1899

14 February
Samoa
Philadelphia lands Marines and sailors at Apia to protect American lives and property during a dispute between two Samoan factions.

24 February
Nicaragua
Marines and seamen from gunboat *Marietta* (PG-15) go ashore at Bluefields during a period of turmoil in Nicaragua.

3 March
Manpower
The President signs legislation increasing the strength of the Marine Corps to 211 officers and 6,000 enlisted men, exclusive of the Marine Band.

1 April
Samoa
British and American forces siding with one of the Samoan parties are ambushed during a raid. Twenty U.S. Marines protect the rear of the outfit as it withdraws to the coast. Sergeants Michael J. McNally and Bruno A. Forsterer and Private Henry L. Hulbert subsequently are awarded the Medal of Honor.

27 April
Guantanamo Bay
A detachment of 80 Marines arrives at Havana, Cuba, to guard the naval base at Guantanamo.

23 May
Philippines
At the request of Admiral Dewey, a Marine battalion of 15 officers and 260 enlisted men arrives at Cavite, Luzon, to protect the naval station from Filipino rebels.

30 June
Manpower
The strength of the Marine Corps on active duty is 76 officers and 3,066 enlisted.

7 August
Guam
A force of five officers and 121 enlisted Marines lands at Agana, Guam, to garrison the Navy's new base.

21 September
Philippines
A second battalion of 16 officers and 362 enlisted Marines reinforces Cavite.

23 September
Philippines
Marines from *Baltimore*, *Charleston*, and gunboat *Concord* (PG-13) land with support of naval gunfire near Olongapo, Luzon, drive off a rebel outfit, and destroy a large-caliber coastal defense gun.

3 October
Philippines
More than a hundred Marines support an army attack on rebel forces near Cavite.

Opposite: *The Marine detachment forms in front of the house of the U.S. consul to Samoa on the island of Upolu in April 1899. (National Archives)*

Right: *USS* Philadelphia *fires practice rounds off Samoa in March 1899. (National Archives)*

8 October
Philippines
In conjunction with Army forces, the Second Marine Battalion under Lieutenant Colonel George F. Elliott assaults the rebel stronghold of Novaleta and takes it with the assistance of naval gunfire from gunboat *Petrel* (PG-2).

28 October
Philippines
Company A of the Sixth Marine Battalion arrives at Manila.

26 November
Philippines
A force of more than 50 Marines deploys ashore to occupy Vigan on the northwest coast of Luzon, in support of an Army offensive.

15 December
Philippines
Major Littleton W. T. Waller's Third Marine Battalion, with 15 officers and 325 enlisted men, lands at Cavite to reinforce the garrison.

1900

1 January
Philippines
The three battalions of Marines in the Philippines are reorganized into two battalions of four companies each and designated as the 1st Regiment.

6 January
Philippines
A small group of Marines burns an insurgent signal station near Olongapo on Luzon.

16 February
Philippines
A party of Marines obtaining water for the outpost at Olongapo is ambushed by rebels and rescued by a relief column.

23 February
Philippines
A company of Marines from Olongapo burns the village of Benectican in retaliation for the ambush.

27 February
Philippines
Olongapo Marines participate in a landing at Perez to rescue prisoners held by the Filipino rebels.

5 March
Philippines
Marines from Olongapo make a landing from gunboat *Nashville* (PG-7) and assist an Army force in capturing the town of Bogac.

29 March
Department of the Navy
Colonel George C. Reid, the adjutant and inspector of the Marine Corps, is the first Marine officer appointed to the General Board of the Navy, the new body of senior officers providing policy advice to the Secretary of the Navy.

29 May
China
Captain John T. Myers, 28 Marines, and a few sailors from *Oregon*, reinforced by cruiser *Newark*'s (C-1) 26 Marines under Captain Newt H. Hall,

land at Taku and proceed to Peking to guard the legation as the anti-foreign Boxers grow more menacing.

10 June
China
U.S. sailors reinforced by a handful of Marines participate in the first relief column destined for the entrapped foreign legations in Peking. The 2,000-man force of several nationalities, under command of British Vice Admiral Edward Seymour, finds slow going against the Chinese.

19 June
China
Major Littleton W. T. Waller and a company of Marines from the Philippines arrive at Taku.

21 June
China
In conjunction with 450 Russian troops, Waller's force attempts to seize Tientsin, but they are driven back. Chinese government forces join Boxers in laying siege to the Legation Quarter in Peking. Meyer's Marine detachment defends the Tartar Wall overlooking the compound.

22 June
China
Seymour's force falls back on a Chinese arsenal six miles from Tientsin.

24 June
China
Waller and his men, now joined with British troops and additional Russians, capture Tientsin against strong resistance.

24–26 June
China
Marines under Waller participate in the relief of Seymour. The combined force of roughly 4,000 men moves back to Tientsin.

27 June
China
A combined force of Russians, British, and American Marines captures an arsenal in Tientsin from a much larger Boxer force. In Peking,

Opposite: *A Marine sergeant balances tote bags on his Krag rifle during the Boxer Rebellion. ("The Old China Hand," Col Charles Waterhouse, USMCR (Ret), Marine Corps Art Collection)*

Top: *"Defense of the Peking Legation," John Clymer, Marine Corps Art Collection*

Right: *"Resupply at Pei-ho River," Col Charles Waterhouse, USMCR (Ret), Marine Corps Art Collection*

THE 1ST MARINE REGIMENT

The Marine Corps formed its first regimental-size unit in 1836 under Commandant Henderson for service in the Seminole War. The next leatherneck regiment, and the first to bear an official designation, was the 1st Regiment, formed in the Philippines from three battalions on 1 January 1900. Although it never took the field as a single entity during the pacification campaign, its battalions participated in the fighting throughout the island chain. That summer the regiment deployed to China, where it served in the expedition to relieve the siege of the Legation Quarter in Peking. Transferred back to the Philippines in October, the 1st Regiment assumed responsibility for the naval station at Olongapo. It largely remained at that base until 1914.

Having just exceeded 4,000 men for the first time in 1900, the Marine Corps was still new to the business of organizing large units. Starting in 1904, things got confusing as Headquarters indiscriminately applied the designation of 1st Regiment to various outfits at overlapping times. A 1st Regiment existed briefly in Panama in 1904. Another came into being for the Cuban occupation in 1906, though it was soon styled as the 1st Provisional Regiment and lasted under that designation until the withdrawal from Cuba in 1909. Four other outfits would bear some variation of the 1st Regiment title during the period 1911 through 1913.

The direct lineal ancestor of the modern 1st Marine Regiment came into existence in November 1913 as the 1st Advance Base Regiment. It participated in the landings at Veracruz, Mexico, in April 1914. A year later it played a major role in establishing order in Haiti. In 1916, it moved next door and repeated the same mission in Santo Domingo. When not engaged in active combat operations, the regiment served with the Advance Base Force and helped develop the concepts that would contribute to the Corps' preeminent role in amphibious warfare from World War II onward.

Throughout its first decade of service, the regiment went through seven variations in title, not to mention an exchange of numbers

with the 2nd Regiment in 1916. After briefly ceasing to exist in mid-1922, it came back to life when the 3rd Regiment was redesignated as the 1st later that year. It went out of existence again in 1924. These bewildering changes in nomenclature came to an end in 1925 with the re-creation of the 1st Regiment on 15 March 1925 in Quantico. From this time forward, each Marine regiment would have a distinct number, no matter its function or its association with higher echelons. On 10 July 1930, the Corps made one more refinement to its method of designating regiments, formally assigning them the simple title of "Marines."

Due to Depression-era cutbacks in defense spending, the 1st Marines was reduced to a battalion in 1931 and ceased to exist altogether in 1932. It came back to life at Culebra, Puerto Rico, on 1 February 1941, as part of the growth of the brand-new 1st Marine Division. With a brief exception, it has served as an element of that famed organization ever since. During World War II, the 1st Marines fought at Guadalcanal, New Britain, Peleliu, and Okinawa. After the war, the regiment participated in the occupation of North China. Deactivated for brief periods in 1947 and 1949, it sprang to life again in August 1950 in time to fight in Korea from the Inchon landing through the armistice in 1953. It battled Communist forces again in Vietnam from 1965 to 1971, serving for a short period in April with the 3rd Marine Amphibious Force during the final withdrawal from that nation. The 1st Marines deployed to Southwest Asia in 1990 for the Gulf war and sent an element to participate in Operation United Shield, the covering force for the withdrawal of United Nations troops from Somalia in 1995.

Opposite: *"Flag Raising, Caribbean," Sydney Riesenberg, Marine Corps Art Collection*

Above: *Marines of the 1st Regiment at Subic in the Philippines in 1901. (Marine Corps Research Center)*

Meyer's Marines fight off a heavy Chinese attack on their position astride the wall.

30 June
Manpower
The strength of the Marine Corps on active duty is 174 officers and 5,240 enlisted.

3 July
China
Meyer's Marines lead a small force of U.S. and British Marines and Russian soldiers in a pre-dawn attack to seize a Chinese tower placed near the American barricade on the wall.

8 July
Taining
A specially trained unit of five officers and 40 enlisted forms the heart of a force that lands from the battleships *Kearsarge*, *Alabama* (BB-8), and *Massachusetts* (BB-2) at Nantucket, Massachusetts. This is the first exercise testing the concept of advance base operations.

10 July
China
The headquarters of the 1st Regiment, one battalion, and an artillery company land at Taku after sailing from the Philippines. Upon reaching Tientsin, the regimental commander, Colonel Robert L. Meade, assumes command of a U.S. brigade composed of his 1st Regiment (including Waller's battalion) and two battalions of the U.S. Army's 9th Infantry Regiment.

13–14 July
China
The allied contingents, now totaling 5,650 men, attack the old, walled, Chinese portion of Tientsin. The Marines fight next to the Royal Welsh Fusiliers and establish a close bond between the two units.

Top: *U.S. and Royal Marines battle the Boxers. ("Blood is Thicker Than Water," H. M. Paget, Marine Corps Research Center)*

Left: *Marine Legation Guard in Peking shortly after they took over the duty in 1905. This would become one of the most sought after posts of the Corps. (Marine Corps Research Center)*

15 July
China
At Peking, Private Dan Daly distinguishes himself in holding a secondary barricade against a strong Chinese attack.

30 July
China
The 4th Marine Battalion of eight officers and 220 enlisted men arrives at Tientsin under command of Major William P. Biddle. Due to the illness of Colonel Meade, Biddle assumes command of the 1st Regiment.

3 August
China
An international relief force of more than 18,000 troops—including 482 men of the 1st Regiment—sets out from Tientsin for Peking.

6 August
China
The 1st Regiment assists an army artillery battery in driving off a Chinese cavalry attack at Yangtsun.

14 August
China
The Marines participate in the attacks that capture Peking and relieve the Legation Quarter.

October
Force Structure
The 1st and 2nd Regiments at Cavite and Olongapo are organized into the 1st Marine Brigade.

3 October
China
The Marines depart Peking and an Army force assumes the role of guarding the U.S. Legation.

Top: *Marines being transported to their next call of duty follow the time-honored shipboard practice of standing in line. (Marine Corps Research Center)*

Right: *"Peking," John J. Capolino, Marine Corps Art Collection*

SERGEANT MAJOR DAN DALY

Daniel Joseph Daly was born in Glen Cove on New York's Long Island on 11 November 1873. After a few years working as a laborer, he enlisted in the Marine Corps on 10 January 1899. At 5 feet, 6 inches and 132 pounds he was not an imposing figure, but his piercing blue-gray eyes and erect posture gave him a military bearing. He did his initial training at the New York Navy Yard, then sailed with the cruiser *Newark* for the Pacific in March 1899. The ship's Marine detachment played a minor role in the Philippine Insurrection in December.

In May of 1900, he and his fellow Marines went ashore in China to help safeguard the U.S. legation in Peking from the Boxers. He helped hold the Tartar Wall of the compound from the onset of the siege on 20 June through relief on 14 August. His biggest contribution came on the night of 15 July, when he and Captain Hall scouted out a location for a new barricade farther along the wall. If it were a viable position, two Marines and Chinese workers were supposed to bring up sandbags to build a bastion. When they didn't appear on time, Hall went back to look for them. Despite the snap of enemy fire, Daly volunteered to hold the advance post until help arrived. For his "courage and fidelity," he would later receive the Medal of Honor.

Although Daly subsequently established a reputation as a "strict disciplinarian," he got in trouble early in his career on at least three occasions due to alcohol. During the detachment's first foray ashore at Vigan in the Philippines, he was determined to be "drunk in the presence of the enemy" (though in fact there was no fighting there). He missed the next landing at Apari because he was confined on the ship. Following his exploits in China, he was twice court-martialed for drunkenness, and each time received 30 days in solitary confinement in irons on bread and water. His conduct improved dramatically thereafter, perhaps in part due to receipt of the nation's highest award for valor in December 1901. His innate courage never changed, however, and he justified many times over the second chance he was given.

In March 1911, while serving on the schooner *Springfield* in Puerto Rico, a drum of gasoline caught fire in the night. He rushed in to help put out the blaze. Four years later he was in Haiti fighting Caco guerrillas. On the night of 24 October 1915, Gunnery Sergeant Daly was with a patrol of 35 enlisted men and five officers, under command of Major Smedley Butler. As the force crossed a stream, a large band of Cacos ambushed it. The Marines fought forward to better ground and formed a perimeter. After taking fire all night long, at first light two officers and Daly each attacked with a squad in different directions. The surprised Cacos fled, leaving their dead and wounded behind. For this action, Daly soon received his second Medal of Honor (making Butler and him the only Marines ever to receive two such awards for separate acts of valor). On 17 November, he participated in the daring assault on Fort Riviere, which required the Marines to crawl through a drainpipe to enter the enemy-held bastion.

During World War I, Daly was the first sergeant for the 73rd Machine Gun Company, 6th Regiment, 4th Marine Brigade. He participated in most of the outfit's engagements, but seemed to be everywhere during the crucial battle at Belleau Wood, where the largely untested Marines of the brigade faced veteran German forces for the first time. On 5 June 1918, he waded into a fire in an ammunition dump and extinguished it. Two days later, under a thunderous bombardment, he moved along the front line visiting his gun crews and reassuring them. At the start of a Marine attack on the 10th, as men hesitated under withering enemy fire, he called for them to follow with a cry that has been enshrined in history: "Come on, you sons of bitches! Do you want to live forever!" Later that day, he single-handedly assaulted a German machine-gun nest with grenades and his pistol. As the fighting subsided, he went back into the open under fire and pulled wounded to safety. For these actions, he received the Navy Cross, the Army Distinguished Service Cross, and the French Croix de Guerre. He also suffered three wounds during his months of combat in Europe.

After 20 years of heroism, Daly went on the inactive list in 1920 and worked as a bank guard in New York. He officially retired from the Marine Corps in 1929 and died in 1937. Smedley Butler lauded his old comrade as "the fightingest Marine I ever knew."

Opposite: *"Private Dan Daly in China," Col Charles Waterhouse, USMCR (Ret), Marine Corps Art Collection*

Right: *The view from the Tartar Wall into the back of the U.S. Legation in Peking. (Marine Corps Research Center)*

Left: *The first Marine Corps Rifle Team at Sea Girt, New Jersey, in 1901. (Marine Corps Research Center)*

Bottom: *Marines originally stationed together on Guam pose at Cavite Navy Yard in the Philippines in December 1900. Two of them would die in the fateful patrol on Samar in 1902. (Marine Corps Research Center)*

10 October
China
With the Boxer Rebellion at an end, the 1st Regiment (the only Marine unit still in China) sails from Taku for the Philippines.

1901

1 May
Expositions
A detachment of Marines assumes guard duty for the Pan-American exposition at Buffalo, New York.

10 June
HQMC
Headquarters Marine Corps moves from Marine Barracks 8th and I to the Bond Building at 14th Street and New York Avenue in Northwest Washington, D.C.

30 June
Manpower
The strength of the Marine Corps on active duty is 171 officers and 5,694 enlisted.

24 October
Samar
A provisional battalion under Waller, composed of three companies from the 1st Regiment and a company from the 2nd Regiment, arrives on the island of Samar in the Philippines. Their mission is to deal with rebellious Moro natives that have massacred an army infantry company.

1–10 November
Samar
Marine patrols on Samar skirmish with numerous enemy bands, driving them back to a rebel stronghold dug into the cliffs along the Sohoton River.

16 November
Samar
Waller's force attacks the Moro bastion at Sohoton and routs the enemy with heavy rifle and machine-gun fire.

24 November
Panama
After a rebel faction stops rail traffic across the Isthmus of Panama, 12 Marine officers and 233 enlisted land from battleship *Iowa* (BB-4) and *Concord* at Panama City.

26 November
Panama
Marines and sailors from gunboat *Machias* (PG-5) and *Marietta* land at Colon to assist in restoring rail transportation. Both elements remain ashore until 4 December.

28 December
Samar
Ordered to map out a telegraph route through the wild heart of Samar, Waller, five officers, 50 men, and a group of native scouts and bearers, depart Lanang on the east coast.

1902

3 January
Samar
With illness and shortages of food debilitating his force, Waller sets out with the strongest Marines to find a way out of the jungle and seek help for the remainder of his beleaguered detachment.

6 January
Samar
Waller's small band reaches a safe haven on the west coast of Samar.

7–17 January
Samar
With fresh Marines, Waller searches in vain for the remainder of his force.

11 January
Samar
Another element of Waller's original patrol makes it back to the east coast of Samar.

15 January
Samar
The last survivors of the Waller expedition make it to the east coast. Ten Marines had died in the interior.

Top: *Lt Dion Williams and his detachment salute Admiral Dewey upon his first visit to the Navy Yard at Cavite, Philippines, 13 June 1898. (Marine Corps Research Center)*

Right: *Marines at Subic in the Philippines in 1901. (Marine Corps Historical Center)*

SAMAR

When the United States took the Philippines away from Spain in 1898, it had to put down a revolt throughout the island chain. The Moro population on the island of Samar proved to be among the toughest opponents. On 28 September 1901, as a company of the Army's 9th Infantry ate breakfast in their mess hall at Balangiga, a Moro force surprised and massacred the soldiers. The Navy soon dispatched Major Littleton W. T. Waller and a battalion of 14 officers and 300 enlisted men to assist in establishing firm control over southern Samar. Two companies under Captain David D. Porter landed at Balangiga in the south on 24 October, while Waller and the other two companies went to Basey a little to the northwest. The blunt instructions from the senior Army general were to destroy the insurgents and anything that might be of assistance to them.

Within days Waller and Porter were patrolling the hinterland and skirmishing with rebel bands. In the course of the campaign they followed Army practice in burning dwellings, boats, and food supplies. They also killed 39 insurgents and captured another 18. Under this pressure, the bulk of the rebel force withdrew into the interior of the island to a system of caves dug into soft rock in cliffs above the Sohoton River.

Waller's command converged there on 17 November. Porter's column reached the scene slightly ahead of Waller and managed to make its way from the rear to the top of the cliff on one side of the river. The Moro soldiers were cooking and working on the opposite bank. Supported by a Colt machine gun, the Marines opened up a devastating fire on the surprised enemy. As the Moros broke and fled, Porter's men rushed down to the river's edge, crossed on canoes and a raft tied up there, and stormed up the opposite rise. They had killed 30 rebels and broken their morale with the daring attack on the supposed bastion. One of the heroes of the assault was John Quick, of Guantanamo fame, since promoted to gunnery sergeant.

Subsequent patrolling inflicted further losses on the rebels, but Waller was intent on showing that he could go anywhere on the island. On 28 December, the battalion commander, four other officers, 50 enlisted men, two native scouts, and 33 porters set out from the east coast to find a route to the west coast. They boated up the Lanang River to its navigable head, then marched along a trail that criss-crossed the swift, swollen waterway. The rough terrain sapped the strength of the Marines, and some of their food proved to be spoiled. By 2 January, a number of men were sick or exhausted, and rations were almost gone. An attempt to construct rafts to go downriver failed for lack of material that would float.

Waller decided to continue westward with 13 of his strongest Marines, in hopes of bringing back a relief party. Porter was to follow with the weaker members of the patrol as best he could. Confusion and disaster ensued. Waller soon found a village and food, but failed to ensure that word got back to Porter. After making it to the west coast on 6 January, Waller retraced his steps the next day and searched for his men without success until the 17th. Porter had turned back and, copying his commander, finally decided to head for the east coast with the seven strongest Marines and obtain help for the others. Before the fiasco was over, 10 Marines were dead, and another had gone insane. Waller, ill and feverish, subsequently had 11 of the native porters executed on charges they had stolen provisions or otherwise undermined the patrol. He was later court-martialed for murder, but was exonerated. Still, the bravery of Sohoton and the bitter tragedy of the cross-island patrol drew admiration. It became customary among Marines in the Philippines to honor the presence of a survivor with the toast: "Stand, gentlemen, he served on Samar."

"Waller's Patrol Crossing Samar," Col Charles Waterhouse, USMCR (Ret), Marine Corps Art Collection

20 January
Samar
Major Littleton W. T. Waller executes 11 Filipinos for alleged treachery associated with his failed expedition.

24 February
Civil Support
Two thousand Marines form the honor guard for Prince Henry of Prussia on his visit to Washington.

2 March
Samar
Waller's battalion returns to Luzon.

16 April
Panama
Marines and sailors from *Machias* go ashore at Boca del Toro in the Isthmus of Panama to protect the American consulate and the shipping port of the United Fruit Company during a civil war.

18 May
Panama
Screw steamer *Ranger* lands her Marines and sailors at Panama City to protect American lives.

30 June
Manpower
The strength of the Marine Corps on active duty is 191 officers and 6,031 enlisted.

July
Commandants
Commandant Heywood is promoted to major general by special legislation, the first Marine to hold that rank.

17 September
Panama
Marines and seamen from cruiser *Cincinnati* (C-7) land at Colon to guard Americans during a rebellion against Colombian rule. U.S. interest in the Isthmus of Panama is heightened by a recent decision to build a canal there to connect the Pacific and Atlantic oceans.

22 September
Panama
A battalion of 17 officers and 325 enlisted Marines arrives at Colon from the United States.

17 November
Panama
Marines withdraw from Panama after Colombian troops restore order in the troubled province.

1903

23 March
Honduras
Marines from *Marietta* and cruiser *Olympia* (C-6) land at Puerto Cortez, Honduras, to protect U.S. interests during a period of civil strife.

28 March
HQMC
Headquarters Marine Corps moves from the Bond Building to the Mills Building at 17th Street and Pennsylvania Avenue in Northwest Washington.

1 April
Santo Domingo
Atlanta sends her Marines ashore at Santo Domingo City in Santo Domingo to protect American lives during political disturbances.

3 May
Training
The School of Application moves from Marine Barracks 8th and I to Annapolis, Maryland.

30 June
Manpower
The strength of the Marine Corps on active duty is 213 officers and 6,445 enlisted.

7 September
Lebanon
Marines and sailors from cruiser *Brooklyn* (ACR-3) land at Beirut, then part of Syria, to defend U.S. interests during a period of unrest.

3 October
Commandants
Major General Heywood retires. Colonel George F. Elliott is promoted to brigadier general and becomes the 10th Commandant of the Marine Corps.

4 November
Panama
A day after Panamanians revolted against Colombia, Marines and sailors from *Nashville* land at Colon to protect American lives and secure the railroad from use by the forces of either side.

5 November
Panama
Major John A. Lejeune's Marine battalion goes ashore at Colon from *Dixie* to reinforce the *Nashville* contingent. Colombian forces withdraw and the Marines re-embark the next day. The United States recognizes the independence of Panama on the 6th.

18 November
Ethiopia
A detachment of 20 Marines lands at Djibouti, French Somaliland, to escort a U.S. diplomatic mission to Addis Ababa for negotiations with the emperor of Ethiopia. They return to the coast on 15 January 1904.

12 December
Panama
Lejeune's battalion goes into camp near Colon.

21 December
Panama
Another expeditionary force of 11 officers and 300 enlisted Marines arrives in Colon, Panama, on board auxiliary cruiser *Prairie*.

Opposite: *Marine drummers and buglers in the Philippines, 1900. (Marine Corps Research Center)*

Right: *These Marines of the relief expedition pause during the hard campaign to rescue the Legation Quarter in Peking. (Marine Corps Research Center)*

1904

3 January
Panama
Two additional battalions of Marines arrive in Panama to ensure the independence of that new nation. Brigadier General Commandant Elliott accompanies them and takes command of the brigade composed of the four Marine battalions in Panama.
Santo Domingo
Cruiser *Detroit* (C-10) lands her Marines at Puerto Plata to help forestall intervention by European creditor nations.

5 January
Korea
A company of Marines from the Philippines lands at Seoul, Korea, to protect the U.S. legation during the Russo-Japanese War.

17 January
Santo Domingo
Marines and sailors from screw sloops *Hartford* and *Detroit* go ashore at Puerto Plata when fighting breaks out near the city.

9 February
Hawaii
Fifty Marines establish a permanent garrison at naval facilities in Honolulu.

11 February
Santo Domingo
Newark and cruiser *Columbia* (C-12) send 300 Marines and sailors ashore at Santo Domingo City after Dominican revolutionaries fire on an American launch.

12 March
Korea
The Marine detachment of *Cincinnati* assists in the evacuation of American nationals from Chemulpo and Seoul during the Russo-Japanese War.

27 April
Samoa
Gunnery Sergeant J. F. Cox arrives at the naval station at Tutuila, Samoa, to become the first drill instructor for the "Fita-Fita" native constabulary.

30 April
Expositions
A Marine unit assumes duties at the Louisiana Purchase Exposition in St. Louis, Missouri, to conduct exhibition drills and guard displays.

May
Midway
Twenty Marines arrive at Midway Island in the Pacific to maintain order among laborers installing a transoceanic cable. The detachment remains there until March 1908.

Left: *Some of the Marines of USS* Columbia *strike a tough pose after their intervention in Santo Domingo in 1904. (Marine Corps Research Center)*

Opposite: *Buglers and drummers of the Marines of the Atlantic Squadron in camp at Pensacola, Florida, April 1898. (Marine Corps Research Center)*

30 May
Morocco
Brooklyn's Marines land at Tangiers as a show of force to convince the Sultan of Morocco to negotiate with rebel leader Ahmed Raisuli for release of an American citizen held for ransom.

30 June
Manpower
The strength of the Marine Corps on active duty is 255 officers and 7,329 enlisted.

20 December
Panama
Marine forces move into Camp Elliott, their permanent base in the Panama Canal Zone. It is located at Bas Obispo, about one-third of the way along the canal from the east coast.

1905

January
Santo Domingo
A Marine expeditionary force sails from Panama for service in politically troubled Santo Domingo.

30 June
Manpower
The strength of the Marine Corps on active duty is 270 officers and 6,741 enlisted.

6 July
Heritage
Marines and sailors from cruisers *Tacoma* (C-18), *Brooklyn*, *Galveston* (C-17), and *Chattanooga* (C-16) land at Cherbourg, France, to escort the body of John Paul Jones from Paris to the United States.

12 September
China
A detachment of 100 Marines previously stationed in the Philippines assumes duties as the Legation Guard in Peking.

December
Russia
Marines are assigned to guard the U.S. embassy at St. Petersburg.

1906

18 April
Civil Support
Marines from the naval stations at Yerba Buena Island and Mare Island aid civilians following an earthquake and fire in San Francisco.

29 May
Panama
A battalion of 229 Marines under Major Lejeune arrives in Panama to deal with civil disturbances in the Canal Zone.

June
Caribbean
A Marine battalion embarks in *Dixie* for service in the Caribbean.

30 June
Manpower
The strength of the Marine Corps on active duty is 278 officers and 7,940 enlisted.

12 September
Cuba
The *Dixie* battalion arrives in Cuban waters as the Cuban government deals with a rebellion.

14 September
Cuba
Marines and sailors from *Marietta* go ashore at Cienfuegos, Cuba, to protect American-owned sugar plantations.

16 September
Cuba
A battalion of 400 Marines sails from Norfolk to reinforce U.S. naval power off Cuba.

18 September
Cuba
Another battalion sails from Philadelphia for service in Cuba. The Marines on board *Dixie* land at Cienfuegos to reinforce the ships detachment there.

25 September
Cuba
Marines and seamen from *Marietta* move inland to protect railroad lines.

28 September
Cuba
A detachment of 31 Marines lands at Havana to guard the Cuban treasury.

29 September
Cuba
Two thousand Marines go ashore at Havana and fan out to garrison various key points in the country.

30 September
Cuba
A fourth Marine battalion departs from Boston for Cuba.

1 October
Cuba
Part of a fifth Marine battalion departs Norfolk for Cuba. A sixth battalion of 804 officers and enlisted, formed from detachments of ships in the Atlantic Fleet, arrives in Havana Harbor. Colonel L. W. T. Waller assumes command of all Marines in Cuba and organizes them into a brigade with two regiments. The eventual strength of the brigade is 97 officers and 2,795 enlisted.

10 October
Cuba
The first U.S. Army units begin arriving in Cuba and relieving Marines from garrisoning various posts.

1 November
Cuba
The remaining 1,000 Marines in Cuba are organized into the 1st Provisional Regiment. It remains there until January 1909.

Opposite: *A recruiting poster from the period around World War I. ("They Shall Not Pass," Marine Corps Art Collection)*

Right: *This pre-WWI Marine Corps recruiting poster clearly states the Corps' universal role in the U.S. military. (Marine Corps Art Collection)*

1907

17 January
Jamaica
Marines and sailors from several U.S. warships land at Kingston, Jamaica, to assist in rescue efforts following a severe earthquake.

18 March
Honduras
Marietta sends her Marine detachment ashore at Truxillo, Honduras, to guard the U.S. consulate during political disturbances.

28 April
Honduras
Marines from *Paducah* (Gunboat No. 18) land at Laguna and Choloma, Honduras, to protect American lives and property during a war between Honduras and Nicaragua.

30 June
Manpower
The strength of the Marine Corps on active duty is 279 officers and 7,807 enlisted.

16 December
Virginia
Marine detachments are part of the Great White Fleet as it sails from Hampton Roads, Virginia, on a 14-month voyage around the world.

1908

21 May
Commandants
The rank of the billet of Commandant is formally established as major general for the first time, resulting in a promotion for Brigadier General Elliott.

28 May
Panama
A battalion of 17 officers and 400 enlisted men arrives in Panama to reinforce the normal Marine garrison during elections. It remains until 6 July.

June
Panama
Another Marine battalion, composed of 19 officers and 706 enlisted men, goes to Panama to assist in maintaining order during elections.

Left: *A Marine crew prepares to fire a round during naval gunnery practice on one of the ships of the fleet in 1912. (National Archives)*

Below: *Marines pose with the colors on board USS* Sheridan *en route to the Philippines in 1910. (National Archives)*

30 June
Manpower
The strength of the Marine Corps on active duty is 283 officers and 8,953 enlisted.

12 November
Roles and Missions
President Theodore Roosevelt signs Executive Order 969, which directs the removal of all Marine detachments from Navy ships. The action is rescinded by Congress in legislation passed on 3 March 1909.

1909

1 January
Training
Marine Officers School (for new lieutenants) moves to the Navy base at Port Royal, South Carolina.

30 June
Manpower
The strength of the Marine Corps on active duty is 328 officers and 9,368 enlisted.

November
Nicaragua
Major Smedley Butler's battalion boards auxiliary cruiser *Buffalo* in Philadelphia for duty in Panama. It ends up in Nicaraguan waters pending the resolution of a civil war in that nation and stays there until 16 March 1910.

December
Nicaragua
A regiment of 750 Marines departs from Philadelphia early in the month for possible duty in troubled Nicaragua. It remains on ship off the west coast port of Corinto until March 1910.

1910

22 February
Nicaragua
Butler and a few Marines land at Corinto to reconnoiter the rail lines.

19 May
Nicaragua
Marines and sailors from *Paducah* go ashore at Bluefields, Nicaragua, to protect American lives and property when revolutionary forces threaten the town.

31 May
Nicaragua
Major Butler and two companies of Marines arrive at Bluefields from Panama and remain there until early September.

30 June
Manpower
The strength of the Marine Corps on active duty is 328 officers and 9,232 enlisted.

30 November
Commandants
Commandant Elliott retires.

1911

3 February
Commandants
Following a long period of political indecision over the selection, President Taft confirms the acting Commandant, Colonel William P. Biddle, as the 11th Commandant of the Marine Corps.

8 March
Force Structure
Colonel George Barnett assumes command of a provisional regiment, which eventually encamps at Guantanamo Bay, Cuba, for possible service in Mexico as a result of a revolution there.

10 March
Force Structure
Colonel Charles A. Doyen activates another provisional regiment at Mare Island, California, for potential expeditionary duty in Mexico.

Above: *Marines applying first aid while on training maneuvers, May 1913. (National Archives)*

Right: *Marines at ease with their rifles at stack arms on the deck of their battleship in 1913. (National Archives)*

MAJOR GENERAL SMEDLEY BUTLER

Smedley Darlington Butler was the product of a prominent line of eastern Pennsylvania families—the Smedleys, Darlingtons, and Butlers. His father went to Congress in 1896 and remained there for 32 years. Despite 16-year-old Smedley's youth, privileged upbringing, and Quaker religion, he rushed to the colors at the outbreak of the Spanish-American War. His father's seat on the House Naval Affairs Committee enabled the son to obtain a Marine commission. He soon reported to the battalion at Guantanamo Bay, but too late to see any action.

In the spring of 1899, Butler deployed to the Philippines with a new battalion. His first battle came in the assault on Novaleta, an important victory in the war against Filipino insurgents. Temporarily in command of a company, he led it against entrenched rebels and routed them. In June 1900, he accompanied Waller's battalion to China. During the initial operations against Tientsin, he distinguished himself by leading a group of six men to rescue a wounded Marine who had been left behind. Not quite 19, he was breveted to the rank of captain for bravery. He was wounded in subsequent fighting, but still participated in the relief expedition to Peking, where he was hit a second time.

Promoted to major in 1908 (at the age of 27), he took command of a battalion in Panama the following year. He twice deployed with his Marines to troubled Nicaragua in 1910 and 1911, but without any fighting. In August 1912 he returned, and this time bluffed his way through rebel forces to open the rail line from the port of Corinto to the capital of Managua. Pushing on to Granada in

September, he and his men were ambushed at Masaya and fought their way through. In early October, Butler's battalion played a major role in defeating the main revolutionary force at Coyotepe. In April 1914, Butler's battalion joined in the landing at Veracruz, Mexico. Once ashore, the Marines and reinforcing sailors had to fight their way house-to-house through the city. For his leadership there, he soon received the Medal of Honor. He tried to refuse it, saying that his conduct had not been sufficiently heroic, but the Secretary of the Navy ordered him to keep it.

A year later, Butler commanded a battalion during the intervention in Haiti. His most spectacular battle was the assault on Fort Riviere. While part of his force covered the approach with fire against the high walls, the major and two dozen men dashed to the face of the bastion. The only entrance through the thick masonry was via a drainpipe about three feet in width. A Caco was at the other end firing down it. Sergeant Ross Iams rushed through, followed by a private and then Butler. The three men bore the initial brunt of the Caco counterattack inside the fort until reinforcements made it through. Each subsequently received the Medal of Honor. The Marine major made no complaint about this award. Promoted to lieutenant colonel, he took on the difficult mission of building the brand-new Haitian constabulary.

Eager to join the fight in World War I, he finally made it to France in September 1918 in command of the 13th Regiment. He was discouraged when the Army broke up the Marine force for service duty and he was made commander of Camp Pontanezen, the reception facility at the port of Brest. The squalid tent city was ravaged with a virulent strain of influenza, which was killing off huge numbers of people around the world. In a matter of weeks, the irrepressible Butler had turned it into a model facility that processed more than 1 million American soldiers for their trip back to the States. The day after the armistice ended the fighting, he had personally led his men in a raid on Army warehouses and liberated tons of duckboards—short wooden slats destined to line trenches—and turned them into sidewalks and tent floors.

By the summer of 1920, Butler was a brigadier general and commander of the main Marine base at Quantico, Virginia. Each year his men marched to a prominent Civil War battlefield and re-enacted the campaign, thus garnering favorable publicity for the Corps during a time when military forces had fallen out of favor. He oversaw the construction of a football stadium by Marine labor and was the head cheerleader when the base team took on college opponents. During a two-year leave of absence in 1924–1925, he served as the incorruptible head of the Philadelphia Police Department. In 1927 he took command of the 3rd Marine Brigade, putting it together and getting it to China, where it protected U.S. interests during the Chinese civil war. In his last years in the Corps, his penchant for speaking his mind brought reprimands from the Navy Department and took away any chance he had of becoming Commandant. He retired in 1931 and undertook a personal crusade against U.S. gunboat diplomacy, writing a book titled *War Is a Racket*. He died in 1940.

Opposite: *A rare photo of the irrepressible Smedley Butler—not out in the field or among his men. (Marine Corps Research Center)*

Right: *Butler's Marines during one of their several forays into strategic Panama. (Marine Corps Research Center)*

Left: *Marines of the Advance Base Force train at Marine Barracks Philadelphia in 1913 with a pedestal-mounted coast defense gun, one of their primary armaments for defending expeditionary bases. The photograph shows how challenging it was to emplace these large, fixed weapons. (National Archives)*

13 March
Force Structure
A third provisional regiment of 22 officers and 666 enlisted men, created from the detachments of the Atlantic Fleet, debarks at Guantanamo Bay. The forces in Cuba are formed into a brigade under Colonel Waller.

20 March
Force Structure
Doyen's regiment lands at North Island in San Diego Bay and establishes a camp there. These Marines remain until July, when the disorders in Mexico come to an end.

April
HQMC
Commandant Biddle creates the billet of Assistant to the Commandant.

26 April
Marine Corps Association
Colonel Franklin J. Moses calls together the officers of the brigade in Cuba for the purpose of forming an association to preserve the Corps. This becomes the genesis of the Marine Corps Association.

1 June
Training
The Marine Corps adds recruit training to the program at the Marine Officers School at Port Royal.

30 June
Manpower
The strength of the Marine Corps on active duty is 328 officers and 9,282 enlisted.

30 August
Training
The Navy establishes a disciplinary barracks at Port Royal. To make room for it, the Marine Officers School is moved to Norfolk, Virginia, while the recruit training function is split between Norfolk and Charleston, South Carolina.

11 September
Training
The Marine Corps moves the year-old Advance Base School from New London, Connecticut, to the Philadelphia Navy Yard.

October
China
A battalion of 15 officers and 360 enlisted Marines sail from the Philippines to Shanghai on board tender *Rainbow* (AS-7), where they serve as a floating reserve for the next several months.

13 October
China
A small detachment of Marines and sailors from gunboat *Helena* goes ashore at Hankow, China, to protect the U.S. consulate and American lives and

businesses following the overthrow of the Manchu Dynasty.

4 November
China
Two dozen Marines land near Shanghai from cruiser *Albany* (CL-23) to protect a cable station.

29 November
China
Cruiser *Saratoga* (ACR-2) departs Shanghai for Taku to protect foreign missionaries.

1912

10 March
China
The Marine battalion from *Rainbow* arrives in Peking to reinforce the Legation Guard and remains there until May.

22 May
Aviation
Lieutenant Alfred A. Cunningham reports for pilot training at the Navy's flying school at Annapolis, Maryland. This marks the birth of Marine aviation.

23 May
Cuba
Within 24 hours of receiving orders to organize the 1st Provisional Regiment, 32 officers and 777 enlisted are gathered and readied for overseas duty at Philadelphia.

28 May
Cuba
The 1st Provisional Regiment arrives at Guantanamo Bay on board *Prairie* to deal with a rebellious force threatening to kill U.S. citizens and destroy American-owned businesses throughout the island.

5 June
Cuba
The 1st Battalion of the 2nd Regiment (totaling 40 officers and 1,252 enlisted) goes ashore at Guantanamo Bay.

10 June
Cuba
The 2nd Battalion of the 2nd Regiment arrives off Havana. The two Marine regiments are formed into a brigade. Marines fan out around Santiago and Guantanamo Bay to guard towns, trains, and plantations. Elements of the brigade remain in Cuba until August.

30 June
Manpower
The strength of the Marine Corps on active duty is 337 officers and 9,359 enlisted.

14 August
Nicaragua
Butler's battalion of 13 officers and 341 enlisted men lands at Corinto and proceeds by rail to Managua to protect the U.S. legation during a civil war.

Right: *Marines practice with a field gun prior to World War I. Note the caisson in the center for carrying ammunition. (National Archives)*

LIEUTENANT COLONEL ALFRED CUNNINGHAM

Like Smedley Butler, Alfred A. Cunningham was eager to go off to the Spanish-American War even though he was quite young. In May 1898, just two months after his 16th birthday, he joined the 2nd Georgia Infantry Volunteers as a corporal. He made it to Cuba in January 1899, far too late for battle, but served four months there before being mustered out. He returned to complete his schooling in his hometown of Atlanta, then entered the real-estate business. In 1903 he became fascinated with aviation and made his first flight in a balloon.

After 10 years of civilian life, Cunningham sought and received a commission in the Marine Corps in 1909. He reported to the school for new lieutenants at Port Royal, South Carolina, where his maturity paid off and he finished fourth in a class of 55 students. After a tour with the battleships of the Navy, he ended up in the Advance Base School at the Philadelphia Navy Yard in November 1911. The lure of flight still held him in its grasp, to the extent that he spent 15 percent of his monthly pay to lease a plane from a local inventor. Despite many attempts, the Marine lieutenant could never get the faulty contraption off the ground. He also developed friendships with members of the local aero club, many of whom possessed a fair amount of wealth and influence. They in turn pressed the Marine Corps (and its Philadelphia-born Commandant, Biddle) to start an aviation arm. Cunningham's efforts paid off on 16 May 1912, when Headquarters ordered him to pilot training. But first there was a brief detour for service afloat related to the creation of expeditionary units for Cuba and Nicaragua.

Although the Navy's fledgling aviation school was based at Annapolis, the three planes available there had all been wrecked, so Cunningham ended up learning to fly with an aircraft builder in Marblehead, Massachusetts. He reported there at the end of July and received a grand total of two hours and 40 minutes of instruction in the air, including two training landings. Then he took off on his own in a seaplane on 20 August 1912. He landed successfully on the bay, thereby becoming the first Marine to solo and the fifth naval aviator. He returned to Annapolis and was assigned Sergeant James Maguire as a mechanic, the first enlisted Marine in leatherneck aviation. In January 1913 the handful of planes and pilots in naval aviation deployed with the fleet for maneuvers off Guantanamo Bay, Cuba, the first use of naval aircraft in an operational environment.

Cunningham's career in flight almost consisted of nothing more than a footnote in history. In August 1913 he asked to be relieved from flight duty because his fiancee would not marry him otherwise. His request was granted, though he remained connected with aviation planning and ground operations. His hiatus from naval aviation proved relatively brief, as he returned to flying (still married) in April 1915. He learned to fly land planes in the summer of 1916 (the second Marine to do so) and attempted the first-ever catapult takeoff from a warship underway. The experiment was a failure, with his seaplane flipping over in the air and crashing in the water. He came away with an injured back.

It was during World War I that Cunningham made his greatest contribution to Marine aviation. In the winter of 1917–1918, he went to Europe to learn about Allied air capabilities and even accompanied British pilots in action against the Germans. He came home with the idea that Navy and Marine aviation units should focus on a campaign against German submarine bases. He eventually assumed command of the 1st Marine Aviation Force and took it to France in July 1918. Christened the Day Wing of the Northern Bombing Group, the Marines ended up going after a wide variety of enemy targets in their de Haviland DH-4 two-seat biplanes. In a few short weeks before the Armistice, Cunningham's force manage to drop more than 27,000 pounds of bombs, shoot down several German aircraft, and even resupply a trapped French infantry unit with food. For his efforts in organizing, training, and leading this first Marine aviation combat outfit, Cunningham received the Navy Cross.

After the war, he served for a time as the first officer in charge of Marine aviation at Headquarters Marine Corps. Following command of a squadron in Santo Domingo, he returned to ground duty, as required at the time following five years of aviation service. Later he served in Nicaragua during the American intervention there in the late 1920s. He never returned to flight status and retired in 1935 due to poor health. He died in 1939. His views of the possibilities of aviation and his drive to bring them to reality had played a major role in establishing Marine air as a vital part of the Corps' capability.

Alfred Cunningham, the father of Marine Corps aviation, poses in front of a plane at the cradle of naval aviation, Pensacola, Florida, in March 1914. (Marine Corps Historical Center)

Left: *Marine guard on board a U.S. battleship assembles for a unit photograph in 1912. (National Archives)*

17 August
Nicaragua
Tacoma puts its Marine detachment ashore at Bluefields, Nicaragua, to guard the U.S. consulate.

20 August
Aviation
Alfred Cunningham completes his solo flight to become the first Marine aviator.

22 August
Manpower
Congress authorizes an increase in the size of the Marine Corps to 348 officers and 9,921 enlisted men. This marks the first time the Corps is allowed to exceed 10,000 personnel.

24 August
China
A Marine force from *Rainbow* lands at Shanghai, China, to protect Americans from revolutionaries.

28 August
Nicaragua
California sends 64 Marines ashore at Corinto to reinforce Butler's battalion.

30 August
Nicaragua
Marines and sailors from *Denver* land at San Juan del Sur, Nicaragua, to guard the cable station.

4 September
Nicaragua
Colonel Joseph H. Pendleton and his provisional regiment of 29 officers and 752 enlisted Marines goes ashore at Corinto from *Buffalo*. He assumes command of all Marine forces in western Nicaragua.

5 September
Nicaragua
More than 300 Marines and sailors from cruiser *Colorado* (CA-7) land at Corinto.

19 September
Nicaragua
While opening the rail lines, Butler's force is ambushed at night on board its train in the town of Masaya. The Marines drive off the Nicaraguan rebels.

3–4 October
Nicaragua
For a day, Butler's battalion shells Nicaraguan rebels entrenched on the adjoining hills of Coyotepe and Barranca outside Masaya. The next morning, reinforced by additional Marines and sailors brought up by Pendleton, the Americans assault the hills. At a cost of 18 Marine casualties, the rebels lose 60 dead (including their commander), and their force disintegrates.

6 October
Nicaragua
Marines and sailors drive rebel forces out of Leon, Nicaragua, bringing the civil war to an end.

November
China
A detachment of 36 Marines from Guam lands in Chefoo to protect U.S. interests during instability in China.

21 November
Nicaragua
Pendleton and Butler's battalion depart Nicaragua for Panama.

1913

17 January
Nicaragua
The remaining battalion of Marines in Nicaragua returns to normal garrison duties in Panama. A force of four officers and 101 enlisted Marines remains behind to guard the legation in Managua. The Legation detachment will remain until August 1925.

25 April
Marine Corps Association
The Marine Corps Association is formally chartered: "For the purposes of recording and publishing the history of the Marine Corps, publishing a periodical journal for the dissemination of information concerning the aims, purposes, and deeds of the Corps, and the interchange of ideas for the betterment and improvement of its officers and men."

30 June
Manpower
The strength of the Marine Corps on active duty is 331 officers and 9,625 enlisted.

7 July
China
Albany lands her Marines at Shanghai during a period of political disturbances.

28 July
China
Marines from *Rainbow* and *Albany* go ashore at Shanghai.

5 September
Mexico
Buffalo's Marines aid in evacuating American citizens from Ciaris, Mexico, during a time of civil strife.

19 December
Commandants
Congress limits the term of the Commandant to four years, with provision for reappointment for an additional four years.

23 December
Force Structure
Colonel Barnett assumes command of the new Advance Base Force at Philadelphia.

27 December
Force Structure
The Aviation Detachment of the Advance Base Force is established with two officers and seven enlisted men. This is the first Marine air-ground team.

Right: *Marines on board USS* California *await the order to "Land the landing force" at Corinto, Nicaragua, on 28 August 1912. (Marine Corps Historical Center)*

THE 1903 SPRINGFIELD RIFLE

Probably no other infantry weapon has ever been more beloved by the Marine Corps than the Model 1903 Springfield rifle. It was designed by the Army, however, in response to the experience of soldiers in the Spanish-American War. A man had to load each cartridge into the American Krag-Jorgenson weapon, whereas his opponent could feed a clip of several rounds into the 1893 Mauser and therefore produce a higher rate of fire. The Spaniards' German-designed rifles also achieved a flatter, and thus more accurate, trajectory. Army ordnance experts copied much of the latest Mauser features and added a few wrinkles of their own. The result was the Model 1903 Springfield, named for the main government arsenal that manufactured it and the year it was adopted.

One of the main advantages of the '03 (as it affectionately came to be known) was its sights. The rear sight was a leaf design—when flipped up, the shooter could adjust it for small increments of elevation and windage. Pushed down flat on the barrel, it provided a much simpler "battle" sight set for accuracy at 550 yards. The front sight was an unusually thin blade. In conjunction with the leaf sight, it allowed a competent

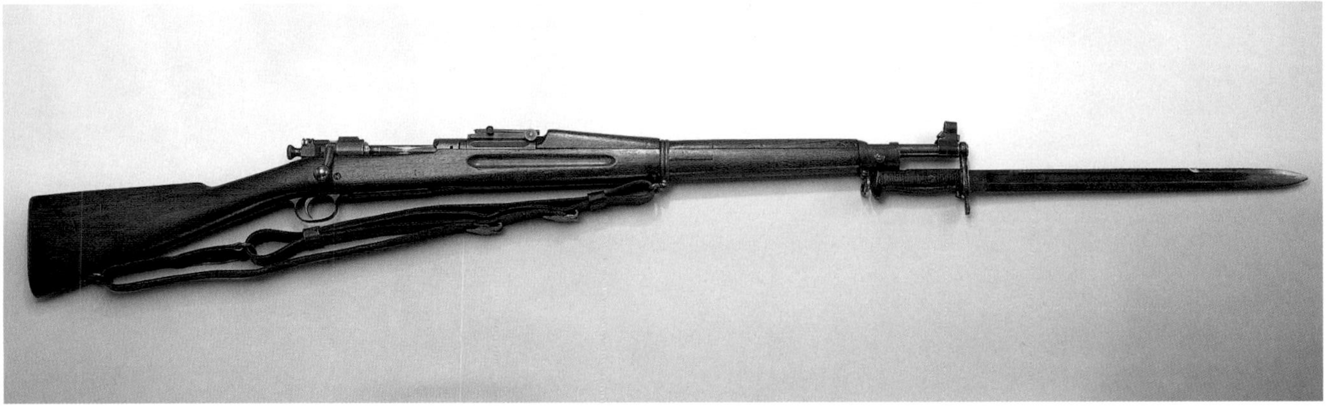

shooter to achieve an unprecedented level of precision in aiming. (The exception was in low-light conditions, when the front sight was more difficult to see than its fatter cousins.) The initial .30-caliber round was improved in 1906 (and quickly dubbed the "30/06") to produce a higher muzzle velocity and flatter trajectory. The combination of rifle and ammunition forged the most accurate weapon of the day. Married with the Marine emphasis on marksmanship training beginning in the first decade of the twentieth century, the result was a body of riflemen who squeezed off rounds rapidly and hit targets at extremely long ranges. (The rear sight was calibrated out to 2,850 yards, though the standard maximum range in actual use was 800 to 1,000 yards).

The Marine Corps began converting to the '03 in 1908. Marines first fired it in combat in Nicaragua in 1912. By the time of the Veracruz landing of 1914, the switch to the new weapon was just about complete. The Springfield earned its everlasting fame in World War I. Beginning on 2 June 1918, victorious German troops swept out of Belleau Wood in pursuit of reeling French forces and promptly ran into the U.S. 2nd Division and its 4th Marine Brigade. The Marines began picking off the advancing enemy soldiers at 800 yards, as veteran NCOs called out the range, and riflemen adjusted their leaf sights. The devastating firepower put a stop to the German offensive and established the legend of Marine combat marksmanship.

During the two decades after World War I, the Marines and their '03s surpassed all their rivals in competitive marksmanship on the firing ranges. The bond—forged in war and peace—was so strong that the Corps was extremely reluctant to replace the bolt-action Springfield with the Army's M-1 Garand at the start of World War II, even though the new semi-automatic rifle provided a significantly higher rate of fire. The finely machined Springfield was unsuited to the mass production required for a global war, however, and that helped seal its demise. Most Marine riflemen who arrived in the first weeks at Guadalcanal were still armed with the trusty '03, but the Garand soon took over. The Springfield continued in service thereafter as a superior sniper rifle and also as a grenade launcher.

Opposite: *Marines put their Springfields to use on the rifle range at Quantico in August 1918. (National Archives)*

Top: *The M-1903 was adapted from a design by German Paul Mauser and manufactured at both Springfield Armory and Rock Island Arsenal. (Marine Corps Historical Center)*

FIRST TO FIGHT

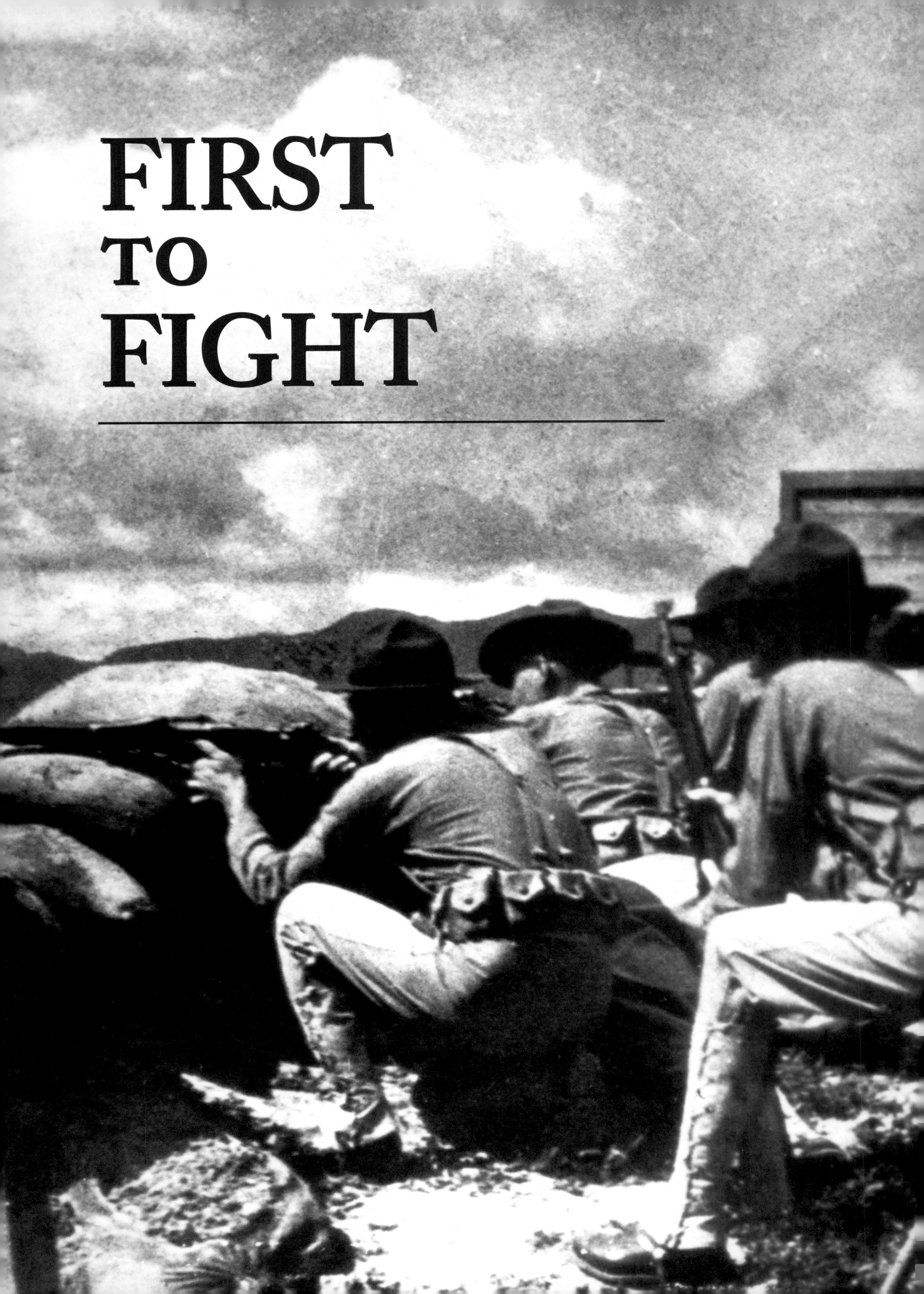

FIRST TO FIGHT

1914–1918

While the Spanish-American War and other events around the turn of the century had given the Corps new missions and helped spur professionalization, the World War I era solidified those changes and established the status of Marines firmly in the hearts of Americans.

The Marine Corps already was fully employed when a nearly global conflict engulfed European nations and their overseas colonies in August 1914. The advent of the Panama Canal, opened that same month, focused the interest of the U.S. Navy and the Marines on protecting this waterway. The canal not only permitted the fleet to shift quickly from one coast to another, it also facilitated transportation of commerce and people from one end of the transcontinental nation to the other. It quickly became U.S. policy to ensure that no other powerful nation placed military forces in a position to interdict this vital link. The most obvious threat would be European encroachment in the Caribbean or Central America, where several chronically impoverished countries provided potentially easy inroads. This strategic situation would lead to two decades of American intervention in this often chaotic region.

The first major deployment of Marines came in 1914. Revolution had engulfed Mexico, and the U.S. government was determined to influence the outcome. When word came that arms were going to be shipped through the port of Veracruz, the United States dispatched forces to forestall this. Elements of the fleet and embarked Marines were the first to arrive and they took control of the city a week before the first units of the U.S. Army reached the scene. This occupation was short lived, but the operation again demonstrated the readiness of the Corps.

A series of revolutions and violent changes in the government of Haiti brought U.S. intervention there the following year. Again, ships' detachments and regiments hastily formed from several Marine barracks provided the means to get American forces on the ground in a hurry. The very next year, 1916, the Marines subdued troublesome elements in Santo Domingo, the other half of the island of Hispaniola. In both cases, the Marines provided almost the entire force to accomplish the mission. And they stayed put, with the mission of bringing long-term stability to these two troubled nations.

Although the Corps already had considerable experience in small wars, Marines brought to bear a new tactic in Hispaniola. In both countries, Marines formed a constabulary force to carry out police and military functions. Marine officers and NCOs served as the leaders for units otherwise composed of recruits from the local population. As these outfits grew in size and capability, they took over most of the responsibility for maintaining order, with regular Marine units serving in the background. Constabularies proved to be an effective tool, since the local soldiers engendered

Pages 158–159: *While World War I in Europe dominates this era, Marines are fighting elsewhere, as well. These Marines are engaged in Santo Domingo in 1916. (National Archives)*

Right: *Training in the Overseas Depot at Quantico in 1917–18 included bayonet and hand-to-hand fighting in preparation for the trench warfare of Europe's western front. (National Archives)*

less resentment among the populace and knew the countryside and the people much better than Marines ever would.

The U.S. declaration of war against Germany on 6 April 1917 catapulted the Marine Corps to an unprecedented level. The United States had not prepared its Army for a war of this scope, so the War Department eagerly accepted the offer of a Marine regiment for service in Europe. Within weeks the 5th Marines was shipped to France as part of a token of U.S. commitment to its allies. By the fall, the 6th Marines and a machine gun battalion joined with the 5th to form the 4th Brigade of Marines, which became an element of the 2nd Infantry Division. Although another Marine brigade and an aviation force eventually would reach Europe, the 4th Brigade would bear the brunt of the Corps' participation in the war. The nearly 10,000 Marines of the brigade eventually were swamped by more than a million U.S. soldiers in Europe, but the small Leatherneck force made an outsize contribution to victory. In a month of fighting around Belleau Wood in June 1918, the 4th Brigade helped stop a German offensive threatening Paris and proved that American infantrymen were more than a match for the vaunted Germans. Although the rest of the 2nd Division also played a prominent role, a fluke in the censorship system gave the Marines the lion's share of publicity for one of the first American victories in the war. The action endeared the Corps to the nation, backed up the Marine claim of being "First to Fight," and created a lasting and bitter rivalry with the Army.

The 4th Brigade lived up to its status as an elite fighting unit throughout the remainder of the war. In battles at Soissons, St. Mihiel, Blanc Mont, and the Meuse-Argonne, the Marines took grievous casualties but still accomplished their mission and often exceeded expectations. By the end of the conflict, the Corps had a well-deserved renown for deadly marksmanship and determined bravery. Marine airmen came late to the struggle and did not serve directly in support of their ground compatriots, but they performed well in battle, too.

World War I did more than simply burnish the standing of the Corps. Strength grew from 10,000 in 1914 to 75,000 at war's end. Although it would drop precipitously after the armistice in November 1918, it would remain double its prewar size. Aviation, previously an experiment, became a major component in the Corps. Artillery and other supporting elements also took on new importance. The Marines acquired the first bases that they could call home, at Parris Island, Quantico, and San Diego. And from its close service with the Army in a major war, the Corps also gained a greater appreciation for doctrine, tactics, and the challenges of controlling organizations at the division level and above. In four short years, in skirmishes in the jungles of the Caribbean and in epic battles in Europe, the Corps had changed dramatically and become a completely modern fighting force with an elite reputation to uphold.

FIRST TO FIGHT

1914–1918

1914

3 January
Training
The 1st Advance Base Brigade sails from Philadelphia for field exercises at Culebra, Puerto Rico.

28 January
Haiti
The Marine detachment of battleship *South Carolina* (BB-26) lands at Port-au-Prince along with British, French, and German forces to protect foreign interests during revolutionary turmoil.

16 February
Haiti
Marines from *Wheeling* (Gunboat No. 14) go ashore at Port-de-Paix to safeguard American citizens as political unrest continues.

21 February
Haiti
Marines from *Wheeling* deploy to Cape Haitien to defend the U.S. consulate.

24 February
Commandants
Commandant William P. Biddle retires after 39 years of service in the Corps.

25 February
Commandants
Colonel George Barnett is appointed as the 12th Commandant of the Marine Corps.

16 April
Force Structure
The 4th Regiment is reactivated on the West Coast of the United States and embarks on ships of the fleet.

21 April
Veracruz
In an effort to forestall delivery of munitions to revolutionary forces in Mexico, lead elements of the 2nd Regiment go ashore at Veracruz, Mexico, from auxiliary cruiser *Prairie*. They are reinforced by Marines and sailors of the fleet. Fighting erupts in the city with Mexican soldiers.

Left: *Marines take a break from field duty in Cuba in 1914, during a period when the restive Caribbean nation was unusually quiet. (Marine Corps Research Center)*

22 April
Veracruz
The 1st Regiment, composed of 24 officers and 810 enlisted men, lands at Veracruz, Mexico, from transport *Hancock* (AP-3). Colonel Lejeune takes command of the Marine Brigade formed from the two regiments.

23 April
Veracruz
Marine and Navy forces complete the seizure of Veracruz.

24 April
Veracruz
The remainder of the 2nd Regiment arrives on board battleship *Mississippi* (BB-23).

29 April
Veracruz
Another Marine regiment created at Philadelphia arrives with 33 officers and 861 enlisted. Army occupation forces begin to go ashore.

1 May
Veracruz
Marine detachments return to the fleet and the Marine Brigade comes under command of the U.S. Army occupation forces, which remain in Mexico until November.

6 May
Santo Domingo
The 44th Company (three officers and 125 enlisted men) arrives off Puerto Plata, Santo Domingo, and remains on ship there for a month for potential deployment due to revolutionary disorder in that country.

30 June
Manpower
The strength of the Marine Corps on active duty is 336 officers and 10,500 enlisted.

Top: *Marine artillerymen train with their light field gun during the Cuban intervention in 1917. (National Archives)*

Right: *Marines on the march toward Camaguay, Cuba. (National Archives)*

Left: *Marines crowd the fantail of a ship as they mount out for the Veracruz expedition in 1914. (National Archives)*

Below: *This photo shows how a Marine carried his field gear during the landing at Veracruz. (Marine Corps Historical Center)*

7 July
Force Structure
The 4th Regiment goes into camp in San Diego after weeks of sailing off the western Mexican coast.

12 August
Force Structure
The newly formed 5th Regiment embarks on *Hancock* at Guantanamo Bay and sails to Hispaniola, where it remains offshore troubled Santo Domingo and Haiti almost continuously through mid-December.

11 December
Expositions
The 4th Regiment headquarters and its 2nd Battalion move into a model camp at the Panama-California Exposition in Balboa Park in San Diego.

17 December
Haiti
Marines from gunboat *Machias* (PG-5) escort the Haitian government's gold stocks from Port-au-Prince onto the ship for transport to New York and safekeeping there.

22 December
Expositions
The 1st Battalion, 4th Regiment embarks from San Diego to sail to Mare Island for subsequent duty with the Panama-Pacific International Exposition in San Francisco Bay.

1915

January
Training
The Marine Corps establishes a field artillery school, its first, at Annapolis.

9 January
Aviation
The Marine Section is established at the Navy Flying School, Pensacola.

16 February
Expositions
The 1st Battalion, 4th Regiment establishes a model military camp at the Panama-Pacific Exposition in San Francisco.

2 June
Department of the Navy
Commandant George Barnett becomes an ex-officio member of the General Board of the Navy.

17 June
Mexico
Three companies of the 2nd Battalion, 4th Regiment in San Diego embark on cruiser *Colorado* (CA-7) and remain on station off the west coast of Mexico for six weeks.

30 June
Manpower
The strength of the Marine Corps on active duty is 338 officers and 9,948 enlisted.

9 July
Haiti
Cruiser *Washington* (ACR-11) lands her Marine detachment to guard a radio station at Cape Haitien. They remain there until 27 July.

28 July
Haiti
A naval regiment from *Washington*, composed of Marines and sailors under command of Marine Captain George Van Orden, goes ashore at Port-au-Prince to protect U.S. lives and property following a severe outbreak of revolutionary violence in Haiti.

29 July
Haiti
A company of Marines from Guantanamo Bay arrives to reinforce the regiment at Port-au-Prince.

Top: *Col L. W. T. Waller and his brigade staff at Veracruz. In the front row (from left) are LtCol Wendell Neville, Col John Lejeune, Waller, Maj Smedley Butler, and Maj Randolph Berkeley. (Marine Corps Research Center)*

Right: *USS* Prairie *sends the first landing party ashore in Mexico on 21 April 1914. (National Archives)*

4 August
Haiti
Five companies of the 2nd Regiment arrive in Port-au-Prince from Philadelphia.

15 August
Haiti
The 1st Regiment and the headquarters of the 1st Marine Brigade reach Port-au-Prince. The mission is to restore order in the chaotic country. The Marines move out to garrison various cities and towns.

17 August
Aviation
Secretary of the Navy Daniels asks the Secretary of War to provide instruction in flying land planes to Marine and Navy aviators. Lieutenant W. M. McIlvain is the first Marine to receive such training.

30 August
Haiti
A Marine artillery battalion joins the forces in Haiti. The brigade now has a strength of 88 officers and 1,941 enlisted.

16 September
Haiti
The United States and Haiti sign a treaty which provides for creation of a constabulary force under Marine supervision. This is the genesis of the Gendarmerie d'Haiti.

20 September
Haiti
Marine patrols engage in the first major battle with Caco bandits in northern Haiti, killing 40 at a cost of 10 wounded Marines.

24–25 October
Haiti
Major Smedley Butler and a 40-man patrol defeats a night ambush by Cacos in northern Haiti. Gunnery Sergeant Dan Daly's heroism will result in his second Medal of Honor.

25 October
Bases
After a hiatus at Norfolk, Virginia, the Marine recruit training depot returns to Port Royal, South Carolina, which is officially turned over to the Marine Corps by the Navy a few days later.

9 November
Mexico
Most of the 4th Regiment deploys at sea off the west coast of Mexico.

18 November
Haiti
Marines under Butler seize Fort Riviere, kill 50 Cacos, and break enemy resistance in northern Haiti.

Left: *"Fort Riviere, Haiti," Maj Donna Neary, USMCR (Ret), Marine Corps Art Collection*

Opposite, top: *"Charge Across the Beach, Caribbean," Sydney Riesenberg, Marine Corps Art Collection*

Opposite, bottom: *A steam launch tows Marines ashore off Santo Domingo in 1916. (National Archives)*

28 November
Mexico
Elements of the 4th Regiment embark on cruiser *San Diego* (ACR-6) and take station off the west coast of Mexico until 3 February 1916.

1916

8 January
Bases
The Navy Department directs the establishment of a permanent Marine Corps base at San Diego, California.

5 May
Santo Domingo
Two companies of Marines from Haiti on board *Prairie* and the detachment of *Castine* (Gunboat No. 6) go ashore at Santo Domingo City to protect the U.S. legation during a revolt. Additional Marines follow during the month. Their ultimate mission is to support the U.S. policy of establishing an effective government for Santo Domingo following years of instability.

1 June
Santo Domingo
The Marine detachments of battleships *Rhode Island* (BB-17) and *New Jersey* (BB-16) lead a naval battalion ashore at Puerto Plata, Santo Domingo.

17 June
Technology
Henderson (AP-1), named for the Marine Commandant and the first transport built specifically to carry Marines, is launched at Philadelphia.

21 June
Santo Domingo
Colonel Pendleton and the 4th Regiment arrive in Santo Domingo at Monte Cristi, then proceed overland toward Santiago.

27 June
Santo Domingo
Pendleton's force, with supporting fire from artillery and machine guns, assaults and seizes the dominating Las Trencheras Ridge against strong rebel opposition.

30 June
Manpower
The strength of the Marine Corps on active duty is 348 officers and 10,253 enlisted.

DE HAVILAND DH-4

An American had been the first to achieve powered flight, but the U.S. aviation community was behind its overseas competitors when the nation entered World War I. Combat had spurred inventiveness in Europe and moved those countries far ahead. Since there was no time for the United States to catch up with its own designs, a group went across the Atlantic to select Allied aircraft for manufacture by American industry. The prime candidate was the British de Haviland DH-4, a biplane bomber. The initial sample plane came to the United States on 27 July 1917. It had no engine, but luckily the newly designed American Liberty motor was a good fit for the airframe and more powerful than its British predecessor. The re-engined sample first flew on 29 October.

Production proved more difficult, in part because the plans had to be converted to standard U.S. measurements. Three companies, all formed by automakers, ended up manufacturing the de Haviland. But the wood-and-fabric DH-4s were nothing like cars, which further slowed the initial building program. Nevertheless, the three firms turned out nearly 5,000 planes at a cost of $5,500 apiece before the war ended. Very few made it to the front in time for combat, however. Among them were some of those employed by the Marine Corps Day Wing of the Northern Bombing Group (which also flew British-built airframes of the same type, plus a modified craft known as the DH-9).

The de Haviland was not particularly well designed. The main gas tank (with a capacity of 67 gallons) was located between the pilot and his observer. The resulting distance between the two men made it difficult for them to converse in flight. The heavy tank also posed a hazard to the pilot in any crash that broke it loose from its moorings. The ease with which it ruptured and caught fire

gave the DH-4 its lasting nickname, "Flaming Coffin." (A major change in the British DH-9 was swapping the location of the pilot's cockpit and the fuel tank.) The location of the wheels left the plane too heavy in front, which gave it a tendency to nose over on landing. A late-war version—the DH-4B—fixed these shortcomings, in part by copying the changes incorporated in the DH-9.

The DH-4 was relatively well-armed for the time. The pilot had two fixed .30-caliber Marlin machine guns firing through the propeller. The observer had a pair of Lewis machine guns on a ring mount. Racks under the lower wing allowed it to carry several bombs, not to exceed a total weight of about 450 pounds. With the added horsepower of the Liberty engine, the DH-4 could achieve a speed of 125 miles per hour and climb to 17,500 feet. Its speed and firepower enabled it to survive against the fighter planes of the day. Of the 196 American-built de Havilands that went into combat, 33 were downed by enemy fire, but the U.S. planes also accounted for 45 enemy aircraft. The Marines lost only one DH-4 in combat and had four confirmed kills and eight more claimed (although some were attributable to the DH-9A).

There were so many surplus de Havilands at the end of the war, and budgets were so tight, that it served as the workhorse of Marine Corps land-based aviation for the next decade. It underwent a number of modifications to improve performance, and Boeing even built its own version with a metal-framed fuselage, designated the O2B-1. The two fixed Marlin guns were also replaced by a single Browning. The airplane proved its worth as late as 1927, when Marines providing close air support at Ocotal in Nicaragua flew the venerable DH-4Bs and O2B-1s into action.

Opposite: *Pilots and ground crew with a DH-4B. (National Archives)*

Top: *"Bombing at Thielt, Belgium," James Butcher, Marine Corps Art Collection*

Right: *A Marine de Haviland in France. (National Archives)*

3 July
Santo Domingo
The 4th Regiment defeats a sizable enemy force at Guayacanas.

5 July
Santo Domingo
Pendleton and his regiment occupy Santiago, Santo Domingo.

29 August
Manpower
The National Defense Act authorizes an increase in the Marine Corps to 597 officers and 14,981 enlisted and also allows the President to expand it further to 693 officers and 17,400 enlisted in case of a national emergency. This legislation also establishes the Marine Corps Reserve and provides money to purchase land for a base in San Diego.

29 November
Santo Domingo
The U.S. declares a military government in Santo Domingo, with the goal of establishing a stable country, thus taking on an extended occupation.

1917

13 February
Aviation
1st Lieutenant Francis T. "Cocky" Evans makes the first successful loop in an N-9 seaplane, in the process determining how to come out of a spin after an initial failed attempt. His spin-recovery technique becomes a standard flying procedure.

25 February
Cuba
Marine detachments from U.S. battleships land at Guacanayabo Bay, Cuba, to guard American-owned sugar plantations and processing mills during a revolution. Sugar is considered a vital commodity, and the Cuban supply is important not only to the United States, but also to prospective allies in Europe.

26 February
Force Structure
1st Lieutenant Alfred Cunningham is ordered to organize an Aviation Company for the Advance Base Force in Philadelphia.

4 March
Cuba
Six companies of Marines from Haiti arrive in Cuba.

8 March
Cuba
Marines from Guantanamo Bay and three warships occupy Guantanamo City, then begin to spread out to other threatened areas. Marine forces remain in Cuban territory until 25 May.

26 March
Manpower
The President issues an executive order allowing expansion of the Corps to its maximum strength under the law passed on 29 August 1916.

29 March
Virgin Islands
Following the purchase of the Virgin Islands from Denmark (to prevent them from being used as German naval bases), a company of Marines occupies St. Croix.

6 April
World War I
The United States declares war on Germany and enters World War I.

7 April
Santo Domingo
Marine patrols defeat a large bandit force at Las Canitas in Santo Domingo.

21 April
Virgin Islands
Two companies of Marines occupy St. Thomas, Virgin Islands, and establish harbor defenses.

27 April
Force Structure
The aviation detachment with the Advance Base Force in Philadelphia is designated the Marine Aeronautic Company.

1 May
Santo Domingo
Marines establish the Guardia Nacional Dominica to begin the process of creating a stable military force for Santo Domingo.

14 May
Bases
The first detachment of Marines, from Annapolis, move to the newly leased base of 5,300 acres at Quantico, Virginia.

19 May
World War I
Secretary of the Navy Josephus Daniels offers a Marine regiment for service in France. The Secretary of War accepts the proposal on 23 May.

22 May
Manpower
Congress authorizes expansion of the Marine Corps to 1,323 officers and 30,000 enlisted.

Opposite: *A WWI Marine prepares to throw a grenade. ("Bombing," Gilbert Gaul, Marine Corps Art Collection)*

Top: *"First in France," John A. Coughlin, Marine Corps Art Collection*

Right: *"Return of the Mayflower," Bernard F. Gribble, U.S. Naval Academy Art Collection*

MARINE CORPS BASE, QUANTICO

Quantico and the surrounding area had been an important site since the early days of the colony of Virginia. The narrow flatlands where Quantico Creek flowed into the Potomac River made an ideal location from which the region's tobacco growers could ship their commodity to markets along the eastern seaboard and in Europe. But a decrease in the importance of tobacco and the silting up of the creek slowly turned Quantico into a backwater during the latter 1800s. Various speculative companies took over the land and periodically tried to market it as a commercial center, a resort destination, and finally a shipyard.

World War I brought a significant increase in the size of the Corps beyond the strength of several thousand that it had maintained since the conflict with Spain. The creation prior to World War I of the Advance Base Force, the first permanently organized peacetime Marine field unit, also brought to the fore a requirement for a place where Marines could train with their growing arsenal of heavier weapons. Simultaneously, the rapid buildup of the Navy after 1914 caused that service to take back facilities aboard naval bases previously provided for the use of Marines. These factors forced Headquarters Marine Corps to search for a suitable base of its own somewhere along the east coast.

The quest became urgent with U.S. entry into the war in April 1917. That same month, a board of senior Marines determined that the Quantico area met just about every need. There was sufficient space for units to fire their weapons and practice maneuvers, a major road and railroad running through the tract, and access for ships on the Potomac. Within days, the Marine Corps leased 5,300 acres from the company that had been trying to sell it for years. Quantico thus became the first Marine Corps base designed specifically for the use of operational units.

Opposite: *During training at Quantico, Marines race into position with crew-served weapons. (National Archives)*

Right: *Marines march through Quantico upon their return from Nicaragua in 1933. (Leatherneck Magazine)*

Other than a tiny village laid out along a single dusty street, there were absolutely no facilities on the largely wooded land. The Marines would have to build their base entirely from scratch. They wasted no time. The first troops arrived from Annapolis in mid-May. A month later, the newly organized 1st Battalion of the 5th Regiment sailed from Quantico for duty in France. Other Marines poured in just as fast as the recruit depots could churn them out. They initially lived in tents pitched in a cornfield. Civilian laborers swarmed over the site erecting single-story wood-and-tarpaper barracks and larger buildings, putting down a concrete road, and creating means to provide fresh water and dispose of waste. By fall 1917, the base was sending additional units to France and elsewhere and training all officer candidates.

Before the war was over, the Marine Corps purchased the land from the development company and even expanded the site to 7,000 acres. When Marine aviation units returned from France in 1919, they established an airfield. Major General Lejeune took command of the base during this period and soon created the Marine Corps Schools for officers. The base did not take on its first permanent character until the late 1920s, when Congress finally appropriated money to replace the temporary wooden structures of the World War. Brick buildings began to spring up in 1928, while work got underway to create a larger airfield on filled land in the Potomac.

Quantico's use as a home for operational units came to an end with the onset of World War II. When the Fleet Marine Force expanded to division and wing strength, there simply no longer were sufficient facilities for organizations of that size. The base expanded dramatically in 1942 with the purchase of 51,000 acres west of U.S. Route 1, but newer bases on the nation's coasts provided more suitable locations for amphibious training. The regiments and aircraft groups soon left for these better sites, never to return. Quantico remained the intellectual heart of the Corps, however. It continues today to provide advanced training and education to Marine officers and senior enlisted men, and it also is home to organizations that oversee the development of doctrine and the acquisition of new equipment for the Corps.

29 May
Force Structure
Secretary of the Navy Daniels orders creation of the 5th Regiment. Commandant Barnett already has begun drawing together forces at Philadelphia from the U.S. and the Caribbean.

4 June
Manpower
The Commandant directs that all future commissioned officers for the World War come from the enlisted ranks of the Marine Corps (with the exception of Naval Academy graduates). The mechanism for turning selected enlisted men into lieutenants is Officers' Training Camp, a three-month course that soon begins at Quantico.

14 June
Force Structure
The 5th Regiment sails for France. It arrives at St. Nazaire on the 26th and comes under command of the American Expeditionary Force (AEF). The regiment is assigned to the U.S. Army's 1st Division in excess of division tables of organization.

15 June
Bases
The Navy purchases 232 acres on San Diego Bay. San Diego donates 500 acres of adjacent tidal land (to be covered by land fill) for a Marine base for the West Coast expeditionary force.

22 June
Bases
The Marine Corps redesignates the base at Port Royal as Marine Barracks, Paris Island. (Spelling would be changed to Parris Island on 3 May 1919.)

30 June
Manpower
The strength of the Marine Corps on active duty is 776 officers and 26,973 enlisted.

4 August
Force Structure
Secretary Daniels orders creation of the 6th Regiment for eventual service with the AEF.

17 August
Force Structure
The 1st Machine Gun Battalion is established at Quantico.

21 August
Force Structure
The newly organized 7th Regiment departs Philadelphia for Cuba to guard U.S. sugar interests.

5 October
Force Structure
Lead elements of the 6th Regiment arrive in France.

9 October
Force Structure
The 8th Regiment is organized at Quantico to serve with the Advance Base Force. It is soon sent to Galveston, Texas, for possible deployment to the Mexican oil fields to protect the fleet's fuel source from disruption.

12 October
Force Structure
The Advance Base Force aviation unit at Philadelphia is divided into the 1st Marine Aviation Squadron and the 1st Marine Aeronautic Company.

14 October
Force Structure
The 1st Marine Aeronautic Company deploys to Cape May, New Jersey, and specializes in seaplanes.

17 October
Force Structure
The 1st Marine Aviation Squadron transfers to Long Island, New York, and specializes in land planes.

23 October
Force Structure
The 6th Regiment joins with the 5th Regiment to form the 4th Marine Brigade. At full strength, the brigade musters 280 officers and 9,164 enlisted.

26 October
Force Structure
The 4th Marine Brigade is joined with Army units to form the 2nd Division.

20 November
Force Structure
The 9th Regiment is organized at Quantico to serve with the Advance Base Force.

25 November
Great Britain
Marine detachments sail from Chesapeake Bay on board the battleships sent to reinforce the Royal Navy's Grand Fleet in British waters.

15 December
Force Structure
Captain Roy Geiger establishes the Aeronautic Detachment at Philadelphia.

Opposite: *World War I recruiting poster. ("First to Fight for Democracy," G. A. Shafer, Marine Corps Art Collection)*

Top: *World War I recruiting poster. ("Be Up To Date, Be A Marine," W. A. Rogers, Marine Corps Art Collection)*

Right: *Marine aviation in the Azores. ("Protect the Convoys," Col Avery Chenoweth, USMCR (Ret), Marine Corps Art Collection)*

PRIVATE ELTON E. MACKIN

Elton Mackin came from a working-class family in western New York, where he was born in 1898. His father died a few weeks later in an accident and his mother eventually remarried. Elton completed high school in the summer of 1917, but did not rush to the colors in the first months after the United States joined the World War. Just before Christmas, inspired in part by an article in a popular magazine of the day, he joined the Marine Corps. Five months later, he arrived in France with the 3rd Replacement Battalion. His group moved up to the front on the evening of 7 June—the second day of the Marine assault on Belleau Wood. They were fed into the lines of the 1st Battalion, 5th Regiment, which had suffered significant losses the prior day while seizing ground west of the main forest. Years later he would recall: "We didn't know how young and scared we were, nor how much we showed it."

Assigned to the 67th Company, Mackin participated in the remaining weeks of fighting to clear Belleau Wood. Near the end of the battle he was offered duty as a battalion runner, considered a suicide billet due to the requirement to frequently traverse fire-swept ground carrying messages. His fear of looking like a coward in front of a senior NCO outweighed his fear of death, and he accepted. In mid-July, he and his battalion were part of the hurried, all-night movement to reach the front lines for the attack at Soissons. The 5th Regiment caught the enemy unprepared and drove them through a wooded area. Its losses were high, but not like Belleau Wood. The St. Mihiel offensive was the easiest of all, with the Army's 3rd Brigade leading the way against a

Left: *During the Meuse-Argonne campaign, Marines pick their way through a heavily shelled landscape. (National Archives)*

Opposite: *"Forced March, Soissons," John W. Thomason, Sam Houston State University*

withdrawing enemy. Blanc Mont in October was the worst. The initial attack was too successful, and the 5th Regiment swept past its objectives in pursuit. The Marines ended up stranded in a wood, with no friendly forces to their flanks and open ground between them and the rear. Heavy German fire savaged the exposed position from three sides, and losses were the heaviest of the war for the regiment. Mackin received the Army Distinguished Service Cross and two citations (subsequently converted to Silver Star medals) for his bravery in this battle. He served as the chief of the battalion runners during the Meuse-Argonne and was one of the lucky, courageous Marines who survived crossing the footbridge over the river under artillery and machine-gun fire during the final night of the war. He also was one of the few men to live through every battle of the Marine Brigade.

Mackin was able to come home before his unit did, mustering out in the States in May 1919. He held several jobs in the 1920s, suffered like most of his countrymen during the Depression, and finally found steady employment as a government clerk with his local draft board in 1939. After World War II, he opened an appliance store, but ended his working life as a schoolbus driver and custodian. Eventually he jotted down his memories of his service, telling the personal story of a young man suddenly thrust into the maw of a cataclysmic war.

He recalled small incidents of great magnitude to those who experienced them. The new replacement, gathering up days-old dead after the battle at Belleau Wood, sickened when he picked up one head-shot Marine, whose brains then slid out of his helmet and on to the feet of the stretcher bearer. A dud shell burrowing at a man's feet, the force of its landing sending him flying through the air, the sheer fright of what might have been leaving

him "twitching horribly, his eyes rolling up and showing white." Marines watching a nearby unit take the brunt of a counterattack, for once feeling a sense of safety, only to have it shattered by the order of the sergeant to "Fix your bayonets" and move forward for their first attempt to kill a man at arm's length. A runner coming across a badly wounded German in a lonely wood and hearing long after the plaintive cries for help as he continues on his mission. A man finally receiving a long-awaited letter from home, but every page an indecipherable blob of water-soaked ink. Looking back, Mackin believed that he and many of his comrades had been "too damned young and under fire too soon," which left an emotional "brittleness that was to mark all the days of our remaining lives." He died in 1974, too soon to see his words published as one of the most searing memoirs of World War I—*Suddenly We Didn't Want to Die.*

Left: *This artist envisioned American troops charging the enemy with the name of a sunken civilian ship as their battle cry. ("Lusitania!" Charles Fouqueray, Marine Corps Art Collection)*

25 December
Force Structure
The 9th Regiment arrives at Guantanamo Bay to further reinforce units guarding U.S. sugar production capability.

28 December
Force Structure
The 1st Machine Gun Battalion arrives in France and is assigned to the 4th Marine Brigade.

1918

January
Force Structure
The 11th Regiment is formed at Quantico as an artillery unit.

1 January
Force Structure
The 1st Marine Aviation Squadron departs Long Island for the Army flying field at Lake Charles, Louisiana.

14 January
Force Structure
The 10th Regiment is organized at Quantico to man tractor-mounted 7-inch naval guns.

20 January
Force Structure
The 1st Machine Gun Battalion is redesignated the 6th Machine Gun Battalion.

21 January
Azores
The 1st Marine Aeronautic Company arrives at the naval base at Ponta Delgado, Azores, and undertakes antisubmarine patrols with its 12 seaplanes and six flying boats.

5 February
Force Structure
Captain Alfred Cunningham convinces the Navy's General Board to order the creation of a bombing group to attack German submarine pens along the Belgian coast.

6 February
Force Structure
The last battalion of the 6th Regiment arrives in France, completing the organization of the 4th Marine Brigade.

7 February
Force Structure
Geiger and his Aeronautic Detachment depart Philadelphia for the Naval Air Station, Miami.

25 February
Commandants
Major General Barnett is reappointed for a second four-year term as Commandant.

17 March
Verdun
The 2nd Battalion, 5th Regiment, becomes the first Marine unit to occupy front-line positions in France, in a sector just south of Verdun.

1 April
Bases
Captain Cunningham's 1st Marine Aviation Squadron arrives at the newly established Marine Flying Field, Miami (recently acquired by Geiger's detachment).

13 April
Verdun
The 4th Marine Brigade suffers its first significant combat casualties when the 74th Company of the 6th Regiment is hit with a barrage of mustard gas prior to dawn while billeted in a reserve area near Verdun. A shell bursting inside a building where many men are sleeping results in unusually heavy casualties. Losses are nearly 300, of whom 40 are killed or subsequently die.

15 April
Force Structure
1st Marine Aviation Squadron becomes 1st Marine Aviation Force with four authorized squadrons.

23 April
Verdun
The first Medal of Honor is earned by a member of the Marine Brigade when Navy dentist Lieutenant Commander Alexander G. Lyle moves through a heavy barrage and renders surgical aid to a wounded Marine.

Top: *The scene of a vicious and bloody 1916 battle became the Marine introduction to the western front in 1918. ("Verdun," Lester G. Hornby, Marine Corps Art Collection)*

Right: *"Chateau-Thierry," Lester G. Hornby, Marine Corps Art Collection*

GENERAL GERALD C. THOMAS

Gerald Carthrae Thomas was a 21-year-old sophomore at Illinois Wesleyan University when the U.S. entered World War I. The 5-foot, 9-inch, 160-pound student had excelled as a lineman on the college football team and managed to achieve decent grades even as he worked to put himself through college. He was eager to serve his nation and tried to join an Army commissioning program. Receiving no response from an overwhelmed bureaucracy, he enlisted in the Marine Corps on 15 May 1917. Following recruit training at Parris Island, he reported to the 1st Battalion, 6th Marines, and shipped with them to France.

Sergeant Thomas participated in his battalion's attack into Belleau Wood on 10 June 1918. He was cited for bravery in brigade orders for leading a squad that wiped out German holdouts in the rear of the Marine position. During the advance at Soissons, he became an acting platoon commander due to heavy losses. Temporarily assigned as a student at a weapons course in the rear, he left without permission to rejoin his battalion when he leaned of its participation in the St. Mihiel offensive. As a newly commissioned officer, he was gassed at the start of the Meuse-Argonne offensive.

After the "war to end all wars," Jerry Thomas soon went to Haiti to help put down the Caco revolt. Initially consigned to a staff job in Port-au-Prince, he nevertheless played a major role in defeating a substantial rebel attack on the capital by establishing a hasty night ambush with a handful of Marines and destroying one of the enemy columns. There followed uneventful tours commanding a ship's detachment, serving in a Stateside Marine barracks, returning to Haiti as a staff officer, getting professional education at the Army Infantry School at Fort Benning and the Field Officers Course at Quantico, and teaching at The Basic School. He developed a reputation as an intelligent planner and confident commander who demanded the best from subordinates and peers and did not suffer fools. His most significant assignment, from a career standpoint, came when he reported in 1935 for duty with the Peking Legation Guard. His superior work as a leader and staff officer in China established him as a valued protege of Colonel Alexander A. Vandegrift. More time as a student and instructor followed.

In 1941, Thomas became the operations officer for the 1st Marine Division. Soon after, Vandegrift took over the division. In August 1942, they led the division in the assault on Guadalcanal. Thomas's resolute performance brought a spot promotion to colonel and chief of staff of the division early in the campaign. The two men were inseparable thereafter. Thomas reprised his role as chief of staff when Vandegrift took command of the I Marine Amphibious Corps and led it in the invasion of Bougainville. When Vandegrift became the Commandant in January 1944, Thomas received a second spot promotion—to brigadier general—and became the director of the Plans and Policies division at Headquarters Marine Corps. From that billet he orchestrated the manpower and materiel needed to fight through the bloody closing campaigns of the war.

Following Japan's surrender, Thomas helped battle for the survival of the Corps during the move to unify the services. He went on to head the last Marine forces in China in the late 1940s and then to serve again in the school house in Quantico. In February 1951, he took command of the 1st Marine Division and saw it through some of the most bitter fighting in Korea. He became General Shepherd's Assistant Commandant in 1952 and pushed through a long-overdue reorganization of Headquarters Marine Corps. A steadfast proponent of professional military education, he closed out his long career in 1954–55 in command of the Marine Corps Schools in Quantico. For his courageous service in the nation's wars, he was promoted to four stars upon his retirement. He died in 1984.

Jerry Thomas as a brigadier general in the 1940s. He wears the fourragere *on his left shoulder, a mark of his service on the western front of World War I with the 4th Brigade. (National Archives)*

7 May
Commanders
General Pershing orders Brigadier General Charles A. Doyen home for health reasons and gives command of the 4th Marine Brigade to the AEF chief of staff, Army Brigadier General James G. Harbord.

9 May
Verdun
French units begin to relieve the 2nd Division in the lines at Verdun, and the division moves to a training area in the rear.

19 May
Training
The Overseas Depot is established at Marine Corps Base Quantico to train units and individual Marines for service with the AEF.

30 May
Belleau Wood
As a major German offensive threatens Paris, the 2nd Division is ordered forward to assist in establishing a new defensive line astride the Paris-Metz road.

1 June
Belleau Wood
The 4th Marine Brigade forms the left sector of the division line near the village of Le Thiolet.

6 June
Belleau Wood
The Marine Brigade launches a counterattack to gain better defensive positions around Belleau Wood. Marine casualties for the day—1,087 killed or wounded—exceed the total losses suffered by the Corps in its entire history up to that point. Belleau Wood is largely taken by 12 June.

13 June
Belleau Wood
Marines repulse a determined German counterattack against the Belleau Wood area.

23 June
Belleau Wood
The Marine Brigade resumes the attack and drives out the last Germans in Belleau Wood by the 25th.

28 June
Russia
Brooklyn lands a detachment of Marines at Vladivostok, Russia, to protect the U.S. consulate and assist other Allied units in taking control of the city from Communist forces.

30 June
Belleau Wood
By order of the French Army, Belleau Wood is officially renamed "Bois de la Brigade de Marine."

Left: *The German offensive of 1918 reached one of its deepest points at Les Mares farm near Belleau Wood in early June 1918. ("Advancing Germans Halted by 2/5," Harvey Dunn, Marine Corps Art Collection)*

Right: *"Oh Lordy, They've Got Us Bracketed," John W. Thomason, Marine Corps Art Collection*

Below: *"1st Marine Aviation Force Insignia, July 1918," John Englehardt, Marine Corps Art Collection*

30 June
Manpower
The strength of the Marine Corps on active duty is 1,503 officers and 51,316 enlisted.

1 July
Manpower
Congress authorizes an increase in the strength of the Marine Corps to 3,341 officers and 75,500 enlisted.

3 July
Force Structure
The 13th Regiment is formed at Quantico.

5 July
Belleau Wood
The Marine Brigade is relieved in the lines by an Army brigade. Total Marine losses for the fighting since 1 June are 4,710.

5 July
Commanders
Brigadier General John A. Lejeune assumes command of the Army's 64th Infantry Brigade of the 32nd Division in France.

14 July
Commanders
Harbord is promoted to major general and assumes command of the 2nd Division. Newly promoted Marine Brigadier General Wendell C. Neville takes charge of the Marine Brigade.

18 July
Soissons
The Marine Brigade leads the assault in the opening of the Soissons offensive. Gunnery Sergeant Louis Cukela later receives both the Army and Navy Medal of Honor for attacking and destroying three German machine-gun positions.

LEWIS MACHINE GUN

The Lewis gun was named after its principal designer, Army Colonel Isaac N. Lewis. The inventive graduate of West Point came up with a number of successful ordnance items during his years of service, starting with an artillery range finder in 1888. Although he spent most of his career as an artilleryman, his passion was automatic weapons. While still on active duty in 1910, he became a consultant for a firm unsuccessfully trying to market a gas-operated, water-cooled machine gun designed by Dr. Samuel N. McLean. Lewis employed some features of this weapon to create an air-cooled version. To ensure wide publicity for its initial public test in 1912, he arranged a demonstration firing from an airplane—the first time a machine gun ever had been used in the air. It proved successful, but senior Army ordnance officials rejected it, reputedly due to a personal feud between the inventor and the chief of the ordnance office.

In 1913, the colonel retired and took his gun to Europe. The government of Belgium, followed soon after by Great Britain, signed orders for it. When World War I erupted in 1914, both nations bought it in large quantities and made it their primary machine gun. By the end of the war more than 100,000 had been produced by the Allies. Beginning in 1917, American firms were manufacturing the weapon for European customers.

The main attraction of the Lewis was its weight. Air cooling and innovative design made it considerably lighter (at 26 pounds) than most of its competitors (the British Vickers weighing in at 68 pounds, for example). Although it could not stand up to a direct duel with a more stable heavy machine gun and its higher rate of fire, the Lewis was much more portable. A single soldier could carry it in an attack and actually employ it while on the move, which made it more of an automatic rifle than a true machine gun. Its light weight also made it ideal for aerial use. Another attractive aspect was its relative simplicity of operation and comparatively low number of parts (62 in all). Distinctive features of the gun were its circular drum magazine, which fed cartridges from atop the weapon, and the long aluminum cooling jacket that surrounded the barrel (often absent from aircraft models). It fired at a rate of 750 rounds per minute, though the capacity of the largest magazine was only 97 rounds.

The U.S. Army ordered its first handful of Lewis guns in 1916, with a .30-caliber chamber to match other American infantry

weapons. A month after the U.S. entered the war, the Navy Department placed its initial order for several thousand. Marines went off to France in 1918 with the Lewis, but soon had to trade them in for the less reliable French Chauchat automatic rifle. Although the reason is not entirely clear, apparently the Army had insufficient Lewis guns to equip its forces, so it adopted the French weapon, and the AEF Marines had to follow suit to maintain uniformity of equipment.

By the time World War I was over, the Browning Automatic Rifle (BAR) and the Browning family of machine guns had appeared and would become mainstays of Marine infantrymen for most of the next four decades. The Lewis still had a niche, however, and remained in use during the 1920s and 1930s in the Corps. It was 10 pounds heavier than the BAR, but it had a higher rate of fire and a larger-capacity magazine. Conversely, it was much lighter and more portable than the Browning machine guns. The Lewis proved to be just the right weapon for the Banana Wars in the Caribbean, where it served as the "heavy" automatic weapon supplementing the BAR with small patrols moving through the jungle and hills of Nicaragua, Haiti, and Santo Domingo. More than one group of Marines or local constabulary soldiers broke enemy ambushes with the devastating fire of a Lewis gun. It also remained a major item in the Marine aerial arsenal until the end of the biplane era.

Opposite: *The Lewis machine gun, with its distinctive drum magazine and cooling jacket. (Marine Corps Historical Center)*

Above: *Marines put a Lewis gun into action during maneuvers. (National Archives)*

Left: *Among the first to enlist, these women (dubbed "Marinettes") took the oath on 17 August 1918. All highly trained clerks and stenographers, they freed male Marines from administrative duties for service overseas. (National Archives)*

Opposite: *A wounded Marine receives first aid on 22 March 1918, probably near Verdun. (National Archives)*

19 July
Soissons
After suffering heavy losses and gaining ground in the face of a German counterattack, the Marine Brigade is relieved. Losses for the two-day attack total 2,091.

26 July
Commanders
General Lejeune assumes command of the 4th Marine Brigade.

28 July
Commanders
Newly promoted Major General Lejeune takes command of the 2nd Division, and Neville resumes command of the brigade.

30 July
France
The personnel of the 1st Marine Aviation Force arrives in Brest, France. The crews soon begin flying missions in British DH-4 and DH-9A bombers with British squadrons.

31 July
Force Structure
The 3rd Brigade headquarters and 9th Regiment depart Cuba for duty in Texas with the 8th Regiment. The continued mission of the force is to be prepared to safeguard the Mexican oilfields.

4 August
France
The 2nd Division takes over a quiet sector of the front and remains there till 12 August.

7 August
Bases
Under authorization from Congress, the Marine Corps takes control of all of Parris Island—a total of roughly 3,000 acres of land and 3,000 acres of marsh. Until this time the government had owned just 78 acres.

8 August
Manpower
By executive order, the President ends voluntary enlistments in the Marine Corps. However, the Corps is authorized to reject draftees that fail to meet its standards, while the inductees in turn are allowed to reject assignment to the Marines. For all intents and purposes, the Marine Corps remains a volunteer service throughout the war. Based on a request from Commandant Barnett, Secretary Daniels authorizes the enlistment of women in the Marine Corps Reserve for clerical duty.

13 August
Manpower
Opha M. Johnson, a civil service employee at Headquarters Marine Corps, becomes the first female to enroll in the Marines. A total of 305 are enlisted during the war.

5 September
Force Structure
The Commandant directs formation of the 5th Marine Brigade headquarters at Quantico. The 11th and 13th Regiments and 5th Machine Gun Battalion are assigned to it.

12 September
St. Mihiel
The 4th Marine Brigade serves as the reserve of the 2nd Division during the U.S. First Army's attack to reduce the St. Mihiel salient. Over the next three days, the brigade participates in reducing German pockets of resistance. Marine losses total 919.

24 September
Force Structure
Lead elements of the 5th Marine Brigade arrive in France. Its units are assigned to guard duty along the lines of communication.

25 September
Force Structure
The 2nd Division is transferred to the French Fourth Army.

28 September
France
While flying with a British squadron, Lieutenant Everett S. Brewster and Gunnery Sergeant Harry B. Wersheimer become the first Marines to shoot down an enemy plane.

1 October
Blanc Mont
The 2nd Division moves into the front lines, with the 4th Marine Brigade occupying the forward trenches.

2 October
France
Marines conduct their first aerial resupply mission, dropping food to a surrounded French regiment.

3 October
Blanc Mont
The 4th Marine Brigade attacks and seizes the Blanc Mont ridge. Corporal J. H. Pruitt and Private John J. Kelly later receive the Medal of Honor for separately destroying German machine-gun nests.

7 October
Commandants
Major General Barnett arrives in France for a month-long tour of Marine units with the AEF.

8 October
Blanc Mont
The brigade takes the village of St. Etienne, its last objective beyond Mont Blanc.

10 October
Blanc Mont
French forces relieve the 2nd Division. Marine casualties in the Blanc Mont battle total 2,369.

THE BATTLE OF BLANC MONT

In late September 1918, General John Pershing, commander of the AEF, loaned his 2nd and 36th Divisions to the battered French Fourth Army on his flank. Major General Lejeune, commander of the 2nd Division, soon learned that the French hoped to use his brigades independently as reinforcements for their weakened outfits. He countered with a bold offer—if the army commander allowed him to employ his division as a unit, he would deliver Blanc Mont in the coming offensive. Given the impregnable reputation of the high chalk ridge, long held by the Germans, the French commander accepted.

Lejeune employed unusual tactics for his attack. The 4th Marine Brigade would jump off from the left half of the division front, while the 3rd Brigade launched its assault from the trench lines of the French division on the right, thus leaving a mile of uncovered ground in between the two American outfits. The Army brigade would move diagonally into the 2nd Division zone during the assault and eventually converge with the Marine brigade. This scheme of maneuver avoided a triangle of terrain that contained the Bois de la Vipere (Snake Woods). The American infantry would avoid strong outposts in concealed positions, focus on the main

Left: *Marines mop up in the Essen Hook. ("Capture of Blanc Mont Ridge," George M. Harding, Marine Corps Art Collection)*

Opposite: *"Marine Mud and Misery," Col Charles Waterhouse, USMCR (Ret), Marine Corps Art Collection*

objective of the ridge beyond, and mop up the bypassed covering defenses later. Although an unusually large aggregation of supporting artillery (48 batteries) was available, the guns would fire only a five-minute preparation—just enough to stun and disorganize the enemy, but not provide them with any warning to move up reserves.

The operation kicked off on the morning of 3 October. The 6th Regiment led off the 4th Marine Brigade in a column of battalions, with 2/6 in the lead. The battalion made rapid progress against weakly held outposts. Two Marines, Private John J. Kelly and Corporal John H. Pruitt, helped spearhead the assault by single-handedly destroying machine-gun nests. By 0830, 2/6 had gained 3,000 yards, climbed the slopes of Blanc Mont, and seized its eastern half. But the French division on the left had not gotten through a strong position immediately to its front. Germans in the Essen Hook, as it was dubbed, poured flanking fire into Marine units moving up to support 2/6. Other enemy outfits threatened to counterattack into the yawning gap on the 4th Brigade's left flank. The 5th Regiment established a line facing perpendicular to the advance to cover this zone. Captain Leroy P. Hunt led his 17th Company against the Essen Hook. By skillful use of machine guns and maneuver, he captured the trench-and-bunker complex and its hundred surviving defenders. He turned it over to the French, who lost it soon after to a German counterattack. The 3rd Brigade achieved equal success to the right of Blanc Mont.

The French high command directed a renewed attack in the afternoon to exploit the rapid advance, but the orders came late, and the Marine brigade elected to postpone the assault until the next morning. That

night the Germans brought up strong reserves to stave off the Americans while other elements withdrew from the main defensive line, now untenable due to the loss of the area's commanding ridge. The 5th Regiment moved through the 6th Regiment and made substantial gains the next morning, but came under intense artillery and machine-gun fire from the fresh German forces on the left flank. (The French still were not keeping pace.) The result was the bloodiest day of the war for the Marines, with more than 1,100 killed or wounded.

In subsequent days of hard fighting, the Marines slogged forward against heavy resistance to clear the remainder of Blanc Mont and seize the town of St. Etienne beyond. The badly depleted 2nd Division was relieved by elements of the 36th Division by 10 October, but Lejeune's outfit had made a major contribution to the Allied offensive.

14 October
Belgium
Captain Robert S. Lytle leads Squadron 9 in the 1st Marine Aviation Force's first independent mission. The five DH-4s and three DH-9As drop 2,218 pounds of bombs on the German-held rail yards at Thielt, Belgium. Lieutenant Ralph Talbot and his observer, Corporal Robert G. Robinson, shoot down two enemy planes before landing their crippled plane. Both men later received the Medal of Honor.

17 October
Haiti
Charlemagne Peralte launches an attack against Marine-led Gendarmerie force at Hinche, Haiti, and is driven off. This marks the opening of the Caco Revolt.

22 October
Belgium
German planes shoot down the bomber of Lieutenant Harvey G. Norman and his observer, Lieutenant Caleb W. Taylor. This is the first Marine aircraft lost to enemy action. Both men die in the crash.

25 October
France
The 2nd Division is reassigned to the U.S. First Army.

1 November
Meuse-Argonne
The 2nd Division, with the 4th Marine Brigade in the lead, joins in the Meuse-Argonne offensive. The brigade attack overruns all German defensive lines and creates a salient forcing an enemy withdrawal all across the front. In pursuit, the division reaches the Meuse River on 9 November.

3 November
Cuba
The 1st Regiment departs Philadelphia for duty in Cuba to deal with revolutionary activity in that country.

10 November
Meuse-Argonne
The 4th Marine Brigade makes a night attack across the Meuse River and gains a foothold on the opposite bank by the next morning. Marine losses in the Meuse-Argonne offensive total 1,263.

11 November
World War I
At 1100, an armistice goes into effect, and World War I comes to an end. Of the roughly 32,000 Marines who served in France, 2,459 died as a result of action, 8,907 were wounded, and 25 had been taken prisoner.

Left: *Marines take a break around the time of the Meuse-Argonne offensive. ("At a Bridge Near Romagne," Lester G. Hornby, Marine Corps Art Collection)*

Opposite: *With peace only hours away, Marines conduct a last attack across the Meuse River. ("The Last Night of the War," F. C. Yohn, Marine Corps Art Collection)*

17 November
Germany
The 2nd Division begins its march toward Germany and reaches the border on 23 November.

20 November
Manpower
The Commandant issues demobilization plans that authorize the immediate release of reservists and those regulars who had enlisted for the duration of the war or who had valid personal reasons for discharge.

1 December
Germany
The 4th Marine Brigade and other Allied forces cross into Germany under the armistice terms. The brigade reaches the Rhine on 9 December.

2 December
Manpower
The Marine Corps resumes reliance on voluntary enlistments for manpower.

6 December
Force Structure
The 1st Marine Aviation Force sails for the U.S.

11 December
Manpower
The Marine Corps reaches its highest strength since its inception, with 2,462 officers and 72,639 enlisted on active duty.

13 December
Germany
The Marines occupy their portion of the bridgehead east of the Rhine, near Coblenz, Germany.

26 December
Force Structure
The battleship force and embarked Marine detachments, deployed in the British Isles for the war, return to New York harbor.

COLONEL JOHN W. THOMASON

John W. Thomason II was born to a well-off family in Huntsville, Texas, on 28 February 1893. His father was a doctor and landowner who expected his son to follow in his footsteps. Young John loved reading and showed a talent for art from his early years, but he disliked school and had no interest in any profession. After mediocre performances at three different colleges, two stints as a teacher, and a year as a reporter, he joined the Marine Corps on the day the U.S. entered World War I. Writing and art would stay with him until the day he died, but he had finally found his niche in life.

Lieutenant Thomason reported to the 4th Marine Brigade in France in April 1918. He led his platoon through the battles of Belleau Wood and Soissons, distinguishing himself in the latter when he and a NCO destroyed a pair of machine guns pinning down their company. He eventually would receive the Navy Cross and an Army Silver Star for that act of bravery. Promoted to XO of the company, he went on to fight at St. Mihiel and Blanc Mont. Only a severe case of the flu prevented him from being one of the rare officers who lasted through to the armistice.

He first tried his hand at serious writing while he was stationed in Cuba in the early 1920s. Editors initially rejected his stories because the public supposedly was tired of reading about war. Transferred to an ammunition depot near New York City, he began to exhibit some of his artwork. A fellow Marine veteran of the great war, Laurence Stallings, launched Thomason into the literary and artistic circles of the metropolis. A national magazine published his first article, about Soissons, in the summer of 1925. "Fix Bayonets!" met rave reviews for its unvarnished depiction of men in combat and its accompanying illustrations. His own stories and his illustrations for the articles of others soon were in high demand. Before long, the Marine captain was earning far more from writing and drawing than he did as an officer, but he chose to stick with the profession of arms and pursue his other talents as a part-time avocation.

For a time, his two worlds merged, as the Commandant assigned him to write a history of the 2nd Division in the World War. But generally Thomason performed duties just like any other Marine officer. He commanded a detachment on a ship in Central American waters, served in the Legation Guard in Peking, attended the Army and Navy War Colleges, and commanded an infantry battalion in the late 1930s. In his spare time, he served as an editor for a major national magazine and published several books, ranging from

collections of short stories, to a biography of J. E. B. Stuart, to a novel.

During the interwar years, he was hospitalized for extended periods on several occasions, usually with a diagnosis of exhaustion. Although the facts are in dispute, alcoholism may have played a part in his poor health. Whatever the cause, his physical condition prevented him from playing a significant role in World War II. He served for a time as a training officer in the States, then as a planner in the Pacific theater on the staff of Admiral Nimitz. The closest he came again to the sound of guns was as an observer during the campaign against Munda Airfield on New Georgia. Invalided home for illness in August 1943, he died in March 1944 at the age of 51.

Thomason's intimate accounts, both fictional and factual, of his fellow Marines in war and peace remain among the very best descriptions of the essence of the Corps. His drawings equally capture in bold fashion the everyday life and sometimes commonplace death of Marines. His ability to translate what he saw and felt into words and art has never been matched by any other leatherneck.

Opposite: *"A small figure in a long gray cloak . . ." John W. Thomason, Sam Houston State University*

Above: *Capt John Thomason, Jr., in a trench, Sino-Japanese War, 1932. (Marine Corps Historical Center)*

THINKERS AND FIGHTERS

THINKERS AND FIGHTERS

1919–1938

The Marine Corps came out of World War I with a sterling reputation, but a bit of a split personality. Where it once had been searching for a mission to keep it relevant, it now had an oversupply of options, each with its own faction of proponents inside and outside the service. Smedley Butler and a number of other leaders were convinced that small wars should be the focus, since they guaranteed full employment for the Corps in what was otherwise a peacetime era. Another group, influenced by the positive impact of Marine success in World War I, emphasized the importance of preparing to fight an extended land campaign alongside the Army. A few harked back to the traditional mission of ships' detachments. General Lejeune, soon to become the Commandant, believed that the advance base mission was the most critical. Some of his adherents (such as Lieutenant Colonel Earl H. "Pete" Ellis) took this a step further, arguing that the bases would have to be seized by amphibious assault, which therefore was the primary role of the Corps.

Through 1933, the Marine Corps prepared itself to carry out all of these missions. The wide range of potential duties was embodied, in part, in a significant organizational change in the early 1920s. The old Advance Base Force disappeared and was replaced by the Marine Corps Expeditionary Forces (MCEF—one at Quantico and another at San Diego). The term "expeditionary" covered any type of overseas operation. To emphasize the point, these permanent air-ground brigades conducted a full range of training exercises in the first several years after World War I; defending advanced bases, simulating amphibious assaults against defended coastlines, and reenacting Civil War land campaigns such as Gettysburg. Meanwhile, the brand-new Marine Corps Schools in Quantico for mid-level officers copied Army doctrine and curriculum, all focused on land operations. The Corps conducted some experiments with equipment for use in amphibious operations, but none of it worked.

While the debates, training, experimentation, and schooling went on in the States, Marines were active overseas, fighting a number of small wars. The situation in Haiti flared into the Caco Revolt in 1919. Both Nicaragua and China exploded into major contingencies in 1927. A full brigade deployed to each locale to deal with civil wars that threatened American citizens and interests. In China, a show of force was enough to achieve U.S. objectives, although a regiment would remain in Shanghai from then until the eve of World War II. In Nicaragua, a committed revolutionary named Augusto Sandino started a guerrilla war that would keep the Marine brigade and another Marine-sponsored constabulary force fully occupied for five years. An expansion of the war between China and Japan would bring another brigade-size deployment to Shanghai in 1937.

These small wars kept the Corps at a high state

Pages 194–195: *During maneuvers in 1923–24, Marines unload a 75mm artillery piece from the "Beetle Boat," an early attempt at an armored landing craft. (National Archives)*

Right: *6th Machine Gun Battalion conducts combat training in Germany. (National Archives)*

of readiness throughout the 1920s and 1930s. They also provided an incomparable level of combat experience and training to a generation of young officers and NCOs. Junior leaders such as Hard Headed Hanneken, Red Mike Edson, Chesty Puller, and Ironman Lee earned more than nicknames in small unit operations deep in the jungle far from any support. Their reputations for courage and daring would help them lead and inspire the new generation of Marines that would fight World War II. In addition, the conflicts served as a laboratory for developing and testing equipment and ideas, such as the birth in Haiti of glide bombing (which eventually became dive bombing). Finally, Marines slowly learned to fight the way they were organized, as an air-ground team, with planes working in support of infantrymen. This combined-arms concept was still at the fledgling stage, but it laid the foundation for great strides during World War II.

With a change in American foreign policy and the end of deployments to Nicaragua (1932) and Haiti (1934), the Marine Corps began to focus itself. The effort was driven in large measure by the Marine Corps Schools, which wanted to create its own doctrine and curriculum. Yet another attempt to merge the Corps into the Army provided an extra spur. And John Russell, who had called for an emphasis on a core mission during his days as a major two decades earlier, added impetus from his position as assistant to the Commandant and then Commandant. The schools shut down for a year and produced the *Tentative Manual for Landing Operations*, which covered both the amphibious assault and the defense of advanced bases. It was the first official doctrine developed by Marines. At the same time, the Corps renamed the MCEFs as the Fleet Marine Forces, which tied them organizationally to the Navy and naval missions. A renewed exercise program (absent for several years due to the press of deployments and the budget reductions of the Depression) focused entirely on amphibious assaults and base defense. Amphibious transport remained a major problem, but the Corps worked around that issue for the time being by acquiring lighter equipment and simulating what it would do when better landing craft became available.

The Corps still hedged its bets to a certain degree, with the schools bringing out the *Small Wars Manual* soon after the first amphibious doctrine. This new publication would receive considerable attention in professional education programs for the remainder of the 1930s. But the *Tentative Manual*, coupled with changes in training and organization, made it clear that the Corps was looking primarily to its naval roots and purposely had moved away from competing directly with the Army's primary missions. For better or worse, Marines had cast their lot on a unique role with little precedent, except for the failed British amphibious campaign at Gallipoli during World War I. It was a bold choice for a small organization that faced possible extinction.

THINKERS AND FIGHTERS

1919–1938

1919

January
HQMC
Major Alfred Cunningham is named the first head of the Aviation Section at Headquarters Marine Corps.

8 February
Force Structure
Elements of the 1st Marine Aviation Force in Miami merge into Squadron D. This marks the birth of what will become Marine Scout Bomber Squadron 231 (VMSB-231). It departs shortly thereafter for Santo Domingo. During this month the 1st Marine Aviation Force is disbanded.

22 February
Force Structure
Squadron E is formed at Miami.

8 March
Santo Domingo
The 15th Regiment and Squadron D arrive in Santo Domingo to reinforce the 2nd Marine Brigade during a time of increasing banditry.

15 March
Bases
Following substantial progress on dredging and filling work, the formal groundbreaking is held for construction at the new Marine Corps base in San Diego.

16 March
Haiti
The chief of the Gendarmerie d'Haiti requests the direct assistance of the 1st Marine Brigade in suppressing the Caco Revolt. The rebellion stems in part from popular discontent with forced labor on road projects.

21 March
Haiti
Sergeant Nicholas B. Moskoff of the gendarmerie becomes the first Marine killed in the Caco Revolt.

25 March
Haiti
The 7th Regiment transfers four of its companies to Haiti to augment the 1st Marine Brigade in response to the Caco Revolt.

Left: *Happy Marines of the 5th Brigade arrive at Newport News, Virginia, on a troopship from Europe. (National Archives)*

Opposite, top: *A Marine inspects a Gendarmerie unit in Haiti, 1919. (National Archives)*

Opposite, bottom: *A grateful nation welcomes the Marines of the 4th Brigade as they parade through Washington, D.C. (National Archives)*

31 March
Haiti
Squadron E arrives in Haiti to provide an aviation element to the 1st Marine Brigade.

4 April
Haiti
A Marine patrol of four officers and 51 enlisted attacks and scatters 500 Cacos near Hinche.

5 May
HQMC
Marine Corps Headquarters moves to the new Navy Building on Constitution Avenue.

20 May
Force Structure
Squadron C of the former 1st Marine Aviation Force arrives in Quantico for duty.

12 June
Bases
Marine Corps Base, Quantico leases a site for its first flying field for land planes, and construction begins on hangars and other supporting facilities.

30 June
Manpower
The strength of the Marine Corps on active duty is 2,270 officers and 46,564 enlisted.

1 July
Force Structure
Squadron C absorbs the Marine Aeronautic Section at Quantico.

11 July
Manpower
Congress completes legislation establishing the enlisted strength of the postwar Marine Corps at 27,400. The next day, Commandant George Barnett promulgates directives to speed up demobilization. The process is largely completed by the end of the year.

Left: *Not every Marine in Haiti used a mule. These men have motorized bicycles for mounts. (Marine Corps Historical Center)*

Below: *Marines load pack mules, a more typical mode of transporting supplies in Haiti, where there were very few good roads. (National Archives)*

21 July
Force Structure
The 15th Separate Battalion is formed at Camp Pontanezan, France, from personnel of the 4th and 5th Marine Brigades, for duty in connection with a plebiscite in Germany.

23 July
Santo Domingo
The first Marine air attack on Dominican bandits is made near Meta de la Palma.

3 August
Force Structure
The 4th Marine Brigade returns to the United States from Europe.

8 August
Force Structure
The 4th Marine Brigade parades through New York City along with its parent 2nd Division. It returns to duty with the Navy Department later that day. The 5th Marine Brigade returns to the United States from Europe.

11 August
Manpower
This is the final day of active service for women Marine reservists enlisted for the World War. A total of 305 women served in clerical billets.

12 August
Force Structure
The 4th Marine Brigade parades for President Wilson in Washington, D.C., and then disbands.

26 September
Force Structure
Squadron A of the former 1st Marine Aviation Force arrives in Quantico after closing down activities at the former Marine Flying Field in Miami.

1 October
Force Structure
The 2nd Advance Base Force is activated to serve as the West Coast Expeditionary Force for the Marine Corps. Its mission is to defend expeditionary overseas naval bases.

7 October
Haiti
Charlemagne Peralte, the most important Caco leader, sends 300 of his men into Port-au-Prince prior to dawn. Marines and gendarmes defeat and drive off the rebels.

31 October
Haiti
Sergeant Herman Hanneken and Corporal William R. Button (respectively a gendarmerie captain and lieutenant) use a ruse to get their patrol into Peralte's camp and kill him.

1 December
HQMC
The Aviation Section is made a part of the newly formed Operations and Training Division at Headquarters Marine Corps.

17 December
Force Structure
The 8th Regiment is reactivated in the States and shipped to Haiti to reinforce the brigade.

23 December
Force Structure
The 15th Separate Battalion arrives in Philadelphia. It is the last Marine unit to return home from World War I.

1920

14 January
Haiti
A few hundred Cacos under Benoit Batraville move into Port-au-Prince during the night in an attempt

Top: *A 1920s recruiting poster. ("Marine on a Jaguar," James Montgomery Flagg, Marine Corps Art Collection)*

Right: *A Marine detachment moves at "doubletime" around the deck of a battleship in 1920. (Naval Historical Center)*

BRIGADIER GENERAL HERMAN H. HANNEKEN

Herman Hanneken was born in St. Louis, Missouri, in 1893. As a young man, he went west and worked as a cow puncher. When U.S. forces seized Vera Cruz, Mexico, in 1914, he enlisted in the Marine Corps in search of greater adventure. He was not disappointed, as he deployed to Haiti at the beginning of the American intervention there in 1915. Subsequently he joined the Gendarmerie d'Haiti as a junior officer, while rising in rank to sergeant in the Marine Corps. In 1919, as disorder heated up

again in Haiti, Hanneken was posted to command of the district of Grande Riviere. He soon devised a scheme to deal with Charlemagne Peralte, the most important leader of the Caco revolt.

Hanneken enlisted two of his gendarmes and a local citizen, Jean Conze, in his plan. Conze left town loudly proclaiming his opposition to the occupation, then installed himself at a abandoned fort and rallied Cacos to join him. Private Jean Francois promptly "deserted" the gendarmerie and joined Conze. Hanneken feigned three attacks on the fort and made it appear he had been wounded during the last fight. Conze's stock with the Cacos rose, and he convinced Peralte to launch a night assault on Grande Riviere. The wily Peralte nearly spoiled the plot when he decided to await the results of the attack at a remote point, surrounded by 700 of his followers. Francois brought word of the change to Hanneken, who lay in wait outside Grande Riviere with Cpl William R. Button and 20 gendarmes, all disguised as Cacos. With Francois providing the password, the group marched on Peralte's camp. They successfully penetrated the well-guarded site. Just as the Caco leader's immediate bodyguards grew suspicious, Hanneken drew out a pistol and shot Peralte. In the confused melee that followed, the gendarmerie outfit fought off two counterattacks. The next day Hanneken brought Peralte's body into the city. When evidence of his death spread around the country, the Caco revolt lost much of its impetus.

Opposite: *Lt Herman "Hard Headed" Hanneken. (National Archives)*

Right: *Col James J. Meade, Capt Hanneken, 2ndLt William R. Button, and 2ndLt H. R. Woods (all gendarmerie ranks) pose after receiving decorations from the president of Haiti. (Marine Corps Historical Center)*

The display of initiative and heroism garnered Hanneken a Medal of Honor and a commission as a lieutenant in the Corps. Five months later he duplicated the daring feat on a smaller scale and killed one of Peralte's primary subordinates, which brought a Navy Cross. In 1929, now deployed in Nicaragua, he succeeded in capturing Simon Jiron, one of the top Sandinista chieftains. The result was a second Navy Cross. His courage and his reserved, almost cold, personality, spawned a nickname that fit his initials—"Hard Headed" Hanneken.

In September 1942, LtCol Hanneken led 2/7 onto Guadalcanal. He and his men fought in the Third Battle of the Matanikau and also in the Battle of Koli Point, but their greatest success came during the Battle for Henderson Field in October. Hastily thrown into position to cover the flank of a regimental-sized combat outpost, 2/7 beat back a strong night attack and inflicted roughly 1,000 casualties on the Japanese. Promoted to colonel in 1943, Hanneken led the Division Special Troops during initial operations at Cape Gloucester, then took command of the 7th Marines in February 1944. For the landing at Peleliu in September, his regiment received responsibility for the right flank. In tough, costly fighting in the first few days, the 7th Marines cleaned out the southern end of the island. Thereafter, he and his unit participated in the bloody reduction of the Japanese pocket in the rugged coral ridges of Umurbrogol Mountain.

Hanneken came back to the States in October 1944 and took command of the Infantry Training Regiment at Camp Elliott in California. Along with Chesty Puller's east coast ITR, Hanneken was responsible for preparing new Marines to join the divisions for the tough battles of Iwo Jima and Okinawa. He retired at the rank of brigadier general in 1948 and died in 1986.

to capture the city. By the next day, Marines and gendarmes have killed, wounded, or captured nearly half of them. Thereafter the number of rebels accepting amnesty increases rapidly.

4 April
Haiti
Sergeant Lawrence Muth of the Gendarmerie d'Haiti is the last Marine killed in action during the Caco revolt, during the ambush of his patrol by Benoit Batraville's band.

11 May
Force Structure
The 16th Regiment is organized at Philadelphia for potential service in Haiti or Santo Domingo.

18 May
Haiti
A Marine patrol attacks Batraville's camp near Los Cahobas and kills him. His death essentially brings the Caco Revolt to an end.

30 June
HQMC
Secretary of the Navy Josephus Daniels relieves Barnett as Commandant and transfers him to be commanding general of the new Department of the Pacific in San Francisco. Major General John Lejeune succeeds him as Commandant. Lejeune is the thirteenth Commandant of the Marine Corps.

30 June
Manpower
The strength of the Marine Corps on active duty is 1,104 officers and 16,061 enlisted.

1 July
Training
In one of his first acts as Commandant, Lejeune renames the Vocational Schools Detachment at Quantico as the Marine Corps Institute and makes its correspondence courses available throughout the Marine Corps.

20 August
Force Structure
A Marine guard is established at the U.S. consulate in Tungchow, China.

12 October
Santo Domingo
Elements of the 4th Regiment help fight a severe fire in Santiago, Santo Domingo.

30 October
Force Structure
Commandant Lejeune approves a new table of organization for aviation that includes four squadrons (designated 1st through 4th), each composed of two smaller units to be known as flights.

1 December
Force Structure
Squadrons A and C at Quantico are disbanded and their personnel and equipment formed into the 3rd Air Squadron. This is the birth of what will become Marine Fighter Attack Squadron 131 (VMFA-131).

1921

1 January
Force Structure
Squadron D is disbanded in Santo Domingo, and its personnel and aircraft are absorbed into the new 1st Air Squadron.

17 March
Force Structure
Flight L, 4th Air Squadron, and its seaplanes arrive in Guam for duty and become the first Marine aviation unit to serve in the Pacific.

30 June
Manpower
The strength of the Marine Corps on active duty is 1,087 officers and 21,903 enlisted.

September
Marksmanship
The Marine Corps shooting team wins all four National Match events (rifle and pistol team and individual) at Camp Perry, the first time it has ever done so.

1 November
Heritage
Commandant Lejeune directs that every Marine be reminded of the honorable service of the Corps on the 10 November birthday of the Marine Corps. He personally wrote out the words, which are repeated every year in ceremonies around the globe.

7 November
Civil Support
President Warren Harding directs the Marine Corps to provide personnel to guard the U.S. mail following a rash of robberies. Fifty-three officers and 2,200 enlisted men are assigned until the following March.

1 December
Bases
Marine Corps Base, San Diego is formally commissioned and occupied by the 5th Brigade (formerly titled the 2nd Advance Base Force).

Opposite: *With an infusion of Marine leadership, training, and spirit, the gendarmerie of Haiti took on all the characteristics of the Corps. ("Gendarme de Haiti," Col John W. Thomason, USMC, Sam Houston State University)*

Right: *While the Army Air Corps focused on the theory of strategic bombing after WWI, Marine aviators practiced close air support in the Caribbean. ("Cunningham in Santo Domingo," John J. Capolino, Marine Corps Art Collection)*

THOMPSON SUBMACHINE GUN

The Thompson submachine gun sprang from the same mind that helped develop the venerable Springfield model 1903 rifle—that of Colonel John Thompson, an Army ordnance expert. In retirement in 1916, Thompson joined forces with John Blish, inventor of the first self-locking blowback operating system for automatic firearms. Their objective was to develop an automatic rifle suitable for the trench warfare of the Western Front in Europe. Thompson thought that a short, lightweight weapon would serve as a "trench broom" and allow soldiers to "sweep" the fortified lines of their enemy with a steady stream of bullets. The two ordnance men decided to build it around a blowback system, which uses the gas pressure from a fired cartridge to push directly back on the bolt and thus prepare the weapon to fire again. It would be simpler and more reliable than a recoil or gas-operated mechanism.

Thompson and Blish hired Oscar Payne (a 23-year-old self-educated engineer) and Theodore Eickhoff (a former Army Ordnance Department employee) to do much of the detailed design work. They were not able to complete a functioning prototype until the end of the war, but it showed considerable promise. The basic model came with front and back pistol grips suited for its intended use of spraying a linear target, but there was an attachable shoulder stock for aimed fire. In the latter role, fired on semi-automatic, it was accurate out to 400 yards. On full automatic, it could spew out bullets at the rate of 800 per minute.

In the years immediately following World War I, the Army and Marine Corps each conducted its own tests of the weapon. The Corps liked the capability offered by the submachine gun, but could not afford to purchase it as budgets dropped precipitously in the face of peacetime parsimony. Oddly enough, the post office provided what the Marines could not afford. In 1926 the President called out the Corps to guard post offices and mail trains in the wake of an epidemic of robberies. To beef up firepower in these close quarters, the postal service provided 250 Thompsons. A year later, when Marine forces went

Opposite: *The Thompson submachine gun provided heavy firepower in a relatively light, compact weapon. (Eric Long)*

Right: *Stationed in Nicaragua in 1931, 1stLt Lewis Puller (second from left) poses with members of the Guardia Nacional, two of whom are carrying Thompsons. (Marine Corps Historical Center)*

ashore in Nicaragua to protect American lives and quell disorder, they took some of the submachine guns with them. The Sandinista rebels liked the Thompson, too, and obtained several in Mexico. The Corps promptly ordered hundreds more to maintain an edge in firepower for patrols that could not carry heavier machine guns into the bush.

By the time World War II arrived, military necessity had resulted in a number of modifications. The stock was no longer detachable, and the mass-produced weapons lacked the adjustable rear sight, semi-automatic selector switch, and fine detailing of the original. The operating system was simplified by doing away with the Blish lock and fixing the firing pin in the face of the bolt. The Thompson now had just two moving parts in the firing action—the bolt and the trigger sear. This model, adopted as the M1A1, could be built more easily and at a lower cost.

In the opening days of the war, the Corps assigned Thompsons to mortar and machine-gun squad leaders and to crewmen manning tanks and other heavy weapons. The submachine guns provided excellent close-in protection in a compact package. The Raiders and parachutists also acquired the M1A1 as a primary weapon well-suited to their lightly equipped, fast-moving, hard-hitting style of warfare. Even the new version of the Thompson was comparatively expensive and heavy, though, and the Corps soon began replacing it with the Reising submachine gun. The cheap substitute proved unreliable, however, and never fully replaced the Thompson in the hearts and hands of Marines.

1922

25 January
Nicaragua
Following growing political unrest in Nicaragua (including a bloody fight between Marines of the Legation Guard and Managua policemen), the Marine detachment of cruiser *Galveston* (C-17) goes ashore at Corinto and proceeds to the capital.

28 January
Civil Support
Marines assist in rescue work after the roof of a theater collapses in Washington, D.C.

11 February
Haiti
President Harding appoints Brigadier General John H. Russell to be the U.S. High Commissioner to Haiti, giving him authority for all American diplomatic and military matters in that country. He holds the post until 12 November 1930.

28 April
China
Cruiser *Albany* (CL-23) lands her Marines in China to reinforce the Legation Guard in Peking.

5 May
China
The Marine detachments of the Asiatic Fleet land at Tientsin for possible duty in Peking. The crisis soon passes, and they return to their ships.
Bases
The air facility at Quantico is named Brown Field in honor of 2nd Lieutenant Walter V. Brown, killed in a crash during a training exercise on 9 June 1921.

19 June
Training
Air units at Quantico begin supporting the maneuvers of the ground elements of the East Coast Expeditionary Force at Gettysburg, Pennsylvania.

Left: *"Marines in Haiti," Donald Dickson, Marine Corps Historical Center*

Opposite, top: *"Mounted Patrol," Col Donald L. Dickson, USMC, Marine Corps Historical Center*

Opposite, bottom: *Marines train with trailer-mounted antiaircraft guns at Culebra around 1924. (National Archives)*

30 June
Manpower
The strength of the Marine Corps on active duty is 1,135 officers and 20,098 enlisted.

1 August
Force Structure
The 3rd and 15th Regiments disband and their personnel transfer to the 4th Regiment and the newly reestablished 1st Regiment.

3 August
Force Structure
The air elements at Quantico are designated the 1st Aviation Group, East Coast Expeditionary Force. This is part of an aviation reorganization that will see the designation of squadrons based on dedicated missions (such as scouting or bombing).

17 August
Force Structure
The 1st Air Squadron is redesignated Marine Observation Squadron 1 (VO-1M).

24 August
Force Structure
The 3rd Air Squadron at Quantico is re-designated Marine Fighting Squadron 1 (VF-1M).

9 September
Expositions
A Marine detachment establishes a model camp at the Brazilian Exposition in Rio de Janeiro.

1923

14 February
China
The Marine detachment of gunboat *Asheville* (PG-21) lands at Masu Island in China to protect U.S. citizens from bandits.

Left: *A 1920s Marine aviation recruiting poster. ("Fly With the Marines," Howard Chandler Christy, Marine Corps Art Collection)*

30 June
Manpower
The strength of the Marine Corps on active duty is 1,141 officers and 18,533 enlisted. Commandant Lejeune's strong relationship with Congress prevents a proposed reduction in personnel to 13,000, a figure that would have been proportional to reductions imposed on the Navy.

11 August
Training
The Marine Corps recruit depot at Mare Island, California, is transferred to San Diego.

15 November
China
A detachment of Marines goes ashore at Tunghan, China, to safeguard American missionaries in the aftermath of factional fighting.

25 December
Training
The 10th Marines and elements of the East Coast Expeditionary Force embark at Quantico on transports *Sirius* and *Chaumont* to serve with the U.S. Fleet during winter maneuvers in the Caribbean.

1924

2 January
Training
The 5th Marines and elements of the East Coast Expeditionary Force embark at Quantico on transport *Henderson* to serve with the U.S. Fleet during winter maneuvers in the Caribbean.

10 January
Training
The 10th Marines begin exercises in Culebra, Puerto Rico, involving the defense of an advanced naval and air base.

14–17 January
Training
The 5th Marines conduct offensive amphibious exercises simulating seizure of the Panama Canal.

31 January
Training
The 5th Marines launch amphibious assaults against the 10th Marines on Culebra. The operation lasts through the next day.

20 February
Training
The East Coast Expeditionary Force conducts a combined-arms amphibious exercise on Culebra for the benefit of dozens of reporters brought from the States to the Caribbean. It brings favorable media comment around the country.

27 February
Honduras
A force of Marines and sailors from cruiser *Denver* (C-14) lands at La Ceiba to protect U.S. interests during revolutionary activity.

3 March
Honduras
Destroyer *Billingsley* (DD-293) lands Marines and seamen at Telas.

4 March
Honduras
Denver lands more Marines and sailors at Puerto Cortez.

30 June
Manpower
The strength of the Marine Corps on active duty is 1,157 officers and 19,175 enlisted.

1 July
Force Structure
The understrength 1st Regiment in Santo Domingo is redesignated as the 3rd Battalion, 6th Regiment.

Right: *Marine aircraft and crewmen line up for inspection at Naval Air Station North Island in San Diego, around 1930. (National Archives)*

12 July
Santo Domingo
Brigadier General Harry Lee ceases to be the military governor of Santo Domingo when the new constitutional government is inaugurated.

18 July
Santo Domingo
VO-1M in Santo Domingo departs for San Diego. The 3rd Battalion, 6th Regiment departs for Cuba.

6 August
Santo Domingo
The 4th Regiment departs Santo Domingo for San Diego.

8 August
Training
The 1st Aviation Group begins supporting the ground elements of the East Coast Expeditionary Force in preparation for the fall maneuvers to be staged at Antietam, Maryland. The operation continues through 18 September.

16 August
Force Structure
VO-1M arrives at Naval Air Station, North Island in San Diego Bay, the first Marine squadron to operate on the West Coast of the United States.

1 September
Training
The East Coast Expeditionary Force begins its maneuvers at Antietam Battlefield in Maryland. The exercise lasts for 12 days.

7 September
Honduras
At the request of the U.S. consul, cruiser *Rochester* (CA-2) lands Marines and seamen at La Ceiba to protect American citizens.

9 September
China
Cruiser *Huron* (CA-9) lands her Marines to reinforce the Peking Legation Guard during factional fighting in north China.

16 September
Santo Domingo
The last elements of the 2nd Marine Brigade depart Santo Domingo by sea, and the American occupation of that country comes to an end.

6 October
China
Asheville lands her Marine detachment and another 101 Marines from the Philippines at Shanghai. The following month they move on to Tientsin.

Left: *During an exercise at Culebra in 1924, Marines build a pontoon causeway. (National Archives)*

Right: *San Diego Marines of the mid-1920s pose around their disassembled machine gun, stowed on a cart for easy transport. (Naval Historical Center)*

1925

15 January
China
The Marine guard of gunboat *Sacramento* (PG-19) goes ashore at Shanghai when the troops of the local warlord mutiny and endanger the foreign settlement.

22 January
China
Three ships deliver 140 Marines from the Philippines to reinforce those already at Shanghai. The Marines remain until February.

20 April
Honduras
Marines land at La Ceiba to protect U.S. interests.

27 April
Training
Drawn from Quantico, San Diego, and the ships of the fleet, 2,500 Marines initiate an amphibious landing against U.S. Army forces on the island of Oahu, Hawaii, as part of annual naval exercises. The Marines simulate two divisions (20 times their number). The one-day operation only serves to prove that ships' boats remain inadequate for making a large-scale amphibious assault against a defended coast.

5 June
China
Marines go ashore at Shanghai from *Huron* when fighting breaks out between rival factions.

9 June
China
Marines land from the commercial ship *Aberenda* to reinforce those already in Shanghai. They remain ashore through August.

30 June
Manpower
The strength of the Marine Corps on active duty is 1,168 officers and 18,310 enlisted.

1 July
Reserve
Legislation goes into effect that re-establishes the Marine Corps Reserve (which had been largely dormant since WW I). Among other features, it provides drill pay for the first time, authorizes an honorary retirement without pay at age 64, and creates two classes of reserves. The Fleet Marine Corps Reserve is composed of company-size units conducting training one evening per week, while the Volunteer Marine Corps Reserve consists of individuals only subject to training upon their own request.

Left: *A Navy launch ferries Marines ashore as sailors man a machine gun in the bow. ("Watercolor #2: Marines in Boats," Col John W. Thomason, Sam Houston State University)*

Opposite: *MajGen Lejeune (far right, saluting) reviews the men of the 5th Marines on the day they depart Quantico for Nicaragua in February 1927. (Marine Corps Historical Center)*

1 August
Nicaragua
Marine Legation Guard withdraws from Managua.

1 September
Force Structure
Division 1 of Marine Fighting Squadron 3 (VF-3M) is activated at San Diego. This is the birth of what will become Marine Fighter Attack Squadron 232 (VMFA-232). VF-1M at Quantico is redesignated VO-4M. VF-8M is activated at Quantico with the delivery of 18 Curtiss F6C-3 Hawk airplanes.

9 November
China
Marines from the Asiatic Fleet go ashore at Tientsin.

30 December
China
A detachment of Marines lands at Shanghai during a renewed period of internecine warfare.

1926

6 May
Nicaragua
The Marine detachment of cruiser *Cleveland* (now redesignated as CL-21) lands at Bluefields to establish a neutral zone during a civil war in Nicaragua. The Marines remain there for a month.

24 June
Reserve
The Fleet Marine Corps Reserve units hold their first field exercise during their first two-week annual training session. Commandant Lejeune and members of Congress view the practice attack.

30 June
Manpower
The strength of the Marine Corps on active duty is 1,178 officers and 17,976 enlisted.

27 August
Nicaragua
Marines, this time from *Galveston*, again occupy Bluefields to keep it out of the hands of both Nicaraguan factions.

1 September
Force Structure
The 1st Aviation Group at Quantico is re-designated Aircraft Squadrons, East Coast Expeditionary Force.

10 October
Nicaragua
Marines and sailors from *Denver* go ashore at Corinto and provide a safe area for a peace conference between contending Nicaraguan leaders. The two sides fail to reach an agreement, and fighting resumes.

20 October
Civil Support
Marines are again assigned to guard the U.S. mail system during a period of increased armed robberies.

12 November
China
Marines go ashore at Chingwangtao, China, from auxiliary ship *Gold Star* (AG-12) to protect U.S. citizens.

22 December
Nicaragua
Rochester lands Marines and sailors to establish a neutral zone at Rio Grande, Nicaragua.

23 December
Nicaragua
Marines from *Cleveland* and *Denver* establish control over Puerto Cabezas, Nicaragua.

1927

5–9 January
Nicaragua
Marines and sailors from the Special Service Squadron land at several points on the Nicaraguan coast to safeguard U.S. interests. *Galveston*'s Marines move inland to protect the U.S. legation in Managua.

10 January
Nicaragua
The 2nd Battalion, 5th Regiment arrives in Bluefields from Cuba. Later in the month, most of the unit shifts by sea to Managua.

9 February
China
Due to factional fighting within the Nationalist Party, a provisional battalion of Marines from Guam lands at Shanghai to safeguard Americans.

19 February
Nicaragua
Marine forces take control of the main railroad line between Corinto and Managua.

21 February
Nicaragua
The Marine detachments of the Scouting Fleet go ashore in western Nicaragua.

24 February
China
The 4th Regiment arrives in Shanghai from San Diego and takes responsibility for a sector of the International Settlement. Other foreign forces assume control over portions of the enclave. The regiment will remain in Shanghai until 1941.

Left: *The Horse Marines pass in review in Peking, China, in 1927. (National Archives)*

26 February
Nicaragua
VO-1M with six DH-4s arrives in Nicaragua to provide an air element to Marine forces there.

4 March
China
A boarding party of Marines and sailors from cruiser *Pittsburgh* (ACR-4) recaptures an American commercial ship from a party of Chinese near Shanghai.

7 March
Nicaragua
The headquarters of the 2nd Brigade and the remainder of the 5th Regiment arrive in Corinto from the U.S.

2 May
China
Brigadier General Smedley Butler, his 3rd Brigade headquarters, the recently organized 6th Regiment, and VF-3M arrive at Shanghai to reinforce the 4th Regiment.

4 May
Nicaragua
Former U.S. Secretary of War Henry Stimson negotiates the Peace of Tipitapa between liberal and conservative factions in Nicaragua. The terms call for all parties to surrender their arms (for a bounty) to the Marines, who will set up a national constabulary and supervise free elections in 1928. Augusto Sandino and some of his Liberal followers reject the peace agreement.

12 May
Nicaragua
Lieutenant Colonel Robert Y. Rhea becomes the first commander of Nicaragua's Guardia Nacional and begins organizing the constabulary force with Marine officers and NCOs serving as officers.

16 May
Nicaragua
Roughly 300 bandits raid the town of La Paz Centro at night. The Marine garrison drives them off and loses two dead in the process.

19 May
Nicaragua
The newly reestablished 11th Regiment and VO-4M arrive in Nicaragua to reinforce the 2nd Brigade and help supervise the peace.

6 June
China
The 6th Regiment and Butler's brigade headquarters shifts to Tientsin as Nationalist forces take over northern China.

11 June
Civil Support
Marines from the Washington Navy Yard assist in handling the crowds welcoming Charles Lindbergh after his historic flight across the Atlantic Ocean.

25 June
Force Structure
VF-3M is redesignated VF-10M in China.

30 June
Manpower
The strength of the Marine Corps on active duty is 1,198 officers and 18,000 enlisted.

July
Nicaragua
About 1,000 Marines are withdrawn from Nicaragua.

1 July
Force Structure
VO-1M is redesignated VO-8M upon its return to San Diego from Nicaragua, while VO-4M in Nicaragua becomes VO-7M.

15–16 July
Nicaragua
The forces of Sandino launch a night attack on the Marine and Guardia barracks in Ocotal. In the morning, two DH-4s of VO-7M strafe the Sandinistas. By noon, five aircraft of the squadron return and conduct dive-bombing and strafing attacks on the enemy. This is often credited as being the first dive-bombing attack in combat. One Marine is killed on the ground, and four Marines and Guardias are wounded. Sandinista losses are estimated at up to 300.

6 September
Nicaragua
The last elements of the 11th Regiment depart for the United States.

18–19 September
Nicaragua
Sandino's forces attack the Marine and Guardia garrison at Telpaneca at night, but are driven off.

8 October
Nicaragua
The Boeing O2B-1 (a metal-fuselage version of the DH-4) of Lieutenant Earl A. Thomas and Sergeant Frank E. Dowdell crashes on Sapotillal Ridge in the rough hinterland of Nueva Segovia province. The accompanying aircraft observes the men exit the wreckage alive, but they are later captured and killed by the Sandinistas.

Right: *The 2nd Battalion, 6th Marines marches down the streets of Teintsin, China, on its way to be inspected by BGen Smedley Butler on 3 May 1928. (National Archives)*

THE BATTLE OF OCOTAL

Augusto Sandino's first attempt to drive U.S. forces from Nicaragua took place in July 1927 at Ocotal, the seat of government for rugged Nuevo Segovia province in the northern highlands. A force of 37 Marines under Captain Gilbert D. Hatfield and a detachment of 47 Guardias led by Marine Lieutenant Grover C. Darnall jointly garrisoned the small town. Each unit had an adobe-walled barracks facing out on the central square. On the night of the 15th, Sandino and about 800 followers filtered into the provincial capital. They even brought additional weapons and armed about 100 local sympathizers.

About an hour after midnight, a Marine sentry spotted movement in the shadows. His verbal challenge was met by fire from the Sandinistas, caught in the act of creeping up on the government forces. With that brief warning, the Marines and Guardias sprang to arms. They exchanged fire for about two hours with the rebels, who then pulled back. Around 0400 the enemy launched an attack, but went to ground when the fire of the defenders proved too intense. The two sides traded shots until shortly after 0800. The firing stopped when a rebel bearing a flag of truce approached the Marine barracks. He carried a demand for surrender from Sandino. Hatfield rejected it.

The sound of the renewed firing was interrupted at midmorning when the normal daily patrol of two planes from Managua came over the town. Since things appeared amiss, Lieutenant Hayne D. Boyden landed briefly at the airstrip outside of town and questioned a local citizen. Meanwhile, his wingman, Marine Gunner Michale Wodarczyk, kept suspicious groups at a

Opposite: *A captured Sandinista flag is displayed at the grave of the Marine killed at Ocotal. (National Archives)*

Right: *Air crew of the Ace of Spades squadron (then VO-8M) flew at Ocotal. (National Archives)*

distance. As Boyden got airborne again, Wodarczyk confirmed the situation when he spotted emergency panels laid out in the courtyard of the Marine barracks. The two pilots briefly strafed the Sandinistas in the streets and returned at top speed to Managua with the news.

Shortly after noon, Major Ross Rowell led the mix of five operational DH-4Bs and O2B-1s of his squadron off the airfield near the Nicaraguan capital. Each of the biplanes carried a full load of 600 rounds for each of its machine guns and four 25-pound bombs (the number limited by the extra gasoline needed for the long flight to Ocotal). They met rough weather crossing the mountains into Nueva Segovia, but skirted around it. Arriving above the town at 1435, the formation circled once around to identify the location of friendly forces and potential targets. Prior to this day, no one in the rebel forces had experienced any aerial action other than a rare nuisance attack by the two antiquated planes of the air force of Nicaragua. Sandino's men thus ignored the droning aircraft above them.

Rowell placed his five planes in line and led them in a dive-bombing assault on enemy groups exposed in the streets of the town. As each pilot bored in from 1500 feet, he fired his fixed machine guns. If the target appeared sufficiently lucrative, he released one of the precious bombs. As the aircraft pulled out of its dive, the observer in back chipped in with his swivel-mounted machine guns. The second pass at lower altitude was enough for the rebels. They streamed from the town in an effort to escape, but in the open terrain they only presented better targets. The aerial assault lasted for 45 minutes, until the planes were low on fuel and had expended their ordnance.

Sandino's casualties were never firmly established, but estimates ranged from 50 to 300. Government losses were just one Marine killed and a total of four Marines and Guardias wounded. Captain Hatfield credited air support with turning the tide. Were it not for the timely support from above, his beleaguered force might have run out of ammunition and supplies long before headquarters realized he was in trouble and a relief force could negotiate the 125 miles of difficult terrain from Managua. In the first true combined-arms action by the Marine Corps air-ground team, it had proven itself to be a formidable combination.

9 October
Nicaragua
A rescue patrol from Jicaro is ambushed at Sapotillal Ridge and forced to withdraw by strong rebel forces.

26–28 October
Nicaragua
Fighting resumes on Sapotillal Ridge when new Marine/Guardia patrols reach the area. The rebels break contact when air support arrives on the 28th.

23 November
Nicaragua
Marine air patrols discover El Chipote, Sandino's fortified mountain base camp, located seven miles from Sapotillal Ridge, and attack it.

4 December
Technology
The first Marine transport plane, a three-engine Fokker, is flown to Nicaragua and put into service primarily to haul cargo to distant, inaccessible outposts.

30 December
Nicaragua
A Marine/Guardia patrol sent to attack El Chipote is ambushed by strong Sandinista forces near Quilali. Captain Richard Livingston and six of his men are killed, and 25 are wounded in driving off the ambushers. His force falls back on Quilali.

Top: *A Marine patrol led by Maj Smedley Butler and GySgt Dan Daly fends off a night ambush by cacos in Haiti in October 1915. ("Cacos Ambush Haiti," Col Charles Waterhouse, USMCR (Ret), Waterhouse Collection)*

Left: *Marines look over rifle barrels from weapons turned in during a bounty drive to disarm Nicaraguan rebels. (National Archives)*

Right: *A Marine patrol on horseback in front of the barracks in Ocotal. (National Archives)*

Below: *Lt Schilt with the plane that he flew onto a street in Quilali. (Marine Corps Historical Center)*

Another Sandinista force attacks a second column, under Lieutenant Merton A. Richal, which breaks through with only one man wounded.

31 December
Nicaragua
Richal's patrol is attacked again near Sapotillal Ridge and loses two killed. It remains surrounded until a relief patrol from Quilali and air support help bring Richal's force into Quilali on 2 January. The two patrols have a combined 31 wounded and are surrounded by rebels.

1928

6–8 January
Nicaragua
Lieutenant Christian F. Schilt makes 10 flights in an O2U Corsair into a dangerous makeshift airstrip in Quilali to bring in a new commander and supplies and bring out the patrol's most seriously wounded. The patrol then withdraws to San Albino. Schilt is awarded the Medal of Honor.

14 January
Nicaragua
Four Marine planes conduct dive-bombing and strafing attacks on El Chipote.

15 January
Nicaragua
The leading elements of the reactivated 11th Regiment return to Nicaragua to reinforce the 2nd Brigade.

19–26 January
Nicaragua
Four companies of Marines and Guardias close in on and seize El Chipote, but the Sandinistas escape the net.

MAJOR GENERAL MERRITT A. EDSON

Merritt Edson made his first real mark in the Corps in 1927, when he led his Marine detachment from the cruiser *Denver* (CL-16) ashore in Nicaragua. He and a handful of his men used native boats to penetrate hundreds of miles up the Coco River into the interior in search of Sandino. Captain Edson's small band fought a number of battles with the rebels (the largest at Iliiquas on 7 August 1928) and rousted them from their previously impenetrable lair. For 14 months the Marines lived off the land and occasional resupplies brought in by boat or plane. When the Coco Patrol finally emerged from the jungle in March 1929, Edson had earned a well-deserved Navy Cross and renown as an aggressive and thoughtful combat leader. The beard he sported also earned him the lifelong nickname "Red Mike."

Born on 25 April 1897, in Vermont, Edson had participated in his first military campaign as a national guardsman called to active duty for the Mexican Border campaign in 1916. He left the University of Vermont for good following his sophomore year in 1917, this time to enlist in the Marine Corps just after the United States entered World War I. He earned a commission soon after, but did not make it to France with the 5th Marine Brigade until the conflict was almost over. In the quiet years of the 1920s, he became a successful competitive marksman, earned his wings as a naval aviator, and lost them a few years later after several crashes revealed a problem with depth perception.

He spent the 1930s teaching tactics at The Basic School, leading Marine Corps shooting teams to some of their most successful seasons ever, and guarding the International

Settlement at Shanghai as the Japanese conquered the Chinese portion of the city. After rewriting the *Small Wars Manual* in 1940, he took command of the 1st Battalion, 5th Marines in June 1941. He immediately became enmeshed in reorganizing his outfit into the lightly equipped, fast-moving, hard-hitting force that was redesignated as the 1st Marine Raider Battalion in early 1942.

In September 1942, Edson gained lasting fame with his epic defense of a coral hogback on Guadalcanal. On the last night of the two-day struggle, he literally stood right in the front lines as the men of his 1st Raiders and the attached 1st Parachute Battalion held off the fierce charges of a numerically superior Japanese brigade. For his courageous leadership in this desperate victory, thereafter known as the Battle of Edson's Ridge, he received the Medal of Honor. As chief of staff of the 2nd Marine Division at Tarawa, and later as the assistant division commander during the conquests of Saipan and Tinian, he continued to display a fatalistic disregard for death in his frequent visits to units in contact with the enemy. Following the end of World War II, Edson went home to serve as the point man in the Corps's battle to survive the Army's plan to unify the military services. Despite President Harry S. Truman's attempts to quash opposition to unification inside the Navy and Marine Corps, Red Mike fought on in the halls of Congress, in interviews with the media, and in speeches to the American public. When the campaign seemed lost, he retired in protest and testified passionately before Senate and House committees. His reputation and his arguments played a key role in getting the missions of the Marine Corps written into the National Security Act of 1947.

In retirement, Edson took on the job of establishing the State Police in Vermont. Later he served as president and executive director of the National Rifle Association. The Marine Corps also called upon him one last time in 1952 to help rescue the troubled foundation charged with erecting the Marine Corps War Memorial. Despite his many successes, Red Mike was often depressed, and he took his own life in August 1955.

Above: *A bearded Capt Edson after his first Coco River patrol. (Library of Congress)*

Opposite: *Edson melded amphibian planes and native boats into an effective force operating deep in the Nicaraguan jungle. (Jon T. Hoffman)*

22 January
Nicaragua
The Eastern Area is established to cover the sparsely inhabited eastern two-thirds of Nicaragua. Its forces come in the following weeks from the Marine detachments of the Special Service Squadron.

28 January
Nicaragua
VO-6M and its six O2B-1s sail from Quantico to reinforce the brigade in Nicaragua.

19 February
Nicaragua
Captain Merritt A. Edson and the 56 Marines of his detachment land from cruiser *Denver* (CL-19) at Puerto Cabezas in eastern Nicaragua.

27–28 February
Nicaragua
Sandinista forces ambush a Marine mule train at Bromaderos. A patrol from the 11th Regiment assists in driving off the enemy. Marine losses are five killed and eight wounded. There are 10 counted enemy dead.

13–14 May
Nicaragua
A Marine and Guardia patrol has a running battle with Sandinistas along the Cua River. Two Marines are killed in driving off the much more numerous enemy.

30 June
Manpower
The strength of the Marine Corps on active duty is 1,198 officers and 17,822 enlisted.

Top: *A Marine slogs through a central American jungle. ("Marines Always Ready," Col John W. Thomason, Marine Corps Art Collection)*

Left: *A patrol prepares to move out in Nicaragua with heavily laden mules. (Marine Corps Historical Center)*

1 July
Force Structure
VF-10M in China is redesignated VF-6M.

26 July
Nicaragua
Edson, 46 Marines, and a corpsman depart Bocay by native boat for a combat patrol up the Coco River toward Sandino's jungle base at Poteca.

7 August
Nicaragua
Edson and his Coco River patrol defeat Sandino and his men at Iliiquas, killing 10 at a cost of one Marine dead and three wounded. Ten days later the patrol occupies Sandino's former lair at Poteca. The Coco Patrol retains control of this site until March 1929.

5 September
Force Structure
In a swap of designations, the utility squadron in Quantico becomes VO-6M, while the old VO-6M in Nicaragua becomes VJ-6M.

1 November
China
VF-6M arrives in San Diego from China. The squadron resumes duty as part of the aviation element of the West Coast Expeditionary Force.

4 November
Nicaragua
Marine forces, with Navy reinforcements, oversee a free and fair election in Nicaragua by preventing interference from Sandinista forces and supervising every single polling place.

Top: *Marines patrol the Coco River, Nicaragua, in 1928. (National Archives)*

Right: *Pilots in front of a trimotor transport (probably a Fokker TA-2) in Nicaragua on 10 November 1928. (Marine Corps Research Center)*

Left: *Observation Squadron 7M in mass formation in the early 1930s. (National Archives)*

Opposite: *Capt John W. Thomason and his 38th Company in Peking in 1930. (Marine Corps Research Center)*

1929

1 January
China
VO-10M returns to San Diego from China.

19 January
China
The 3rd Brigade is disbanded, and its units (primarily the brigade headquarters and 6th Regiment) are withdrawn from Tientsin, China, over the remainder of the month.

3 February
Nicaragua
Lieutenant Herman Hanneken and a small patrol of Marines capture Manuel Jiron, one of Sandino's most effective generals.

1 March
Force Structure
Headquarters Detachment 7M of Aircraft Squadrons, West Coast Expeditionary Force, is redesignated as Marine Utility Squadron 7. This is the birth of what will eventually become Marine Aerial Refueler Transport Squadron 252 (VMGR-252).

5 March
Commandants
Major General Lejeune retires, and Wendell C. Neville is elevated to become the Major General Commandant. He is the 14th Commandant of the Marine Corps.

3 April
Nicaragua
The last Marines from the Special Service Squadron return to their ships as part of a general drawdown of Marine forces in Nicaragua.

30 June
Manpower
The strength of the Marine Corps on active duty is 1,181 officers and 17,615 enlisted.

August
Nicaragua
The 11th Regiment departs Nicaragua and is disbanded as it sails for the United States.

5 December
Aviation
Captain Alton N. Parker, USMCR, becomes the first man to fly over the Antarctic continent, during the Byrd Expedition to the South Pole.

31 October
Reserve
Commandant Neville initiates a "New Reserve" policy, which merges the Fleet Marine Corps Reserve and Volunteer Reserves into battalions and regiments, with participants bearing all costs on their own and receiving no drill pay.

31 December
Force Structure
The only balloon squadron in the Marine Corps

(ZKO-1M) is disbanded at Quantico. This was the last use by Marines of lighter-than-air craft for manned flight.

1930

31 May
Aviation
Captain Arthur H. Page wins the Curtiss Marine Trophy Race at Anacostia Naval Air Station in the District of Columbia.

19 June
Nicaragua
Marine aircraft discover a large concentration of rebels near Jinotega, Nicaragua, and attack. Numerous casualties are inflicted, among them Sandino, who is wounded by shrapnel.

30 June
Manpower
The strength of the Marine Corps on active duty is 1,208 officers and 18,172 enlisted.

1 July
Force Structure
VF-6M in San Diego is redesignated VF-10M. VO-10M is absorbed into VO-8M.

8 July
Commandants
Commandant Neville dies following a severe stroke suffered in March 1930.

9 July
Commandants
Ben H. Fuller is promoted to Major General and named Commandant. He is the 15th Commandant of the Marine Corps.

10 July
Force Structure
Regiments are henceforth formally designated by the title "Marines" (as in "1st Marines").

21 July
Aviation
Captain Page establishes the world record for the longest instrument flight, from Omaha, Nebraska, to Anacostia Naval Air Station. (Page dies in September in a crash during an air race in Chicago.)

August
Force Structure
VF-5M, first activated in 1925 as VF-2M, is re-designated VF-9M at Quantico.

12 December
Nicaragua
Gunnery Sergeant William A. Lee and his Guardia patrol fight off an attack by a Sandinista force several times their number at Vencedora.

31 December
Nicaragua
A patrol of 10 Marines repairing the telephone

COLONEL WILLIAM A. LEE

Like many of the most successful Marine "Banana Warriors," Bill Lee had joined during World War I to fight the Germans, but did not make it to France in time to do so. He mustered out when that conflict was over, then enlisted again in 1921, just shy of his 21st birthday. Serving in typical peacetime billets, including a tour aboard the battleship *Arkansas*, he rose to the rank of gunnery sergeant. His first combat service came when he deployed with Marine forces to Nicaragua in 1928.

A Massachusetts native, Lee had spent a lot of his youth in western North Carolina, where he came in contact with Cherokee Indians. From them he absorbed the ways of the wilderness, learning to hunt and trap animals and survive in the woods. The tall, athletic Marine returned to Nicaragua in early 1930 to serve as a lieutenant in the constabulary. His skill in tracking men and animals—coupled with his energy, endurance, and determination—were perfectly suited to the task of ferreting the wily Sandinistas from their jungle lairs. The assignment of Lee to serve as second-in-command of Company M, and the arrival soon after of the ever-aggressive Chesty Puller as his commander, produced an unbeatable combination.

Lee proved his physical prowess and courage in his first battle alongside Puller. As the constabulary unit moved along a trail, an enemy force opened fire from an ambush position located on the crest of a long hill above the government troops. Puller headed up the slope and yelled for his men to follow. Lee and a private overtook him and reached the top first, dodging Sandinista bullets and dynamite bombs as they went. Their furious dash was so rapid the guerrillas could not break contact fast enough or carry away their

Opposite: *GySgt "Ironman" Lee (second from right, standing) in 1928 in Nicaragua, where he earned three Navy Crosses. (Marine Corps Historical Center)*

Right: *"Banana War Ambush," Col Charles H. Waterhouse, USMCR (Ret), Marine Corps Art Collection)*

casualties. Company M recovered seven rebel bodies. For his bravery and "extreme physical exertion" in this and several subsequent engagements that summer, Lee received his first Navy Cross.

Whenever Puller was absent, Lee took Company M to the field. He led the intrepid unit in one of its toughest battles of the war, at Vencedora in December 1930. The 20 Guardias and their lieutenant attacked a force of roughly 200 Sandinistas and were nearly overwhelmed, but in the end routed the enemy. By summer 1931, Lee had earned a second Navy Cross, as well as Puller's assessment: "There are few better field soldiers in any military organization." An unprecedented third Navy Cross came in the fall of 1932, when Lee was wounded in the head and knocked unconscious in the opening fusillade of an ambush. After 15 minutes, he came to his senses. Still groggy and weak, he struggled to a pack mule and retrieved the unit's lone Lewis machine gun. He employed it with immediate impact and, despite receiving a second wound in the arm, suppressed the enemy fire. That allowed the rest of Company M to charge and break the ambush. The small force of Guardias had several other casualties to carry back over dozens of miles of rough terrain, so Lee walked under his own power. Puller gave Lee a lifelong nickname when his after-action report lauded his subordinate's toughness: "In the days of wooden ships, he would have been an iron man."

Lee became a standout on the legendary Marine Corps marksmanship teams of the mid-1930s. He was promoted to warrant officer in 1935 and was in charge of the ranges for the Legation Guard in China on 7 December 1941. Forced to surrender his small outfit to overwhelming odds, his legendary toughness enabled him to survive 44 months of hardship as a Japanese prisoner. After World War II and now a lieutenant colonel, he commanded the rifle range at Quantico. "Iron Man" Lee retired in 1950 as a colonel and died in 1998.

line outside Ocotal is ambushed by Sandinistas, and eight Americans are killed. The incident fuels a decision by President Herbert Hoover to withdraw all Marines from Nicaragua by the end of 1932.

1931

21 February
Nicaragua
The ground force of the 2nd Brigade in Nicaragua is reduced to a single battalion of the 5th Marines.

24 February
Force Structure
The Marine squadron on Guam is withdrawn after 10 years of service there.

31 March
Nicaragua
A major earthquake devastates Managua and starts fires that rage throughout the city. Roughly 15 percent of the population is killed or injured. Marine and Guardia forces provide emergency assistance throughout the stricken city.

1 April
Force Structure
VO-6M absorbs VF-8M.

12 May
Nicaragua
All Marine forces, with the exception of officers and enlisted men serving in the Guardia Nacional, are withdrawn into Managua.

30 June
Manpower
The strength of the Marine Corps on active duty is 1,196 officers and 17,586 enlisted.

26 October
Mishap
Colonel Thomas C. Turner, the director of Marine aviation, is severely injured by a turning propeller in Haiti and dies two days later.

2 November
Aviation
Squadron VS-14M reports on board *Saratoga* (CV-3), and VS-15M joins *Lexington* (CV-2), the

Top: *LtCol Roy Geiger, commander of Aircraft One, in Quantico in 1936. (National Archives)*

Left: *Marines go ashore in Shanghai from a Navy launch in 1930. (National Archives)*

Right: *A Vought O2U-2 Corsair of VS-14M flies past* Saratoga *in the early 1930s. (Naval Historical Center)*

Below: *A survivor of the 31 December 1930 ambush near Ocotal is airlifted to Managua on a Fokker transport. (National Archives)*

first Marine aviation units to deploy with Navy aircraft carriers. They remain with these ships for three years.

December
Training
A Marine battalion reinforced by an artillery battery and embarked on the old battleships *Arkansas* (BB-33) and *Wyoming* (BB-32) participates in fleet maneuvers in the Caribbean.

1932

28 January
China
Japanese troops garrisoning their portion of the International Settlement launch a major attack on Chinese forces in the remainder of Shanghai. The 4th Marines establishes defensive positions on the perimeter of the U.S. enclave of the settlement.

February
Training
A regimental headquarters and an infantry battalion participate in the Joint Army-Navy Exercise on Oahu in Hawaii.

3 February
China
Cruiser *Houston* (CL-30) lands her Marine detachment to reinforce the 4th Marines in Shanghai. Another 334 officers and men from other Pacific commands also arrive around this time.

5 February
China
The Army's 31st Infantry Regiment arrives from the Philippines to join the 4th Marines in Shanghai.

13 June
China
The state of emergency in Shanghai finally is declared over. Chinese forces had conducted an orderly withdrawal from the city in March, ending the battle with the Japanese, who then returned to their former lines inside the International Settlement.

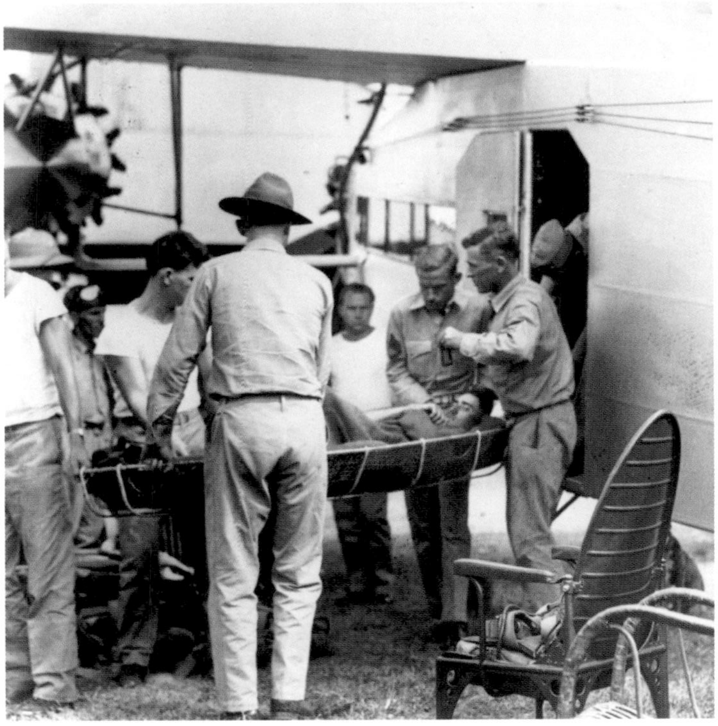

Left: *Marines man a hasty bunker in Shanghai in March 1932, with a Browning water-cooled .30-caliber machine gun peering out from the firing port. (National Archives)*

27 June
Technology
The Marine Corps conducts its first flight of an autogiro (an aircraft using a propeller for forward motion and a horizontal rotor rather than a wing for lift). The Pitcairn OP-1 is flown in Nicaragua.

30 June
Manpower
The strength of the Marine Corps on active duty is 1,196 officers and 15,365 enlisted. Depression-era budget cuts are driving down the size of the Corps.

26 September
Nicaragua
Captain Lewis B. Puller, Bill Lee, and Guardia Company M defeat a Sandinista ambush near La Pavona, killing 10 rebels at a cost of two dead.

6 November
Nicaragua
Marine and Guardia forces oversee the free and fair election of a new Nicaraguan president.

15 December
Nicaragua
All Marine leaders are withdrawn from the Guardia Nacional and concentrated in Managua in preparation for the return of all Marines in Nicaragua to the United States.

26 December
Nicaragua
Puller and six other Marines volunteer to lead a patrol of 64 Guardias to secure the new rail line between Leon and El Sauce. Their train is ambushed. At a cost of three Guardias killed and three wounded, the government force inflicts the largest confirmed loss (31 dead) on the Sandinistas since the battle of Ocotal in 1927.

December
Manpower
President Hoover calls for a reduction in Marine strength to 13,600 men.

1933

2 January
Nicaragua
The last Marines of the 2nd Brigade depart Corinto, Nicaragua. Marine deaths as a result of enemy action during the course of the six-year intervention totaled 47. VO-7M returns to Quantico.

12 January
Doctrine
The Joint Army and Navy Board issues a small doctrinal pamphlet titled *Joint Overseas Expeditions*, which sets forth a few broad principles on amphibious operations.

30 June
Manpower
The strength of the Marine Corps on active duty is 1,192 officers and 14,786 enlisted.

1 July
Force Structure
VF-10M in San Diego is redesignated as Marine Bombing Squadron 4 (VB-4M). VO-8M is disbanded.

8 December
Force Structure
Commandant Fuller (implementing a Navy authorization signed the previous day) orders the establishment of the Fleet Marine Force (FMF). This essentially is a renaming of the Expeditionary Forces.

1934

January
China
Marines from gunboat *Tulsa* (PG-22) land at Foochow to protect the consulate during a period of fighting between Chinese factions. They remain ashore until Nationalist forces retake control of the city.

8 January
Force Structure
Aircraft Squadrons, West Coast Expeditionary Force is redesignated as Aircraft Two, FMF.

17 January
Force Structure
The headquarters of the FMF is organized at Quantico. At the same time, the designation of the 1st Battalion, 7th Marines (1/7) is changed to 1st Battalion, FMF, in Quantico. The 2nd Battalion, 7th Marines (2/7), is redesignated 2nd Battalion, FMF, while it is on board *Wyoming* in Havana Harbor, Cuba.

18 January
Force Structure
Aircraft Squadrons, East Coast Expeditionary Force is redesignated Aircraft One, FMF.

28 February
Commandants
Major General Commandant Fuller retires at the mandatory age of 64 and is replaced by newly promoted Major General John Russell. He is the 16th Commandant of the Marine Corps.

Right: *A patrol checks out a street in the Legation Quarter of Peking in December 1929. (Marine Corps Research Center)*

LIEUTENANT GENERAL LEWIS B. PULLER

Long before Lewis Puller's distinguished career was complete, he would be the preeminent icon of the Corps and the archetypical Marine—hard as the frontal armor of a tank, tenacious as a bulldog, courageous to a fault, and scornful of anyone or anything that did not wear the eagle, globe, and anchor insignia. But when he arrived in Nicaragua in 1928, even though he already had 10 years in the Marines, he was still a relatively obscure junior officer. Other than a few minor skirmishes in Haiti,

his service consisted of a failed attempt at flight school and the usual peacetime tours of garrison duty. He was not a gifted athlete and, at 5 feet, 8 inches and 144 pounds, was not physically imposing. His barrel chest, square-blocked face, and out-thrust jaw were his most impressive visible features. His voice was his distinctive trademark; he spoke slowly with a touch of Southern accent, underpinning his own unique and butchered pronunciations with a deep-throated, gravelly intonation. When the situation warranted, he could "shout commands with all the vigor and carrying power of an angry bull."

At first his tour in Nicaragua promised more of the same anonymity. He spent 18 months as a personnel officer and quartermaster before being posted to command of Company M, a special outfit freed from garrison duties so it could pursue the rebels wherever they went. Puller's aggressiveness and fearlessness were perfectly suited to the task of making long patrols into enemy territory without any units on his flanks or any fire support. He and his native soldiers doggedly swept the hinterland for signs of the Sandinistas and quickly began to rack up an impressive string of victories against superior numbers.

After a yearlong hiatus in the U.S. for schooling at Fort Benning, Puller returned to Nicaragua and Company M in 1931. He wasted no time in picking up where he left off. In a single operation he and his men fought six battles with the rebels and bested them each time. The patrolling and fighting continued right up until the withdrawal of the Marines from the Central American nation. Puller's most spectacular victory, at El Sauce, took place on 26 December 1932, five days before he and his compatriots boarded a ship for the States. In his two tours in Nicaragua, the Marine lieutenant had received two Navy Crosses for valorous leadership under fire and earned two nicknames. To Nicaraguans, he was "El Tigre"—the Tiger. To fellow leathernecks, he was now "Chesty."

During the 1930s Puller served tours in China in the cruiser *Augusta* (CA-31), with the legation guard in Peking (for a time commanding the famed Horse Marines), and with the 4th Marines in Shanghai. Sent to Guadalcanal in September 1942 with the 7th Marines, he led 1/7 through a series of vicious battles that helped secure the island and netted him a third Navy Cross. He landed at Cape Gloucester as regimental executive officer and earned a fourth Navy Cross for leading two battalions after their commanders became casualties. Promoted to colonel, he took the 1st Marines into the meatgrinder of Peleliu. When the North Koreans invaded South Korea in 1950, Chesty reformed the 1st Marines and fought with it at Inchon, Seoul, and the Chosin Reservoir, resulting in a fifth Navy Cross. As a brigadier, he served as ADC of the 1st Marine Division and led it briefly as the acting division commander during the Central Front campaign. He was forced to retire for medical reasons in 1955. In 1968, his only son—Lewis B. Puller, Jr.—was grievously wounded in Vietnam, but survived to make his own courageous fight against crippling injuries and alcoholism. Chesty Puller passed away in 1971. His son died in 1995.

Although Puller was well-known for his bravery and medals, it was his reputation as a leader that made him a legend. He was always out in front with his men in the thick of the fight, whether it was with the enemy or the bureaucracy. He made their welfare his greatest interest. And he always inspired them to follow his example and give everything they had.

Opposite: *"Chesty" Puller at Camp Lejeune in July 1945. (National Archives)*

1 March
Soviet Union
A Marine detachment of one officer and six enlisted men assumes responsibility for guarding the U.S. embassy in Moscow, Soviet Union.

May
Manpower
Commandant Russell succeeds in convincing Congress to pass legislation allowing officer promotions by selection, rather than seniority.

24 May
Force Structure
The 2nd Battalion, FMF, returns to Quantico after spending months in the Caribbean on board various ships of the fleet.

14 June
Reserve
The Marine Corps authorizes a resumption of drill pay for reserve training. During this period, the Corps also does away with the regimental echelon and relies on separate battalions as its largest reserve units.

30 June
Manpower
The strength of the Marine Corps on active duty is 1,187 officers and 15,174 enlisted.

15 August
Force Structure
Personnel just returned from Haiti are organized into 1/6, for eventual transfer to San Diego to establish a West Coast ground element of the FMF.

21 August
Haiti
The last elements of the 1st Marine Brigade withdraw from Haiti, ending the 20-year U.S. intervention in that country.
Force Structure
The 1st Marine Brigade and most of its supporting elements (including the 2nd Regiment) are deactivated. VO-9M (formerly Squadron E) transfers to the Virgin Islands.

1 September
Force Structure
In a reorganization of the FMF, the headquarters of the 6th Marines is reactivated to serve as an element of the West Coast FMF. The San Diego-based force will also include 1/6, an artillery battery, and Aircraft Two. The 1st and 2nd Battalions, FMF, at Quantico are redesignated 1/5 and 2/5, and the regimental headquarters of the 5th Marines is reestablished to serve as the ground element on the East Coast. The overall headquarters of the FMF, Aircraft One and an

Left: *Pilots show off the cup they won at the Miami air races flying the Curtiss F7C-1 Sea Hawk. (National Archives)*

Right: *The Horse Marines patrolling the countryside in northern China. (Marine Corps Research Center)*

artillery battalion (1/10) are also at Quantico. As part of the redesignations, the previous system of identifying companies by numbers is ended, and letters are substituted.

15 November
Force Structure
VO-8M is reactivated by combining the personnel and planes remaining at the deactivation of VS-14M and VS-15M.

1935

19 January
Training
FMF Marines (air and ground) participate in Fleet Landing Exercise 1 at Culebra and Vieques Islands in the Caribbean. This is the first of several annual FLEXs designed to train forces in the new amphibious doctrine. FLEX 1 continues through 13 March.

1 February
Force Structure
The 2nd Battalion, 10th Marines is organized at San Diego as an artillery outfit.

15 April
Manpower
Legislation creates the rank of aviation cadet in the Marine Corps Reserve and provides a means to commission these prospective pilots in the Reserve once they have successfully completed flight training.

29 April
Training
West Coast FMF units participate in Fleet Problem XVI, which includes a landing operation against Midway Island and the establishment of an advance base. The exercise continues through 12 June.

25 May
Doctrine
The Chief of Naval Operations approves Navy use of the draft manual for landing operations created by the Marine Corps Schools in 1934.

5 June
HQMC
The Aviation Section is removed from the Division of Operations and Training and made an independent office within Headquarters Marine Corps reporting directly to the Commandant.

30 June
Manpower
The strength of the Marine Corps on active duty is 1,163 officers and 16,097 enlisted.

THE "TENTATIVE MANUAL FOR LANDING OPERATIONS"

In a 1916 article in the *Marine Corps Gazette* titled "A Plea for a Mission and Doctrine," Major John H. Russell argued that "a military organization to be efficient and powerful must be so indoctrinated as to acquire a uniformity of mind and action on fundamental truths." For the next 15 years Marines struggled to determine which of their possible missions should receive primary focus. By the early 1930s, there was growing agreement that the tasks of seizing and defending advance naval bases would probably be the most important in the looming strategic competition with Japan. Instructors at the Marine Corps Schools in Quantico undertook the work in 1930 of developing doctrine for these two missions. Over the next two years deadlines for completing it passed while officers tried to keep up with their primary job of teaching students (using Army textbooks and curricula to impart Army doctrine). In 1933, now Brigadier General Russell, assistant to the Major General Commandant, wrote again in the *Gazette* and complained that Marines had done little more about doctrine for the amphibious mission than "write canned articles, make an occasional address, refer mechanically to them in a dry report."

Things finally began to change in September 1933 when Brigadier General James C. Breckinridge, the head of the schools, recommended that classes be cancelled for the academic year just underway and that instructors and students turn full time to developing doctrine for landing operations and small wars (the term applied to counterguerrilla actions such as the ongoing war the Marines were fighting in Nicaragua). He received a positive reply from Headquarters Marine Corps, where Russell had the influence to determine policy. The two senior officers maintained frequent contact over the next few months. On 1 March 1934, Russell became the 16th Commandant of the Marine Corps, with full power to implement his longheld views about doctrine and the importance of the amphibious mission.

The students and faculty of the schools, with assistance from officers at Headquarters in Washington and with the operating forces stationed at Quantico, forged ahead. By the spring of 1934, the schools had completed their work on amphibious doctrine and compiled a book of several hundred pages, titled "Tentative Manual for Landing Operations." It was the first formal doctrinal publication created by the Marine Corps. It actually went far beyond its title. Fully one-third of it covered methods for defending advance bases (whether seized or simply occupied), while other sections dealt with general topics such as staff principles and logistics. The new head of the schools proclaimed in May 1934: "For the first time since the founding of the Marine Corps Schools the entire course of instruction is based on *our* missions and *our* jobs."

Russell was pleased, but not content. At the end of July 1934, he approved a series of changes in the manual, one of them taking into account the broad contents of the book. He retitled it the "Manual for Naval Overseas Operations." He also approved the establishment of a board to undertake

revisions to the doctrine based on input from those using it to teach and to train. He had taken another far-reaching step in late 1933, convincing Commandant Fuller to rename the Marine Corps Expeditionary Forces (which had largely existed as skeletons for several years) as the Fleet Marine Forces (FMF). This change in title had real meaning, as well, tying the operating forces of the Marine Corps to those of the Navy.

The change in emphasis of the schools and organization of the Marine Corps presaged—and provided the basis for—the amphibious assaults that would become the hallmark of the Marine Corps during and after World War II. The Marines of the 1930s had done more than simply prepare to fight, they had readied themselves for the right war at the right time. As a result, the institution would grow in prestige and size far beyond what anyone could have envisioned prior to 1941.

Above: *Marines wade through the surf at Culebra during rudimentary amphibious exercises in 1923–24. (National Archives)*

Left: *Men of Company H, 4th Marines, practice on the rifle range in China in 1937. (National Archives)*

Below: *"Horse Marine, 1937," Col Charles H. Waterhouse, USMCR (Ret), Marine Corps Art Collection*

1 July
Force Structure
Marine Bombing Squadron 6 (VB-6M) is established at Quantico.

8 July
Manpower
The first Platoon Leaders Class training camp begins. This program allows college students who participate in two six-week summer training camps to obtain commissions as lieutenants in the Reserve upon graduation.

9 July
Doctrine
The Marine Corps Schools formally publishes the "Tentative Manual for Landing Operations," the first detailed written doctrine for amphibious operations against defended coastlines.

9 August
Force Structure
The overall headquarters of the FMF is transferred from Quantico to San Diego to be near the largest concentration of the U.S. fleet.

1 September
Force Structure
The 1st Marine Brigade is reactivated to serve at Quantico as the headquarters of the East Coast element of the FMF. FMF headquarters in San Diego still commands West Coast elements.

1936

4 January
Training
Marines participate in FLEX 2 in the Caribbean, which continues through 24 February.

1 April
HQMC
The Aviation Section is elevated to division status within Headquarters Marine Corps.

30 June
Manpower
The strength of the Marine Corps on active duty is 1,208 officers and 16,040 enlisted.

1 July
Force Structure
The 2nd Marine Brigade is activated at San Diego to serve as the headquarters of the West Coast element of the FMF. FMF headquarters in San Diego now is in charge of a brigade on each coast.

14–16 November
Training
The 2nd Marine Brigade conducts training with the fleet at San Clemente Island.

1 December
Commandants
Major General Russell retires upon reaching the statutory age limit, and Brigadier General Thomas Holcomb is promoted to become the Major

Top: *"Horse Marine," Charles Wilbourn, Marine Corps Art Collection*

Right: *Men of the 4th Marines practice their combat drill in the streets of Shanghai in 1937. (National Archives)*

General Commandant. He is the 17th Commandant of the Marine Corps.

1937

1 January
Force Structure
Marine Fighting Squadron 4 (VF-4M) is organized at San Diego to form a part of Aircraft Two.

27 January
Training
Marines and the Army's 1st Expeditionary Brigade participate in FLEX 3 at San Clemente Island off the southern coast of California. The exercise continues through 10 March. It marks the first time that the FMF units from both coasts operate together, to include Aircraft One (the aviation component of the east coast FMF) following its cross-country flight from Quantico.

6–8 May
Civil Support
Marines join civil forces in performing rescue and security duties following the fiery crash of the German airship *Hindenburg* at Lakehurst, New Jersey.

30 June
Manpower
The strength of the Marine Corps on active duty is 1,312 officers and 16,911 enlisted.

1 July
Force Structure
Marine squadrons undergo wholesale redesignation in accordance with new Navy nomenclature. At Aircraft One in Quantico, VF-9M becomes Marine Fighting Squadron 1 (VMF-1), VO-7M becomes Marine Scouting Squadron 1 (VMS-1), VB-6M becomes Marine Bombing Squadron 1 (VMB-1), and Marine Utility Squadron 6 (VJ-6M) becomes Marine Utility Squadron 1 (VMJ-1). At Aircraft Two in San Diego, VF-4M becomes VMF-2, VO-8M becomes VMS-2, VB-4M becomes VMB-2, and VJ-7M becomes VMJ-2. VO-9M in the Virgin Islands is redesignated VMS-3. The ten Marine Reserve squadrons are redesignated as VMS-1R through VMS-10R.

4 August
Marine Corps League
The Marine Corps League, in existence since 1923, receives its formal charter from Congress.

8 August
China
The Japanese seize Peiping from Chinese forces, leaving the Marine Legation Guard surrounded in unfriendly territory.

12 August
China
In an expansion of the undeclared war between Japan and China, Japanese forces launch an offensive to seize control of the Chinese portion of Shanghai. The 4th Marines establishes defensive positions around the U.S. sector of the International Settlement. Cruiser *Augusta* (CA-31) places her Marines and some sailors ashore to augment the regiment.

19 August
China
A company of 104 Marine officers and enlisted men arrives in Shanghai from the Philippines.

Opposite: *PFC D. D. Pomerleau rides Vesper Belle in Peiping in 1937. (National Archives)*

Right: *Marines at the ready at a sandbagged emplacement in Shanghai. The man in the foreground has a BAR; the others aim bayonet-tipped Springfields. (National Archives)*

26 August
China
A second company of Marines reaches Shanghai to reinforce the 4th Marines.

19 September
China
The 2nd Marine Brigade headquarters and the 6th Marines arrive in Shanghai to reinforce the 4th Marines during the fighting between Japanese and Chinese forces.

1 December
Force Structure
The 3rd Marines, a reserve regimental headquarters since December 1925, is disbanded.

12 December
China
Japanese naval aircraft sink the U.S. gunboat *Panay* (PR-5) on the Yangtze River above Nanking. The Japanese government issues a formal apology two days later.

1938

13 January
Training
Marines participate in FLEX 4 at Culebra, Puerto Rico. The exercise continues through 15 March.

18 February
China
The 2nd Brigade headquarters and 6th Marines depart Shanghai after the Chinese are forced from the city by the Japanese, and the threat to the International Settlement is reduced.

28 February
China
Following the withdrawal of the Army's 15th Infantry Regiment from Tientsin, a detachment of about 200 Marines is sent from the Legation Guard at Peiping to establish a post at the former Army barracks.

15 March
Training
Marine units participate in Fleet Problem XIX in Hawaii, practicing the occupation of an advance base.

23 June
Manpower
President Roosevelt signs legislation providing that the active duty strength of the Marine Corps should be 20 percent of the active-duty enlisted strength of the Navy. That act adds 97 billets to the 27,400 already authorized for the Marine Corps. Congress does not provide sufficient funding for that number, however.

25 June
Reserve
The Naval Reserve Act reorganizes the Marine Reserve into three groups: Fleet Marine Corps Reserve (now consisting of active-duty retirees still subject to recall), the Organized Marine Corps Reserve (units), and the Volunteer Marine Corps Reserve (individuals).

30 June
Manpower
The strength of the Marine Corps on active duty is 1,359 officers and 16,997 enlisted.

HOLDING THE LINE

1939 – MAY 1943

HOLDING THE LINE

1939–MAY 1943

When World War II erupted on 1 September 1939, the United States officially stayed neutral, but began preparing slowly for the worst. The isolationist mood of the American public hampered the buildup, but the Corps came up with an idea to create defense battalions, using a name that implied no overseas entanglements. Marine leaders thus succeeded in obtaining some additional force structure. The mission of the defense battalion, of course, was to protect advance expeditionary bases, most likely occupied or seized as part of an offensive campaign.

As the war engulfed more of the globe, the amphibious assault mission grew increasingly dominant in Marine thinking. Simultaneously, the Corps grew more and more frustrated by shortcomings in transports and landing craft. This spurred further Leatherneck creativity. In addition to the acquisition of lighter equipment (such as 75mm pack howitzers initially intended for transport on mules), the Corps began to focus on light units specifically designed for easy and rapid deployment across the beach. One idea—parachutists and gliders—came from the spectacularly successful German use of these capabilities in May 1940. Another organizational adaptation soon turned into the raider battalions. Meanwhile, amphibious exercises steadily grew larger and more challenging. The Marines eventually found the landing craft they needed by adapting products on the civilian market, though Andrew Higgins's landing boat and Donald Roebling's tracked landing vehicle would not become available in significant numbers until after the United States was in the war. The Corps did take one step backward, breaking up its air-ground teams around the time the brigades expanded into divisions and wings. They would remain largely separate throughout the war.

The Japanese raid on Pearl Harbor brought the United States into the global conflict with a thirst for vengeance. Marine heroics could not overcome surprise, and aviation units in Hawaii suffered like everyone else. Small Marine outfits in China and Guam had to surrender against overwhelming odds. The 4th Marines won a brief respite with a late November 1941 transfer from Shanghai to the Philippines, but the regiment eventually went down swinging at Bataan and Corregidor. One of the few bright spots in the early weeks of the war was the gallant defense of Wake Island. The Marine garrison turned back one Japanese amphibious assault, though it eventually succumbed to another. At Midway in June 1942, the Marines lent a hand in the Navy's defeat of the Japanese fleet.

The dispatch of a brigade to defend Iceland and two to hold Samoa depleted the Corps at a time when it needed to train cohesive divisions for future offensives. When the 1st Marine Division received orders to land on Guadalcanal, it was ill-prepared to do so. Many of the young enlisted men and officers had barely a few months in the

Pages 244–245: *"U.S. Marines Patrolling, Guadalcanal," John Hamilton, Naval Art Collection*

Right: *Marines come ashore on Guadalcanal. (National Archives)*

service. A shortage of transports caused the division to leave behind much of its heavy equipment. But General Alexander A. Vandegrift accepted his orders and led his men ashore on 7 August 1942. They took the incomplete airstrip and a small perimeter around it, as well as several nearby small islands. It was not a very stern test of Marine amphibious capability, but the land-sea-air campaign to hold these gains would become an epic of courage, determination, and resourcefulness. The challenges began almost immediately, when the quick departure of the fleet following a Japanese naval counterattack left the division with very few supplies.

The aviation units that began arriving on the island soon after did not belong to the 1st Marine Division, but their commander, Brigadier General Roy S. Geiger, wisely placed his organization at Vandegrift's disposal. Geiger's polyglot Cactus Air Force, composed of fliers from all U.S. services and a couple of other countries, flew few close air support missions, but the aviators performed mightily in blunting Japanese air and naval attacks. The 1st Marine Division, later reinforced by the 2nd Marine Division and Army units, beat back a number of fierce Japanese counteroffensives during the first few months of the campaign. In a few cases, such as the Battle of Edson's Ridge in mid-September and the Battle for Henderson Field in late October, the outcome could have gone either way. Despite limited air, naval, and logistics support during the opening weeks, the Marines were determined not to lose, even when disease and malnutrition sapped their physical and mental endurance.

While the forward elements turned the tide of the war, the rest of the Marine Corps geared up for the long march that would take the United States from the outer ring of Japanese defenses right through to the home islands. From less than 20,000 men in 1939, the Corps grew to 300,000 in mid-1943. The expansion not only placed a severe strain on the training establishment, it also dramatically changed personnel policies. For the first time since the last three months of World War I (and only the second time in its history), the Corps was forced by presidential directive to accept draftees. The Marines (again with some reluctance) began taking in women. In a major modification from policy in World War I, these prospective female Leathernecks went through recruit and officer candidate training to earn the title Marine. They went on to serve in a much wider array of billets, as well. President Roosevelt also decreed that the Marine Corps would enlist African Americans, something it had not done since the Revolutionary War. The Corps responded to this new range of diversity in time-honored fashion. Everyone, no matter how they joined and who they were, completed Marine training with the spirit of the Corps deeply imbued and went on to share the burdens of winning the largest conflict in the experience of mankind.

HOLDING THE LINE

1939–MAY 1943

1939

January
Aviation
The General Board of the Navy approves a formal mission statement for Marine aviation: "To be equipped, organized, and trained primarily for the support of the Fleet Marine Force in landing operations and in support of troop activities in the field; secondarily as replacements for carrier-based naval aircraft."

3 January
Bases
The Hepburn Board (a Navy fact-finding group led by Adm Arthur Hepburn) reports to Congress

about base expansion in the Pacific. It calls for construction of bases and defenses at Midway, Wake, Johnston, and Palmyra Atolls. This work will eventually be facilitated by the 1st, 3rd, and 6th Defense Battalions.

13 January
Training
Marine units participate in FLEX 5 in the Caribbean. The exercise continues until 19 March.

15 March
Technology
Following tests of Andrew Higgins's Eureka boat during FLEX 5, Marines enthusiastically endorse it as the best landing craft available. The Higgins boat is finally adopted by the Navy in 1940. Later improved with a bow ramp, it becomes the standard U.S. landing craft of World War II. Higgins soon develops larger models to carry tanks.

21 April
HQMC
The Division of Operations and Training of Headquarters Marine Corps is renamed the Division of Plans and Policies.

1 May
Force Structure
Aircraft One (Quantico) and Aircraft Two (San Diego) are renamed respectively 1st and 2nd Marine Aircraft Groups.

30 June
Manpower
The strength of the Marine Corps on active duty is 1,380 officers and 18,052 enlisted.

1 September
World War II
World War II begins when Germany invades Poland. France and Great Britain declare war on Germany two days later.

Opposite: *A 1942 recruiting poster. ("Want Action?" James Montgomery Flagg, Marine Corps Art Collection)*

Right: *Machine-gun squads of the 4th Marines move through Shanghai. (National Archives)*

5 September
World War II
The U.S. proclaims its neutrality in the war in Europe.

8 September
World War II
President Franklin D. Roosevelt proclaims a limited national emergency.
Manpower
Roosevelt orders an increase in the strength of the Marine Corps to 25,000 enlisted men. He also authorizes the recall of retired officers and enlisted.

17 September
World War II
The Soviet Union invades Poland. Organized resistance in Poland ends on 27 September, and the country is divided by the Soviets and the Germans.

3 October
World War II
The Declaration of Panama establishes the Western Hemisphere below Canada as a neutral zone.

10 October
Force Structure
The 3rd Defense Battalion is established at Parris Island. The mission of this new type of unit is to provide fixed defenses for expeditionary bases against air and surface attacks. The primary armament is antiair artillery and machine guns, and coast defense guns, though some later units also include infantry and tank elements.

1 November
Force Structure
The 1st Defense Battalion is organized at San Diego.

4 November
World War II
The Neutrality Act of 1939 repeals a 1937 total arms embargo and allows other nations to purchase U.S. armaments, as long as they transport them. That effectively permits only Great Britain and France to take advantage, since Germany's coast is effectively blockaded by Allied naval power.

20 December
Midway
CNO Adm Harold Stark directs the establishment of a Marine detachment on Midway Atoll.

1940

11 January
Training
The 1st Marine Brigade and the 1st Marine Aircraft Group participate in FLEX 6 in the Caribbean.

1 February
Force Structure
The 4th Defense Battalion is organized at Parris Island.

1 March
Force Structure
The 2nd Defense Battalion is organized at San Diego.

Left: *Marines during maneuvers at Guantanamo Bay, Cuba, in August 1941. (National Archives)*

Opposite: *A sentry stands a lonely watch on a hill above a Marine camp in Iceland in October 1941. (National Archives)*

1 April
Force Structure
The 8th Marines is reactivated at San Diego and assigned to the 2nd Marine Brigade.

9 April
World War II
Germany occupies Denmark and invades Norway. With some Allied help, Norway holds out until 10 June before finally surrendering.

9 May
Iceland
British troops occupy Iceland due to its key location along sea lanes in the Atlantic.

10 May
World War II
Germany invades France, Belgium, the Netherlands, and Luxembourg. A key element of the offensive is a glider-borne attack that seizes the important Belgian fortress of Eben Emael. Other airborne assaults aid in the rapid conquest of these countries. Winston Churchill becomes Prime Minister of Great Britain upon the resignation of Neville Chamberlain.

14 May
Doctrine
Impressed by German success with airborne operations, Commandant Holcomb orders his staff to "prepare plans for the employment of parachute troops."

28 May
World War II
The British begin the amphibious evacuation from Dunkirk.

June
Force Structure
Congress authorizes the Navy Department to begin a program to build 10,000 new planes, of which 1,167 will go to the Corps. The Marine planes will form four aircraft groups of 11 squadrons each.

10 June
World War II
Italy declares war on Great Britain and France.

22 June
World War II
France concludes an armistice with Germany, bringing its participation in the war to an end.

30 June
Manpower
The strength of the Marine Corps on active duty is 1,732 officers and 26,545 enlisted.

3 July
World War II
British naval forces attack French naval forces at various locations to prevent the French fleet from falling into the hands of Germany and Italy.

8 July
Martinique
The Joint War Planning Committee earmarks the 1st Marine Brigade for a projected mid-July occupation of Martinique, the most important of the French colonies in the Caribbean. The operation never is executed.

20 July
Force Structure
The Two Ocean Navy Act authorizes a vast expansion in the size of the fleet and naval aviation. Under this plan, Marine aviation will increase to 1,500 aircraft.

10 August
China
Great Britain announces the withdrawal of all its forces from Shanghai and North China, leaving the U.S. Marines as the only non-Axis western force in those areas.

2 September
Carribean
The U.S. agrees to give Britain 50 World War I-era destroyers in exchange for leases on British bases in the Caribbean, including the Bahamas, Jamaica, Antigua, Saint Lucia, Trinidad, and British Guiana. Marine detachments later occupy these bases.

10 September
Force Structure
Marine Observation Squadron 1 (VMO-1) is activated in Quantico.

12 September
North Africa
Italian forces from Libya attack British forces and invade Egypt. This opens the North African campaign.

MARINE CORPS RIFLE BOARD 1940

John C. Garand designed his first semi-automatic rifle in 1920. Near the end of the decade, following a competition with other weapons of this type, the Army selected the gas-operated Garand model for further development. In 1936, the Department of War adopted it as the basic service rifle and designated it the M1. That bold step placed the Army far ahead of its rivals around the globe. Even by the end of World War II, only the Germans had fielded a workable semi-automatic rifle, but it remained merely a supplement to the standard bolt-action model they had been using since World War I.

The Marines might have been expected to follow the Army's lead, but they did not, at least not immediately. Although Headquarters outfitted an entire battalion (1/6) with M1s in the summer of 1939, this was a test and not a decision to replace the M1903. The Corps hesitated in part due to its tremendous confidence in the accuracy and reliability of the Springfield. The M1 also underwent a number of growing pains when first fielded in the Army. Another factor was the appearance in 1936 of a competing semi-automatic. Melvin Johnson, a Marine reservist, had fashioned a recoil-operated weapon fed by a rotary magazine that was potentially more reliable, more accurate, and simpler than the Garand. The Bostonian inventor also had political backing in Congress. In late May 1940, as France fell to the Germans, the Senate Military Affairs Committee held hearings on the Johnson rifle. The Army, already heavily invested in the Garand, testified strongly against its competitor. Lieutenant Colonel Merritt Edson, the director of target practice, spoke for the Corps. He indicated that the Corps normally desired compatibility with Army weapons, with the caveat that they had to be rugged enough for landing operations. He said Marines regarded the Johnson as perhaps better suited in those conditions, but they had not yet made field comparisons of the various semi-automatic models: "And, after all, that is the final test of any piece."

Spurred on by Congressional interest in appropriating large sums of money for new weapons (and the fact that no more M1903s would be produced), the Corps established a formal competition in November 1940. The board members were all officers and mainly highly regarded team shooters, to include Edson. They were assisted by 40 enlisted men with a purposely wide range of

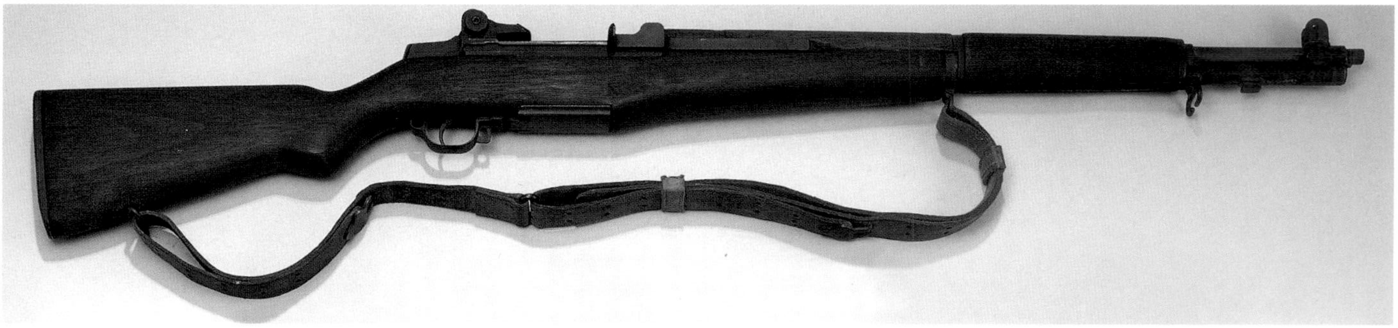

Opposite: *The M1 Garand rifle proved superior during the 1940 Marine Corps rifle tests. (Eric Long)*

Right: *Marines took to the M1, and it soon became the beloved weapon of Marine infantrymen. (Marine Corps Historical Center)*

experience. The candidate weapons were the Garand, the Johnson, and a gas-operated, magazine-fed Winchester model. The Springfield joined them as a benchmark comparison. Two of each model went through the program. Due to the amount of procurement dollars involved and the critical role of the rifle in the Corps, Commandant Holcomb proclaimed: "The work of this board is the most vital thing going on in the Marine Corps at this time."

The 37 separate tests were multifaceted and rigorous. Some were simple, such as standard range firing. The abuse tests were demanding—dragging the weapons through surf and over a beach, immersing them in a mud bath, placing them under sprinklers for 14 hours to simulate rain, and soaking them in seawater for 10 hours. After each such ordeal, the rifles were fired from a bench rest. Altogether, each weapon fired 12,000 rounds over four weeks.

The Johnson proved to be the least accurate of the competitors, though the differences between them were insignificant. The Garand was the most reliable; it suffered one-half the malfunctions and had one-third the number of broken parts as the Johnson. The board concluded that the Garand was the best choice for the Corps. The wild card in this process was the state of the two Johnson test models. They were the only such rifles in existence, and each had fired as many as 15,000 rounds in previous sales demonstrations. They obviously came to the competition already well-worn, but the board could only lament: "It is impossible to determine what effect, if any, this previous firing had in relation to the malfunctions which occurred."

The Marine Corps formally adopted the Garand soon after. The Army, eager to seal the deal before any other challenges could arise, immediately allocated a substantial portion of its own production to the Corps. When Johnson won a contract for his rifle from the Dutch government, the Department of War even tried to withhold machine tools to produce it. The weapons were eventually manufactured, but too late to be of use in the Dutch East Indies, conquered by Japan in December 1941. The Marine Corps picked up some of these to outfit its parachute units, since the Johnson's barrel could be quickly removed or put back on, making it easier to carry in a jump. Few made it to combat in the Pacific, however, and improvements in the M1 already had endeared the Garand to Marine infantrymen.

16 September
Manpower
Congress and President Roosevelt approve the Selective Service and Training Act, the first peacetime draft in the history of the United States. It authorizes the induction of 900,000 men into the Army for one year and the activation of the 270,000 men of the National Guard.

26 September
World War II
President Roosevelt declares an embargo on the export of scrap iron and steel to any country other than Britain outside the Western Hemisphere. It is aimed at Japan, which depends heavily on these U.S. commodities.

27 September
World War II
Japan becomes the third Axis power when it signs a military alliance with Germany and Italy.

29 September
Midway
The Midway Detachment arrives on Midway Atoll and begins setting up defenses. It consists of nine officers and 168 enlisted and one-third of the equipment of the 3rd Defense Battalion.

October
Technology
The Marine Corps receives its first prototype of Donald Roebling's Alligator, a tracked aluminum vehicle capable of swimming in the water and crawling onto land.

1 October
Training
Marine units of the East Coast FMF participate in Landing Operation 2 in the Caribbean. It lasts until 9 December. Following the exercise, the 1st Marine Brigade goes into camp at Guantanamo Bay, Cuba.

5 October
Manpower
Secretary of the Navy Frank Knox orders the Organized Reserve to active duty by 9 November. These units add 236 officers and 5,009 enlisted men to the strength of the active Marine Corps.
Bases
An airstrip is opened at Parris Island to serve as an outlying field for Quantico-based aviation units.

26 October
Training
Volunteers already serving in the Corps report to Lakehurst to form the first class of trainees for eventual Marine parachute units.

1 December
Commandants
Major General Holcomb is appointed to a second term as Comandant.

Left: *A Marine formation in Reykjavik, the capital of Iceland. (National Archives)*

Opposite: *British officers view Marine weapons. While a gun crew readies a 75mm pack howitzer in the foreground, a truck with twin .50-caliber machine guns sits in the background. (National Archives)*

Force Structure
The 5th Defense Battalion is organized at Parris Island.

16 December
Force Structure
The 7th Defense Battalion is established at San Diego.

27 December
Force Structure
The 10th Marines is reactivated as an artillery regiment at San Diego, to serve with the 2nd Marine Brigade.

1941

January
Force Structure
2nd Marine Aircraft Group deploys from San Diego to Hawaii.

1 January
Force Structure
The 7th Marines is reactivated at Guantanamo Bay to serve as the second infantry regiment in the 1st Marine Brigade.

27 January
Midway
The CNO orders the remainder of the 3rd Defense Battalion to Midway Atoll, the advance echelons of the 1st Defense Battalion to Johnston and Palmyra, and the 6th Defense Battalion to Pearl Harbor.

1 February
Force Structure
The 1st Marine Brigade is redesignated the 1st Marine Division as it sails from Guantanamo Bay to Culebra for exercises. Simultaneously, the 2nd Marine Brigade in southern California is redesignated the 2nd Marine Division. The 2nd Marines is reactivated at San Diego to serve as the third infantry regiment of the 2nd Marine Division. The 4th Defense Battalion arrives at Guantanamo Bay to garrison that base.

3 February
Bases
A Marine Corps Air Station is established at Oahu's Ewa Mooring Mast Field (originally constructed for dirigibles in the 1920s) when the 2nd Marine Aircraft Group deploys there from Ford Island.

14 February
Midway
The remaining elements of the 3rd Defense Battalion reach Midway Atoll.

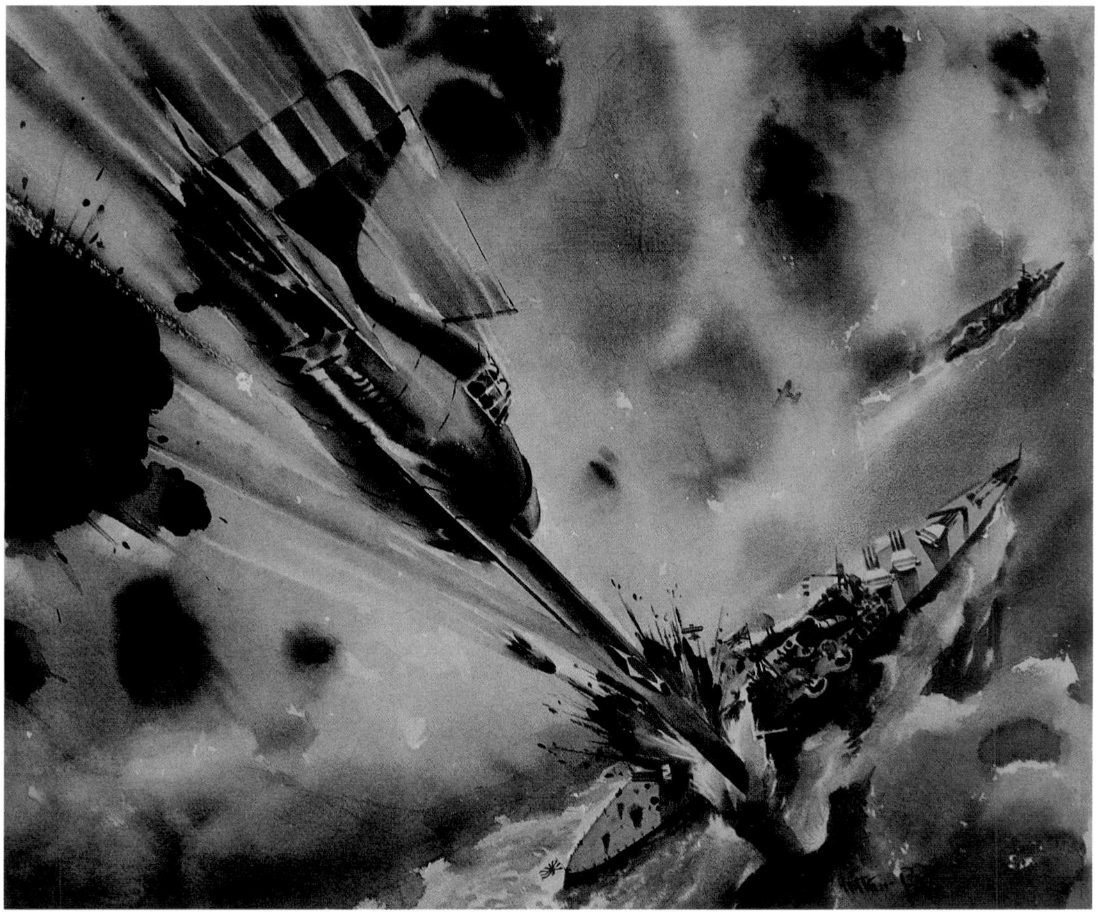

Left: *Japanese ships, here a destroyer, come under fire from Marine and Navy planes off Wake Island on 23 December 1941. ("Wake Island," Arthur Beaumont, Marine Corps Art Collection)*

Opposite: *The weapons of the 1st Marine Defense Battalion take a toll of the enemy during the siege of Wake Island. ("Wake Island," E. Franklin Wittmack, Marine Corps Art Collection)*

15 February
Bases
Congress approves the purchase and construction of a new Marine Corps base at New River, North Carolina. It is selected to provide sufficient room for training a division.

1 March
Force Structure
The 1st Marines and 11th Marines (an artillery regiment) are reactivated at Guantanamo Bay to serve with the 1st Marine Division. The 6th Defense Battalion is formed at San Diego.

3 March
Johnston
The advance echelon of the 1st Defense Battalion lands at Johnston Atoll.

11 March
World War II
President Roosevelt approves the Lend-Lease Act, which allows the transfer of armaments and vital commodities to Allied nations without payment.

15 March
Force Structure
The FMF is administratively divided, with the 1st Marine Division reporting to the Atlantic Fleet and the 2nd Marine Division reporting to the Pacific Fleet.

18 March
Samoa
The 7th Defense Battalion reaches American Samoa and secures naval and air facilities on the island of Tutuila.

22 March
Force Structure
The 2nd Parachute Company is formed as part of the 2nd Marine Division. It is the first Marine Corps parachute unit and becomes the nucleus for the 2nd Parachute Battalion.

6 April
World War II
Germany launches an invasion of Yugoslavia and Greece, which fall within the space of a few weeks.

13 April
World War II
The Soviet Union and Japan sign a neutrality treaty.

14 April
Palmyra
Elements of the 1st Defense Battalion arrive.

18 April
Wake Island
Admiral Husband E. Kimmel, commander of naval forces in the Pacific, asks the CNO for a Marine defense battalion for Wake Island.

1 May
Bases
Marine Barracks, New River, North Carolina, is formally established. The base will eventually be named Camp Lejeune.

20 May
World War II
German airborne forces invade the island of Crete in the Mediterranean. The island falls on 1 June.

21 May
Technology
Based on tests in Louisiana, a bow-ramp version of the Higgins boat is determined to be fully functional and preferable to the non-ramp boats previously being built for the Navy. This design goes into production and becomes the forerunner of the Landing Craft Vehicle, Personnel or LCVP.

27 May
World War II
President Roosevelt proclaims an unlimited state of national emergency.

28 May
Force Structure
The 1st Parachute Battalion is established at Quantico.

29 May
Force Structure
The Joint Board approves a plan for a landing force of 28,000 troops (half Marine and half Army) under command of Major General

MARINE CORPS RECRUIT DEPOT, SAN DIEGO

Marines first came to San Diego on 29 July 1846, when they helped seize the town after war began with Mexico. The large harbor, the location near troubled Mexico, and the ready access to the Pacific made it an ideal location for an expeditionary force poised for future contingencies. Marines put it to that use for the first time in 1911, with the 4th Regiment setting up camp on North Island while revolution flared in Mexico. By 1914, the Navy Department was eying San Diego as a site for the West Coast Advance Base Force. Assistant Secretary of the Navy Franklin Roosevelt inspected the area that year and deemed it desirable. In July, a reincarnated 4th Regiment landed again on North Island and went into bivouac. This time the Marines were in San Diego to stay.

In December 1914, over half of the 4th Regiment shifted to Balboa Park in the city of San Diego, to participate in an international exposition. The following August, Commandant Barnett personally surveyed the region and determined that the best available site for a base was a relatively cheap expanse of land near the north end of the bay. The city, eager to see the development of a military installation, offered the adjacent tidal lands for free. With the backing of the local congressman, the House and Senate approved the deal in 1916. The Navy Department acquired the land in 1917, filled in the tidal flats to provide a total of more than 700 acres, and began construction of permanent buildings in 1919. The Spanish Renaissance-style barracks and support buildings rose out of the otherwise barren area, and by 1 December 1921, sufficient facilities were complete to place the base in commission.

The Advance Base Force no longer existed, but its successor, the 5th Brigade of the Marine Corps Expeditionary Force, occupied the brand-new installation. In 1923, it was joined by the recruit depot for the western United States, which moved to San Diego from Mare Island. That same year, the Navy acquired the land immediately to the west and established its own training facility there. In 1927, the city began filling other tidal land just to the east of the Marine Base and developed its new airport—Lindbergh Field—on the site. A decade later, as part of an expansion of the airport, the city traded 544 acres adjacent to the base's outlying rifle range at La Jolla for 60 acres of the main Marine base. There was a similar transfer of another 60 acres to Lindbergh Field in 1940. The only other changes to the base since the completion of the main buildings in 1926 had been the paving of the drill field.

Throughout the 1920s and 1930s, the installation continued its dual role as a recruit depot and home to operating forces. The 4th Regiment deployed from there to mail guard duty in 1926, then to China in 1927. The outfit that replaced them at San Diego—the 6th Marines—deployed from the base to reinforce the 4th Marines in Shanghai during the 1937 crisis. The major shortcoming of the facility, however, was the lack of suitable field training sites. The San Diego base had operated the rifle range near La Jolla (several miles due north) since early in its existence. Formally designated Camp Matthews in 1942 (for a distinguished Marine marksman), it remained in use until 1964, when urban development necessitated the construction of new range facilities for the recruit depot at Camp Pendleton. (Camp Matthews then provided the land for the University of California San Diego.)

Another outlying installation was Camp Kearney to the northeast. Initially acquired in the 1920s as a site for Navy dirigibles, in the first half of the 1940s it served as the nexus for a huge Marine satellite base which grew just to the east. Dubbed Camp Elliott, these 32,000 acres provided the maneuver room for field training. Although a few FMF units continued to come to life and temporarily reside at the main base, most everything related to the FMF shifted to Kearney, Elliott, and Pendleton. After World War II, Kearney became Naval Air Station, Miramar, only to return to the hands of the Corps near the end of the century. Parts of Elliott were subsumed into Miramar, while the rest returned to civilian use.

The main base underwent a construction boom beginning in 1939 to provide facilities for the vast expansion in recruit training and the FMF. When World War II ended, all FMF activities concentrated at Camp Pendleton, leaving the San Diego base entirely devoted to recruit training and a few small, specialized training facilities (such as Sea School). On 1 January 1948, in recognition of the new focus of the installation, it formally became Marine Corps Recruit Depot, San Diego. The Korean War brought more construction, mainly in the form of Quonset huts for recruit living quarters. As in World War II, and again during Vietnam, many Korean-era recruits also resided in tents due to the shortage of buildings. In the latter 1960s, the base began putting up large permanent barracks to replace tents and Quonset huts. All of the former and most of the latter were gone by 1974. Although much has changed since the base first appeared in the early 1920s, its original Spanish Renaissance architecture remains its distinctive trademark.

Right: *Current day recruits. (Rick Mullen)*

Holland M. Smith to occupy the Portuguese Azores. Although the plan is never executed, it becomes the basis for the first Marine-Army joint command of the war.

1 June
Bases
The 2nd Marine Division begins moving to Camp Elliott. Located on Kearney Mesa in the vicinity of the current Marine Corps Air Station, Miramar, part of this area had been rented from the city of San Diego since 1934. The government would purchase and use a total of 32,000 acres here before the end of World War II.

13 June
Force Structure
General H. M. Smith relinquishes command of the 1st Marine Division to become commander of the newly created I Corps (Provisional), composed of his old division and the Army's 1st Infantry Division. This force changes its name several times and ultimately is renamed the Amphibious Force Atlantic Fleet; it focuses on training for amphibious assaults.

16 June
Iceland
Following a 5 June decision by President Roosevelt to commit American forces to the defense of Iceland, the 1st Marine Brigade (Provisional) is established at Charleston, South Carolina. It is formed around the reinforced 6th Marines, newly arrived by sea from California and originally destined to reinforce the 1st Marine Division for the Azores operation. The other major elements of the brigade are the 5th Defense Battalion and the 2nd Battalion, 10th Marines. The brigade sails on 22 June. Marines receives the mission because U.S. law prevents draftees and National Guardsmen from serving overseas.

22 June
World War II
Germany invades the Soviet Union.

24 June
Force Structure
VMF-121 is organized at Quantico.

30 June
Manpower
The strength of the Marine Corps on active duty is 3,339 officers and 51,020 enlisted.

1 July
Force Structure
New designations are applied to existing squadrons: VMF-1 and 2 respectively become VMF-111 and 211; VMS-1 and 2 are now respectively Marine Scout Bombing Squadron 131 (VMSB-131) and 231; VMB-1 and 2 are now VMSB-132 and 232; VMO-1 becomes VMO-151; VMJ-1 and 2 are redesignated VMJ-151 and 252. VMS-3 in the Virgin Islands is not redesignated.

7 July
Iceland
The 1st Marine Brigade (Provisional) arrives in Iceland.
Force Structure
The 1st Marine Aircraft Wing (1st MAW) is established at Quantico by the addition of a headquarters squadron to the 1st Marine Aircraft Group.

Opposite: *Marines watch their lone F4F-3 take off to battle the Japanese on 22 December 1941. ("The Last Plane," Col John W. Thomason, Marine Corps Art Collection)*

Right: *Marine Corps Grumman Wildcats helped stem the tide in the Pacific war. (Marine Corps Historical Center)*

10 July
Force Structure
The 2nd Marine Aircraft Wing (2nd MAW) is established at San Diego by the addition of a headquarters squadron to the 2nd Marine Aircraft Group (in Hawaii).

11 July
Force Structure
VMF-221 is organized at San Diego.

15 July
London
A Marine detachment is established to guard the U.S. Embassy in London, England.

24 July
World War II
Japanese forces occupy French Indochina. In retaliation two days later, President Roosevelt orders the freezing of all Japanese funds in the United States, which brings all trade to a halt. A formal embargo on oil and aviation fuel follows on 1 August.

26 July
Philippines
President Roosevelt nationalizes the armed forces of the Philippines and places them under command of General Douglas MacArthur, commander of all U.S. forces in the Far East.

28 July
Force Structure
2nd Marine Aircraft Group is redesignated Marine Aircraft Group 21 (MAG-21).

1 August
Force Structure
The 1st Marine Aircraft Groups is redesignated Marine Aircraft Group 11 (MAG-11).

12 August
Manpower
By a one-vote margin, the House of Representatives approves the bill continuing Selective Service and extending the service of Army draftees for 18 months.

16 August
Samoa
The first man is enlisted in the 1st Samoan Battalion, Marine Corps Reserve. Its purpose is to provide an infantry element to reinforce the 7th Defense Battalion on Tutuila.

18 August
Bases
The command that will become Marine Corps Air Station, Cherry Point, North Carolina, is established. The first air operations will commence in March 1942. Cherry Point will become one of the primary Marine airfields on the East Coast.

19 August
Wake Island
The advance echelon of the 1st Defense Battalion arrives at Wake Island.

September
Training
VMSB-131 participates in the Army's Louisiana Maneuvers.

11 September
Midway
The 6th Defense Battalion relieves the 3rd Defense Battalion on Midway Atoll.

24 September
Iceland
The 1st Provisional Marine Brigade is detached from the Department of the Navy for service with the Army.

1 October
Force Structure
The 1st and 2nd Barrage Balloon Squadrons are organized at Parris Island.

17 October
World War II
General Hideki Tojo becomes Japan's premier and minister of war in a reorganization of the government.

1 November
Force Structure
The 2nd Joint Training Force is established at Camp Elliott, California, under command of Marine Major General Clayton B. Vogel. A West-Coast counterpart of the Amphibious Force Atlantic Fleet, it is composed of the 2nd Marine Division, 2nd MAW, and the Army's 3rd Infantry Division.

2 November
Wake Island
Additional elements of the 1st Defense Battalion reach Wake Island, bringing the Marine force to 15 officers and 373 enlisted men.

3 November
Pearl Harbor
The staff of the Imperial Japanese Navy approves the plan for the attack on the U.S. Pacific Fleet at Pearl Harbor.

10 November
China
The U.S. Asiatic Fleet receives permission to withdraw gunboats and Marines from China.

26 November
Pearl Harbor
The Pearl Harbor attack force departs Japanese waters.

27 November
World War II
The War and Navy Departments send warnings of imminent war to U.S. commanders in the Pacific.

27–28 November
Philippines
The 4th Marines embarks and sails from Shanghai for the Philippines. The regiment arrives at Olongapo on the 30th.

30 November
Manpower
Total strength of the active Marine Corps has grown to 65,881 officers and enlisted.

November
Aviation
Marine officers begin training as glider pilots in civilian schools to form the cadre of a Marine glider program for carrying troops into combat.

1 December
Wake Island
The 2nd and 4th Defense Battalions arrive at Pearl Harbor, destined for eventual employment at Wake Island.

Force Structure
VMO-251 is organized at San Diego.

4 December
Wake Island
Twelve F4F-3 Grumman Wildcat fighter planes of Marine Fighter Squadron 211 (VMF-211) fly from *Enterprise* to Wake Island. They begin aerial patrols the next day.

7 December
Pearl Harbor
Japanese carrier-borne aircraft attack U.S. forces on Oahu, sinking 19 ships, destroying 188 planes, killing 2,280, and wounding 1,109. Marines losses are 111 killed or missing, 75 wounded, 33 aircraft destroyed, and 12 damaged. Two Japanese destroyers bombard Midway, inflicting 14 Marine casualties.

8 December
World War II
The United States declares war on Japan. Japanese forces invade Thailand and Malaya.
Pacific
Japanese aircraft attack Wake Island (destroying seven F4F-3s), Guam, and the Philippines.
China
Marine detachments in Peiping, Tientsin, and elsewhere in China surrender to superior Japanese forces.

9 December
Guam
Japanese air attacks continue against Guam.
Wake Island
Japanese aircraft attack the island for the second day in a row and continue to do so daily until it is captured by the Japanese on 23 December.
Force Structure
MAG-11 begins moving to San Diego from Quantico.

Opposite: *A portrait of an emaciated prisoner of the Japanese, by a Wake Island defender who survived the experience. ("The Long Dark," Capt James R. Brown, USMC (Ret), Marine Corps Art Collection)*

Right: *A view of a Japanese prisoner of war camp in Shanghai, China. ("Kiang Wong," Capt James R. Brown, USMC (Ret), Marine Corps Art Collection)*

GRUMMAN F4F WILDCAT

The Grumman F4F almost didn't make it into active service, but it went on to become the mainstay of Marine fighter squadrons during the first two years of World War II. The plane emerged from a Navy design competition launched in 1935. The Grumman Corporation of Long Island, New York, initially placed its hopes on a biplane model, but switched to a monoplane in July 1936. The resulting XF4F-2 first flew on 2 September 1937. The sole prototype suffered from engine problems, culminating in a crash that damaged the plane in April 1938. Although it was a bit faster than its competitor, the Grumman airframe lost out to the then-more-effective Brewster F2A Buffalo, which received the Navy contract in June 1938.

Later that year, the Navy decided the F4F had sufficient promise to warrant development of a new version, the XF4F-3. Among the main changes were a better powerplant and larger, square-tipped wings. The prototype made its maiden flight in February 1939. With a few modifications, it went into production six months later as a supplement to the Buffalo. The Marine Corps received its first F4F-3 in May 1941 with the formation of VMF-111, 121, and 211.

The Wildcat, as it was dubbed, weighed in at 5,238 pounds empty, had a wingspan of 38 feet, and a length of 28 feet, 9 inches. Its main and emergency fuel tanks held 144 gallons, giving it a range of 860 miles. The Pratt & Whitney 1,200-horsepower engine produced a rate of climb of 2,300 feet per minute and a maximum speed of 331 miles per hour (40 mph faster than the initial model and 50 mph more than the Brewster Buffalo). It had a service ceiling of 37,000 feet. It was armed with four wing-mounted, .50-caliber machine guns, and it could carry a

Opposite: *Outnumbered Grumman F4F Wildcats duel with Japanese Zeros over Wake Island in December 1941. ("Cat and Mouse over Wake Island," Marc Stewart, Stewart Studios)*

Left: *The Wildcat proved a sturdy plane early in WWII. (Marine Corps Historical Center)*

100-pound bomb under each wing. The pilot had to hand crank its retractable landing gear. The Navy Department ultimately purchased 380 F4F-3 variants, of which about four dozen went to the Marines.

The Wildcat saw its first aerial combat action at Wake Island (most of them at Pearl Harbor being destroyed on the ground). The Marine F4Fs on Wake shot down several Japanese planes and sank a destroyer before that battle ended with the island overrun. One of the pilots, Captain Henry T. Elrod, later received the Medal of Honor posthumously for his bravery in the air and on the ground. Other Marine Wildcats at Midway shot down more enemy aircraft in June.

By the time of the Guadalcanal campaign, the Marines were receiving a new model, the F4F-4. The main changes were folding wings for carrier service, an additional two wing-mounted, .50-caliber machine guns, and better armor. Although the Wildcat was significantly slower than the Japanese Zero in airspeed and rate of climb, the tough Grumman fighter could take a beating and bring its pilot home. Dueling with the Japanese in the immediate environs of Henderson Field, as the Marines often did, brought additional advantages. Before long, intrepid Marine pilots were racking up kills, even against the vaunted Zero.

Captain Marion E. Carl of VMF-223 became the first leatherneck ace after he shot down three enemy planes on 24 August (he already had downed two fighters at Midway). Ultimately 26 Marine pilots flying the F4F shot down five or more Japanese aircraft during the course of the war. Six of them received Medals of Honor: Lieutenant Colonel Harold W. Bauer (posthumous), 1st Lieutenant Jefferson J. DeBlanc, Captain Joseph J. Foss, Major Robert E. Galer, Major John L. Smith, and 1st Lieutenant James E. Swett. The leading Wildcat aces were Foss (26), Smith (19), Carl (16.5 in the F4F), Galer (13), and William P. Marontate (13). In one of the most spectacular aerial engagements of the war, on 7 April 1943, Swett shot down seven Japanese Val dive bombers in one mission while defending shipping around Guadalcanal. On 31 January 1943, DeBlanc downed five Zeros while escorting a bombing raid in the central Solomons. Both men had to ditch their badly damaged planes.

Although U.S. factories churned out a total of nearly 8,000 Wildcats before the war was over, the F4F was largely superseded by late 1943 by the Grumman F6F Hellcat and the Chance Vought F4U Corsair. Nevertheless, the sturdy Wildcat had served the Marines well when the odds were toughest.

10 December
Guam
A Japanese force of nearly 6,000 men lands at three points. The 153 Marines of the garrison and the 80 Chamorros of the Insular Guard, armed with rifles and four machine guns, fight back for a time, but the U.S. Navy governor of the island soon surrenders to avoid useless casualties. Marine losses are four killed and 12 wounded.
Philippines
Japanese forces land in northern Luzon.
Gilberts
The Japanese seize Makin Island.

11 December
World War II
Germany and Italy declare war on the United States.
Wake Island
The Wake Island defense force defeats an attempted Japanese amphibious assault, sinking two enemy destroyers and damaging three cruisers, two destroyers, a destroyer-transport, and a transport. Marine losses are a handful of wounded.

12 December
Philippines
Japanese forces land in southeastern Luzon. Enemy air attacks begin against Olongapo.

15 December
Johnston
Two Japanese ships bombard Johnston Island. The Marines suffer no casualties.

Above: *A 1942 recruiting poster. ("Fly With the Marines," Marine Corps Art Collection)*

Left: *Col Samuel Howard decorates two men on Bataan. He would lament at the end of the siege of Corregidor: "My God . . . and I had to be the first Marine officer ever to surrender a regiment." (National Archives)*

17 December
Midway
Led by a Navy patrol bomber, 17 SB2U-3 Chance-Vought Vindicator dive bombers of VMSB-231 make the longest mass overwater single-engined flight recorded until then, covering the 1,137 miles from Oahu to Midway Island in 9 hours and 45 minutes. They represent the first combat aircraft on the island.

20 December
Commanders
Admiral Ernest King is appointed commander-in-chief of the U.S. Fleet (COMINCH).
Philippines
The commander of the Asiatic Fleet places the 4th Marines under command of General MacArthur. Japanese troops invade Mindanao.

21 December
Force Structure
1st MAW arrives in San Diego.
Wake Island
Japanese carrier planes destroy the last remaining aircraft of VMF-211 on the island.
Philippines
Japanese forces land at Lingayen Gulf on Luzon and move toward Manila.

23 December
Wake Island
Following a dawn landing by a Japanese Special Naval Landing Force and 12 hours of fighting, the battered garrison of Wake Island surrenders. Total Marine casualties during the campaign are 56 killed and 44 wounded. A U.S. Navy relief expedition carrying VMF-221 and the 4th Defense Battalion turns back to Pearl Harbor.
Philippines
General MacArthur decides to withdraw his forces into the Bataan Peninsula.

24 December
Force Structure
The 2nd Marine Brigade is reactivated at Camp Elliot, California. It consists of the 8th Marines, the 2nd Battalion of the 10th Marines, and the 2nd Defense Battalion.
Midway
Elements of Batteries A and C of the 4th Defense Battalion reinforce the garrison on Midway.

25 December
China
The British defenders of Hong Kong surrender following a Japanese assault.

Right: *Filipino soldiers learn the intricacies of the Browning water-cooled machine gun from a Marine crew. (National Archives)*

Left: *A Marine enjoys a fresh ration of cigarettes, about the only thing besides Japanese fire that was plentiful on Corregidor. (National Archives)*

Below: *A Marine humps a machine-gun tripod up a ridge on Guadalcanal. (National Archives)*

Midway
The 14 F2A-3 Brewster Buffalo fighter planes of VMF-221 fly off *Saratoga* and land on Midway.

26 December
Midway
Battery B of the 4th Defense Battalion and the ground elements of VMF-221 arrive at Midway.
Philippines
The 4th Marines begins moving to its assigned defensive positions on the fortress island of Corregidor guarding the entrance to Manila Bay. The deployment is completed two days later. Two antiaircraft batteries of 3/4 (recently created from units of the former Marine Barracks, Cavite Navy Yard) remain on Bataan.

29 December
Philippines
Japanese aircraft begin daily attacks on Corregidor and slowly destroy its fixed fortifications.

30 December
Panama Canal
The 1st Barrage Balloon Squadron arrives in the Panama Canal Zone to assist in defending it.

31 December
Pacific Theater
Admiral Chester Nimitz assumes command of the U.S. Pacific Fleet.

1942

10 January
Force Structure
The Glider Detachment is formed at Parris Island.

15 January
Samoa
Brigadier General Henry L. Larsen (commanding general of the 2nd Marine Brigade) is appointed the first military governor of American Samoa.

Above: *Four Marines bring in a wounded buddy on Guadalcanal. (Marine Corps Research Center)*

Right: *F4F Grumman Wildcats lined up at Ewa Field in Hawaii. (National Archives)*

20 January
Commandants
Legislation authorizes the promotion of Commandant Holcomb to lieutenant general, the first Marine of that rank.

23 January
Samoa
The 2nd Marine Brigade reaches American Samoa and joins with the 7th Defense Battalion in protecting that territory.
New Britain
Japanese forces land on the island and take the harbor of Rabaul from its small Australian garrison.

24 January
Borneo
Four destroyers score the first surface victory of the U.S. Navy since 1898, sinking four transports and a patrol vessel during a night attack on a Japanese force invading Borneo at Balikpapan Bay.

27–28 January
Philippines
Dozens of Marines from two batteries of 3/4 assist a provisional naval battalion and Philippine units in containing a Japanese amphibious landing against the Bataan coast near Mariveles.

1 February
Bases
The airfield at Parris Island is designated a full-fledged Marine Corps Air Station.
Force Structure
The 9th Defense Battalion is organized at Parris Island.

9 February
Joint Chiefs of Staff
The first formal meeting of the new military policy body, the Joint Chiefs of Staff, is held. The members are General George C. Marshall (Chief of Staff of the Army), Lieutenant General Henry H. "Hap" Arnold (Chief of the Army Air Corps), Admiral Stark (CNO), and Admiral King (COMINCH).

10 February
Midway
VMF-221 aircraft drive off a Japanese submarine after it fires two rounds from its deck gun against the atoll.

12 February
Force Structure
The 9th Marines is reactivated at Camp Elliott. The regiment is initially assigned to the 2nd Marine Division to replace the absent 6th and 8th Marines.

Opposite: *Marines ford a river on Guadalcanal. (Marine Corps Research Center)*

Right: *This range finder helps direct the fire of defense battalion heavy guns on Guadalcanal. (Marine Corps Research Center)*

15 February
Singapore
The British garrison surrenders Singapore to the Japanese following an assault on the island and its naval bases (once thought to be impregnable).

16 February
Force Structure
The 1st Separate Battalion (formerly 1/5) is redesignated the 1st Raider Battalion at Quantico. The 2nd Separate Battalion at Camp Elliot (formed from scratch two weeks earlier) is redesignated the 2nd Raider Battalion on 19 February.

17–18 February
Philippines
Sailors without specific shipboard duties are assigned to augment the ranks of the 4th Marines on Corregidor. Survivors of other units eventually swell the Marine regiment to almost 4,000 men (four times its pre-war size). The 4th Marines is responsible for the beach defenses of the island.

19 February
Cuba
The 9th Defense Battalion arrives at Guantanamo Bay to assume responsibility for protecting that base.

23 February
California
A Japanese submarine shells an oil refinery near Santa Barbara.

27 February
Java Sea
The Allied naval force in the South Pacific is badly beaten by the Japanese in the Battle of the Java Sea. Over the next two days, in the Battle of Sunda Strait, the remainder of the Allied force is sunk.

1 March
Force Structure
Various elements of MAG-11 provide nuclei for four new MAGs: MAG-12, MAG-14, and MAG-15 are established at Camp Kearney, California; MAG-13 comes into being at San Diego. VMF-112 and VMJ-153 are formed at San Diego; VMF-122, VMSB-141, and VMSB-142 at Kearney. MAG-21 provides squadrons and personnel to form the basis for three other MAGs: MAG-22 is organized on Midway; MAG-23 and MAG-24 are formed at Ewa Field in Hawaii. VMF-212 is commissioned at Ewa. VMF-222 and VMSB-241 and 242 are organized at Midway.

8 March
Iceland
The 1st Marine Brigade (Provisional) is relieved by U.S. Army forces and departs Iceland.

Left: *An 81mm mortar crew fires in support of operations west of the Matanikau River in early November 1942. (Marine Corps Research Center)*

New Guinea
Japanese troops land at Lae and Salamaua.

10 March
Bases
The government purchases the 132,000 acres of Santa Margarita Ranch on the Pacific coast between Los Angeles and San Diego for use as a new Marine Corps base. It is named Camp Pendleton soon after.

11 March
Force Structure
VMJ-253 is organized at Ewa, Hawaii.

12 March
Department of the Navy
The President combines the offices of CNO and COMINCH, giving Admiral King complete authority over the Navy.
New Caledonia
U.S. forces occupy New Caledonia in the South Pacific and begin building an air base at Tontouta.

15 March
New Hebrides
Elements of MAG-24 depart Ewa Field, Hawaii, for Efate, New Hebrides, to assist in establishing an airfield there.

17 March
Commanders
General MacArthur arrives in Darwin, Australia, following his recall from the Philippines. He assumes command of the Southwest Pacific Area.
Samoa
Engineers complete the airfield on Tutuila, American Samoa.

20 March
Samoa
The United States assumes responsibility for defending Western (or British) Samoa.
Commanders
Army Lieutenant General Jonathan M. Wainwright assumes command of all forces remaining in the Philippines.

21 March
Force Structure
The 3rd Marine Brigade is established at New River, North Carolina. Its major elements are the 7th Marines and 1/11. Its mission will be to garrison Western Samoa.

25 March
Force Structure
The 1st Marine Brigade (Provisional) arrives in New York Harbor, and the headquarters element is disbanded.

28 March
Samoa
The 7th Defense Battalion moves from American Samoa to the island of Upolu, Western Samoa.

29 March
New Hebrides
The 4th Defense Battalion and VMF-212 arrive at Efate.

1 April
Force Structure
The 8th Defense Battalion is organized on Samoa. Marine Photographic Squadrons 1 and 2 (VMD-1 and 2) are organized at San Diego.

2 April
Samoa
The first flight echelon of MAG-13 flies into Tutuila and assumes responsibility for the air defense of American Samoa.

3 April
Commanders
Admiral Nimitz is given a second responsibility as Commander-in-Chief of the Pacific Ocean Area (CINCPOA—command over a geographic theater) in addition to his existing billet as Commander-in-Chief of the Pacific Fleet (CINCPAC—command over naval forces).

9 April
Philippines
U.S. and Filipino forces on Bataan surrender to the Japanese. Battery C of the 4th Marines escapes to Corregidor. Japanese heavy artillery begins bombarding Corregidor.

12 April
Philippines
Sailors are formed into a unit designated as 4th Battalion, 4th Marines.

16 April
Force Structure
The 3rd Barrage Balloon Squadron is formed at Parris Island.

18 April
Japan
Army Lieutenant Colonel James H. Doolittle and his 16 B-25 bombers fly off carrier *Hornet* (CV-8) and bomb targets in major Japanese cities.
Palmyra
VMF-211 flies onto the island from carrier *Lexington.*

20 April
Training
The Fleet Marine Force Training Center is established at Camp Elliott. Although its initial

Right: *A wounded Marine is loaded on board a landing craft for evacuation from Guadalcanal. (Marine Corps Research Center)*

effort is training battalions, it becomes the primary place to train men in individual skills prior to their assignment to a combat unit.

24 April
Force Structure
Glider Group 71 (MLG-71) and Marine Glider Squadron 711 (VML-711) are formed from the Glider Detachment at Marine Corps Air Station, Parris Island.

25 April
Technology
In tests conducted at Norfolk, Andrew Higgins's 50-foot tank lighter (a larger version of his bow-ramp landing craft) proves superior to a Navy-designed craft. It goes into production and is designated the Landing Craft Mechanized or LCM. The LCM provides the first practical means to get medium tanks from ship to shore during an amphibious assault.

28 April
Samoa
Major General Charles F. B. Price and his staff arrive in Samoa and establish the Headquarters Samoan Area Defense Force. The 1st Raider Battalion and 2nd Barrage Balloon Squadron also reinforce the Samoan garrison.

1 May
Samoa
The 8th Defense Battalion arrives at Wallis Island to garrison this outpost west of the Samoas.

Force Structure
VMF-223 and 224 and VMSB-233 and 234 are organized at Ewa, Hawaii.

3 May
Solomons
The Japanese 3rd Kure Special Naval Landing Force captures Tulagi and Gavutu Islands in the southern Solomons.

5–6 May
Philippines
A Japanese regiment lands on Corregidor. The reserve elements of the 4th Marines counterattack, but are unable to defeat the enemy. Wainwright surrenders the island on the second day. Colonel Samuel L. Howard, commander of the 4th Marines, orders the national and regimental colors burned to prevent them from falling into Japanese hands. Total Marine casualties during the Philippines campaign are 331 killed and 357 wounded. Another 239 will die while prisoners of war.

Left: *Marines extinguish flames on a Wildcat fighter following a Japanese bombardment on Guadalcanal. (Marine Corps Research Center)*

Opposite: *Col Clifton B. Cates, CO of the 1st Marines at Guadalcanal, stands near the wreckage of a Japanese bomber. (Marine Corps Research Center)*

7–8 May
Coral Sea
Japanese and U.S. carrier planes attack each other's fleets in the Coral Sea. Although U.S. forces sustain slightly higher losses, they forestall Japan's planned invasion of Port Moresby, New Guinea. The Battle of the Coral Sea is the first major sea engagement conducted entirely by air.

8 May
Samoa
The 3rd Marine Brigade arrives at Tutuila and begins building an airfield and defenses. It takes control of the 7th Defense Battalion.

11 May
Iceland
Marine Barracks, Fleet Air Base Iceland is established.

20 May
Bases
Cunningham Field is commissioned at Cherry Point, North Carolina. It is capable of supporting a MAW.

23 May
Training
The Training Center, FMF, is established at New River, North Carolina. During the course of the war, the base becomes the home of numerous schools and training programs.

24 May
New Hebrides
The headquarters of MAG-24 departs Efate for Santa Barbara, California.

25 May
Midway
Companies C and D of the 2nd Raider Battalion and the 37mm antiaircraft battery of the 3rd Defense Battalion arrive in Midway to reinforce the garrison.

26 May
Midway
More elements of the 3rd Defense Battalion, as well as 16 SBD-2 Douglas Dauntless dive bombers and seven F4F Grumman Wildcat fighters of MAG-22, reinforce Midway.

1 June
Manpower
In accordance with the orders of President Roosevelt and Secretary of the Navy Knox, the Marine Corps begins recruiting African Americans. The initial enlistees are Alfred Masters and George O. Thompson. They are the first African Americans to join the Marine Corps since the Revolutionary War.
Force Structure
MAG-25 is organized at Camp Kearney. The 10th Defense Battalion is established at San Diego. The 4th Barrage Balloon Squadron is formed at Parris Island and soon deploys to Samoa.

OPERATION WATCH TOWER—THE FIRST DAY

The Joint Chiefs of Staff decided on 24 June 1942 to launch Operation Watchtower, an amphibious assault into the lower Solomon Islands. The initial target was Tulagi, a small island with an enemy seaplane base. The goal was to stop the southward expansion of Japanese power, which was threatening the Allied lifeline to Australia. When evidence came to light of an airfield under construction on nearby Guadalcanal, it also became an objective. Planners subsequently added the enemy-occupied, conjoined islets of Gavutu and Tanambogo guarding the approaches to Tulagi.

A number of issues complicated preparations for this first offensive designed to take back territory from the Japanese. The 1st Marine Division received the assignment on 25 June, but it had one infantry regiment in New Zealand, another at sea, and the remainder of its elements (including the just-attached 2nd Marines) spread around the Pacific. All units would not come together until the rehearsal at sea, just one week before the 7 August D-Day. There also was very little intelligence and only a poor map cobbled together from aerial photos at the last minute. Sketchy information indicated there were a few hundred enemy on Tulagi, about as many on Gavutu-Tanambogo, and perhaps several thousand on Guadalcanal. Finally, there was too little shipping and too few of the latest amphibious landing craft to fully support the assault force.

The division operations officer, LtCol Gerald C. Thomas, and his assistant, LtCol Merrill B. Twining, were responsible for crafting a workable plan in this difficult situation. Both men saw Guadalcanal and its airfield as the primary objective, but they were more concerned about the other islands. These were defended by the Imperial Navy's special landing forces—sailors trained to fight ashore like Marines. They likely would be dug in on terrain overlooking the limited landing sites available on these confined targets. Consequently, Thomas and Twining arranged for the bulk of the force (11,000 men) to take Guadalcanal. The best units (in terms of training and leadership) would attack the smaller objectives. The 1st Raider Battalion, with 2/5 in support, would take Tulagi, while the 1st Parachute Battalion would seize Gavutu-Tanambogo. The 2nd Marines would provide the reserve and execute supporting landings on nearby Florida Island to protect the raiders and parachutists from possible flanking fire.

The most difficult problem was choosing landing sites, given the possible nature of enemy defenses and the limitations of the wooden-hulled Higgins boats, which needed beaches free of coral reefs or other obstacles. On Guadalcanal, the prime alternative was Lunga Point, which was very close to the airfield. Here the coast also was convex in shape; that meant Japanese gunners on one flank would lose sight of boats coming ashore on the opposite flank. Thus enemy firepower would be less effective. Although Twining favored this site, Thomas opted for Red Beach, located four miles to the east. Doctrinally it was a poor site, since it was concave and provided excellent fields of fire to any defender. The distance from the airfield also meant that it would take additional time for the assault force to reach the objective, while supplies dumped ashore would be far from their eventual destination. Thomas gambled that there would be no defenders this far from the airfield, and any counterattack would take longer to arrive, thus giving the assault force time to get ashore and get organized without opposition.

Tulagi was a long, slender island consisting mainly of a wooded ridge running right down to the water, except for a small saddle near its southeastern end. The only suitable beaches were on the northeastern coast at this saddle, since the rest of the island was fringed by coral. Aerial reconnaissance indicated that the Japanese had concentrated all their defenses against the obvious landing site. American planners decided to take on coral and rough terrain instead of the enemy. They would go ashore about halfway up the southwestern coast, which meant that they would have to wade in once the boats touched the reefs and they would not be able to bring artillery or other heavy equipment ashore. There was no alternative to avoid enemy defenses on Gavutu-Tanambogo, so the parachutists would have to land under enemy fire across a seaplane ramp on Gavutu. This attack would go in four hours after the 0800 assaults on Guadalcanal and Tulagi, to allow maximum naval gunfire support.

The operation went off much as the division planned it. The raiders got ashore on Tulagi without opposition, got organized, and were ready for the hard fight for the southern end of the island, which lasted for two days. The 1st and 5th Marines also landed on Guadalcanal unmolested and took the airfield the next day with little fighting. Only Gavutu went awry, since the Japanese defenders had four hours to get ready. Once they recovered from the pre-landing naval bombardment, they savaged the second wave of landing craft. The parachutists eventually seized the high ground by evening, but took heavy casualties. Elements of 3/2 came ashore the next day to help finish the job and then take adjacent Tanambogo.

It would take six months of sometimes intense fighting before Guadalcanal was entirely secured. In the first test of the amphibious doctrine developed in the 1930s, however, the 1st Marine Division and supporting naval forces had proven that they could successfully execute these techniques against a real enemy. The Pacific campaign would bring forth many changes in amphibious tactics and technology, but the daring, pioneering efforts of the men engaged in Watchtower gave American leaders the confidence to move on to subsequent objectives all across the war-torn globe.

Above: *Marines coming ashore on 7 August from nonramp Higgins boats. (National Archives)*

3 June
Aleutians
Japanese forces attack the Aleutian Islands as a diversion from the planned assault on Midway. Ground forces eventually occupy Attu and Kiska Islands, Alaska.
Force Structure
VMSB-243 is organized at Santa Barbara.

4 June
Midway
In the initial aerial attacks of the Battle of Midway, 108 Japanese planes strike the atoll. VMF-221 loses most of its Brewsters and Wildcats, though they destroy or damage about 40 of the enemy. VMSB-241 also suffers heavy losses among its dive bombers, but fails to achieve hits on the enemy fleet. Captain Richard E. Fleming's aircraft crashes into cruiser *Mikuma*. He subsequently receives the Medal of Honor. U.S. Navy aircraft sink four Japanese carriers, and the enemy abandons the planned invasion of the atoll. Over the next two days, American planes from carriers sink and damage more Japanese ships as they withdraw. One U.S. carrier is sunk.

14 June
New Zealand
The advance echelon of the 1st Marine Division arrives in New Zealand.

15 June
Force Structure
The 11th Defense Battalion is formed at Parris Island.

16 June
Force Structure
The 3rd Marines is reactivated at New River, North Carolina.

19 June
Commanders
Vice Admiral Robert L. Ghormley assumes command of the South Pacific Area (a subset of Nimitz's Pacific Ocean Area).

26 June
Guadalcanal
The 1st Marine Division receives the warning order for an amphibious assault against the Guadalcanal-Tulagi area in the Southern Solomons.

30 June
Manpower
The strength of the Marine Corps on active duty is 7,138 officers and 135,475 enlisted.

June
Ireland
Marine Barracks, Londonderry is established in Northern Ireland to protect naval facilities.

1 July
Force Structure
VMF-213 and 214 are commissioned at Ewa, Hawaii. The 5th Barrage Balloon Squadron is organized at Parris Island.

10 July
Bases
Marine Corps Air Station, El Centro, California, is established.

11 July
New Zealand
The last elements of the 1st Marine Division arrive in New Zealand.

14 July
Force Structure
The 21st Marines, an infantry regiment, is organized at New River, North Carolina.
Bases
The Marine Corps Glider Base, Edenton, North Carolina, is established.

15 July
New Hebrides
Elements of the 4th Defense Battalion arrive at Espiritu Santo to help protect an air base there.

20 July
Force Structure
The 23rd Marines, an infantry regiment, is established at New River.

21 July
New Zealand
The 1st Base Depot establishes an advance echelon in New Zealand. Its mission is to provide logistics support to units in the area.

22 July
New Guinea
Japanese forces land at Buna on the north coast of New Guinea to begin an operation to cross the Owen Stanley Mountains and seize Port Moresby with a ground assault.

1 August
Force Structure
The 12th Defense Battalion is organized at San Diego.

2 August
New Hebrides
The first F4F-3 long-range photographic planes of Marine Observation Squadron 251 (VMO-251) land on the recently completed airfield at Espiritu Santo.

7 August
Solomons
In the southern Solomons, the 1st Marine Division (less the 7th Marines) and reinforcing elements (2nd Marines, 1st Raider Battalion, 1st Parachute Battalion, 3rd Defense Batalion) conduct Operation Watchtower, the first Allied offensive amphibious operation in the Pacific. The objectives of Tulagi, Gavutu-Tanambogo, and the half-finished airfield on Guadalcanal are all taken by the next day.

Opposite: *A 1945 recruiting poster depicts a Marine wading across a river at Guadalcanal. ("Enlist Now," Sgt Tom Lovell, Marine Corps Art Collection)*

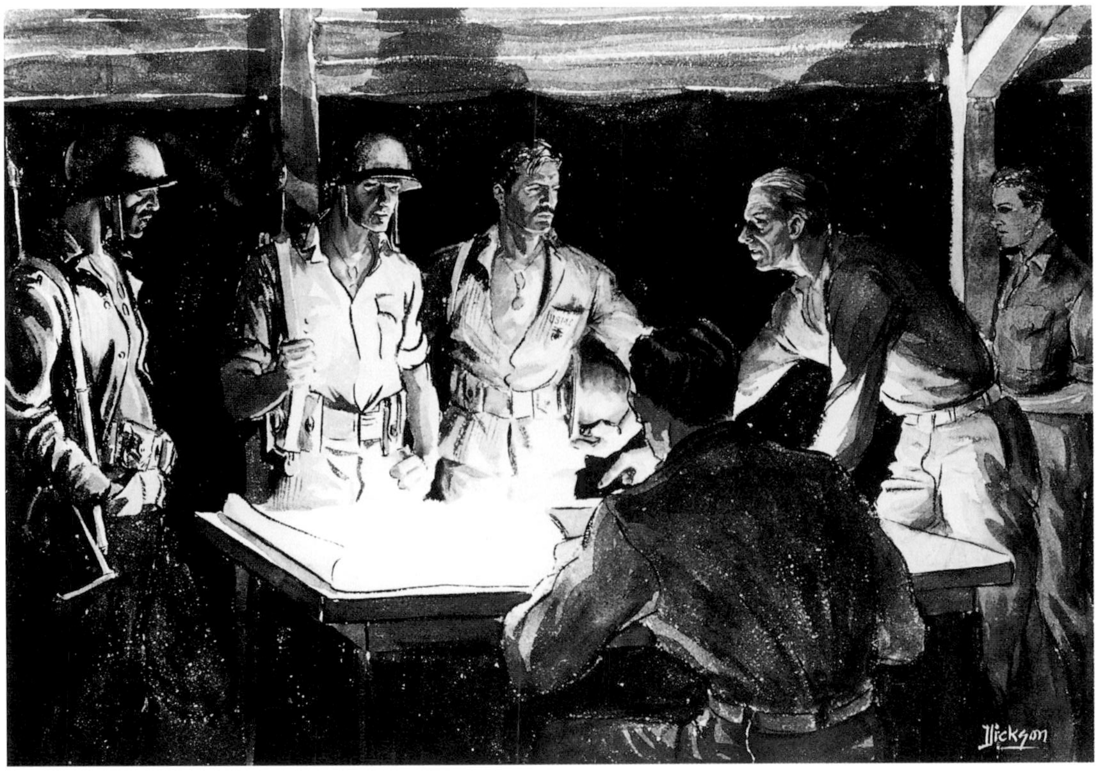

Right: *A Marine briefs members of a patrol on their mission at Guadalcanal in 1942. ("Final Instructions," Col Donald L. Dickson, USMCR, Marine Corps Art Collection)*

8 August
Guadalcanal
During the night Japanese surface forces attack the Allied naval task force off Guadalcanal, sinking four cruisers and damaging one destroyer.

9 August
Guadalcanal
The naval task force withdraws from the lower Solomons without completing the unloading of Marine supplies and forces. The Marines ashore are short of critical items, including food, and begin subsisting on two meals a day to stretch out meager stocks.

12 August
Guadalcanal
Lieutenant Colonel Frank Goettge, 1st Marine Division intelligence officer, leads a 25-man patrol to the Matanikau River area of Guadalcanal to check out reports of Japanese willing to surrender. The patrol is attacked, and only three Marines escape alive.

13 August
Bases
Marine Corps Air Station, Santa Barbara, California, is established.

15 August
Force Structure
Marine Aircraft Wings, Pacific, is organized at San Diego to provide administrative and logistic oversight for all MAWs.
Guadalcanal
CUB One, a Navy aviation ground support unit, arrives on Guadalcanal to provide the initial maintenance echelon for Marine aircraft.

Top: *A Marine cleans his rifle. ("Marine's Best Friend," Col Donald L. Dickson, USMCR, Marine Corps Art Collection)*

Left: *"8 August 1942, Night Action off Savo," William Draper, Navy Art Collection*

Opposite, top: *"Weary Trail," Kerr Eby, Navy Art Collection*

Opposite, bottom: *"Down the Slot: Landing of Japanese Troops on Guadalcanal," John Hamilton, Navy Art Collection*

17 August
Gilberts
Companies A and B of the 2nd Raider Battalion land from submarines on Makin Atoll to destroy enemy installations and conduct a diversionary raid in support of the Guadalcanal offensive. The Marines defeat the garrison, but heavy surf disrupts their withdrawal and delays it until the next night. Marines casualties during the raid are 18 dead, 16 wounded, and 12 missing. Of the latter, nine are captured soon after and beheaded on Kwajalein by the Japanese. Major James Roosevelt, son of the President, participates in the raid as XO of the 2nd Raiders.

18 August
Guadalcanal
Marines complete the airstrip on Guadalcanal and name it Henderson Field after Major Lofton Henderson, who died leading his Marine dive bombers against the Japanese at Midway.
Force Structure
The 51st Defense Battalion is activated at Montford Point, New River, North Carolina. It is destined to train the first African American recruits and become the first African American operational unit in the Marine Corps.

19 August
Guadalcanal
Three companies of the 5th Marines conduct attacks against Japanese forces around Matanikau and Kokumbona villages.

20 August
Guadalcanal
The first echelons of MAG-23 and 1st MAW (19 F4Fs of VMF-223 and 12 SBD-3s of VMSB-232) land on Henderson Field.

BRIGADIER GENERAL EVANS F. CARLSON

Evans Carlson got an early start in his career as a maverick. He ran away from his home in Vermont in 1910 at the age of 14, and two years later bluffed his way past the recruiters to enlist in the Army. He served four years, went into the reserves, and was recalled for duty during the Mexican Border campaign. When the United States entered World War I in 1917, he already had five years of active service under his belt. He soon won a commission, but served on the staff of a division in France that never saw combat. After the war he tried to make it as a salesman, but gave that up in 1922 and enlisted in the Marine Corps. In a few months he earned a commission again. Other than a failed attempt at flight school, his first several years as a Marine lieutenant were unremarkable.

In 1927 Carlson went over to Shanghai with the 4th Marines. There he became regimental intelligence officer and developed a deep interest in China that would shape the remainder of his days. Three years later, commanding an outpost of the Guardia Nacional in Nicaragua, he had his first brush with guerrilla warfare. That became the second guiding star of his career. In his only battle, he successfully engaged and dispersed an enemy band in a daring night attack, for which he received a Navy Cross. There followed a tour with the Legation Guard in Peking, and a stint as executive officer of the presidential guard detachment at Warm Springs, Georgia. In the latter job Carlson developed a friendship with President Franklin D. Roosevelt.

Captain Carlson arrived in Shanghai for his third China tour in July 1937. Along with "Red Mike" Edson, he watched the Japanese seize control of the city. Detailed to duty as

Left: *On 30 September 1942, on Guadalcanal, Admiral Nimitz presents a Navy Cross to LtCol Carlson for his leadership of the Makin Raid. MajGen Vandegrift is on the far left. To the right of Carlson are BGen William H, Rupertus, Col Edson, LtCol Edwin A. Pollock, and Maj John L. Smith. (Marine Corps Research Center)*

Right: *Carlson cuts a "good luck" cake in the wardroom of USS* Nautilus *on the way to Makin. The submarine's skipper, R. W. H. Brockman, Jr., looks on. (National Archives)*

an observer, Carlson sought and received permission to accompany the Chinese Communist 8th Route Army, which was fighting against the Japanese. For the next year he divided his time between the front lines and the temporary Chinese capital of Hangkow. During that time he developed his ideas on guerrilla warfare and military leadership. When a senior naval officer censored him for granting newspaper interviews, Carlson returned to the States and resigned so that he could speak out about the situation in China. He believed passionately that the United States should do more to help the Chinese in their war with Japan.

During the next two years Carlson spoke and wrote on the subject, to include two books ("The Chinese Army" and "Twin Stars of China"), and made another trip to China. With war looming for the United States, he sought to rejoin the Corps in April 1941. Commandant Holcomb granted his request, made him a major in the reserves, and promptly brought him onto active duty. Ten months later he created the 2d Raider Battalion. In August 1942, he led two companies of his outfit on a submarine-borne raid against Makin Atoll far behind the Japanese outer defensive ring. The operation did not go according to plan, but the Marines destroyed the enemy garrison and their audacious action boosted morale on the home front. In November and December that year, he and his battalion conducted a long patrol in the jungles of Guadalcanal and inflicted nearly 500 casualties on the Japanese. For these two campaigns, he received his second and third awards of the Navy Cross.

After his departure from the raiders in 1943, Carlson served as operations officer of the 4th Marine Division. He made the Tarawa landing as an observer and participated with his division in the assaults on Kwajalein and Saipan. In the latter battle he received severe wounds in the arm and leg while pulling his wounded radio operator out of the line of fire of an enemy machine gun. After the war Carlson retired from the Marine Corps and ran briefly in 1946 for a seat in the California Senate before poor health forced him out of the campaign. He died in May 1947.

21 August
Guadalcanal
The roughly 900 Japanese soldiers of the Ichiki Force attack the 1st Marines along what was thought to be the Tenaru River (actually the Ilu River). After repulsing the assault, Marines cross the river and envelop the remaining enemy, almost completely wiping out the attackers. Captain John L. Smith of VMF-223 scores the first aerial kill for a Guadalcanal-based fighter, shooting down a Japanese Zero.

22 August
Force Structure
The 4th Marine Base Defense Air Wing is organized at Ewa, Hawaii. It is eventually redesignated 4th MAW.
Guadalcanal
The first Army Air Forces aircraft arrive at Henderson Field—five Bell Airacobra P-400 fighter planes of the 67th Fighter Squadron.

24 August
Guadalcanal
Marine fighter planes of VMF-223 have their first big aerial battle with the Japanese, downing 16 enemy at a cost of four of their own aircraft. Captain Marion E. Carl becomes the first Marine ace of the war after he destroys three enemy planes. Air battles become an almost-daily occurrence hereafter. Eleven Navy SBDs from damaged *Enterprise* (CV-6) land at Henderson Field to temporarily reinforce what is now referred to colloquially as Cactus Air Force.
Training
General H. M. Smith turns over command of the Amphibious Force Atlantic Fleet to the Army. Smith and his staff then form the Amphibious Training Staff, FMF.
Force Structure
MAG-25 begins arriving in Hawaii.

25 August
Guadalcanal
The dive bombers of VMSB-232 assist in sinking a Japanese destroyer and a transport in the Battle

Above: *Maj John L. Smith, Maj Robert E. Galer, and Capt Marion E. Carl (left to right) after receiving Navy Crosses for aerial victories over the Japanese. (Marine Corps Research Center)*

Left: *Casualties departing Guadalcanal, August 1942. ("The Wounded," Dwight Shepler, Naval Art Collection)*

of the Eastern Solomons, which turns back an enemy effort to land troops on Guadalcanal.

26 August
Manpower
The first African American recruits arrive at Montford Point to begin training.

27–28 August
Guadalcanal
Landing craft place 1/5 ashore near Kokumbona, leading to two days of inconclusive fighting with Japanese forces near the Matanikau River.

30 August
Guadalcanal
Captain John Smith shoots down four Zeros, temporarily making him the leading Marine ace, with nine kills. VMF-224 and VMSB-231 arrive on Henderson Field. The Kawaguchi Brigade begins landing on Guadalcanal.

1 September
Guadalcanal
Elements of the 6th Naval Construction Battalion arrive, primarily to assist in maintaining Henderson Field.
Force Structure
The 12th Marines is reactivated as an artillery regiment at San Diego.

3 September
Guadalcanal
Brigadier General Roy S. Geiger and the command echelon of 1st MAW reach Guadalcanal via a MAG-25 R4D transport and assume control of all air elements on the island.
Force Structure
MAG-25 begins shifting from Hawaii to New Caledonia. (MAG-25 will become the nucleus of South Pacific Combat Air Transport Command or SCAT, which will remain in existence until February 1945.)

Above: *Guadalcanal, 1942. ("Rifleman," Col Donald L. Dickson, USMCR, Marine Corps Art Collection)*

Right: *Edson's Ridge on Guadalcanal, after the mid-September 1942 battle. (Marine Corps Research Center)*

4 September
Guadalcanal
Two companies of the 1st Raider Battalion sweep Savo Island for reported enemy, but find nothing.

7 September
Force Structure
VMF-123 and VMSB-144 are organized at San Diego and VMF-124 and VMSB-143 at Kearney.

8 September
Guadalcanal
The 1st Raider Battalion and attached 1st Parachute Battalion conduct an amphibious raid at Tasimboko and defeat the rear echelon of the Kawaguchi Brigade. Elements of the 3rd Barrage Balloon Squadron arrive on Tulagi.

12–14 September
Guadalcanal
The 1st Raider Battalion and 1st Parachute Battalion defend a low coral ridge south of Henderson Field during two nights of assaults by the Kawaguchi Brigade. Toward the end of the second night, 2/5 is brought up to reinforce the raiders and parachutists. The Japanese are turned back after suffering heavy casualties in what becomes known as the Battle of Edson's Ridge.

14 September
Samoa
The 3rd Marines arrives at Tutuila.

Above: *Marine ingenuity—a cook prepares pancakes on a Japanese safe turned into a stove. (Marine Corps Research Center)*

Left: *A 40mm antiaircraft gun trained up to the sky. (National Archives)*

Right: *A Marine carrying a .30-caliber, air-cooled machine gun fords a stream in the South Pacific. (National Archives)*

Below: *A Stuart light tank, nicknamed "The Blizzard" by its crew, is hoisted from a cargo ship for transfer ashore at Guadalcanal. (Marine Corps Research Center)*

Force Structure
VMSB-242 and VMSB-244 swap designations.

15 September
Force Structure
VMO-151 is redesignated VMSB-151. VMD-1 and 2 become respectively VMD-154 and 254 (and soon after swap designations with each other). The new VMSB-242 becomes VMF-215.

16 September
Force Structure
The 3rd Marine Division is activated at Camp Elliott. It is initially composed of the 9th Marines, 21st Marines, 23rd Marines, 12th Marines (artillery), and 19th Marines (an engineer regiment). The 3rd Parachute Battalion is organized in southern California.

18 September
Guadalcanal
The 7th Marines land and return to the 1st Marine Division. The same ships depart with the depleted 1st Parachute Battalion.

19 September
Bases
Marine Corps Air Station, Eagle Mountain Lake is established at Fort Worth, Texas, to serve as a glider training base.

20 September
Force Structure
The 3rd Raider Battalion is organized in Samoa.

BRIGADIER GENERAL JOSEPH J. FOSS

Joe Foss grew up near Sioux Falls, South Dakota, coming to maturity during the bleak Depression years of the early 1930s. Following his father's death in Joe's junior year in high school, he ran the family farm until his brother was old enough to take over. Despite the economic hard times, he put himself through college. He also played sports in school and served in the National Guard during his senior year. The curly headed six-footer had yearned to be a flier, however, and had even paid out some of his hard-earned dollars for private pilot lessons. After graduating from college in the summer of 1940 at the age of 25, he enlisted in the Marine Corps Reserve, then soon earned an appointment as an aviation cadet. He won his wings and his commission in March 1941.

A natural pilot, Foss found himself assigned to instructor duty. His requests for transfer to a squadron got him into a photo reconnaissance unit. Finally he managed to join VMF-121 in the fall of 1942. Already a captain, he served as the executive officer. On 9 October, Foss and the 20 F4F-4s of his squadron reached Guadalcanal. He wasted no time in making his presence felt. On his fourth day, he shot down his first enemy plane—a Zero. He also almost met his own end that day. Three other Japanese fighters jumped him and shot up his oil pump. He managed to reach Henderson Field and make a dead-stick landing. That night, Japanese battleships pounded the airstrip and destroyed a majority of Cactus Air Force's planes. Foss and others gamely withstood the

Left: *"Joe Foss Downs a Zero," Robert T. Horvath, Marine Corps Art Collection*

Opposite: *Maj Joe Foss in the spring of 1944 as a squadron commander. (National Archives)*

bombardment. The next day he was aloft again and downed his second Zero. Within a few days, he added three more to his credit in a single mission—becoming an ace in his first few days of combat.

The intrepid Marine captain continued ringing up an impressive score. On 23 October he knocked down four Zeros while fending off a Japanese bomber raid. Two days later, he claimed two enemy during an initial attack, and three more in a subsequent battle that day. He had been on the island two weeks and had 16 kills. On 7 November, Foss and several of his fellow Wildcats launched with bombs under their wings to assist in attacking a reported convoy. Instead they came across six floatplane versions of the Zero. Foss got one, while his wingmates downed the others. Coming out of that melee, he saw a float biplane. The enemy pilot maneuvered deftly, giving his rear gunner a good shot. Foss's Wildcat took a beating, but gave more than it got, as the enemy aircraft went down. Limping back toward base, he destroyed a third Japanese floatplane. His engine finally gave out, and he landed on the water near the island of Malaita. Again luck was with him, as he had to scramble out of his plane after it had sunk below the surface. A missionary and natives in a dugout rescued him that night from the water.

Foss was evacuated from Guadalcanal on 19 November with a severe case of malaria. He left with 20 kills, the largest tally of any American pilot to date in the war. On the last day of 1942, he returned to Henderson Field still full of fight, but 37 pounds lighter. In the next six weeks he downed six more enemy aircraft, tying him with America's leading ace in World War I, the legendary Eddie Rickenbacker. Called back to the States, Foss received the Medal of Honor for his feat. Although he later formed VMF-115—a Corsair outfit—and took it into battle in the Central Solomons, he found few enemy left there and did not add to his score. At the end of the war, his 26 kills ranked second among Marine aces only to Gregory "Pappy" Boyington's 28 (six of them as a Flying Tiger in China).

Following the war, Foss rose to the rank of lieutenant colonel in the reserves, but in 1947 he transferred to the Air National Guard, where he soon took command of a fighter squadron in his home state. He served in the South Dakota legislature, returned to active duty for two years during the Korean War, was elected to two terms as governor, and went on to be commissioner of the American Football League and president of the National Rifle Association. He eventually closed out his time in the Guard as a brigadier general.

22 September
New Caledonia
The 5th Barrage Balloon Squadron arrives on New Caledonia.

23–27 September
Guadalcanal
In the 2nd Battle of the Matanikau, 1/7 is briefly trapped behind enemy lines following an amphibious landing, while strong enemy defenses prevent the 1st Raider Battalion and 2/5 from crossing the river. Lieutenant Colonel Lewis B. Puller oversees a fighting amphibious withdrawal of 1/7.

24 September
Bases
Marine Corps Air Station, Mojave, California, is established.

25 September
Guadalcanal
Elements of VMF-121 arrive on the island.

Force Structure
The 13th Defense Battalion is organized at Guantanamo Bay.

1 October
Force Structure
General H. M. Smith's Amphibious Training Staff, FMF is disbanded and takes over the duties of the headquarters element of the Amphibious Corps, Pacific Fleet at San Diego. The I Marine Amphibious Corps is formed at San Diego under Major General Clayton B. Vogel. VMO-155 and VMF-441 are organized on Samoa.

3 October
Guadalcanal
Lieutenant Colonel Harold W. Bauer of VMF-212 shoots down four enemy planes and becomes an ace while making an inspection visit to Guadalcanal.

4 October
Force Structure
Headquarters, Marine Aircraft Wing, Pacific arrives at Ewa from San Diego.

October 7–9
Guadalcanal
In the 3rd Battle of the Matanikau, 3/2, 2/7, and 1/7 cross the upper Matanikau and attack toward the coast, destroying a Japanese battalion, while 2/5, 3/5, and the 1st Raider Battalion defeat a Japanese company holding the mouth of the river.

9 October
Guadalcanal
VMF-121 arrives on Henderson Field.

11 October
Guadalcanal
In the Battle of Cape Esperance, a U.S. naval force defeats a Japanese bombardment group in a night surface action.

13 October
Guadalcanal
A convoy deposits the Army's 164th Infantry regiment at Guadalcanal and takes off the depleted 1st Raider Battalion for recuperation in New Caledonia. That night, two Japanese battleships bombard Henderson Field, destroying

Opposite: *"Marine Airman," Kerr Eby, Navy Art Collection*

Right: *Marines hunker down in a bomb shelter during a Japanese bombardment. ("Naval Gunfire," Col Donald R. Dickson, USMCR, Marine Corps Art Collection)*

Below: *"Japanese Naval Bombardment of Henderson Field," John Hamilton, Navy Art Collection*

half of Cactus Air Force and large quantities of aviation gasoline.

14 October
Guadalcanal
Japanese planes and artillery bomb and shell Henderson Field by day, then two cruisers bombard the airstrip that night.

15 October
Guadalcanal
Cactus Air Force gets a few planes aloft to attack Japanese transports landing men and supplies on the island.

16 October
Guadalcanal
Bauer and his VMF-212 arrive after a flight from Efate, just as a Japanese air attack is ending. Despite being nearly out of fuel, Bauer engages the enemy and shoots down four dive bombers. For this feat he eventually receives the Medal of Honor. MAG-14 relieves MAG-23 as the aviation administrative and logistics element on Guadalcanal.

18 October
Commanders
Vice Admiral William F. Halsey replaces Ghormley in command of the South Pacific Area.

GUNNERY SERGEANT JOHN BASILONE

John Basilone was born on 4 November 1916 in Buffalo, New York, where his Italian-born father worked as a tailor. Later, the family moved to his mother's hometown of Raritan, New Jersey. Basilone attended a Catholic grade school, but never finished high school. After working for a few years, he joined the Army at 19 and spent his three-year tour in the Philippines. Back in civilian life in 1939, he became a truck driver in Maryland. With the war in Europe looking bleak in July 1940, Basilone went to the recruiting station in Baltimore and enlisted in the Marines. The veteran soldier soon bore the nickname "Manila John" (based on his prior service) and quickly moved up the ranks in the Corps. He made private first class in two months, corporal in eight more, and sergeant in another eight.

From the first, Basilone served with the water-cooled, .30-caliber Browning heavy machine guns of Company D, 1st Battalion, 7th Marines. His battalion commander after the summer of 1941 was none other than the already famous "Chesty" Puller. After a few months on Samoa in 1942, the 7th Marines rejoined the 1st Marine Division at Guadalcanal in September. Although Basilone and his guns missed out on the desperate fighting of the 2nd Battle of the Matanikau, he and the heavies would more than make up for it at the Battle for Henderson Field. On the night of 24–25 October, 1/7 was defending the southern zone of the Marine perimeter—a sector normally held by two battalions. It was lightly guarded because the Japanese were supposed to be attacking elsewhere. Instead, the infantrymen of the Sendai Division launched assault after assault against the Marine lines.

Basilone was leading two sections of machine guns near the left-center of 1/7's position. The Marines had one advantage—they had hacked out clear fields of fire from the jungle that fronted their position. General Vandegrift considered it to be "a machine gunner's paradise." As the Japanese swarmed forward in company-size attacks that night, Basilone's guns cut them to ribbons. When enemy grenades knocked out the two crews of one of his sections, the sergeant rushed through the fire to their gun pits carrying a fresh weapon. He got the survivors organized to man it, then put one of the original guns back into action himself. One of his fellow Marines observed the sergeant using his pistol whenever the Japanese got too close to bring the machine gun to bear. As reserves from a nearby Army regiment fed into the line to beef it up, Basilone turned over the gun to others and went back across the exposed, fire-swept ground to bring up badly needed ammunition.

The last of the enemy attacks that night petered out at dawn. During the day, the intermingled Army and Marine battalions disentangled, with 1/7 shifting to the right to concentrate on defending Edson's Ridge. That night the Japanese renewed their attack, but concentrated largely on the zone now held by the Army's 164th Infantry. But when the lines had been thinnest, Basilone and a few other stalwart Marines had held against the odds. A few days later, Puller recommended just one man—the machine gun sergeant from New Jersey—for a Medal of Honor for this critical battle that saved Henderson Field.

The Marine Corps promoted Basilone to platoon sergeant and brought him home to receive the Medal of Honor from the President. Along with other surviving heroes of early campaigns, he toured the country to help sell war bonds and motivate industrial workers. He ended up with easy duty at the Marine barracks in the Washington Navy Yard, where he could have sat out the remainder of the war. Instead, he insisted on going back to the infantry. In January 1944, he got his wish and transferred to the 1st Battalion, 27th Marines. While stationed at Camp Pendleton with the 5th Marine Division, he was promoted to gunnery sergeant and also met and married Lena Riggi, a sergeant in the Women's Reserve.

On 19 February 1945, he was in one of the early waves of the landing on Iwo Jima. When a blockhouse barred the way forward for his company, he worked his way around to the flank under continuous fire from machine guns, mortars, and artillery. He finally reached it, clambered on top, and tossed a demolitions charge and grenades into the firing ports to silence it. Later he came upon a tank trapped in a minefield. Braving more indirect fire, he guided it back to safer ground. As his outfit moved up onto the exposed apron of an airfield, a heavy barrage came down, killing three men instantly and mortally wounding Basilone. He died soon after. For his feats that day, he was awarded the Navy Cross.

Manila John Basilone. (National Archives)

23 October
Guadalcanal
Marine antitank guns and artillery crush a diversionary Japanese tank and infantry assault across the Matanikau.
Captain Joseph J. Foss shoots down four Zeros.
Force Structure
The 4th Raider Battalion is organized in southern California.

24–26 October
Guadalcanal
In the Battle for Henderson Field, the Sendai Division attacks the position of 1/7 south of the airstrip. Elements of the 164th Infantry reinforce Marine lines during the night and assume responsibility for the threatened zone the second night. The Japanese are repulsed with heavy losses. Another diversionary attack across the Matanikau is defeated by 2/7. At sea, U.S. naval forces turn back a Japanese fleet in the Battle of Santa Cruz. In the air on the 25th, Joe Foss shoots down five enemy planes during two sorties, bringing his total kills to 16.

28 October
Force Structure
The I Marine Amphibious Corps (I MAC) arrives at Noumea, New Caledonia. It is initially purely an administrative command to control Marine units in rear areas of the South Pacific command.

31 October
Guadalcanal
On this day and the next, elements of VMF-211 and VMSB-132 reach Henderson Field.

November
New Hebrides
MAG-11 moves to Espiritu Santo.

1 November
Guadalcanal
VMF-112 arrives on the island.

1–3 November
Guadalcanal
With support from the division scout-snipers and 3/7 screening the flank, the 5th Marines attack

Opposite, top: *Supplies are brought ashore at Lunga Point, Guadalcanal. ("Disgorging Stores off Lunga Point," John Hamilton, Naval Art Collection)*

Opposite, below: *A Guadalcanal Marine airs his feet and cleans his Springfield. (National Archives)*

Right: *LtCol Carlson and his son, Lt Evans Carlson, both of the 2nd Raiders. (Marine Corps Research Center)*

west across the Matanikau and destroy a pocket of Japanese around Point Cruz. The 2nd Marines and 1/164 move past Point Cruz to establish a new defensive line to the west.

2 November
Guadalcanal
A battery each of Marine and Army 155mm guns arrive on the island.

3–9 November
Guadalcanal
The Battle of Koli Point opens with 2/7 skirmishing with Japanese reinforcements arriving by sea to the east of the Marine perimeter. The 164th Infantry and 1/7 move up to assist and help destroy part of the enemy, with the rest escaping inland.

Right: *Marines and soldiers offload aviation ordnance from a landing craft at Guadalcanal. (Marine Corps Research Center)*

Left: *Marines wait on the beach for a trip out to transports that will take them away from Guadalcanal in January 1943. (National Archives)*

Opposite: *A soldier bids farewell to departing Marines as the Guadalcanal campaign draws to a close. (Marine Corps Research Center)*

4 November
Guadalcanal
The 8th Marines and 1/10 arrive at Lunga Point. Two companies of the 2nd Raider Battalion secure a new beachhead at Aola Bay and are joined by the 1st Battalion, 147th Infantry, a battery of Army artillery, and a Seabee unit.

6 November
Guadalcanal
The 2nd Raider companies set out from Aola to track down enemy elements escaping the encirclement at Koli Point.

7 November
Manpower
The Marine Corps Women's Reserve is authorized by the Commandant, although actual enlistments are not taken until February 1943.

8 November
North Africa
Operation Torch begins, with U.S. and other Allied forces landing at several points along the coast of North Africa. Marine detachments serve on board the larger U.S. Navy warships and a handful of Marines participate in the landings.

9 November
Force Structure
The 6th Barrage Balloon Squadron is formed at New River.

10 November
Guadalcanal
Three more companies of the 2nd Raider Battalion land at Tasimboko and move to join the rest of the battalion.
Force Structure
The 3rd MAW is organized at Cherry Point. The 16th Defense Battalion is activated on Johnston Island.

11 November
Guadalcanal
Elements of the 2nd and 8th Marines and the 164th Infantry pull back from the Point Cruz area to the eastern side of the Matanikau in preparation for an anticipated Japanese assault on the main American perimeter. The 2nd Raider Battalion engages Japanese forces at Asamama.

12 November
Guadalcanal
Captain Foss shoots down three Japanese planes, making him the first American pilot to achieve 20 kills in the war. VMSB-131 and 142 arrive.

12–15 November
Guadalcanal
In the naval battle for Guadalcanal, U.S. surface forces drive back a Japanese bombardment group on the night of the 12th, U.S. aircraft destroy most of a large troop convoy during daylight hours on the 14th, another U.S. surface fleet beats back a Japanese bombardment force that night, and U.S. artillery and aviation destroy the remaining transports on the 15th. This is the last major Japanese attempt to retake Guadalcanal.

13 November
New Georgia
Japanese troops arrive at Munda Point, New Georgia, in the central Solomons to begin building an airfield. This will allow Japanese fighter planes to spend more time above Guadalcanal, since it is much closer to Henderson Field than existing Japanese bases at Rabaul.

16 November
Force Structure
The first Marine night fighter squadron, VMF(N)-531, is organized at Cherry Point.

18 November
Guadalcanal
MAG-23 arrives in San Diego following its stint at Guadalcanal.

24 November
Force Structure
MLG-71 moves from Parris Island to MCAS, Eagle Mountain Lake.

30 November
Guadalcanal
The 2nd Raider Battalion surprises and routs a Japanese force on the slopes of Mount Austen. A U.S. Navy task force loses one cruiser sunk and three heavily damaged while turning back a resupply run by Japanese warships in the Battle of Tassafaronga. The Japanese lose one destroyer.

1 December
Force Structure
VMF-311 is organized at Cherry Point, North Carolina.

Left: *Cpl John Miller instructs Marines of the Women's Reserve in aircraft-engine maintenance procedures at the Naval Air Technical Training Center. More than 1,000 female Marines served in aviation maintenance during the war. (National Archives)*

5 December
Manpower
President Roosevelt orders the end of voluntary enlistments for those 18–37 years old for all services effective in January. Those 17, or older than 37, are still allowed to enlist. Thereafter, Marine liaisons at the draft induction centers work to arrange for draftees who want to serve in the Corps to do so.

9 December
Guadalcanal
General Vandegrift turns command of Guadalcanal over to the Major General Alexander M. Patch of the Army's Americal Division. The 1st Marine Division begins its movement to Australia, with the 5th Marines departing this day, followed soon after by the 1st Marines.

15 December
Guadalcanal
The 2nd Raider Battalion departs Guadalcanal for Espiritu Santo.

17 December
New Georgia
The Japanese complete an airstrip at Munda Point.

20 December
Bases
Marine Barracks, New River is renamed Camp Lejeune.

22 December
New Caledonia
The 1st and 6th Barrage Balloon Squadrons arrive on New Caledonia.

29 December
New Hebrides
MAG-12 begins moving to Efate. The entire group will be there by 28 January 1943.

1943

1 January
Force Structure
Marine Base Defense Air Group 41 (MBDAG-41) and VMF-113 are organized at El Toro. MBDAG-42 and VMF-422 are established at San Diego. MBDAG-43, VMF-216, and VMSB-235 are activated at El Centro. MBDAG-44, VMF-225, and VMSB-236 are formed at Mojave. VMSB-331 is organized at Cherry Point.

4 January
Guadalcanal
The command echelon of the 2nd Marine Division and the 6th Marines arrive on the island.

11 January
New Caledonia
The 2nd Parachute Battalion arrives on the island.

13 January
Guadalcanal
The 2nd Marine Division begins a coordinated attack with the Army's 25th Division to destroy remaining Japanese forces west of the American perimeter on Guadalcanal. The advance continues through 17 January.

15 January
Guadalcanal
Joe Foss shoots down three enemy planes, giving him 26 kills and tying Army Captain Eddie Rickenbacker's World War I American record. The 2nd Marines leave Guadalcanal for New Zealand.

Force Structure
The 14th Defense Battalion is organized on Tulagi.
Manpower
Anne A. Lentz becomes the first Marine woman reservist when she is commissioned a captain following her civilian work in designing the uniforms for the Women's Reserve program.

20 January
Guadalcanal
The 6th Marines and the 2nd Marine Division artillery are joined with Army elements to form the CAM (Composite Army-Marine) Division. This organization participates in attacks designed to destroy the remaining enemy forces in western Guadalcanal. The operation continues through 8 February, when American forces reach Tassafaronga Point.
Force Structure
MAG-24 departs California for Ewa Field.

Right: *A Stuart light tank on the ramp of a tank lighter. The Marine Corps relied on these light models early in the war because amphibious landing craft were not yet capable of bringing in heavier tanks during an assault. (National Archives)*

29 January
HQMC
Ruth Cheney Streeter is commissioned a major and named as director of the Marine Corps Women's Reserve.

31 January
Guadalcanal
1st Lt Jefferson J. DeBlanc of VMF-112 shoots down five enemy Zeros in a single mission over the central Solomons, giving him a total of eight kills. For this feat he will receive the Medal of Honor.

1 February
Force Structure
MAG-31, 32, 33, and 34, VMF-321, and VMSB-341 are organized at Cherry Point.

9 February
Guadalcanal
The island is declared secured. Total Marine casualties during the campaign are 1,504 killed and 2,916 wounded. Losses among Navy personnel serving with Marines units are 36 killed and 101 wounded.

13 February
Manpower
The first women are enlisted into the Marine Corps for World War II.

15 February
Solomons
All land-based aircraft in the southern Solomons are placed under a single new command, Aircraft Solomons (AirSols). This is a joint (multiservice) and combined (multinational) force.

20 February
Force Structure
The 4th Barrage Balloon Squadron is deactivated on Samoa.

21 February
Russells
The 3rd Raider Battalion makes an unopposed landing on Pavuvu Island in the Russells. The 11th Defense Battalion follows the 43rd Infantry Division ashore on nearby Banika Island.

1 March
Force Structure
VMO-351 and VMB-413 (the Marine Corps' first medium bomber squadron) are organized at Cherry Point.

Bases
Marine Corps Air Base Kearney Mesa is established adjacent to Camp Elliott, California.

8 March
Force Structure
The 1st Marine Depot Company is formed, with primarily African American enlisted Marines. It is the first of 51 such units, which have the mission of unloading supplies at the beach and moving them inland during an amphibious assault.

12 March
Technology
The first Marine F4U Chance-Vought Corsair fighter planes enter combat when VMF-124 arrives at Henderson Field.

13 March
Manpower
The first women officer candidates report for training at Mount Holyoke College in Massachusetts.

14 March
Russells
MAG-21 begins deploying to Banika Island.

15 March
Force Structure
The 1st Raider Regiment is established to command all four raider battalions. The 3rd and 4th Raider Battalions arrived in Espiritu Santo during February.

16 March
Force Structure
VMJ-353 is organized at San Diego.

17 March
Bases
Marine Corps Air Station, El Toro is formally commissioned in southern California.

Opposite, top: *Lt Merrill B. Twining. As a LtCol at Guadalcanal, he would help mastermind the operations of the 1st Marine Division. (Marine Corps Historical Center)*

Opposite, bottom: *Lt Mitchell Paige, who received the Medal of Honor as a machine-gun section leader on Guadalcanal. (National Archives)*

Top: *Lt Jim Swett. (Marine Corps Historical Center)*

Left: *Master Gunnery Sergeant Leland "Lou" Diamond, the expert mortarman of the 1st Marine Division on Guadalcanal. (Marine Corps Historical Center)*

Left: *Thin, hungry Marines man a 75mm pack howitzer on Guadalcanal. (National Archives)*

Opposite: *Marine Wildcats lined up on the fighter strip at Guadalcanal in April 1943, ready to carry the war further into Japanese-occupied territory. (National Archives)*

20 March
Bougainville
Marine Torpedo-Bomber Squadron 143 (VMSB-143) conducts the first aerial mine-laying mission in the South Pacific, near Bougainville.

21 March
New Georgia
A small group of Marine scouts from the Raiders land at Segi Plantation on New Georgia to reconnoiter landing beaches for a planned invasion.

24 March
Manpower
The first women recruits report for boot camp at Hunter College in New York City. The Marine Women's Reserve training facility is co-located with the Navy's WAVEs training program at this prestigious university.

26 March
Force Structure
The 24th Marines, an infantry regiment, is organized at Camp Pendleton.

31 March
Samoa
The 2nd Marine Brigade is disbanded in Samoa.

1 April
Guadalcanal
The Japanese launch the I Operation, an aerial offensive against Guadalcanal. It lasts until 16 April.
Force Structure
MAG-51, the first Marine night fighter group, and VMF(N)-532 are established at Cherry Point. The 1st Parachute Regiment is organized at New Caledonia with the 1st, 2nd, and recently arrived 3rd Parachute Battalions.

2 April
Force Structure
MAG-35 and VMJ-352 are formed at Cherry Point. The 4th Parachute Battalion begins organizing in southern California.

4 April
Guadalcanal
MAG-12 moves to Guadalcanal in place of MAG-14, which shifts to New Zealand.

7 April
Guadalcanal
Allied fighters repel the largest Japanese air raid (about 170 planes) on Guadalcanal in months. 1st Lt James E. Swett of VMF-221 shoots down seven dive bombers before crash landing his damaged plane in the water. For this he receives the Medal of Honor.

9 April
New Caledonia
The 3rd Barrage Balloon Squadron arrives at New Caledonia.

17 April
Aleutians
Part of VMO-155 goes on board *Nassau* (CVE-16) to participate in the reconquest of Attu.

18 April
Bougainville
Army P-38s shoot down Admiral Yamamoto's transport plane over Bougainville. Marine aviators participate in planning the operation.

1 May
Force Structure
The 25th Marines, an infantry regiment, is organized at Camp Lejeune. VMSB-133 is organized at El Toro and VMTB-134 at Santa Barbara.

11 May
Aleutians
U.S. Army forces land on Attu in the Aleutians. The seizure of the island is completed on 3 June.

13 May
Solomons
1st Lieutenant Kenneth A. Walsh of VMF-124 shoots down three Zeros in the Solomons, giving him a total of six and making him the first Corsair ace.
North Africa
Allied forces complete the North African campaign following the defeat and withdrawal of the last Axis forces.

19 May
Bougainville
VMSB-143 conducts another aerial mine-laying mission in the waters around the island. Two TBF torpedo bombers are lost to heavy antiaircraft fire. Repeat attacks on 20 and 23 May complete the mission without further loss.

29 May
Force Structure
The Marine glider program is disestablished.

31 May
Force Structure
VMSB-143 is redesignated VMTB-143.

ON THE OFFENSIVE

ON THE OFFENSIVE

JUNE 1943–SEPTEMBER 1945

By the summer of 1943 the Marine Corps and the nation had passed through the most difficult phases of mobilization. Now it was time to switch over to full-scale offensive operations. The Corps found itself involved in two major and distinct campaigns. The first was a continuation of operations in the South Pacific theater. From Guadalcanal, U.S. and Allied forces would move north to reduce the Japanese air and naval bastion at Rabaul, on the eastern end of New Britain Island. This also would facilitate Army General Douglas MacArthur's push through New Guinea and on to the Philippines. The other main effort for the Corps was in the Central Pacific, which featured a drive straight across the Pacific toward the Japanese homeland.

The South Pacific campaign was fought on the ground mainly by the 1st and 3rd Marine Divisions, raiders, parachutists, and some of the defense battalions. The Central Pacific, which ultimately involved much bigger battles, employed all six Marine divisions. During the middle part of the war, Marine aviation was primarily engaged in the South Pacific. By the final year, Leatherneck squadrons were playing a larger role in the Central Pacific, but also supporting the Army in the Philippines and operating off Navy carriers. A smattering of Marines participated in other battles around the globe, including the campaigns in North Africa and Europe.

The Marines almost found themselves on the sidelines in the South Pacific, due to an unaggressive corps commander. An Army division was the main show on New Georgia starting in June 1943, though the raiders and defense battalions provided significant support. A revitalized I Marine Amphibious Corps (later redesignated III Amphibious Corps—IIIAC) and 3rd Marine Division spearheaded the November landing at Bougainville. The 1st Marine Division conducted the main assault on the west end of New Britain in December, then fought one of its toughest battles ever at Peleliu in September 1944 in support of MacArthur's offensive into the Philippines.

The Central Pacific campaign opened in November 1943 with the 2nd Marine Division's assault on Tarawa Atoll. Here, for the first time, tracked landing vehicles were used as amphibian troop carriers. They won their spurs hauling the initial waves of Marines across the shallow reef that guarded Betio Island. The frightful price of over 1,000 dead for the half-square-mile lump of sand shocked the American public, especially after the government released photos of Marine bodies floating off the beach. Nevertheless, the bloody battle proved that the Corps had developed the right doctrine and equipment to enable it to overcome even the strongest enemy resistance at the water's edge. The 4th Marine Division opened the Marshalls campaign in January 1944. The V Amphibious Corps (VAC—2nd and 4th Marine Divisions and Army 27th Infantry Division) landed on Saipan in June 1944, and followed up with Tinian in July. IIIAC (3rd Marine Division,

Pages 304-305: *Reinforcements flow ashore from Higgins boats during the early days of the Bougainville campaign in November 1943. (National Archives)*

Right: *A view of the Tarawa landing by a combat artist who observed it firsthand. ("Bullets and Barbed Wire," Kerr Eby, Naval Art Collection)*

1st Provisional Marine Brigade, and Army 77th Infantry Division) assaulted Guam in July. VAC (now the 3rd, 4th, and 5th Marine Divisions) launched the epic battle of Iwo Jima in February 1945. IIIAC (now the 1st, 2nd, and 6th Marine Divisions) landed on Okinawa as part of Tenth Army in April. While both Leatherneck corps prepared in late summer for the invasion of Japan, the atomic bomb helped bring the war to an end. The cost had been high, but the Marine divisions and their supporting units had relentlessly carried the war to the enemy and rooted determined warriors out of some of the most formidable defenses ever devised.

During the last two years of the war, the Corps underwent a number of changes. As better amphibious transports and landing craft became available, the Marines acquired much heavier equipment and utilized more and more firepower. Some specialized combat forces such as the raiders, parachutists, and most of the defense battalions disappeared to free up manpower for the six divisions. Other new types of units came into being, such as the ammunition and depot companies needed to maintain the flow of material into the maw of corps-sized operations. Tables of organizations of units changed significantly, too. One of the most important innovations was the shift from the prewar unitary 8-man rifle squad to the 13-man outfit built around the revolutionary concept of the 4-man fireteam. After the demise of the raiders, the Corps developed a new light unit devoted to amphibious reconnaissance, which later would become the forerunner of force reconnaissance. Training grew more specialized, with most every skill from cooks to communicators having a separate school. There was a training program after boot camp for infantrymen, as well, but the high rate of casualties in the latter stages of the war prevented the manpower system from letting most new Marines complete the full syllabus.

Marine aviation made use of improving communications equipment to make dramatic advances in doctrine and techniques for close air support. Regrettably, there were few opportunities to provide this tremendous capability to Marines on the ground. At Okinawa, for instance, where Marine air formed a large portion of the aviation element supporting Tenth Army, most Leatherneck fighter squadrons were assigned to combat air patrols. In many other cases, Navy squadrons on carriers supported the amphibious assaults. The Corps finally managed to get squadrons dedicated to close air support on escort carriers, but not until very late in the war. Marine air made its finest showing in the close air support role in the Philippines, perfecting the new methods in combat and setting a standard that left Army ground commanders begging for more. The Marine air-ground team was never effectively re-formed after the breakup of 1941, but the two parts were each honed to a keen edge of excellence at the end of the war.

ON THE OFFENSIVE

JUNE 1943 – SEPTEMBER 1945

1943

June
Force Structure
VMSB-131 and 232 are redesignated VMTB-131 and 232.

1 June
Force Structure
The 14th Marines (an artillery regiment) is activated at Camp Lejeune. VMF-312 is formed at Parris Island. VMSB-332 is organized at Cherry Point.

7 June
Guadalcanal
The Japanese make an unusually large aerial attack against Guadalcanal in an effort to erode growing U.S. power on the island. Allied fighter planes turn back the attack and inflict heavy enemy losses. Similar large Japanese air attacks on 12 and 16 June meet the same fate.

13 June
New Georgia
Reconnaissance patrols including men from the Marine Corps, Navy, and Army go ashore on New Georgia to survey possible landing sites for the planned invasion of the Central Solomons island.

15 June
Force Structure
The 20th Marines (a regiment of engineers and pioneers) is established at Camp Lejeune. VMJ-952 is formed at Camp Kearney.

21–22 June
New Georgia
The 4th Raider Battalion (less two companies) and two Army infantry companies land at Segi Point, New Georgia, to stave off a Japanese advance against a coastwatcher. This marks the earlier-than-planned opening of the campaign to seize the island.

26 June
Force Structure
The Army agrees to assume responsibility for all barrage balloon missions in the Pacific. The six Marine balloon squadrons gradually begin to shift over to operating 90mm anti-aircraft guns.

27 June
New Georgia
The 4th Raider Battalion (less two companies) moves by boat and overland from Segi to support a planned amphibious landing at Viru Harbor. The Raiders have several skirmishes along the way.

Left: *By the end of 1943, the gull-winged Corsair was rapidly becoming the Corps' premier fighter plane. ("F4U Corsair," 2ndLt Jesse G. Evans, USMC, Marine Corps Art Collection)*

Right: *Marines wade to the narrow Bougainville beach late on D-Day. In the foreground is a machine gun mounted on the starboard gunwales of an LCVP. (National Archives)*

30 June

New Georgia

The amphibious transports attempting to land an Army force at Viru Harbor are turned back by shore batteries. Army units secure Rendova Island, and the 9th Defense Battalion establishes positions there to support the pending assault against Munda Airfield on New Georgia. AirSols aircraft drive off heavy enemy air attacks against U.S. ships off Rendova. Marine fighter planes claim 58 of the 101 reported kills, with 1st Lieutenant Wilbur J. Jones of VMF-213 getting four Zeros.

Vangunu

Companies N and Q of the 4th Raider Battalion land unopposed on Vangunu Island in the Central Solomons as the vanguard for the Army's 2nd Battalion, 103rd Infantry. The two units succeed in defeating Japanese forces on the island over the next three days.

Manpower

The strength of the Marine Corps on active duty is 21,384 officers and 287,139 enlisted.

July

Manpower

The Women's Reserve officer candidate school and recruit training programs are transferred from civilian institutions to Camp Lejeune.

1 July

New Georgia

The 4th Raiders defeat the Japanese defenders of Viru Harbor.

Commanders

Major General Vandegrift takes command of I MAC in place of Major General Vogel.

Force Structure

VMF-114 and VMSB-245 are organized at El Toro, VMF-115 at Santa Barbara, VMF-217 and VMTB-242 at El Centro, VMF-218 at Mojave, and VMF-322, VMSB-342, and VMD-354 at Cherry Point.

Manpower

The Navy Department establishes the V-12 program at various universities to train enlisted sailors and Marines for commissioning.

COLONEL RUTH CHENEY STREETER

Ruth Cheney Streeter might have seemed an unlikely choice to be the first director of the Marine Corps Women's Reserve in 1943. Born to an established Boston family in 1895, she had married a successful banker and lawyer during her last year at an elite women's college, and had never held a paying job in her life. Beyond that snapshot biography, however, was a capable, determined leader. Her two brothers had joined the Army in World War I, one serving as an engineer in France and the other dying in an aviation accident. Two of her sons were Navy officers and the third had enlisted in the Army. She knew full well the cost of war. Throughout the Depression years of the 1930s, she had been active in organizations devoted to improving public health programs and assisting the elderly, the poor, and orphans—as she put it, "working with people." When World War II broke out in Europe, she prepared to do her part in a conflict that many knew would eventually embroil the United States. She learned to fly in 1940 at the age of 45, helped organize the Civil Air Patrol in New Jersey in the summer of 1941, and earned her commercial pilot's license in April 1942. Despite being a dozen years over the age limit, she tried five times to join the Women Air Service Pilots, a quasi-military group that ferried planes from factories to bases. She next looked into the Navy's reserve outfit, but rejected their limitation that she could only be a ground instructor in the aviation field. The Marines were not going to let her fly either, but they did offer her the chance to build their Women's Reserve program from the ground up. She jumped at the challenge.

The Secretary of the Navy swore in Streeter as a major on 29 January 1943. She was the second female Marine officer (the honor of being first went to Anne A. Lentz, commissioned a captain on 15 January). Major Streeter selected six other women for direct commissions as captains to fill key staff billets in her organization. Another 19 women transferred from the Navy to serve as recruiters. The Corps formally announced the establishment of its Women's Reserve on 13 February and began accepting volunteers that day. The decision to send them to formal recruit training and officer candidate programs marked a departure from World War I, when the Corps had simply given uniforms to women who already possessed the desired administrative skills. Now the Corps would train them to be Marines first, and then assign them to advanced schooling in a much wider range of occupational specialties. Major Streeter set the tone from the very first when she informed a correspondent on 14 February that there would be no catchy title (such as the Navy's WAVES) for the Corps' Women's Reserve. Commandant Holcomb seconded her instincts a few weeks later: "They are Marines. They don't have a nickname and they don't need one."

Major Streeter soon realized the limitations of her billet as director of the Women's Reserve. She would recall years later a brief conversation with her boss, the director of Reserve. To her complaint that "I've got so much responsibility and no authority," he replied: "You have no responsibility, either." Indeed, female Marines belonged to their units and the chain of command did not run

Col Streeter arrives at Marine Corps Air Station Eagle Mountain Lake, Texas, for a visit with some of her Women Marines. (Marine Corps Historical Center)

through the director. Nevertheless, Streeter performed important functions. She spent much of her time traveling the country and visiting female Marines, looking out for their welfare and inspiring them by her own example. She also advocated an expanded role for women throughout the Corps. By the time the war was over, female Marines had broken into 225 specialties in 16 of the 21 functional fields in the Corps. The one thing that Streeter found aggravating—women could work on the Corps' planes, but still not fly them.

The director of the Women's Reserve made colonel in early 1944 as the number of females on duty expanded, eventually reaching 820 officers and 17,640 enlisted. That freed enough men from stateside jobs to man an entire Marine division. With the end of the war, the temporary requirement for women also disappeared. Colonel Streeter oversaw the initial shift to demobilization, then left active duty herself on 6 December 1945. One of her last official acts was to compile a history of the Women's Reserve. She carefully presented the lessons of her tenure to make it easier to repeat the process again. Little did she know that the Corps would end up creating a permanent female presence before it quite completed demobilizing the temporary outfit of World War II.

Colonel Streeter remained active in her community after she left the Marine Corps. Among other public service duties, she served as a chief of civil defense and even donated a bomb shelter to her New Jersey township after the onset of the Cold War. She died in 1990.

Right: *The strong surf at Bougainville has pinned this Higgins boat against the beach. An unseen craft is trying to pull it free. (National Archives)*

Below: *A Marine Gunnery Sergeant wipes blood from his bayonet with a Japanese flag. ("Gunnery Sergeant," A. Mulford, Navy Art Collection)*

Opposite: *A few Marines admire a pin-up as their landing craft heads toward smoke-enshrouded Betio Island at Tarawa Atoll. (National Archives)*

2 July
New Georgia
The Army's 43rd Division conducts an amphibious assault on New Georgia to launch its attack on Munda airfield. Although the landing is successful, the division makes slow progress against determined Japanese resistance. The 9th Defense Battalion provides supporting artillery fire from Rendova throughout this campaign.

Technology
VMF-123 is the last of the eight Marine fighter squadrons in the South Pacific to convert from the Wildcat to the Corsair.

4 July
New Georgia
Anti-aircraft units from the 9th Defense Battalion move forward to New Georgia to support the 43rd Division. Marine guns on Rendova turn back a sizable Japanese air raid.

5 July
New Georgia
The 1st Raider Regiment headquarters and the 1st Raider Battalion spearhead the landing at Rice Anchorage on New Georgia. Two Army battalions join them ashore. There is no enemy opposition on the beach. The force immediately moves overland toward their objective, a large base at Enogai Inlet.

9 July
New Georgia
The 1st Raider Battalion launches its attack on Japanese defenders at Enogai. The Marines finish cleaning out the position on 11 July.

10 July
Bases
Marine Corps Air Station El Centro, California, is placed in commission.
New Georgia
The 4th Raider Battalion elements at Viru Harbor return to Guadalcanal.
European Theater
British and U.S. forces begin the invasion of Sicily in the Mediterranean.

12 July
Vangunu
The 4th Raider Battalion companies at Vangunu return to Guadalcanal.

13 July
Bases
The Marine Corps Glider Base at Edenton, North Carolina, is redesignated as a Marine Corps Air Station.
Force Structure
MAG-61 is organized at Cherry Point.

14 July
New Georgia
The light tank platoon and anti-aircraft guns from the 9th Defense Battalion follow Army infantry ashore at Laiana Beach, just a few miles from Munda Airfield. For the next five days, the Marine tanks spearhead the Army attack to wrest the landing field away from the Japanese.

17 July
Bougainville
AirSols executes a 192-plane strike against shipping concentrated at the southern end of Bougainville Island. Marine fighters claim 41 of the 52 enemy planes shot down. Marine dive bombers assist in hitting four destroyers.
New Georgia
Elements of the 9th Defense Battalion repulse a Japanese night attack against the American beachhead supporting the drive on Munda Airfield.

18 July
New Georgia
The 4th Raider Battalion arrives at Enogai from Guadalcanal, to reinforce the 1st Raider Regiment for the drive on Bairoko Harbor.

20 July
Choiseul
Marine land-based aircraft sink a Japanese destroyer and damage a cruiser south of Choiseul Island in the northern Solomons.

20–21 July
New Georgia
The 1st Raider Regiment, supported by the Army's 3rd Battalion, 148th Infantry, attacks enemy forces holding Bairoko Harbor. After fierce fighting against strong Japanese defenses, the Americans pull back with heavy losses. The withdrawal is covered by 250 AirSols sorties, one of the largest air operations of the Central Solomons campaign.

Left: *The dense jungle of Bougainville and other islands in the Solomons could conceal an enemy just yards away. (National Archives)*

Opposite: *Surrounded by casualties from the intense Japanese fire, a machine gun team prepares to leave the cover of an amtrac and Betio's seawall. (Marine Corps Research Center)*

22 July
Bougainville
Marine torpedo bombers sink a Japanese seaplane carrier with a load of tanks.
Vella Lavella
A six-man patrol of Marine, Army, and Navy officers lands near Barakoma, Vella Lavella Island, to scout the area for a proposed amphibious operation.

25 July
European Theater
Premier Mussolini is replaced as head of the Italian government.

26–28 July
New Georgia
The light tanks of the 9th and 10th Defense Battalions lead the Army assault against Japanese bunkers near Munda Airfield. Marine and Navy aircraft attack Bibilo Hill overlooking Munda Airfield on 25 and 26 July.

1 August
New Georgia
Marine planes of AirSols participate in a major strike against Japanese positions holding up the advance on Munda Airfield.
Force Structure
VMF-323 and VMSB-333, 334, and 343 are organized at Cherry Point.

4–5 August
New Georgia
The light tanks of the 9th, 10th, and 11th Defense Battalions help Army forces defeat the final Japanese positions around Munda Airfield.

6 August
New Georgia
The major elements of 9th Defense Battalion begin moving from Rendova Island to the Munda Airfield area to protect the newly captured landing strip.

9 August
New Georgia
A light anti-aircraft battery of the 11th Defense Battalion arrives at Enogai.

13–19 August
New Georgia
9th Defense Battalion 155mm guns support the Army seizure of Baanga Island near Munda Airfield.

14 August
New Georgia
VMF-123 and 124 begin operating from Munda Airfield. They are followed in the coming weeks by VMSB-144, 234, and 244, and VMTB-143 and 232. The headquarters of 2nd MAW and MAG-14 also shift to Munda.

15 August
Vella Lavella
The 4th Defense Battalion follows Army forces ashore in an amphibious landing on Vella Lavella Island. Marine fighters from Munda provide cover and shoot down 17 enemy planes.

16 August
Force Structure
The 4th Marine Division is activated at Camp Pendleton. It primarily consists of the 23rd, 24th, and 25th Marines (infantry), 14th Marines (artillery), and 20th Marines (engineers and pioneers).

18 August
European Theater
Axis resistance in Sicily ceases.

19 August
Force Structure
The 4th Marine Base Defense Aircraft Wing departs Hawaii for the central Pacific.

21 August
Force Structure
The 2nd Barrage Balloon Squadron is

disestablished and its personnel join the 2nd Defense Battalion on Samoa.

25 August
Force Structure
Major General H. M. Smith's Amphibious Corps, Pacific Fleet, at Camp Elliott, is redesignated V Amphibious Corps (VAC) in preparation for its employment as a tactical headquarters. Its training mission is passed to the newly established Troop Training Unit, Pacific Fleet.

27 August
Ellice Islands
The 2nd Marine Airdrome Battalion and Seabee units occupy Nukufetau Atoll in the Ellice Islands to build an airfield in support of future operations in the Gilbert Islands.

28 August
New Georgia
The 1st Raider Regiment is withdrawn from New Georgia and sails to Guadalcanal. Total Marine casualties during the New Georgia campaign are 221 killed and 415 wounded. Losses among Navy

personnel serving with Marines units are three killed and 11 wounded.
Bougainville
Lieutenant Alvin J. Jensen of VMF-214 destroys 24 enemy aircraft on the ground at Kahili Airfield on southern Bougainville.
Gilberts
The 7th Defense Battalion occupies Nanomea Island, where Seabees will construct an airfield to support subsequent operations in the Gilberts.

30 August
Rabaul
Lieutenant Ken Walsh shoots down four Zeros while escorting bombers over Rabaul, bringing his total kills to 20. Although forced to crash land his plane in the water due to damage, he survives and becomes the first Corsair pilot to receive the Medal of Honor.

September
New Hebrides
MAG-24 headquarters departs Ewa Field for Efate.

2 September
Bases
Marine Corps Air Base Kearney Mesa, California, is renamed Marine Corps Air Depot Miramar.

3 September
European Theater
The British Eighth Army invades the Italian mainland at the toe of the peninsula.

4 September
Guadalcanal
MAG-12 departs Guadalcanal for New Zealand.

8 September
European Theater
Italy surrenders to the Allies. German forces subsequently occupy and defend much of the peninsula.

9 September
European Theater
The U.S. Fifth Army makes an amphibious landing at Salerno in southern Italy.

11 September
Russells
VMF(N)-531 arrives in Banika and begins flying night intercept missions.

15 September
Commanders
Major General Charles D. Barrett takes command of I MAC in place of General Vandegrift.
Force Structure
The 2nd Marine Division in New Zealand is attached to VAC for the upcoming assault on Tarawa. VMB-423, 433, and 443 are commissioned at Cherry Point.

16 September
Bougainville
Major Gregory Boyington of VMF-214 shoots down five Zeros near southern Bougainville.
Arundel
The light tank platoons of the 9th, 10th, and 11th Defense Battalions land on Arundel Island in the Central Solomons to reinforce Army units. The Marine tanks continue in operation until the island is secured five days later.

19 September
Force Structure
MAG-23 arrives at Ewa Field from El Toro.

20 September
Force Structure
The 4th Marine Division is assigned to VAC.

Opposite: *A Marine machine gunner takes a quick break for chow. ("Mess on Machine Gun Watch," A. Draut, Marine Corps Art Collection)*

Above: *Two Marines sprint forward from Red Beach on Betio. (National Archives)*

Right: *Sherman tanks move along the beach at Bougainville. (National Archives)*

Left: *On D-Day at Tarawa Atoll, heavily laden Marines move inland from the coconut-log seawall. (Marine Corps Research Center)*

22 September
Choiseul
Two patrols comprised of Marine and Navy officers and New Zealanders scout Choiseul Island and the vicinity in the northern Solomons. The patrols complete their work on 30 September.

23 September
Bougainville
A Navy-Marine patrol lands from submarine *Gato* (SS-212) on the northeast coast of Bougainville. After four days of scouting, they determine the area is unfavorable for an amphibious landing. A similar reconnaissance element goes ashore at Empress Augusta Bay on the west coast from submarine *Guardfish* (SS-217). It finds the area lightly defended and suitable for construction of an airfield.

24 September
New Britain
Marines from the 1st Marine Division are part of a patrol landing on western New Britain to scout the area. They remain ashore until 6 October.

25 September
Vella Lavella
Elements of I MAC establish a forward staging area on the island.

27 September
Vella Lavella
Marine aircraft land at Barakoma Airfield on Vella Lavella and begin operating from that base. It becomes the home of VMF-212, 215, and 221.

1 October
Force Structure
The 1st Marine Ammunition Company is formed at Montford Point. It is the initial one of 12 such units, which have the mission of moving and storing ammunition during an amphibious assault. The baptism of fire of the ammunition and depot companies in battle comes at Saipan. VMF-313 is organized at El Centro. VMF-314 and 324; VMF(N)-533 and 534; VMB-611, 612, 613, and 614 are commissioned at Cherry Point.

Right: *From flooded fighting holes along Bougainville's Piva Trail, men of the 2nd Marine Raider Battalion repel repeated Japanese attacks. (National Archives)*

Below: *A 40mm anti-aircraft gun crew on Bougainville sports Japanese flags on the barrel, one for each enemy plane shot down. (MacArthur Memorial)*

6 October
Samoa
MAG-31 begins operations in Samoa after its move from the United States.

8 October
Commanders
Major General Vandegrift reassumes command of I MAC following the accidental death of Major General Barrett.

Left *Marines wait for the word to move out on Tarawa Atoll. (National Archives)*

Opposite, top: *A Tarawa veteran portrays the cost of taking the Japanese bastion. ("The Last Full Measure," Richard M. Gibney, Marine Corps Art Collection)*

Opposite, bottom: *A Christmas Eve memorial service honors fallen comrades on Bougainville. (National Archives)*

13 October
European Theater
Italy declares war on Germany, although it provides no forces to join in the Allied war effort.

20 October
Force Structure
The 1st Joint Assault Signal Company (1st JASCO) is activated at Camp Pendleton. Its mission is to coordinate the fire of supporting arms, including air, during amphibious operations.
New Georgia
The commander of AirSols displaces his headquarters from Guadalcanal to Munda.
New Hebrides
The headquarters of 2nd MAW moves to Efate in the New Hebrides and begins to serve primarily as a training command.

27 October
Bougainville
The 8th New Zealand Brigade makes diversionary landings on the islands of Mono and Stirling southwest of Bougainville.
Force Structure
Marine Observation Squadron-1 (VMO-1) is activated at Quantico.

28 October
Choiseul
The 2nd Parachute Battalion makes an unopposed night landing from destroyer transports on the northwest coast of Choiseul to divert enemy attention from the pending assault on Bougainville.

30 October
Choiseul
Two companies of the 2d Parachute Battalion attack and destroy a Japanese barge staging point on the coast.

31 October
Force Structure
The 22nd Marines is detached from the Defense Force, Samoan Group, and assigned to VAC.

November
New Hebrides
MAG-12 moves from New Zealand to Efate.

1 November
Bougainville
Following air and naval bombardments (including attacks by Marine air based at Munda), the

reinforced 3rd Marine Division conducts an amphibious assault at Cape Torokina, Empress Augusta Bay, on the west coast of Bougainville. The 3rd and 9th Marines and the 2nd Raider Battalion make the main landing, while the 3rd Raider Battalion goes ashore on Puruata Island. The Marines (under command of I MAC) overwhelm the enemy company defending the Cape Torokina area and establish a beachhead perimeter. The 3rd Defense Battalion comes ashore, as well.

Force Structure

VMO-2 is commissioned at Quantico.

2 November

Choiseul

Elements of the 2d Parachute Battalion make a mortar attack on Japanese installations on Guppy Island off the coast of Choiseul. Two Navy torpedo boats (one commanded by Lieutenant junior grade John F. Kennedy) assist in returning the Marines to their main perimeter.

Bougainville

A Navy task force defeats a Japanese attempt to attack the Bougainville beachhead prior to dawn.

4 November

Choiseul

Before first light, the 2nd Parachute Battalion conducts an unopposed amphibious withdrawal from the island.

6 November

Bougainville

The second echelon of the 3rd Marine Division, including a battalion of the 21st Marines, arrives by sea at Cape Torokina.

GENERAL ROY S. GEIGER

Since the time of World War I the Marine Corps has prided itself on being the consummate air-ground team, with these two dimensions of combat power being more closely wedded than in any other armed force around the globe. One Marine more than any other epitomized that status. Roy S. Geiger not only helped lead Marine aviation to its prominent position in the Corps, he also is the only Leatherneck to ever command a field army in battle.

Geiger grew up in a small town in Florida and initially followed in his father's footsteps as an educator. Not content with that, he put himself through school to earn a law degree. A few months later he decided to look for something more adventurous. He wanted a commission in the Marine Corps, but failed the physical examination. Determined to try another route, he enlisted in the Corps a few weeks shy of his 23rd birthday in November 1907. He quickly won promotion to corporal, then a shot at taking the tests to qualify for a commission. He passed, received waivers for his physical defects, and put on his lieutenant's bars in February 1909.

There followed the usual tours with ship detachments and overseas garrisons. In late 1915, he applied for pilot training, but his physical status still dogged him. Alfred Cunningham, the first Marine aviator, listed Geiger as the sixth choice for orders to flight school, but noted that he would "place him No. 1 on the list if he can pass the physical examination." Geiger got the nod from the doctors and eventually became the fifth Marine to earn his wings. That qualification came just in time, as the United States was entering World War I. In the summer of 1918 he took command of a squadron of the 1st Marine Aviation Force. He and his outfit made it to France, but he saw almost no action, in part due to his own fault. Planes were hard to come by for the Marine unit; having just received the first for his squadron, he promptly crashed it attempting to impress British airmen with a showy take-off. Just before the end of the war, he was grounded for a time for insubordination. He received a Navy Cross, however, for his contributions as a determined leader and planner.

After the war, Geiger spent two tours in Haiti, where he had his first chance to use his planes in support of Marines on the ground. As the commander of Aircraft One (all Marine squadrons on the east coast) in the mid-1930s, he and his pilots were at the center of the development and testing of the new amphibious assault doctrine. In addition to other stints with Marine aviation units, he graduated from the Army's Command and General Staff College, the Army War College, and the Naval War College.

His fearlessness in the air and his forceful personality were just the traits required to build a small force of planes and pilots into the 1st Marine Aircraft Wing in the summer of 1941. Far more important was his clear sense that aviation's value lay not in independent action, but in working hand in glove with surface forces. The man and the moment came together at Guadalcanal in September 1942. When Geiger arrived on the island the situation was grim. His dirt landing strip suffered alternately from enemy explosives and rain. His aircraft were barely adequate to challenge the more nimble planes of the enemy. His pilots fell far short of the flying hours and combat experience of their opponents. The logistics pipeline provided only a trickle of ammunition, fuel, parts, and food. His squadrons came from all over—the Marines, the Army, the Navy, and even New Zealand. But perhaps most challenging, there was no clear chain of command. Geiger might have concentrated on his own problems and goals, but instead he melded his polyglot wing into the Cactus Air Force and placed it at the disposal of General Vandegrift. His planes fought to achieve command of the air over Guadalcanal, but they focused even more on sinking enemy ships bringing reinforcements to the island and on striking those Japanese that got ashore. The close cooperation between ground and air, in contrast with Japanese interservice rivalry, contributed significantly to ultimate victory and brought him another Navy Cross.

Geiger's ability to work with other arms and services, and his understanding of the entire spectrum of warfare, made him the only Marine aviator to command a major ground force in combat. He succeeded Vandegrift in charge of I Marine Amphibious Corps at Bougainville in late 1943 and took his outfit (redesignated III Amphibious Corps) through Guam and Peleliu the following year. In 1945 he led it into battle at Okinawa. Near the end of the campaign, he fleeted up to temporarily head the Tenth Army when the commanding general was killed. During the last few months of the war, he commanded the entire Fleet Marine Force.

He succumbed to lung cancer while on active duty in January 1947. In recognition of his outstanding service to Corps and country, a special act of Congress promoted him posthumously to the four-star rank of general.

MajGen Geiger (right) with Army LtGen Simon Bolivar Buckner, Jr., on Okinawa. Upon Buckner's death near the end of the campaign, Geiger became the only Marine ever to command a field army in combat. (National Archives)

Left: *Marines and corpsmen tend a casualty on Tarawa. ("A Wounded Buddy," Kerr Eby, Naval Art Collection)*

Below: *A Tarawa Marine. ("Moving Forward," Richard M. Gibney, Marine Corps Art Collection)*

7 November
Bougainville
A Japanese battalion lands from destroyers just west of the Marine perimeter and attacks. Artillery and the Marines of 3/9 and 1/3 turn back the enemy at the Koromokina River.

7–10 November
Bougainville
The 2nd and 3rd Raider Battalions and elements of the 9th Marines battle for control of the Piva Trail, the only route into or out of the jungle-choked eastern end of the Bougainville perimeter. Marine dive bombers support the final attack on Piva Village on 10 November.

8 November
Force Structure
The 3rd Marine Brigade on Samoa is deactivated.

9 November
Bougainville
Major General Roy S. Geiger assumes command of I MAC and the Bougainville campaign in place of Lieutenant General Vandegrift.

13–14 November
Bougainville
In the Battle of the Coconut Grove, 2/21 defeats a Japanese force and gains control of an important trail junction on the eastern side of the Bougainville perimeter. VMF(N)-531 makes its first successful night intercept and shoots down a Japanese Betty bomber near Bougainville.

17 November
Bougainville
A Japanese air attack on a convoy results in the sinking of destroyer transport *McKean* (APD-5) and the loss of personnel from the 21st Marines.

18 November
New Hebrides
MAG-21 moves to Efate from the Russells.

19–20 November
Bougainville
In the first phase of the Battle of Piva Forks, 2/3 and 3/3 expand the perimeter to the east and seize a key ridge in the face of strong Japanese opposition.

20 November
Gilberts
The 2nd Marine Division launches an amphibious assault against Betio Island in Tarawa Atoll, Gilbert Islands, with the 2nd and 8th Marines leading the way into murderous Japanese fire. Only the use of amphibian tractors (LVTs) allows the leading waves to get through the shallow water covering the coral shelf around the island. The Marines establish a beachhead at great cost. A regiment of the Army's 27th Infantry Division makes an amphibious assault on Makin Atoll.
Commanders
Major General Ralph J. Mitchell assumes command of AirSols.

21 November
Gilberts
The 2nd and 8th Marines continue the attack on Betio and reach the opposite shore, cutting the Japanese force in two. 1/6 gets ashore relatively unscathed that evening to reinforce the assault. 2/6 lands on nearby Bairiki Island to clear it for the use of artillery. The VAC Reconnaissance Company seizes an island on Apamama Atoll in the Gilberts against light resistance.

Above: *Inside an amphibious tractor hit by a Japanese shell at Tarawa. ("Grapes of Wrath," Kerr Eby, Naval Art Collection)*

Right: *A Marine winds up to throw a grenade on Betio. (National Archives)*

21–25 November
Bougainville
During the final phase of the Battle of Piva Forks, the 3rd Marines, 2nd Raider Battalion, and 1/9 further expand the perimeter and establish firm control over the dominating high ground.

22 November
Gilberts
Reinforced by the landing of 3/6, the 2nd Marine Division seizes all of Betio except for a small pockets near the original landing beaches and the long narrow tail of the island. That night 1/6 repels enemy counterattacks coming out of the Betio tail. Organized Japanese resistance on Makin Atoll ceases.

23 November
Gilberts
The 2nd Marine Division completes the seizure of Betio.
Bougainville
The 1st Parachute Battalion arrives at Cape Torokina from Vella Lavella.

24–27 November
Gilberts
The 2nd Marine Division Scouts and 2/6 complete the conquest of Tarawa Atoll. Total

Above: *A Corsair downs a Japanese fighter. ("What a Helluva Thing," Paul J. Clinkenbroomer, Marine Corps Art Collection)*

Left: *"Dangerous Duty," George Harding, Marine Corps Art Collection)*

Marine casualties for the battle are 1,085 dead or missing and 2,233 wounded. Losses among Navy personnel serving with Marines units are 30 killed and 59 wounded.

24 November
Gilberts
The 2nd and 8th Marines depart Tarawa for a new base camp in Hawaii. The 2nd Defense Battalion arrives on Tarawa from Samoa.

25 November
Gilberts
The VAC Reconnaissance Company completes its conquest of Apamama Atoll.

29 November
Bougainville
The 1st Parachute Battalion, reinforced by Company M of the 3rd Raider Battalion, makes an amphibious raid at Koiari, about 10 miles east of the Bougainville perimeter. They encounter a large Japanese force and make an amphibious withdrawal under pressure late in the day.

30 November
Gilberts
The scout company of 2nd Tank Battalion searches for enemy on Abaiang and Makakei

Above: *On Christmas Day 1943, Marines climb up cargo nets onto a transport to sail away from Bougainville. (National Archives)*

Right: *Marine reinforcements march toward the battle for Hill 660 at Cape Gloucester on New Britain. ("Moving Up," Master Technical Sergeant Victor P. Donahue, USMC, Marine Corps Art Collection)*

Left: *"Tank-Infantry Team, Cape Gloucester," Master Technical Sergeant Victor P. Donahue, Marine Corps Art Collection*

Opposite, top: *A 105mm howitzer crew serves their piece on Bougainville. (National Archives)*

Opposite, below: *Marines of the Gilnit Group move down a trail hacked out of the New Britain jungle. (MacArthur Memorial)*

Atolls north of Tarawa and finds only five Japanese. The first Marine aircraft (six SBDs of VMSB-331) arrive on the Betio airstrip (named after 1st Lieutenant William D. Hawkins, posthumous recipient of the Medal of Honor for his actions in the battle).

December
Manpower
The first Reserve Officer Class is formed for newly commissioned women lieutenants.

1 December
Gilberts
The scouts of 2nd Tanks land at Maiana Atoll and determine it is not occupied by enemy forces.
Force Structure
Making use of lightweight search radars, the Marine Corps creates the first air-transportable air warning squadron, AWS(AT)-5, at Cherry Point. VMO-3 is organized at Quantico.

3 December
Bougainville
The 1st Marine Parachute Regiment headquarters and weapons company and its 3rd Battalion arrive at Cape Torokina.

7–15 December
Force Structure
The 1st, 3rd, 5th, and 6th Barrage Balloon Squadrons are deactivated and most of their personnel are assigned to defense battalions.

9 December
Bougainville
The ground echelons of VMF-212 and 215 reach Bougainville and move to the airstrip under construction at Cape Torokina.

9–10 December
Bougainville
The 1st Parachute Regiment and its 3rd Battalion begin an attack to seize Hellzapoppin Ridge, a

heavily defended spur east of the Bougainville perimeter. The parachutists are relieved by 1/9 and 1/21 on the night of 10 December.

10 December
Bougainville
The Cape Torokina Airfield is declared operational. The F4U Corsairs of VMF-216 fly in to make it their home, but for the near future, aircraft based in New Georgia will simply stage through this intermediate base for refueling.

11–18 December
Bougainville
The 21st Marines take Hellzapoppin Ridge in eight days of fighting, with the help of close air support by Marine planes on 13, 14, 15, and 18 December.

15 December
New Britain
The campaign on New Britain begins with Marine amphibian tractors from the 1st Marine Division carrying the Army's 112th Cavalry Regiment in the assault against Arawe Peninsula

on the southern coast of the large island. The Army's XIV Corps headquarters assumes command of the Bougainville campaign in place of I MAC.

Force Structure
The 52nd Defense Battalion is formed at Montford Point.

LANDING VEHICLE, TRACKED

As the Marine Corps grew increasingly interested in amphibious operations after World War I, it wrestled with the need for special craft and vehicles to carry men and equipment from ocean-going transports to the shore. While the primary focus was always on boats that could land and retract at the waterline, there was occasional interest in a machine that could swim in the water and then drive right up onto the beach—a true amphibian. The first significant experiment in the latter realm came in 1924, when the Marines tested an amphibian tank invented by J. Walter Christie. It used a propeller in the water and tracks on land, but was not sufficiently seaworthy for actual use in a landing.

The Marine Corps proved to be more lucky than prescient when it came to amphibian vehicles. Following a devastating hurricane in Florida in 1932, Donald Roebling (grandson of the builder of the Brooklyn Bridge) started designing a vehicle that could perform rescue operations in swampy terrain. Within two years he built a prototype consisting of a buoyant aluminum hull that relied on cleated tracks to propel itself on water and land. By 1937 he had perfected a version that could achieve a speed of eight miles per hour in the water. The Marines discovered his work when a national magazine printed a story about the vehicle that fall. Initially the inventor had no interest in dealing with the military, but following the outbreak of war in September 1939, he agreed to develop a more advanced model. It rolled out of his shop in 1940 and participated in maneuvers in Culebra. A steel version, designated the Landing Vehicle, Tracked (LVT-1), went into production at the Food Machinery Corporation (FMC) factory in Dunedin, Florida, in 1941. The vehicle was 21 feet, 6 inches long, and 9 feet, 10 inches wide, weighed in at 18,500 pounds, and could carry a load of 4,500 pounds. A subsequent design based on early experience in training resulted in creation of the LVT-2, though it would not join the Marines for duty in significant numbers until 1943.

The Marine Corps acquired the LVT-1 for a very specific purpose—to reduce the onerous requirement for men to unload supplies from landing craft at the beach and manhandle them into trucks for transport to where they were needed ashore. The amphibian LVT could be loaded at the ship, cross the beach, and drive inland to its destination, saving precious time and manpower. The tables of organization provided a battalion of amphibians (100 vehicles) for each division.

As early as the summer of 1941, the Marine Corps decided that the amphibian tractor could serve as a fire support vehicle during a landing. Roebling and FMC designed the LVT(A)1, which added light armor, plus the 37mm gun and turret of the Stuart light tank to the basic LVT-2 model, but it didn't get into production until mid-1943. It was not until the 2nd Marine Division began its planning for the invasion of Tarawa Atoll in August 1943, however, that Marines first saw the most important tactical role of the LVT. Confronted with a coral reef surrounding the main objective of Betio Island, the senior leaders of the division realized that traditional landing craft could not get the troops anywhere close to the beach. Their tentative answer was the

An amphibious tractor deposits Marines on dry land during the assault on Guam in July 1944. This model had no stern ramp, so infantrymen had to leap over the tall sides. (National Archives)

LVT. Once Marines tested and proved its ability to rumble over a coral reef, the amphibian assault vehicle was born.

The 2nd Marine Division did not have enough LVTs to carry even two battalions, and many of these had seen hard service and were badly worn. Eventually the division obtained 50 brand-new LVT-2s from the States, but these would have to meet it on D-Day. The LVT-1 could carry 18 men, the LVT-2 could handle 20. On the morning of 20 November 1943, these tractors carried the three leading waves of the 2nd and 8th Marines across the reef at Betio and into intense fire. Thereafter they returned to the edge of the reef to ferry in subsequent boat-borne echelons. That process soon broke down due to losses among the amphibians, and their importance quickly was revealed by the high casualties sustained in reinforcing battalions as men had to wade in across the reef through a murderous hail of shrapnel and bullets. Tarawa proved to be a watershed and henceforth the LVT would serve as the primary Marine assault transport while landing craft were relegated to bringing in supplies or reserves once the beach was secured.

The amphibian tractor continued to develop during and after the war. At the Army's behest, FMC built an armor-plated version of the LVT-2 troop-cargo vehicle known as the LVT(A)2. The Borg-Warner Corporation came up with a major innovation in 1944 with the LVT-3, which provided a stern ramp (thus allowing troops to disembark without having to jump over the exposed, 8-feet-high sides of previous models). It also could carry 12,000 pounds of cargo. FMC followed with a similar stern-ramp model dubbed the LVT-4. It could handle 8,000 pounds of cargo or 35 troops. This became the classic version that carried many Marines (and soldiers) into the later assaults of the war; it accounted for nearly half of the 18,000 amphibian vehicles produced through 1945. The final WWII variant was the LVT(A)4, the basic LVT-4 mounting a turreted 75mm gun to replace the much lighter-armed LVT(A)1. Subsequent models of tracked landing vehicles (later dubbed assault amphibian vehicles or AAVs) have served the Corps ever since World War II and remain at the heart of the Marine capability for storming an enemy-held coast.

17 December
Rabaul
Major Gregory Boyington of VMF-214 leads the first fighter sweep against Rabaul. Results are disappointing since few Japanese planes rise from the ground to challenge the 76 U.S. Marine and Navy and New Zealand aircraft.

20 December
Force Structure
VMO-4 is commissioned at Quantico.

21–22 December
New Britain
Two Marine patrols scout beaches near Tauali in preparation for the assault on western New Britain.

22-23 December
Bougainville
Elements of the 21st Marines seize Hill 600A overlooking the Torokina River. This is the last significant action by the 3rd Marine Division on Bougainville.

23 December
Rabaul
Boyington leads another fighter sweep of 48 planes against Rabaul. This time claimed kills total 30, at a cost of three American planes. Boyington gets four, to bring his tally to 24.

Gilberts
Five VMSB-331 SBDs from Tarawa participate in the attack against enemy shipping at Jaluit Atoll.

25 December
Bougainville
The Army's Americal Division begins relieving the 3rd Marine Division.
Gilberts
The 4th Marine Base Defense Aircraft Wing headquarters arrives on Tarawa.

26 December
New Britain
The 1st Marine Division launches its amphibious assault on Cape Gloucester at the northwestern end of New Britain. The 7th and 1st Marines (less 2/1) go ashore near the Japanese airfields at the cape, while 2/1 lands on the western coast to block trails. The heaviest ground fighting comes when a Japanese battalion counterattacks the lines of the 7th Marines that night. Marine aircraft of VMF-214, 216, 222, 223, and 321 provide cover for the operation.

27 December
Bougainville
The Army's 164th Infantry replaces the 9th Marines at Bougainville. The regiment and the 3rd Parachute Battalion sail for Guadalcanal the next day.

Left: *A patrol makes its way through the difficult terrain around Cape Gloucester. ("Wading Through the Mud," Master Technical Sergeant Victor P. Donahue, Marine Corps Art Collection)*

Right: *An LCI (Landing Craft Infantry) disembarks Marines at Cape Gloucester. (MacArthur Memorial)*

Below: *A rifleman smokes a cigarette during a brief break on New Britain. (National Archives)*

Rabaul
AirSols conducts fighter sweeps over Rabaul this day and the next.

28 December
New Britain
The Marines of 3/1 destroy Japanese forces fighting from a bunker complex, dubbed Hell's Point, astride the path to the Cape Gloucester airfields.
Bougainville
Army forces relieve the last elements of the 3rd Marines in the lines at Bougainville.

29 December
New Britain
The 5th Marines comes ashore to reinforce the drive on the Cape Gloucester airfields. That night, 2/1 defeats a counterattack on its lines at Tauali by elements of a Japanese battalion.

30 December
New Britain
The 1st and 5th Marines overrun the final enemy defenses and seize the airfields at Cape Gloucester.
Force Structure
Commandant Holcomb issues an order abolishing the Marine parachute and raider programs.

31 December
Commandants
Commandant Holcomb retires and is promoted to the rank of general (four stars). Lieutenant General Alexander A. Vandegrift becomes the 18th Commandant of the Marine Corps.

1944

1 January
Force Structure
VMF-511 is organized at the Marine Corps airfield at Oak Grove, North Carolina.
VMSB-344 is commissioned at Cherry Point, North Carolina.

1–2 January
Bougainville
Army forces relieve the 21st Marines from positions on the perimeter.

2 January
New Britain
The 7th Marines and 3/5 attack across Suicide Creek to enlarge the beachhead perimeter at Cape Gloucester and also stave off an enemy night attack against Target Hill.
Vella Lavella
The 2nd Parachute Battalion sails from Vella Lavella to Guadalcanal to rejoin the 1st Parachute Regiment.
Force Structure
MAG-32 departs Cherry Point for Hawaii.

3 January
Rabaul
Boyington shoots down three enemy planes during a fighter sweep over Rabaul, only to be shot down himself soon after. His claimed kills give him 28, two more than the number achieved by Joe Foss.

Above: *A Marine armed with a BAR (Browning Automatic Rifle) keeps a wary eye on the jungle as he searches for the enemy on New Britain on 8 January 1944. (National Archives)*

Left: *"Pavuvu Island Scene," Col H. Avery Chenoweth, USMCR (Ret), Marine Corps Art Collection*

Boyington spends the rest of the conflict as a prisoner of war. AirSols maintains a daily schedule of heavy attacks on Rabaul throughout the month.

6–11 January
New Britain
The 7th Marines and 3/5 seize Aogiri Ridge to expand the Cape Gloucester perimeter.

6 January
France
Marine Captain Peter J. Ortiz, a former member of the French Foreign Legion, parachutes into southeastern France with two Allied officers to assist the French in establishing additional guerrilla units. His team remains on the ground until early May.

7 January
Rabaul
Marine and Navy dive bombers and torpedo bombers from New Georgia, supported by fighters from Bougainville, stage a large raid against Rabaul. A similar attack is repeated two days later.

10 January
Force Structure
The 26th and 27th Marines (infantry) and 13th Marines (artillery) are organized at Camp Pendleton for duty with the soon-to-be-created 5th Marine Division.

Above: *After losing his tail rudder in a dogfight over Rabaul, Maj Thomas M. Coles managed to bring his plane back to its home field. (National Archives)*

Right: *Camouflage-clad crewmen work their 75mm pack howitzer on New Britain. (National Archives)*

Left: *Lt Edward Rust of the 5th Marines displays a Japanese flag from the quarters of MajGen Iwao Matsuda, commander of the Japanese garrison in western New Britain, until Marines routed him from his lair in January 1944. (MacArthur Memorial)*

11 January
New Britain
A company of the 1st Tank Battalion is deployed to Arawe to reinforce Army units holding the peninsula.

12 January
Bougainville
The 2nd Raider Regiment embarks and sails to Guadalcanal.

13 January
New Georgia
The 9th Defense Battalion begins to move from New Georgia to the Russell Islands.

13–14 January
New Britain
The 7th Marines seize Hill 660, the last piece of terrain needed to complete the Cape Gloucester perimeter.

16 January
Bougainville
The last elements of the 3rd Marine Division return to Guadalcanal. Marine casualties during the Bougainville campaign total 732 dead and 1,249 wounded. Losses among Navy personnel serving with Marine units are 12 killed and 30 wounded.
New Britain
Marine tanks spearhead a successful Army assault that drives off Japanese forces threatening the perimeter at Arawe.

18 January
Rabaul
1st Lieutenant Robert M. Hanson of Torokina-based VMF-215 shoots down five Japanese planes in a single mission.
Force Structure
The 1st and 2nd Parachute Battalions sail from Guadalcanal for San Diego.

21 January
Force Structure
The 5th Marine Division is officially activated at Camp Pendleton.

22 January
New Britain
The 1st Marine Division begins aggressive patrolling of the interior of western New Britain.
European Theater
U.S. and British army forces make an amphibious assault at Anzio to outflank strong German defenses south of Rome. They fail to exploit an initial advantage and become trapped against the coast by enemy counterattacks.

24 January
Gilberts
The 23 Corsairs of VMF-422 fly out of Hawkins Field on Betio bound for Funafuti, 700 miles distant. Due to bad weather, 22 of the planes land in the water and six pilots die.

Force Structure
The 1st Raider Regiment arrives on Guadalcanal from New Caledonia. The 2nd Raider Regiment and its battalions are recombined with the 1st.

27 January
European Theater
Soviet forces break the German siege of Leningrad, which has lasted for 880 days.

28 January
Force Structure
The 16th Marines (an engineer regiment) is activated at Camp Lejeune for eventual duty with the 5th Marine Division.

30 January
Rabaul
Lieutenant Hanson shoots down four Japanese planes, giving him a total of 25 kills, 20 of them in the course of six missions over the past 13 days. He dies during a mission on 3 February, but eventually

Right: *Men of the 2nd Battalion, 1st Marines pay their last respects to their fallen comrades at Cape Gloucester on 29 December 1943. (MacArthur Memorial)*

receives the Medal of Honor for his incredible run of victories. His tally remains the highest of any Marine Corsair pilot during the war.

New Britain

The Gilnit Group is formed under command of Lieutenant Colonel Lewis Puller. Composed of elements of all three regiments of the 1st Marine Division, it is tasked with clearing all enemy forces in the interior of western New Britain. The group continues operations until 18 February.

Force Structure

The 1st Parachute Regiment headquarters and the 3rd Parachute Battalion sail from Guadalcanal for San Diego.

Rabaul

Total AirSols sorties over Rabaul for the month are 873 by light bombers and 1,850 by fighters. They claim 503 enemy aircraft destroyed, at a cost of 65 planes lost.

31 January

Marshalls

Against light resistance, the 25th Marines seizes the islands of Mellu, Ennuebing, Ennumennet, Ennubir, and Ennugarret in the northern end of Kwajalein Atoll. The 14th Marines places artillery here to support the 4th Marine Division's landings scheduled for the next day on Roi-Namur.

The VAC Reconnaissance Company occupies Majuro Atoll in the Marshalls. Elements of the Army 7th Infantry Division capture outlying islands in southern Kwajalein Atoll in preparation for their attack on Kwajalein Island.

1 February

Marshalls

The 23rd Marines assaults Roi and overruns the entire island by late afternoon. The 24th Marines attacks Namur and captures about two-thirds of the island by nightfall. The 7th Infantry Division lands on Kwajalein Island.

Force Structure

The 1st Raider Regiment is redesignated as the 4th Marines, resurrecting the regiment that had disappeared when the Japanese overran Corregidor in 1942. MBDAG-45 is organized at Santa Barbara. VMJ-953 is formed at Camp Kearney.

2 February

Marshalls

The 24th Marines completes the seizure of Namur. When mopping-up actions are finished a few days later, the 4th Marine Division's casualties in the Kwajalein/Majuro campaign total 387 killed and 631 wounded.

Left: *Corpsmen treat their patients in a true field hospital on New Britain. (MacArthur Memorial)*

Opposite: *A patrol uses a rubber raft to scout along the Natamo River in western New Britain. (Marine Corps Research Center)*

4 February
Marshalls
The 7th Infantry Division completes the conquest of Kwajalein Island.

5 February
New Britain
The 5th Marines begins an advance eastward along the north coast of New Britain using landing craft for shore-to-shore movements.
Marshalls
Based on the quick conquest of Kwajalein Atoll, senior leaders decide to use the VAC reserve, Tactical Group 1 (built around the 22nd Marines), to attack Eniwetok Atoll months ahead of schedule. D-Day ultimately is set for 17 February.

7 February
Marshalls
Ground elements of the 4th Marine Base Defense Air Wing arrive at Roi.

8 February
Marshalls
The 4th Marine Division begins to depart Kwajalein Atoll. The 25th Marines is temporarily detached to remain behind as the garrison force.
Force Structure
The 28th Marines is organized at Camp Pendleton to round out the 5th Marine Division.

12 February
Marshalls
A Japanese air raid strikes an ammunition dump on Roi. The resulting explosions kill 26, wound 130, and destroy large quantities of supplies.

15 February
Marshalls
The first aircraft of MAG-31 arrive on Roi. They include 10 planes of VMF-224 and seven of VMF(N)-532.
Force Structure
VMF-451 and 452 are commissioned at Mojave. VMF-512 and 513 are organized at Oak Grove. VMF(N)-541 is formed at Cherry Point. VMO-5 is established at Quantico

17 February
Marshalls
The VAC Reconnaissance Company and the scout company of the 4th Tank Battalion occupy three small islands in Eniwetok Atoll. Marine and Army artillery batteries follow and setup to support the main landings the next day.

Left: *A Marine on patrol has his Thompson submachine gun at the ready. The firepower of the Thompson was particularly useful in the type of surprise encounters at close quarters experienced in the South Pacific jungles. (National Archives)*

18 February
Marshalls
The 22nd Marines assaults Engebi Island in Eniwetok Atoll and overrun it by mid-afternoon.

19 February
Marshalls
Two battalions of the Army 106th Infantry assault Eniwetok Island. During the afternoon, 3/22 goes ashore to lend support. The ground echelon of MAG-22 goes ashore on Engebi Island, with the rest of the group to follow later.
Rabaul
In the last significant aerial battle over Rabaul, an AirSols 139-plane strike tangles with 30 enemy fighters and claims 23 kills. The Japanese withdraw their remaining planes from Rabaul. Air attacks continue for the remainder of the war against ground targets at the sprawling Japanese base complex.

20 February
Marshalls
3/22 and 1/106 complete their task of clearing the southern end of Eniwetok Island. 3/106 continues the attack to capture the northeastern end.
Force Structure
VMF-514 is organized at Cherry Point.

21 February
Marshalls
Army units complete the seizure of Eniwetok Island. VMSB-231 flies onto the airfield at Majuro Atoll.
Rabaul
AirSols bombers sink two Japanese merchant ships attempting to evacuate ground crews.

22 February
Marshalls
The 22nd Marines, reinforced by a 500-man provisional infantry battalion formed from elements of the 10th Defense Battalion, assaults Parry Island. The Marines overrun Japanese defenders that day, completing the seizure of Eniwetok Atoll. Marine casualties during the Eniwetok campaign total 254 killed and 555 wounded. Losses among Navy personnel serving with Marines units at Kwajalein, Majuro, and Eniwetok are six killed and 36 wounded.

24 February
New Britain
Elements of the 5th Marines seize the Iboki Plantation on the north-central coast of New Britain.

25 February
Marshalls
The 10th Defense Battalion assumes garrison duties for Eniwetok Island.

26 February
Marshalls
VMSB-331 arrives on Majuro Atoll. The 22nd Marines arrives on Kwajalein Atoll to relieve the 25th Marines from garrison duty there.

27 February
Ellice Islands
The 51st Defense Battalion relieves the 7th Defense Battalion in the Ellice Islands.

29 February
Force Structure
The 1st Parachute Regiment and its subordinate battalions officially disband. Their personnel are transferred to form the core of the infantry regiments of the 5th Marine Division.

1 March
Marshalls
MAG-22 planes begin to arrive on Engebi Island.
Force Structure
MBDAG-46 and VMSB-454 (later redesignated VMTB-454) are commissioned at El Toro.

2 March
Ellice Islands
The 5th Defense Battalion departs the Ellice Islands for Hawaii.
Gilberts
The headquarters of MAG-15 departs San Diego for Apamama.

4 March
Marshalls
The 4th Marine Base Defense Air Wing, recently arrived in Kwajalein, begins its campaign against Wotje, Jaluit, and other atolls in the eastern Marshalls with attacks by VMSB-331. The aerial neutralization campaign continues until the surrender of Japan.

Above: *Marines take cover as a water-cooled M1917A1 machine gun duels with the Japanese on Parry Island. (National Archives)*

Right: *Infantrymen of the 22nd Marines scan for snipers on Parry Island on 22 February 1944. (MacArthur Memorial)*

MONTFORD POINT MARINES

A small handful of black men served in the Continental Marines during the Revolutionary War. When Congress formally reestablished the Corps in 1798, the first regulations specifically forbid the enlistment of African and Native Americans. No such rules applied to the Army and the Navy, and both of those services included racial minorites in their ranks for most of their history, though almost always in segregated units or in strictly limited specialties. Although the Corps had not created the initial policy of exclusion, senior leaders never made an effort to alter it, despite the successful record of Marines training, leading, and fighting alongside Caribbean blacks and Indians in the constabularies of Santo Domingo, Haiti, and Nicaragua.

Things began to change within the Marine Corps only after President Franklin Roosevelt directed on 25 June 1941 that "all departments of the government, including the Armed Forces, shall lead the way in erasing discrimination over color or race." The Corps bowed to this decree and initially planned to recruit 1,200 blacks, who would train at Montford Point, a part of what would soon be called Camp Lejeune. The first men enlisted on 1 June 1942 and began reporting to the North Carolina base in late August.

The ultimate objective was to form the men into the 51st Defense Battalion, which would be led by white officers but otherwise would consist entirely of black enlisted men. This policy of unit segregation did possess one positive aspect, since it ensured the creation of black NCOs at a pace faster than might be expected otherwise. White sergeants trained the first recruit platoons in the fall of 1942. By April 1943, new black NCOs were leading the recruit platoons. Many of these first NCOs had prior service in the Army or Navy or advanced education and were thus more than ready for the responsibility despite

Left: *African American recruits drill at Montford Point, North Carolina, in March 1943. (Library of Congress)*

Opposite: *Marines in the depot and ammunition companies saw duty in the thick of the fighting at Peleliu (pictured here) and elsewhere. (National Archives)*

their short time as Marines. Men such as Gilbert H. Johnson and Edgar R. Huff would go on to distinguished careers and rise to the very top of the enlisted ranks of the Corps. The Marine Corps began sending black enlisted Marines to officer training programs in 1944, with some going to the Navy's V-12 program and others to the Platoon Commanders Class in Quantico. It was not until November 1945, however, that a black Marine, PFC Frederick C. Branch, was able to overcome all the hurdles in his path and earn his commission as a second lieutenant.

The end of voluntary enlistments in all the services in December 1942 radically changed the plans of Headquarters Marine Corps. From then on, about 10 percent of all recruits would be black, a number reflecting the makeup of the population. To absorb this much greater influx, the Corps soon established the 52nd Defense Battalion, plus a large number of depot and ammunition companies, and a stewards' branch, as well. The depot units would provide a labor pool to unload supplies from landing craft during amphibious assaults, while the ammunition outfits would handle the flow of that critical commodity into the beachheads. As fate would have it, these logistics outfits would be the ones that saw the most action.

By the time the defense battalions made it overseas in 1944, their capability had limited utility. There was still a requirement to garrison captured bases, but the likelihood of Japanese counterattacks against them was remote. The 51st served in the Ellice Islands and then at Eniwetok and Kwajalein, but never fired a shot in combat. The 52nd went to Guam, where its patrols did engage small bands of Japanese soldiers still hiding out on the island. In contrast, depot and ammunition companies landed on the first day of amphibious assaults against Saipan, Tinian,

Guam, Peleliu, Iwo Jima, and Okinawa. They did far more than heavy labor, often serving as stretcher bearers in the front lines, or repelling enemy counterattacks and mopping up infiltrators and bypassed defenses. They took their share of casualties and performed heroically, earning a number of unit and individual awards.

The end of World War II did not bring an end to the policy of segregation within the Corps. Recruit training continued at Montford Point and graduates went to a handful of remaining units manned entirely by black enlisted men. It took another president, Harry Truman, to force the next step forward. On 26 July 1948, he ordered the military services to end bias against minorities in their ranks. By the fall of 1949, the Corps had ended segregated recruit training, accepted the first black women, and ordered black Marines to previously all-white units. The most symbolic turning point came when the recruit training facility at Montford Point ceased to exist on 9 September 1949. The Marines who had gone through their transformation from civilian life there had mixed emotions about its demise, but all could look back with pride on the pioneering role they had played. There was more for the Corps to do to achieve complete integration, but the process finally was well on its way.

Left: *Marines pick their way around a dead Japanese soldier and the debris of battle during the seizure of Namur Island. (National Archives)*

Below: *A crew gets its .50-caliber machine gun into action on Namur Island, Kwajalein Atoll. (National Archives)*

6 March
New Britain
The 5th Marines, with 1/5 in the lead, conducts an amphibious assault against the Willaumez Peninsula in north-central New Britain. In three days of fighting, the regiment clears the area of Japanese forces.
Force Structure
VMF(N)-542 is organized at Cherry Point.

9 March
Ellice Islands
The 7th Defense Battalion departs the Ellice Islands for Hawaii.

12 March
Force Structure
The JCS direct the return of the 1st Marine Division from MacArthur's Southwest Pacific Area to control of CINCPAC.

15 March
Commanders
Major General Mitchell ends his tour as commander of AirSols; the billet goes to an Army Air Forces general.
Emirau
Admiral Halsey, commander of the South Pacific area, orders the seizure of Emirau Island on 20 March. Located 230 miles northwest of Rabaul, it would complete the mission of surrounding the Japanese bastion. The 4th Marines receives the assignment, draws up plans, and embarks within two days.
Force Structure
MAG-52 is organized at Cherry Point. VMF-461 is organized at El Centro.

20 March
Emirau
The 4th Marines lands on Emirau without opposition.
Marianas
Plans for the invasion of the Marianas assign VAC (with the 2nd and 4th Marines Divisions) the mission of seizing Saipan and Tinian, while

Right: *Marines with fixed bayonets prepare to advance during the assault on Roi in the Marshall Islands, February 1944. (National Archives)*

Below: *A rifleman scans the blasted terrain of Eniwetok Island for the enemy. (MacArthur Memorial)*

IMAC (3rd Marine Division and 1st Provisional Marine Brigade) tackles Guam. Major General H. M. Smith doubles as overall commander of Expeditionary Troops (both corps) and commander of VAC. The Army's 27th Infantry Division is tasked as the Expeditionary Troops reserve, while the Army's 77th Division is held in Hawaii as the theater reserve.

21 March
Marshalls
3/22 seizes Ailinglapalap Atoll in the southern Marshalls after a brief fight.

22 March
Force Structure
The 1st Provisional Marine Brigade headquarters is activated at Pearl Harbor. The primary components of the brigade will be the 4th Marines (on Emirau) and the 22nd Marines (on Kwajalein).

23 March
Marshalls
Elements of 3/22 attack Ebon Atoll and clear it of the enemy.

28 March
Marshalls
A reinforced company of 2/22 lands on Bikini Atoll and raises the U.S. flag.

29 March
Force Structure
Admiral King, COMINCH/CNO, authorizes Major General Smith to exercise administrative and logistical control over all FMF units in the Central Pacific. This is the beginning of the establishment of a FMF Pacific headquarters.

31 March
Force Structure
MacArthur asks to retain the 1st Marine Division until late June.

1 April
Force Structure
The 9th MAW is established at Cherry Point. Its mission is to train and equip aviation units for deployment to combat theaters. MAG-61 departs Cherry Point, ultimately bound for the Pacific. MAG-93 is organized at Bogue Field. VMF-521 and 522 are formed at Cherry Point.

5 April
Emirau
The lead elements of MAG-12 arrive on Emirau.

Force Structure
VMF-481 is organized at El Toro.

6 April
Force Structure
VAC orders establishment of a Marine Administrative Command, composed of a headquarters and the Marine Supply Service, to perform administrative and logistical services for both VAC and IMAC. This marks the birth of the command that will later be called FMF Pacific.

7 April
Force Structure
VMF-482 is organized at El Toro.

10 April
Force Structure
The Marine Administrative Command is created. VMSB-474 and 484 are organized at El Toro. VMB-621, VMF-924, and VMSB-944 are formed at Cherry Point.

11 April
Emirau
Army forces arrive to relieve the 4th Marines on Emirau and the regiment begins its movement back to Guadalcanal.

Above: *Curtiss SB2C Helldivers based on Eniwetok Atoll cruise high over the Pacific. (National Archives)*

Left: *Marines clamber over the carcass of a Japanese twin-engine bomber destroyed on the ground at Eniwetok Atoll. (MacArthur Memorial)*

12 April
Force Structure
Major General H. M. Smith divides his VAC headquarters into two staffs, one for his role as VAC commander and the other for his role as Expeditionary Troops commander.

14 April
Marshalls
VMF(N)-532 flew its first successful night intercept in its F4U fighters near the Marshalls.

15 April
Force Structure
IMAC is redesignated III Amphibious Corps (IIIAC). VMF-462 is formed at El Centro. VMSB-464 is organized at El Toro. VMF(N)-543 and VMSB-931 are commissioned at Cherry Point.

22 April
New Guinea
Company A, 1st Tank Battalion, 1st Marine Division, supports Army assault forces in the landing at Tanahmerah Bay, part of MacArthur's campaign around Hollandia, New Guinea.

23 April
New Britain
The Army's 40th Division begins to arrive at Cape Gloucester to relieve the 1st Marine Division.

24 April
New Britain
The 1st Marines sails from Cape Gloucester for Pavuvu Island in the Russells.

27 April
Force Structure
MAG-35 arrives at the newly designated Marine Corps Air Facility Corvallis, Oregon.

Above: *Another view of SB2C Helldivers, underpowered dive bombers that came to the Corps in the middle of the war, but never performed well. (National Archives)*

Right: *A Navy chaplain reads the funeral service as the burial party prepares to bury fellow Marines at sea. (Marine Corps Historical Center)*

Left: *A Japanese tank, dug in as an anti-boat gun, lies destroyed on Engebi Island. (MacArthur Memorial)*

Below: *A Marine leader motions for his men to stay low in a shell hole, which provides temporary cover during their attack on Namur Island. (National Archives)*

28 April
New Britain
The 1st Marine Division hands over responsibility for western New Britain to the 40th Division.

May
Force Structure
The 29th Marines (infantry) is organized at Camp Lejeune.

1 May
Force Structure
VMF(N)-544 is formed at Cherry Point.

2 May
Emirau
VMF-115 is the first flight element of MAG-12 to arrive on Emirau.

4 May
New Britain
The last elements of the 1st Marine Division sail for Pavuvu. Marine casualties for the New Britain campaign totaled 275 dead and 948 wounded. Losses among Navy personnel serving with Marine units are 12 killed and 30 wounded. The 12th Defense Battalion remains on New Britain.

5 May
Force Structure
The Marine Corps promulgates the new F-series tables of organization for its divisions. The main changes include enlargement of the rifle squad from 12 to 13 and the adoption of the four-man fire team, removal of the amphibian tractor battalion, deletion of the infantry battalion weapons company (with its machine guns and mortars dispersed to other companies), and abolition of the engineer regiments (though not its component engineer and pioneer battalions). The divisions implement the changes over the coming months. VMF-523 is formed at Cherry Point.

Right: *A gun crew stands by with their M1919A4 Browning on Namur Island. (MacArthur Memorial)*

Below: *Marines climb down a cargo net from their Navy transport into a waiting landing craft. (National Archives)*

8 May
Force Structure
3rd MAW arrives in Hawaii and assumes control of all Marine aviation units there. MAG-23 departs Hawaii for Midway.

10 May
Force Structure
VMF-524 and VMB-622 are organized at Cherry Point.

15 May
Force Structure
VMF-471 is organized at El Centro. VMB-623 and VMSB-932 are formed at Cherry Point.

20 May
Force Structure
VMS-3 is deactivated on the Virgin Islands.

21 May
Mishap
Following amphibious exercises, a Landing Ship Tank (LST) carrying ammunition explodes in Pearl Harbor and destroys five adjacent LSTs. Just over 200 men in the 2nd and 4th Marine Divisions are killed or wounded.

23 May
Bougainville
Marine and Navy torpedo bombers from Cape Torokina mine the waters off the Japanese-held southern end of Bougainville.

25 May
Force Structure
The 16th Marines is disbanded as part of the reorganization of the Marine divisions.

27 May
New Guinea
MacArthur's forces land on Biak Island off New Guinea and soon run into a tough fight for the island.

1 June
Force Structure
VMF-472 is organized at El Centro.

3 June
Force Structure
The designation of Marine transport squadrons is changed from VMJ to VMR.

4 June
European Theater
The U.S. Fifth Army enters Rome.

5 June
Force Structure
Admiral King designates Major General H. M. Smith as commander of all Marine ground forces in the Pacific theater and authorizes establishment of a headquarters FMF Pacific (FMFPAC), to include an Administrative Command, FMFPAC.

6 June
Normandy
The largest amphibious operation of the war begins, with General Dwight D. Eisenhower's Allied army landing on the Normandy Peninsula of France. Marine ships detachments participate from their stations in the fleet, while a number of officers are assigned as observers with various army and naval commands.

12 June
Force Structure
The Marine Administrative Command of VAC becomes the Administrative Command, FMFPAC. Two days later, the Marine Supply Services, VAC, becomes Supply Services, FMFPAC.

15 June
Saipan
The 2nd and 4th Marine Divisions launch their amphibious assault on the west coast of Saipan. They meet strong resistance, including an unusually profuse Japanese employment of artillery. Following an amphibious feint against the north coast of Saipan, the reserve regiments of both divisions are committed ashore. Despite heavy casualties (over 2,000 dead and wounded), the divisions seize a firm beachhead by nightfall, then drive off enemy counterattacks.
Japan
China-based Army Air Forces B-29 bombers launch their first attacks on Kyushu, thus opening an air offensive against the Japanese home islands.
Pacific Theater
The South Pacific theater is revamped, with some forces and territory going to MacArthur's command.

Left: *A Coast Guard-manned LCVP takes a boat-load of Marines toward shore during the assault on Saipan. (MacArthur Memorial)*

Right: *Men of the 2nd Marine Division under heavy fire on the beach at Saipan. An LVT(A)4, with its short-barreled 75mm howitzer, sits in the background. (National Archives)*

Force Structure
AirSols is redesignated as Aircraft, Northern Solomons. Its new commander is Major General Ralph Mitchell. Of its 40 flying squadrons, 23 are Marine.

16 June
Guam
Vice Admiral Raymond A. Spruance, overall commander of the Marianas operation, cancels the Guam landing planned for 18 June upon learning that the Japanese fleet has sortied from the Philippines.
Saipan
The 2nd and 4th Marine Divisions expand their beachhead against continuing fierce resistance. As part of the redeployment of the fleet for battle, most transports are due to withdraw on 17 June, so Smith orders two-thirds of the 27th Infantry Division landed. That night, the Japanese launch a major counterattack against the 2nd Marine Division with 44 medium tanks and 500 infantrymen. The enemy are repulsed with a loss of 31 tanks and 300 men.

17 June
Saipan
American forces on Saipan resume their attack, with the Army's 165th Regiment taking over the right flank of the 4th Marine Division zone. Progress remains slow and averages a thousand yards across the extended front.

18 June
Saipan
The 105th Infantry enters the fight on the right flank of the 165th Infantry, placing all eight U.S. infantry regiments on Saipan on the front lines. The 4th Marine Division reaches the east coast at Magicienne Bay, thus cutting the Japanese garrison in two, while the 27th Infantry Division captures Aslito Airfield.

19–20 June
Marianas
In the Battle of the Philippine Sea (also called the Marianas Turkey Shoot), Spruance's Task Force 58 decisively defeats the Japanese fleet in an aerial battle. American planes shoot down 424 enemy aircraft and sink a carrier and tanker.

20 June
Saipan
The 4th Marine Division reorients its lines to drive north on Saipan in conjunction with the 2nd Marine Division. The 27th Infantry Division's third regiment comes ashore and the division continues its attack to the southeast against enemy bottled up in Nafutan Point.
Tinian
An Army artillery battery on Saipan opens the bombardment against Tinian. By the time Marine forces launch the Tinian assault, 13 battalions of artillery will be executing preparation fires on that objective.

Left: *Marines leap from the side of an amphibious tractor near the beach on Namur Island. (National Archives)*

Below: *A Marine takes aim at the enemy on Roi Island, Kwajalein Atoll. (National Archives)*

Force Structure
MAG-91 and VMB-624 are organized at Cherry Point. VMSB-933 is formed at Eagle Mountain Lake.

21 June
Bougainville
The 3rd Defense Battalion departs Bougainville; it had been the last Marine ground unit in action there.

22 June
Saipan
Following a day of consolidation, the 2nd and 4th Marine Divisions gain ground in their drive north

on Saipan and come up against the enemy's new defensive line. The 6th Marines seizes Mount Tipo Pale. The 105th Infantry holds its position around Nafutan Point, while the remainder of the 27th Infantry Division becomes the corps reserve. The Army Air Forces 19th Fighter Squadron lands on Aslito Airfield.

23 June
Saipan
The 27th Infantry Division assumes responsibility for the center of the corps zone on Saipan. All three divisions make minimal progress.

24 June
Saipan
The 4th Marine Division wheels east to clean out Kagman Peninsula on Saipan. Disappointed by the performance of the 27th Infantry Division, Major General H. M. Smith relieves its commander, Army Major General Ralph C. Smith.

25 June
Saipan
The 2nd Marine Division captures Mount Tapotchau, the key point for observers controlling Japanese artillery fire on Saipan. The 4th Marine Division completes its mission of destroying enemy forces in the Kagman Peninsula. U.S. destroyers disperse a Japanese attempt to reinforce Saipan from Tinian with 11 troop-laden barges.

Force Structure
VMB-453 is organized at Cherry Point. VMF-911 is formed at Kinston, North Carolina.

26 June
Saipan
During the night, 500 Japanese troops infiltrates the lines of the Army battalion at Nafutan Point and conduct attacks against Aslito Airfield, artillery positions, and a Marine regiment in reserve. The enemy force is destroyed by dawn the next day.

27 June
Saipan
The 4th Marine Division resumes its position on the right flank of the corps front on Saipan.

30 June
New Hebrides
The headquarters of 2nd MAW moves from Efate to Espiritu Santo.
Manpower
The strength of the Marine Corps on active duty is 32,788 officers and 442,816 enlisted.

July
Bougainville
The headquarters of MAG-25 moves to Bougainville from New Caledonia.

1 July
Force Structure
VMSB-943 is formed at Santa Barbara.

3–4 July
Saipan
Following the enemy's withdrawal the previous day from his main defenses, VAC forces make significant progress on Saipan. The town of Garapan falls to the 2nd Marine Division, which then is pinched out of the corps front.

6 July
Guam
Major General H. M. Smith attaches the 77th Infantry Division to IIIAC for the Guam operation.

Above: *Red Beach 2 on Roi Island shows the effects of the heavy pre-landing bombardment. (National Archives)*

Right: *The crew of a Browning air-cooled machine gun waits for orders on the beach at Namur Island. (National Archives)*

7 July
Saipan
Prior to dawn, about 3,000 Japanese launch a last-ditch banzai attack that falls primarily on the 105th Infantry. After overrunning the Army positions, the enemy strike batteries of the 10th Marines. Marines and soldiers defeat the attack by noon, but American casualties exceed 1,000.

8 July
Saipan
The 2nd Marine Division passes through the 27th Division and reassumes responsibility for the left flank of the corps front.

9 July
Saipan
The 4th Marine Division reaches Marpi Point, the northern end of Saipan, and all organized Japanese resistance is finished. Among the Japanese dead is Admiral Chuichi Nagumo, leader of the Pearl Harbor raid.

10 July
Marshalls
The Army's 305th Regimental Combat Team (305th RCT) on Eniwetok is assigned to the 1st Provisional Marine Brigade.
Force Structure
VMF-912 is organized at Cherry Point.

10–11 July
Tinian
Elements of the VAC Amphibious Reconnaissance Battalion and Underwater Demolitions Teams 5 and 7 scout the Tinian landing beaches.

12 July
Command
Major General H. M. Smith relinquishes command of VAC to Major General Harry Schmidt and becomes the first commander of FMFPAC.
Emirau
MAG-61 departs Espiritu Santo for Emirau, where it will remain for the rest of the war.

Above: *Marines carry in the body of a dead buddy on Saipan. (National Archives)*

Left: *Action on Saipan, 6–7 July 1944. ("Counterattack by Japanese Troops Defending Saipan," John Hamilton, Naval Art Collection)*

Right: *The morning after the Japanese banzai charge on Saipan. ("Aftermath of Battle, Saipan," William Draper, Naval Art Collection)*

Below: *These three Marines, all Navajo Indians, served as "code talkers" on Saipan. Selected words in their language provided an unbreakable code for tactical communications. (National Archives)*

13 July
Saipan
3/6 conducts a shore-to-shore amphibious assault and seizes Maniagassa Island off the coast of Saipan. The 2nd and 4th Marine Divisions begin recuperating and preparing for the Tinian assault. Marine casualties on Saipan total 3,152 dead and 8,575 wounded. Losses among Navy personnel serving with Marines units are 77 killed and 337 wounded.

15 July
Force Structure
VMF-913 is commissioned at Greenville, North Carolina. VMSB-941 is organized at Bogue Field.

18 July
Japan
As a result of the loss of Saipan, the cabinet of Premier Tojo leaves office and a new government is installed in Japan.

20 July
Force Structure
VMB-463 is commissioned at Cherry Point.

21 July
Guam
IIIAC (also designated the Southern Troops and Landing Force) assaults the west coast of Guam. The 3rd Marine Division goes ashore north of Orote Peninsula with all three regiments abreast, while the 1st Provisional Marine Brigade lands to

Left: *Marines get briefed on their mission just prior to the invasion of Guam. (MacArthur Memorial)*

Below: *Marines display an American flag recaptured on Guam, while a Japanese battle standard lies in the dust. (MacArthur Memorial)*

Opposite, top: *Marines use flamethrowers to rout out entrenched enemy on Tinian. (National Archives)*

Opposite, bottom: *A wounded Marine doubles over as others react to sniper fire on Saipan. (MacArthur Memorial)*

the south of the peninsula with the 4th and 22nd Marines in the lead and the 305th RCT in reserve. By the end of the day, the corps has two separate beachheads on either side of Orote. The brigade fights off a strong Japanese counterattack that night.

22 July
Guam
Elements of the 9th Defense Battalion land on Guam to provide assistance to other IIIAC forces.

23 July
Guam
Elements of the 3rd Marine Division complete the seizure of Cabras Island off the coast of Guam. The 14th Defense Battalion assumes control of the island. The 77th Infantry Division begins going ashore and replacing elements of the Marine brigade in the southern perimeter.

24 July
Tinian
The 4th Marine Division conducts an amphibious assault on the northwest coast of Tinian, while the 2nd Marine Division makes an amphibious feint in the south. The Japanese conduct a major banzai attack against the beachhead that evening and suffer severe losses.

25 July
Tinian
The 2nd Marine Division comes ashore and begins to assume responsibility for the eastern half of the corps zone. The 8th Marines captures Ushi Point Airfield.
Guam
The Marine brigade seals off the base of Orote Peninsula and positions itself with both Marine

regiments abreast to assault the peninsula the next day. The 77th Infantry Division assumes complete responsibility for the rest of the southern beachhead facing toward the remainder of Guam. That night, the Japanese launch a strong counterattack, mainly against the northern beachhead, but the 3rd Marine Division repulses it.

Force Structure

MAG-94 and VMB-473 are commissioned at Cherry Point. VMSB-934 is organized at Bogue Field.

26 July

Guam

The Marine brigade launches its assault on Orote Peninsula.

Tinian

The 2nd and 4th Marines Divisions drive south on Tinian, with the latter organization seizing Mount Lasso, the highest terrain on the island.

27 July

Tinian

Ushi Point Airfield goes into operation.

28 July

Guam

The 22nd Marines captures the old Marine Barracks on Orote Peninsula. The 3rd Marine Division and 77th Infantry Division expand their beachheads and link them in one solid perimeter. The 395th Infantry captures Mount Tenjo.

29 July

Guam

The Marine brigade defeats the last organized Japanese resistance on Orote Peninsula.

30 July

Tinian

The 4th Marine Division captures Tinian Town.

Guam

The airfield on Orote Peninsula goes into operation when aircraft from VMO-1 land on it.

31 July

Tinian

The 2nd and 4th Marine Divisions meet stiff resistance along an escarpment in southern Tinian. By the end of the day, the 8th Marines has a toehold on the high ground.

THE BATTLE OF TINIAN

Most Pacific theater battles in the latter stages of World War II pitted American foot soldiers and firepower against Japanese fortifications and fatalism. U.S. forces won every time, but always at a high cost in lives. The conquest of Tinian was a welcome exception to that rule.

Geography had made Tinian a strategic objective of the first order by 1944. The new long-range B-29 bombers of the Army Air Forces could reach distant Tokyo from this 50 square mile mesa of an island in the middle of the Pacific. Its level surface and location thus made it a massive aircraft carrier awaiting only a little engineering, some planes, and their supporting elements to become a mortal threat to the Japanese homeland.

Geography also partially accounted for the relative ease with which Marines would seize the island. Its northern end was only four miles south of Saipan, which V Amphibious Corps had captured in a bitter battle that ended on 9 July 1944. From that close range, U.S. forces executed a pre-landing bombardment against Tinian and its 9,000 defenders that was unmatched in scope and ferocity. Naval forces had begun their preparation fires on Tinian on the same day that the assault forces went ashore at Saipan—11 June. Once the latter island was secured, the fleet turned the full fury of its guns and carrier planes on their second objective. In addition to that 44-day blitz from the sea, the Americans were able to bring to bear artillery and land-based air once the southern end of Saipan was cleared early in that battle. By 24 July, 13 battalions of artillery were focusing their attention across the narrow waters. Planes took off regularly from a hastily rehabilitated airfield and flew the short distance south to drop their loads, which included a new munition—napalm-filled canisters. The jellied gasoline burned off concealing vegetation even when it didn't inflict casualties.

Vigilant Marines try to coax Japanese soldiers out of a bunker on Tinian. (MacArthur Memorial)

What really made Tinian unique in the latter stages of the Pacific campaign, however, was the scheme of maneuver employed by the assault forces. During the planning stages, Vice Admiral Richmond Kelly Turner (commander of the amphibious task force) had wanted to land on the best available site along the southwest coast. This followed usual practice—getting as many men and as much materiel ashore as rapidly as possible—which required a wide swath of relatively open beach. The Japanese were well aware of American proclivities and they had placed nearly all their defenses there. Reconnaissance by Navy underwater demolition teams and the Corps amphibious recon unit revealed heavy fortifications, numerous minefields, and a forest of obstacles along that part of the coastline.

Major General Holland Smith was drawn to an alternate idea. There were two small landing sites at the northwestern end of Tinian. White Beach One was 60 yards wide. White Two stretched for 160 yards, but more than half of it was blocked by boulders or rock ledges just in from the water. These two small gaps in the cliffs that otherwise formed the northern coast seemed like such unlikely places for an American landing that the Japanese had not bothered to give them much attention. Turner initially rejected this option, but finally gave in to the strong arguments of Smith. The naval commander still maintained that he could not get enough men and supplies ashore through such a narrow bottleneck.

The battle opened on 24 July with the 2nd Marine Division feigning a landing against the southwestern beaches. That brought forth a fierce response from Japanese coastal guns that had survived weeks of bombardment. The defenders scored a total of 28 hits on the battleship *Colorado* (BB-45) and the destroyer *Norman Scott* (DD-690), while mortars and artillery peppered the empty amphibian tractors making a showy approach toward shore. With the enemy's attention focused on the south, the 4th Marine Division stormed ashore over the White Beaches. A few Japanese soldiers and mines were the only opposition. By the end of the day, all the combat units of the 4th Division and the lead elements of the 2nd had streamed through the two choke points. More than 15,000 Marines had gotten ashore with only 15 killed and 225 wounded—10 percent of the losses for the opening day of the Saipan landing.

According to plan, the assault units stopped early in the afternoon despite the lack of serious resistance. Pre-loaded amtracs appeared at the front with extra ammunition and enough concertina wire to enclose the entire beachhead. Tanks, 75mm halftracks, and 37mm anti-tank guns bolstered every infantry battalion. When the inevitable banzai counterattack took place that night, the Marines handily beat it back. The Marines suffered less than 100 casualties and destroyed five enemy tanks and killed 1,200 Japanese. It took eight more days for the two Marine divisions to reach the southern end of Tinian. Along the way, they enveloped the formidable southwestern beach defenses from the rear, but the enemy had already abandoned these fortifications facing uselessly out to sea. In the course of the entire battle, the landing force suffered 328 killed and 1,571 wounded—the cheapest conquest of the Pacific war for an island defended as strongly as this one.

Although the unusually heavy application of firepower had played a role in minimizing friendly losses on Tinian, the bold choice to attack where the enemy least expected it was primarily responsible for the favorable outcome. The operation remains a classic of Marine ingenuity and daring.

Guam
The 3rd Marine Division captures Agana, the capital, while the 77th Infantry Division reaches the eastern coast of the island, cutting it two. Most Japanese forces have withdrawn to the north.

1 August
Tinian
The 2nd and 4th Marine Divisions reach the southern coast of Tinian and all organized Japanese resistance is finished. Marine casualties on Tinian total 368 dead and 1,921 wounded. Losses among Navy personnel attached to VAC are 26 killed and 40 wounded.

Guam
The 1st Provisional Marine Brigade assumes responsibility for clearing the southern sector of Guam while the 3rd Marine Division and the 77th Infantry Division advance abreast to the north.
Force Structure
VMSB-236 and 241 are decommissioned.
France
Major Peter Ortiz and Marine Sergeants John P. Bodnar, Jack R. Risler, and Frederick J. Brunner parachute into German-occupied southeastern France. They are part of a seven-man team from the Office of Strategic Services (a forerunner of the Central Intelligence Agency) inserted to assist French guerrilla units. All but Brunner are captured by German forces on 16 August.

3 August
Force Structure
MBDAG-48 is organized at Santa Barbara.

4 August
Guam
VMF(N)-534 is the first squadron of MAG-21 to arrive on Guam, followed soon after by VMF-216, 217, and 225. The 77th Infantry Division captures Mount Barrigada.

Above: *Some enterprising Marines acquire fresh meat on Guam. (MacArthur Memorial)*

Left: *Marines wade ashore on the rocky Tinian beaches as the sun sets. (MacArthur Memorial)*

5 August
Guam
The 3rd Marine Division smashes through the Japanese defensive line around the town of Finegayan.

6 August
Tinian
The 2nd and 4th Marine Divisions begin embarking, with the 2nd headed for Saipan and the 4th for Hawaii. The 8th Marines assumes responsibility for mopping up Tinian.

7 August
Guam
The 1st Provisional Marine Brigade reenters the corps front on the left flank (western coast of Guam), with the 3rd Marine Division in the center and the 77th Infantry Division on the right. IIIAC launches its final attack to seize northern Guam. VMF-225 launches the first combat air patrol and close air support missions from Orote Airfield.

8 August
Guam
The 77th Infantry Division captures Mount Santa Rosa.

10 August
Guam
The 3rd Marine Division destroys and captures the last handful of Japanese tanks on Guam and reaches the northern coast. IIIAC declares the island secure, although mopping-up operations will continue until the end of the war. Marine casualties during the assault phase on Guam total 1,568 dead and 6,933 wounded. Losses among Navy personnel serving with IIIAC are 51 killed and 206 wounded.
Force Structure
MAG-92 is organized at Cherry Point.

Above: *A Marine rifleman employs a Japanese sniper suit for camouflage on Tinian. (MacArthur Memorial)*

Right: *Cooks dole out the first hot meal during the operation on Guam on 21 July 1944. (MacArthur Memorial)*

Left: *A Navy corpsman administers life-saving blood plasma near the frontlines on Saipan. (National Archives)*

Below: *A machine gun crew checks the field of fire from the window of a destroyed building on Guam. (MacArthur Memorial)*

12 August
Guam
Major General Roy Geiger departs Guam for Guadalcanal. His IIIAC headquarters begins to follow the next day. Geiger and his staff assume responsibility for planning the Palaus campaign, slated to begin on 15 September.

13 August
Marianas
VAC assumes command of all Marine ground units remaining in the Marianas that are not under control of the recently established island garrison commands.

14 August
Force Structure
VMF-914 is organized at Greenville.

15 August
Guam
Marine Major General Henry L. Larsen and his Island Command headquarters takes complete control of Guam.

18 August
Northern Ireland
Marine Barracks Londonderry is disbanded and most of the Marines sail for the States. An 80-man detachment remains behind to guard the Naval Radio Station.

21 August
France
Marine Second Lieutenant Walter W. Taylor, working with an OSS team in front of Allied lines in southern France, is captured by German forces.
Guam
The 1st Provisional Marine Brigade begins embarking on ships for transport to Guadalcanal.
Force Structure
VMF-921 and 922 are formed at Cherry Point.

22 August
Guam
The 3rd Marine Division is assigned to Guam Island Command to continue mopping up operations. Numerous Japanese holdouts resist until December 1945. The last of them come out of hiding in 1960.

Above: *Two Marine captains of an amphibious tractor battalion hoist Old Glory on a boat hook eight minutes after the first wave touches shore on Guam. (MacArthur Memorial)*

Right: *This Marine take a breather with some of the local produce on Saipan. (National Archives)*

24 August
Force Structure
Administrative Command FMFPAC is redesignated Provisional Headquarters FMFPAC. VMSB-942 is organized at Bogue Field.

25 August
European Theater
Paris is liberated by Allied forces.

26 August
Force Structure
VMB-483 is formed at Cherry Point.

29 August
France
As part of the Allied invasion of southern France, the Marine detachments of the cruisers *Augusta* (CA-31) and *Philadelphia* (CL-41) land on islands in Marseilles harbor and oversee the surrender and disarmament of the German garrisons.

31 August
Force Structure
The Commandant directs that FMFPAC will consist of Headquarters Troops, IIIAC, VAC, FMF Supply Service, and other supporting elements. The future chain of command of Marine aviation units in the Pacific theater remains unresolved. The 20th Marines is disbanded as 4th Marine Division shifts to the new tables of organization.

5 September
Force Structure
MAG-51 moves from Oak Grove, North Carolina, to Mojave, California.

7 September
Force Structure
The 1st Provisional Marine Brigade headquarters is deactivated on Guadalcanal and its units (primarily the 4th and 22nd Marines) are absorbed by the 6th Marine Division, organized the same day. The other main elements of the

Above: *A Marine reaches through the fence of a refugee camp on Tinian to give a child some candy. (Marine Corps Research Center)*

Left: *A war dog unit moves up toward the frontlines on Guam. (MacArthur Memorial)*

division are the 29th Marines (infantry) and 15th Marines (artillery).

8 September
Ellice Islands
The 10th Defense Battalion relieves the 51st Defense Battalion in the Ellice Islands.
Marshalls
The 51st moves forward to Eniwetok Atoll.

9 September
Ulithi
MBDAG-45 departs California for Ulithi, where it will provide air protection to the fleet anchorage.

15 September
Peleliu
Based on input from Admiral Halsey and General MacArthur, the JCS ordered MacArthur to forego his scheduled 15 November invasion of Mindanao in the southern Philippines and instead attack Leyte in the central Philippines in mid-October. The Peleliu operation, originally designed to support the Mindanao strike, goes forward as planned. On this day, the 1st Marine Division launches its assault on the southwest coast of Peleliu in the Palau Islands. The three infantry regiments of the division sustain heavy casualties in fighting their way ashore, but withstand a Japanese tank-led counterattack late in the afternoon. The lead echelon of MAG-11 goes ashore.

Force Structure
VMF-923 is organized at Parris Island.

16 September
Peleliu
The 7th Marines completes its turning movement to the right and isolates the southern promontory. The 5th Marines in the center drives straight across the island, seizing the airfield and reaching the opposite shore. The 1st Marines wheels left into a widening zone and begins the assault toward the rugged coral ridges that constitute the heart of the Japanese defenses.

Above: *Marines on the beach during the early hours of the assault on Peleliu, 15 September 1944. (National Archives)*

Right: *Dug-in Marines await an expected Japanese counterattack on Peleliu. (National Archives)*

Left: *A badly wounded Marine is passed down out of the broken coral of Umurbrogol Ridge. A Marine with a rifle grenade at the ready is in the foreground. (Marine Corps Research Center)*

17 September
Peleliu
The 7th Marines continues its assault on the southern promontory, while the 1st Marines and 2/7 batter their way into the nightmare terrain in the north. Two regiments of the 81st Infantry Division assault Angaur Island just south of Peleliu.
Force Structure
The "Provisional" label is dropped from the title of FMFPAC headquarters.

18 September
Peleliu
The 7th Marines completes the seizure of the southern promontory of the island.

19 September
Peleliu
The 5th Marines nearly completes the conquest of the eastern flatlands, while the 1st Marines presses deeper into the coral ridges. Two light planes of VMO-3 are the first to land on Peleliu's airfield.

20 September
Philippines
The seven dive-bombing squadrons of the 1st MAW are slated to support Army forces in the upcoming Luzon campaign.

21 September
Peleliu
The 7th Marines assumes responsibility for the center of the 1st Marine Division zone and takes up the assault on the coral ridges. The 1st Marines focuses its remaining combat power on the narrow plain on the west coast of Peleliu. Elements of the 5th Marines occupy two small islands off the northeast coast of Peleliu. On Angaur, the 81st Infantry Division has conquered all but the northwest corner of the island.
Marshalls
The 52nd Defense Battalion departs San Diego for the Marshalls, where detachments will guard Roi-Namur and Majuro Atoll.

23 September
Peleliu
The 321st RCT, temporarily detached from the 81st Infantry Division, arrives on Peleliu from Angaur and begins replacing the 1st Marines in the lines.

24 September
Peleliu
The 321st RCT begins a drive up the west coast of the island designed to surround the coral ridges. The 7th Marines continues the assault against the ridges from the south and west. The first aircraft of VMF(N)-541 arrive on Peleliu. The headquarters of 2nd MAW arrives on Peleliu.
Ulithi
The 323rd RCT of the 81st Infantry Division secures Ulithi Atoll, northeast of the Palaus.

25 September
Peleliu
The 5th Marines is committed to exploit the lack of significant enemy resistance on the west coast of Peleliu. While the 321st RCT drives across the island north of the coral ridges to isolate the Japanese strongpoint, the 5th Marines continues north with the objective of seizing the less-rugged ground at that end of the island.
Force Structure
VMD-954 is organized at Cherry Point.

26 September
Peleliu
VMF-114 flies into the Peleliu airfield.

28 September
Peleliu
3/5 conducts a shore-to-shore amphibious assault from northern Peleliu to seize Ngesebus Island off the coast.

29 September
Peleliu
While 3/5 completes the conquest of Ngesebus, the rest of the 5th Marines wipes out the last significant Japanese positions in northern Peleliu. All enemy resistance is now bottled up in the central ridges, an area roughly one-half mile long by one-quarter mile wide and henceforth known as the Umurbrogol Pocket. The 7th Marines assumes responsibility for squeezing out this position. The 321st RCT begins mopping up operations in northern Peleliu.

Right: *Pilots of Pappy Boyington's famed Blacksheep Squadron (VMF-214) on Vella Lavella in 1944. (National Archives)*

October
Force Structure
MAG-35 moves from Corvallis to El Centro, California.

1 October
Peleliu
VMF-122 and the rest of VMF(N)-541 arrive on the island. The 322nd RCT of the 81st Infantry Division has compressed the remaining Japanese into a small pocket on Anguar. Thereafter the regiment primarily uses heavy firepower rather than infantry assault to reduce these well-fortified positions.

2 October
Peleliu
The remnants of the 1st Marines depart Peleliu for Pavuvu.

3 October
Peleliu
The 7th Marines seizes Walt's Ridge and Boyd Ridge, further compressing the Umurbrogol Pocket.

Above: *A rifle grenade launches toward Japanese positions behind a low ridge. (Marine Corps Research Center)*

Left: *A Marine checks a casualty slumped against the side of a trench on Peleliu. (National Archives)*

4 October
Technology
The Germans employ the Me 262, the first jet combat plane, in its first fighter mission against Allied bombers.

5 October
Peleliu
The 5th Marines relieves the 7th Marines around the Umurbrogol Pocket.

8 October
Ulithi
MBDAG-45 arrives from the States with the mission of protecting this vital anchorage.

10 October
Peleliu
Elements of the 5th Marines seize Old Baldy, a key terrain feature in the Umurbrogol Pocket.
Force Structure
VMSB-334, 342, 344, 941, 942, and 944 and VMF-472, 481, 482, 921, 922, 923, and 924 are decommissioned.

Above: *A weary Marine pauses during mopping up operations. ("Not for the Glory of War," G. Corriero, Marine Corps Art Collection)*

Right: *Marine dead are gathered for temporary burial in a shallow grave. The intense heat and high casualties on Peleliu were additional parts of the nightmare. (Marine Corps Research Center)*

11 October
Force Structure
Command relationships are formalized for FMFPAC. General Smith is given the status of a type commander for all operational Marine forces; as such he reports to COMINCH/CNO (Admiral King). Aircraft FMFPAC is a component of FMFPAC, but under operational control of the commander of Air Force Pacific Fleet (an admiral).

12 October
Peleliu
The assault phase of the Peleliu operation is declared over, but IIIAC continues to control the battle to reduce the Umurbrogol Pocket. Marine Brigadier General Harold D. Campbell and his Island Command assume responsibility for the remainder of Peleliu. Among his forces is the 12th Antiaircraft Artillery Battalion.

13 October
Iwo Jima
VAC headquarters moves from the Marianas to Hawaii to begin planning for the Iwo Jima operation.

14 October
Force Structure
VMSB-144 is redesignated VMTB-144.

Above: *One Marine can still smile after weeks of fighting on Peleliu. (National Archives)*

Left: *Machine gunners get a welcome delivery of mail during a break in the battle for Peleliu. (Marine Corps Research Center)*

15 October
Peleliu
The 321st RCT begins replacing the 5th Marines in the lines around the Umurbrogol Pocket. This Japanese zone is now no larger than 400 yards by 500 yards.
Saipan
Aslito Airfield is now capable of handling B-29s, the large bombers that will launch strikes on the Japanese homeland from the Marianas.
Force Structure
VMSB-132 is redesignated VMTB-132.

16 October
Peleliu
The 321st RCT completes its relief of the 5th Marines, which goes into reserve.

17 October
Philippines
The Army's 6th Ranger Battalion seizes islands in Leyte Gulf in preparation for the Leyte campaign. Four Marine aviation officers, including Major General Ralph Mitchell, accompany the force as observers.

20 October
Peleliu
The 322nd Infantry wipes out the last pocket of Japanese resistance on Angaur. The 81st Infantry Division assumes responsibility for ground operations on Peleliu in place of IIIAC and the 1st Marine Division. Both Marine commanders and their senior staffs depart the island by air; IIIAC to Guadalcanal and the division to Pavuvu. The 5th Marines remains ashore attached to the 81st Division.
Philippines
Sixth U.S. Army begins the invasion of Leyte Island.

21 October
Philippines
VAC Artillery (a headquarters element and a battalion each of 155mm guns and howitzers) goes ashore on Leyte to support Sixth U.S. Army.
Carrier Air
Marine Carrier Groups headquarters is established at Santa Barbara, California, as a subordinate echelon of Aircraft FMFPAC. This marks the beginning of the process of establishing Marine squadrons on Navy carriers for the first time in World War II.

Right: *A war dog handler reads a message just delivered by his faithful companion. (Marine Corps Research Center)*

Left: *A Marine prepares for a rush forward under the intense enemy fire at Peleliu. (National Archives)*

22 October
Ulithi
VMF-321 and VMTB-232 arrive to join MBDAG-45. VMF(N)-542 joins soon after.

23 October
Philippines
The Battle of Leyte Gulf begins, the last-ditch effort of the Imperial Navy to defeat the U.S. Navy. It lasts through 26 October and results in the virtual annihilation of the remaining Japanese surface fleet, with the loss of four carriers, three battleships, 10 cruisers, nine destroyers, and a submarine.

25 October
Tinian
1/8 assumes responsibility for mopping up Tinian when the rest of the 8th Marines departs for Saipan.

30 October
Peleliu
The 5th Marines and the last elements of the 7th Marines depart Peleliu for Pavuvu. Marine casualties for the operation total 1,336 dead or missing and 5,450 wounded. Losses among Navy personnel serving with Marines units are 61 killed and 249 wounded.

1 November
Force Structure
MAG-34 and 94 swap designations. The old MAG-92 redesignated as MAG-91. Upon its arrival at Walnut Ridge, Arkansas, MAG-52 is redesignated as the new MAG-92.

4 November
Force Structure
Marine Base Defense Air Group 48 at Santa Barbara and MAG-51 at Mojave are redesignated as Marine Air Support Groups (MASG). Each will be composed of four carrier air groups (MCVG). An MCVG will operate from a single escort carrier with a fighter squadron and a torpedo bomber squadron. The mission of the MASGs is to provide close air support to ground troops during an amphibious assault and subsequent fighting ashore.

7 November
Force Structure
MAG-24 and 32 and VMSB-133, 142, 236, 241, 243, 244, and 341 are assigned to the operational control of Fifth Air Force for the upcoming Luzon campaign.

10 November
Force Structure
The 4th Marine Base Defense Aircraft Wing is redesignated 4th MAW and its groups (MBDAG-41, 42, 44, 45, and 46) are redesignated as MAGs. MAG-44 is moving from California to Hawaii. VMSB-235 is decommissioned.

13 November
Peleliu
The final elements of the 1st Marine Division, mainly amphibian tractors, depart Peleliu for Pavuvu.

20 November
Force Structure
VMO-6 is commissioned at Quantico. VMSB-943 is redesignated VMTB-943 at El Toro.

24 November
Saipan
B-29s operating from the island bomb Tokyo. This marks the first attack on the Japanese capital by land-based aircraft.

27 November
Peleliu
The 81st Infantry Division reports the end of organized Japanese resistance in the Umurbrogol Pocket.

Above: *Peleliu. ("Marines Advance Under Fire," Walter A. Jones, Marine Corps Art Collection)*

Right: *A Marine on Peleliu—the intensity of the battle etched on his face. (National Archives)*

29 November
New Hebrides
MAG-33 arrives at Espiritu Santo.

30 November
Philippines
Four Corsair squadrons of 1st MAW are ordered to Leyte under operational control of Fifth Air Force to free Navy carriers for duty elsewhere.

December
Carrier Air
VMF-221 goes on board carrier *Bunker Hill* (CV-17).
Peleliu
The headquarters of 2nd MAW shifts from Peleliu to Hawaii.

2 December
Manpower
The first Women's Reservists report for duty in Hawaii following authorization for them to serve outside the continental limits of the United States.

3 December
Philippines
VMF(N)-541 moves from Peleliu to Tacloban Airfield on Leyte, to provide faster fighters than those of the Army Air Forces, which could not catch Japanese bombers. MAG-12 and its squadrons (VMF-115, 211, 218, and 313) begin arriving at Tacloban from Emirau and become part of Fifth Air Force.
Carrier Air
Due to the threat of Japanese kamikaze attacks, the number of fighter planes on Navy carriers is increased. Since no additional Navy fighter pilots are available, Marine squadrons are rushed in to fill the gap. VMF-112 goes on board carrier *Bennington* (CV-20).

7 December
Philippines
MAG-12 aircraft participate in attacks to destroy Japanese convoys bringing more troops to Leyte. The effort continues through 12 December and results in 10 ships sunk or damaged and the end of enemy reinforcement efforts.

10 December
Force Structure
MBDAG-43 is redesignated MAG-43.

11 December
Philippines
MAG-12 Corsairs shoot down 19 Japanese aircraft either attacking U.S. ships or defending their own against Marine air attacks.

12 December
Philippines
VMF(N)-541 downs 11 enemy planes and prevents an air attack on a U.S. convoy just after dawn.

13 December
Philippines
A kamikaze strikes cruiser *Nashville* (CL-43) during the movement of Army forces to Mindoro. Among the 135 dead on the ship are 28 men of her Marine detachment. VAC Artillery departs Leyte for Guam.

14 December
Philippines
MAG-12 attacks enemy airfields on Luzon and Masbate Islands to reduce Japanese aerial opposition to the pending Mindoro landing.

Opposite: *"First Toll at Guam," William Draper, Naval Art Collection.*

Above: *Col John Walker, LtGen Holland M. Smith, MajGen Roy S. Geiger, and Adm Raymond A. Spruance (left to right) on Guam. (MacArthur Memorial)*

Right: *On the opening day of the Bougainville landing, these Corsairs at Barakoma Airfield on Vella Lavella are ready to sortie to cover the beachhead. (National Archives)*

Left: *Joe Rosenthal's immortal photo of the second flag-raising on Mount Suribachi. (AP Wide World)*

Opposite, top: *The first flag is taken down as the second one is fixed in place on Iwo Jima. (National Archives)*

Opposite, below: *The first salute rendered to Old Glory on the summit of Mount Suribachi. (National Archives)*

15 December
Philippines
Planes of MAG-12 and VMF(N)-541 provide combat air patrol over the landing of Sixth Army on Mindoro Island.
Okinawa
The headquarters of 2nd MAW moves from Peleliu to Hawaii. It subsequently serves as the nucleus for Tactical Air Force, the aviation component of Tenth Army, which will conduct the invasion of Okinawa.

Force Structure
VMO-7 is organized at Quantico.

26 December
Philippines
Sixth Army declares Leyte secured.

28 December
Carrier Air
VMF-124 and 213 join *Essex* (CV-9) at Ulithi Atoll and become the first Marine aircraft to operate from carriers during World War II (beating out the program already underway to place them on their own escort carriers to support amphibious assaults).
Force Structure
VMO-8 is commissioned at Quantico.

30 December
Tinian
B-29s begin using airfields on Tinian.

31 December
Carrier Air
VMF-123 joins *Bennington*.

1945

1 January
Marianas
1/8 departs Tinian to rejoin the 2nd Marine Division on Saipan.

2 January
Philippines
MAG-14, VMF-212, 222, and 223, and VMO-251 begin deploying from the Solomons to an airfield on the island of Samar. The movement of aerial echelons is complete by 24 January.

3 January
Carrier Air
Marine aircraft on *Essex* participate in their first missions from the carrier, during strikes on Okinawa, and shoot down their first Japanese plane.

6 January
Philippines
MAG-12 aircraft participate in raids to destroy key bridges on Luzon. The attacks continue through 9 January.

9 January
Philippines
Sixth Army conducts an amphibious assault at Lingayen Gulf on Luzon.

10 January
Philippines
Advance parties of MAG-24 and 32 go ashore at Lingayen.

11 January
Philippines
VMF(N)-541 departs Leyte for Peleliu.

12 January
Carrier Air
Marine aircraft on *Essex* participate in major strikes along the coast of French Indochina.

20 January
Carrier Air
Marine Lieutenant William McGill from *Essex* shoots down three Japanese aircraft as the U.S. fleet exits the South China Sea.

24 January
Carrier Air
Planes of VMF-451 go on board *Bunker Hill.*

25 January
Philippines
The first planes of VMSB-133 and 241 arrive at newly built Mangalden Airfield on Luzon. They are the lead echelon of MAG-24 and 32, which are titled Marine Air Groups Dagupan. Within six days, seven squadrons are present.

Above: *A 5th Division Marine wounded by mortar fragments is helped to the rear. (National Archives)*

Left: *Stretcher bearers carry their precious load over the blasted volcanic landscape of Iwo Jima. (National Archives)*

Right: *Marines turn a captured Japanese Taisho 3 Model 1914 machine gun (a modified Hotchkiss) against its former owners. (National Archives)*

Below: *Men of the 4th Marine Division climb toward the Quarry on the right flank of the Iwo Jima landing beaches. (National Archives)*

27 January
Philippines
VMSB-241 flies its first sorties in support of Army ground forces on Luzon. MAG-32 arrives at Mangalden Airfield.

31 January
Force Structure
VMO-155 is redesignated VMF-155 on Kwajalein. VMO-251 is redesignated VMF-251 on Samar. VMB-621 is redesignated VMTB-621 at Cherry Point.

1 February
Philippines
The Army's 1st Cavalry Division launches a rapid attack from Lingayen Gulf designed to free internees near Manila. MAG-14 provides air liaison parties on the ground and continuous sorties overhead during the daytime to cover the flanks and front of the fast-moving ground columns. The Marine dive bombers help the division reach Manila on 3 February and achieve its mission.

3 February
Carrier Air
VMF-216 and 217 begin going on board carrier *Wasp* (CV-18) at Ulithi, as part of the program to add fighter planes to fleet carriers to deal with the kamikazes. VMF-511 goes aboard escort carrier *Block Island* (CVE-106), the first results of the program to provide Marine air support for amphibious assaults.

8 February
Carrier Air
Forward echelon of VMF-452 joins carrier *Franklin* (CV-13).

CORPORAL TONY STEIN

Tony Stein was born in Dayton, Ohio, on 30 September 1921. After graduating from Kiser High School, he became a toolmaker. Just eight days shy of his 21st birthday in 1942, he enlisted in the Marines. He quickly sought out the most hazardous duty, volunteering for the parachutists. By April 1943, he was in the South Pacific as a demolitions man with the 3rd Parachute Battalion (oddly enough at Camp Kiser on New Caledonia). He and his battalion deployed to Bougainville in early December and participated in the hard fighting at Helzapoppin Ridge during 7–10 December. Stein and his demolitions platoon were called on to plug a gap in the regiment's lines and stop a Japanese attack on the 9th.

He returned to the United States in January 1944 along with the rest of the 1st Parachute Regiment. Upon the disbandment of the parachute program the following month, he became part of the cadre of the brand-new

Tony Stein, pictured here as a PFC wearing his jump wings. The intrepid Marine seemed to be everywhere during the first few days of the battle on Iwo Jima. (National Archives)

5th Marine Division, ending up in Company A, 1st Battalion, 28th Marines. In July he got married, just before the division moved to Hawaii for final training for the Iwo Jima landing. In Hawaii, the former toolmaker obtained a stripped-down machine gun of the type used on fighter planes. He modified it into his own unique handheld infantry weapon, which he dubbed the "stinger."

The 28th Marines formed the very left flank of the amphibious assault on Iwo Jima on 19 February 1945. The 1st Battalion led the way ashore, with B and C Companies charging across the narrow neck toward the opposite shore. Company A landed behind them, then turned left to protect the flank against enemy forces holding Mt. Suribachi. Although initial opposition was not especially heavy, the Japanese opened an increasingly severe bombardment with mortars and artillery as subsequent waves crowded into the narrow beachhead. In the move toward the looming height at the southern end of the island, Company A also encountered the band of pillboxes guarding Suribachi's approaches.

Corporal Stein used the heavy firepower of his stinger to cover his platoon as it moved forward. When intense machine-gun fire from the defenders pinned down his fellow Marines, the former paratrooper stood up, fully exposed to bullets and shrapnel, to pinpoint the source. As the enemy zeroed in on him, he dashed forward and single-handedly attacked the fortifications one by one, until he had killed 20 Japanese soldiers and enabled his unit to regain the initiative. In the process, he exhausted his ammunition for his special weapon. Without hesitation, he stripped off his helmet and shoes to improve his mobility, picked up a wounded Marine, and took him to the beach. Then he returned with enough rounds to resume the fight. Before the day was over, he made seven more trips to the rear under fire, each time carrying or assisting a wounded Marine to the beach and bringing back a fresh supply of ammunition. When a halftrack arrived on the scene, he moved alongside the vehicle to direct its fire and assist in destroying another Japanese fortification. By the time evening approached, his furious assault had carried the platoon into exposed territory, so he covered its withdrawal to the company's night position with his unerring fire. Twice during the course of the day, bullets had knocked the stinger from his hands, but he had not received a scratch.

For his "aggressive initiative, sound judgment, and unwavering devotion to duty in the face of terrific odds" on D-Day, he later would be awarded the Medal of Honor. At the moment, though, there was still plenty of fighting before the battle would be won. The next day his luck temporarily ran out and he was struck by a bullet. He sustained another hit on 21 February and finally reported to the beach for treatment. The wounds to his neck and right arm were not serious, however, and he was back in the front lines three days later.

He remained undaunted by the heavy enemy fire that met every attack on the island. On 1 March, his company tried to attack through a draw toward Nishi Ridge, which was holding up the advance of the regiment. Pinned down by positions cleverly concealed in a cliff forming one side of the draw, Stein volunteered to lead 20 men to root out the opposition. Only seven returned from the unsuccessful mission. Corporal Stein was among the dead, from a gunshot wound in the right side of his chest.

Tony Stein's body came home to Dayton, Ohio, in December 1948, for permanent burial. In 1970, his audacious courage in the bloodiest battle of the Corps was honored when the Navy commissioned a brand-new destroyer escort USS *Stein* (DE-1065).

10 February
Carrier Air
Task Force 58 (TF 58) sails from Ulithi. Four of its fast carriers host 144 Marine Corsairs (16 percent of the fighter planes in the task force).
Force Structure
VMB-623 is redesignated VMTB-623.

13 February
Kwajalein
MAG-94 arrives on Kwajalein.

15 February
Force Structure
VMB-624 is redesignated VMTB-624.

16 February
Philippines
U.S. Army parachute troops assault Corregidor.

16–17 February
Carrier Air
Marine planes of TF 58 participate in air strikes in the Tokyo area. Marine pilots claim 21 Japanese aircraft shot down and another 60 destroyed on the ground.

19 February
Iwo Jima
Under the overall command of Lieutenant General H. M. Smith's Expeditionary Troops headquarters, VAC's 4th and 5th Marine Divisions lead the amphibious assault on the southeast coast of Iwo Jima. The 28th Marines reaches the western shore at the narrow neck of the island and seals off Mt. Suribachi before the end of the day, while the 27th and 23rd Marines make it to the edge of Airfield No. 1. Heavy Japanese artillery, mortar, and rocket fire, aided by mines and machine guns, inflicts over 2,400 casualties on the assault divisions. Marine aircraft aboard TF 58 participate in air strikes in support of the landing, and continue to do so through 22 February.
Philippines
Forty-eight Marine aircraft from Mangaldan strike derelict ships in Manila harbor to silence enemy opposition to Army forces.

20 February
Iwo Jima
The 28th Marines begins the assault on Mt. Suribachi. The 4th Marine Division and the remainder of the 5th Marine Division capture Airfield No. 1 as they begin the drive north.

Left: *Marines patrol the rugged terrain of Iwo Jima in search of Japanese survivors on 8 April 1945. (National Archives)*

Right: *A flame-throwing tank in action. These modified Sherman tanks were one of the key weapons in defeating Japanese burrowed deep into Iwo Jima's volcanic rock. (National Archives)*

Force Structure
VMB-453 is decommissioned at Cherry Point.

21 February
Iwo Jima
VAC commits the 21st Marines of the 3rd Marine Division from corps reserve to reinforce the 4th Marine Division. That night, the Japanese launch the only major kamikaze attack of the campaign, against the U.S. fleet off Iwo Jima.

22 February
Iwo Jima
Elements of the 8th Field Depot begin going ashore on Iwo Jima to manage the flow of supplies onto the island.
Philippines
Marine air liaison parties join up with Filipino guerrillas operating behind Japanese lines in northern Luzon.

23 February
Iwo Jima
Elements of the 28th Marines seize the crest of Mt. Suribachi and hoist an American flag over the summit. Soon after, five Marines and a corpsman replace it with a larger national ensign. Joe Rosenthal's photograph of this flag raising electrifies the United States and becomes the symbol for the 7th War Bond drive.
Philippines
VMF-115 Corsairs sink a midget submarine off Cebu. MAG-32 headquarters and its squadron ground echelons (the squadrons now assigned are VMSB-142, 236, 243, and 341) begin to move from Mangaldan for sea transport toward Zamboanga on the island of Mindanao in the southern Philippines.

24 February
Iwo Jima
The 3rd Marine Division (less the 21st Marines already ashore and the 3rd Marines still held as Expeditionary Troops reserve) begins to go ashore on Iwo Jima.

25 February
Iwo Jima
The 3rd Marine Division assumes responsibility for the center of the corps front on Iwo Jima, with the 4th Marine Division on its right and the 5th Marine Division on the left. VAC slugs its way slowly forward through the heaviest belt of Japanese defenses.

Carrier Air
Marine aircraft participate in TF 58 strikes around Tokyo.

26 February
Iwo Jima
Two planes from VMO-4 land on Airfield No.1 to begin spotting for artillery and naval gunfire.

27 February
Iwo Jima
The 9th Marines completes the seizure of Airfield No. 2 and also takes Hill Peter and Hill 199 Oboe, key terrain dominating the exposed strip. Army forces of the Island Command begin to come ashore. Planes of VMO-5 begin arriving.

28 February
Iwo Jima
The 21st Marines captures Motoyama Village and the high ground overlooking Airfield No. 3 on the northern plateau of Iwo Jima.
Force Structure
VMB-463 is decommissioned.

Above: *A Marine of Easy Company, 9th Marines, dashes across the open terrain leading to Iwo's Airfield #2. Men armed with flamethrowers were primary targets for Japanese gunners. (National Archives)*

Left: *A squad from 3/28 attacks up a rocky slope on Iwo Jima. (Marine Corps Research Center)*

1 March
Carrier Air
Marine aircraft participate in TF 58 strikes on Okinawa.
Iwo Jima
Transport planes of VMR-952 make the first Marine air drops of supplies on Iwo Jima. VMR-253 and 353 join in over the next few days.
Force Structure
VMSB-332 is redesignated VMTB-332. VMF-472 is reactivated at Mojave.

2 March
Iwo Jima
The 28th Marines captures Hill 362-A, the heavily fortified western anchor of the Japanese main cross-island defensive belt. Elements of the 24th Marines seize Hill 382, the highest elevation in northern Iwo Jima.

3 March
Iwo Jima
The 3rd Marine Division clears Airfield No. 3 and captures Hills 357 and 362B.

Above: *Marines bow their heads in prayer at the dedication of the 4th Marine Division cemetery on Iwo Jima. (National Archives)*

Right: *A rifle, stuck in the ground by its bayonet and topped by a helmet, marks the hasty grave of a Marine near the frontlines. (National Archives)*

Left: *A chaplain gives communion on Iwo Jima. (National Archives)*

Below: *A wounded man moves to the rear with the aid of a fellow Marine. (National Archives)*

Opposite, top: *A Marine crouches low as he dashes forward under fire on Iwo Jima. (Marine Corps Research Center)*

Opposite, below: *A tank lumbers up Iwo's sandy beaches with Suribachi looming in the background. (National Archives)*

Philippines
The U.S. Sixth Army wrests the last of Manila from the Japanese.

4 March
Iwo Jima
Although Marine gains have been measured in yards on Iwo Jima, at this point in the battle VAC has blasted and bled its way through most of the main Japanese defensive line. The first B-29, damaged during a strike on Japan, lands on Iwo Jima.

5 March
Iwo Jima
Lieutenant General H. M. Smith orders his Expeditionary Troops reserve, the 3rd Marines, to sail for Guam, despite the pleas of the VAC commander for use of the fresh regiment.

6 March
Iwo Jima
Following a day to consolidate and incorporate replacements, all three divisions of VAC renew the offensive behind a massive artillery, air, and naval bombardment. Gains remain small and hard-won in the extremely broken terrain falling away from Iwo Jima's northern plateau. Army Air Forces fighter squadrons begin to arrive on Iwo Jima.
Carrier Air
VMF-512 joins escort carrier *Gilbert Islands* (CVE-107) in San Diego.

7 March
Iwo Jima
Hill 362-C falls to the 9th Marines.

8 March
Iwo Jima
Army Air Forces fighter planes on Iwo Jima begin to assume combat air patrol over the island and to fly some close air support missions. Elements of VMTB-242 also arrive from Tinian to assist. Aircraft from VMR-253, 353, and 952 begin landing on Iwo's airstrips to deliver supplies and evacuate wounded. That night, the 4th Marine Division repulses a large-scale enemy counterattack, the first since the battle began.

9 March
Iwo Jima
Patrols from the 3rd Marine Division reach the northeast coast of the island.

10 March
Iwo Jima
The 4th Marine Division eliminates the Amphitheater-Turkey Knob salient that has been holding it up in the center of its zone since 25 February and makes substantial gains. The 3rd Marine Division largely clears the remainder of its zone. Navy escort carriers depart Iwo Jima, leaving aerial support in the hands of Army squadrons on the island.
Philippines
Elements of U.S. Eighth Army land at Zamboanga on Mindanao. MAG-12 furnishes air support for the operation, while forward elements of its ground echelons go ashore to begin manning an existing airfield.
Carrier Air
VMF-124 and 213 are detached from *Essex* and depart for the United States. A portion of the maintenance crews remain on board to service replacement Navy squadrons in subsequent operations.

11 March
Iwo Jima
The 3rd and 4th Marine Divisions drive to the coast in their respective zones, leaving only a few pockets of organized resistance remaining on the island.

12 March
Iwo Jima
The 9th Marines surrounds and compresses Cushman's Pocket, one of the last major Japanese strongholds on the island. Operations continue against this zone for the next several days.

13 March
Carrier Air
At Ulithi, VMF-216 and 217 are detached from *Wasp*, although some maintenance personnel remain on board.

14 March
Iwo Jima
As the official flag raising on Iwo Jima is held at the VAC command post, the flag raised on 23 February over Suribachi is lowered. Army aircraft fly the last close air support mission on the island since the remaining areas under Japanese control are too small to permit further attacks.
Carrier Air
TF 58 sails from Ulithi Atoll. With the addition of *Franklin* and her two Marine Corsair squadrons (VMF-214 and 452), there are six Marine squadrons in the task force.

15 March
Philippines
VMF-115 aircraft of MAG-12 land on San Roque airfield at Zamboanga and begin operations the next day.

Force Structure
MAG-92 and VMB-473 and 483 are deactivated.

16 March
Iwo Jima
The 9th Marines completes the reduction of Cushman's Pocket, while the 21st Marines cleans out the approaches to Kitano Point. The 4th Marine Division overruns the last area of resistance in its zone along the eastern coast. Iwo Jima is declared secure, though combat operations are not yet entirely complete.

17 March
Iwo Jima
The 26th Marines reaches the coast near Kitano Point, thus closing the ring on Death Valley, the gorge where the Japanese commander is holding out with the last of his forces. VAC Artillery units complete embarkation and depart Iwo Jima.

18 March
Carrier Air
Marine aircraft participate in TF 58 strikes against Kyushu Island, Japan. Marine pilots claim 14 of the 102 Japanese planes shot down, plus a share of 275 destroyed on the ground.

19 March
Carrier Air
Franklin is hit by bombs from a Japanese plane and is severely damaged. Among the 772 dead in her crew, 65 are Marines from the two Corsair squadrons. Marine planes from other carriers shoot down 18 enemy aircraft. VMTB-233 (formerly VMSB-233) goes aboard *Block Island*, which sails from San Diego.
Iwo Jima
The 4th Marine Division completes embarkation and departs Iwo Jima for Hawaii.

20 March
Iwo Jima
The 147th Infantry arrives on Iwo Jima as the garrison force and is temporarily attached to the 3rd Marine Division.

21 March
Commandants
Commandant Vandegrift is promoted to general, the first Marine to hold four-star rank on active duty.

Opposite: *Volcanic steam piped to the surface by Japanese engineers provides hot coffee for two Marines during a break in the fighting on Iwo Jima. (Marine Corps Research Center)*

Right: *A Marine throws a grenade while his team provides covering fire. (National Archives)*

23 March
Carrier Air
Marine aircraft of TF 58 participate in air strikes against Okinawa.

24 March
Philippines
The four squadrons of MAG-32 begin flying to Zamboanga to marry up with their ground echelons and support the Eighth Army campaign in the southern Philippines. The movement is complete two days later.

25 March
Iwo Jima
The 5th Marine Division wipes out the last resistance in Death Valley. This marks the end of organized Japanese control of any terrain on Iwo Jima.
Gilberts
MAG-15 begins transferring to Ewa Field, Hawaii.

26 March
Iwo Jima
Prior to dawn, over 200 Japanese launch a surprise attack on Marine, Navy, and Army rear-area elements on the island. Marine units involved are the 5th Pioneer Battalion and the 8th Field Depot. The pioneers, including many black Marines, provide the first organized resistance and lead the effort to destroy the infiltrators after first light. VAC turns over control of the island to the Army and begins departing.
Okinawa
Elements of the Army's 77th Infantry Division seize islands in the Kerama Reto group off the coast of Okinawa.
Philippines
MAG-14 planes support the landing of the Americal Division on Cebu.

26–27 March
Okinawa
The FMF Reconnaissance Battalion lands on four islets of Keise Shima near Okinawa, finds no enemy, and reembarks.

27 March
Iwo Jima
The 3rd and 5th Marine Divisions begin departing the island. Total Marine casualties during the battle are 5,931 dead and 17,272 wounded. Losses among attached Navy personnel are 209 dead and 641 wounded.

28 March
Carrier Air
Marine aircraft participate in TF 58 strikes against Kyushu.
Force Structure
VMD-954 is redesignated VMD-254.

29 March
Okinawa
The 77th Infantry Division completes the conquest of the Kerama Retto group. The FMF Reconnaissance Battalion scouts two islands between Kerama Retto and Keise Shima.
Philippines
MAG-14 supports the landing of the 40th Infantry Division on Negros Island.

30 March
Philippines
VMB-611 arrives on Mindanao.

April
Carrier Air
VMF-351 (formerly VMO-351) joins escort carrier *Cape Gloucester* (CVE-109).

1 April
Okinawa
Tenth Army launches its amphibious assault against the west coast of Okinawa, with IIIAC taking the left or north beaches and the Army's XXIV Corps attacking the right or south beaches. Within IIIAC, the 1st Marine Division lands on the right and the 6th Marine Division is on the left. The 2nd Marine Division conducts an amphibious feint off the southeast coast of the island. The initial landing is lightly opposed with casualties totaling about 150. The 4th Marines seizes Yontan Airfield and the XXIV Corps takes Kadena Airfield. VMF-221 and 451 fly missions to soften up the landing beaches prior to the assault.

2 April
Okinawa
XXIV Corps elements reach the eastern coast of Okinawa, cutting the island in two. One Yontan airstrip is made ready and a light plane from a Marine observation squadron is able to land. The Tactical Air Force (TAF) headquarters begins setting up ashore. The 2nd Marine Division repeats its amphibious feint off the southeast beaches. MAG-43 (formerly MBDAG-43) headquarters arrives on Okinawa to provide the administrative echelon of the Air Defense Command for TAF.
Philippines
The ground echelons of MAG-24 begin moving to the coast for transport by sea to Mindanao.

3 April
Okinawa
The 1st Marine Division reaches the east coast of the island and seals off the base of the Katchin Peninsula. *Bunker Hill*'s Marine Corsairs down 11 Japanese aircraft attempting to raid the Okinawa beachhead. Spotter planes from VMO-2, 3, and 6 are operating from Yontan airfield.

4 April
Okinawa
The 1st Marines clears out the Katchin Peninsula while the 6th Marine Division completes its wheel to the left and begins its drive north. XXIV Corps continues its drive south.
Iwo Jima
The 147th Infantry assumes responsibility for the ground defense of the island and the 9th Marines begins departing.

5 April
Okinawa
XXIVth Corps begins to meet serious resistance in the south as it runs up against the outposts of the main Japanese defenses, known as the Shuri Line. The 1st Marine Division begins mopping up rear areas while the 6th Marine Division exploits light opposition and moves rapidly northward. The FMF Reconnaissance Battalion lands on Tsugen Shima off the east coast and uncovers significant enemy defenses, then withdraws.
Japan
The Japanese cabinet installed after the defeat on Saipan resigns.

Opposite: *An amphibious tractor loaded with men of the 8th Marines heads for Iheya Shima off Okinawa. (National Archives)*

Right: *A unit of the 5th Marines lands in the fourth wave at Okinawa on 1 April 1945. (National Archives)*

Below: *Marines in later waves transfer from an LCVP into an LVT for the run into the beach. (National Archives)*

6 April
Carrier Air
The Japanese begin launching large-scale kamikaze attacks against U.S. ships around Okinawa. Marine planes of TF 58 shoot down 22 of the enemy. The Japanese suicide missions recur on a frequent basis over the next few weeks. One Marine pilot from *Bennington* achieves a bomb hit on battleship *Yamato*, which sinks under a rain of Navy bombs and torpedoes as it sorties toward Okinawa.

7 April
Okinawa
The FMF Reconnaissance Battalion scouts the remaining islands off the east coast of Okinawa and finds them free of the enemy. IIIAC artillery begins providing support to XXIV Corps along the southern front. The first Marine aircraft of TAF (MAG-31's VMF-224, 311, and 441 and VMF(N)-542) begin operating ashore on Okinawa.
Iwo Jima
Army P-51s from Iwo Jima provide the first land-based fighter escort for B-29s bombing the Japanese home islands.

8 April
Okinawa
The 6th Marine Division seals off the base of the Motobu Peninsula on the northwest coast.

Left: *"1st Marine Division in Assault Craft Pass the Battleship* North Carolina,*" John Hamilton, Naval Art Collection*

Opposite: *Two Marines take on a Japanese bunker at close range on Okinawa. ("Grenade Throwers," John R. McDermott, Marine Corps Art Collection)*

9 April
Okinawa
The 22nd and 29th Marines launch patrols to determine the disposition of the strong Japanese force defending the Motobu Peninsula. The 11th Marines begins moving south to add its fires in support of XXIV Corps. Kadena Airfield is opened for operational use by MAG-33 (VMF-312, 322, and 323 and VMF(N)-543).
Philippines
Marine aircraft support the landing of the Army's 41st Infantry Division on Jolo Island.

10 April
Iwo Jima
VMB-612 arrives on Iwo Jima and begins making night anti-shipping attacks as far away as Japan.
Force Structure
VMSB-933 is decommissioned.

11 April
Okinawa
The 2nd Marine Division departs Okinawan waters and sails back to Saipan

12 April
United States
President Roosevelt dies and Vice President Harry S. Truman is sworn in as his successor.
Carrier Air
Marine Corsairs of TF 58 shoot down 51 kamikazes, while squadrons based on Okinawa get 16 more. Major Herman A. Hansen, Jr., the 25-year-old CO of VMF-112, destroys three, making him an ace. Major Archie Donahue scores five kills, giving him a total of 14. Over the remainder of the month, Marine planes on the carriers rack up 30 additional kills. VMTB-143 goes on board *Gilbert Islands.*
Iwo Jima
The last elements of the 9th Marines depart after assisting in mopping up operations.

13 April
Okinawa
Patrols from the 6th Marine Division reach the northern tip of Okinawa. The FMF Reconnaissance Battalion occupies Minna Shima, an island off the northwest coast. TAF flies its first close air support missions for Tenth Army.

14 April
Okinawa
The 4th and 29th Marines launch an attack to destroy enemy forces concentrated around Mt. Yae Take on the Motobu Peninsula.
Philippines
The aircraft of MAG-24 begin their movement from Luzon to Mindanao. They arrive at Malabang on that island on 20 April.

15 April
Okinawa
Another large kamikaze assault begins and lasts through the next day.

16 April
Okinawa
The 4th Marines seizes Mt. Yae Take. The 77th Infantry Division launches an amphibious assault on Ie Shima, off the west coast of Okinawa. TAF Marine pilots score 38 kills and carrier-based Marines get another 10. VMF-441 claims 17 of the enemy. Lieutenant William W. Eldridge kills four, while Captain Floyd C. Kirkpatrick and Lieutenant Selva E. McGinty get three each.

18 April
Okinawa
Transport planes of VMR-252 make their first flight to Okinawa with vital supplies. VMR-253, 353, and 952 join in over the next four days.

19 April
Okinawa
XXIV Corps launches a major assault on the Shuri Line, employing three divisions abreast.

20 April
Okinawa
The 6th Marine Division completes the reduction of enemy defenses on the Motobu Peninsula.

21 April
Okinawa
The 77th Infantry Division completes the conquest of Ie Shima.

22 April
Okinawa
VMTB-232 (formerly VMSB-232) arrives on the island. Marine pilots of TAF down 33 enemy planes during a kamikaze attack. Major Jefferson D. Dorroh gets six, while Major George C. Axtell, Jr. and Lieutenant Jeremiah J. O'Keefe score five each.
Philippines
MAG-32 aircraft conduct a major close air support mission for the Army 41st Infantry Division that breaks the center of Japanese resistance on the island of Jolo. MAG-24 launches its first missions from the Malabang Airfield.

24 April
Okinawa
The 1st Marine Division is assigned the role of Tenth Army reserve. Prior to dawn, the Japanese withdraw to the second layer of their Shuri Line defenses.

26 April
Okinawa
XXIV Corps opens a three-division assault against the second ring of Shuri Line defenses.

28 April
Okinawa
During another large kamikaze attack at Okinawa, TAF Marines shoot down 35 planes, while Marines on the carriers get another 14.
European Theater
Benito Mussolini is killed by Italian partisans.

30 April
Okinawa
The 1st Marine Division is attached to XXIV Corps and begins moving forward to replace the 27th Infantry Division in the front lines. The 77th Infantry Division replaces the 96th Infantry Division at the same time.
European Theater
Adolf Hitler commits suicide as Berlin is being overrun by Soviet forces.

May
Force Structure
VMSB-141 is redesignated VMTB-141.

1 May
Okinawa
With the 1st Marines on the right and the 5th Marines on the left, the 1st Marine Division is in position on the right of the XXIV Corps front.

2 May
Okinawa
The 1st Marine Division launches its first attacks against the Shuri Line.
European Theater
Berlin falls to the Soviets. German forces in Italy surrender.

3 May
Okinawa
In the evening, a massive Japanese kamikaze attack begins against the U.S. fleet, designed to coincide with the upcoming ground assault on Okinawa. TAF Marines splash 60 enemy planes, with Lieutenants Robert Wade, John W. Rushman, Joseph V. Dillard, and William P. Brown getting four each.

4 May
Okinawa
The Japanese launch a major daylight counterattack against XXIV Corps and continue into the night, but the Marines and soldiers defeat it and inflict heavy casualties on the enemy.
Guam
The 52nd Defense Battalion arrives on the island.

5 May
Okinawa
The 1st Marine Division reaches its initial objective, the northern banks of the Asa River.

Above: *Marines move past a dead Japanese soldier on Okinawa. (National Archives)*

Left: *Infantrymen negotiate a destroyed stone wall. (National Archives)*

Opposite, top: *LtCol Richard P. Ross, Jr., plants the U.S. flag on the ramparts of Shuri Castle. (National Archives)*

Opposite, below: *Marines get a welcome ride on a tank during the dash into northern Okinawa. (National Archives)*

Tenth Army orders IIIAC to assume responsibility for the right half of the Shuri front lines by 7 May.

6 May
Okinawa
The 1st Marine Division begins attacking the Awacha Pocket.

7 May
Okinawa
The 1st Marine Division returns to IIIAC control. VMO-7 begins to arrive on Okinawa.
Force Structure
Admiral King approves "Base Post-War Plan No. 1," which calls for an FMF in the Pacific theater consisting of a Marine division and aircraft wing in California and a brigade and aircraft group in the western Pacific.

8 May
Okinawa
The 1st Marine Division shifts into the left of its previous frontage. The 6th Marine Division moves into position on the Asa River between the 1st Marine Division and the western coast.
European Theater
The war in Europe ends following Germany's surrender.

9 May
Okinawa
After darkness sets in, the 6th Engineer Battalion builds a foot bridge over the Asa. Four companies

of the 22nd Marines cross before the Japanese blow it up early the next morning.

10 May
Okinawa
The 5th Marines seizes control of Awacha Draw. In a determined attack against a Japanese reconnaissance plane flying at high altitude, VMF-312's 1st Lieutenant Robert R. Klingman's guns freeze, but he uses his propeller to cut away the enemy's tail and send it into the sea. VMF(N)-533 arrives on Okinawa following a long flight from Eniwetok Atoll.
Carrier Air
Block Island and its Marine squadrons join the fleet off Okinawa. VMTB-234 (formerly VMSB-234) joins escort carrier *Vella Gulf* (CVE-111).

11 May
Okinawa
In another large-scale kamikaze attack, *Bunker Hill* is hit by two planes and severely damaged. Her two Marine squadrons (VMF-221 and 451) suffer 29 dead. TAF Marines pilots shoot down 19 enemy, with Lieutenants Edward C. Keeley and Lawrence N. Crawley (both of VMF-323) getting four each. Tenth Army launches a coordinated offensive all across its front. The 5th Marines wipes out the final enemy resistance in the Awacha Pocket.

Left: *A Marine shares his rations with an Okinawan child. (National Archives)*

Opposite, top: *A Marine and his war dog stand watch on Okinawa as evening approaches. (National Archives)*

Opposite, below: *A 6th Division Marine pauses to say farewell to a fallen buddy on Okinawa. (National Archives)*

12 May
Okinawa
The attack of the 22nd Marines runs up against a ridge, quickly dubbed Sugar Loaf, that forms the western anchor of the Japanese Shuri Line. Admiral Nimitz removes the 2nd Marine Division (less the 8th Marines) on Saipan from Tenth Army reserve and makes it the theater reserve. That part of the division finally debarks from transports and goes ashore on Saipan. The 8th Marines remains under control of Tenth Army.

15 May
Philippines
MAG-14 ends combat operations on Samar in preparation for its shift to Okinawa.
Force Structure
VMB-622 is redesignated VMTB-622 at Mojave.

18 May
Okinawa
The 29th Marines captures Sugar Loaf after four days of bitter, see-saw fighting. Lieutenant Robert Wellwood of VMF(N)-533 shoots down three enemy bombers in one night.

19 May
Okinawa
The 4th and 22nd Marines seize the Horse Shoe, another formidable position just beyond Sugar Loaf.

21 May
Okinawa
The aircraft of MAG-22 (VMF-113, 314, and 422) arrive on Ie Shima from Engebi and begin supporting Tenth Army.
Carrier Air
VMTB-132 goes on board *Cape Gloucester* at San Diego.

24 May
Okinawa
As part of a larger kamikaze raid that night, six Japanese transport planes loaded with commandos attempt to land on Yontan Airfield. Five are shot down by antiaircraft fire, but one makes it to the ground and the enemy soldiers destroy eight planes and cause other damage. Lieutenant Albert F. Dellamano of VMF(N)-533 shoots down three enemy planes during the night. The 8th Marines sails from Saipan for Okinawa. *Gilbert Islands* and her Marine squadrons arrive off Okinawa.

25 May
Okinawa
Marine fighters from TAF claim 39 of 75 Japanese planes downed in aerial combat during a mass kamikaze attack. Captain Herbert J. Valentine is credited with five kills and Lieutenant William Farrell gets four.

26 May
Okinawa
Frontline observers report the rearward movement of Japanese forces and call in massive air, artillery, and naval firepower. Nevertheless, over the next four days much of the enemy's remaining firstline strength is able to withdraw to the final defensive line in the escarpments along the Kiyamu Peninsula. Second-echelon forces come up to fight a delaying action in the Shuri defenses.

27 May
Okinawa
The 6th Marine Division captures Naha, the capital city of Okinawa.

28 May
Okinawa
American fliers deal with yet another massive kamikaze raid against the fleet. Marine pilots claim 32 of the 49 enemy downed.

29 May
Okinawa
The 5th Marines seizes the crest of Shuri Ridge and against light opposition takes Shuri Castle, the heart of the Shuri Line defenses. VMTB-131 lands on Ie Shima and begins supporting Tenth Army.
Manpower
President Truman increases the authorized strength of the Marine Corps to 503,000.

31 May
Okinawa
The 1st Marine Division cleans out final enemy resistance in Wana Draw.

1 June
Okinawa
Gilbert Islands and its Marine squadrons join the fleet off Okinawa. VMO-7 begins operating on Okinawa.
Force Structure
The FMFPAC Supply Service is redesignated Service Command. VMF-251 and 313 are decommissioned. VMSB-464 is redesignated VMTB-464.

2 June
Okinawa
Elements of the 8th Marines occupy Iheya Shima north of Okinawa to provide a base for early warning radar.

3 June
Okinawa
Elements of the 8th Marines occupy Aguni Shima west of Okinawa to provide a base for early warning radar. The Japanese launch another mass kamikaze attack, which lasts through 7 June. During the four-day aerial battle, Marine pilots of TAF claim 35 of the 118 enemy aircraft shot down.

4 June
Okinawa
The 6th Marine Division launches a shore-to-shore amphibious assault against the Oroku Peninsula in southwest Okinawa.

6 June
Okinawa
The 4th Marines completes the capture of Naha Airfield on the Oroku Peninsula.

7 June
Philippines
MAG-14 begins its movement from Samar to Okinawa.

8 June
Carrier Air
Bennington departs the operational theater around Okinawa, the last fast carrier with Marine squadrons. VMF-112 and 123 had been in action almost continuously with the ship since 16 February.
Okinawa
MAG-14 (VMF-212, 222, and 223) arrives on Okinawa.

11 June
Okinawa
The 1st Marine Division comes up against Kunishi Ridge, the western anchor of the final Japanese defensive line on Kiyamu Peninsula. In a night attack, the 7th Marines seizes the crest of part of the ridge, though the Japanese retain control of the area all around it for several more days.

13 June
Okinawa
The 6th Marine Division completes the reduction of enemy positions on Oroku Peninsula. In another night attack, elements of the 1st Marines take more of Kunishi Ridge.

14 June
Marshalls
A detachment of the 51st Defense Battalion moves from Eniwetok Atoll to Kwajalein.

15 June
Okinawa
The 8th Marines comes ashore on Okinawa and is attached to the 1st Marine Division.

16 June
Okinawa
The 1st Marine Division captures most of the rest of Kunishi Ridge.

17 June
Okinawa
The 6th Marine Division moves up to assume responsibility for the right half of the 1st Marine Division zone of action. XXIV Corps captures the commanding ground along the Yaeju Dake-Yuza Dake Escarpment on the eastern side of the Kiyamu Peninsula. VMF-513 joins *Vella Gulf* at San Diego.

18 June
Okinawa
Prior to dawn, the 8th Marines moves into position and assumes responsibility for the right half of the 1st Marine Division frontage. While observing the regiment in action that morning, Lieutenant General Simon B. Buckner, commander of Tenth Army, is killed by Japanese fire. Tanks and 2/5 wipe out the last enemy resistance on Kunishi Ridge.

19 June
Okinawa
Roy Geiger is promoted to lieutenant general and designated as commander of Tenth Army. He becomes the first Marine to command a field army.

21 June
Okinawa
Organized resistance in IIIAC's zone ends when the 1st Marine Division takes Hill 81 and the 6th Marine Division reaches the southernmost point of Okinawa. General Geiger announces that the island is secure that afternoon.

23 June
Okinawa
Army General Joseph W. Stilwell arrives on the island and assumes command of Tenth Army in place of General Geiger. The 1st and 6th Marine Divisions participate in a mop up of southern Okinawa, in which the five assault divisions turn about and slowly begin to sweep over the ground they had taken in preceding weeks. In the evening, the Japanese launch their tenth wave of kamikaze attacks.

30 June
Okinawa
The mop up of southern Okinawa is completed. Marine casualties during the campaign are 3,443 dead and 16,017 wounded. Losses among Navy personnel serving with Marines units are 118 killed and 442 wounded. At sea, the Navy loses nearly 10,000 personnel killed and wounded, almost entirely due to kamikaze attacks.
Manpower
The strength of the Marine Corps on active duty is 37,067 officers and 437,613 enlisted.

1 July
Okinawa
Marine Corsairs escort the first Army Air Forces medium bomber attack on the Japanese home islands since the carrier-launched Doolittle Raid of April 1942. The 8th Marines departs Okinawa to rejoin the 2nd Marine Division on Saipan.
Carrier Air
Marine pilots and MASG-48 headquarters on *Block Island* and *Gilbert Islands* support the landing of the Australian 7th Division on Balikpapan in Borneo.
Force Structure
VMTB-453 is organized at El Toro.

2 July
Okinawa
IIIAC is released from mop up operations on Okinawa.

4 July
Okinawa
The 6th Marine Division begins moving from Okinawa to Guam. *Cape Gloucester* and her two Marine squadrons arrive off Okinawa.

Opposite: *A Thompson submachine gunner covers the forward rush of a BAR man on Wana Ridge. (National Archives)*

Right: *A wounded Marine awaits evacuation from the frontlines of Okinawa by a Consolidated OY-1 Grasshopper. (National Archives)*

13 July
Okinawa
Many IIIAC corps-level units begin re-deployment to Guam. The 1st Marine Division, IIIAC Artillery, and the 1st Armored Amphibian Battalion remain on Okinawa and go into rehabilitation camps on the Motobu Peninsula.

14 July
Okinawa
TAF is dissolved and all Marine aircraft in the Okinawa area revert to control of 2nd MAW.

15 July
Force Structure
IIIAC is detached from Tenth Army and comes under control of FMFPAC. The corps headquarters begins displacing to Guam. VMTB-463 is organized at Santa Barbara.

16 July
Technology
The first atomic bomb is successfully tested at Alamogordo, New Mexico.
Force Structure
VMSB-133 and 241 of MAG-24 are decommissioned.

24–26 July
Carrier Air
Marine squadrons on board *Vella Gulf* fly sorties against Pagan and Rota Islands north of Guam.

29 July
Okinawa
The medium bombers of VMB-612 arrive on Okinawa and begin flying anti-shipping missions off Kyushu.

31 July
Force Structure
MAG-43 and MAG-62 are deactivated.

1 August
Okinawa
Most of 2nd MAW passes under the control of the Far East Air Forces (FEAF).
Carrier Air
Cape Gloucester and her Marine squadrons sail from Okinawa for the East China Sea to cover minesweeping operations and launch strikes near Shanghai.
Philippines
MAG-32's four dive bomber squadrons cease tactical operations in the Philippines and prepare for return to the United States.
Force Structure
VMTB-473 is organized at El Centro. VMF-481 is reactivated at Santa Barbara.

6 August
Japan
A B-29 drops an atomic bomb on Hiroshima, Japan.

Left: *A flamethrower team moves forward into the smoke. (National Archives)*

Opposite: *Cpl Robert E. Lowe and Dutch, veterans of Peleliu and Okinawa. During the latter battle, Dutch alerted his Marines to a hidden platoon of Japanese at a range of 150 yards. (National Archives)*

8 August
Japan
The Soviet Union declares war on Japan.

9 August
Japan
A B-29 drops an atomic bomb on Nagasaki, Japan.
Rabaul
Marine PBJ bombers of VMB-413, 423, and 443 conduct the last Marine air strikes on Rabaul.
China
Soviet forces invade Manchuria.

10 August
Pacific Theater
Japan offers to surrender unconditionally. FMFPAC directs the 6th Marine Division to provide a regimental combat team to the Third Fleet for possible occupation duty in Japan.

11 August
Japan
A Fleet Landing Force headquarters is formed with a Marine staff for future occupation duty. IIIAC makes preliminary plans for Task Force Able, to consist of an infantry regiment, an amphibian tractor company, and a medical company.

12 August
Carrier Air
VMTB-144 goes on board *Salerno Bay* (CVE-110).
Manpower
Plans are initiated for the establishment of separation centers at Great Lakes, Illinois, and Bainbridge, Maryland, to speedily demobilize eligible personnel.

13 August
Wake Island
Marine aircraft make their last raid on Wake Island's Japanese garrison.

14 August
Pacific Theater
President Truman announces that a cease fire is in effect with Japan. He also appoints General MacArthur as Supreme Commander Allied Powers, with authority to accept the surrender of Japan on behalf of the United States, the Soviet Union, Great Britain, and the Republic of China.

15 August
Manpower
The Commandant and the Undersecretary of the Navy approve a point system to guide demobilization. Points are awarded for time in service, for time deployed overseas, for combat awards, and for minor children. Those with the most points will be separated from active duty first.

16 August
Vietnam
Ho Chi Minh, leader of the Viet Minh movement, declares an independent Democratic Republic of Vietnam. His guerrilla forces have gained control of the northern half of the country from the defeated Japanese. British, Indian, and Free French forces soon occupy the southern half of the country, a pre-war French colony.

19 August
Japan
Task Force 31 is formed in Guam for the mission of occupying Japan. The headquarters of 1st MAW and MAG-61 complete their movement to the Philippines.

20 August
Force Structure
The reinforced 4th Marines joins TF 31 in Guam.

23 August
Japan
Aircraft FMFPAC assigns MAG-31 on Okinawa as the air component of the Marine occupation force for Japan.

NORTH AMERICAN B-25 MITCHELL

Marine aviation in World War II is best known for its top-notch fighters such as the Chance Vought F4U Corsair and its workhorse dive bombers such as the Douglas SBD Dauntless. Almost forgotten are the 12 squadrons that operated the North American B-25 Mitchell, the only medium bomber ever flown in combat by the Corps.

The plane (named for Billy Mitchell, the Army general who was court-martialed in the 1920s for his outspoken advocacy of air power) is often credited as being the best medium bomber in World War II. It was developed on a crash basis as conflict loomed on the horizon. The Army requested ideas for a two-engine bomber in March 1939, North American began designing it in August of that year, it first flew in August 1940, and the Army immediately adopted it for service and placed it in production. It gained widespread attention in April 1942 when Army Lieutenant Colonel Jimmy Doolittle flew a squadron of them off the aircraft carrier *Hornet* to bomb Japan. Although it underwent a number of changes during the war, the basic airframe was twin-engined and twin-tailed, with a wing span of 67 feet, and a length of 53 feet. It had a top speed of 284 miles per hour, a ceiling of 24,000 feet, and a range of 1,500 miles. Depending on the variant, it could carry up to 4,400 pounds of bombs and 13 .50-caliber machine guns. The B-25H model boasted a 75mm cannon in the nose.

The United States produced the Mitchell in such numbers (nearly 10,000 before the war ended) that the Army Air Forces could not use all of the airframes flowing off the assembly lines. The Marines gladly absorbed some of the excess as the Corps' aviation arm expanded exponentially in 1943. Redesignated the PBJ-1 in Marine service, the first squadron (VMB-413) organized at Cherry Point on 1 March 1943. It had 15 planes and 30 aircrews of six men each. Equipped with the B-25D, it deployed to the Treasury Islands in March 1944 and participated in the ongoing neutralization of Rabaul. It subsequently moved to other locations in the northern Solomons to operate against other bypassed Japanese garrisons. Colloquially dubbed "milk runs," these missions were hardly easy or safe. The squadron lost five planes and 32 men in its first three months in action. VMB-423, 433, and 443 all made it to the South Pacific in 1944 and conducted similar neutralization attacks until the end of the war. VMB-611 arrived in Emirau in December 1944 and flew against Rabaul until March 1945, when it shifted to the airfield at Zamboanga in the Philippines to support operations by the U.S. Army and Filipino guerrillas. VMB-613 made it to Kwajalein in December 1944 and launched attacks against enemy-held portions of the Marshalls until the end of the war.

VMB-612 drew the most complicated and challenging mission of all the PBJ squadrons. Formed on 1 October 1943 at Cherry Point, it was equipped with H and J models. These received special modifications including the addition of a nose-mounted radar and launching rails for eight rockets under the wings. The squadron trained for the mission of attacking Japanese shipping at night. The

commander for most of the outfit's life was Lieutenant Colonel Jack R. Cram. He had achieved fame in the Corps piloting General Geiger's personal PBY-5A Catalina flying boat at Guadalcanal. During the desperate fighting of mid-October 1942, Cram's ground crew affixed two torpedoes under the wings of the lumbering amphibian and he fought through anti-aircraft fire and a fighter screen to loose them at Japanese transports delivering reinforcements to the island. Now in command of VMB-612, he finally had a proper steed for hunting enemy ships.

Cram's squadron arrived on Saipan in October 1944. To give his planes the range and endurance to operate around Iwo Jima, the top turret and other equipment was removed to reduce weight. From November until the invasion of Iwo Jima in February 1945, VMB-612 flew 334 missions to slow the flow of men and supplies into the critical island. These flights produced 49 contacts and the crews claimed two ships sunk and another 27 hit. The cost was three planes and 13 men lost. Once Iwo Jima was secured, the squadron moved onto its airfields in April and began operating in waters around the Japanese home islands. In a third of the 251 sorties from Iwo, VMB-612 found targets. The squadron estimated hits on 53 ships and it lost seven more planes. At the end of July, Cram moved his outfit forward to Okinawa to continue its mission. They flew 31 sorties and claimed 20 hits before the end of hostilities arrived.

During the course of the war, the VMB squadrons collectively lost 45 of their PBJs (26 of them in combat operations) and a total of 173 crewmen. With the exception of VMB-612, their activities were not particularly glamorous, but they had performed significant missions and contributed to the ultimate victory over Japan.

A PBJ of VMB-611. ("Marine Bombers Over Emirau," Robert T. Horvath, Marine Corps Art Collection)

27 August
Philippines
The forward echelon of VMB-611 departs the Philippines for Peleliu to join 4th MAW there.

28 August
Japan
The ships of TF 31 enter Tokyo Bay and anchor off the naval base at Yokosuka.

29 August
China
Plans are issued for IIIAC to move to northern China, with a tentative departure date of 15 September.
Japan
Naval forces begin operations to rescue Allied prisoners of war held by the Japanese.

30 August
Japan
The 4th Marines, the Fleet Marine Landing Force (a three-battalion regiment composed of the 2,000 men in the fleet's Marine detachments), U.S. and British sailors, and Royal Marines go ashore at Yokusuka, while the Army's 11th Airborne Division lands at Atsugi Airfield. General MacArthur lands at Atsugi Airfield. As SCAP, he becomes the virtual ruler of Japan.

31 August
Force Structure
The Headquarters and Service Battalion of FMFPAC is disbanded.
Japan
A company of 3/4 lands at Tateyama Naval Air Station at the mouth of Tokyo Bay.

1 September
Bases
Marine Barracks Guantanamo Bay is redesignated as a Marine Corps Base.

2 September
Pacific Theater
Japanese representatives sign the formal surrender documents on board battleship *Missouri* (BB-63) in Tokyo Bay. The ship's Marine detachment and Marines on several senior staffs are present.
Manpower
The Marine Corps is at its peak strength of the war (and all time) with a total of 485,833 officers and men.
Japan
U.S. Army occupation forces begin to arrive in Tokyo Bay. Japanese garrisons all over the Pacific begin surrendering.

Left: *Men of the 6th Marine Division cast shadows on a damaged LVT as they march past on Okinawa. The special tracks that power the vehicle on land and water are clearly visible at right. (National Archives)*

Opposite: *A night patrol of 3/29 is silhouetted on an Okinawan ridge as it prepares to depart. (National Archives)*

4 September
Marianas
A force of Marines and Seabees moves on to Rota Island in the Marianas and begins repairing its airstrip.
Wake Island
The Japanese garrison on Wake Island formally surrenders to Brigadier General Lawson H. M. Sanderson, commander of 4th MAW.
Carrier Air
VMF-511 and VMTB-233 on *Block Island* assist in rescuing Allied prisoners of war from Formosa.
Force Structure
The Marine Corps replaces the F-series tables of organization (adopted in early 1944) with the G series. The change increases the size of a full-strength division by 1,700 men (much of it due to beefed-up service and support elements in light of the planned disbandment of corps-level reinforcing units).

6 September
Japan
Nearly all elements of the Fleet Marine Landing Force have been relieved of occupation duties and returned to their ships. The 4th Marines parades for 120 former members of the regiment who had survived Japanese imprisonment since the fall of Corregidor.

7 September
Japan
The headquarters of MAG-31 and the planes of VMF-441 fly onto the Yokosuka Airfield and become the first U.S. aviation unit to operate from Japan. They are followed in the next few days by VMF-224, VMF-311, VMF(N)-542, and VMTB-131.

10 September
Force Structure
Over the course of the next two weeks, the Marine Corps decommissions MASG-51, VMD-154, VMSB-142, 243, 341, and 484, and VMF-112, 123, 221, 451, 462, 471, 481, 521, and 522.

20 September
Japan
The advance echelons of MAG-22 fly onto Omura Airfield on Kyushu.

22 September
Japan
The VAC headquarters and the 5th Marine Division arrive at the Sasebo naval base on Kyushu Island, Japan. The 5th Marine Division assumes responsibility for occupying the northern half of the island.
China
1st MAW begins to move from Mindanao to China via Okinawa.

23 September
Japan
The lead squadron of MAG-22, VMF-113, lands on Omura airfield. It is followed in the next few days by VMF-314 and 422 and VMF(N)-543. The 2nd and 6th Marines land at Nagasaki and relieve the Marine detachments of the cruisers *Biloxi* (CL-80) and *Wichita* (CA-45). The 2nd Marine Division has responsibility for occupying the southern half of Kyushu Island. VAC assumes command of the 2nd and 5th Marine Divisions.

24 September
Japan
The 8th and 10th Marines and VMO-2 come ashore at Nagasaki. The U.S. Sixth Army assumes control of all ground forces in Japan.

30 September
China
IIIAC arrives at Tangku, China. 2/7 lands and secures the city. 3/7 goes ashore and boards a train for Tientsin.

HOT OPENING TO A COLD WAR

OCTOBER 1945–1953

HOT OPENING TO A COLD WAR

OCTOBER 1945–1953

At the end of World War II, the Marine Corps had attained a strength of a half million, but those numbers melted away quickly in the postwar drawdown. The 3rd and 4th Marine Divisions and the 3rd, 4th, and 9th MAWs disbanded almost immediately. The 1st and 6th Marine Divisions and 1st MAW moved into China to oversee the surrender of Japanese forces, while the 2nd and 5th Marine Divisions occupied Japan and 2nd MAW remained on Okinawa. Within weeks of the end of the war, even the occupation forces began to go home, and the last Marines left Japan in June 1946. A few months later, the Corps had reached its planned peacetime force level of 7,000 officers and 100,000 enlisted. Simultaneously, Marine Corps Reserve units slowly came back into existence and began rebuilding.

Despite its outstanding wartime contributions—in terms of doctrine, equipment, and battlefield success—the Marine Corps found itself threatened institutionally as soon as the guns fell silent. An Army plan to unify the services would have resulted in air, sea, and ground forces, but no dedicated amphibious element. In secret papers exchanged between the War and Navy Departments, Army leaders envisioned a Corps limited, if it existed at all, to operating landing craft. An impassioned speech by General Vandegrift in May 1946 temporarily delayed Congressional action, but it took a strong lobbying and public relations effort the following year to secure language protecting the Corps in the 1947 National Security Act. President Truman, a strong proponent of the merger, never forgave Marines for blocking his aims. Congress had to step in again in 1949 to prevent aviation from being stripped out of the Corps.

Internally, Marines knew they had to develop new methods if they wanted to maintain the viability of the amphibious assault in the face of nuclear weapons. The result was a new doctrine based on helicopters, even though there were then no machines capable of carrying a payload. The Corps was again operating on blind faith that technology would catch up, as it had in the late 1930s. Budget constraints also caused the Corps to continue shrinking, to the point where it numbered less than 75,000 officers and enlisted in the spring of 1950. In addition, manpower policies changed significantly with the partial integration of women into the regular component and the complete racial desegregation of the armed forces. Despite the challenges seemingly affecting all aspects of the Corps, the Marines pursued the amphibious mission with single-minded determination. Marine ground units began deploying as a ready landing force in the Mediterranean, and the air wing pressed forward with the development of helicopters and associated tactics.

A shrinking Marine presence in North China in the late 1940s attempted to stem the civil war going on there, but in the first hints of what would become the Cold War, the Chinese

Pages 406–407: *Marines trudge along the narrow mountain road on 9 December 1950 as they fight their way south from the Chosin Reservoir. (National Archives)*

Right: *Company E of 2/1 attacks North Korean positions on 13 September 1951. ("Assault on Hill 749," Col Charles Waterhouse, USMCR (Ret), Marine Corps Art Collection)*

Communists proved uncooperative and initiated several skirmishes with Marines. The Soviet Union, meanwhile, raised the Iron Curtain and divided Europe. This tense atmosphere exploded into war in June 1950 when Communist North Korea invaded the South in an attempt to reunify the peninsula by force. A wider war might have ensued, but the Chinese and Soviets initially stood by as the United States and elements of the United Nations rushed forces to save South Korea. In a sign that the Corps was determined not to repeat what had happened in World War II, it formed the air-ground 1st Provisional Marine Brigade for immediate deployment to Korea. Marines had doggedly maintained a high state of preparedness for combat throughout the period after the defeat of Japan and it showed as the brigade mounted out in a hurry and then played a major role in staving off defeat in the Pusan Perimeter. The rebuilding of the skeletonized 1st Marine Division and its sterling performance in the dramatic amphibious assault at Inchon turned the tide of the war and enshrined the Corps as the nation's premier force in readiness. The Reserves, heavily salted with World War II veterans, played a significant part, but only as individuals fleshing out regular units. The eventual result would be major changes in the reserve program, including attendance at boot camp and specialty training for reserve recruits and weekend drill training thereafter, so that reserve units could be mobilized ready to fight.

Marine performance on the battlefields of Korea more than matched the success and courage of earlier generations of Leathernecks. The brigade's counterattacks along the Naktong River, the division's landing at Inchon, the drive through Seoul, the fighting breakout from Chinese encirclement at the Chosin Reservoir, and the close air support provided by 1st MAW all added to the sterling reputation of the Corps. In the see-saw fighting along the central front during the last two years of the war, the 1st Marine Division proved itself to be the most powerful and successful outfit in Korea. Regrettably, the Air Force pursued its doctrine for centralized control of aviation and diverted much of the effort of 1st MAW during this period to deep interdiction missions, but Leatherneck airmen continued to perfect close air support tactics and techniques whenever they could. Marine innovation also came to the fore again as the Corps conducted the first tactical helicopter operations in combat and deployed the first infantry flak jackets and effective cold weather boots.

President Truman's criticism of the Corps early in the war only served to highlight for the public what Marines had accomplished. In June 1952, their elected representatives further strengthened the Corps by legislating a minimum size of three divisions and three wings, emphasizing its status as a separate service within the Navy Department, and giving the Commandant more of a role in the Joint Chiefs of Staff.

HOT OPENING TO A COLD WAR

OCTOBER 1945–1953

1945

1 October
China
1/7 arrives at Chinwangtao and arranges a halt in fighting between Communist Chinese forces and Japanese troops and their allies (forces of the former Japanese puppet government in north China). 3/7 arrives in Tientsin to secure the city. The 1st Marines follows soon after to assume occupation of Tientsin. The primary mission of Marine forces in north China is to accept the surrender of Japanese forces and oversee their repatriation to Japan. Marines also assume security for the vital coal trains that carry fuel to power the urban areas of China. They become involved inevitably in the ongoing Chinese civil war between the Nationalists and Communists, each of whom hopes to take over Japanese-controlled territory and arms.

6 October
China
The 5th Marines begins landing at Tangku and moving out toward Peiping. Headquarters of 1st MAW shifts to Tientsin from Okinawa. IIIAC, in command of Marine forces in north China, accepts the surrender of 50,000 Japanese troops in the Tientsin-Tangku-Chinwangtao area. An engineer unit and a rifle platoon of the 1st Marines are fired upon by Chinese Communist forces on the road to Peiping.

7 October
China
A stronger Marine force removes roadblocks on the road to Peiping without opposition. The 5th Marines reaches the Chinese capital. Transport aircraft of MAG-25 (VMR-152 and 153) begin arriving at Tientsin.
Japan
MAG-31 at Yokosuka is returned to naval control by Fifth Air Force.

8 October
Okinawa
A typhoon strikes Okinawa and damages many 1st MAW planes over the next two days.

10 October
Manpower
Marine separation centers are established at Navy training bases in Bainbridge, Maryland, and Great Lakes, Illinois.

Left: *6th Marine Division tanks roll through the streets of Tsingtao on 13 October 1945 as Chinese civilians look on. (National Archives)*

Opposite: *Marines prepare to disembark as they pull alongside the dock at Taku, China, on 1 October 1945. (National Archives)*

Japan
1/3 begins landing on Chichi Jima as part of the occupation of the Bonin Islands.

11 October
China
The 6th Marine Division (less the 4th Marines in Japan) begins going ashore at Tsingtao, China.

12 October
China
Aircraft of VMO-6 land at an airfield near Tsingtao.

13 October
China
Elements of the 1st Marines disperse Chinese mobs attacking Japanese civilians in Tientsin.

15 October
Force Structure
VMF-155, VMF-324, VMF-523, VMF-524, and VMSB-934 are deactivated.

17 October
China
VMF(N)-533 and 541 of MAG-24 begin operating from an airfield at Peiping.

18 October
China
Marines guarding the rail lines to Peiping kill six Chinese Communist soldiers firing at their train.

19 October
Force Structure
The 26th Marines is detached from the 5th Marine Division and placed under direct control of FMFPAC.
Roles and Missions
The Senate Military Affairs Committee begins hearings on proposed legislation that would merge the War and Navy Departments into a single agency. First proposed by Army Chief of Staff General Marshall in 1942 and again on 19 September 1945, this unification of the services poses a threat to the continued existence of the Corps, since Marines supposedly duplicate the capabilities of the Army.

21 October
Peleliu
The 26th Marines (less the 2nd Battalion, which is to be disbanded on 30 October) departs Sasebo for the Palau Islands.
China
The flight echelons of MAG-32 arrive at Tsingtao.

25 October
China
MAG-12 (VMF-115, 211, and 218) flight echelons arrive at Peiping.
Japan
MAG-22 at Sasebo is returned to naval operational control by Fifth Air Force.

26 October
Peleliu
The 26th Marines arrives on Peleliu and relieves the Army's 111th Infantry of garrison duties. The Marines will oversee repatriation of Japanese troops located throughout the Palaus and the Western Carolines.

31 October
Force Structure
Marine Air Support Group 42 (formerly MBDAG-42) and MAG-41 (formerly MBDAG-41) are deactivated, as is VMO-4.

November
Force Structure
The 51st Defense Battalion departs Eniwetok Atoll for the United States. VMF-111 is deactivated.

1 November
Japan
Eighth Army gives control of the 4th Marines to the U.S. Navy command at Yokosuka.
Force Structure
VMSB-333 is deactivated.

3 November
Force Structure
The last elements of the 4th Marine Division arrive in the United States from Hawaii. Its units are disbanded over the course of the month at Camp Pendleton.

6 November
China
The 6th Marine Division provides 1/29 to reinforce 1st Marine Division rail guards on the lines near Peiping.

Left: *A Navy landing ship brings Marines into the harbor at Tangku, China. They will oversee the disarmament and repatriation of Japanese forces. (National Archives)*

Opposite: *Men of the 1st Marine Brigade rest on 22 August 1950 during a brief respite from the fighting in Korea's Pusan Perimeter. They have just driven North Korean troops out of the Naktong Bulge. (MacArthur Memorial)*

9 November
China
1/29 takes up station in Peitaiho.
Force Structure
VMTB-132 and VMF-351 are deactivated.

10 November
Manpower
Frederick C. Branch is commissioned a second lieutenant. A veteran of the 51st Defense Battalion, he is the first black Marine to achieve officer rank in the Corps.

12 November
Force Structure
The Marine detachment at Londonderry, Northern Ireland, is disbanded.
Japan
After flying their Corsairs to Okinawa for storage and returning to Kyushu, the pilots and ground personnel of MAG-22 sail from Japan.

13 November
Force Structure
VMF-215 and VMTB-332 are deactivated.

14 November
China
Chinese Communist troops fire on a train carrying the 1st Marine Division commander.

16 November
Force Structure
VMTB-131 and 232 and VMO-7 are deactivated in California.

17 November
Force Structure
VMSB-245 is deactivated at San Diego.

21 November
Force Structure
VMSB-331 and VMB-613 are deactivated.

23 November
Japan
As U.S. Army forces arrive to assume the primary role in the occupation of Japan, the 5th Marine Division begins to reduce its area of responsibility on Kyushu and transfer its personnel to the 2nd Marine Division.

Left: *Marines get a rare break in Korea in 1953—a ride to the front lines on armored vehicles. (National Archives)*

Force Structure
VMTB-242 is deactivated at San Diego.

25 November
Truk
2/21 arrives to occupy the island, formerly the main Japanese fleet base in the Pacific. The battalion will garrison the key naval installation and repatriate Japanese troops.

28 November
Force Structure
The 4th Marine Division is disbanded at Camp Pendleton. MAG-45 is decommissioned.

30 November
Force Structure
MAG-13, recently returned to San Diego from the Marshall Islands, is deactivated. VMO-8, VMB-413, VMB-423, VMB-433, VMB-443, and VMB-611 are decommissioned.

1 December
Japan
1/4 sails from Yokosuka for the United States, where it will be disbanded.

5 December
Japan
MAG-22 arrives in the United States from Japan. Elements of the 5th Marine Division begin sailing for home.

6 December
China
Following frequent incidents of ground fire against Marine aircraft on reconnaissance flights over north China, IIIAC issues authorization for return fire, albeit on a very restricted basis.

8 December
Mishap
Six SB2C-5s of VMSB-343 are lost while flying in a snowstorm in north China. Ten of the 12 crew members die in the crashes.

9 December
Force Structure
VMTB-144 and VMF-514 are deactivated.

15 December
Force Structure
The 3rd Marines (less 1/3) arrives at Camp Pendleton.

19 December
Japan
The last elements of the 5th Marine Division sail from Sasebo for the United States.
Roles and Missions
President Truman addresses Congress and advocates the merger of the War and Navy Departments. The Secretary of the Navy orders Navy and Marine officers not to speak out against unification. Following a backlash in the media, the directive is modified the next day to allow service personnel to voice their concerns if they are stated as personal views.

20 December
Force Structure
The 21st Marines is deactivated on Guam.

24 December
Force Structure
VMF-472 and VMB-621 are deactivated.

28 December
Force Structure
The 3rd Marine Division is disbanded on Guam, with discharge-eligible Marines and some unit flags returning to the States, while Marines with obligated service remaining head to China as replacements. The exceptions are 1/3 in the Bonin Islands and 2/21 on Truk. VMB-614 is deactivated.

31 December
Force Structure
3rd MAW is decommissioned in Hawaii. The 9th Marines is deactivated at Camp Pendleton.
Japan
The U.S. Eighth Army assumes command of all occupation forces in Japan and formally relieves VAC headquarters of its occupation responsibilities. The 2nd Marine Division now reports to the Army's I Corps headquarters.

1946

1 January
Japan
3/4 assumes all security duties at Yokosuka in place of the 4th Marines.
Force Structure
2/4 sails for the United States and disbandment.

Right: *A Marine fires his M3 submachinegun at a target in the upper story of a building during street fighting in Seoul in September 1950. (National Archives)*

6 January
Japan
The headquarters element of the 4th Marines departs Yokosuka for Tsingtao, China.

8 January
Japan
The last corps-level elements of VAC sail from Japan, with most returning to the States and a few units shifting to Guam. The 2nd Marine Division continues on occupation duty and gradually assumes complete responsibility for all of Kyushu.
Force Structure
The 12th Marines is deactivated at Camp Pendleton.

10 January
China
General George Marshall (former Amy chief of staff and now the U.S. special envoy to China) mediates a cease fire agreement between the Chinese Nationalists and Communists. It is to take effect at midnight on 13 January.
Manpower
Imitating the widespread unrest in the Army over the pace of demobilization, a group of Marine NCOs in Hawaii present a petition to General Geiger (commanding general of FMFPAC) calling for a speedier return to civilian life. Geiger demotes all of them to private on the spot. There are no recurrences of unrest anywhere in the Corps.

11 January
Civil Support
Marines from Marine Barracks 8th and I serve as the honor guard for the ceremony in which the Magna Carta is removed from its storage vault at the Library of Congress in Washington, D.C. (where it was kept for safety during the war) and presented to the British Ambassador for return to Great Britain.

13 January
Force Structure
The 3rd Marines is deactivated at Camp Pendleton.

14 January
Wake Island
A Marine detachment is activated to garrison Wake Island.

15 January
China
MAG-25 transports assist in moving truce teams around China and dropping leaflets announcing the cease fire.

22 January
Force Structure
Commandant Vandegrift orders the organization of a special infantry brigade at Quantico to stand in readiness for possible expeditionary service in troubled parts of the Caribbean.

28 January
Force Structure
The headquarters of the 1st Special Marine Brigade and two battalions are formed at Quantico, while a third battalion forms at Camp Lejeune. The battalions are designated as the 1st, 2nd, and 3rd Battalions; there is no regimental headquarters. VMF-321 and VMTB-454 are deactivated.

31 January
Force Structure
The 51st Defense Battalion is disbanded at Montford Point. VMO-5, VMF-124, VMTB-622, VMF-913, VMF-914, VMSB-932, VMSB-931, and VMD-954 are decommissioned.

4 February
Force Structure
Brigadier General O. P. Smith assumes full control of the 1st Special Marine Brigade, which also now includes MAG-11.
Japan
Elements of the British Commonwealth Occupation Force begin arriving on Kyushu to assist the 2nd Marine Division in controlling the island.

5 February
Force Structure
With most of its subordinate elements already disbanded, the 5th Marine Division headquarters is deactivated at Camp Pendleton.

10 February
Wake Island
The Wake Island Marine detachment is ordered to shift to Eniwetok and remain there through the completion of upcoming atomic bomb tests at Bikini Atoll.

15 February
Force Structure
VAC headquarters is disbanded at San Diego and the corps ceases to exist. The headquarters of 2nd MAW departs from Okinawa for Marine Corps Air Station Cherry Point. VMR-353 is deactivated.
Japan
In Yokosuka, 3/4 is redesignated as the 2nd Separate Guard Battalion (Provisional), with primary duty as the security force for the naval base.
Okinawa
MAG-14 and 33 depart for the United States from Okinawa.

19 February
Reserve
The Secretary of the Navy authorizes establishment of the Marine Air Reserve Training Command (MARTC) to administer and direct the training of Marine Corps Reserve aviation units.

26 February
Reserve
MARTC is activated at Glenview Naval Air Station in Illinois.

27 February
Force Structure
2/21 sails from Truk for Guam, where it will be disbanded on 5 March.

Opposite: *Chow and smokes lift the spirits of Marines taking a break as the chill of winter settles on North Korea late in 1950. (National Archives)*

Right: *Sgt Roger J. Hooper, SSgt Frank C. Kerr, and Cpl Robert L. Miller warm themselves and heat coffee over a fire on 6 November 1950. (National Archives)*

Left: *A patrol marches through a South Korean village during the Pohang Guerrilla Hunt in early 1951. (MacArthur Memorial)*

8 March
China
The headquarters of the 4th Marines is formally rejoined to the 6th Marine Division in north China. Its subordinate elements will be gradually reconstituted from personnel of other division units that are disbanded.

10 March
Force Structure
VMTB-143, VMF-216, VMF-217, VMTB-233, VMTB-464, VMF-511, and VMB-624 are deactivated.

13 March
Force Structure
The 52nd Defense Battalion and the headquarters of 4th MAW depart Guam for the United States.

15 March
Force Structure
The 26th Marines is deactivated on Peleliu. Some personnel are reformed as a provisional Marine detachment to continue garrisoning the island. MAG-46, VMB-612, and VMF-912 are decommissioned.

20 March
Force Structure
VMSB-231, VMTB-234, VMTB-463, VMTB-473, VMTB-623, and VMF-911 are deactivated.

22 March
Force Structure
The Marine Corps issues Basic Post-War Plan No.2. It sets the desired strength of the Corps at 100,000 enlisted and 8,000 officers (8 per 100 enlisted—an increase from the prewar ratio of 5 per 100). The FMF will consist of two subordinate headquarters, one each for the Pacific (FMFPAC) and Atlantic (FMFLANT) fleets. The ground forces will be comprised of two divisions (one each at Camp Lejeune and Guam) and a brigade at Camp Pendleton. Marine aviation will have two wing-size commands. Aircraft FMFPAC will control all ground-based squadrons in the Pacific, while another headquarters will be responsible for six Marine carrier groups.

26 March
Force Structure
4th MAW headquarters arrives in San Diego and is disbanded.

31 March
Force Structure
9th MAW headquarters is disbanded at Cherry Point. 1/29 is disbanded in China.

April
China
MAG-12 headquarters returns to the United States from China. The group's former squadrons remaining in China transfer to MAG-24.

Manpower
Congress sets the postwar strength of the Marine Corps at 7,000 officers and 100,00 enlisted.

1 April
China
The 6th Marine Division is deactivated and replaced in north China by the newly activated 3rd Marine Brigade. It consists of the 4th Marines and supporting units—all the remaining elements of the 6th Marine Division.

11 April
Force Structure
VMF(N)-543 is deactivated.

15 April
Force Structure
The provisional Marine detachment on Peleliu is designated a Marine barracks. To achieve peacetime manning levels, the 1st Marine Division disbands one battalion in each of its three infantry regiments and one firing battery in each of the four battalions of the 11th Marines.

20 April
Force Structure
VMF(N)-544 is deactivated.

24 April
Force Structure
VMF-213 is deactivated.

30 April
Force Structure
Following their return from China, VMTB-134 and VMF(N)-541 are deactivated at San Diego. VMF-422 is decommissioned.

May
China
MAG-32 returns to the United States from China.
Training
The 1st Special Marine Brigade conducts the Corps' first postwar training exercise (the only one in 1946), an operation in the Caribbean.

1 May
China
Operational control of Marine forces shifts from the theater command, which is dissolved, to the U.S. Seventh Fleet.
Reserve
Marine Corps Reserve Bulletin No. 1 advises all personnel being released from active duty that they can retain their connection to the Corps through membership in its reserve component.

Right: *Marines question a Korean about the enemy. (National Archives)*

2 May
Civil Support
Marines assist civilian police in putting down a prison riot in the federal penitentiary on Alcatraz Island in San Francisco Bay.

6 May
Roles and Missions
Commandant Vandegrift testifies before the Senate Naval Affairs Committee against the unification bill. In his presentation he argues against an emasculated role for the Marines:

> "The bended knee is not a tradition of our Corps. If the Marine as a fighting man has not made a case for himself after 170 years of service, he must go. But I think you will agree with me that he has earned the right to depart with dignity and honor, not by subjugation to the status of uselessness and servility planned for him by the War Department."

His powerful words help stop consideration of the proposed legislation for that session of Congress. In response to a question, he also reveals the existence of the classified 1478 papers, in which Army leaders had plainly stated their desire to reduce the Marine Corps to a small force operating landing craft.

10 May
Force Structure
VMF-512 is deactivated.

15 May
Force Structure
The 52nd Defense Battalion is redesignated the 3rd Antiaircraft Artillery Battalion at Montford Point.

20 May
Force Structure
The 8th Military Police Battalion (Provisional) is redesignated Marine Barracks Okinawa.

21 May
China
In one of the rare instances of fighting involving Marines since the onset of the truce in China, Communist forces clash with a 1st Marines patrol near Tientsin and one Marine is killed. He is the only fatal combat loss in the first six months of 1946 in China. Violations of the truce between the Communists and Nationalists grow more frequent as summer approaches.

1 June
Force Structure
1/3 is disbanded on Chichi Jima in the Bonin Islands. The 1st Base Headquarters Battalion becomes Marine Barracks Guam.

6 June
China
MAG-25 departs Tsingtao for El Toro.

Left: *This North Korean soldier, a casualty of the fighting along the Naktong River in late summer 1950, has been booby trapped with a grenade placed beneath his head. Marines had to be wary, even of the dead. (National Archives)*

Right: *Marine Corporal G. G. Pendas, nicknamed "Peepsight" for his skill as a sniper with George Company, 3/1, aims in on a target in Korea in November 1950. ("The Sniper," Col Charles Waterhouse, USMCR (Ret), Marine Corps Art Collection)*

10 June
China
The headquarters of IIIAC is disbanded and the headquarters of the 1st Marine Division assumes a dual role as Marine Forces, China. The headquarters of the 3rd Marine Brigade in Tsingtao is also disbanded, with the 4th Marines (Reinforced) assuming its functions.
Force Structure
The 5th Military Police Battalion (Provisional) is redesignated Marine Barracks Saipan. VMSB-343 is deactivated.

13 June
Japan
The first elements of the 2nd Marine Division (primarily the 2nd Marines) begin sailing from Kyushu for the United States.

15 June
Japan
The 2nd Marine Division turns over responsibility for the occupation of Kyushu to the Army's 24th Infantry Division. The 8th Marines departs Japan for the United States. The 2nd Separate Guard Battalion (Provisional) at Yokosuka becomes a Marine Barracks.

20 June
Japan
MAG-31 embarks at Yokosuka for the United States. It is the last Marine occupation unit on Honshu.
Force Structure
The Marine Detachment (Provisional) in Samar is redesignated as a Marine Barracks.

23 June
Japan
The 10th Marines sails for the United States.

24 June
Japan
The headquarters of the 2nd Marine Division sails from Kyushu for the United States.

25 June
Force Structure
VMSB-142 is reestablished as VMF-142 in the Reserve at Miami.

27 June
Reserve
In a move boosting the status of the Marine Corps Reserve, the Division of Reserve is moved from the Personnel Department and now reports directly to the Commandant.

Left: *With their M-1s at the ready, Marines search a Korean building. The 1st Marine Division had to master urban warfare during the drive through Seoul in the fall of 1950. (National Archives)*

30 June
Manpower
The strength of the Marine Corps on active duty is 14,208 officers and 141,471 enlisted. The Marine Corps' participation in the Navy's V-12 officer program comes to an end.

1 July
Technology
The U.S. conducts its first test of an atomic bomb at Bikini Atoll, to determine the effectiveness of an air burst against surface ships and other military targets.
Japan
Elements of the 6th Marines sail from Kyushu for the United States.
Force Structure
VMF-112, 121, 124, 321, 251, 351, and 451 and VMTB-132, 144, and 234 are reactivated as Reserve fighter squadrons. Marine Corps Air Station Eagle Mountain Lake in Texas is deactivated and several auxiliary strips around the country are also closed.
Manpower
Draftees and reservists with 30 months of active duty become eligible for discharge regardless of the number of points they possess.

2 July
Japan
The last major elements of the 2nd Marine Division depart for the United States.

4 July
Japan
MAG-31 returns to the United States from Japan.

5 July
Force Structure
VMTB-141 is reactivated as a Reserve fighter squadron.

7 July
China
The Chinese Communist Party issues a manifesto attacking U.S. support of the Nationalist government.

11 July
Force Structure
VMF-441 is deactivated.

13 July
China
Communist forces capture seven Marines visiting

a village near Peitaiho. Five days of patrolling by elements of the 7th Marines fail to turn up any sign of them.

Force Structure

Elements of the 2nd Marine Division begin to arrive at Camp Lejeune, its new permanent home station.

15 July

China

1st MAW reports aircraft availability at 20 percent due to a lack of trained maintenance personnel. The last ship repatriating Japanese nationals from China sails from Tangku. Over two million troops and civilians had moved back to Japan, more than a quarter of them from north China.

16 July

HQMC

In accordance with reorganization plans emanating from the President's office, Headquarters Marine Corps abolishes the Paymaster Department and renames the Quartermaster Department the Supply Department.

24 July

China

Negotiations result in the release of the seven Marines captured by Communist forces near Peitaiho.

25 July

Technology

The second Bikini atomic test utilizes the first-ever underwater explosion of a nuclear device.

29 July

China

Communist forces ambush a supply convoy on the road to Peiping. Marines from 1/11 and the 1st Marines hold off the attacking force throughout the afternoon, until the enemy breaks contact. Marine losses are four killed and 10 wounded.

1 August

Force Structure

The Commandant fixes Marine aviation strength at a wing and a group, all concentrated on the west coast of the United States or in the Pacific region. Proposed manpower for all FMF elements is set at 2,149 ground and 1,498 aviation officers, and 36,493 ground and 11,848 aviation enlisted personnel.

7 August

Manpower

The Commandant authorizes the retention of 100 Women Reservists on active duty until 30 June 1947 to perform administrative tasks at Headquarters Marine Corps in connection with new laws providing benefits to demobilizing personnel. Soon after this number is increased to 300.

Right: *A fire team crouches behind rubble as it waits for the word to move up in a North Korean town. (National Archives)*

8 August
Force Structure
VMTB-233 is reestablished as a Reserve fighter squadron.

19 August
Cuba
Marine Corps Base Guantanamo Bay is redesignated Marine Barracks, Naval Operating Base Guantanamo Bay.

21 August
Doctrine
General Geiger, chief Marine observer at the Bikini atomic tests, reports that nuclear weapons will make it impossible to conduct future amphibious assaults with the tactics of World War II, which relied upon concentrated naval and ground forces to obtain superiority at the landing point. He recommends an urgent effort to develop new amphibious techniques.

28 August
Bikini
The Marine detachment at Bikini Atoll is disbanded following the completion of atomic tests there.

31 August
Force Structure
The 1st Special Marine Brigade and its units are deactivated at Camp Lejeune and Quantico.

3 September
China
The 4th Marines (less 3/4) embark at Tsingtao, China, for the United States, where they will join the 2nd Marine Division. 3/4 comes under command of the Naval Port Facilities, Tsingtao.

6 September
China
Marine guards are henceforth assigned only to trains transporting American personnel or supplies. The Chinese Nationalist Army assumes responsibility for protecting all other rail traffic, including the coal trains previously guarded by Marines.

10 September
Roles and Missions
Following the failure to pass unification legislation in the previous session, President Truman orders the Secretaries of War and Navy to negotiate a compromise bill that can be submitted to Congress.

Left: *A rifleman takes aim in the bloody streets of Seoul as other Marines remain at the ready. (National Archives)*

Right: *A Marine steadies his BAR on the wall of a Communist rice bag fort in the midst of the battle for Seoul. (National Archives)*

11 September
Force Structure
The regimental echelons of the 6th Marines are redesignated as the headquarters and weapons companies of the 3rd Marine Brigade at Camp Pendleton.

13 September
Doctrine
Commandant Vandegrift directs the formation of the Special Board, charged with developing "broad concepts and principles" for adapting amphibious assault tactics to the nuclear battlefield. The senior members of the board are Major General Lem Shepherd (Assistant Commandant), Major General Field Harris (Assistant Commandant for Air), and Brigadier General O. P. Smith (Commandant of the Marine Corps Schools).

1 October
Manpower
The Marine Corps essentially reaches its postwar planning levels with a strength of 95,000 regulars (out of 100,000 planned) now serving on peacetime contracts.

3 October
China
Communist forces make a night raid on the 1st Marine Division's main ammunition supply point at Hsin Ho. The guard force drives them off without losing a man.

4 October
Manpower
Headquarters Marine Corps directs the release of those few remaining enlisted personnel still on duty who had come into the Corps as reservists or through the draft or whose regular enlistment periods had expired. This essentially completes the process of demobilization.

15 November
Force Structure
VMSB-235 is reestablished as VMF-235, a Reserve squadron at Squantum, Massachusetts.

1 December
Manpower
The Marine Corps reforms its enlisted rank structure, which had developed numerous designations in the same grades during World War II. There now would be a single rank for each of the seven existing pay grades. The ranks are

Left: *Marine infantrymen rush across open ground under enemy fire in Seoul. (National Archives)*

private, private first class, corporal, sergeant, staff sergeant, technical sergeant, and master sergeant.

Bases

The Marine Barracks at Parris Island is formally redesignated as the Marine Corps Recruit Depot.

10 December

Force Structure

The provisional detachments at Wake Island and Eniwetok Atoll are disbanded. The Kwajalein unit is redesignated a Marine Barracks.

Mishap

A Marine R5C transport disappears during a flight over Washington State with 32 Marines on board. The wreckage is discovered in July 1947 on the South Tahoma Glacier.

16 December

Force Structure

The headquarters of Fleet Marine Force Atlantic (FMFLANT) is established, with the commander of the 2nd Marine Division initially dual-hatted with both responsibilities. FMFLANT reports to the commander of the Atlantic Fleet.

Doctrine

General Shepherd submits the report of his board charged with studying the impact of atomic weapons on the future of the amphibious assault. The study concludes that dispersal at sea is necessary to avoid giving the enemy a target and that helicopters, seaplanes, and other means of rapid mobility are required to concentrate the landing force only at the last minute at the actual point of attack on the shoreline. The Shepherd report calls for the creation of an experimental helicopter squadron to begin developing this capability.

1947

1 January

Force Structure

The Marine detachment in the Philippines is redesignated Marine Barracks Sangley Point.

Training

The Marine Corps reinstitutes the pre-World War II practice of paying extra money for marksmanship proficiency.

5 January

China

The 7th Marines, 3/11, 4/11, VMO-6, and the ground echelon of VMF(N)-533 sail from Chinwangtao. The aircraft of VMF-115 and VMF(N)-533 have already flown out of the country to Hawaii.

6 January

China

President Truman orders an end to U.S. participation in truce enforcement efforts.

13 January
Training
The 2nd Marine Division begins amphibious maneuvers with the fleet in the Caribbean. The exercises will last through 28 March.

16 January
Roles and Missions
Truman submits a new unification bill to Congress based on input from the secretaries of the War and Navy Departments. In an attempt to placate supporters of the Marine Corps, he promises to issue an executive order that will spell out the roles and missions of the services.

18 January
China
The remainder of the 11th Marines, 1st Tank Battalion, and the ground echelon of VMF-115 sail from Chinwangtao.

31 January
Manpower
The Navy Department announces that naval services lost a total of 88,939 dead and missing during World War II, of which 24,479 were Marines.

3 February
China
The 1st Marine Division receives orders to cover the withdrawal of U.S. personnel from Peiping and prepare for its own departure from the country.
Force Structure
The first Volunteer Training Unit (VTU) is formed in Chicago. The VTU allows reservists not joined to a tactical unit to conduct some individual training, usually in staff or specialist fields.

16 February
Force Structure
VMSB-236 is reestablished as VMF-236, a Reserve squadron in Denver, Colorado.

5 March
Force Structure
The 7th Marines is disbanded at Camp Pendleton and most of its personnel transfer to the 3rd Marine Brigade.

10 March
China
Elements of the 1st Pioneer Battalion depart for Guam, where they will begin building a camp for the soon-to-be-established 1st Marine Brigade.

Right: *A heavily laden BAR man helps clear a building in Korea. (National Archives)*

THE HELICOPTER REVOLUTION

The idea for a rotary-wing aircraft goes back as far as Leonardo da Vinci in the 15th century. It wasn't until 1937, however, that the first practical helicopter appeared, in Germany. The U.S. Army Air Corps issued its first contract for such a machine in 1940. Igor Sikorsky's helicopter flew in early 1942. The Navy and Army funded improved models during World War II, but few made it overseas and they were used sparingly in such roles as carrying messages. Payloads remained minimal, while speed and range also were a fraction of the capability of fixed-wing aircraft. Although the Marine Corps had experimented in Nicaragua in the early 1930s with an autogiro (a hybrid of the helicopter and a conventional plane), it did not acquire any rotary-wing aircraft during the war.

An entirely different type of technical revolution spurred the Corps to speed into helicopters at full throttle. The advent of the atomic bomb promised to put an end to the type of amphibious assault, based on massed combat power, that the Marines had pioneered during World War II. General Roy Geiger's August 1946 report on the atomic tests at Bikini Atoll called for new tactics based on dispersion, surprise, speed, and smaller forces. Commandant Vandegrift immediately convened a high-level panel to develop an outline for future doctrine. The Shepherd Board completed its work in December. It called for the use of helicopters and flying boats to transport ground forces from distant bases and widely dispersed ships at sea to objective areas ashore. Helicopters, in particular, would allow the assault commander to get his forces into the rear of the enemy position instead of launching a traditional attack through his beach defenses.

There was as yet no helicopter in the world capable of lifting more than its pilot and two passengers, and there was little money for new aircraft in the barebones postwar budgets. But the Corps forged ahead with the new doctrine in spite of the lack of suitable equipment (just as it had done prior to World War II with the original amphibious concept). Even though no aircraft were available, the Marines formed an experimental helicopter squadron at Quantico in December 1947. Major Armond H. DeLalio, the first Marine qualified to pilot helicopters, became the instructor for the Marines of HMX-1 as they awaited delivery of their aircraft. The first machines, two Sikorsky HO3S-1 utility helicopters, arrived at Quantico in February 1948. The small helicopter had a payload of 500 pounds, a speed of 103 miles per hour, and a range of 80 miles. In August, HMX-1 received the Piasecki HRP-1. Nicknamed the "Flying Banana" due to its shape, the twin-rotor aircraft had a payload of 900 pounds and a speed of 100 miles per hour.

During May 1948, the small Sikorsky aircraft embarked in the escort carrier *Palau* and participated in Operation Packard II along the North Carolina coast. In the first amphibious helicopter assault in history, HMX-1 ferried a few dozen Marines ashore in a day-long airlift. It was a mere simulation of what could be done, but it was enough to allow the Marine Corps Schools to finalize the first written doctrine for heliborne amphibious operations that November. The following spring, the bigger Piasecki aircraft lifted more men in a much shorter period of time in Operation Packard III. Other exercises demonstrated the ability of the HRP-1s to carry 75mm pack howitzers and supplies.

War intervened long before the equipment and doctrine were perfected, but the Marines were quick to put into practice what they had learned with the aircraft they had on hand. Personnel from HMX-1 quickly joined VMO-6 as part of the mobilization of the brigade for Korea. The pilots and their HO3S-1s performed wonders during the next few months. The small utility helicopters enabled commanders to reconnoiter the ground before operations, rapidly visit far-flung units, quickly evacuate casualties, and get emergency supplies to outfits in dire need. Other aviation units also benefited when VMO-6 helicopters plucked downed pilots from the sea or enemy territory. These missions were valuable, but they were not new and were not the reason the Corps had invested so much in the new capability.

The true value of the helicopter began to come in reach on 15 January 1951 when the Marine Corps formed its first transport helicopter squadron, HMR-161. Three months later, it took delivery of its initial aircraft, three Sikorsky HRS-1 transports. Like its older but smaller brother, the HO3S-1, it had a main rotor overhead supplemented by a small vertical tail rotor. Its maximum speed was 90 knots and it could carry nearly 1,500 pounds or six combat-equipped infantrymen. Four months later (August 1951), with a full strength of 15 helicopters, 43 officers, and 244 enlisted, the squadron departed San Diego for Korea. The outfit was set up at a forward airfield in the battlezone on 10 September. Two days later, it was busy training with personnel of the 1st Marine Division. On the 13th, it executed Operation Windmill I, resupplying a battalion fighting in mountainous terrain. The helicopters brought forward a team to control the landing zone, then dropped off sling loads of badly need items and picked up casualties from steeply sloped high ground inaccessible to any other form of transport. The first troop lift took place on 21 September, as HMR-161 moved the division reconnaissance company to a hill in a remote, barren, mountainous section of the front. The landing zones were so small and rough that the initial security and landing support personnel had to debark by rope lines as the aircraft hovered above ground. Missions grew in scale and complexity week by week, until the squadron was transporting an entire infantry battalion and even moving troops at night. The helicopter had finally arrived on the battlefield as something more than a glorified jeep. Thanks to the pioneering efforts of the Corps, it was now a tactical arm that added an entirely new dimension to warfare.

Marines board an HRS-1 of HMR-161 in Korea in 1951 for one of the first heliborne troop movements in combat. (National Archives)

17 March
Peleliu
Sixty-two Marines from Hawaii and Guam are airlifted to Peleliu to help deal with 12 Japanese holdouts that threw a grenade at a Marine patrol.
Manpower
Technical Sergeant Mary F. Wancheck becomes the first female Marine to rate a "hashmark" (service stripe) on her uniform for completing four years of service.

26 March
China
The planes of VMF-218 depart for Guam.

27 March
China
At the end of a month of air drops, VMR-153 has delivered 750,00 pounds of relief supplies in support of United Nations relief efforts in north China.

31 March
Manpower
The wartime draft law expires.

3 April
Peleliu
A Japanese naval enlisted man surrenders to Marine Forces and provides information on other holdouts.

4 April
Manpower
The Navy Department reactivates the Reserve Officer Training Corps at college campuses.

5 April
China
Prior to dawn, a strong Communist force again attacks the ammunition supply point at Hsin Ho, while another element ambushes the relief company immediately dispatched by the 5th Marines. Marine losses are five killed and 16 wounded. The Chinese leave behind six dead.
Peleliu
Twenty-five more Marines from Guam arrive on Peleliu to reinforce the drive against Japanese soldiers still at large.

20 April
Peleliu
A Japanese lieutenant and 26 enlisted men surrender to American forces. Seven more surrender the next day, bringing to an end the last organized Japanese force on the island.

22 April
Roles and Missions
Commandant Vandegrift appears before the Senate Armed Services Committee regarding the unification bill and returns to complete his

Left: *Following a napalm strike on a hill in central Korea in March 1951, Marine infantrymen charge through the smoke and onto the objective. (National Archives)*

Right: *Elements of the 5th Marines and supporting tanks deploy from the road and return fire against Chinese troops on a ridge line. (National Archives)*

testimony two days later. In contrast to his ringing 1946 defense of the Corps, he expresses only mild concerns about the president's unification bill.

24 April
Force Structure
The advance echelons of the headquarters of 1st MAW and MAG-24 arrive in Guam as part of the withdrawal from China.

30 April
Force Structure
MAG-32, VMF-113, and VMF-314 are deactivated.

1 May
China
Fleet Marine Force Western Pacific (FMFWESPAC) is activated at Tsingtao to control remaining forces in China following the departure of the 1st Marine Division and 1st MAW.

9 May
Force Structure
The last elements of the headquarters of MAG-24 transfer from China to Guam.

12 May
China
The last elements of the 5th Marines depart Peiping and the regiment (less 1/5) sails for Guam.

23 May
China
Marines evacuate civilians (including 66 Americans) from Peitaiho Beach after they had fled Chinese Communist troops attacking the surrounding area.

24 May
China
1/5 sails for Guam.

26 May
China
The 1st Pioneer Battalion, the last Marine unit in Peitaiho, departs for Tientsin.

30 May
Force Structure
VMF(N)-532 is deactivated.

31 May
Force Structure
MAG-25, MAG-31, VMR-253, VMF(N)-534, VMJ-952, and 953 are deactivated.

1 June
Force Structure
The 1st Marine Brigade is reactivated on Guam. Its main elements are the 5th Marines and a supporting artillery battalion (1/11).

Left: *Marines regroup after dealing with a minor ambush on the central front in June 1951. (National Archives)*

17 June
Roles and Missions
After submitting his request for retirement, Brigadier General Merritt Edson testifies before the House Committee on Expenditures in the Executive Departments, strongly opposing the unification bill because of a perceived threat to civilian control of the military.

20 June
China
The remainder of the 1st Marine Division (less elements of the 1st Marines and 3/4) sails for California. Only the 1st Marines (consisting of headquarters and 2/1), 3/4, two squadrons (VMR-153 and VMF-211), and 12th Service Battalion remain at Tsingtao. 1/1 continues to garrison Tientsin. Their mission is to guard naval installations there and protect the remaining American citizens in China.

23 June
Roles and Missions
In response to criticism from some congressmen, Secretary of the Navy James V. Forrestal issues a message to the naval services indicating that officers are free to express their private views on the unification bill before Congress. A number of senior leaders then go on record against the unification bill in its present form.

30 June
Manpower
The strength of the Marine Corps on active duty is 7,506 officers and 85,547 enlisted. This is far short of the 108,200 officers and men authorized, due to budget constraints as the government seeks to reduce spending in the aftermath of the huge expenditures for World War II.
Manpower
President Truman signs special legislation posthumously promoting Lieutenant General Roy Geiger to four-star rank.

4 July
Guam
The 1st Marine Brigade cantonment is formally named Camp Witek after Private Frank P. Witek, who received the Medal of Honor posthumously for his actions during the recapture of the island in 1944.

6 July
Force Structure
The headquarters of the 1st Marine Division arrives at Camp Pendleton, which will become its permanent home station.

7 July
Manpower
The first postwar Platoon Leaders Class officer training course convenes at Quantico.

16 July
Roles and Missions
Under the guidance of its chair, Representative Clare Hoffman, the House Committee on Expenditures in the Executive Departments reports a modified version of the President's unification bill that spells out the roles and missions of the Marine Corps and minimizes the merger of the War and Navy Departments. This bill is subsequently passed by the entire House and it goes to conference with the Senate-passed version backed by Truman.
Force Structure
The 3rd Marine Brigade disbands at Camp Pendleton, with its personnel and equipment being absorbed by the 1st Marine Division.

22 July
Civil Support
A detachment of 26 Marines begins duty as the official guard of the Freedom Train, which will tour the United States for over a year carrying treasured documents and artifacts of American history.

25 July
Roles and Missions
After the conference committee agrees on a bill largely following the House version and both chambers pass it, President Truman signs the National Security Act of 1947 into law. Although the law creates a National Defense Establishment to oversee the services, it leaves intact the Departments of the Navy, Army, and Air Force (the latter two newly created from the former War Department) as intervening echelons with significant powers. The law gives the Marine Corps several specific missions, to include primary responsibility for developing amphibious warfare capability, confirms that it is a separate service within the Navy Department, and provides that the Corps will include ground combat, aviation, and service elements. The act also formalizes the Joint Chiefs of Staff (the military heads of the Army, Navy, and Air Force) and gives them a Joint Staff limited to 100 officers. The Commandant is not a member of the JCS.

26 July
Roles and Missions
President Truman nominates Secretary of the Navy Forrestal to be the first Secretary of National Defense.

Right: *A Marine dashes up with extra mortar rounds during a fire fight in July 1951. (National Archives)*

7 August
Commandants
A new law establishes the permanent rank of the billet of Commandant of the Marine Corps at four stars.

25 August
Aviation
Major Marion Carl, a test pilot assigned to the Patuxent Naval Air Test Center, sets a new world air speed record of 650.6 miles per hour in a Douglas D-558 Skystreak jet over Muroc Lake, California.

27 August
China
1/1 departs Tientsin for Camp Pendleton. The only Marine outpost in China is now FMFWESPAC, located at Tsingtao.

15 September
Force Structure
The Marine Corps begins implementing the J-series tables of organization. In order to stretch limited manpower further, infantry regiment headquarters are eliminated and battalion landing teams (an infantry battalion and reinforcing elements) are redesignated using the former regimental system. As an example, 2/1 and 3/4 in China will respectively become the 1st and 3rd Marines.

17 September
Department of Defense (DOD)
The National Security Act of 1947 is implemented, with James Forrestal becoming the Secretary of National Defense, John L. Sullivan replacing him as Secretary of the Navy, and W. Stuart Symington, the former Assistant Secretary of War for Air, becoming the first Secretary of the Air Force. The title Secretary of National Defense will soon be routinely shortened to Secretary of Defense. The overarching executive department titled the National Military Establishment will formally change its name to the Department of Defense in 1949.

30 September
Force Structure
The 8th Ammunition Company and the 49th Depot Company, both the last Marine units of their type still on duty, are deactivated on Guam.

1 October
Force Structure
The headquarters of 1st MAW moves to El Toro from Guam. The 9th Marines is reactivated on Guam. The 3rd Marines is reactivated at Tsingtao, China.

Left: *A heavy machinegun team of 2/7 moves out to its position just after helicopters dropped the Marines on Hill 884 in the first heliborne combat troop lift in history on 21 September 1951. (National Archives)*

Right: *Artillerymen shield their ears as a barrage of 4.5-inch rockets launch toward Communist positions. (National Archives)*

10 October
Manpower
The first contingent of American war dead returns to the United States from Pacific battlefields on the Army transport *Honda Knot*.

12 October
Philippines
Corregidor Island is formally returned to control of the republic of the Philippines.

24 October
Force Structure
VMF-122, the first Marine jet squadron, is organized at Cherry Point under command of Major Marion Carl. It is equipped with McDonnell FH-1 Phantoms.

10 November
Training
The 1st Marine Division begins a large-scale amphibious exercise off the coast of southern California that lasts for five days.

14 November
Korea
Despite a Soviet boycott, the United Nations approves establishment of the Korea Commission to hold elections in Korea (currently divided into two zones based on postwar occupation by Soviet forces in the north and American troops in the south).

1 December
Force Structure
The first experimental Marine helicopter squadron, HMX-1, is commissioned at Quantico. It is eventually equipped with the Sikorsky HO3S-1 (a utility/observation helicopter) and the Piasecki HRP-1 (a small transport helicopter dubbed the "Flying Banana" for its unusual shape).

25 December
China
Five Marines on a hunting expedition cross into territory controlled by the Communists. In a subsequent firefight, one is killed and the others are taken prisoner.

31 December
Commandants
General Alexander A. Vandegrift relinquishes his post and General Clifton B. Cates becomes the 19th Commandant. Vandegrift will remain on active duty until 1 April 1949.

MAJOR GENERAL MARION E. CARL

Marion Carl came from a determined, unflinching family. His parents had gotten their start in life living in a tent on wooded land in the untamed Willamette Valley of Oregon. They slowly cleared acreage for farming and a dairy herd, until they finally could afford to build a house. Mister Carl died when Marion and his two siblings were still young. They pitched in to help their mother not only keep the farm going, but make it even more successful. In turn, she made sure all of them went off to college.

Marion helped put himself through school with summer jobs, but also found time to participate in the Army's Reserve Officer Training Corps. In the fall of 1937, he took private flying lessons and soloed. Upon graduation in 1938, the Army gave Carl and all his contemporaries reserve commissions, because it obtained all the regular officers it needed from West Point. The Marine Corps took advantage of the situation throughout the latter 1930s and offered the top Army ROTC graduates regular commissions and orders to active duty. Carl was one of those who jumped at the chance. He then earned his wings at Pensacola in late 1939.

Already a captain by May of 1942, he was flying one of the handful of VMF-221 Wildcat fighters at Midway Island during the Japanese attempt to take it in June of that year. In a large-scale melee with enemy fighters and bombers, he led his section against a numerically superior force of much-vaunted Japanese Zeros, shooting down one and damaging two others. Transferred to VMF-223, he and his squadron flew into Guadalcanal on 20 August, the first element of what would become Cactus Air Force. In his first successful action on the island, just four days later, he shot down two Betty bombers and a Zero. On 26 August, he got two more fighter planes, making him the first Marine Corps ace in history. He raised his score to nine by the end of the month with three more Zeroes.

His rapid rise as an ace nearly came to an end on 9 September. Just recuperating from a bout with dysentery, he led a flight against a formation of bombers attacking U.S. shipping in Ironbottom Sound. He and his men broke up the attack and he got two bombers, but his Wildcat was crippled by a Zero in the process. He bailed out and ended up in the water far away from friendly lines. He managed to stay afloat until rescued by natives in a canoe. There were too many Japanese troops around the perimeter to get back by land, so ultimately he made it home in a small boat powered by a decrepit engine, which he had to put in working order himself. In the intervening five days, his squadron mates had written him off for dead. By the end of the month, he had claimed two more enemy planes and joined in destroying a third. He also received his first Navy Cross, for his actions during the current campaign. He scored his last kill at Guadalcanal on 3 October, downing another Zero.

The Marines brought him back to the States soon after to take advantage of the fame he had gained as a leading ace. During a national tour selling war bonds, he proved to be equally successful in love as in war—meeting, wooing, and marrying Edna Kirvin,

Maj Marion Carl during his second combat tour in the Pacific in January 1944. He had just run up his score to 18 kills. (Marine Corps Historical Center)

a New York model. Before he headed back overseas in command of his old squadron, he also was promoted to major and given a second Navy Cross, for his daring intercept at Midway. Now flying the much more powerful Corsair out of Vella LaVella, he fought several aerial battles over Rabaul and raised his total score to 18 planes by out-dueling three more enemy pilots. In early 1944 he turned over command of his squadron and eventually transferred back to the States. Not content to rest on his two Navy Crosses, three Distinguished Flying Crosses, and 13 Air Medals, he became a test pilot. With just seven years in the military, he made lieutenant colonel in September 1945.

Carl continued his pioneering ways after the war. He became one of the first jet pilots in the Corps. In a remarkable show of the range of his aerial skills, he also became one of the earliest Marine helicopter pilots (and the first one formally designated as such). He earned his fourth Distinguished Flying Cross in 1947 while piloting a test jet to a world speed record. After a stint in command of the Corps' first jet squadron, he returned to head a test unit at the Navy's Patuxent River facility. In 1953, piloting a rocket-powered craft dropped from a bomber, he set an unofficial world altitude record of 83,235 feet. In the process, he successfully tested a special pressurized flight suit and gained a fifth Distinguished Flying Cross.

The intrepid pilot went on to command the air-ground 1st Marine Brigade and the 2nd MAW. He retired in 1973 with 13,000 flight hours and moved back to Oregon. In 1998, an intruder broke into his home. General Carl stepped between the armed man and his wife of 55 years and was killed by a shotgun blast. He died at the age of 82, courageous to the very end.

1948

1 January
Bases
Marine Corps Base San Diego is redesignated as Marine Corps Recruit Depot San Diego.

5 January
Mediterranean
The 2nd Marines (a reinforced infantry battalion under the J-series T/O) departs Morehead City, North Carolina, on the Navy transports *Bexar* and *Montague* for extended service in the Mediterranean Sea. Once in the Mediterranean, the Marines will shift to carrier *Midway* (CVB-41) and cruisers *Portsmouth* (CL-102), *Providence* (CL-82), and *Little Rock* (CL-92). They will remain afloat until 12 March. This initiates what will become a routine and near-continuous deployment of a Marine landing force as an element of the Sixth Fleet.

7 January
Mediterranean
Fleet Admiral Chester Nimitz announces that the presence of the 2nd Marines with the Sixth Fleet will serve as a warning to Yugoslavia not to menace the 5,000 U.S. Army troops in the Free Territory of Trieste.

11 January
Reserve
As part of the rebuilding of its reserve forces after WWII, the Marine Corps holds a rally and celebration in Philadelphia to inaugurate National Marine Corps Reserve Week and spur reserve recruiting.

31 January
China
A Marine patrol engages in a firefight with Chinese Communist forces near Tsangkou airfield, the home of the aviation elements of FMFWESPAC.

February
China
Early in the month, Marine transport planes evacuate U.S. and British nationals from Changchun in Manchuria, just before it falls to Communist forces.

9 February
Technology
HMX-1 receives the first Marine helicopters, two Sikorsky HO3S-1s.

13 February
China
Communist forces confirm that they had captured five Marines on 25 December 1947 and that one of them had died soon after of wounds received. The Chinese demand an official apology for what they claim was U.S. participation in the ongoing civil war with the Nationalists.

20 February
Mediterranean
The 8th Marines (a reinforced battalion) departs Morehead City as the intended relief on station for the 2nd Marines deployed with the Sixth Fleet. They will remain afloat until 28 June.

11 March
Roles and Missions
Forrestal and the Joint Chiefs of Staff (JCS) meet in Key West, Florida, to discuss the roles and missions of the services. Four days later, they

complete the Key West Agreement. It stipulates that the Corps will not form a second land army, will not expand beyond four divisions in wartime, and will not command units larger than a corps.

17 March
Manpower
Speaking before a joint session of Congress, President Truman urges a return to the draft and adoption of universal military training. He also calls for speedy passage of what will become the Marshall Plan, designed to aid the recovery of the European economies. These initiatives recognize the growing discord between the democracies of the West and the Soviet Union.

25 March
Manpower
Commandant Cates joins the Secretary of Defense, the three service secretaries, and the members of the JCS in testifying before Congress in favor of the requirement for a quick return of the draft and eventual implementation of universal military training.

27 March
Roles and Missions
Secretary Forrestal announces the provisions of the Key West Agreement.

1 April
China
The Communists release the four Marines taken prisoner on the previous Christmas Day.

10 April
China
Communist forces capture four Marine airmen after their transport plane makes a forced landing for mechanical reasons in Communist-controlled territory. Troops fire on Marine aircraft reconnoitering the scene of the crash.

19 May
Aviation
HMX-1 embarks on *Palau* (CVE-122) for an exercise, the first time Marine helicopters go to sea.

Opposite: *A Marine fires his air-cooled M1919A4 from the hip. ("Solo Machine Gunner," G. Corriero, Marine Corps Art Collection)*

Right: *"Village Near Hagaru," John Groth, Marine Corps Art Collection*

23 May
Training
In the first-ever amphibious use of Marine helicopters, HMX-1 ferries 66 men and their equipment from *Palau* to an objective inland during Operation Packard II at Camp Lejeune.

1 June
Mediterranean
The 21st Marines (a reinforced infantry battalion) sails from Morehead City as the relief on station for the 8th Marines. The 21st will remain afloat until 2 October.
Force Structure
VMF-111 and VMSB-231 are reactivated as fighter squadrons in the Marine Corps Reserve.

2 June
Manpower
Congress passes the Women's Armed Services Integration Act, which authorizes the armed services to enlist up to 20,045 women in their regular components. Previously women had only served in reserve components on active duty. The act is signed by President Truman and goes into effect on 12 June. The Marine Corps portion of this allotment is 1,100. It obtains the first women regulars in November by rejoining veterans of the World War II Women's Reserve.

3 June
Force Structure
VMTB-232 is reactivated as VMF-232 in the Reserve.

24 June
Manpower
President Truman signs the new draft act into law.

30 June
Manpower
The strength of the Marine Corps on active duty is 6,907 officers and 78,081 enlisted. The number of personnel continues to decline due to budget constraints.
Reserve
President Truman signs into law the Reserve Retirement Bill, which for the first time permits members of the reserve establishment to receive retirement pay for reserve service.

2 July
China
Communist forces release the four Marine airmen held since their plane crashed on 5 April.

18 July
Middle East
The 21st Marines provides a provisional Marine Consular Guard for service in Jerusalem to protect

Left: *Marines wait to lift off on the first night combat heliborne troop lift in Korea. (National Archives)*

Right: *Sgt Anthony Barbosa (left) and PFC Thomas Brooks helped drive off an enemy attack in April 1952. (National Archives)*

the U.S. Consul General during the First Arab-Israeli War, which had broken out on 14 May following the departure of British forces and the declaration of the creation of the state of Israel.

20 July
Manpower
President Truman issues a proclamation calling on all U.S. males between the ages of 18 and 25 to register for the draft between 30 August and 18 September. The first inductions will take place on 1 October.

22 July
Manpower
The Marine Corps announces that voluntary enlistments are meeting its requirements and it will not need any draftees in the coming year.

26 July
Manpower
President Truman issues an executive order that bans racial bias in the military services.

9 August
Training
For the first time since World War II, all services are represented in the annual CAMID amphibious exercise at Camp Lejeune.

15 August
Technology
HMX-1 takes delivery of its first Piasecki HRP-1. The twin-rotor "Flying Banana" has a payload of 900 pounds and a speed of 100 miles per hour.
Korea
Following U.N.-supervised elections, Syngman Rhee establishes a prowestern Republic of Korea in South Korea. The Soviet Union did not permit elections in North Korea.

25 August
Manpower
Second Lieutenant John Earl Rudder, the first black Marine officer commissioned in the regular Marine Corps, begins his training at the Basic School in Quantico.

9 September
Korea
Kim Il-sung, a former member of the Soviet Army during World War II, proclaims the establishment of Communist People's Democratic Republic in North Korea.

13 September
Mediterranean
The 4th Marines (a reinforced infantry battalion) departs Morehead City to become the landing force of the Sixth Fleet. The 4th will remain afloat until early 1949.

Left: *A tank rolls off an LST during the movement of the 1st Marine Division to the left flank of the U.N. line in March 1952. (National Archives)*

Opposite: *A sniper uses binoculars to search for a target in early 1952. (National Archives)*

1 October
Reserve
The Marine Corps Reserve achieves a strength of 116,000, with 37,742 men and women serving in units.

4 October
Training
Joint service maneuvers begin on both coasts. Instead of the traditional scenario of defending against an attack on the United States, these exercises involve practice for a surprise attack on enemy territory.

18 October
HQMC
Colonel Katherine A. Towle reports for duty as the Director of Women Marines and the first to head the regular female component of the Corps.

November
Doctrine
The Marine Corps publishes *Amphibious Operations—Employment of Helicopters (Tentative)*, its first doctrine on the subject. Its short title is *Phib-31*.

10 November
Manpower
Commandant Cates personally enlists the first eight women (all former reservists) to join the regular component of the Corps.

14 November
China
Small detachments of Marines move to Peiping and Tientsin to assist in evacuating American citizens desiring to leave before Communist forces overrun those cities. They remain there for four days.

17 November
China
Secretary Forrestal announces that an additional 1,250 men from Guam will be sent to Tsingtao to reinforce the 3,000 men of FMFWESPAC. A platoon of Marines from Tsingtao deploys the same day to Nanking to protect the U.S. Embassy as the city appears ready to fall to Communist forces. The platoon will remain there until 21 April 1949. American military family members in China are ordered out of the country and FMFWESPAC begins shipping out extra supply stocks.

18 November
Middle East
A detachment of 62 Marines is stationed in Haifa, Israel, as part of the U.S. Military Observer Group involved in truce supervision.

28 November
China
In accordance with Secretary Forrestal's announcement, BLT-9 (the 9th Marines—a battalion-sized force—plus additional reinforcing elements) sails from Guam on transport *Bayfield* (APA-33). Its mission is to assist in the evacuation of 2,500 Americans from Shanghai, which is in danger of falling to the Communists. After a stopover at Tsingtao, the BLT will arrive at Shanghai on 16 December.

15 December
China
The U.S. Army general directing the military advisory group in China reports that the Nationalist Army is no longer making effective resistance to the Communists and can be expected to lose control of the country.

16 December
China
The acting secretary of state announces that the U.S. has not changed its hands-off policy toward the Chinese civil war and Marines will not go into action at Shanghai unless American lives are threatened.

31 December
Manpower
The number of women on active duty in the Marine Corps totals 24 officers and 300 enlisted.

1949

3 January
Mediterranean
The 2nd Marines (a reinforced battalion) departs Morehead City to take over as the landing force of the Sixth Fleet. The 2nd will remain afloat until 24 May.
Middle East
A Marine Guard is formally organized for the long-term protection of the U.S. Consulate in Jerusalem.

21 January
China
VMF-211 departs China. The fighter squadron transfers to carrier *Rendova* (CVE-114) and remains in the western Pacific.

29 January
China
The last elements of VMR-153 depart China for Cherry Point.

8 February
China
Most of the ground elements of FMFWESPAC sail from Tsingtao for the United States, with only a portion of the 3rd Marines (a battalion-sized force) remaining ashore. For the time being, the city remains a Nationalist island in Communist-controlled north China.

23 February
Manpower
The 3rd Recruit Battalion is activated at Parris Island to train new female enlistees. Up to this point, women regulars had been obtained from veterans of the Women's Reserve. The first female recruits arrive at Parris Island five days later.

Left: *Infantrymen move up past a knocked-out U.S. tank. (National Archives)*

25 February
Training
A Navy-Marine Corps task force numbering 20,000 personnel completes a month-long amphibious exercise in Alaska.

26 February
Force Structure
FMFWESPAC officially dissolves at Camp Pendleton and its personnel are absorbed by the 1st Marine Division.

28 February
Roles and Missions
The Hoover Commission on the Organization of the Executive Branch recommends that the Secretary of Defense receive stronger authority over the branches of the armed forces to end interservice rivalry and effect unification.

March
Force Structure
The 1st Marine Brigade and MAG-24 depart Guam for the United States, leaving behind 3/5 and VMF-218.

2 March
Training
U.S. Marines and soldiers and three Canadian platoons conduct the largest amphibious exercise since WWII on Vieques Island in the Caribbean.

5 March
Roles and Missions
President Truman proposes significant changes to the National Security Act of 1947 in order to strengthen the Secretary of Defense and the National Military Establishment at the expense of the service departments.

17 March
China
The 3rd Marines sails from Tsingtao for Shanghai, leaving one rifle company behind.

28 March
Department of Defense
Louis A. Johnson succeeds James Forrestal as Secretary of National Defense.

30 March
China
BLT-9 departs Shanghai for the United States, with the 3rd Marines assuming its mission of protecting American citizens.

April
Roles and Missions
Army Secretary Kenneth C. Royall testifies before a Senate committee and proposes that Congress abolish the Marine Corps.

1 April
Aviation
The designation of Marine Fighting Squadrons is changed to Marine Fighter Squadrons, but the VMF initials remain the same.

20 April
China
A Royal Navy frigate moving up the Yangtze River to protect British citizens in Nanking is shelled and forced aground. A cruiser and another frigate are damaged in an unsuccessful effort to aid the first ship. British losses are 40 killed and 78 wounded.

21 April
China
In response to the increased threat, the U.S. naval commander in China orders the withdrawal by air of the Marine platoon in Nanking. The 7th Marines sails from California as a planned relief for the 3rd Marines.

26 April
Roles and Missions
Secretary Johnson announces that he is planning to transfer Marine aviation to the Air Force.

28 April
Roles and Missions
Representative Carl Vinson, chairman of the House Armed Services Committee, discusses Marine aviation with Secretary Johnson and makes it clear that any change in its status must be approved by Congress in view of the National Security Act of 1947.

29 April
China
After the departure of the last American civilians, the 3rd Marines sails from Shanghai. The only remaining Marine force in China is the rifle company in Tsingtao.

1 May
China
Due to the deteriorating situation in China, the 7th Marines is turned back at Pearl Harbor and only a rifle company is sent forward to reinforce the ships detachments of the U.S. squadron in Chinese waters.

2 May
Mediterranean
The 8th Marines sails from Morehead City to assume the mission of landing force for the Sixth Fleet. It will remain afloat until 26 September.

Right: *A Marine sniper and his spotter work together. (National Archives)*

4 May
Force Structure
VMF-211 arrives in the United States from its duty in Chinese waters. It eventually settles at MCAS Edenton, North Carolina.

9 May
Training
HMX-1 conducts a simulated heliborne amphibious assault at Quantico for visiting members of Congress. Eight HRP-1s carry 56 Marines in a single lift. A second lift brings in 75mm pack howitzers and their gunners.

10 May
Force Structure
The 1st Marine Brigade is deactivated after its arrival at Camp Pendleton. Its personnel are absorbed into the 1st Marine Division.

16 May
China
Company C, 3rd Marines, departs Tsingtao for the United States.
Force Structure
The 9th Marines arrives at Camp Lejeune and becomes a part of the 2nd Marine Division.

20–21 May
Training
HMX-1 participates in Operation Packard III at Camp Lejeune. Its eight HRP-1s lift infantry units from ship to shore during the amphibious exercise.

24 May
Force Structure
The 3rd Marines arrives in Hawaii following completion of its duty in China. It is on its way to Camp Pendleton.

25 May
China
Shanghai falls to Communist forces.

26 May
China
Cruiser *Manchester* (CL-83) and her reinforced Marine guard depart Tsingtao when it is obvious the Nationalists there will surrender within days. This marks the end of the post-World War II involvement of Marines in China.

30 June
Manpower
The strength of the Marine Corps on active duty is 7,250 officers and 78,715 enlisted.

1 July
Force Structure
Due to cuts in the number of personnel available for the FMF, the Marine Corps plans a reduction in the number of infantry battalions during the coming fiscal year from 11 to eight and in aviation squadrons from 23 to 12.

10 August
Roles and Missions
President Truman signs legislation amending the National Security Act of 1947. It renames the National Military Establishment as the Department of Defense (DOD), enhances DOD's powers by reducing the Departments of the Army, Navy, and Air Force from executive departments reporting directly to the president to subordinate elements of DOD, creates a chairman of the JCS, and more than doubles the Joint Staff to 210 officers. In a small victory for the Marine Corps, it also

Opposite: *An HRS-1 helicopter skims over the mountainous terrain of central Korea. (National Archives)*

Right: *"On The Deck," Col H. Avery Chenoweth, USMCR (Ret), Marine Corps Art Collection*

specifically prohibits any alteration in the missions of the services assigned in the original act of 1947.

11 August
Middle East
Marine Brigadier General William E. Riley is assigned as chief of staff of the United Nations Palestine Truce Mission, which oversees the truce between Israel and her Arab neighbors.

20 August
Force Structure
VMO-3 is deactivated.

6 September
Mediterranean
The 21st Marines departs Morehead City to become the landing force of the Sixth Fleet. It will remain afloat until 26 January 1950.

8 September
Manpower
Annie E. Graham becomes the first black female to enlist in the Marine Corps.

9 September
Manpower
Montford Point Camp is deactivated at Camp Lejeune and black Marines located there are transferred to other units on the base. At roughly the same time, black recruits are integrated into regular training platoons at Parris Island.

1 October
Force Structure
The Marine Corps replaces the J-series tables of organization, reestablishing true regiments and reverting infantry units to historic nomenclature. The 1st Marine Division converts first, with the 1st, 6th, and 7th Marines (J-series battalions) being re-formed into the headquarters of the 5th Marines, 1/5, and 2/5. The 3rd Marines is deactivated at Camp Pendleton.
China
Mao proclaims the People's Republic of China in Peking (formerly Peiping). The last territory in southern China falls into Communist hands before the end of the month, with the Nationalists retreating to the island of Formosa.

11 October
Aviation
Brigadier General Vernon A. Megee, assistant director of Marine Corps aviation, tells the House Armed Services Committee that the Air Force is neglecting the close air support mission.

12 October
Manpower
Congress passes the Career Compensation Act. Among other provisions, it turns the existing enlisted pay grade structure on its head. Henceforth privates are E-1s and master sergeants E-7s, instead of the other way around.

17 October
Force Structure
The 2nd Marine Division sheds the J-series T/O. The 4th and 9th Marines (J-series battalions) are deactivated at Camp Lejeune to fill out the 2nd Marines to full regimental strength. The 6th Marines is reactivated as a skeleton regiment.
Roles and Missions
Commandant Cates testifies before Congress that the Marine Corps is being reduced to irrelevance despite the intent of the National Security Act of 1947. He argues that without a Marine voice in the JCS, the budget and manpower of the Corps are being drastically curtailed. Under current limitations, the Corps will have only 67,000 men by June 1950 and will be able to field only six infantry battalions. The Navy also is dedicating all the training time of its amphibious ships in the coming year to Army exercises and attempting to relegate the Commandant to the equivalent of one of the Navy bureau chiefs subordinate to the CNO.

21 October
Roles and Missions
Secretary Johnson assures Congress that the Marine Corps will continue in existence. There is conflicting testimony over the reason for the forced resignation of former Navy Secretary John

L. Sullivan, who claims he was pushed out in April 1949 because he was opposed to the abolition of Marine and Navy aviation and the "slow death" of the Marine Corps.

25–26 October
Training
In the largest post-WWII amphibious exercise to date, Navy, Army, and Marine forces launch a simulated assault on Hawaii to liberate it from an aggressor.

30 October
Manpower
DOD announces that a number of Navy ships will be placed in mothballs in line with plans to reduce Navy and Marine Corps personnel by nearly 55,000 by 1 July 1950. To accommodate the reductions, Marine infantry battalions shrink to two rifle companies of two rifle platoons each.

5 November
Aviation
Marine enlisted pilots begin training in jet aircraft at El Toro, flying the Lockheed TO-1 Shooting Star.

18 November
Manpower
The Marine Corps issues policy to implement Truman's executive order banning racial discrimination in the military services. One of the primary points is the adoption of assignment to units without regard for race, which spells the formal end of segregated outfits in the Corps.

30 November
Force Structure
VMF-322 is deactivated.

31 December
Force Structure
VMF-218, VMF-222, and VMF-452 are deactivated.

Opposite: *Marines lift a wounded buddy onto a Bell HTL-4 for a quick trip to a hospital in the rear. (National Archives)*

Right: *A Marine fires a 3.5-inch rocket launcher against an enemy bunker. (National Archives)*

1950

5 January
Force Structure
The last FMF units (3/5 and VMF-218) depart Guam for their new home stations in California.

6 January
Mediterranean
1/6 (Reinforced) sails from Morehead City to become the landing force of the Sixth Fleet. It will remain afloat until 23 May.

9 January
Manpower
President Truman's budget for the fiscal year beginning in July 1950 reduces Marine Corps personnel by about 10,000 to 74,396.

14 January
Training
Air Force, Navy, and Marine flyers stage the first unified air maneuvers in Miami.

1 February
Force Structure
MAG-25 is reactivated at El Toro to control VMR-152 and 352.

3 February
Force Structure
3/5 rejoins the 5th Marines at Camp Pendleton and VMF-218 reports to El Toro.

25 February
Training
U.S. forces begin their first large-scale amphibious-airborne peacetime exercise, PORTEX, which involves an assault on Vieques Island in the Caribbean. It is also the largest peacetime amphibious exercise to date, with 80,000 personnel from all four services, 160 ships, and over 700 planes. The exercise concludes on 11 March. During its course, seven personnel die in various accidents.

28 February
Force Structure
VMF-461 is deactivated.

1 March
Roles and Missions
The House Armed Services Committee issues a report calling for the inclusion of the Commandant of the Marine Corps on the JCS, more joint training, and the assignment of important air warfare roles to naval aviation.

10 March
Force Structure
The Marine Corps Schools at Quantico are reorganized into the Marine Corps Development Center (focusing on new equipment and doctrine) and the Marine Corps Educational Center (focusing on education and training programs).

4 May
Mediterranean
3/6 (Reinforced) departs Morehead City to become the landing force of the Sixth Fleet. It is scheduled to remain at sea until 18 August.

9 May
China
The Communist government releases two airmen (including a Marine) it had been holding since 19 October 1948, when their plane had gone down in Manchuria.

9 June
Aviation
Secretary Johnson announces that due to budget limitations, the armed forces will not participate in the National Air Races.

15 June
Roles and Missions
In an attempt to convince President Truman that the Corps is deserving of a bigger budget, Marine infantrymen and aviators put on a demonstration of a helicopter assault for him at Quantico.
Force Structure
VMR-253 is commissioned at El Toro.

25 June
Korea
Eight divisions of the Communist North Korean People's Army (NKPA) sweep over the 38th Parallel into South Korea and begin to roll over their weaker neighbor.

27 June
Korea
The United Nations Security Council authorizes member states to help South Korea repel the invasion. President Truman immediately orders air and naval forces to intervene under the command of General Douglas MacArthur in Japan.

28 June
Korea
The NKPA captures Seoul.

30 June
Korea
Truman authorizes the use of U.S. ground forces in South Korea and air attacks against North Korea. Congress also approves the call-up of reserve forces for up to 21 months of active duty.
Manpower
The strength of the Marine Corps on active duty is 7,254 officers and 67,025 enlisted.

1 July
Force Structure
VMF-216 is reactivated.

Opposite: *"That Way," Col H. Avery Chenoweth, USMCR (Ret), Marine Corps Art Collection*

Right: *The 1st Marine Brigade moves up to the front in early August 1950. (National Archives)*

Left: *Tankers load up for the next battle in the Pusan Perimeter. (National Archives)*

Opposite: *Marines look down on the Naktong. (National Archives)*

2 July
Korea
General MacArthur requests immediate dispatch of a Marine Corps regimental combat team and associated aviation for duty in Korea. FMFPAC issues a warning order to the 1st Marine Division to prepare for embarkation. The first U.S. Army ground troops arrive in Korea from occupation duty in Japan, lightly armed and ill-trained. Senior commanders feed these and subsequent units into battle piece-meal over the next several days and they are overrun by the NKPA.

3 July
Korea
The JCS agree to meet MacArthur's request for a Marine air-ground force.

5 July
Force Structure
1st MAW forms the 1st MAW (Forward Echelon), built around MAG-33, under the command of Brigadier General Thomas J. Cushman.

7 July
Force Structure
The 1st Provisional Marine Brigade is activated at Camp Pendleton under command of Brigadier General Edward A. Craig (ADC of the 1st Marine Division). Its components are the 5th Marines (the sole infantry unit of the division), 1st MAW (Forward Echelon), and supporting elements. The three battalions of the 5th each have only two rifle companies hurriedly brought up to normal strength of three rifle platoons each. HQMC directs HMX-1 to transfer pilots and maintenance men to VMO-6 to provide a helicopter element to the observation squadron and the brigade.
Korea
The United Nations authorizes the United States to establish a combined command for U.N. forces in Korea. Truman names MacArthur to command this headquarters.

10 July
Korea
MacArthur asks for additional reinforcements, to include a complete Marine division and associated aviation support.

12 July
Korea
The 1st Provisional Marine Brigade begins sailing from California for Korea. The last ships will depart on 14 July. On the battlefield, the NKPA have occupied half of South Korea and U.S. and South Korean forces continue to retreat. MacArthur names Army Lieutenant General Walton H. Walker commander of Eighth Army, which controls all U.S. ground forces in Korea.

15 July
Korea
FMFPAC warns the 1st Marine Division to prepare for expansion to full strength. The Marine Corps provides two transport squadrons to support airlift operations to Korea.

16 July
Korea
The Republic of Korea (ROK) places all its military forces under control of Eighth Army.

19 July
Manpower
President Truman calls the Organized Marine Corps Reserve to active duty.

22 July
Korea
Commandant Cates directs the formation of third rifle companies and the provision of individual replacements to bring the 1st Provisional Marine Brigade to full strength. They are to be ready to depart California by 10 August.

25 July
Korea
The JCS approves MacArthur's request for a full Marine division, but it will include the brigade already on its way to Korea. The Commandant orders the 1st Marine Division brought to full war strength, in preparation for departure for Korea beginning on 10 August. Units of the 2nd Marine Division (primarily the 2nd Marines, 1/6, and supporting elements) depart Camp Lejeune for Camp Pendleton, where they will form the base for rebuilding the 1st Marine Division. The CNO authorizes a 50 percent reduction in the strength of Marine security forces at Navy bases, with this manpower going to the 1st Marine Division and 1st MAW.

27 July
Manpower
President Truman signs legislation lifting the legal limit on the size of the U.S. armed forces and extending for one year enlistments due to expire in the next 12 months.

31 July
Japan
MAG-33 begins to arrive in Kobe. VMF(N)-513 sets up at Itami Airfield, its initial base of operations.
Force Structure
President Truman authorizes the Marine Corps to expand to its two divisions to full war strength (about 23,000 men each). Secretary Johnson approves an increase in Marine aviation to 18 squadrons.

2 August
Korea
The ground elements of the Marine brigade arrive at the port of Pusan in southeast Korea and begins unloading.

3 August
Korea
MAG-33's day fighter squadrons will operate from Navy carriers to reduce their range to the battlefield. VMF-214 flies from Itami airfield in Japan on to escort carrier *Sicily* (CVE-118). After refueling and arming on the ship's deck, eight of the Corsairs launch the first Marine offensive against the North Koreans, bombing and strafing Communist forces that evening. The brigade moves out from Pusan and assumes defensive

positions near the southwest corner of what is dubbed the Pusan Perimeter. It is the 60-mile-wide by 90-mile-long toehold of U.N. forces in the southeast corner of the country, its western flank mainly by the Naktong River.

Force Structure

Infantry units begin arriving at Camp Pendleton by train from Camp Lejeune. The next day, they are redesignated to form the reactivated 1st Marines, under command of Colonel Chesty Puller. The regiment is filled out to war strength by regulars reporting in from other duties and by reservists.

The 1st Marines also forms and takes under its wing the third rifle companies for the 5th Marines.

4 August
Korea

The HO3S-1 observation helicopters and light OY planes of VMO-6 begin to support the brigade. The helicopters evacuate their first casualties.

5 August
Korea

Sicily moves into the Yellow Sea and VMF-214 makes the first Marine attacks on the Inchon-Seoul region. VMF-323 flies from Itami airfield on to escort carrier *Badoeng Strait* (CVE-116). It launches its first air strikes the next day.

7 August
Korea

On the eighth anniversary of the Guadalcanal landings, the Marine brigade launches its first counterattack, to relieve pressure on the southern flank of the Pusan Perimeter. The Marines move southwest to clear a peninsula, while Army units drive due west on their right flank. The objective is the town of Chinju, 25 miles to the west. The offensive runs right into NKPA soldiers resuming their attack on the perimeter.

Manpower

The Marine Corps alerts its 80,000 individual reservists for call up to active duty. The first men and women will report on 15 August.

Above: *The 1st Marine Brigade moves up to the Naktong again. (MacArthur Memorial)*

Left: *Marine Corsairs over Mt. Fuji, Japan. (National Archives)*

Right: *Col "Chesty" Puller presents the first flag raised over Seoul to Commandant Cates on 3 October 1950. (Marine Corps Research Center)*

8 August
Korea
An HO3S-1 helicopter of VMO-6 makes the first night evacuation of a casualty from a brigade aid station near Chindong-ni.

10 August
Korea
The first Marine heliborne rescue operation takes place when a VMO-6 bird picks up a Marine pilot forced to ditch his aircraft after the engine fails. The 1st Marine Division begins embarking on ships at San Diego. The last elements of the 1st Marines will sail by 22 August. The 7th Marines, yet to form, will not complete embarkation until 1 September.

11 August
Korea
A Marine artillery bombardment rousts a large North Korean motorized force from the town of Kosong. Marine air destroys roughly 100 trucks, jeeps, and motorcycles retreating along the road. The brigade takes the town that morning.

12 August
Korea
The Marine brigade advances to the village of Changchon, several miles south of Chinju. Although the Army-Marine counterattack is short of its objective, it is called off as a Communist attack pierces the Naktong River line and threatens the Pusan Perimeter.

14 August
Korea
The Marine brigade begins a movement by truck, train, and ship to the Naktong Bulge, the NKPA salient on the eastern side of the river, about halfway up the Pusan Perimeter.

16 August
Korea
MacArthur forms X Corps, under command of his chief of staff, Army Major General Edward S. Almond. It consists of the 1st Marine Division and the Army's 7th Infantry Division, and reports directly to MacArthur, not Eighth Army. Its mission is to conduct an amphibious assault at Inchon and outflank NKPA forces around the Pusan Perimeter.

17 August
Korea
The Marine brigade opens a counterattack to regain the Naktong Bulge and drive the NKPA back across the river. The Army's 24th Division attacks on the Marine right flank.
Force Structure
The 7th Marines begins forming around remaining elements (the regimental headquarters and one

under-strength battalion) of the redesignated 6th Marines. 3/6, then afloat in the Mediterranean, will join at sea off Korea to provide the basis of the 7th's third infantry battalion.

18 August
Korea
The 5th Marines complete the seizure of Obong-ni Ridge, the first objective of the counterattack, at mid-morning. The enemy break under the fierce pursuit of Marine infantrymen and Corsairs, and the Marines sweep forward to take their second and most of their third objective. Major General O. P. Smith, commander of the 1st Marine Division, arrives in Japan by air to confer with Eighth Army planners. He learns for the first time that his division will spearhead an amphibious assault at Inchon, Korea, on 15 September.
Manpower
To spur enlistments, the Marine Corps reduces the minimum contract from four years to three, and also recruits men into the Volunteer Reserve for immediate active duty, which will allow the enlistees to revert to reserve status as soon as the war is over.

19 August
Korea
The 5th Marines cleans out the remainder of the Naktong Bulge.

20 August
Korea
The Marine brigade reverts to Eighth Army reserve and moves to the coastal town of Masan, where it goes into bivouac in a field, soon to be dubbed the Bean Patch.

24 August
Korea
Elements of the remainder of 1st MAW begin sailing from San Diego for Japan and Korea.

27 August
Indochina
A dozen Marines arrive in Saigon to guard the U.S. Embassy.
Force Structure
Representative Carl Vinson, Chairman of the House Armed Services Committee, announces that he believes the Corps should have four divisions and 26 squadrons.

29 August
Korea
The first elements of the 1st Marine Division arrive in Japan and go ashore to conduct training prior to the Inchon landing.
Technology
HMX-1 conducts the first test firing of a 3.5-inch rocket from a bazooka mounted on the landing skid of a Bell HTL-3 utility helicopter.

1 September
Korea
Elements of four NKPA divisions force another crossing of the Naktong River and begin driving the Army's 2nd Division out of the Naktong Bulge. That afternoon, the Marines are on the move back to the bulge. The last elements of 1st MAW ship out from California for Japan and Korea.
Mediterranean
3/6 detaches from the Sixth Fleet and sails through the Suez Canal toward its eventual rendezvous with the 7th Marines.
Force Structure
President Truman announces a plan to expand U.S. military forces from 1.5 million personnel to 3 million.
Roles and Missions
Representative Gordon L. McDonough inserts in the Congressional Record a letter he received from

Opposite: *A tank covers an enemy bunker on Wolmi-do. (National Archives)*

Right: *A flame thrower burns out a Communist position on Wolmi-do. (National Archives)*

President Truman in response to McDonough's plea that the Commandant be made a part of the JCS. Truman wrote: "The Marine Corps is the Navy's police force and as long as I am President that is what it will remain. They have a propaganda machine that is almost equal to Stalin's." Release of the letter brings widespread calls for an apology from the President.

3 September
Korea
The Marine brigade opens a counterattack to stop the enemy offensive in the Naktong Bulge. As elements of the 1st Marine Division combat load their ships in Japan, a typhoon rolls in and soaks much of their supplies on the docks (an eerie repeat of the rain that disrupted the division's embarkation in New Zealand for Guadalcanal in 1942).

5 September
Korea
The 5th Marines halt their attack just short of Obong-ni Ridge, in preparation for a return to the coast to embark for the Inchon landing. Before the regiment can disengage, it has to defeat a determined NKPA counterattack in the afternoon. That night an Army regiment takes over the positions of the Marines and the brigade begins a movement to Pusan.

6 September
Force Structure
Itami airfield is designated as the operational base for 1st MAW, which reassumes command of its Forward Echelon.
Roles and Missions
President Truman personally gives a letter of apology to Commandant Cates and sends another to the Marine Corps League, to be read at the national convention then in session in Washington, D.C.

9 September
Korea
Captain Leslie E. Brown flies the first Marine combat mission in a jet while piloting an F-80 as an exchange officer with an Air Force squadron.

10 September
Korea
1st Marine Division elements in Japan sail out of port toward Korea for the Inchon landing.

11 September
Force Structure
3/6 is redesignated as 3/7 to finish out the 7th Marines.

Left: *"Road To Seoul," John Groth, Marine Corps Art Collection*

Below: *North Korean troops killed some prisoners. ("Execution," John Groth, Marine Corps Art Collection)*

12 September
Department of Defense
President Truman forces Louis Johnson to resign as Secretary of Defense and appoints retired Army Chief of Staff General George C. Marshall in his place.

13 September
Korea
The 1st Marine Brigade sails from Pusan for the Inchon landing. It is deactivated and its forces are absorbed into the 1st Marine Division.

14 September
Korea
1st MAW headquarters and elements of MAG-12 (its other air group) begin to arrive in Japan to join the rear echelon of MAG-33 at Itami airfield.

15 September
Korea
In the morning, 3/5 lands on Wolmi-do Island in the harbor of Inchon and seizes it against light opposition. That afternoon, the remainder of the 5th Marines and the 1st Marines assault Inchon itself and seize beachheads by nightfall.

16 September
Korea
Eighth Army launches an offensive from the Pusan Perimeter, with a view to crushing the NKPA between there and X Corps positions around Inchon and Seoul.

18 September
Korea
The 5th Marines completes the seizure of Kimpo Airfield.
Force Structure
VMF-235 is brought onto permanent active duty from the reserves.

19 September
Korea
MAG-33 (VMF(N)-542, VMF-212, and VMF-312) begins deploying to Kimpo Airfield in support of X Corps. The 7th Infantry Division moves up to assume position on the right flank of the 1st Marine Division for the drive on Seoul.

20 September
Korea
The 5th Marines attacks across the Han River and establishes a bridgehead eight miles northwest of Seoul. In subsequent days the regiment is engaged in heavy fighting in well-defended hills outside the South Korean capital. The 1st Marines begin an attack on Yongdungpo, an industrial suburb of Seoul on the west bank of the Han River.

21 September
Korea
The 7th Marines comes ashore at Inchon and moves toward the frontlines.

22 September
Korea
The 1st Marines completes the seizure of Yongdungpo.

24 September
Korea
The 1st Marines crosses the Han River and links up with the 5th Marines. Bypassing the hills in which the 5th is still fighting, elements of the 1st reach the suburbs of Seoul by late afternoon and raise the American flag.

25 September
Korea
The 1st and 5th Marines launch a coordinated attack to take the capital. That night, X Corps orders the Marines to pursue enemy "fleeing" Seoul. The 1st Marine Division's cautious urban

Above: *A Marine prepares to defend himself in close combat. ("Bayonet Charge," John Groth, Marine Corps Art Collection)*

Right: *"Street Fighting," John Groth, Marine Corps Art Collection*

night attack runs into a determined NKPA counterattack and annihilates it.

26 September
Korea
The 7th Marines joins the fighting as it moves to protect the north flank of the 5th Marines.
Manpower
The Marine Corps reports the completion of mobilization of its entire Organized Reserve.

27 September
Korea
Elements of the 1st Marines raise the American flag over the U.S. Consulate in Seoul, while the 5th Marines does the same over Korean government buildings in its zone. Both regiments reach the eastern outskirts of the city. Except for mopping up, the liberation of the South Korean capital is complete. President Truman authorizes MacArthur to conduct operations north of the 38th Parallel to destroy the NKPA. The goal of those operations is to destroy the remaining NKPA, with the likely result of reunifying the country.

1 October
Korea
The 7th Marines attacks northward toward the town of Uijongbu and captures it two days later. Elements of the South Korean Army cross the 38th Parallel into North Korea in pursuit of Communist forces.
Roles and Missions
Following an auction, Representative McDonough sells President Truman's letter about the Marine Corps for $2,500, which he donates to the Marine Corps League for welfare efforts.

5 October
Korea
After being relieved in place by other forces, the 1st Marine Division moves back to Inchon in preparation for further action. The division's losses in the Inchon-Seoul campaign total 411 dead and missing and 2,029 wounded.

6 October
Technology
An HMX-1 Piasecki transport helicopter drops a bomb from an altitude of 8,000 feet in experiments at Edgewater Arsenal, Maryland.

8 October
Korea
The Fifth Air Force assumes operational control of 1st MAW and begins to dictate how its sorties will be used.

9 October
Korea
Despite warnings from Communist China that it will intervene in the war if any non-Korean forces enter North Korea, the President and the U.N. authorize U.S. elements of Eighth Army to cross the 38th parallel. Army units move into North Korea this day.

15 October
Korea
The 1st Marine Division embarks for movement to the city of Wonsan on the east coast of North Korea. Originally slated to be an amphibious

Opposite: *1st Marine Division cemetery at Inchon. (National Archives)*

Right: *Marine tanks moving up toward the Chosin Reservoir. (National Archives)*

assault, ROK forces already had taken the objective by land on 10 October. VMF-312, VMF(N)-513, and ground crews of MAG-12 had begun flying into the city's airfield on 14 October.

21 October
Korea
General MacArthur publicly announces that the end of the war is near.

26 October
Korea
Following two weeks of mine clearing offshore by the Navy, the 1st Marine Division makes an administrative landing at Wonsan. The mission of X Corps is now to assist ROK forces in clearing northeast Korea, while Eighth Army does the same in northwest Korea.

27 October
Korea
The 5th Marines assumes responsibility for controlling the 50 miles of territory between Wonsan and the port of Hungnam to the north. The 7th Marines moves north to relieve ROK forces at Sudong, 30 miles northwest of Hungnam. 1/1 relieves Korean soldiers in the town of Kojo, 25 miles south of Wonsan. That night, NKPA forces attack 1/1. Losses in the fighting total 27 dead and missing and 47 wounded.

28 October
Korea
3/1 moves 30 miles west of Wonsan to occupy the town of Majon-ni. ROK forces engage Chinese Communist forces (CCF in American parlance of the time) at Suding and capture 16 prisoners.

2 November
Korea
NKPA forces attack a Marine patrol near Majon-ni and ambush a Marine convoy bringing supplies to the town. Losses are 25 killed and 41 wounded. For the moment, 3/1 is isolated. The 7th Marines relieves ROK forces near Sudong and begins an advance up a narrow mountain road to the Chosin Reservoir (also known as the Changjin Reservoir). That night, CCF elements launch strong attacks on the positions of the 7th Marines, but are repulsed.

4 November
Korea
In moving upward as the road rises through Funchilin Pass, the 7th Marines encounters the 124th CCF Division. The regiment fails to dislodge the enemy in three days of heavy fighting, but the Chinese withdraw on the night of 6–7 November. Marine losses total about 50 killed and 200 wounded, while Chinese casualties are estimated at 2,000.

PRIVATE FIRST CLASS HECTOR A. CAFFERATA, JR.

Hector Cafferata was born in New York City on 4 November 1929, but his family soon moved to New Jersey. Too young to fight in World War II, he went to work at the age of 14, spending his evenings in a factory making aircraft instruments while his father was in the Army in the European theater. Following the war, the strapping youngster played tackle for his high school football team, then went on to a semi-pro league when he graduated in 1948. He enlisted in the Marine Corps Reserve the same year. In those days, reserve recruits learned how to be Marines in on-the-job instruction during drill meetings and summer camp. An avid fisherman and hunter, he at least knew his way around in the backwoods.

Cafferata's unit was mobilized in early September 1950 and reported to Camp Pendleton. He had far less than the minimum reserve training needed to go oversees and was slated for transfer to boot camp, but he already had missed one war and wasn't about to let another pass by him. A sympathetic sergeant got him on the ship for Korea. He arrived there as a replacement in October 1950 and joined the 2nd Battalion, 7th Marines, as a rifleman as it fought its way up to the Chosin Reservoir. He got his infantry training the hard way, under real fire in combat.

On 27 November, 2/7's Fox Company received the mission of holding an outpost in critical Toktong Pass as the 5th and 7th Marines moved forward in the attack from Yudam-ni. The company commander, Captain William E. Barber, picked a hill just off the road. He assigned his 3rd Platoon to hold the summit, while the other platoons tied in on the flanks and carried the lines down toward the road. The 2nd Platoon, including Cafferata, was on the left. Reinforcing detachments of heavy weapons from the rest of the battalion held the part of the perimeter along the road. The Marines fortified their lines as best they could, since the ground was too frozen for digging. As darkness came on, they hunkered down against the cold as the temperature dropped below zero.

Cafferata, Private First Class Kenneth R. Benson, and two other men had been sent a little ways forward of the lines as a listening post. While two men watched, the other two tried to sleep. Around 0230 the sound of close-in gunfire snapped the New Jersey reservist awake. By the time he got out of his bag, he saw Chinese all around him, rushing toward the Marine perimeter. He and Benson crawled back toward friendly lines and into a small gully that served as a trench for some 3rd Platoon Marines. In his haste, he had left behind his shoe pacs (the ineffective cold weather boot then being used by Marines).

The four Marines already in the position were wounded. The Chinese, attempting to break through the seam between the 2nd and 3rd Platoons, were focusing their attack just to the left of the gully. Cafferata and Benson fired as fast as they could load and threw every grenade they had. To obtain a better field of fire, the 6 foot-3 inch Cafferata stood upright in the shallow depression as he engaged the onrushing enemy. He killed at least 15 of them and helped drive off the determined assault.

After a lull, the Chinese renewed the attack. When a grenade came flying into the gully, Cafferata grabbed it and threw it back. As it left his hand it exploded, tearing some flesh from the end of his finger. He ignored the minor wound and kept on fighting. Benson tossed back another enemy grenade, but he wasn't so lucky. The ensuing blast close at hand knocked off his glasses and blood in his eyes temporarily blinded him. As Cafferata kept up the battle, Benson sat in the hole, pressing clips into an M-1 rifle and handing it up to his partner.

The Chinese pulled back by dawn. After first light, Cafferata went forward in search of his missing shoes pacs, his feet encased in frozen socks. The enemy finally got him, drilling him in the arm and chest. He crawled back the way he had come the night before, this time dragging a useless hand that felt like he was gripping a live electric wire. Marines carried him to the company aid station, where the corpsmen did the best they could for him.

In one night of action, Fox Company had lost 20 dead and 54 wounded, but had held off a Chinese regiment. The saga was not yet over. The enemy would come back every night, until 1/7 reached Fox Hill from Yudam-ni and linked up with the beleaguered outfit around noon on 2 December. Captain Barber, himself wounded, had suffered total casualties of 29 killed or missing and 89 wounded—half of his 237-man outfit. Many others suffered from varying degrees of frostbite or weather-induced ills. Cafferata and the other casualties finally were evacuated. The badly wounded private ended up in Japan, then all the way back in the States. The Marine Corps retired him medically as a private first class on 1 September 1951. A little over a year later, the Nation recognized his valiant actions at Toktong Pass with its highest award, the Medal of Honor.

PFC Hector Cafferata received the Medal of Honor for his heroic defense of his post at Toktong Pass. (National Archives)

Left: *A Charlie Company tank splashes ashore from an LSU at Wonsan in October 1950. (National Archives)*

5 November
Korea
After having been repulsed the day before, Captain Robert Barrow's Company A, 1st Marines, destroys the North Korean roadblock on the way to Majon-ni, killing 51 enemy.

9 November
Sweden
The Marine detachments of *Columbus* (CA-74) and *Furse* (DD-882) participate in the funeral of King Gustav V in Sweden.

10 November
Korea
The 7th Marines occupies the village of Koto-ri at the top of Funchilin Pass. From here a plain leads to the Chosin Reservoir several miles to the north.
Heritage
To celebrate the 175th anniversary of its birth, the Marine Corps opens an exhibit of its historical documents and artifacts at the Navy Museum in the Washington Navy Yard. Colonel Katherine Towle wears the first evening dress uniform for women to the HQMC birthday ball. It is patterned after the male uniform.

15 November
Korea
The 7th Marines occupies Hagaru-ri, at the southern end of the Chosin Reservoir. The remainder of the division is slowly beginning to close up behind the 7th, on the single road (dubbed the Main Supply Route or MSR) from Hungnam to the reservoir.

20 November
Korea
41 Independent Commando of the Royal Marines (a company-sized force commanded by Lieutenant Colonel Douglas B. Drysdale) is attached to the 1st Marine Division.

23 November
Korea
1/1 assumes the mission of garrisoning Chinhung-ni, a town on the MSR just north of Sudong.

24 November
Korea
The 5th Marines moves up the eastern side of the Chosin Reservoir. The headquarters of the 1st Marines and 2/1 take over responsibility for protecting Koto-ri.

25 November
Korea
The 7th Marines reaches Yudam-ni, a village west of the Chosin Reservoir. Charlie and Fox Company of the 7th each hold outposts in Toktong Pass, about halfway between Hagaru-ri and Yudam-ni. An Army battalion relieves the 5th Marines east of the Chosin Reservoir and the regiment begins to move through Hagaru-ri and up toward Yudam-ni. Chinese forces attack II ROK Corps on the right flank of Eighth Army (in the center of the country, about 70 miles west of Yudam-ni) and practically destroy it.

26 November
Korea
3/1 (less G Company) becomes the defensive force for Hagaru-ri, site of the forward division command post, supply dumps, and an airfield under construction. The Chinese attack extends all along the front of Eighth Army, which begins to retreat in the face of overwhelming numbers and an open right flank. The U.S. Army 2nd Division is ambushed on the road as it withdraws in a massive convoy and suffers grievous losses in men and equipment.

27 November
Korea
2/5 attacks west from Yudam-ni in accordance with X Corps orders. It meets strong Chinese resistance and makes little headway. The remainder of the 5th Marines joins the 7th Marines in the town during the day. That night, as the temperature drops to 20 below zero, eight Chinese divisions (with four more in reserve) open a counterattack against U.S. positions in the reservoir area. The 5th and 7th hold on against heavy assaults, as do the two company outposts in Toktong Pass but Army units (two infantry battalions and reinforcing elements) east of the Chosin suffer heavy losses and are partially overrun. Throughout the Chosin Reservoir campaign, Marine aviators, sometimes reinforced by Navy and Air Force pilots, support the division with attacks against the CCF.

28 November
Korea
Smith halts his division's attack beyond Yudam-ni and concentrates the efforts of his Marines in opening up the MSR, now cut in several places by the Chinese. 1/7 succeeds in linking up with its C Company and bringing it back into the Yudam-ni perimeter. That night, the Chinese hit Hagaru-ri and renew their attacks on Fox Company. In addition to 3/1, division support elements and small numbers of U.S. soldiers man the Hagaru-ri perimeter and largely hold off the CCF, although losing some ground on East Hill (the key terrain feature dominating the town).
Heritage
As U.S. and British Marines fight together in Korea, the Royal Marines present the Canton Bell, captured by them in China in 1875, to the U.S. Marine Corps for display in the museum at Quantico.

29 November
Korea
1/1 launches a spoiling attack to drive off enemy forces gathering outside Chinhung-ni. Task Force Drysdale (41 Commando, 3/1's G Company, Marine tanks, and an Army infantry company) attempts to escort a convoy of headquarters and support elements from Koto-ri to Hagaru-ri. The convoy and the Army company are stopped on the road that night and overrun by the Chinese. The Communists attack Koto-ri, but are beaten back by 2/1.

Right: *Men of the 7th Marines get mail as they move up through Koto-ri in November 1950. (National Archives)*

30 November
Korea
MAG-12 and its squadrons begin shifting from Wonsan to Yonpo airfield, near Hungnam. The move is completed the next day. The Chinese again make a night attack on Hagaru-ri, but without success.

1 December
Korea
The 5th and 7th Marines begin their break-out from Yudam-ni toward Hagaru-ri. That night, 1/7 begins a cross-country night attack to relieve Fox Company in Toktong Pass. The first C-47 cargo plane lands on the partially completed runway at Hagaru-ri. Thereafter daily runs bring in replacements and needed supplies and take out wounded. East of the Chosin Reservoir, the Army force (dubbed Task Force Faith) is overrun by the Chinese during its attempt to reach Hagaru-ri. Of the original strength of 2,500 on 27 November, barely 1,000 survivors make it to Marine lines, and only 40 percentof those are still in condition to fight.

2 December
Korea
Prior to dawn, the rear guard Marines at Yudam-ni defeat CCF attacks against the perimeter. 1/7 links up with Fox Company, which has lost more than half its men killed and wounded during nightly attacks by the Chinese.

3 December
Korea
The 5th and 7th Marines link up with 1/7 and Fox Company in Toktong Pass. By evening, the head of the column reaches Hagaru-ri. There is constant fighting along the MSR as the CCF seeks to prevent the Marines from reaching the sea at Hungnam.

4 December
Korea
The tail end of the 5th and 7th Marines column reaches Hagaru-ri. VMF-212 flies out of Yonpo to Itami to re-equip with newer model Corsairs.

6 December
Korea
The 1st Marine Division launches its attack down the MSR from Hagaru-ri. Its vehicle train numbers over a thousand. Marine, Navy, and Air Force air support sorties now reach 200 per day. To control them, a Marine R5D transport plane is rigged as a flying tactical air direction center, to relieve ground units of that burden. It is the first-ever use of a transport plane in this role. That night, Marines and soldiers beat back a fierce CCF assault on East Hill.

Opposite, top and bottom; and right: *The bitter sub-zero cold of the Chosin Reservoir was as bad as anything American fighting men had experienced since Valley Forge. (National Archives)*

7 December
Korea
The tail of the 1st Marine Division column reaches Koto-ri. Air Force cargo planes drop bridging sections for the division to span a blown bridge in Funchilin Pass. Engineers install the bridge when the site is retaken on 9 December. VMF-214 flies out of Yonpo and returns to *Sicily*.

8 December
Korea
The 1st Marine Division continues its push south, with the lead elements fighting their way out of Koto-ri. 1/1 meanwhile attacks north into Funchilin Pass to help clear the way.

10 December
Korea
The front of the 1st Marine Division column reaches Chinhung-ni while the rear guard is still in Koto-ri. That night, the brakes of a tank lock on the one-lane road and ultimately seven M-26 Pershings are abandoned at the tail of the column. VMF-311 arrives at Yonpo airfield and flies the first Marine Corps jet combat missions with its F9F-2 Panthers.

11 December
Korea
The last elements of the 1st Marine Division reach the Allied perimeter at Hungnam. As part of an amphibious withdrawal, the division begins embarking the next day.

12 December
Korea
VMF-212 flies on to carrier *Bataan* (CVL-29), joining VMF-214 on *Sicily* and VMF-323 on *Badoeng Strait* in providing support to X Corps during the evacuation of Hungnam.

14 December
Korea
VMF-311 shifts from Yonpo to K-9 airfield near Pusan.

15 December
Korea
With the exception of the 1st Amphibian Tractor Battalion, the last elements of the 1st Marine Division depart Hungnam.

16 December
Korea
The 1st Marine Division command post opens at the Bean Patch in Masan, the same rest area used by the 1st Provisional Marine Brigade during the Pusan Perimeter campaign. Most elements of the division immediately begin patrolling a wide belt around the town to search for bandits and guerrillas in the area.

17 December
Korea
Remaining MAG-12 units depart Yonpo airfield for South Korea. Marine losses during the fighting from 26 October until this date total 908 dead and missing, 3,508 wounded, and 7,313 nonbattle casualties (mostly frostbite or severe illness due to the weather). Enemy losses approach 40,000.

18 December
Korea
The 1st Marine Division is assigned to Eighth Army reserve.

23 December
Korea
General Walker dies in a traffic accident. Lieutenant General Matthew B. Ridgway is appointed to succeed him as commander of Eighth Army and arrives in country on Christmas Day.
Indochina
The United States signs a mutual defense agreement with France, Vietnam, Cambodia, and Laos to provide indirect U.S. military aid to the three countries of Indochina. France is still fighting Ho Chi Minh's Viet Minh, which dominates the countryside of northern Vietnam.

24 December
Korea
Elements of the 1st Amphibian Tractor Battalion are the last to depart Hungnam at the completion of the Allied amphibious withdrawal from that port city.

28 December
Aviation
Marine R5Ds fly their first mission transporting other aircraft, bringing Bell HTL helicopters from the States to Japan for eventual use in Korea.

31 December
Korea
Eighth Army and X Corps occupy a defensive line roughly along the 38th parallel. That night, Communist forces attack the ROK 1st Division and drive it back. This forces the U.N. line to withdraw below Seoul starting on 3 January. The Marine squadrons on the escort carriers and at K-9 fly missions in support of forces on the ground throughout this period, though under Air Force direction, most strikes are against the enemy rear rather than along the frontlines.

Left: *Dead Marines await burial in the frozen ground at Koto-ri in December 1950. (National Archives)*

Right: *1st MAW aviators provide unerring support to Marines on the ground during the fighting withdrawal from the Chosin Reservoir. (National Archives)*

1951

1 January
Korea
VMF-212 and its carrier shift from the east coast of Korea to the west to help stem the Communist onslaught in that area.

2 January
Department of Defense
Congress passes a supplemental defense appropriation bill adding $20 billion to the DOD's budget of $14 billion for fiscal year 1951.

3 January
Force Structure
The JCS authorize the Marine Corps to add three aviation squadrons for a total of 21.

4 January
Korea
General Ridgway orders a fresh withdrawal to Line D, roughly 50 miles south of the 38th parallel. Communist forces capture Seoul as U.N. troops fall back. Eighth Army and X Corps are in position on 7 January.

7 January
Korea
The three carriers hosting Marine squadrons withdraw from Korean waters. VMF-212 and *Bataan* return within a week, but VMF-214, 323, and 311 end up at Itami, mainly due to the lack of good airfields in the remaining territory under U.N. control.

8 January
Korea
A Communist attack near Wonju in east-central Korea forces the U.S. 2nd Division to fall back The U.N. line now has a salient roughly 20 miles deep. Large numbers of North Korean soldiers penetrate the gap and begin operating as guerrillas in the U.N. rear. Ridgway alerts the 1st Marine Division for movement toward this threatened zone.

10 January
Korea
The 1st Marine Division begins a movement north from the Bean Patch to the vicinity of Pohang, a port on the east cost of South Korea. A major airlift effort, much of it provided by VMR-152 and 352, brings over a thousand replacements for the division from the States to Korea.

12 January
Korea
The U.N. cease-fire committee floats a proposal to end the fighting in Korea.

Left: *The pioneers—Marines ride into history during the first heliborne troop lift in combat. (National Archives)*

15 January
Department of Defense
President Truman asks Congress to authorize another defense budget supplement of $41.4 billion.
Force Structure
Marine Helicopter Transport Squadron 161 (HMR-161) is organized at El Toro. It is the first nonexperimental squadron of its type in the world.

16 January
Korea
Due to continuing severe maintenance problems, the jets of VMF-311 are grounded pending trouble-shooting by the manufacturer.

17 January
Korea
China rejects the U.N. peace proposal of 12 January.

18 January
Korea
The 1st Marine Division begins operating in a 1,600-square-mile area north and west of Pohang with the missions of keeping the main road open, clearing out Communist guerrillas, and being prepared to counterattack any penetration of the U.N. line in that region. The division assigns each of its regiments and combat support elements a zone of action. Combat patrols search for enemy forces.

21 January
Korea
The 1st Korean Marine Corps (KMC) Regiment is attached to the 1st Marine Division.

22 January
Korea
VMF(N)-513 begins operating from K-9 in place of grounded VMF-311. China makes its own peace offer, which is rejected by the United States.

23 January
Korea
MAG-33 and VMF-312 move to newly rebuilt Bofu airfield in Japan, which places them in reasonable range of Korea. 1st MAW and VMF-214 and 323 arrive the next day.

24 January
Korea
The most substantial fighting of the Pohang guerrilla hunt occurs after North Koreans attack the 7th Marines command post on the night of the 24th and the regiment pursues them over the next two days. The 7th Marines kills or captures 168 enemy.

25 January
Korea
Eighth Army launches an offensive on the left flank of the U.N. line that gains ground. By the

28th, all Marine squadrons in Korea and Japan are supporting the advance.

8 February
Korea
VMF-323 flies into K-1 airfield, near Pusan. VMF-214 and 312 follow over the next two days.

10 February
Korea
The U.S. 24th Division recaptures Inchon and Kimpo Airfield.

11 February
Korea
A Communist counter-offensive in the middle of the line defeats two ROK divisions and forces the retreat of the IX Corps. The drive wanes soon after.

12 February
Korea
The 1st Marine Division receives orders to begin moving to Chungju in preparation for an attack (part of Operation Killer) to regain the ground lost along the central front. Marine losses during the Pohang guerrilla hunt total 36 dead and missing and 148 wounded.

13 February
Korea
MAG-33 sets up its command post at K-3 airfield near Pohang. The squadrons at K-1 soon transfer there. VMF-311 and its jets, restored to good condition after a month of work, also begin moving to K-3. VMF(N)-513 and 542 are scheduled to arrive at the field before the end of the month.

21 February
Korea
The 5th Marines leads off the division attack from Wonju. The objective is high ground near the town of Hoengsong. There is no significant fighting until 23 February and the division seizes its objective on the 24th despite rain and heavy mud.

24 February
Korea
The commanding general of IX Corps dies in a helicopter accident and is temporarily replaced by Marine Major General O. P. Smith. Brigadier General Chesty Puller moves up to temporary command of the 1st Marine Division.

1 March
Korea
Eighth Army resumes Operation Killer. The 1st Marine Division jumps off from its positions near Hoengsong and after some heavy fighting achieves its objectives beyond the town on 4 March. This battle highlights the shortcomings of the Air Force's Joint Operations Center, which centralizes control of all air missions, most of which it directs toward deep targets. Requests for close air support

Right: *Under fire, Marines peer over the crest of a ridge as they advance in central Korea. (National Archives)*

Left: *Reinforcements catch a ride on supply trucks. (MacArthur Memorial)*

Opposite: *A Marine Corsair bombs the enemy as infantrymen move into the attack. ("Close Air Support, Korea, 1951," MSgt John DeGrasse, Marine Corps Art Collection)*

missions by the Marines on the ground go largely unmet, and 1st MAW's skill in that area is not utilized. Marine commanders discuss the issue with the commander of Fifth Air Force, who begins to divert more Marine aircraft to the support of the division.

Force Structure

VMF-451 is reassigned from the Reserve to permanent active duty.

5 March

Korea

An Army general arrives to assume command of IX Corps and Smith returns to the 1st Marine Division.

Mediterranean

2/6 departs Morehead City to become the landing force for the Sixth Fleet. It will remain afloat until 6 July.

7 March

Korea

Eighth Army launches a new offensive dubbed Operation Ripper. The 1st Marine Division's mission is to capture the town of Hongchon, north of Hoengsong. Opposition is relatively light at the Communists fight small delaying actions and withdraw.

12 March

Korea

VMF(N)-542 departs for the United States, where it will transition to F3D all-weather jet fighters.

14 March

Korea

The 1st Marine Division takes Hongchon. ROK forces retake abandoned Seoul.

15 March

Force Structure

MAG-13 is reactivated at El Toro.

15–16 March

Korea

The 1st and 7th Marines encounter tough resistance in a series of hills north of Hongchon, but seize them in close-in combat with grenades.

31 March
Korea
U.S. Army forces cross to the north of the 38th parallel for the first time since the retreats of December.

1 April
Force Structure
Force Troops, FMFLANT, is organized at Camp Lejeune to provide combat and support units to reinforce a Marine division for extended operations.

5 April
Force Structure
HMR-261 is established at Cherry Point.

7 April
Korea
1st MAW receives responsibility for the air defense of the Pusan-Pohang area.

8 April
Korea
After a period of increased support to the 1st Marine Division, the JOC again begins to divert nearly all 1st MAW sorties to other missions.

10 April
Manpower
DOD issues an order lowering the intelligence standards for enlistment in the Air Force, Navy, and Marines to those of the Army. The plan also calls for these three services to also take draftees for the first time since WWII.

11 April
Korea
President Truman relieves General MacArthur of command following his repeated statements undermining U.S. official policy in the war. Ridgway is elevated to replace MacArthur as the theater commander. Army Lieutenant General James A. Van Fleet takes charge of Eighth Army.

15 April
Manpower
The Marine Corps convenes its first Officer Candidate School since World War II, at Parris Island.

21 April
Korea
In the first Marine air-to-air action of the war, Captain Philip C. DeLong of VMF-312 and *Bataan* shoots down two Communist Yak fighters and his wingman, 1st Lieutenant Harold D. Daigh, gets another. DeLong had scored 11 kills during World War II. Chinese anti-aircraft grows increasingly effective. During the first three weeks of this month, 16 Marine aircraft are downed by ground fire, with the loss of nine pilots killed and one captured.

22 April
Korea
The 1st Marine Division and attached 1st KMC regiment reach the Hwachon Reservoir, an advance of 45 miles since the inception of Operation Killer in February. That night, the Chinese launch their spring offensive. They rout the ROK 6th Division on the immediate left of the Marines. The 7th Marines and 1st KMC hold against heavy enemy attacks while the 1st Marines refuses the division's left flank.

23 April
Korea
Eighth Army orders the 1st Marine Division and other units to withdraw due to the holes in the U.N. line. 1st MAW launches 205 sorties all along the front, of which the Marine division receives an unusually high 42. That night the Chinese come on again and 1/1 fights a fierce battle to hold Horseshoe Ridge.

26 April
Force Structure
VMF-251, recently brought back onto permanent active duty from reserve status, is redesignated as VMA-251.

30 April
Korea
The U.N. withdrawal ends. The 1st Marine Division is now near Hongchon, roughly half of the way back to Wonju, where it had started in February.

1 May
Force Structure
VMF(N)-543 is reactivated at NAS Glenview, Illinois.

5 May
Roles and Missions
Despite strong opposition from the Navy and Army, the Senate unanimously passes a bill calling

Left: *Marines of Dog Company, 2/5, take cover in a ditch. (National Archives)*

Opposite: *A Marine moves up through the smoke of battle. (National Archives)*

for a 400,000-man ceiling for the Corps and giving the Commandant a non-voting seat on the JCS when issues arise concerning the Corps. Soon after, the House votes 253–30 for a bill giving the Corps a strength of 300,000 and the Commandant full membership in the JCS. Both bills die when Congress adjourns its session without being able to reach a compromise.

9 May
Korea
1st MAW Corsairs and Panthers participate in a raid by more than 300 U.S. aircraft against Sinuiju, North Korea's temporary capital and the site of key bridges spanning the Yalu River to China.

15 May
Force Structure
VMF-121 is redesignated VMA-121. It is equipped with the Douglas AD Skyraider, a propeller attack plane that can carry over 5,000 pounds of bombs.

16 May
Korea
The Communists launch an offensive focused on two ROK divisions to the east of Marine positions. The South Koreans are defeated and the Chinese soon create a hole 20 miles wide and 30 miles deep in the U.N. line. The 1st Marine Division defeats two regimental-sized attacks in its zone.

20 May
Korea
Eighth Army reserves stabilize the Chinese penetration.

23 May
Korea
Eighth Army counterattacks against Communist forces weakened by losses sustained in their spring offensives. The 1st Marine Division drives north in a zone just to the east of the Hwachon Reservoir. Opposition is sporadic and large numbers of the enemy surrender. Within days, U.N. forces regain and cross much of the 38th parallel. Fifth Air Force begins Operation Strangle, which focuses on shutting down Communist supply lines deep behind the front. 1st MAW receives the mission of shutting down key roads in the Iron Triangle, the area near the formal North Korean capital city Pyongyang. In the next seven weeks, 20 Marine aircraft are downed by flak, with 14 pilots killed or captured. Only a third of 1st MAW sorties go to close air support during this period.

27 May
Korea
VMF-214 and 323 begin using the K-46 dirt strip near the front lines as a forward base, rotating up to a dozen Corsairs there from the main K-1 base, as a means to cut down response time for close air support missions. 1st MAW also begins to use transport aircraft to drop flares at night in support of Marines on the ground.

31 May
Legal
The new Uniform Code of Military Justice replaces separate Army-Air Force and Navy-Marine legal systems.

1 June
Force Structure
As part of an authorized buildup beyond its current two divisions, the Marine Corps establishes the 3rd Marine Brigade at Camp Pendleton. It will be built around the 3rd Marines.

Manpower
The Marine Corps begins to release mobilized reservists. Nearly 2,200 officers and men are allowed to return to civilian life during this first month of the program.

6 June
Korea
The 1st Marines opens the fight for a dominating ridge north of the Hwachon Reservoir. The division is engaging primarily North Korean forces during this period.

10 June
Korea
Using well-coordinated artillery and close air support from VMF-214 during the day and VMF(N)-513 at night, the 1st Marines finally seizes the ridge near the Hwachon Reservoir in close combat with grenades and bayonets. After six days of inconclusive fighting for key terrain overlooking the Punchbowl (a gigantic volcanic crater), the 1st KMC conducts a night attack that sweeps away the NKPA defenders. The 7th Marines is engaged in equally tough fighting to capture the ridgeline between the 1st Marines and the 1st KMC.

14 June
Mediterranean
1/8 (Reinforced) departs Morehead City to become the landing force of the Sixth Fleet. It will return on 30 September.

15 June
Training
FMFPAC units conduct an amphibious exercise dubbed Operation LEX in southern California.
Force Structure
VMR-253 is reactivated at El Toro.

16 June
Korea
Having gained the most defensible terrain along a line running from the Hwachon Reservoir northeast to the Punchbowl, the 1st Marine Division receives orders to dig in and hold.

19 June
Manpower
President Truman signs legislation lowering the draft age to 18 years and 6 months.

20 June
Mishap
During a 2nd Marine Division training exercise at Camp Lejeune, eight Marines are killed and 25 injured when two mortar shells fall short into a battalion command post.
Force Structure
The 3rd Marines is reactivated at Camp Pendleton as part of the 3rd Marine Brigade.

25 June
Korea
The Chinese publicly endorse the idea of truce talks.

30 June
Korea
A Marine F7F Tigercat of VMF-513 achieves the Corps' first kill by this aircraft, shooting down an enemy biplane making night nuisance raids against U.N. forces near Seoul.
Manpower
The strength of the Marine Corps on active duty is 15,150 officers and 177,770 enlisted.
Force Structure
HMR-162 is activated at Santa Ana, California.

6 July
Manpower
President Truman extends for a year the enlistments of more than 300,000 personnel due to expire before 1 July 1952.
Force Structure
VMF-322 is reactivated as a Reserve squadron at Squantum, Massachusetts.

10 July
Korea
Truce talks begin between military representatives of the two sides at Kaesong.

Manpower
The Marine Corps is forced to make arrangements to take 7,000 draftees during August, its first since WWII, because voluntary enlistments are slowing just as the Corps is trying to build up its strength.

Opposite, top and bottom: *Marines pause during the battle in June 1951. (National Archives)*

Above: *A flamethrower burns off cover. (National Archives)*

Right: *Marine artillery in action. (National Archives)*

Left: *Men of the 5th Marines present arms. (National Archives)*

Opposite: *Maintenance Marines of the Black Sheep Squadron at work in October 1951. (National Archives)*

14 July
Korea
MAG-12 ceases use of K-46 airfield because the dirt runway causes too many maintenance problems. The group shifts its forward base to K-18, on the east coast near the 38th parallel.

15 July
Korea
The U.S. 2nd Division begins relieving the 1st Marine Division in the front lines and the Marines go into reserve for X Corps.

25 July
Korea
The truce talks produce an agenda for further discussion. The main items were decision on a line of demarcation and the return of prisoners of war.

18 August
Korea
1st MAW aircraft evacuate to Japan for three days due to a typhoon threatening the Korean Peninsula.

23 August
Korea
The Communists break off the truce talks.

27 August
Korea
The 1st Marine Division begins moving back into the lines southeast of the Punchbowl.

31 August
Korea
The 1st Marine Division launches an attack to seize a high ridge forming the northeast rim of the Punchbowl. The objective is achieved on 3 September by the 1st KMC and 7th Marines. HMR-161 arrives in Korea with 15 HRS-1 helicopters, each capable of carrying about 1,500 pounds of cargo or four to six troops. In the next ten days it moves to airfield X-83 close to the front lines, sharing it with VMO-6.

1 September
Force Structure
HMR-262 is established at Cherry Point.

2 September
Mediterranean
1/6 departs Morehead City to assume duty as the landing force of the Sixth Fleet. It will remain afloat until 12 February 1952.

7 September
Vietnam
The United States signs an agreement to provide economic assistance to the French-controlled government of Vietnam.

11 September
Korea
The division opens a new assault to take the next ridgeline to the north. After getting bogged down

part way up the forward slope, the 7th Marines sends 2/7 in a night move between the two assault battalions to infiltrate the enemy rear. The left half of the position falls to the Marines the next day, but at a cost of 250 casualties. The enemy has used the lull of the truce talks to build strong defenses. The Communists also now bring to bear almost as much mortar and artillery fire as American forces.

13 September
Korea
The 1st Marines renew the attack to seize the right half of the ridgeline. In a battlefield first, HMR-161 brings ten tons of supplies up to the frontlines to help keep the offensive moving forward. It simultaneously removes 74 casualties.

16 September
Korea
The 5th Marines passes through the division lines and keeps up the pressure, taking Hill 812 the next day.

20 September
Korea
The 1st Marine Division ends the attack begun on the 11th. Although it is not known at the time, this marks the end of true offensive warfare on the part of U.S. forces in Korea. Henceforth the only assaults made are to gain local positional advantage to better defend front lines existing on this date. The division also begins to assume control of terrain on its right flank in relief of the ROK 11th Division. This extends the division front by 9,000 yards to a total of nearly 23,000 yards (13 miles). VMF-323 debarks from *Sicily* and moves in the next two days to Pusan.

21 September
Korea
In another helicopter first, HMR-161 transports 224 men of the division reconnaissance company, reinforced by a heavy machine gun platoon of 2/7, to occupy Hill 884. The helicopters deposit men and supplies in two very small zones on the rugged terrain, accomplishing in less than four hours what would have required 15 hours of difficult overland movement. VMF-212 departs Itami on board *Rendova*.

26 September
Manpower
DOD announces plans to increase the number of women in the armed forces. Current Marine numbers of 63 officers and 2,187 enlisted are projected to rise to 100 and 2,900 respectively.

27 September
Korea
The division rehearses its plan to bring a reserve company from the rear by helicopter to reinforce any threatened point on its long front. The night troop movement of 223 men is made in two hours and 20 minutes.

29 September
Manpower
The draft calls scheduled for November and December are supposed to provide a total of 19,900 men for the Corps, which has grown to 211,000 personnel since June 1950. President Truman has authorized a fresh increase to 236,000.

30 September
Korea
Fighting through enemy defensive positions during September brought the third highest monthly casualties of the war (2,416), exceeded only by December 1950 and June 1951.
Technology
Marines introduce the use of the MPQ-14 radar system to drop bombs based on guidance from the ground-based radar.

1 October
Doctrine
The Joint Landing Force Board is formed at the Marine Corps Schools. The first president of the board is Marine LtGen Franklin A. Hart.

11 October
Korea
In 156 sorties, HMR-161 makes the first battalion-sized troop lift in history, moving the 958 men of 3/7 over 17 miles from a reserve position to the front lines, to effect the relief in place of another battalion.

13 October
Technology
Tests of a flak jacket designed to protect the wearer from shrapnel and low-velocity bullets are completed with a handful of Marines and soldiers in Korea. The Navy-designed vest is soon slated for production.

21 October
Commandants
General Cates announces that he will not retire at the completion of his term as Commandant. At 58, he is short of the statutory retirement age of 62.

22 October
Korea
VMA-121 arrives at K-3 airfield from the U.S.
Force Structure
VMF-441 is reestablished as a reserve squadron at Niagara Falls, New York.

25 October
Korea
For the first time, a flight of Corsairs on a mission over North Korea encounters enemy MIG jets.

2 November
Manpower
DOD issues a large draft call of nearly 60,000 men for January. 11,650 will go to the Corps.

4 November
Korea
Captain William F. Guss of VMF-311 becomes the first Marine pilot to shoot down a Chinese MIG jet.

8 November
Korea
VMF-214 embarks for return to U.S. from Japan.

10 November
Heritage
A limestone version of Felix de Weldon's statue of the Iwo Jima flag raising is unveiled at the front gate of the Quantico base. The sculptor is working on a much larger-scale casting for what will become the Marine Corps War Memorial in Arlington, Virginia.

15 November
Technology
The 1st Marine Division finishes issuing the new thermal boot to all its personnel. This footgear has a pocket of air between two layers of rubber, which helps retain the wearer's body heat. The bulky boots are awkward for marching, but prevent frostbite and are especially effective in the static tactical situation facing the division.

27 November
Korea
The truce talks yield one point of agreement, the line of demarcation, should hostilities be brought to an end. It largely will be the current line of contact. Beyond that, little progress is being made.

1 December
Force Structure
HMR-163 is activated at Santa Ana, California.

8 December
Manpower
The announced draft call for February of 55,000 men will provide 14,000 to the Corps.

Opposite: *"Drag To Safety," Col Charles Waterhouse, USMCR (Ret), Marine Corps Art Collection*

Top: *"Communicators," Col H. Avery Chenoweth, USMCR (Ret), Marine Corps Art Collection*

Right: *"Helicopter Relief of Lines," MSgt John DeGrasse, Marine Corps Art Collection*

Left: *Marine artillerymen prepare to fire another round from their 105mm howitzer. (National Archives)*

31 December
Korea
The division maintained patrol operations and made occasional trench raids throughout the month, but casualties declined markedly, totaling only 171.
Commandants
General Lemuel C. Shepherd, Jr., assumes duty as the 20th Commandant of the Marine Corps. Cates returns to the rank of lieutenant general and takes command of the Marine Corps Schools.

1952

2 January
HQMC
In an early move, Commandant Shepherd orders a partial adoption of a general staff system (G-1, 2, 3, 4) at HQMC in place of the old Division of Plans and Policies, but other divisions such as Aviation and Personnel remained.

7 January
Korea
HMR-161 successfully completes Operation Muletrain, during which it provides all supplies required for a frontline battalion for a week.
Force Structure
The 3rd Marine Brigade is redesignated the 3rd Marine Division. Its regiments will be the 3rd, 4th, 9th, and 12th Marines (the latter an artillery outfit). Only the 3rd Marines is fully formed as of this date.

8 January
Mediterranean
Battalion Landing Team 3/8 sails from Morehead City to assume duty as the landing force Sixth Fleet. It will return on 20 May.

31 January
Technology
The first 500 of the new flak vests are delivered to the 1st Marine Division in Korea and put into immediate use by troops most exposed to enemy fire. They immediately prove their worth.
Training
In Operation HELEX I, HMR-261 and 262 lift 1/8 from *Siboney* (CVE-112) and place it ashore at Camp Lejeune in an elapsed time of four hours and 25 minutes.

1 February
Force Structure
3rd MAW and VMF-314 are reactivated at Cherry Point.

10 February
Korea
The entire Eighth Army front conducts Operation Clam-Up, which involves a feigned withdrawal in order to lure enemy patrols to positions from which prisoners can be taken. That night Marine elements engage such patrols and inflict casualties, but get no prisoners.

11 February
Korea
VMF-312 leaves Itami airfield and goes on board *Bairoko* (CVE-115), which deploys to the west coast of Korea. It is replaced the next day by the lead elements of VMF-115, which soon joins MAG-33 at K-3 airfield near Pohang, Korea.

23 February
Training
LEX Baker One begins in southern California with the reinforced 3rd Marines and HMR-162. It is the largest amphibious exercise on the West Coast since 1949 and a major test of employing helicopters in that role.

25 February
Force Structure
The 1st MAW photographic unit is redesignated as Marine Photographic Squadron 1 (VMJ-1).

26 February
Korea
VMF-115 arrives at K-3 airfield.

28 February
Force Structure
HMR-361 is activated at Santa Ana, California.

1 March
Force Structure
VMF-312 in Korea is redesignated as Marine Attack Squadron 312 (VMA-312). MAG-16 is activated at Santa Ana, California.
Aviation
Following the second hard landing of an HMR-161 helicopter due to mechanical failure, the entire squadron is grounded for two weeks until re-designed tail pylons are received.

11 March
Manpower
The Marine Corps announces that it will no longer take draftees after 30 June because voluntary enlistments are again beginning to meet its requirements. By the end of this month, the Corps will have taken in 73,430 draftees.

12 March
Korea
1st Marine Division receives orders to prepare to shift its position from the east-central front to the west. This is part of a larger switch involving many elements of Eighth Army.

17 March
Korea
The 1st Marine Division commences its 140-mile move to the west with the 1st KMC regiment.

Right: *An infantryman awaits the helicopter that will take him up to the front lines in January 1952. (National Archives)*

Left: *A heliborne medevac. (National Archives)*

Opposite, top: *Marines of 3/5 work on their bunker in March 1952. (National Archives)*

Opposite, bottom: *Easter services 1952. (National Archives)*

Force Structure
The 9th and 12th Marines are reactivated at Camp Pendleton as part of the 3rd Marine Division. VMA-324 is reactivated at Cherry Point.

22 March
Force Structure
The Corps activates six battalions and a new air group on the west coast to reach its full complement of three divisions and three wings.

25 March
Korea
The 1st Marine Division is completely established in its new position astride the primary route of attack toward Seoul. As part of the shift, the division is now part of I Corps. The division front totals 32 miles, but much of the left portion of this is along the Han and Imjin rivers, which provide a substantial defensive barrier. Chinese forces man the opposite trench lines in this sector, which also includes the truce corridor at Panmunjom.

30 March
Korea
VMF(N)-513 begins redeploying from the east coast of Korea to K-8 airfield near Kunsan, on the west coast about 100 miles below Seoul.

1 April
Korea
Chinese forces launch strong attacks against the KMC portion of the 1st Marine Division line and are repulsed.

5 April
Korea
HMR-161 and 2/7 conduct Operation Pronto, which simulates a reserve force counterattacking an enemy landing along the coast.

15 April
Korea
In what will become a hallmark of the last year of the war, a platoon of Easy Company of 2/5 defeats a Chinese attempt to seize its outpost on a hill forward of the main line of resistance (MLR). The reinforced platoon loses 11 killed and missing and 25 wounded, while inflicting more than 70 casualties on the enemy. Before the month is over, the 1st Marine Division withdraws its permanent outposts and shifts to a policy of occupying them only during the day.

19 April
Mediterranean
3/6 departs Morehead City to become the new landing force of the Sixth Fleet. It will return on

20 October. This marks the first extension of this deployment to six months, which later will become the standard.

20 April
Korea
MAG-12 shifts to K-6 airfield near Pyongtaek.

21 April
Korea
VMA-312 shifts from *Bairoko* to *Bataan*, but continues to operate off the west coast of Korea.

23 April
Force Structure
VMA-331 and VMA-332 are reactivated at Miami.

24 April
Korea
MIGs attack two Marine photographic reconnaissance planes, which escape unharmed, marking the first air-to-air encounter of the year.

26 April
Aviation
All of HMR-161's HRS-1 helicopters are grounded due to a defect in the tail rotor driveshafts. They do not resume flying until mid-May.

30 April
Korea
Seven VMF-311 jets on an interdiction mission engage eight MIGs and damage one.

Force Structure
3rd MAW departs Cherry Point for its new home at MCAS Miami, Florida.

1 May
Training
In Exercise Desert Rock IV at Yucca Flats, Nevada, 2,000 Marines from the 3rd Marine Division hunker down in trenches just 7,000 feet from the blast point of an atomic bomb dropped by an Air Force bomber. After the explosion, the ground troops conduct simulated offensive operations.

2 May
Manpower
Star Boston Red Sox baseball player and Marine Reserve Captain Ted S. Williams is recalled to active duty. He will serve in Korea flying Panther jets with VMF-311. He is not the only major league star to serve. Jerry Coleman of the New York Yankees switches from his World War II Dauntless to the Corsair and flies 63 missions in Korea.

8 May
Force Structure
MAG-32 and VMA-333 are reactivated at Miami as part of 3rd MAW.

9 May
Korea
Most of 1/5 conducts a raid to destroy Chinese forces that have occupied an outpost abandoned earlier by the division. Marines lose seven killed and 66 wounded, but inflict greater losses on the enemy.

15 May
Force Structure
VMR-353 is reactivated at Miami.

19 May
Korea
Fifth Air Force temporarily relaxes strict limits on the number of close air support missions to allow Marine planes to train in this specialty along the front held by the 1st Marine Division.

28 May
Korea
1/7 launches a raid to destroy enemy occupying another outpost beyond the MLR. Marine casualties total nine killed and 107 wounded.

31 May
Force Structure
VMA-334 is reactivated at Miami.

2 June
Force Structure
MAG-36 and HMR-363 are activated at Santa Ana, California.

7 June
Korea
1Lt Jon W. Andre of VMF(N)-513 becomes an ace when he shoots down a YAK-9. He had scored his first four kills against the Japanese during WWII.

10 June
Force Structure
VMF-212 in Korea is redesignated as VMA-212.
Korea
HMR-161 participates in a practice amphibious operation (dubbed MARLEX-1) conducted by the 1st Marine Division's reserve element. In the absence of a carrier, an offshore island is used to simulate amphibious shipping. The MARLEX is repeated frequently thereafter.

15 June
Force Structure
VMF-225 is redesignated as VMA-225.

16 June
Force Structure
MAG-26 is activated at Cherry Point as a helicopter group. HMR-263 is established as one of its squadrons.

23–24 June
Korea
In a change in air strategy, Fifth Air Force turns briefly from interdicting supply lines to hitting strategic targets. MAG-12 and MAG-33 each conduct a group strike and destroy two hydroelectric plants.

24 June
Korea
Chinese forces attack several platoon-sized daylight-only outposts of 2/5, using artillery and mortar fire to pin them in place for an evening infantry assault. All of them manage to hold.

28 June
Reserve
Congress passes the Armed Forces Reserve Act of

1952, which reorganizes the Marines Corps Reserve into a Ready Reserve, Standby Reserve, and Retired Reserve. It also establishes a Reserve Policy Board to advise the Secretary of the Navy on reserve affairs.

30 June
Korea
The 11th Marines publishes a standard operating procedure for using artillery to suppress anti-aircraft fire while planes conduct close air support missions. These tactics result in an immediate and significant decrease in losses of aircraft. The procedure later will become known as SEAD (suppression of enemy air defenses).
Roles and Missions
President Truman signs the Douglas-Mansfield Act. It authorizes a three-division, three-wing structure for the Corps (enshrining what Truman already had approved in practice), sets a 400,000-man peacetime ceiling (to quiet fears of the Corps becoming a second land army), and gives the Commandant the right to attend JCS meetings and vote on any issue he deems of interest to the Corps. The law also clearly states that the Marine Corps is a separate service within the Navy Department.
Manpower
The strength of the Marine Corps on active duty is 16,413 officers and 215,544 enlisted.
Force Structure
VMF-211 and 323 are redesignated as VMA-211 and 323.

3 July
Korea
G Company of 3/7 launches a night raid against Hill 159 and finds it defended by a battalion. It loses 44 men before disengaging.

6 July
Korea
In a battalion night raid on Hill 159, 1/7 suffers 102 casualties.

3 August
Korea
Due to complaints from the Eighth Army that the 1st Marine Division is getting more close air support than other outfits, Fifth Air Force ends the three-month-old program of allowing Marine aircraft to "train" for close air support with the division.

6 August
Korea
MAG-33 flies 141 sorties, a new daily record for the group.

9 August
Korea
Following the 1st Marine Division's resumption of a policy of permanently occupying outposts, the

Opposite: *Marines wait out the atomic blast at Desert Rock IV in May 1952. (Marine Corps Historical Center)*

Right: *Machine gunners burn through another belt of ammo on the central front. (National Archives)*

Left: *Fox Company, 2/1, on Bunker Hill. (National Archives)*

Opposite, top: *A machine gunner of Hotel Company, 2/7. (National Archives)*

Opposite, bottom: *On watch. (National Archives)*

Chinese attack and seize outpost Siberia just after midnight. The 1st Marines gains it back and loses it twice more by morning the next day. Marine losses are 17 killed and 243 wounded.

11 August
Korea
The 1st Marines launches a complex night attack and captures Bunker Hill, which dominates Siberia. The fighting continues through the afternoon of 15 August, with the Chinese making determined attempts to regain the position. 1st MAW conducts numerous missions for the division during this period. American casualties exceed 38 killed and 268 wounded, in part due to increasingly heavy enemy use of artillery. The division estimates Chinese losses at 3,200.
Manpower
The Combat Duty Pay Act goes into effect, providing extra compensation for personnel in a combat zone.

19 August
Korea
In another Marine innovation, Operation Ripple uses HMR-161 helicopters to move the division's 4.5-inch rocket battery into firing position and then displace it before enemy counterbattery fire strikes.

20 August
Korea
Marine aircraft participate in a mass aerial attack on the Communist supply area at Changpyng-ni on the west coast.

22 August
Equipment
The Army adopts the Marine flak vest and orders 25,000 copies.

25 August
Mediterranean
3/2 departs Morehead City to assume duty as the landing force of the Sixth Fleet. It will return on 4 February.

1–2 September
Korea
The 1st Marine Division conducts MARLEX VII, another in its series of amphibious exercises, with HMR-161 flying off *Sicily* (CVE-118) and delivering 1/7 to its assigned objective.

2 September
Aviation
1st MAW pulls its Douglas F3D-2 Skynight jet night fighters out of combat operations due to the possibility of engine explosions.

Force Structure
The 4th Marines is reactivated at Camp Pendleton. Its final battalion is not formed until the end of November, at which point the 3rd Marine Division is finally filled out.

4 September
Korea
The outpost war flares up with a Chinese attempt to retake Bunker Hill. Fighting is particularly intense in a subsidiary attack to seize Outpost Bruce. That battle is renewed on the following two nights, but the Marines hold.

10 September
Korea
Captain Jesse G. Folmar of VMA-312 (flying off *Sicily*) becomes the first American pilot of a propeller plane (an F4U-B) to shoot down a MIG jet, after eight of them attack him and his wingman. He is shot down in the melee, but is rescued at sea. During an instrument-guided landing in foggy weather at K-2 airfield, six F9F-4s of VMF-115 crash into a mountain.

15 September
Force Structure
Marine Composite Squadron 1 (VMC-1) is commissioned to perform electronic countermeasures in support of U.N. air operations.

28 September
Korea
While on exchange duty with an Air Force squadron, Marine Major Alexander J. Gillis shoots down two MIGs before he himself goes down in the Yellow Sea. He is rescued within a few hours.

1 October
Korea
Navy and Marine aircraft are slowly able to begin reemphasizing close air support missions over deep interdiction sorties.

2 October
Korea
The Chinese make night attacks against Outposts Warsaw and Seattle, taking both objectives. Marine counterattacks before dawn the next day regain Warsaw, but not Seattle. The division's losses are 13 killed and 88 wounded.

6 October
Korea
The 7th Marines makes another attempt to get back Outpost Seattle and loses 12 dead and 44 wounded without achieving the goal. That night the Chinese attack and seize Outposts Detroit and Frisco. A dawn counterattack on 7 October retakes Frisco, but division decides to abandon the exposed position. The night and morning of fighting costs the Marines 32 killed and missing and 128 wounded.

THE BATTLE FOR THE HOOK

Truce negotiations had been going on in Korea for quite some time by the fall of 1952, but the fighting had not slackened to any significant degree. The war had long since settled into a stalemate along a trace of opposing trench lines eerily reminiscent of World War I. The Communists were too lacking in air power and logistics to defeat the United Nations forces, which in turn were unwilling to pay the price to attack and drive their enemies out of the Korean peninsula. The Chinese, however, were determined to achieve an advantage at the bargaining table by demonstrating their ability to inflict unbearable casualties on the United States and South Korea. Until the bitter end, they would launch repeated local attacks with that goal in mind. One such fight was the battle for the Hook.

The Hook was a U-shaped protrusion in the right sector of the 1st Marine Division lines. About 100 yards in width at its base, it jutted out 300 yards north into the zone between the trench lines. Friendly lines tying in on either side of it ran off to its rear flanks, which left it dangerously exposed. The only reason the Marines maintained this tenuous position was the high ridge it encompassed. From there one could see all the way into the division rear around the Imjin River. In enemy hands, it would be an observation post to control artillery fires that would wreak havoc. In early October, the Chinese had wrested ownership of Outpost (OP) Seattle from the Marines; it was just 400 yards northwest of the Hook. A squad of the 7th Marines held OP Ronson (midway between Seattle and the Hook), a platoon was on OP Warsaw (600 yards northeast of the Hook), and Charlie Company occupied the Hook and the adjoining trenches at its base.

On 24 October, the Chinese opened a steady and increasingly heavy bombardment against the 7th Marines. Shortly after nightfall on the 26th, a Communist battalion attacked. One element immediately overran lightly defended Ronson. A company hit Warsaw and broke into the Marine position. The defenders called in air-burst artillery on themselves and that temporarily checked the assault. Lieutenant Sherrod E. Skinner, Jr., the forward observer, continued to bring in the fires even after he was hit twice. When a Communist grenade tumbled into his bunker, he unhesitatingly jumped on it to shield the others. He would receive a posthumous Medal of Honor for his selfless sacrifice.

The fierce Chinese bombardment and ground attack soon drove Charlie Company out of the Hook and the trenches immediately adjacent to it. The survivors formed perimeters that contained the penetration. The battalion committed Able Company to the fight in the dark, but its counterattack regained only a small portion of the objective before it ground to a halt under intense Communist small arms and artillery fire. The 7th Marines chipped in its reserve, How Company, just before dawn. A platoon commander, Lieutenant George H. O'Brien, Jr., led his men forward in a dash. A bullet felled him, but he got up and kept moving. Once he hit the trenches, he methodically knocked out several strongpoints with grenades and his carbine. In the process, he killed three Chinese in hand-to-hand fighting. A flurry of concussion grenades finally stopped him, but he refused evacuation to remain in command of his platoon. He also would receive the Medal of Honor. Despite such heroics, the Marines of Able and How could only hold on to a small portion of their gains due to heavy losses.

During daylight hours on 27 October, the Air Force allowed 1st MAW to provide an unusually heavy number of sorties to the division, nearly all of them pounding the Hook. Division in turn provided the 7th Marines with Item Company of 3/1 from its reserve force. This fresh outfit launched a new counterattack that afternoon behind a heavy artillery bombardment. Chinese artillery and mortar fire answered. The Marines made a slow but steady advance through the blasted terrain, reducing pockets of resistance one by one. Baker Company of the 7th Marines went after the main trenches to the left of the Hook that evening. Initially stopped, a renewed attack at 0300 succeeded. By daylight on the 28th, the Hook was back in U.N.

hands. During the course of the day, the 7th Marines recaptured Ronson and Warsaw.

The two days of heavy combat cost the 1st Marine Division 79 killed, 435 wounded, and 39 missing. (The Chinese had captured a number of the missing Marines when they overran the OPs.) The regiment counted 369 Communist bodies around the scene and estimated it had inflicted another 1,000 casualties. The Chinese artillery fire was almost certainly the fiercest and most concentrated bombardment Marines had faced since World War I. In a 36-hour period, the enemy had fired as many as 34,000 shells into the small objective area. It was a complete reversal from the earlier days of the war at the Chosin Reservoir, where they had relied almost entirely on small arms and a few mortars—and been slaughtered by the Marines. Nevertheless, the 1st Marine Division had held onto the key real estate, and demonstrated U.S. resolve in the process.

Opposite and top: *Digging bunkers and calling in artillery—trench warfare 1952. (National Archives)*

Left: *Tanks wait to move up to the front lines for a fire mission. By 1952, tanks frequently served as additional artillery. (National Archives)*

24 October
Korea
U.S. forces in Korea face limits on the amount of artillery fire they can use due to shortages of shells. The Chinese use their temporary advantage in fire power to begin directing heavy bombardments against the Hook, a ridge forming a U-shaped salient in front of the lines of the 7th Marines. This high terrain affords views deep into the Marine rear area and is thus key terrain.

26 October
Korea
Following an extremely heavy bombardment, Chinese troops attack the Hook and nearby Outposts Ronson and Warsaw. They take all three. The 1st Marine Division receives unusually heavy air support, much of it from 1st MAW, and makes determined counterattacks throughout the 27th and 28th that finally succeed in regaining all the lost ground. Chinese attacks against other outposts along the division line are repulsed. The enemy is estimated to have fired as many as 34,000 shells during this battle, a level far exceeding anything the Marines faced in World War II. Marines losses over the two days total 118 killed or missing and 435 wounded. The outpost war quiets down hereafter as winter settles in. The division uses the respite to alter its defensive tactics, moving defensive positions from the military crest to the topographical crest, digging deeper, and employing better barbed wire obstacles.

30 October
Korea
HMR-161 sets a record with 365 aerial medical evacuations (medevacs) in October. 1st MAW flew its second highest monthly total of sorties of the war with 3,765, of which 36 percent are dedicated to close air support.

1 November
Korea
VMF(N)-513 gains full operational status following incorporation of upgrades to its F3D-2 Skynight jets. Soon after it assumes responsibility for escorting Air Force B-29 night bombing raids over North Korea.

3 November
Korea
Major William T. Stratton and Master Sergeant Han C. Hoglind, flying a Douglas F3D-2 Skynight of VMF(N)-513, make the first night kill

of an enemy jet (a YAK-15) using on-board radar, near Sinuiju.

8 November
Korea
Captain Oliver R. Davis and Warrant Officer Dramus F. Fessler of VMF(N)-513 score the first night kill of a MIG jet for the squadron.

3 December
Korea
President-elect Dwight D. Eisenhower and JCS Chairman General Omar Bradley visit the 1st Marine Division command post.

1953

5 January
Force Structure
To test alternative tables of organization for the infantry regiment, 3/4 adds a fourth rifle company and 4/4 is formed.

7 January
Mediterranean
2/8 sails from Morehead City to become the landing force of the Sixth Fleet. It will remain afloat until 20 May.

9 January
Department of Defense
President Truman asks Congress for a defense budget of more than $46 billion for fiscal year 1954.

19 January
Force Structure
The 1st Provisional Air-Ground Task Force is activated at Kaneohe Bay on the island of Oahu in Hawaii.

3 February
Korea
1/5 conducts a daylight raid against Hills 31 and 31A, inflicting an estimated 400 casualties at a loss of 41 killed and 91 wounded.

12 February
Korea
HMR-161 suffers its first casualties when an HRS-1 crashes into the sea with its two crewmen near Pusan.

16 February
Korea
Following his participation in a massive air raid, Ted Williams crash lands his jet near his base. He is able to walk away from the wrecked Panther.

Right: *Maj John Glenn can smile after he brought this damaged Panther jet back for a safe landing in March 1953. (Marine Corps Historical Center)*

18–19 February
Korea
Colonel Robert Shaw, commander of MAG-33, leads 208 Marine and Air Force jets in a sustained strike totaling 379 sorties against North Korean positions around Pyongyang. It is the largest mission controlled aloft by a Marine commander.

25 February
Korea
2/5 makes a pre-dawn raid covered by smoke against former Outpost Detroit.

5 March
Soviet Union
Communist dictator Joseph Stalin dies.

19 March
Korea
The Chinese launch company-sized night assaults against outposts Hedy and Esther and the MLR in the 1st Marines sector. The attacks are beaten back.

25–30 March
Korea
Just after dark, a Chinese regiment attacks the Nevada Cities complex in front of the 5th Marines sector. Outposts Vegas, Reno, and Carson are each held by a platoon, while a squad defends Reno Block. Under a rain of an estimated 14,000 artillery shells, all but Carson fall to the enemy and piecemeal Marine counterattacks cannot regain the other outposts. The fighting rages back and forth, mainly at Vegas, through 30 March. In the end, the 5th Marines takes back only Vegas. Fifth Air Force allows 1st MAW to provide unusually heavy close air support, with 100 sorties alone on 28 March. Division losses in the battle are 214 killed and missing and 801 wounded. Chinese casualties counted and estimated are around 2,300.

12 April
Korea
The 1st Marine Division and 1st MAW pioneer a successful technique to use searchlights to illuminate targets for night close air support missions.

17 April
Korea
In a planned effort, MAG-12 and 33 complete a total of 262 sorties in this 24-hour period. The two jet squadrons of MAG-33 set records for sorties flown and ordnance dropped. The 30 pilots and 23 planes of VMF-115 tally 114 sorties and expend 120 tons of bombs.

18 April
Training
Nearly 2,200 Marines participate in a nuclear exercise (Desert Rock V) at Yucca Flats. The trenches of the two infantry battalions are a little over two miles from the blast site. After the bomb goes off at 0300, the four helicopter squadrons of MAG-16 participate in offensive exercises in the area by lifting some troops to an objective barely a thousand yards from the location of the detonation. The simultaneous use of 39 helicopters marks the largest operation of its type in the United States until that time.

20 April
Korea
Operation Little Switch, an exchange of sick and wounded prisoners between the two sides, begins. Of the 684 U.N. personnel returned, 15 are

Marines and four are Navy corpsmen. The rest of MAG-12 (VMA-212 and 323) shift to K-6, near Pyongtaek about 30 miles below the capital.

Training

The 3rd Marine Division begins PACPHIBEX-II, a full-division amphibious exercise that lasts until 10 May. It includes helicopters, simulated use of atomic weapons by both sides, and a rehearsal landing on the Silver Strand at Coronado Island off San Diego.

Mediterranean

2/6 (Reinforced) leaves Morehead City on its way to becoming the landing force of the Sixth Fleet, It will return on 26 October.

29 April

Manpower

Colonel Katherine Towle becomes the first female line officer to retire from the U.S. military. She is succeeded as director of Women Marines by Lieutenant Colonel Julia E. Hamblet.

30 April

Department of Defense

President Eisenhower submits a defense reorganization plan to Congress designed to strengthen the power of the Secretary of Defense.

1 May

Korea

The U.S. 25th Division begins relieving the 1st Marine Division on the MLR. The shift is complete on 4 May, except that the 11th Marines and the 1st Tank Battalion remain to provide fire support for the soldiers. The 1st Marine Division becomes the corps reserve and begins a period of recuperation and training at Camp Casey, 15 miles behind the lines.

13 May

Korea

As part of the division training program, the 5th Marines conducts an amphibious exercise. Other regiments take their turns soon after.

25–29 May

Korea

The 1st Marines and division reconnaissance company move up toward the MLR as a reserve force during extremely heavy Chinese attacks in and around the Nevada Cities complex. VMA-121, 212, and 323 fly numerous missions in support of the 25th Division, while the 11th Marines and 1st Tank Battalion add their weight to the battle. To avoid greater casualties, Eighth Army gives up these hotly contested outposts on 29 May.

Opposite: *A white phosphorous shell ("willie pete") bursts in front of Marine lines. (National Archives)*

Right: *Tanks still proved their worth even in the hilly terrain of Korea. (National Archives)*

29 May
Korea
VMA-332 arrives in Korea from MCAS Miami to replace VMA-312 on *Bairoko*. The relief is completed on 10 June.

10–17 June
Korea
As Communist forces launch a large offensive against ROK forces in the center of the U.N. line, 1st MAW squadrons conduct an unusually high number of sorties, including a one-day record of 283 on 15 June.

18 June
Korea
Marines help stop anti-Communist POWs from breaking out of a U.N. prison camp near Inchon.

24–30 June
Korea
During another Communist offensive against ROK forces, 1st MAW breaks its sortie record with 301 on 30 June, accounting for 28 percent of Fifth Air Force close air support missions and 24 percent of interdiction attacks.

30 June
Manpower
The strength of the Marine Corps on active duty is 18,731 officers and 230,488 enlisted.

3 July
Korea
VMA-323 depart Korea for rotation back to the United States.

6 July
Korea
The 1st Marine Division begins moving back into its old positions on the west flank of the Eighth Army line.

7–8 July
Korea
After dark, a Chinese battalion attacks Outposts Berlin and East Berlin while Marines are relieving the Turkish troops defending them. The Marines and Turks fight side by side and hold Berlin. A morning counterattack on the 8th recaptures East Berlin. That night the Marines turn back fresh assaults. The 7th Marines loses 21 killed or missing and 140 wounded.

Left: *Weary Marines of 3/1 just after a stint at the Boulder City outpost. (National Archives)*

Opposite: *A DUKW-load of 3/7 Marines ride up the ramp of an LST following a 1953 amphibious exercise in Korea. (National Archives)*

11 July
Korea
Major John F. Bolt becomes the first (and only) jet ace in the Marine Corps when he shoots down his fifth and sixth MIGs while flying with an Air Force squadron. He had downed six Japanese Zeroes during World War II.

12 July
Korea
VMA-251 joins MAG-12 in Korea as the replacement for VMA-323.

17 July
Mishap
A Marine C-119 transport plane crashes near Milton, Florida, claiming the lives of the four crewmen and 38 NROTC midshipmen.

19 July
Korea
A Chinese battalion conquers the Berlins in a night attack, completely destroying the two Marine platoons defending them. Following the loss of these two outposts, the Marine division begins to adopt a defense-in-depth, relying on supplementary positions behind the lines to block penetrations rather than relying on outposts in front of the lines to blunt attacks before the MLR.

20 July
Korea
Major Thomas M. Sellers, flying on an exchange tour with the Air Force, brings down two MIG-15s before he himself is shot down and killed.

22 July
Korea
Major John H. Glenn, flying with an Air Force squadron, downs his third MIG in 10 days, tying him with Major Gillis as the second-leading Marine scorer in Korea.

24–27 July
Korea
On the night of 24–25 July, two Chinese battalions attack Boulder City, a hill on the MLR, while other units strike Outposts Esther and Dagmar elsewhere along the Marine line. All assaults are repulsed. They come back again the next two nights, again without success. Marine losses are 43 killed and 316 wounded.

25 July
Force Structure
President Eisenhower announces that the 3rd Marine Division and MAG-11 of 3rd MAW will move to Japan to provide a ready amphibious force in the Far East.

27 July
Korea
At 1000 the two sides sign the armistice agreement at Panmunjom. The cease fire goes into effect at 2200 that night. The accord establishes a 4,000-yard-wide demilitarized zone (DMZ) between the frontlines and sets the stage for political talks to achieve a peace agreement. (No such agreement is ever signed.) During the course of the war, Marine units had lost 4,262 killed in battle and 26,038 wounded. Their sacrifice paved the way for an independent and eventually democratic South Korea.

28 July
Korea
The 1st Marine Division reorganizes its defenses, with one regiment manning the forward line and the remainder (including the 1st KMC) providing a defense-in-depth.

Left: *Marines catch a breather after working on Panther jets at an airfield in Korea. (National Archives)*

29 July
Department of Defense
Congress passes a defense budget of more than $34 billion for fiscal year 1954.

5 August
Korea
Operation Big Switch begins. The Communists return 157 Marines—129 from the division and the rest from 1st MAW—plus six corpsmen. Of the 221 Marines believed to have been captured during the war, 20 had escaped, 174 had been released, and 27 died in captivity. Nearly a quarter of these men had fallen into enemy hands on 29–30 November during the attempt of Task Force Drysdale to reach Hagaru-ri.

6 August
Manpower
The Marine Corps extends the standard tour of duty with units in Korea to 14 months from 11.

7 August
Manpower
Staff Sergeant Barbara O. Barnwell becomes the first female Marine to earn the Navy-Marine Corps Medal for Heroism, by saving a fellow Marine from drowning.

13 August
Japan
The headquarters of the 3rd Marine Division departs Camp Pendleton for Japan. Its subordinate elements also shift during the month. MAG-16 (a helicopter transport group) arrives in Japan with HMR-162 and 163, both flying the HRS-2.
Force Structure
As part of the transfer to Japan, the 4th Marines disbands 4/4 and the fourth rifle company in 3/4.

16 August
Japan
VMR-253 arrives at Naval Air Station Atsugi. The squadron is equipped with R4Q Fairchild Packets, which can carry 42 Marines.

14–19 August
Greece
BLT 2/6, with the Sixth Fleet, assists in rescue and relief operations following an earthquake in the Ionian Isles of Greece.

6 September
Korea
The exchange of POWs willing to be repatriated is completed.

10 September
Japan
MAG-11 arrives at Atsugi. Its three squadrons, VMF-222, 224, and 314, are all equipped with F9F Panther jets.
Mediterranean
1/2 (Reinforced) departs Morehead City to serve as the landing force of the Sixth Fleet. It will return on 4 February 1954.

30 November
Manpower
The total strength of the Marine Corps is 251,770, its maximum during the Korean War era.

Top: *Machine gunners provide long-distance support to advancing infantry. (National Archives)*

Right: *Sgt Sylvester Jarvis of 2/5 test fires his flame thrower. (National Archives)*

WATERHOUSE

THE LONG WAR

1954–1975

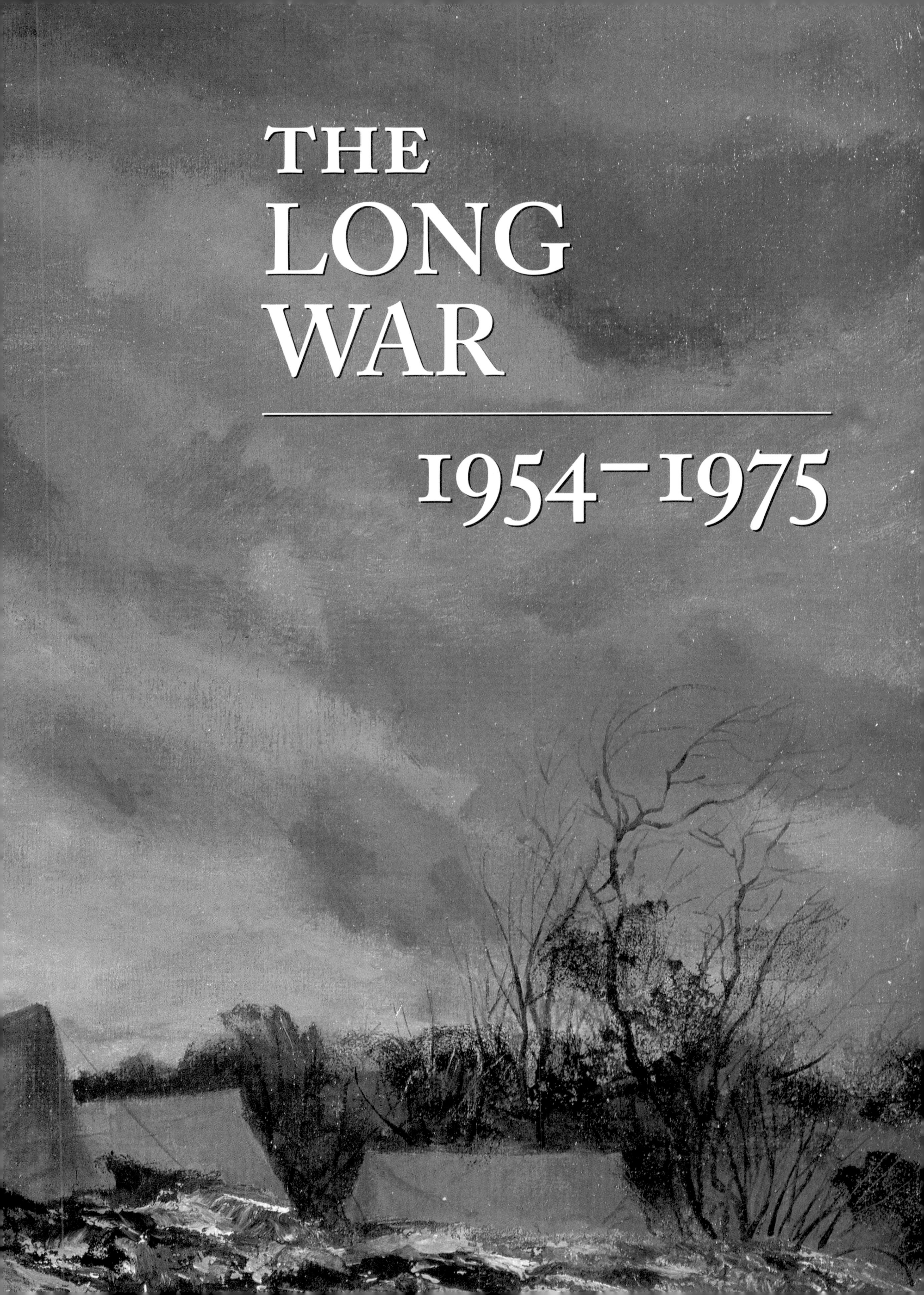

THE LONG WAR

1954–1975

The Marine Corps came out of the Korean War with a sterling reputation and a determination to further improve. It benefitted from the fact that, for the first time in its history, the United States did not unilaterally slash its military forces to a bare bones level in the aftermath of conflict. The Cold War was in full swing and America kept its guard up. The Corps, working with the Navy, made large strides toward its goal of a heliborne amphibious assault capability. The Navy converted an escort carrier into its first helicopter carrier in 1956 and began building a new class of ships designed for the purpose. The Marines placed their first helicopter squadron on ship for an operational deployment the very next year. In July 1955, the Corps organized the 1st Provisional Marine Air Ground Task Force in Hawaii. Although it would be redesignated as a brigade, the acronym MAGTF was born and the concept embodied therein would henceforth dominate the way Marines organized their forces. For a 1959 training exercise, the Corps created the 1st Marine Expeditionary Force (MEF), a temporary headquarters to control a division and wing. Another exercise force in 1960 involving a regiment and an aircraft group was dubbed a Marine Expeditionary Brigade (MEB). A squadron and a battalion deploying for a Caribbean contingency the same year operated as a Marine Expeditionary Unit (MEU). It would be some time before these MAGTFs became permanent organizations, but the Corps was fully committed to keeping its aviation and ground elements firmly wedded. In 1959, the Seventh Fleet in the Pacific also began copying the Mediterranean Sixth Fleet in keeping an amphibious force almost constantly deployed and ready at a moment's notice to respond to crisis. To relieve the hardship of overseas tours unaccompanied by families, and to enhance the cohesiveness of units, the Corps initiated the transplacement program in 1959. This rotated battalions and squadrons from the U.S. to Okinawa and Japan for a year at a time.

The Marine Corps faced a major crisis in 1956 when a drill instructor took his platoon of recruits on a punishment march through a tidal estuary and six drowned. Ultimately the Corps emerged stronger than ever, reassuring the American public by its openness, maintaining a tough training program, and reining in the potential for abusive conduct. At the same time, the Corps continued to emphasize the vital leadership role of NCOs. A major development in 1957 was the creation of the billet of Sergeant Major of the Marine Corps.

Potential combat operations flared in Lebanon in 1958 and during the Cuban Missile Crisis in 1962, but both situations were resolved peacefully. The Cold War was turning hot in Indochina, however. Marine helicopter squadrons began deploying there in April 1962 to support the South Vietnamese military in its war against Communist insurgents (known as the Viet Cong or VC) and

Pages 500-501: *"Night Watch," Col Charles Waterhouse, USMCR (Ret), Naval Art Collection*

Right: *"Mine On Patrol," John Steele, Naval Art Collection*

the North Vietnamese Army (NVA). American involvement grew steadily and exploded into full-scale war in March 1965, when the 9th MEB went ashore at Da Nang as the first increment of U.S. ground forces to play a direct combat role. The commitment of American troops mushroomed. By May, the Marines had III MEF (soon renamed III Marine Amphibious Force or III MAF) in country, controlling the 3rd Marine Division and 1st MAW. The 1st Marine Division followed soon after. III MAF eventually took control of the northernmost provinces in South Vietnam, an area dubbed I Corps Tactical Zone. Here the Marines faced not only local VC and NVA infiltrating along the Ho Chi Minh Trail, but also major conventional forces from north of the border.

In one of its first major operations, III MAF conducted a regimental-sized amphibious and heliborne envelopment against Communist forces and trapped them against the coast. Operation Starlite stunned the VC, who were unprepared for fighting a mobile combined-arms foe, and inflicted heavy casualties on the insurgents. The Communist forces would learn from early defeats and adapt to the American way of war. The Marines, schooled by their long experience in small wars, had no intention of relying purely on conventional tactics. They instituted the Combined Action Program, which paired a Marine squad with a local militia platoon in each village. The Marines provided training and access to fire support, while the South Vietnamese contributed knowledge of the area and a desire to protect their homes. It was a formidable combination that echoed the constabulary units of Haiti, Nicaragua, and Santo Domingo. The Army theater command, however, was wedded to an offensive strategy of seeking out Communist forces wherever they might be. III MAF thus had to devote nearly all its resources to repeatedly capturing villages and hills from enemy units that often could decide when it was in their best interest to fight or melt away.

The Corps added to its long roll of victories such names as Khe Sanh, Hue City, and the Tet Offensive. But most Marines experienced day after day of small-scale battles involving booby traps, ambushes, patrols, search and destroy missions, and short but intense bombardments. Marine aviation occasionally participated in Operation Rolling Thunder and other strategic air campaigns against the North, but for once it was largely able to concentrate its efforts on providing close air support to fellow Leathernecks on the ground. The constant toll of casualties with no apparent decisive result led to political division at home and eventual withdrawal. The last Marine combat units left Vietnam in May 1971. Ultimately Marine amphibious forces had to evacuate the last Americans from Cambodia and South Vietnam when those nations succumbed to Communist invasions in 1975.

THE LONG WAR

1954–1975

1954

7 January
Mediterranean
BLT 1/8 leaves Morehead City, North Carolina, to become the landing force of the Sixth Fleet. It will return on 26 May. This continues the practice begun in 1948 of keeping at least one reinforced battalion of the 2nd Marine Division afloat in the Mediterranean at all times.

15 January
Korea
3/4 provides guards on ships carrying 14,500 Chinese prisoners who have refused repatriation to Communist China and asked to become citizens of the Republic of China on Taiwan.

21 January
Mishap
Twenty-seven Marines and two corpsmen of the 4th Marines drown when their landing craft is struck by a ship and sinks in icy waters off Inchon, Korea.

13 April
Indochina
Pilots of VMA-324 ferry planes from carrier *Saipan* (CVL-48) to Tourane airfield, where the aircraft are turned over to French forces battling Communist insurgents. Ground crews serve ashore until 10 May to assist in the transfer.

7 May
Indochina
Communist Viet Minh forces complete the seizure of the French base at Dien Bien Phu in northern Vietnam. This military failure weakens French will to continue the fight and strengthens the hand of the Communists in the Geneva Conference. In Geneva, Switzerland, France, the Viet Minh, the United States, Communist China, and other parties meet to discuss means of restoring peace in Indochina.

7 June
Caribbean
Following amphibious exercises, 2/8 remains afloat on board *Mellette* (APA-156) off the coast of Guatemala, prepared to evacuate American citizens during an attempt by other forces to overthrow the pro-Communist government of Guatemala. The Marines remain there until 1 July.

22 June
Heritage
President Eisenhower signs an executive order formally adopting an official seal for the Marine Corps.

Opposite: *A Vought F-8E Crusader of VMF (AW)-235 flies close air support in the spring 1967 fights around Khe Sanh. ("Gates of Hell," Ned Conlon, Marine Corps Art Collection)*

Right: *A patrol of the 26th Marines moving down a Vietnamese stream. (National Archives)*

30 June
Manpower
The strength of the Marine Corps on active duty is 18,593 officers and 205,275 enlisted.

12 July
Indochina
The 3rd Marine Division in Japan is placed on a 48-hour alert status for possible deployment to assist the French. The alert is cancelled five days later.

21 July
Indochina
The parties at the Geneva Conference reach an agreement that establishes a pro-Communist zone north of the 17th parallel in Vietnam and an anti-Communist zone in the south. Although the Viet Minh and the French-installed Bao Dai government will respectively administer the two zones, they are not meant to be sovereign states. The agreement calls for elections of a government within two years to control a unified Vietnam. Nevertheless, the two zones soon become the de facto nations of North and South Vietnam. The French agree to withdraw their forces from Indochina. The United States begins supplying military and financial support to the Bao Dai government.

2 August
Vietnam
Lieutenant Colonel Victor J. Croizat arrives in country to become the first Marine assigned to the U.S. Military Assistance Advisory Group (MAAG).

THE MARINE CORPS WAR MEMORIAL

Joe Rosenthal's sensational photograph of the flag raising on Mount Suribachi had inspired the nation in 1945. It also had roused an equally strong reaction in Felix de Weldon, an enlisted Navy Seabee who had emigrated to the United States in 1937 from Austria. The already well-known artist immediately sensed the possibilities of the image and feverishly produced a wax model for a heroic sculpture. The Navy Department liked the final product and put him to work on a life-size version. He completed the plaster statue (coated to look like bronze) in June 1945. It was formally unveiled in front of the Navy Department Building in Washington, D.C., on 10 November, and a copy went on national tour to spur the purchase of war bonds.

The Marine Corps soon saw de Weldon's creation as the centerpiece of a memorial to honor all Marines killed in action throughout the history of the Corps. Congress authorized such a monument in mid-1947. Three years later, the corporation formed to raise the money and oversee the project contracted with the artist to create a bronze casting four times life size. The estimated cost was $350,000. None of the members of the Marine Corps War Memorial Foundation had experience in this arena, however, and the fund-raising effort ran into a series of difficulties. In 1952, Gen Lem Shepherd, the Commandant, brought in retired MajGen Red Mike Edson to reinvigorate the endeavor. Edson got the foundation on a better footing, while Shepherd spurred active-duty Marines to contribute from their meager pay. A large chunk of the funds came from newly minted officers and enlisted men and women as they passed through initial training at Quantico, Parris Island, and San Diego. In the end, 96 percent of the final cost of $850,000 came from Marines.

The foundation and the Corps fought a different battle to acquire their chosen site, a 27-acre tract adjacent to Arlington National Cemetery. The Lincoln Memorial was just across the river, with the Mall, the Washington Monument, and the Capitol marching eastward from there. Eventually the Corps won the authority to land on the site and claim it as their own.

While Marines raised the money, de Weldon labored on the centerpiece of the monument in his Washington, D.C., studio. He began with a full-size plaster model. The

Opposite: *The massive bronze figures being assembled at Arlington. (MacArthur Memorial)*

Right: *Sculptor Felix De Weldon and his full-scale plaster model. (MacArthur Memorial)*

three surviving flag raisers sat for the artist, who shaped 5-foot likenesses of their heads in clay and then cast them in plaster. Photographs had to suffice for capturing the image of the other three men killed on Iwo Jima. Other Marines donned the correct uniforms and equipment to pose in action for the sculptor, who shaped the six forms around a skeleton of steel. Once de Weldon finished the full-scale model, he painstakingly cut it into 106 pieces for shipment to the foundry in New York. From the plaster sections, craftsmen created molds and then poured the molten bronze. Artisans welded the pieces together into one of three sections (subdividing the statue so it could be transported to its final home).

Shepherd and Edson officiated at the ground-breaking ceremony on 19 February 1954, the ninth anniversary of the Iwo Jima landing. On 10 November—the 179th anniversary of the Corps—President Dwight D. Eisenhower presided at the dedication of the completed memorial. The heroic scale of the bronze sculpture, reputedly the largest in the world, fittingly reminds the nation of the sacrifices made to preserve freedom. Its black-granite base, ringed with a list of the major campaigns of the Corps, honors the Marine dead of every war with Fleet Admiral Chester W. Nimitz's famous tribute to the men who fought on Iwo Jima: "Uncommon valor was a common virtue."

Left: *USS* Thetis Bay *(CVHA-1), converted to a helicopter carrier in 1956, was the Navy's first contribution to the Marine Corps' new idea for an amphibious assault*

17 August
Vietnam
U.S. naval forces begin the transfer of anti-Communist refugees from Hanoi and Haiphong in the north to the south.

8 September
Southeast Asia
The United States, Australia, France, Great Britain, New Zealand, Pakistan, the Philippines, and Thailand sign a collective defense treaty (known as the Southeast Asia Treaty Organization or SEATO).

4 October
Technology
The Convair R3Y-2 Flying LST lands Marines on Coronado Beach, California, marking the first use of this huge flying boat in an amphibious role.

11 October
Vietnam
The Viet Minh formally assume control of North Vietnam.

13 October
Vietnam
The South Vietnamese government orders the creation of a Marine Corps (VNMC) of 1,137 men.

24 October
Vietnam
President Eisenhower informs Premier Ngo Dinh Diem of the Bao Dai government that the United States will hereafter provide assistance directly rather than through the French.

10 November
Heritage
On the 179th anniversary of the Marines, the Corps dedicates sculptor Felix de Weldon's heroic bronze statue of the Iwo Jima flag raising as the Marine Corps War Memorial. It is located adjacent to Arlington National Cemetery.

December
Manpower
The Marine Corps reestablishes the rank titles of first sergeant and sergeant major, though both are in pay grade E-7, the highest then available. Although all three ranks are paid the same, the order of seniority is sergeant major, first sergeant, and then master sergeant.

20 December
Force Structure
The Secretary of Defense announces that the 1st Marine Division will be replaced in Korea by an Army division and return to Camp Pendleton.

1955

26 January
Training
The Navy and Marine Corps begin a series of amphibious exercises dubbed TRAEX 2-55 that will continue through 6 May. They take place at Camp Lejeune and the Caribbean and involve elements of the 2nd Marine Division and 2nd MAW. The operations simulate surprise raids to destroy guided missile launching sites.

3 February
Force Structure
The 3rd Engineer Battalion moves from Japan to its new home base on Okinawa. This marks the beginning of a gradual shift of 3rd Marine Division from Japan to Okinawa, which is still under U.S. administration.

4 February
Force Structure
The 4th Marines arrives at Kaneohe Bay, Hawaii, from Japan. This location on the island of Oahu will be its new duty station.

12 February
Vietnam
Following French relinquishment of command authority over Vietnamese armed forces, U.S. MAAG takes over the training of the army in South Vietnam.

19 February
Southeast Asia
SEATO extends its collective protection guarantee to Vietnam, Cambodia, and Laos.

17–18 March
Korea
The U.S. 24th Division completes its relief of the 1st Marine Division along the demilitarized zone.

20 May
Vietnam
The U.S. Navy, with assistance from Marine forces, completes the transfer of nearly 300,000 anti-communist refugees from North Vietnam to South Vietnam.

25 May
Force Structure
The final elements of the 1st Marine Division depart Korea for Camp Pendleton.

31 May
Force Structure
MAG-33 returns from Korea to El Toro following five years in the Far East.

2 June
Force Structure
The 9th Marines moves from Japan to Okinawa.

Right: *A Marine HRS-1 helicopter makes the first landing on* Thetis Bay *on 19 July 1956. (National Archives)*

20 June
Manpower
The Senate rejects a House-passed cut in the strength of the Corps from 215,000 to 193,000. The Senate prevails in the final legislation.

30 June
Manpower
The strength of the Marine Corps on active duty is 18,417 officers and 186,753 enlisted.

1 July
Force Structure
The 4th Marines and MAG-13 are formed into the 1st Provisional Marine Air Ground Task Force at Kaneohe Bay.

7 July
Vietnam
Communist China announces an agreement to provide economic aid to North Vietnam.

18 July
Vietnam
The Soviet Union announces an aid agreement with North Vietnam.

10 August
Force Structure
3rd MAW begins moving from Miami to El Toro, its new permanent duty station. The move is completed on 29 August.

13 August
Reserve
President Eisenhower signs an executive order directing the Army and Marine Corps to begin enlisting personnel under the Armed Forces Reserve Act of 1955. The law authorizes an initial six-month active-duty training program for new reservists. For the first time, reserve enlistees now must complete recruit training and initial specialty training in the same fashion as enlistees in the regular component.

18 August
Civil Support
Helicopters from HMR-261 and 262 and HMX-1, along with reserve ground units, assist in relief work in Connecticut and Pennsylvania following Hurricane Diane.

8 September
Commanders
Lieutenant General William O. Brice assumes command of FMFPAC. He is the first aviator to command this organization since General Geiger.

10 September
Training
The Marine Corps team completes a clean sweep of the National Trophy Rifle Matches by winning the National Trophy, the Pershing Trophy, the Daniel Boone Trophy, the Rattlesnake Trophy, and the Infantry Trophy.

Left: *A Douglas A-4 Skyhawk. (National Archives)*

Opposite: *SSgt McKeon (center) with his attorney, Emile Zola Berman, at Parris Island. (National Archives)*

16–30 September
Training
BLT 3/4 and HMR-161 conduct a field exercise in Hawaii to train in counter-guerrilla, mountain, and night attack operations.

20 September
Civil Support
Some 600 Marines from the 2nd Infantry Training Regiment at Camp Pendleton help battle fires in Los Padres National Forest near Santa Barbara, California.

2–13 October
Mexico
Elements of 2nd MAW, including HMR-153 and 252, aid in rescue work in Tampico, Mexico, following a flood.

26 October
Vietnam
Following elections, Ngo Dinh Diem proclaims the Republic of Vietnam in the south and becomes its first president.

7–18 November
Training
The 1st Marine Division and 3rd MAW participate in a major fleet training exercise (PACTRAEX 56L) at Camp Pendleton. Opposition forces are provided by Force Troops.

18 November
Heritage
Commandant Shepherd dedicates a memorial at Belleau Wood to the 4th Marine Brigade.

2 December
Civil Support
Marine firefighters from Camp Lejeune and Camp Geiger assist the Jacksonville, North Carolina, fire department in putting out a major fire in the downtown section of the city.

13 December
Doctrine
The Marine Corps publishes *Landing Force Bulletin Number 17*, which postulates that the assault echelons of an amphibious force will eventually be landed entirely by helicopter.

25–27 December
Civil Support
HMR-152 and 352, stationed at El Toro, fly food, clothing, and medical supplies to flood-stricken areas of northern California.

31 December
Commandants
General Lemuel C. Shepherd, Jr., retires and is replaced by General Randolph McCall Pate, the 21st Commandant of the Marine Corps.

1956

31 January
Force Structure
MAG-25 is decommissioned at El Toro.
Bases
Headquarters FMFPAC dedicates its new home base, Camp H. M. Smith, at Halawa Heights on the island of Oahu.

8 April
Mishap
Staff Sergeant Matthew C. McKeon marches Platoon 71 of Company A, 3rd Recruit Training Battalion into Ribbon Creek, a tidal estuary at Parris Island. The night march is designed to discipline the recruits. Six of them drown.

Left: *Commandant Pate meets SSgt McKeon at the court martial that caught the attention of the nation in 1956. (National Archives)*

1 May
Force Structure
The 1st Provisional Marine Air Ground Task Force at Kaneohe Bay is redesignated the 1st Marine Brigade.
Training
The Commandant establishes recruit training commands at Parris Island and San Diego that are separate from the base command structure. They are commanded by brigadier generals and report directly to him. He also creates a new post, Inspector General of Recruit Training. These changes are in response to the Ribbon Creek incident.

14–18 May
Training
RCT 1 from Camp Pendleton takes part in an exercise at 29 Palms, California, involving simulated atomic weapons.

22 May
Technology
The CNO and the Commandant agree to a five-year shipbuilding plan that calls for the construction of five helicopter landing ships (LPH) and the conversion of five escort carriers to that class.

4 June
Force Structure
The FMF Organization and Composition Board (known as the Hogaboom Board) meets at Quantico to study changes to the FMF. Its work continues through 1 December.

30 June
Manpower
The strength of the Marine Corps on active duty is 17,809 officers and 182,971 enlisted.

5 July
Force Structure
1st MAW moves from Korea to Japan, its new home base.

20 July
Technology
The Navy commissions its first assault helicopter carrier, *Thetis Bay* (CVHA-1), converted from an existing escort carrier. It can accommodate 20 HRS helicopters. (In 1959, it will be reclassified as LPH-6.)

4 August
Legal
The court martial of SSgt McKeon is completed at Parris Island. He is convicted of negligent

homicide and drinking on duty in the incident that took the lives of six recruits.

17 August
Manpower
The title of Marine Gunner is restored for warrant officers serving in nontechnical fields.

29 October
Morocco
A company of Marines from 2/2 flies to Port Lyautey to reinforce the Marine Barracks at the Naval Air Station there during a period of friction between the French and Moroccans.

30 October
Suez
Following the Israeli invasion of the Sinai Peninsula the day prior, RLT-2 goes on alert for possible deployment to reinforce 3/2 in the Mediterranean. The alert for RLT-2 ends on 27 November.

1 November
Suez
After British and French forces begin attacking Egypt on 31 October, BLT 3/2 and the Sixth Fleet evacuate over 1,500 people (mostly U.S. citizens) from Alexandria, Egypt, as well as a U.N. observer force from the Gaza Strip.

11 November
Morocco
BLT 3/3 on Okinawa is dispatched for Port Lyautey to further reinforce the base as tensions rise due to the Suez crisis. Before the Marines make it to the Mediterranean, a ceasefire ends the fighting in Egypt and BLT 3/3 is diverted to a goodwill tour of Asian ports.

31 December
Force Structure
The HMR squadrons are redesignated as Marine Light Helicopter Squadrons—HMR(L)—in anticipation of the acquisition of larger "medium" helicopters.

1957

January
Technology
VMA-224 receives the Marine Corps' first Douglas A-4 Skyhawks. The small delta-wing attack planes prove to be nimble and rugged.

7 January
Force Structure
The report of the Hogaboom Board is accepted by Commandant Pate. Its main recommendations are to add a fourth rifle company to the infantry battalion, shift the tank battalion from the division to Force Troops, and add an antitank battalion of 45 Ontos vehicles (small tracked vehicles mounting six 105mm recoilless rifles) to the division. This new M-series table of organization, designed to enhance the helicopter transportability of the division, is fully implemented by fall 1958.

Right: *Four jets of VMA-214 fly over the mountains of Japan in 1958. The squadron is flying the North American FJ-4 Fury, a naval version of the Air Force's F-86. (National Archives)*

MARINE CORPS RECRUIT DEPOT PARRIS ISLAND

Parris Island opened its recorded history as a military installation. French troops landed there in 1562 and built a small fort. They lasted only a few months before heading back to Europe, but Spanish soldiers followed a few years later. The Union Navy was next on the scene, taking over nearby Port Royal early in the Civil War and maintaining a small naval station in the area through the 1880s. In searching for a place to build permanent facilities, the Navy settled on Parris Island in 1883, purchasing 37 acres for $5,000. The first Marines, a small guard detachment, set foot on the base on 26 June 1891. In a foretaste of the island's future reputation as a tough environment for recruits, these men lived in tents until winter set in and a number of them became sick. The Navy then transferred them to quarters in a coal shed for a year before finally building a barracks.

The Corps' first major activity on the island began on 1 January 1909, when the Marine Officers School (what would later become The Basic School) moved there. On 1 June 1911, the east coast recruit training program shifted to Parris Island from Norfolk. That lasted only a few weeks, as the Navy decided to turn the base into a disciplinary barracks. Both new officers and recruits departed on 30 August 1911, transferring back to Norfolk. A Marine detachment remained to guard the base and its prisoners.

Recruit training returned to Parris Island for good on 25 October 1915. The Navy was closing down its facilities, and it completely turned over ownership of the base to the Corps three days later. With the arrival of World War I, the Marines needed much more than the 78 acres they had. Pursuant to legislation passed 1 July 1918, the President ordered the government to take over the entire island and reimburse its owners. There were 6,000 acres in all, about half of it in marsh land. (As occurred at the base in San Diego, much of this swampy ground would be filled in over the years.) The Navy Department put up more than 500 temporary structures. The recruits pouring onto the island provided the labor to create the rest of the base, building roads and other facilities as part of the process of building their muscles and stamina. At the height of the war, Parris Island had 13,286 men in training, compared to its prewar level of 835. The burgeoning base underwent name changes, as well. It had started out as Port Royal, after the nearby town, but became Paris Island to avoid confusion in mail delivery, only to switch soon after to the correct spelling of Parris Island.

After World War I, boot camp varied in length depending on the circumstances; from a high of 12 weeks during the doldrums of the 1920s, to a low of 24 days during the expansion of the Corps in the late 1930s. One of the biggest changes on the island took place in 1928 upon the completion of a causeway and bridge to connect it to the mainland. Before that, enlistees arrived on the island by barge. Preparations for war prior to Pearl Harbor enlarged a program already underway to replace the temporary buildings of World War I with permanent brick barracks and support facilities. Up through World War

Recruits at Parris Island learn the basics of marksmanship with M1 rifles as they prepare for the rifle range. (Marine Corps Historical Center)

II, the base also hosted an airfield and occasionally a number of FMF units.

The onset of American participation in World War II brought another staggering increase to recruit training. In January 1942, 22,686 men joined the Corps, 11 times the number of enlistees in November 1941. Boot camp was temporarily reduced to five weeks in duration and many recruits went to Quantico to shoot for qualification. The cycle eventually returned to 12 weeks. To accommodate the influx in personnel, the base received a new wave of temporary buildings, this time metal Quonset huts.

The base received another name change shortly after World War II. As its role outside recruit training declined to insignificance, its status as a Marine barracks disappeared. On 1 December 1946, it became simply Marine Corps Recruit Depot, Parris Island.

Parris Island received unwelcome notoriety in April 1956 following the drowning deaths of six recruits in Ribbon Creek. The resulting national attention brought significant changes in recruit training. The Commandant established recruit training commands headed by general officers at both Parris Island and San Diego. The selection and schooling of drill instructors also became more intense.

In the last decades of the 20th century, new waves of construction brought numerous new structures to the island, replacing many of the temporary facilities of four major wars. But the building of Marines at Parris Island (and San Diego) has remained unchanged in most respects— the depots still take in young men and women and turn out well-disciplined, motivated, toughened privates more than capable of handling the nation's foes.

12 January
Force Structure
The Marine Corps forms its first medium helicopter squadron, HMR(M)-461, at New River, North Carolina. It will receive the Corps' first medium helicopters, the Sikorsky HR2S-1 (later redesignated the CH-37). By far the largest U.S. helicopter to date, it can carry nearly 8,000 pounds of cargo or 23 Marines at a speed of 100 knots.

30 January
Morocco
Company H of 3/6 flies to Port Lyautey to replace Company E, 2/2.

1 February
Bases
29 Palms, located in the desert of southeastern California, becomes a Marine Corps base.

13 February
Technology
The Corps takes delivery of its first Sikorsky HUS-1 utility helicopters, which can carry nearly 6,000 pounds of cargo or 12 Marines at a speed of 90 knots.

14 February
Indonesia
The 3rd Marines and HMR-162 take up station 550 miles northeast of the island of Sumatra in readiness to evacuate U.S. citizens during a rebellion there.

17 March
Philippines
HMR(L)-162 assists in rescue operations after an aircraft carrying Philippine President Ramon Magsaysay crashes on a flight from Cebu to Manila.

15 May
Training
The 4th Marine Provisional Exercise Brigade (composed of BLT 2/5, MAG 26, and VMA 223) takes part in atomic exercise Operation Plumbbob at Desert Rock, Nevada. The operation continues through 5 July.

18 May
Morocco
Company D, 2/2 lands at Port Lyautey to relieve Company H, 3/6 of security duties there. It will remain there until 1 October.

23 May
Sergeants Major
Sergeant Major Wilbur Bestwick is appointed as the first Sergeant Major of the Marine Corps, the Commandant's senior enlisted advisor.

Left: *Dominican Republic 1965. ("Checkpoint Charlie," John Groth, Marine Corps Art Collection)*

Opposite: *Sgt Duane T. MacBeth of 3/6 in Lebanon. (Marine Corps Historical Center)*

1 June
Spain
Marine Barracks Rota is established at the Spanish port.

19 June
Force Structure
The 1st Amphibious Reconnaissance Company at Camp Pendleton is redesignated the 1st Force Reconnaissance Company.

30 June
Manpower
The strength of the Marine Corps on active duty is 17,434 officers and 183,427 enlisted.

16 July
Aviation
Major John H. Glenn, Jr., breaks the transcontinental speed record by crossing from Los Alamitos, California, to Floyd Bennett Field, New York, in 3 hours and 23 minutes in a Chance Vought F8U-1P Crusader (photo reconnaissance variant).

12 August
Manpower
Due to budget constraints, the Secretary of the Navy directs a reduction in strength in both the Navy and Marine Corps over the next two fiscal years. The Corps is slated to end up with 175,000 personnel by mid-1959.

20 August
Mediterranean
In an unusually large deployment, the headquarters of the 6th Marines, HMR(L)-261, and HMR(L)-262 depart Morehead City, North Carolina, for duty with the Sixth Fleet. This marks one of the first deployments afloat for Marine helicopter squadrons.

30 August
Mediterranean
The remainder of the 6th Marines sails for duty with the Sixth Fleet. The regiment will return to Camp Lejeune on 18 November, but 1/6 will remain with the fleet until 6 February 1958.

22 September
Training
RLT 6, MAG-26, VMF-312, and the 2nd Amphibious Reconnaissance Company conduct a landing exercise at Saros Gulf, Turkey.

16 October
Spain
HMR(L)-262, flying from *Lake Champlain* (CV-39), evacuates flood victims and distributes emergency supplies at Valencia.

3 November
Force Structure
HMR(M)-462 is commissioned at Santa Ana.

December
Technology
VMF(AW)-122 takes delivery of the Marine Corps' first Chance Vought F8U Crusader.

1 December
HQMC
The duties of Assistant Commandant and Chief of Staff are divided into two separate billets, each held by a lieutenant general.

18 December
Indonesia
RLT 3 and HMR(L)-162 deploy from Okinawa toward the waters off Indonesia for possible

Left: *A Marine patrol in Lebanon, 1958. (Marine Corps Historical Center)*

Opposite: *A Howtar on Okinawa in 1964. (National Archives)*

evacuation of U.S. citizens during continued unrest there. RLT 3 remains offshore until 6 January 1958.

26 December
Ceylon
HMR(L)-162 is temporarily diverted from Indonesia on board *Princeton* (CV-37) to assist flood victims in Ceylon over the next few weeks.

31 December
Bases
The Marines assume command of Naval Air Station Iwakuni, transforming it into a Marine Corps facility.

1958

16 January
Force Structure
The 3rd Antitank Battalion, equipped with the Ontos, is activated at Camp Hansen, Okinawa.

21 January
Venezuela
When mob violence erupts in Caracas during the overthrow of dictator Perez Jimenez, a provisional company of Marine Barracks Guantanamo embarks on *Des Moines* (CA-134) and deploys off the coast to protect American interests. It remains offshore for a week.

25 January
Bases
The Marine Corps breaks ground for the construction of Camp Futema, which will house MAG-16, presently stationed in Oppama, Japan.

28 January
Training
RLT 2 and MAG-24 participate in PHIBTRAEX 1-58 at Vieques, Puerto Rico. The amphibious exercise continues through 17 March.

11 February
Training
RLT 3 and MAG-16, with 3/1 acting as aggressors, conduct PHIBLEX 58M in the Philippines. The exercise lasts until 13 March.

14 February
Civil Support
The 6th Truck Company, a reserve unit located in Scranton, Pennsylvania, assists in the rescue of motorists stranded on the Pennsylvania Turnpike by a severe blizzard.

9 March
Indonesia
Company C, 1/3, VMA-332, and HMR(L)-163 deploy with elements of the Seventh Fleet off Indonesia to protect U.S. citizens and interests.

10 April
Training
RLT 4 begins a three-day anti-guerrilla field exercise in the Kahuku Training Area in northern Oahu, Hawaii.

23 April
Reserve
Commandant Pate orders the formation of 12 helicopter (HMR-761 through HMR-772) and 9 fixed-wing (VMF-131, 133, 134, 413, 511, 534, and VMA-243, 341, 611) squadrons in the Marine Corps Reserve. The helicopter squadrons are the first of their type in the Reserve

25 April
Civil Support
Company M, 3/2 helps fight brush and forest fires in Hyde County, North Carolina.

1 May
Mediterranean
BLT 2/2 and HMR(L)-262 deploy as the landing force Sixth Fleet. This marks one of the infrequent deployments of helicopters with the landing force. The two units will return home on 17 October.

13 May
Venezuela
BLT 1/6 and elements of MAG-26 and MAG-35 deploy with a naval task force off the coast to protect Vice President Richard M. Nixon and party after Venezuelan mobs threaten them during a state visit.

14 May
Mediterranean
Due to deteriorating political conditions in Lebanon, BLT 1/8 remains on station at the conclusion of its normal tour with the Sixth Fleet to reinforce newly arriving BLT 2/2.

1 June
Force Structure
The 2nd Amphibious Reconnaissance Company at Camp Lejeune is redesignated the 2nd Force Reconnaissance Company.

27 June
Cuba
A group of Marines and sailors returning from liberty are kidnaped by Raul Castro, brother of rebel leader Fidel Castro. The Americans are held until 18 July.

30 June
Manpower
The strength of the Marine Corps on active duty is 16,471 officers and 172,754 enlisted.

1 July
Bases
Marine Corps Air Station Miami is closed.

12 July
Civil Support
More than 1,500 Marines from the 1st Marine Division and Camp Pendleton help Forest Service personnel in fighting fires in California's Cleveland National Forest.

14 July
Lebanon
President Camille Chamoun appeals to the United States and Britain for assistance in combating Syrian influence in his country and preventing civil war between Christian Maronites and Muslims.

President Eisenhower orders the three Marine BLTs afloat in the Mediterranean to intervene.

15 July
Lebanon
BLT 2/2 lands at Red Beach, just south of Beirut. The rifle companies set up a perimeter just inland at the city's international airport. BLT 2/8 begins an air movement toward Lebanon.

16 July
Lebanon
BLT 3/6 goes ashore at Red Beach and assumes control of the airport, as BLT 2/2 moves north to take over the port facilities and secure the U.S. Embassy and key bridges.

18 July
Lebanon
BLT 1/8 lands near Juniyah, four miles north of Beirut. BLT 2/8 and the Army's 24th Airborne Brigade begin arriving at the airport.

21 July
Lebanon
BLT 3/3 sails from Okinawa for the Mediterranean, but never goes ashore in Lebanon.

14 August
Lebanon
Following elections on 31 July that ease tensions, BLT 2/2 goes back on board ships and reconstitutes the landing force of the Sixth Fleet.

23 August
Heritage
The Marine Corps Drum and Bugle Corps, the Marine Corps Recruit Depot Parris Island band, and a ceremonial troop unit deploy to Scotland to participate in the annual Edinburgh Tattoo. The Marines return home on 13 September.

1 September
Force Structure
HMR(M)-463 is commissioned at Santa Ana, California.

2 September
Training
RLTs 1 and 5, 3/7, and MAGs 33 and 36 participate in PHIBLEX 2-59 at Camp Pendleton. The exercise lasts through 14 September.
Force Structure
HMR-773 and 774 are activated as part of the Marine Corps Reserve.

8 September
Taiwan
Elements of MAG-11 deploy from Japan to Taiwan to reinforce the island's air defenses after Communist China begins a heavy bombardment of the Nationalist-held islands of Quemoy and Little Quemoy off the coast of mainland China.

10 September
Lebanon
A Marine company in surface craft and an Army airborne company in Marine and Army helicopters conduct a joint amphibious exercise 20 miles north of Beirut.

12 September
Japan
MAG-13 deploys from Hawaii to Naval Air Station Atsugi to replace MAG-11 during its stay on Taiwan.

15 September
Lebanon
BLTs 1/8 and 2/8 depart for the United States.

29 September
Lebanon
The 6th Marines' headquarters and BLT 2/6 go ashore. They relieve BLT 3/6, which departs the next day.

13 October
Aviation
VMA-212 and 214 fly 4,800 miles from Hawaii to Japan, the first ever squadron-strength trans-Pacific flight by Navy or Marine fighter-type aircraft.

18 October
Lebanon
BLT 2/6 and the headquarters of the 6th Marines depart, ending the deployment of U.S. combat forces to Lebanon.

10 November
Aviation
The first permanent Marine aviation detachment afloat is activated on board *Boxer* at Norfolk, Virginia, to provide supply, maintenance, and flight deck control to Marine helicopter squadrons assigned to the ship.

2 December
Civil Support
The 2nd Infantry Training Regiment deploys 650 Marines to assist in fighting a forest fire near Malibu, California.

6 December
Civil Support
64 Marines of 3/8 help fight a forest fire near Pungo Lake, North Carolina.

14 December
Civil Support
Nearly 700 Marines of the 2nd Infantry Training Regiment fight brush fires in the San Juan Capistrano area of California.

Opposite: *"Patrol Approaching Marble Mountain," Edwin C. Brewer, Marine Corps Art Collection*

Left: *A Marine of 1/9 during Operation Georgia. ("Combat Patrol," John Steele, Naval Art Collection)*

Left: *Marines ride a Mule in the Dominican Republic in May 1965. The motorized cart was designed to carry ammunition and crew-served weapons. (Marine Corps Historical Center)*

1959

1 January
Manpower
Following legislative authorization to add the pay grades of E-8 and E-9, the Marine Corps institutes major changes to its enlisted rank structure. The reform is needed after the percentage of NCOs in the ranks rises to 58 percent from its pre-World War II share of 25 percent. To ensure that no one is reduced in rank (such as a former E-3 corporal having to become a new E-3 lance corporal), a dual rank structure is allowed for a transitional period. The new ranks are fully implemented by mid-1963. The new structure is: private, private first class, lance corporal, corporal, sergeant, staff sergeant, gunnery sergeant, first sergeant or master sergeant, and sergeant major or master gunnery sergeant. The replacement of technical sergeant with gunnery sergeant revives a historic rank that had disappeared. The ranks of master sergeant and master gunnery sergeant are provided for technical specialists, while first sergeant and sergeant major are reserved for leadership billets.
Civil Support
Marines from 1/1 and 1st Force Service Regiment provide assistance in putting out forest fires near Santa Monica, California.
Bases
The Marine Corps auxiliary airfield at Edenton, North Carolina, is deactivated.
Cuba
Dictator Fulgencia Batista flees and Fidel Castro and his revolutionary forces take control of the government. The United States puts Cuban territory off limits to its military personnel and perimeter security is heightened at the naval base at Guantanamo Bay.

10 January
Bases
The Marine Corps acquires Vincent Air Force Base in Yuma, Arizona, and activates it as an auxiliary airfield for El Toro.

30 January
Technology
Boxer is reclassified as LPH-4.

12 February
Bases
The Marine Corps training camp at Vieques, Puerto Rico, is named for PFC Fernando Luis Garcia, a Puerto Rican-born Marine Medal of Honor recipient.

2 March
Technology
Princeton is reclassified as LPH-5.

17 March
Force Structure
1/1 departs Camp Pendleton for a one-year tour of duty with the 3rd Marine Division on Okinawa. It is the first infantry battalion in the transplacement program, which will rotate such units through Okinawa for the next several years.

1 April
Force Structure
HMR(L)-776 is activated as part of the Marine Corps Reserve.

10 April
Aviation
Lieutenant Colonel John Glenn is one of the first seven men selected for astronaut training.

13 April
Mediterranean
VMA-225 deploys from Cherry Point on board *Essex* (CV-9) for duty with the Sixth Fleet.

18 April
Training
RLT 3, MAG-12, and the Korean Marine Corps' RLT 2 conduct amphibious training in Korea. The exercise continues through 9 May.

4 May
Aviation
Two Marine A4D-2 Skyhawks become the first single-engine jets to fly nonstop across the Atlantic (2,270 miles from Argentia, Newfoundland, to Rota, Spain) using a technique known as "buddy refueling."

8 May
Civil Support
Elements of the 8th Marines assist in putting out forest fires in Camden County, North Carolina.

18 May
Training
The 1st Marine Division and 3rd MAW, joined together as the 1st Marine Expeditionary Force, conduct amphibious training at Camp Pendleton. In Indonesia, RLT 9, elements of MAG-16, and HMR(L)-362 participate in amphibious training in British North Borneo. Both exercises continue through 12 June.

Right: *A Marine of 1/8 takes cover behind a car when small arms fire breaks out in the Dominican Republic. (Marine Corps Historical Center)*

Left: *An ONTOS of the 2nd Tank Battalion on outpost duty in the Dominican Republic. (Marine Corps Historical Center)*

19 May
Berlin
BLT 1/2 and HMR(L)-262 are alerted for deployment to Berlin during Communist threats to renew the blockade of the divided city. They remain on alert through 4 June.

1 June
Vietnam
The Vietnamese Marine Corps increases to nearly 3,000 men when it adds a third landing battalion to its structure.

2 June
Training
BLT 2/6 sails from Morehead City for a two-month cruise through the newly opened St. Lawrence Seaway to the Great Lakes. During its time in the Great Lakes, it will conduct five amphibious demonstration landings for the public.

14 June
Camp Lejeune
Marines and Forest Service personnel battle a forest fire on the base.

20 June
Training
BLT 3/2 joins with British Royal Marine Commandos for a week-long landing exercise in Gufo di Bomba, Libya.

30 June
Force Structure
HMR(L)-264 is commissioned.
Manpower
The strength of the Marine Corps on active duty is 16,065 officers and 159,506 enlisted.

11 July
Manpower
The Marine Corps resumes participation in the aviation cadet program at Pensacola after a hiatus of 18 years, since it is having difficulty obtaining enough pilots through other commissioning sources.

13 July
Training
The 1st Reconnaissance Battalion begins a 175-mile foot march from Death Valley (the lowest point in the continental United States) to Mount Whitney (the highest).

30 July
Mediterranean
BLT 3/8, VMA-225, and a detachment of HMR(L)-262 depart North Carolina to serve as the landing force of the Sixth Fleet. They will return on 8 February 1960. Helicopter squadrons do not become a routine part of the landing force until 1963.

28 August
Sergeants Major
Sergeant Major Francis D. Bauber succeeds Sergeant Major Bestwick and becomes the second Sergeant Major of the Marine Corps.

5 September
Pacific
RLT 9 and elements of MAG-16, organized as the 3rd Marine Expeditionary Force, sail from Okinawa to serve as the first landing force of the Seventh Fleet, stationed in the western Pacific.

10 September
Manpower
The title of Marine Gunner is eliminated, although those currently holding it are allowed to retain it.

2 November
Training
BLT 1/9, Company H of 2/9, and the 1st Force Reconnaissance Company participate in a winter amphibious exercise in Alaska. The training continues through 10 December.

5 November
Civil Support
200 men of the 5th Marines aid the Forest Service in fighting a fire in Cleveland National Forest in California.

20 November
Civil Support
More than 300 Marines from various Camp Pendleton units fight fires in Las Pulgas and Alysso Canyon areas in and near the base.
Cuba
The 4th Provisional Marine Force is deployed from Camp Lejeune and Cherry Point to stand by to protect U.S. citizens during a period of increasing tensions with Cuba's Castro regime. The units remain away from their home bases until 15 February 1960.

30 November
Cuba
About 100 Marines from Camp Lejeune arrive at Guantanamo Bay to reinforce the security element already there. They remain ashore until 15 January 1960.

3–7 December
Aviation
Elements of MAG-13 returning from the Far East to California make the first flight by naval single-engine jets (North American FJ-4B Fury models) between Hawaii and the mainland.

31 December
Commandants
General Randolph McCall Pate retires and Lieutenant General David M. Shoup is promoted

Right: *Marines search for a sniper, 8 May 1965, in Santo Domingo City. (Marine Corps Historical Center)*

to become the twenty-second Commandant of the Marine Corps. Shoup had received the Medal of Honor for his courageous leadership at Tarawa.

Force Structure

Manpower cuts during the preceding year had forced a reduction in the number of infantry battalions in the Corps from 27 to 21.

1960

2 January

Bases

Marine Corps Air Facility Futema is placed into commission on Okinawa.

20 January

Training

BLT 1/5 participates in SNOWFLEX II-60 at the Cold Weather Training Center, Bridgeport, California. The exercise lasts until 11 February.

21 January

Space

Helicopters from MAG-26 are instrumental in recovering the nose cone of the fourth Project Mercury space shot, from Wallops Island, Virginia.

30 January

Training

The 8th Provisional Marine Brigade conducts amphibious exercises at Vieques to test new heliborne amphibious assault techniques and modifications to *Boxer*. The operation lasts through 19 February.

3 February

Force Structure

Commandant Shoup announces that due to increased personnel stability arising from the success of the four-year enlistment program, it will be possible to reactivate two of the recently disbanded six infantry battalions.

Left: *Marines help evacuate foreign citizens caught in the wartorn Dominican Republic. (National Archives)*

Right: *Men of 9th MEB run ashore from a Navy LCM-6 landing craft at Da Nang in March 1965. (National Archives)*

10–12 February
Cuba
VMF-122 and 312 from Beaufort, South Carolina, deploy to Naval Air Station Leeward Point in Cuba.

1 March
Morocco
Marines stationed at Port Lyautey aid in rescue and relief operations following an earthquake at Agadir.
Bases
The auxiliary air station at Beaufort, South Carolina, is redesignated a Marine Corps Air Station.

4 March
Technology
The chief of staff of the Army presents Commandant Shoup with the Marine Corps' first M-14 rifle, which will replace the WWII-era M-1 Garand.

7 March
Training
Elements of 3rd Marine Division, 1st Marine Brigade, 1st MAW, the Seventh Fleet, and the Nationalist Chinese Navy and Marine Corps conduct a large-scale exercise in Taiwan. It involves the first helicopter lift of Nationalist Marines and the establishment of a Short Expeditionary Landing Field (SELF). The exercise lasts through 10 April.

14–30 March
Training
The 5th Marines (less 3/5), with support from VMO squadrons, conducts a 150-mile foot march in the desert at 29 Palms.

2 May
Force Structure
The 1st Light Antiaircraft Missile Battalion (1st LAAM) is activated as part of Force Troops at 29 Palms. It is armed with the HAWK (Homing All the Way Killer) missile.

5 May
Vietnam
At the request of the Vietnamese government, the United States agrees to more than double the number of military advisors to 685.

6 June
Training
The 9th Provisional Marine Brigade (composed of RLT 9, MAG-12, and KMC RLT 3) conducts amphibious exercises in Korea. The 17-day operation includes a helicopter assault by 4,600 troops.

Left: *1/26 in 1966. ("Firefight DMZ," Capt Jack T. Dyer, Jr., USMCR, Marine Corps Art Collection)*

Opposite: *A door gunner in a UH-34 looks out over the Vietnamese countryside as a CH-46 flies alongside. (National Archives)*

10 June
Japan
White House Press Secretary James C. Hagerty and Ambassador Douglas MacArthur II are rescued from a stone-throwing crowd in Tokyo by a Marine helicopter.
Training
The 2nd Marine Expeditionary Brigade (2nd MEB—composed of BLTs 2/6, 3/6, 3/2, and 3/8, VMA-225, and Provisional MAG-30) deploys to the Caribbean for a training exercise.

30 June
Force Structure
The Department of the Pacific headquarters, in existence since 1920 in San Francisco, is deactivated. The Marine Barracks for the Naval Ammunition Depot in Bremerton, Washington, is disestablished.
Manpower
The strength of the Marine Corps on active duty is 16,203 officers and 154,418 enlisted.

1 July
Force Structure
The headquarters of Air FMFLANT is merged into the FMFLANT headquarters, both located at Norfolk, Virginia. This saves billets and ties Marine air more closely to the ground forces.

9 July
Congo
Following Congo's declaration of independence from Belgium on 30 June and the secession of the province of Katanga, the U.N. authorizes a peacekeeping force for the African nation. Company L of 3/2 and a detachment of HMR(L)-261 on board *Wasp* (CVS-18) deploy there.

14 August
Pacific
BLT 2/5 embarks on *Lenawee* (APA-195) and *Thomaston* (LSD-28) for service as the landing force of the Seventh Fleet. The plan is to rotate other units out of Okinawa for this duty every three months. 1st MAW also assigns an attack squadron to the fleet carriers.

9 August
Cuba
VMA-225 is deployed to the airfield at Leeward Station on alert. It remains there until 12 September.

13 August
Force Structure
Commandant Shoup announces that plans are on track to reactivate the remainder of the six infantry battalions deactivated in Fiscal Year 1959.

15 August
Caribbean
The 8th Marine Expeditionary Unit (composed of BLT 3/8, VMA-331, VMF-122, HMR(L)-261, and HMR(M)-461) deploys to the Caribbean for potential operations in Cuba. The units remain there until 29 November.

22–24 August
Training
Operation Charger, the largest reserve exercise conducted to date, takes place at 29 Palms. It involves 13 ground units and 9 squadrons, plus regular forces from Force Troops, 1st Marine Division, and 3rd MAW.

5 September
Aviation
LtCol Thomas H. Miller sets a new world speed record of 1,216.78 miles per hour over a 500-kilometer course in a McDonnell F4H-1 Phantom II.

11 September
Mishap
Hurricane Donna causes a half million dollars of damage to Camp Lejeune.

12 September
Heritage
The Marine Corps Museum is officially opened at Quantico.

14 September
Caribbean
VMF-122, already deployed in support of the 8th Marine Expeditionary Unit, takes up station at Roosevelt Roads, Puerto Rico, and remains there until 11 June 1961.

17 September
Technology
The Navy launches *Iwo Jima* (LPH-2), its first helicopter carrier built from the keel up. In addition to an entire squadron of helicopters, it can carry 2,000 Marines.

1 October
Force Structure
VMA-242 is reactivated at Cherry Point.

6 October
Manpower
Unaccompanied tours (without dependents) with FMF units in the Far East are reduced from 15 months to 13.

12 October
Force Structure
1st Force Reconnaissance Company begins to deploy elements as part of the transplacement rotation of units to Okinawa.

20 October
Caribbean
BLT 2/2, VMA-331, and HMR(L)-261 depart for standby duty at Vieques. They will return to North Carolina on 17 January 1961.

15 November
Force Structure
The 24th Expeditionary Unit is activated at Camp

Lejeune. It consists of an infantry battalion and a provisional MAG with a light helicopter squadron and a fixed-wing attack squadron.

30 November
Africa
Company G of 2/6 and HMR(L)-264 sail from North Carolina to conduct Operation Solant Amity, a goodwill tour of the continent. They will return to the United States on 15 May 1961.

15 December
Training
The Marine Corps abolishes drill based on eight-man units (the old squad prior to WWII) and reestablishes drill as conducted in the Landing Party Manual.

23 December
Technology
VMF-334 receives the Marine Corps first 2N model of the Chance Vought F8U Crusader.

1961

1 January
Force Structure
In a change to the transplacement rotation system, infantry battalions joining the 3rd Marine Division in Okinawa must now swap designations with the unit they are replacing. Although it solves the confusion inherent in a battalion serving with a different regiment (such as 1/5 under the 3rd Marines), it undercuts the traditional ties between personnel and an identified unit history.

3 January
Cuba
The United States formally terminates diplomatic relations with the Castro regime, as a result of ever-increasing tensions with the Caribbean nation. President Eisenhower already has vowed to defend the base at Guantanamo Bay with force, if necessary.

18 January
Manpower
Bertha L. Peters becomes the first female Marine promoted to the rank of sergeant major.

20 January
Congo
Elements of the Solant Amity task force assist in famine relief work at Matad, unloading supplies by helicopter from *Hermitage* (LSD-34).
Civil Support
400 Marines from Camp Pendleton help fight brush fires in Orange County, California.

31 January
Manpower
The number of Women Marines on active duty is 124 officers and 1,486 enlisted.
Mediterranean
VMA-225, the first Marine squadron equipped with the new Douglas A4D-2N Skyhawk, deploys on board *Shangri-La* (CVA-38) with the Sixth Fleet.

1 February
Manpower
President Kennedy revokes the existing order limiting dependents accompanying military personnel overseas.

Congo
Helicopters of HMR(L)-264 evacuate U.N. troops (Guineans) from Matadi to *Hermitage*. The ship drops them off Conakry, Guinea, a week later.

6 February
Aviation
Lieutenant Colonel W. D. Patterson, commanding officer of VMF(AW)-114, lands his Douglas F4D-1 Skyray on the Short Expeditionary Landing Field at Vieques. It is the first jet to use the expeditionary airfield.

1 March
HQMC
The Marine Corps Emergency Actions Center is established as a part of the G-3 division.
Technology
VMR-352 becomes the Corps' first in-flight refueling squadron when it takes delivery of its Lockheed GV-1 Hercules aerial tanker.

3 April
Training
Operation Greenlight, a series of amphibious exercises, begins in southern California. It ultimately involves 50,000 personnel, 150 ships, and 300 Navy and Marine Corps aircraft and lasts through 8 June.

Opposite: *Elements of BLT 3/9 come ashore at Da Nang in LVTP-5 tractors March 1965. (National Archives)*

Right: *Marines of 9th MEB March 1965. (National Archives)*

12 April
Mediterranean
The 16th MEB headquarters and BLT 3/6 sail from North Carolina for duty with the landing force of the Sixth Fleet. BLT 1/2, already deployed in the Mediterranean, falls under the brigade upon its arrival overseas. The MEB and BLT 3/6 will remain afloat until 11 October.

14 April
Training
The 5th MEB (consisting of RLT 9 and HMR(L)-162) conducts a SEATO exercise in Borneo that lasts through 4 May.

17 April
Cuba
Anti-Castro forces totaling 1,500 men land at the Bay of Pigs in an attempt to overthrow the Castro regime. The amphibious operation is defeated in three days. During the fighting, Marine forces at Guantanamo Bay take added security precautions.

18 April
Africa
Company F of 2/2 and a detachment of HMR(L)-262 sail from North Carolina for a goodwill tour of North African ports, dubbed Solant Amity II.

27–30 April
Training
The 16th MEB conducts an amphibious exercise at Porto Scudo, Sardinia.

30 April
Force Structure
VMA-343 is deactivated at El Toro, after just having been recommissioned on 1 October 1960.

May
HQMC
Commandant Shoup names a Headquarters Marine Corps Reorganization Board and charges it to provide a report by 1 August. Members are Lieutenant General Robert H. Pepper, Major General Alpha M. Bowser, and Colonel Norman Anderson.
Vietnam
The Corps institutes the On The Job Training (OJT) program. It sends 20 junior officers and SNCOs per month to Vietnam to observe that country's counter-guerrilla operations.

3–5 May
Training
2/12 conducts a live-fire artillery exercise from positions on the beach at Zambales, Luzon Island, Philippines.

Left: *A 9th MEB ONTOS rolls along the beach at Da Nang. (National Archives)*

Right: *Elements of BLT 1/3 board a Sikorsky UH-34 Seahorse in April 1965. (National Archives)*

5 May
Vietnam
President Kennedy announces he is considering using U.S. forces, if necessary, to aid South Vietnam in resisting Communist aggression.
Space
A helicopter from HMR(L)-262 retrieves America's first man in space, Commander Alan B. Shepherd, from the ocean and deposits him and his Mercury capsule on the deck of *Lake Champlain*.

15 May
Indochina
BLT 3/9 and HMR(L)-162 deploy from Okinawa to serve as the Seventh Fleet landing force off Southeast Asia.

20 May
Turkey
HMR(L)-262 and BLT 3/6 provide assistance following an earthquake at Marmaris, Turkey.

25 May
Manpower
President Kennedy requests funds from Congress so that manning in the Marine Corps can increase from 175,000 to 190,000.

12 June
Heritage
President Kennedy decrees that the U.S. flag will be flown 24 hours a day at the Marine Corps War Memorial in Arlington.
Indochina
BLT 1/3 deploys from Okinawa to serve as the Seventh Fleet special landing force in Southeast Asian waters.

15 June
Caribbean
The 8th Marine Expeditionary Unit (BLT 1/8, Provisional MAG-20, VMA-242, and HMR(L)-262) deploys at sea on standby until 1 August. During this period, it conducts training emphasizing counter-guerrilla and riot-control operations.

30 June
Manpower
The strength of the Marine Corps on active duty is 16,132 officers and 160,777 enlisted.

17 July
Force Structure
The Marine Corps Schools' standby infantry unit, 2/8, is redesignated 2/22.

August
Manpower
Due to an increase in voluntary enlistments and the response of reservists to voluntary call up to active duty, the Corps announces that its buildup to 190,000 will be achieved six months earlier than planned.

1 August
Manpower
In response to rising tensions with the Soviet Union over Cuba and Berlin, Congress authorizes the president to activate reserve forces totaling up to 250,000 for up to one year.
Force Structure
Helicopter units, beginning with HMR(L)-362, begin participating in the transplacement rotation to Okinawa.

2 August
Vietnam
President Kennedy declares that the United States will do all it can to save South Vietnam from Communism.

10 August
Indochina
BLT 2/3 and HMR(L)-261 deploy as the landing force of the Seventh Fleet in Southeast Asian waters.

13 August
Berlin
East Germany seals off the border between East and West Berlin and soon after begins erecting permanent concrete and barbed wire barriers, dubbed the Berlin Wall.

30 August
Training
31 Marines of 1st Force Reconnaissance Company make the first-ever night parachute jump from a Marine GV-1 propjet transport, over Camp Horno on board Pendleton.

1 September
Force Structure
HMR(L)-364 is activated at Santa Ana, California.

6 September
Africa
The 500 Marines who participated in Solant Amity II return to North Carolina after traveling 30,191 miles and visiting 17 African ports.

12 September
Civil Support
About 400 Marines from the 2nd Marine Division and MAG-26 assist in rescue operations in Texas and Louisiana following Hurricane Carla.

14 September
Africa
Company F, 2/6 departs North Carolina to conduct another goodwill tour in Africa, Solant Amity III.

October
Manpower
Four enlisted Marines, including two as voting members, serve on the gunnery sergeant selection board, the first time enlisted Marines participate in making selections for promotion.

1 November
Force Structure
MAG-31 is reactivated at Beaufort.

1–17 November
British Honduras
HMR(L)-264, flying off *Antietam* (CVS-36), aid the victims of Hurricane Hattie.

18 November
Dominican Republic
Following the resignation and departure overseas of General Rafael L. Trujillo, Jr., a U.S. Navy task force with embarked Marines takes station off the coast to discourage a possible coup d'etat by Trujillo supporters

11 December
Vietnam
Two Army helicopter companies and 400 men, the first U.S. forces deployed for direct combat support of the South Vietnamese, arrive in Vietnam.

31 December
Manpower
The combined strength of the Marine Corps on active duty is 100,708 officers and enlisted.

1962

January
Vietnam
Detachment A, 1st Radio Company, FMF arrives in country to reinforce an Army communications unit.

1 January
Vietnam
The Vietnamese Marine Corps is expanded to brigade strength and over 6,000 officers and men.

9 January
Training
The 5th Marines and other elements of the 1st Marine Division and 3rd MAW conduct a four-day counter-guerrilla exercise at Camp Pendleton.

15 January
Aviation
All 18 F8U-2n Crusaders of VMF(AW)-451 fly across the Pacific, refueling enroute from GV-1 tankers of VMR-153, 253, and 352. It is the first trans-Pacific crossing by an entire single-engine jet squadron.

Opposite: *3rd Marine Division Marines in Vietnam in 1965. (National Archives)*

Right: *Marines of Charlie Company 1/3 wait in the zone for helicopters on 25 April 1965. (National Archives)*

20 January
Vietnam
CINCPAC authorizes MAAG advisors to accompany their Vietnamese units into combat. Soon after, President Kennedy authorizes the advisors to return fire if fired upon.

31 January
Force Structure
VMR-253 becomes VMR-152.

1 February
Force Structure
HMR(L) squadrons begin redesignation to medium helicopter squadrons (HMM), HMR(M) squadrons become heavy helicopter squadrons (HMH), and fixed-wing transport squadrons become aerial refueler transport squadrons (VMGR).

5 February
Technology
Marine Captain L. K. Keck and Navy Lieutenant R. W. Crafton fly a Sikorsky SH3A jet-powered helicopter to a world-record speed of 210.6 miles per hour.

8 February
Vietnam
The U.S. Military Assistance Command, Vietnam (USMACV) is established with the mission of providing support to South Vietnam in its war against Communist forces. MAAG is absorbed into the new command, which comes under the operational control of CINCPAC.

Technology
In a test of the new XRE-1 Cataport (a portable catapult), an A4D Skyhawk is launched from less than 1,000 feet of runway at Lakehurst, New Jersey. Combined with portable arresting gear, the capability is dubbed the Short Airfield for Tactical Support (SATS). It allows aircraft to operate from an austere expeditionary airfield.

20 February
Space
John Glenn becomes the first American to orbit the earth, doing so three times in his Mercury capsule, *Friendship 7*.

28 February
Caribbean
The 34th Marine Expeditionary Unit, with BLT 2/8, sails from Morehead City for duty afloat in the Caribbean.

8 March
Civil Support
HMM-263 provides assistance along the Outer Banks of North Carolina following one of the worst storms to ever hit the area.

4 April
Civil Support
More than 400 Marines help combat forest fires around Jacksonville, North Carolina.

9 April
Vietnam
The leading elements of Marine Task Unit 79.3.5 (code-named Shufly) begin arriving in transport aircraft at the Soc Trang airstrip (just west of the Mekong Delta). The major element of the force, the helicopters of HMM-362, fly off *Princeton* six days later. The mission is to provide assault transport to Vietnamese combat units.

14 April
Training
President Kennedy watches Marines storm ashore at Onslow Beach, North Carolina, during LANTPHIBEX 1-62.

Opposite: *Troops rush from their helicopters into the landing zone. (National Archives)*

Right: *A patrol searches a village for Viet Cong in 1965. (National Archives)*

22 April
Vietnam
On Easter Sunday, HMM-362 conducts its first combat operation, lifting elements of the Vietnamese 7th Division.

23 April
Vietnam
HMM-362 makes its first sorties in support of Vietnamese Marines.

28 April
Sports
Marine Dave Tork of Camp Pendleton sets a world record in the pole vault with a jump of 16 feet, 2 inches, at the Mt. San Antonio Relays in Walnut, California.

9 May
Vietnam
Eight Marine helicopters are hit by small arms fire during a landing on the Ca Mau Peninsula.

12 May
Indochina
In response to an alarming string of Communist military victories during May in Laos, President Kennedy orders U.S. forces toward Southeast Asia.

18 May
Indochina
The 3rd MEB begins arriving in Thailand as part of the task force sent to Indochina in response to the deteriorating situation in Laos. The first elements on the ground at the Udorn airfield are the 20 A4 Skyhawks of VMA-332, which fly in from the Philippines. The Seventh Fleet landing force (BLT 3/9 and HMM-261) goes ashore at Bangkok and moves to Udorn.

1 June
Force Structure
1/22 is reactivated at Camp Lejeune.

29 June
Sergeants Major
Sergeant Major Thomas J. McHugh succeeds Sergeant Major Bauber as the third Sergeant Major of the Marine Corps.
Technology
VMF(AW)-314 at El Toro is the first Marine squadron to receive the F4H-1 Phantom II fighter.

30 June
Manpower
The strength of the Marine Corps on active duty is 16,861 officers and 174,101 enlisted.

1 July
Reserve
The entire Marine Corps Reserve is restructured from independent battalions and squadrons to form a complete 4th Marine Division and 4th MAW that can be activated as fully manned complements to the three regular division-wing teams. Among the newly reestablished units are the division and wing headquarters, the 23rd, 24th, and 25th Marines (infantry), the 14th Marines (artillery), and MAG-41, 43, and 46.
Indochina
Roughly 1,000 Marines of 3rd MEB in Thailand move back on board their ships as part of negotiations for a settlement in Laos.

14 July
Okinawa
Camp Koza, former home of the 3rd Pioneer Battalion, is returned to civilian control and use.

27 July
Indochina
As part of a settlement guaranteeing the future neutrality of Laos, U.S. forces resume their withdrawal from Thailand. The last Marines depart three days later.

1 August
Vietnam
HMM-163 replaces HMM-362 as the Shufly squadron.

4 September
Vietnam
The Shufly force begins displacing to Da Nang in the I Corps Tactical Zone in northern South Vietnam. The move is complete on the 20th.
30 September
Force Structure
HMM-265 is commissioned at New River.

6 October
Vietnam
Five Marines and two Navy medical personnel die in an accidental crash of a Shufly helicopter. They are the first Marines to die in the Vietnam War.

19 October
Cuba
Following the discovery of Soviet offensive nuclear missiles in Cuba, Marine units begin to receive alert orders. Nine hours after that order, 2/1 is ready to fly from El Toro and it does so the next day.

21 October
Cuba
Elements of the 1st and 2nd Marine Divisions begin arriving at Guantanamo Bay to reinforce the garrison there.

22 October
Cuba
President Kennedy publicly announces a quarantine to force Soviet withdrawal of missiles

Left: *A patrol from 2/3 moves along a shallow river in Vietnam. (National Archives)*

Opposite: *Marines sweep toward a Vietnamese village in June 1965. (National Archives)*

from Cuba. The 5th MEB (over 11,000 troops) is prepared to sail from San Diego for the Caribbean.

28 October
Cuba
5th MEB sails from San Diego. Most of the 2nd Marine Division and major elements of MAG-14, 24, 26, 31, and 32 are deployed to Key West and the Caribbean for a possible invasion of Cuba.

2 November
Aviation
Lieutenant Colonel John Glenn is the first recipient of the Cunningham Trophy, presented by the First Marine Aviation Force Veterans Association to the outstanding Marine pilot of the year.

13 November
Guam
400 Marines of 3/4 fly from Hawaii to Guam to provide assistance following a typhoon.

20 November
Cuba
The United States ends the naval quarantine following an agreement for the withdrawal of Soviet offensive missiles. Marine units deployed for the Cuban Missile Crisis soon begin returning to their home stations.

1963

11 January
Vietnam
HMM-162 replaces HMM-163 in the Shufly force.

6 February
Heritage
As part of his emphasis on national physical fitness, President Kennedy challenges Marine officers to fulfill President Theodore Roosevelt's 1908 executive order that Marine officers serving in Washington complete a 50-mile hike within 20 hours of marching over three days. Twenty officers at Camp Lejeune immediately make plans to take on the challenge.

13 February
Africa
Fifty-three Marines from Camp Lejeune deploy on board *Spiegal Grove* (LSD-32) for a 14-week goodwill tour of the continent dubbed Solant Amity IV.

29 March
Force Structure
VMGR-353 is deactivated at Cherry Point. It is reactivated on 3 August as a reserve squadron.

13 April
Vietnam
Marine transport helicopters conduct their first mission with U.S. Army UH-1B helicopter gunships.

30 April
Haiti
The Marine Corps training mission is withdrawn at the request of the Haitian government.

4 May
Haiti
BLT 2/2, while on a training cruise in the Caribbean, takes station off the coast of Haiti during political unrest there. It remains in the area for five days.

8 June
Vietnam
HMM-261 replaces HMM-162 as the Shufly force.

15–24 June
Training
The 11th MEB, including RLT 3 (USMC) and RLT 2 (KMC), conducts a joint amphibious exercise around Pohang, South Korea.

30 June
Manpower
The strength of the Marine Corps on active duty is 16,737 officers and 172,946 enlisted.

1 July
Force Structure
VMF(AW)-114 is deactivated in Japan. HMM-365 is activated at Santa Ana.

1 August
Force Structure
Marine all-weather squadrons equipped with the F4B Phantom are redesignated as fighter/attack squadrons. They become VMFA-314, 513, and 531.

2 October
Vietnam
HMM-361 replaces HMM-261 as the Shufly force.

7 October
Bases
The Marine Corps' Cold Weather Training Center at Bridgeport, California, is renamed the Mountain Warfare Training Center.

Left: *Marines take a knee as they approach suspected Viet Cong positions. (National Archives)*

Opposite: *Sgt David K. Costa of 3/4 crosses a foot bridge near Phu Bai. (National Archives)*

20 October
Haiti
HMM-162 arrives in Port-au-Prince Bay on board *Thetis Bay* to deliver food and supplies to hurricane-stricken areas of southern Haiti.

1 November
Vietnam
The government of South Vietnam is overthrown in a military coup and President Diem is killed.

15 November
Vietnam
USMACV announces that 1,000 of the 16,575 U.S. military personnel in Vietnam will be withdrawn due to progress made in training the South Vietnamese armed forces. The first 220 servicemen depart on 3 December.

24 November
Vietnam
Two days after President Kennedy's assassination, President Lyndon B. Johnson affirms continued military support for South Vietnam against Communist aggression.

31 December
Commandants
General Shoup retires and is replaced by General Wallace M. Greene, Jr., the 23rd Commandant of the Marine Corps. One of Greene's first official duties is a trip to South Vietnam.

1964

1 February
Vietnam
HMM-364 replaces HMM-361 as the Shufly force.

6 February
Cuba
The Cuban government cuts off the water supply to the U.S. base at Guantanamo Bay.

3 March
Training
VII MEF (composed of units from the 1st and 3rd Marine Divisions, the 1st Marine Brigade, and 1st MAW) joins with Nationalist Chinese forces to conduct Exercise Backpack in Taiwan.

23 March
Training
The 1st Marines engage in a 12-day counter-guerrilla exercise on board Camp Pendleton.

April
Technology
The mortar batteries of 1/12 and 3/12 on Okinawa receive the new M98 107mm mortar, dubbed the Howtar for its artillery-like wheeled mount.

27 April
Vietnam
HMM-364 lifts Vietnamese troops during Operation Sure Wind 202 in northern II Corps.

30 April
Heritage
The last Marine officer to serve during WWI retires. Chief Warrant Officer Percy L. Smith had enlisted in April 1916 at the age of 16.

20 May
Vietnam
Marine Advisory Team One arrives in Vietnam. Headed by Major Alfred M. Gray, Jr., its 30 communicators and 76 infantrymen (the latter of Company G, 2/3) become the first Marine ground unit to operate as a unit in the Vietnam War. It provides radio support to South Vietnamese forces.

1–20 June
Training
Company I, 3/6 participates in a NATO exercise dubbed Northern Express in Norway, 300 miles above the Arctic Circle.

4 June
Training
A massive amphibious and airborne assault on the island of Mindoro caps SEATO Exercise Ligta. U.S. Marines and troops from Australia, France, New Zealand, the Philippines, and Great Britain participate.

20 June
Commanders
Army Lieutenant General William C. Westmoreland assumes command of USMACV in Vietnam.

21 June
Vietnam
HMM-162 replaces HMM-364 as the Shufly force. The latter squadron turns over all its helicopters to a Vietnamese air force squadron.

28 June
Aviation
VMFA-531 arrives for duty in the Far East after flying from its home station of Cherry Point, with stops at El Toro, Hawaii, and Wake Island, and aerial refueling across the rest of the Pacific.

30 June
Manpower
The strength of the Marine Corps on active duty is 16,843 officers and 172,934 enlisted.

1 July
Force Structure
HMM-164 is activated at Santa Ana, California. It will receive the new Boeing CH-46 Sea Knight helicopter.

7 July
Vietnam
HMM-162 participates in the relief of the Nam Dong Special Forces Camp.

17 July
Vietnam
Marine Advisory Team One fends off a Communist assault on its perimeter atop Tiger Tooth Mountain.

28 July
Vietnam
The United States announces it will send an additional 5,000 troops to South Vietnam.

30 July
Cuba
The Guantanamo Bay Navy base dedicates a new plant that produces fresh water.

1 August
Training
The Marine Corps Schools renames the Senior Course as Command and Staff College and the Junior Course as Amphibious Warfare School.

2–5 August
Vietnam
North Vietnamese patrol boats attack U.S. warships in what will become known as the Tonkin Gulf Incident.

Opposite: *A Marine from 2/9 searches a house south of Da Nang in 1965. (National Archives)*

Right: *A sniper with a Winchester Model 70 rifle scans for a target. (National Archives)*

5 August
Vietnam
In retaliation for the naval attacks, U.S. aircraft bomb North Vietnamese naval targets and an oil storage depot.

7 August
Vietnam
Congress passes the Tonkin Gulf Resolution, which authorizes President Johnson to use military force in Vietnam.

17 August
Bases
Edson Range opens at Camp Pendleton as a replacement for Camp Calvin B. Matthews, closed four days later due to urbanization around the San Diego area weapons training facility.

13 September
Vietnam
Marine Advisory Team One dissolves and departs the country.

8 October
Vietnam
HMM-365 replaces HMM-364 as the Shufly force.

14 October
Sports
First Lieutenant Billy Mills wins the gold medal in the 10,000 meter race at the Tokyo Olympics.

26 October
Training
Exercise Steel Pike I begins in Spain with 22,000 Marines, 33,000 sailors, and 2,000 Spanish Marines.

17–23 November
Vietnam
HMM-365 off *Princeton* and HMM-162 assist flood victims in central South Vietnam.

26 November
Egypt
A mob protesting U.S. policies in the Congo attack the U.S. Embassy compound, burning portions of, including the Marine Guard facility.

Left: *Echo Company, 2/4, advances across a rice paddy, July 1965. (National Archives)*

Opposite: *Searching for tunnel entrances in a village. (National Archives)*

1965

1 February
Training
Operation Snowfex-65 begins at Fort Drum, New York, and lasts for a month. It is billed as the largest Marine Corps cold weather training exercise on the east coast since the 1940s. Participating units are 1/8, VMGR-252, and HMM-265.
Force Structure
MAG-42 is reactivated at Alameda, California, as part of 4th MAW.

8 February
Da Nang
Following Viet Cong attacks on U.S. forces and camps in South Vietnam, President Johnson orders the deployment of the 1st LAAM Battalion to the Da Nang area. Battery A arrives this day.

12 February
Training
In the largest Marine exercise since WWII, 25,000 Marines and 20,000 sailors conduct Operation Silver Lance at Camp Pendleton. It lasts through 9 March.

17 February
Vietnam
HMM-163 relieves HMM-365 as the Shufly force. A company of the 7th Engineer Battalion arrives in Da Nang.

8 March
Da Nang
The 9th MEB begins arriving in Vietnam with the mission of defending the airbase at Da Nang. BLT 3/9 comes by sea and BLT 1/3 follows by air from Okinawa. The MEB is the first U.S. ground combat unit in country.

9 March
Da Nang
HMM-163 of Shufly and 1st LAAM Battalion are placed under operational control of the MEB. HMM-162 arrives. All three units become part of MAG-16.

29 March
Saigon
Following a bomb explosion outside the U.S. Embassy, the Marine Security Guard detachment restores order and safeguards the compound.

10 April
Da Nang
BLT 2/3 goes ashore to reinforce 9th MEB, while VMFA-531 flies onto the airfield. A company of 2/3 helicopters to the airbase at Phu Bai, about 50 miles north of Da Nang, near Hue City.

12 April
Da Nang
The headquarters of the 3rd Marines joins the brigade to serve as the command element of the BLTs.

13 April
Vietnam
VMFA-531 flies its first combat missions in Vietnam.

14 April
Phu Bai
BLT 3/4 arrives and relieves the company of 2/3 around the air base.

16 April
Da Nang
The electronic countermeasure EF-10B Skyknights of Marine Composite Reconnaissance Squadron 1 (VMCJ-1) arrive.

20 April
Vietnam
General Westmoreland authorizes 9th MEB forces to conduct aggressive patrolling and prepare to act as a mobile reaction force. The MEB now numbers more than 8,600 men.

22 April
Da Nang
In 9th MEB's first significant contact, a patrol engages Viet Cong forces, killing one enemy and suffering one wounded. A company of 1/3 sent to reinforce the patrol makes the first Marine helicopter assault of the war.

27 April
Dominican Republic
Following a coup and fighting, HMM-264 evacuates 556 American citizens to U.S. warships off the coast.

28 April
Dominican Republic
Elements of BLT 3/6 goes ashore by helicopter to guard the U.S. Embassy and protect American lives in the city of Santo Domingo. The remainder of the BLT lands the next day. U.S. Army forces also begin to deploy soon after.

30 April
Dominican Republic
Two Marines are killed in street fighting as BLT 3/6 seeks to clear part of the city of Dominican fighters.

1 May
Dominican Republic
4th MEB begins arriving by sea and air from North Carolina. It brings the total Marine force in country to over 5,500 men. Another Marine is killed and three wounded.

3 May
Dominican Republic
The Marine detachment of *Newport News* goes ashore to reinforce 3/6. It is the first ship's detachment to land in a combat role since 1945.

6 May
Vietnam
9th MEB dissolves and III MEF assumes command of Marine forces in the I Corps zone. The 3rd Marine Division headquarters assumes command of ground elements. The MEF is redesignated as III Marine Amphibious Force (III MAF) the next day. Amphibious is substituted for expeditionary in all Marine designations as a result of a request from General Westmoreland due to the connotations of the French Expeditionary Force in an earlier Vietnam intervention.

7 May
Chu Lai
The 3rd MAB (RLT 4, MAG-12, 3rd Reconnaissance Battalion, and Naval Mobile Construction Battalion 10) begins landing at Chu Lai, on the coast about 50 miles south of Da Nang. The MAB will construct an expeditionary airfield here.

11 May
Da Nang
Elements of 2/3 clear the village of Le My and establish a civic action program to assist the population. The 1st MAW headquarters arrives to assume command of Marine aviation elements.

12 May
Chu Lai
With the arrival of BLT 3/3, all of 3rd MAB is in country. It is dissolved and its forces assigned to III MAF. Marine forces in Vietnam now total over 17,500.

25 May
Dominican Republic
U.S. mediation leads to a truce between Dominican factions. Marine units begin departing the next day.

1 June
Chu Lai
Skyhawks of VMA-225 and 311 land on the recently completed SATS field, the first use of this concept in a combat theater. They conduct air strikes from their new base this same day.

3 June
Dominican Republic
President Johnson orders the withdrawal of the 2,100 Marines remaining in country. Total Marines casualties during the intervention were nine dead and 30 wounded.

4 June
Commanders
Major General Lewis W. Walt assumes command of III MAF and 3rd Marine Division.
Vietnam
In several company-sized actions around Da Nang and Phu Bai, Marines engage in their first major ground combat. At a cost of two dead and 19 wounded, they kill 79 Viet Cong.

15 June
Da Nang
VMFA-513 relieves VMFA-531, which departs Vietnam.

17 June
Da Nang
1/9 relieves 3/9, which returns to Okinawa.

21 June
Da Nang
HMM-261 relives HMM-163, which becomes the transport squadron for the Special Landing Force at sea.

25 June
Mishap
A Vietnam-bound military transport plane crashes after takeoff from El Toro, killing 79 Marines.

30 June
Manpower
The strength of the Marine Corps on active duty is 17,258 officers and 172,955 enlisted. There are 18,156 Marines in Vietnam, with a total U.S. deployment there in excess of 50,000.

1 July
Da Nang
Under the cover of a mortar barrage, Communist sappers break into the perimeter of the airbase and severely damage six USAF aircraft.
Qui Nhon
The Special Landing Force (BLT 3/7 and HMM-163) go ashore to protect a major logistics base in II Corps Zone.
Force Structure
HMM-165 is commissioned at Santa Ana.

6 July
Da Nang
RLT 9 headquarters and BLT 2/9 arrive to join III MAF.

8 July
Qui Nhon
2/7 flies in from Okinawa to relieve BLT 3/7, which returns to its amphibious ships.

10 July
Da Nang
VMFA-542 flies into the airbase. Within a few days, MAG-11 arrives to take command of VMFA-542 and 513.

14 July
Dong Ha
Elements of the 3rd Marine Division move to Dong Ha, site of an airfield just a few miles south of the DMZ, as well as bridges crossing the Cua Viet River.

16 July
Sergeants Major
Sergeant Major Herbert J. Sweet succeeds Sergeant Major McHugh as the fourth Sergeant Major of the Marine Corps.

28 July
Vietnam
President Johnson announces that an additional 50,000 U.S. troops will go to Vietnam.

1 August
Phu Bai
3/4 begins the Combined Action Program, which will eventually be adopted throughout III MAF. It uses a Marine infantry squad to reinforce a local Vietnamese militia unit. These Combined Action Platoons are each permanently assigned to protect a village.

Opposite: *A new Marine arrives at Da Nang in August 1965. (National Archives)*

Right: *Marines come ashore near Vihn Gaing. (National Archives)*

3 August
Da Nang
A CBS news team films Marines setting fire to huts in the village of Cam Ne. Aired soon after on the evening news in the United States, it creates public controversy

10 August
Manpower
The Marine Corps is authorized to expand to 223,100 personnel, which will include the creation of three new infantry battalions.

11 August
Technology
Marine aircraft make their first combat use of the cluster bomb unit (CBU) in Vietnam.

14 August
Manpower
The Navy Department involuntarily extends the enlistments of all Marines and sailors by four months to help meet personnel requirements.

15 August
Vietnam
The headquarters of the 7th Marines and 1/7 land at Chu Lai, while 3/9 returns to Da Nang from Okinawa.

18–24 August
Operation Starlite
III MAF fights the first Marine regimental-size battle since Korea when the 7th Marines (1/7, 2/4, and 3/3) launches heliborne and amphibious attacks against the a VC Regiment around Van Tuong south of Chu Lai. BLT 3/7 of the SLF eventually joins the fight. Marine casualties are 51 dead and 203 wounded. There are 623 counted Viet Cong bodies, with more casualties probably sealed in caves and bunkers.

28 August
Da Nang
1/1 arrives and relieves 1/3, which departs soon after for the States. BLT 2/26 comes ashore.

1 September
Manpower
The Marine Corps reduces recruit training from 12 to eight weeks in order to process increased numbers without expanding the instructor cadre.
Operation Golden Fleece
The 9th Marines launches a series of cordons and patrols to deny the rice harvest to the Viet Cong. This operation lasts through 27 October. All subsequent III MAF operations for this purpose bear the same name.

2 September
Chu Lai
MAG-36 begins arriving in Vietnam with an HMH, three HMMs, and a VMO squadron.

7 September
Manpower
Although the number of volunteers is increasing, the Marine Corps announces it will have to resort to the draft in January to meet its expanded strength.

7–10 September
Operation Piranha
The 7th Marines (1/7 and 3/3) attack a Viet Cong concentration in the Batangan Peninsula, a few miles south of Van Tuong, killing 163 enemy.

25–26 September
Operation Dagger Thrust
The Seventh Fleet SLF uses helicopters and amphibious craft to launch a raid against suspected Viet Cong locations on the coast south of Qui Nhon. This is the first of a series of SLF amphibious raids.

28 October
Vietnam
Viet Cong attacks at Chu Lai and Marble Mountain (near Da Nang) result in a few sappers getting into the airbases and the destruction of two jets and 19 helicopters.

3 November
Chu Lai
During a search and destroy operation south of the Marine base, well known correspondent Dickie Chapelle is killed by a booby trapped mortar round while with Marines.

7 November
Qui Nhon
BLT 2/7 boards ships and permanently departs the II Corps Zone, rejoining its parent regiment at Chu Lai a few days later.

17–18 November
Hiep Duc
After the Viet Cong overrun the garrison of the town in the Que Son Valley, 30 UH-34 helicopters of MAG-16 and MAG-36 lift two Vietnamese Army (ARVN) battalions to the scene, while attack aircraft provide support. Seventeen of the helicopters are hit by ground fire and one Marine is killed.

3 December
Manpower
The Marine Corps' share of the January draft call is scheduled to be 8,980 men, the first Marine draftees since the Korean War.

8–29 December
Operation Harvest Moon
Working with three ARVN battalions, 2/7, 3/3, and 2/1 sweep through an area between Chu Lai and Da Nang. Marine air and artillery and four Air Force B-52 strikes provide fire support. At a cost of 51 Marines dead, 256 wounded, and one missing, the operation accounts for 407 Viet Cong killed and 33 captured.

22 December
Vietnam
USMACV orders a 30-hour truce over Christmas. American and South Vietnamese forces announce they will only fight if attacked.

31 December
Vietnam
There are 39,092 III MAF Marines in country, of a total U.S. deployment of 181,000. Since 8 March 1965, 342 Marines have died in action, 2,047 have been wounded, and 18 are missing. They have killed 2,627 of the enemy.

Opposite: *Rice paddy water cools an M60 machine gun. (National Archives)*

Above: *LCpl Ralph H. McWilliams and his scout dog Major. (National Archives)*

1966

3–15 January
Commandants
General Greene tours Marine units in the Western Pacific and Vietnam.

15 January
Cuba
After a reduction in strength, 2/8 deploys to Guantanamo Bay to become the ground defense force for the naval base.

18 January
Chu Lai
The headquarters of the 1st Marines arrives in Vietnam.

20 January
Force Structure
President Johnson requests additional funds from Congress to add a fourth active-duty division to the Corps.

28 January
Da Nang
VMFA-314 deploys into Vietnam.

28 January–17 February
Operation Double Eagle I
Task Force Delta (4th Marines headquarters, 2/9, BLT 2/3, BLT 3/1, BLT 2/4, and supporting elements) launches one of the largest operations of the war to date, in southern Quang Ngai Province. It includes a two-battalion amphibious assault. By the time it is over on 17 February, the Marines have killed 312 enemy and captured 19 at a cost of 24 Marines killed and 156 wounded.

23 February
Vietnam
Elements of the 1st Marine Division headquarters and the 11th marines begin arriving in country.

1 March
Force Structure
The 26th Marines (infantry) is reactivated at Camp Pendleton as the lead element of the revived 5th Marine Division. After a hiatus of 7 years, HMH-463 is reactivated at Santa Ana. The 9th MAB is activated on Okinawa to command all Western Pacific ground units not deployed in Vietnam.

4–7 March
Operation Utah
The attack begins with MAG-11 and 12 jets supporting MAG-36 helicopters as they place the 1st ARVN Airborne Battalion into a landing zone in the face of heavy antiaircraft fire. 2/7, 3/1, and 2/4 join the effort against a North Vietnamese Army (NVA) regiment. Nearly 600 Communists are killed, while the Marines lose 98 dead and 278 wounded. ARVN casualties are 30 killed and

Left: *An alert Marine of Lima Company, 3/4, moves through the jungle north of Con Thien in January 1966. (National Archives)*

Right: *Two Marines stand ready to fire their M79 grenade launchers. (National Archives)*

120 wounded.

7 March
Manpower
Secretary of Defense Robert McNamara requests an increase in the Corps to 278,184 Marines by mid-1967. If approved, this would make the Corps the only service to grow larger than its maximum size during the Korean War.

8 March
Da Nang
HMM-164 arrives in country with the first CH-46 helicopters to reach Vietnam.

8–17 March
Training
3/6 operates above Norway's Arctic Circle in Winter Express, the largest cold weather exercise held by NATO to date.

9–12 March
A Shau Valley
Communist forces overrun a Special Forces camp. Helicopters of HMM-163 and VMO-2 take losses in pulling out many of the survivors under heavy antiaircraft fire.

10 March
Vietnam
Following the dismissal of the Vietnamese general commanding I Corps Zone, political unrest sweeps over South Vietnam. It lasts into June and seriously hampers the war effort.

15 March
Vietnam
III MAF stands up Force Logistics Command, composed of the 1st and 3rd Service Battalions and elements of 3rd Force Service Regiment, to support Marines in country.

20–25 March
Operation Texas
Along with an ARVN regiment, 3/7, 2/4, and 3/1 engage elements of two Communist regiments deeply entrenched in a village northwest of Quang Ngai. With the assistance of air and artillery support, the Marines kill 283 enemy at a cost of 99 dead and 212 wounded.

26 March
Operation Jack Stay
The SLF, BLT 1/5, conducts the first Marine ground action in the Saigon area, clearing enemy from the river delta southeast of the Vietnamese capital. The heliborne and riverine operation lasts through 6 April.

29 March
Chu Lai
The 1st Marine Division headquarters formally begins to operate in Vietnam. For the first time since WWII, the Corps has two of its divisions

SERGEANT MAJOR EDGAR R. HUFF

A natural leader, SgtMaj Edgar Huff served in combat in WWII, Korea, and Vietnam and earned a lasting reputation as one of the outstanding staff noncommissioned officers in the long history of the Corps. (National Archives)

Edgar Huff was born on 2 December 1919 near Gadsden, Alabama. His father, who had served in the Army Signal Corps in World War I, died soon after from complications arising out of being gassed in combat. Huff grew up in poverty, and had to quit school at 16 to help out when his mother fell ill. He was walking five miles to work each day at a steel mill in 1942 when President Roosevelt decreed that the Marines would begin enlisting African-Americans. Huff was one of the first to join. When things seemed toughest in the first few days at Montford Point, North Carolina, and drill instructors dared the new enlistees to quit, the tall burly Alabaman convinced his fellow recruits to persevere with the vow that he himself would "stick to it like a bulldog to a bone." His natural leadership resulted in his being selected shortly after graduation to become a drill instructor. By 1944 he held the billet of field sergeant major for recruit training at Montford Point.

In November 1944 he sewed on first sergeant stripes and transferred to become the senior enlisted man of the 5th Depot Company. He went overseas with the logistics unit and prepared it on Saipan for the subsequent invasion of Okinawa. In addition to hauling supplies from landing craft to inland dumps, the men often ended up on the front lines as stretcher bearers. Huff and his company then participated in the disarmament of Japanese troops in North China at the end of the war.

Upon his return from the Pacific, Huff resumed his old billet at Montford Point, although he was now formally called the noncommissioned officer in charge of recruit training. (By virtue of the altered 1946 rank structure in the Corps, he also became a master sergeant when first sergeants disappeared.) He remained there until integration brought the closure of Montford Point in 1949. After a stint with a Marine barracks, he joined the 1st Marine Division in Korea in May 1951. Assigned as the company gunnery sergeant for Weapons Company, 2/1, he participated in the bitter fighting around the Punch Bowl and later on the western end of the U.N. line after the Marines shifted there in early 1952.

Back in the States in late 1952, he assumed duty as the first sergeant of Weapons Company, 2/8. His division commander, Chesty Puller, ultimately recommended him for promotion to warrant officer, proclaiming Huff to be a "highly capable, intelligent, and outstanding noncommissioned officer" who "invoked the respect and set a fine example for all the junior noncommissioned officers." But Huff was content to stay a master sergeant, where he was "closer to the ranks." With the reestablishment of the titles first sergeant and sergeant major in 1955, Huff was promoted successively to each on 30 and 31 December of that year.

In subsequent tours, he served as the sergeant major for Marine Barracks Port Lyautey in Morocco, 2nd Force Service Regiment at Camp Lejeune, Landing Force Training Unit in Little Creek, 3rd Force Service Regiment on Okinawa, 1st Infantry Training Regiment at Camp Geiger, and Marine Corps Base Camp Pendleton. In 1967 he went to Vietnam to become the top enlisted man with the 1st Military Police Battalion. During the Tet Offensive, when a mortar barrage struck his unit's position, Huff covered a severely wounded Marine in the open with his own body and was in turn struck by shrapnel from ensuing rounds. That action brought his second Purple Heart and second Bronze Star. In May 1968, he moved up to become the senior enlisted Marine in Vietnam as the sergeant major of III MAF. After a stint in the States with 2nd MAW, he returned for a second Vietnam tour as sergeant major of the MAF.

Huff went back to North Carolina in 1971 to serve as the sergeant major of Marine Corps Air Station New River and retired in 1972. He went on to a career in the government and retired for good in 1981. He remained a leader in the Montford Point Marine Association, until his death at the age of 74 on board Camp Lejeune. The man who had stuck to the Corps "like a bulldog to a bone" had left his own substantial mark on the institution. One of his fellow drill instructors from World War II said of Huff: "He was a giant. I'm not just talking about size, either. You just don't meet many men like him."

simultaneously engaged in combat.

5 April
Force Structure
The 13th Marines (artillery) is reactivated at Camp Pendleton to serve with the 5th Marine Division.

13 April
Chu Lai
2/5 arrives in country.

21–23 April
Operation Hot Springs
A sweep northwest of Quang Ngai by the 7th Marines kills over 150 enemy.

8 May
Vietnam
1/5 arrives in country.

11 May
Aviation
For the first time in history, jet aircraft launch from a land-based catapult in combat. Four Skyhawks of VMA-311take off from the field at Chu Lai, using just 1,400 feet of the 8,000 foot runway.

17 May
Manpower
The first Marine-oriented Junior Naval ROTC program is instituted, at Jesuit High School in New Orleans, Louisiana.

21 May
Cuba
A Marine sentry kills a Cuban soldier attempting to climb the fence into the naval base at Guantanamo Bay.

25 May
Cuba
Marine fire drives off five Cuban soldiers who had infiltrated into the Guantanamo base.

27 May
Chu Lai
The 5th Marines headquarters arrives in country.

1 June
Force Structure
The 5th Marine Division headquarters and two battalions of the 27th Marines (infantry) are reactivated at Camp Pendleton, while 1/27 is reestablished at Kaneohe Bay, Hawaii, as part of the 1st Marine Brigade.

18–27 June
Operation Deckhouse I
BLT 3/5 (the Seventh Fleet SLF) conducts an amphibious assault and subsequent ground operations in Phu Yen Province in II Corps Zone. The SLF makes three more landings under the same code name over the remainder of 1966.

25 June
Operation Jay
2/4 and 3/1 conduct heliborne assaults northwest of Hue in an effort to trap a Communist force. The main fighting occurs this day, but the operation continues through 2 July. Marines losses are 23 dead and 58 wounded. They recover 82 enemy bodies and estimate 200 additional dead.

26 June
Vietnam
Sergeant James S. Dodson and Lance Corporal Walter Eckes, captured by the Viet Cong in May, manage to escape and return to friendly forces.

30 June
Manpower
The strength of the Marine Corps on active duty is 20,512 officers and 241,204 enlisted.

4 July
Operation Macon
Following contact between two companies of 3/9 and a Viet Cong battalion, the 9th Marines (3/9, 1/3, and 3/3) launches an operation to clear the An Hoa area south of Da Nang. The main fighting is over by 14 July, but sweeps and patrols continue through 27 October. At a cost of 24 dead and 172 wounded, the regiment kills roughly 380 enemy.

7 July
Operation Hastings
In the largest Marine operation to date in Vietnam, five battalions of infantry (2/1, 1/3, 2/4, 3/4, and 3/5) and an artillery battalion (3/12) attack the NVA 324B Division, which has infiltrated across the Demilitarized Zone (DMZ) between North and South Vietnam into Quang Tri Province. Following a reconnaissance effort, the main fighting begins on 15 July and lasts through 3 August in the area north of the Rockpile. Marines losses are 126 killed and 448 wounded, with supporting ARVN units losing 21 killed and 40 wounded. Enemy dead exceed 700. During the operation MAG-16 helicopters fly almost 10,000 sorties, while attack aircraft add another 1,677. Reconnaissance teams operating in the area call in frequent air and artillery missions on Communist troops flushed by the Marine battalions. The use of recon teams to call in fire is dubbed "Stingray" at the end of this battle.

20 July
Vietnam
The Seventh Air Force initiates Operation Tally Ho, air strikes directed against targets in southern North Vietnam. 1st MAW provides numerous sorties to this campaign.

21 July
Vietnam
All CH-46 helicopters are grounded until air and fuel filters are retrofitted to deal with the dust generated in the primitive operating conditions of I Corps Zone.

Opposite: *Waiting to board a helicopter on USS* Princeton *in March 1966. (National Archives)*

Right: *Wounded Marines of 3/1 being placed on a HMM-363 helicopter. (National Archives)*

1 August
Force Structure
VMO-3 is reactivated at Cam Pendleton. It will be subsequently redesignated in 1968 as HML-367.

3 August
Operation Prairie
III MAF opens a reconnaissance effort and uses Stingray tactics in the area south of the DMZ. This effort continues through 13 September, as part of Operation Prairie, an effort to stop the penetration of two NVA divisions into Quang Tri Province.

6 August
Operation Colorado
The 5th Marines and South Vietnamese forces conduct a search and destroy operation in the Que Son Valley. It lasts until 22 August and temporarily drives the 2nd NVA Division from the area.

18 August
Chu Lai
The 2nd Korean Marine Brigade begins arriving in the I Corps Zone, positioning itself on the Batangan Peninsula south of Chu Lai.

20 August
Force Structure
The headquarters of the 26th Marines arrives on Okinawa and becomes a part of 9th MAB.

28 August
Da Nang
BLT 2/26 arrives in country.

6 September
Manpower
The Marine Corps asks for Women Marines to volunteer to serve in the Far East. By February 1969, more than 100 women are stationed in Japan, Okinawa, and South Vietnam.

13 September
Operation Deckhouse IV
As part of Operation Prairie, the SLF (now BLT 1/26) makes an amphibious assault just south of the DMZ. In 12 days the BLT has several significant fights and kills more than 200 enemy at a cost of 36 killed and 167 wounded.

16 September
Operation Prairie
Two companies of 1/4 are ambushed as they move toward the Nui Cay Tre ridgeline (later named Mutter Ridge for the call sign of 3/4). This opens a series of intense fights around the Rockpile, Mutter Ridge, and another feature called the Razorback that involve 1/4, 3/4, and 2/7. The battle lasts until 4 October, but the overall operation continues.

25 September
Chu Lai
MAG-13 begins arriving from Japan.

Left: *Marines rush to board helicopters on USS* Princeton *on 26 March 1966 as part of Operation Jackstay. (National Archives)*

Right: *A Marine of Charlie Company, 1/1, moves through elephant grass during Operation Virginia in April 1966. (National Archives)*

27 September
Vietnam
1/26 arrives in country.

29 September
Khe Sanh
Marine KC-130 transports land 1/3 and an artillery battery of 1/13 at the airfield of Khe Sanh, a Special Forces base camp southwest of the Rockpile.

6 October
Vietnam
The 3rd Marine Division begins moving north to assume responsibility for Quang Tri and Thua Thien, the two northernmost provinces of South Vietnam. The division CP opens at Phu Bai on 10 October. The 1st Marine Division assumes responsibility for the other three provinces of I Corps Zone (Quang Nam, Quang Tin, and Quang Ngai).

14–16 October
Mexico
Marines participate in a joint-service task force airlifting food to victims of Hurricane Inez in Tampico.

17 October
Manpower
To meet its needs in Vietnam, the Marine Corps defers the resignation and retirement requests of 500 pilots and aviation maintenance officers.

1 November
Da Nang
VMA(AW)-242 arrives, bringing with it the first Marine Grumman A6 Intruders.
Mishap
Four Marines die while fighting a brush fire in the Piedro de Lumbre Canyon area of California.

11 December
Dong Ha
3/26 arrives in country and is assigned to the 4th Marines.

15 December
Force structure
VMO-5 (a helicopter unit) is activated at Camp Pendleton. It will subsequently be redesignated as HML-267.

31 December
Vietnam
III MAF strength has risen to 65,789 Marines (including 18 infantry battalions, eight artillery battalions, two tank battalions, 11 fixed-wing squadrons, and 10 helicopter squadrons). Marine casualties for the year total 1,692 dead and 10,270 wounded. There are 385,000 U.S. troops in Vietnam. There are 281,709 officers and men on active duty in the Corps, which took in 14,980 draftees during the year.

Left: *Marine tractors in the water during Operation Deckhouse V. (National Archives)*

Opposite: *A recon team exits a CH-46 in January 1967. (National Archives)*

1967

5 January
Da Nang
BLT 2/4 arrives in country and relieves 3/9, which returns to Okinawa. This is part of an ongoing rotation program, in which a fresh Okinawa battalion joins the SLF, the old SLF battalion goes into Vietnam, and the unit it replaces goes back to Okinawa to rebuild.

6 January
Cuba
1/8 departs Camp Lejeune to relieve 1/ 2 as the defense force at Guantanamo Bay.

8 January
Technology
HMH-463 brings the first Sikorsky CH-53A Sea Stallion heavy helicopters into Vietnam, at Marble Mountain. The CH-53A can lift 8,000 pounds internally or 12,000 externally.

16 January
Manpower
The Marine Corps reinstitutes the practice of giving battlefield commissions to qualified enlisted men who have demonstrated exceptional leadership.

Training
The 10th Marines departs Lejeune for a one-month field firing exercise at Vieques, where it will work with elements of the 6th and 8th Marines, the 2nd Field Artillery Group, and 2nd MAW.
Vietnam
USMACV completes planning for the construction of a fortified line along the DMZ designed to prevent the infiltration of NVA units from the North.

17 January
Force Structure
The 28th Marines is reactivated as part of the 5th Marine Division at Camp Pendleton.

26 January
Operation DeSoto
The 7th Marines conducts search and destroy operations against Viet Cong units in southern Quang Ngai Province. By the time it ends on 7 April, it accounts for 383 Communist troops killed at a cost of 69 dead and 556 wounded.

31 January
Operation Prairie
After 182 days, the operation is terminated. Marine losses over the period total 239 killed and

1,214 wounded. Enemy casualties are 1,397 dead and 27 captured.

1 February
Operation Prairie II
With the start of this new operation, the 3rd Marine Division maintains one infantry battalion conducting mobile operations immediately south of the DMZ while elements of two other battalions and supporting units hold the combat bases scattered throughout the area.

8–12 February
Vietnam
A ceasefire is declared for Tet, an important Vietnamese holiday. Although there are numerous small violations, there is no major fighting.

10 February
Force Structure
The Marine Security Guard Battalion is created to train and administer the embassy guard detachments around the world. It is located at Quantico.

12–22 February
Operation Stone
The 1st Marines conduct sweeps through Quang Nam Province, starting with Go Noi Island. At a cost of nine dead and 76 wounded, the regiment estimated over 400 enemy dead, plus 74 captured.

13 February
Technology
Some Marine training establishments in the United States begin receiving the M-16 rifle, which will replace the M-14. The rifle is already being fielded to III MAF.

16 February
Operation Deckhouse VI
The SLF (BLT 1/4 and HMM-363) makes an amphibious assault at the southern tip of Quang Ngai Province. Although it does not meet strong resistance, Stingray teams call in supporting arms to kill more than 200 of the enemy moving out of the area. The SLF withdraws to its ships on 26 February and conducts a new assault the next day a little farther north. The operation terminates on 3 March. Marine casualties total seven dead and 111 wounded, while enemy losses are about 280.

21 February
Hue
Bernard B. Fall, a noted author on Vietnam, is killed by an enemy mine while accompanying a Marine patrol north of the city.

25 February
Operation Prairie II
III MAF asks for and receives permission to begin firing artillery into and across the DMZ. This leads to an escalation in the fighting as Communist forces respond. By the time the operation ends on 18 March, the enemy have lost 694 killed and 20 captured. Marine casualties are 93 killed and 483 wounded.

27 February
Da Nang
Communist forces launch 51 140mm rockets into the airbase area, killing 11 men, wounding 97, and damaging 18 aircraft. In this first use of large rockets by the enemy, 72 Vietnamese civilians are also casualties.

16 March
Khe Sanh
During patrols in the vicinity of the base, two platoons come under heavy fire. The Marines lose 19 dead and 59 wounded and confirm only 11 enemy killed.

Left: *Golf Company, 2/9, attacks a Viet Cong-held hamlet. (National Archives)*

Opposite: *A recon Marine searches for the enemy. (National Archives)*

18 March
Manpower
Master Sergeant Barbara J. Dulinsky becomes the first Woman Marine to report to Vietnam. She works at the USMACV headquarters in Saigon.

19 March
Operation Prairie III
The 3rd Marine Division employs five infantry battalions and four artillery battalions in search and destroy operations near Dong Ha and Cam Lo. At the end of the operation on 19 April, the Marines have killed 252 enemy and lost 55 dead and 529 wounded.

20 March
Operation Beacon Hill
The SLF (BLT 1/4) makes an amphibious assault northeast of Dong Ha and remains ashore through 1 April. It accounts for 334 NVA soldiers killed at a cost of 29 dead and 230 wounded.

22–25 March
Operation New Castle
A three-day search and destroy operation in Quang Nam province kills 118 enemy.

12 April
Vietnam
Commandant Greene tells a Congressional committee that III MAF will need 40,000 more Marines to accomplish its mission.

15 April
Vietnam
At the direction of USMACV, III MAF begins building the barrier line just south of the DMZ.

20 April
Operation Prairie IV
The 3rd Marine Division opens a new series of search and destroy operations around Dong Ha and Cam Lo. They continue through 31 May, resulting in 489 enemy killed and nine captured at a cost of 164 Marines dead and 999 wounded.
Chu Lai
A U.S. Army brigade begins relieving Marine forces in southern I Corps Zone for redeployment to the north against NVA divisions crossing the DMZ.

22 April
Operation Union
Three Marine and three ARVN battalions conduct sweeps 30 miles south of Da Nang. By the conclusion of the operation on 17 May, 110 Marines die and 473 are wounded while killing 865 of the enemy and capturing another 173.

24 April
Khe Sanh
Company B, 1/9 (the Khe Sanh defense force) encounters strong enemy forces on Hill 861 near the base. 3/3 arrives at the base the next day and 2/3 on the 26th. The fight to defeat two NVA regiments

dug in on Hills 861, 881 South, and 881 North lasts through 13 May. The Marines kill 940 enemy and capture six at a cost of 155 dead and 425 wounded. 1st MAW flies over 1,100 close air support sorties, while artillery units fire 25,000 rounds.

26 April
Vietnam
The headquarters of the 26th Marines arrives in country.

28 April
Operation Beaver Cage
SLF Alpha (one of two now afloat with the Seventh Fleet) makes a landing into the Que Son Valley. BLT 1/3 and HMM-263 sweep the area through 12 May, accounting for 181 enemy killed and 66 captured. Marines casualties are 55 killed and 151 wounded.

8 May
Con Thien
North Vietnamese forces attack the Marine base near the DMZ on the 13th anniversary of their victory at Dien Bien Phu. Elements of 1/4 drive off the enemy, killing 197 and capturing eight at a cost of 44 dead and 110 wounded.

13 May
Khe Sanh
The 26th Marines headquarters and 1/26 assume the defense of the base. They launch Operation Crockett to prevent the NVA from building up forces in the area. It lasts until 16 July and kills 206 enemy. Marines losses are 52 dead and 255 wounded.

18 May
DMZ
Marine forces launch three simultaneous operations to make their first sweep through the southern half of the DMZ. SLF Alpha (BLT 1/3 and HMM-263) lands under the code name Beau Charger along the coast. 2/26, 2/9, 3/9, and 3/4 begin a sweep of the area around Con Thien under the code name Hickory. Two days later, SLF Bravo (BLT 2/3 and HMM-164) lands northeast of Con Thien under the code name Belt Tight. The operations wind up on 26 May. The Marines kill 447 enemy but lose 142 killed and 896 wounded.

Operation Rolling Thunder
VMA(AW)-242 flies the first Marine mission in support of Seventh Air Force's strategic bombing campaign in North Vietnam.

25 May
Operation Union II
The 5th Marines and the ARVN 1st Ranger Group conduct search and destroy operations in Quang Nam and Quang Tin Provinces. By the time it ends on 6 June, it accounts for 701 enemy killed. Marine losses are 110 dead and 241 wounded.

31 May
Commanders
Lieutenant General Robert E. Cushman takes over III MAF in place of Lieutenant General Walt.

23 June
Mishap
Twenty Marines die when two helicopters collide over Camp Lejeune.

30 June
Manpower
The strength of the Marine Corps on active duty is 23,592 officers and 261,677 enlisted.

Left: *Marines use Vietnamese sampans in January 1967. (National Archives)*

2 July
Operation Buffalo
1/9 conducts a sweep north from Con Thien and makes heavy contact. Both SLF Alpha (1/3) and Bravo (2/3) and 3/9 move to reinforce. By the time the battle dies out on 14 July, the Marines have killed 1,301 of the enemy and lost 113 dead and 290 wounded.

7 July
Manpower
To meet the need for captains, time-in-grade for first lieutenants to become eligible for promotion drops from two years to one.

15 July
Da Nang
More than 50 122mm rockets hit the airbase early in the morning, killing eight, wounding 175, and destroying or damaging 42 aircraft.

16 July
Operation Kingfisher
The 3rd and 9th Marines launch a series of sweeps in the vicinity of Dong Ha and Cam Lo that last through 31 October. At a cost of 340 Marines dead and 1,461 wounded, the operation killed 1,117 enemy.

24 July
Operation Rolling Thunder
Marine jets strike the Thai Nguyen power plant 30 miles north of Hanoi.

31 July
Training
In one of the largest amphibious landings ever conducted at Camp Pendleton, regular and reserve units conduct Exercise Golden Slipper to test the integration of the two.

1 August
Vietnam
There are now about 78,000 Marines in country.

19 August
Vietnam
Captain Stephen W. Pless, flying a Huey gunship, rescues four American soldiers from a beach where they are being attacked by dozens of Viet Cong. After driving back the enemy with low-level strafing runs, he lands and picks up the men, then strikes the water four times as he struggles to get the overloaded helicopter safely airborne. He subsequently receives the Medal of Honor for his intrepidity, while his three crewmen receive the Navy Cross.

28 August
Vietnam
The enemy makes heavy artillery and rocket attacks on Dong Ha and the airbase at Marble Mountain. Ten marines die and 49 aircraft are damaged or destroyed.

30 August
Phu Bai
An enemy mortar attack damages 18 helicopters and causes 57 Marine casualties.

September
Aviation
All CH-46s are grounded due to unexplained accidents, which turn out to result from structural failure in the aft rotor pylon. The situation is not resolved until December.

3 September
Dong Ha
A Communist artillery barrage destroys the ammunition dump and fuel farm and damages 17 helicopters of HMM-361. Thereafter no more helicopters are based here.

4–15 September
Operation Swift
A 5th Marines search and destroy operation in the Que Son Basin kills 571 enemy at a cost of 127 dead and 352 wounded.

18 September
Vietnam
Monsoon rains and resulting floods kill 10 Marines and make it difficult to supply bases near the DMZ.

25 September
Con Thien
In one of the heaviest Communist barrages of the war, more than 1,000 artillery rounds strike the base. Although 202 Marines are wounded, only two are killed.

4 October
Vietnam
More Marine units shift north toward the DMZ when a brigade of the Army's 1st Air Cavalry Division replaces them in Quang Tin and Quang Ngai Provinces.

5 October
Mishap
Marine astronaut Maj Clifton C. Williams, Jr., dies when his T-38 jet trainer crashes in Florida.

24 October
Operation Rolling Thunder
Marine jets participate in a joint-service raid on Phuc Yen Airfield in North Vietnam. The attack destroys 10 MIGs.

27 October
Manpower
DOD announces a plan to double the number of African-American officers in the Marine Corps, from its present 155 (less than one percent).

Right: *A M60 machine gunner takes the enemy under fire. (National Archives)*

GUNNERY SERGEANT JIMMIE E. HOWARD

Jimmie Earl Howard had made the all-state high school football squad in Iowa in the late 1940s. The 6-foot, 3-inch, 235-pound tackle earned a college scholarship, but dropped out of school after one year to enlist in the Marines just after the Korean War broke out in 1950. He performed so well at boot camp that he was promoted to PFC at graduation and made a drill instructor. He joined the 1st Marine Regiment in Korea in 1952 as a mortar forward observer. In 13 months of bitter trench warfare with the Chinese, he earned two Purple Hearts, as well as a Silver Star for bravery in the fight for the combat outpost at Bunker Hill. During the relatively peaceful dozen years that followed, he alternated tours in reconnaissance with stints coaching Marine football teams.

Staff Sergeant Howard joined Company C, 1st Reconnaissance Battalion, 1st Marine Division, in Vietnam in 1966. He was serving as an acting platoon commander when helicopters dropped him and 17 other men on a peak west of Chu Lai on 13 June. Their orders were to watch for enemy infiltration in the rugged area and call in air or artillery to strike the Communist formations. They successfully carried out that mission for the next two days, but a North Vietnamese battalion moved into position around the base of the mountain during the afternoon and evening of the 15th. Alerted to the danger by an Army Special Forces patrol, the recon team prepared for an onslaught that night.

The enemy launched their first attack at 2200. The Marines repelled that assault, and then another, but most of them had been hit by bullets or shrapnel by now. They also were running low on ammunition. Senior leaders in the rear arranged for strong aerial support, which arrived around 0100. Under Howard's direction and the light of flares, jets and Huey gunships alternated attacks on the hundreds of North Vietnamese arrayed on the slopes of the mountain. Bombs, napalm, rockets, and machine guns battered the Communist infantrymen. In the lulls between Marine air attacks, South Vietnamese artillery blasted the approaches to the summit.

Hit in the back by a bullet around 0300, Howard refused a morphine injection so he could stay alert and remain in command. He continued to encourage his men as he had all night. In between the first two major enemy assaults, he had urged his Marines to laugh out loud in response to the shouted threats and taunts of the surrounding Communists. When the Marines ran short of grenades, he had them throw rocks to simulate the explosive missiles. A little before first light, he called out to his surviving men: "OK, you people, reveille goes in 35 minutes."

A company from the 5th Marines landed by helicopter near Howard's Hill after sunrise. They quickly swept through scattered resistance to reach the peak, where the recon platoon commander directed their subsequent operations until the entire position was secure. Six recon Marines had died, along with two men from the relief company and two helicopter crewmen. But together, the Marine infantrymen and aviators had savaged a North Vietnamese battalion.

Cpl Jimmie Howard receives a Silver Star for bravery in the fight for Bunker Hill in Korea. Nearly 15 years later he would earn the Medal of Honor for more courage on another hilltop, this time in Vietnam. (Marine Corps Historical Center)

Ricardo Binns, John Adams, Jerrald Thompson, and Navy Corpsman Billie Don Holmes received Navy Crosses, while every other member of the patrol was awarded a Silver Star. Howard received the Medal of Honor in a White House ceremony. In praising the feat of the small band of Marines, President Lyndon Johnson harked back to the famous last stands of the Spartans at Thermopylae and the Texans at the Alamo. This time, though, the defenders had won. For his part, Howard gave all the credit to his men, "That's the guys who did it."

Howard volunteered to return for another tour in Vietnam in 1969. He retired from the Corps in 1972 and worked as a counselor for the Veterans Administration. He died in 1993.

1November
Da Nang
During a visit to III MAF, Vice President Hubert Humphrey presents the presidential Unit Citation to 3rd Marine Division for its performance along the DMZ.
Operation Lancaster
The 9th Marines launches a series of search and destroy operations around Camp Carroll that last through 20 January 1968.

6 November
Operation Essex
A search and destroy operation by 2/5 in Antenna Valley near An Hoa kills 72 enemy at a cost of 37 Marine dead and 122 wounded.

8 November
Manpower
President Johnson signs a bill giving women equal promotion opportunity in the military services.

13–30 November
Operations Foster and Badger Hunt
3/7 and BLT 2/3 sweep the area west of An Hoa, killing 125 enemy. Marine losses are 21 dead and 137 wounded.

14 November
Mishap
Major General Bruno A Hochmuth, commander of the 3rd Marine Division, dies in a helicopter crash near Hue.

13 December
Khe Sanh
3/26 arrives at the base to reinforce it during a period of increasing enemy activity.

17 December
Vietnam
Captain Doyle D. Baker, flying an exchange tour with the Air Force's 13th Tactical Fighter Squadron, destroys a MIG-17 with cannon fire and a missile while escorting a bombing mission over North Vietnam. He is the first Marine pilot to score an aerial victory in the war.

26 December
Operation Rolling Thunder
Marine jets attack targets near Hanoi and Dong Hoi.

31 December
Vietnam
Of the 478,000 U.S. troops in country, 81,249 are Marines. III MAF has 114,158 personnel, of which

Left: *"Secondaries at Khe Sanh," Larry Zabel, Naval Art Collection*

Opposite: *"Marine Bombers at Twilight," John Steele, Naval Art Collection*

76,616 are Marines. Marine casualties during the year total 3,461 dead and 25,525 wounded. The III MAF effort to build a strongpoint barrier system along the DMZ, directed by USMACV, has consumed more 757,000 man-days during 1967.

Commandants

General Greene retires and is replaced by General Leonard F. Chapman, Jr., the 24th Commandant of the Marine Corps. He departs on 3 January for an inspection trip of Marine forces in Vietnam.

1968

6 January
Khe Sanh

General Westmoreland begins Operation Niagara, a plan to use heavy firepower to destroy enemy units building up around the Marine combat base.

8 January
Mishap

A CH-53 crash kills 36 Marines and five others in Vietnam.

11 January
Mishap

A Quantico-based transport crashes in Nevada, killing all 19 Marines on board.

16 January
Khe Sanh

2/26 flies into the base, placing the entire 26th Marines there.

Vietnam

The North Vietnamese state that they will not begin negotiations to end the war until the United States halts the bombing of North Vietnam.

Cuba

In a change of policy, 2/8 moves to Guantanamo Bay to become the permanent defense force. Instead of rotating battalions every 90 days, personnel will now be rotated into 2/8.

19 January
Khe Sanh

A platoon patrolling toward Hill 881 North has to withdraw in the face of strong enemy opposition. This marks the beginning of the siege of the remote combat base.

20 January
Khe Sanh

Company I, 3/26 kills an estimated 100 NVA and loses seven killed and 35 wounded in an attempt to clear Hill 881 North. The company is withdrawn after an NVA lieutenant comes into the main perimeter and reveals plans for a major assault beginning in the next few days.

21 January
Vietnam

General Westmoreland orders a temporary halt to work on the McNamara Line, the strongpoint barrier system along the DMZ. The 4th Marines begins Operation Lancaster II around Camp Carroll. The 3rd Marines begins Operation Osceola around the base at Quang Tri.

Khe Sanh

Company K, 3/26 defeats a Communist night attack on Hill 861. The NVA begins a bombardment of the combat base just before dawn. The Marines will receive incoming shells and rockets every day for the next 77 days. One shell sets off the main ammunition dump, raining exploding ordnance over much of the perimeter.

22 January
Khe Sanh
1/9 arrives to reinforce the 26th Marines.

23 January
Korea
North Korean naval forces seize the U.S. intelligence ship *Pueblo* (AGER-2) in international waters off their coast.

27 January
Vietnam
A seven-day truce begins for the Tet holiday. The ARVN 37th Ranger Battalion arrives at Khe Sanh.

30 January
Tet Offensive
Communist forces launch an offensive that spreads throughout South Vietnam by the next day. Attacks come against most major cities and province capitals. By infiltration and assault, they take control of most of Hue, the former imperial capital. An attempt to seize the U.S. Embassy in Saigon is thwarted by the Marine guards. Facilities at Da Nang are hit by rockets, mortars, and a ground assault.

1 February
Hue
1/1 and 2/5 begin operations to recapture the city. The Marines focus on the area south of the Perfume River, while the 1st ARVN Division is responsible for the Citadel, the old city north of the river. HMM-165 provides lift for ARVN forces into the city. The battle quickly devolves into typical building-to-building fighting.

5 February
Khe Sanh
Guided by ground sensors, Marine artillery blasts an enemy troop concentration, and shortly after Company E, 2/26 defeats a Communist attempt to take Hill 861A.

6 February
Hue
Marines capture the province headquarters building in Hue, pull down the Communist flag, and run up the Stars and Stripes.
Da Nang
Marines beat back another round of Communist attacks against installations and units in the area.

7 February
Khe Sanh
NVA forces using PT-76 amphibious tanks capture the Special Forces camp at Lang Vei, west of the Marine base.

8 February
Khe Sanh
Company A, 1/9 defeats an enemy attempt to capture a platoon outpost.

10 February
Hue
The 1st Marines (1/1 and 2/5) finish clearing the city south of the Perfume River. Marine casualties are 38 dead and 320 wounded, while the enemy loses over 1,000. 1/5 begins to reinforce the 1st Marines.

13 February
Hue
1/5 starts its attack on the Citadel and is soon joined by two battalions of Vietnamese Marines.

17 February
Vietnam
As part of a reinforcement package resulting from the Tet Offensive, the 27th Marines and 2/13 depart California for Vietnam.

24 February
Khe Sanh
In an effort to cut down the number of helicopters being hit by enemy fire during resupply missions to the hill posts, 1st MAW institutes the Super Gaggle.

Opposite: *"Flushing Out Snipers, Hue," Ned Conlon, Marine Corps Art Collection*

Right: *"Walking Wounded," Col Houston Stiff, USMC (Ret), Marine Corps Art Collection*

It typically involves a KC-130 refueler, eight or more CH-46 helicopters carrying sling loads, up to 12 A-4s and four Huey gunships providing fire support, and a two-seat TA-4 with the backseater coordinating the mission. The attack aircraft would suppress enemy antiaircraft positions with napalm and tear gas, lay smoke on both sides of the helicopter path, then attack with bombs and guns anything that fired as the helicopters swooped in to drop their loads.

25 February
Hue
1/5 and Vietnamese forces complete the seizure of the Citadel, bringing the battle for the city to an end, except for mopping up operations. Total friendly casualties for the entire battle are more than 600 dead and almost 3,800 wounded, of which Marine losses are 142 dead and nearly 1,100 wounded. The number of enemy killed exceeds 1,000 and is estimated as high as 5,000.

27 February
Khe Sanh
A CH-46 is shot down near the base, resulting in 22 Marines dead and one wounded.

28 February
Khe Sanh
Two NVA battalions attempting to attack the 37th Ranger Battalion sector of the perimeter are hit by artillery fire and air support as they assemble.

6 March
Khe Sanh
Antiaircraft fire downs an Air Force C-12 transport, killing 43 Marines and five others.

10 March
Vietnam
1st MAW's fixed-wing aircraft are placed under the operational control of Seventh Air Force as the "single manager" for tactical aviation in Vietnam.

15 March
Force Structure
HML-167 is commissioned at Marble Mountain in Vietnam.

22 March
Manpower
The Marine Aviation Cadet program, which had allowed men without college degrees a chance to earn their wings, comes to an end.

Left: *Marines of Kilo Company, 3/5, carry a casualty toward a helicopter landing zone. (National Archives)*

30 March
Khe Sanh
Company B, 1/9 conducts a dawn attack against enemy trenches and bunkers, inflicting significant casualties. The siege is essentially ended as much of the NVA force has withdrawn. Marine casualties between 1 November 1967 and now total 205 dead and 1,668 wounded. Enemy confirmed dead are 1,602, with estimates of total casualties exceeding 10,000.

31 March
Vietnam
President Johnson announces a partial halt to the bombing of North Vietnam in an attempt to begin negotiations to end the war. He also declares an end to his campaign for reelection.

1 April
Khe Sanh
The 1st Air Cavalry Division and the 1st Marines launch Operation Pegasus to open a road link to the Marine base.

5 April
Civil Support
Three companies of Marines from Quantico and the Marine Barracks assist in quelling severe riots in Washington, D.C., following the assassination of Dr. Martin Luther King, Jr.

8 April
Khe Sanh
The siege is officially over when elements of the 1st Air Cavalry Division reach the area by road.

16 April
Force Structure
MAG-39 is activated at Quang Tri, Vietnam, as part of 1st MAW.

18 April
Khe Sanh
The 26th Marines is relieved by the 1st Marines and it moves back to Dong Ha and Camp Carroll.

30 April
Dai Do
BLT 2/4 attacks 4 NVA battalions dug in around the village of Dai Do and interdicting the Cua Viet River. The battle lasts until 3 May. Marines losses are 81 dead and almost 300 wounded, while estimated enemy dead exceed 500.

4 May
Operation Allen Brook
The 7th Marines begins a series of search and destroy missions to clear the area south of Da Nang. It last through 23 August and results in 1,017 enemy dead. Marine losses are 172 killed and 1,124 wounded.

5 May
Vietnam
In a miniature repeat of the Tet offensive, Communist forces launch rocket and mortar attacks against 119 towns and cities.

13 May
Vietnam
Peace talks begin in Paris between the United States, South Vietnam, and North Vietnam.

18 May
Operation Mameluke Thrust
The 1st Marine Division conducts search and destroy operations in central Quang Nam Province that last through 23 October, killing 2,728 enemy. Marine losses are 269 killed and 1,730 wounded.

21 May
Dong Ha
An NVA division makes an attempt to infiltrate south from the DMZ toward Dong Ha. In 10 days of fighting, the 3rd and 9th Marines drive the enemy back, killing more than 770 and taking 61 prisoners. Marine and ARVN losses are 112 dead and 446 wounded.

22 May
Technology
1st MAW makes the first use of the North American OV-10A Bronco, a light observation plane.

28 May
Khe Sanh
Companies E and F, 2/3 defeat an NVA attempt to take a hill along Route 9 near the base. At a cost of 13 dead and 44 wounded, the Marines kill 230 enemy. This is only one of a series of small battles around the base in the weeks after the siege.

1 June
Go Noi Island
In an effort to burn away the island's foliage in support of Operation Allen Brook, nine C-130s drop 31,000 gallons of fuel in drums.

26 June
Iwo Jima
The island is returned to Japanese control.

27 June
Khe Sanh
The Marine garrison begins to dismantle defenses and withdraw from the base, to be abandoned under a new operations plan for northern I Corps Zone.

30 June
Manpower
The strength of the Marine Corps on active duty is 24,555 officers and 282,697 enlisted.

1 July
Commanders
General Creighton W. Abrams replaces General Westmoreland as commander of USMACV.

Right: *Echo Company, 2/7, during Operation Arizona south of Da Nang in June 1967. (National Archives)*

LIEUTENANT VINCENT R. CAPODANNO, JR., USNR

The Capodanno family came from strong Italian roots. Vincent, Sr., arrived in the United States in 1900 at the age of 16, while the family of his wife, Rachel Basile, had immigrated two generations earlier. They married in New York in 1907 and moved to an Italian-American community on Staten Island. They had ten children. The last one was Vincent, Jr., born on 13 February 1929. Although Vincent grew up in a devoutly Catholic family, his initial ambition during his years in public school was to be a doctor. After graduating from high school in 1947, he went to work as a clerk with an insurance company and attended college at night. It was only in 1949 that he decided to become a priest. He was ordained in 1958 as a Maryknoll, becoming part of a society of priests dedicated to missionary work in foreign lands. It was a life that called for dedication and, not infrequently, bravery. He spent the next seven years in Taiwan and Hong Kong, mainly in remote villages.

In July 1965, he sought to join the Navy as a chaplain, specifically requesting service with the Marine units that had only recently deployed to Vietnam. He was not a complete stranger to the service, since all three of his older brothers had served during WWII, one of them in the Corps. After initial training in the Navy, and with the Field Medical School at Camp Pendleton, Lieutenant Capodanno reported to the 1st Battalion, 7th Marines at Chu Lai in April 1966.

Tall, wiry, quiet Father Capodanno wasted no time establishing a reputation as a field Marine and soon earned the nickname "Grunt Padre." As the only Catholic chaplain in the regiment, he spent much of his time rotating between the 12 rifle companies and accompanying them on operations. He explained at the time, "I want to be available in the event anything serious occurs, to learn firsthand the problems of the men, and to give them moral support, to comfort them with my presence. I feel I must personally witness how they react under fire—and experience it myself—to understand the fear that they feel." The tall, spare priest carried a load on the march just like the men. In battle, he had no hesitation in moving forward under fire to minister spiritually and physically to the wounded and dying. For numerous actions during his months with the 7th Marines, he subsequently received the Bronze Star. When he was not out in the field, he spent his time writing letters to the families of casualties and working with the villagers protected by Marine CAP units.

In December 1966, Capodanno was transferred to the 1st Medical Battalion and its field hospital near Chu Lai. Although he might have stayed exclusively in this somewhat more secure environment, he still spent a lot of time forward with combat units. Before the end of his tour in Vietnam, he requested and received a six-month extension. In July 1967 he transferred to the 5th Marines, then fighting in the Que Son Valley. Soon after he submitted paperwork for another six-month extension.

In the pre-dawn hours of 4 September, two companies of 1/5 became involved in a tough fight in Thang Binh District. By mid-morning, two companies of 3/5 helicoptered

Father Vince Capodanno, a Catholic priest and Navy chaplain, earned the nickname "Grunt Padre" for his selfless service with field Marines in Vietnam. (National Archives)

into position to reinforce the beleaguered Marines of 1/5. Chaplain Capodanno went out with them. As the men of 3/5 advanced from their landing zone to link up, they ran into strong enemy resistance. When one platoon was pinned down under heavy fire and in danger of being overrun, he went forward to their aid. He pulled a radio operator to safety, then proceeded to move through the fusillade to minister to the Marines. After being wounded in the hand, arm, and leg by mortar shrapnel, he refused aid and braved automatic weapons fire to drag a wounded sergeant to cover. Seeing a corpsman severely wounded by a machine gun just 15 meters away, Capodanno rushed forward to his assistance, placing himself between the enemy weapon and the casualty. Within moments, the chaplain was cut down and killed.

For his courageous devotion to his Marines that day, Lieutenant Capodanno was awarded the Medal of Honor, one of three Navy chaplains to receive the nation's highest decoration during the Vietnam War. He exemplified all those Navy doctors, chaplains, and corpsmen who have selflessly served the Corps.

Left: *An ONTOS fires at night from the Rockpile. (National Archives)*

Opposite: *Hue City. (National Archives)*

Operation Thor
Air, artillery, and naval surface fires blanket the Cap Mui Lay area of southern North Vietnam in an effort to destroy long-range artillery located there. The operation continues through 7 July.

5 July
Khe Sanh
The combat base is closed and the last Marines depart.

22 August
Da Nang
Communist forces launch their third phase offensive with attacks on bridges, mortar barrages, and ground assaults in the area around Da Nang. They are driven off in each case before causing serious damage.

29 August
Operation Sussex Bay
The 5th and 7th Marines conduct operations to hunt down Communist forces involved in the recent attacks around Da Nang. The campaign ends on 9 September, with an estimated 2,000 enemy dead stemming from the initial Communist offensive and its aftermath.

5 September
Vietnam
Typhoon Bess strikes I Corps Zone with 50-knot winds and heavy rain. Operations are suspended for two days and defensive positions are washed out.

10 September
Vietnam
The 27th Marines begins departing Vietnam for Camp Pendleton. It is the first Marine unit to leave the war on a nonrotational basis.

16 September
Vietnam
Communist forces hit the command group of 2/26 with two mortar barrages, killing 22 and wounding 146.

29 September
Vietnam
Battleship *New Jersey* (BB-62) arrives on station off I Corps Zone and fires her first missions in support of Marines in the Vietnam War.

1 October
Manpower
Since the inception of the battlefield commissioning program in June 1965, more than 8,000 enlisted Marines have become officers.

3 October
Manpower
DOD announces that the Marine Corps will receive 2,500 of the 17,500 men to be drafted in December. This marks the first time since May that the Corps needed to resort to the draft.

5 October
Vietnam
The number of U.S. troops in country reaches 540,000, of which 84,000 are Marines.

6–19 October
Operation Maui Peak
The 7th Marines relieves the Special Forces camp Thuong Duc, in the process killing 202 enemy at a cost of 28 Marines killed and 143 wounded.

11 October
Space
One of the three astronauts on Apollo VII during its 11-day space voyage is Marine Reserve Major Walter Cunningham.

23 October
Operation Henderson Hill
The 5th Marines launches a series of search and destroy operations south of Da Nang. When the operation winds up on 6 December, the regiment has killed 700 enemy and lost 35 Marines dead and 272 wounded.

31 October
Vietnam
President Johnson announces a complete halt to the bombing of North Vietnam.

20 November
Operation Meade River
In support of a South Vietnamese pacification program, the 1st Marines launches a cordon and search operation designed to encircle the entire Dodge City area, 36 square miles of flat farming land south of Da Nang. The effort involves seven Marine infantry battalions. It ends on 9 December with 1,023 enemy dead and 123 prisoners. Marine losses are 108 dead and 510 wounded.

23 November
Operation Lancaster II
The series of 4th Marines search and destroy missions comes to an end. Reported Enemy casualties are 1,800, while 359 Marines have been killed and another 2,101 wounded.

9 December
Operation Napoleon/Saline
A 13-month-old series of search and destroy operations by the 3rd Marines in the northeast quadrant of Quang Tri Province comes to an end. The effort resulted in 3,495 enemy killed and 106 captured, while Marine losses totaled 395 dead and 2,134 wounded.

23 December
Korea
North Korea releases the crew of *Pueblo* after 11 months. Two Marines, Staff Sergeant Robert J. Hammond and Sergeant Robert J. Chicca, are part of the group.

28 December
Camp Carroll
Marines abandon the combat base, which they had been using for two years.

31 December
Vietnam
During the course of the year, III MAF inflicted 31,691 reported casualties on the enemy. Marine losses were 4,634 dead and 29,319 wounded. 1st MAW flew 47,436 fixed-wing sorties and 639,194 helicopter sorties.

1969

6 January
Department of the Navy
President-elect Richard M. Nixon announces his selection of Rhode Island governor John H. Chafee as the new Secretary of the Navy. Chafee served in the Marine Corps during WWII and Korea.

22 January
Operation Dewey Canyon
The 9th Marines and supporting artillery units are helicoptered into the A Shau Valley for a search and destroy mission.

1 February
Force Structure
The 5th LAAM Battalion is deactivated at Yuma following the return of the 2nd LAAM Battalion from Vietnam.

25 February
Manpower
Since the summer of 1965, more than 30,000 Marines have voluntarily extended their tours in Vietnam for six or more months. That equates to a battalion a month. During December 1968, 3,200 of the 8,000 men scheduled to come home volunteered to remain in country.

28 February
Operations Kentucky and Scotland II
The 3rd Marine Division ends these two long-term operations. Kentucky had started on 1 November 1967 and focused on search and cordon operations in the area between Cam Lo, Dong Ha, and Con Thien. The division suffered 52 dead and 3,079 wounded while killing 3,921 enemy. Scotland II had begun on 14 April 1968 and encompassed the region around Khe Sanh. Marine losses were 463 dead and 2,555 wounded, most suffered in the numerous small battles after the siege. Communist dead numbered 3,311.

March
HQMC
Plans are finalized for a law enforcement branch in the headquarters to oversee training and other issues related to military police. It will come into existence during fiscal year 1970.

2 March
Vietnam
The South Vietnamese hold village elections throughout the country without serious disruption from Communist forces.

3 March
Technology
The Marines receive their first Sikorsky CH-53D, an improved model of the Corps' heavy lift helicopter.

Left: *"Northeast of the Rockpile," Ned Conlon, Marine Corps Art Collection*

Opposite: *"The Hill At Thuong Duc," Col Charles Waterhouse, USMCR (Ret), Marine Corps Art Collection*

9 March
Operation Taylor Common
The 1st Marine Division closes out an operation initiated on 7 December 1967. In the area southwest of An Hoa, Marine battalions killed 1,398 enemy and captured 610, while losing 156 dead and 1,327 wounded.

10 March
Dewey Canyon
Secretary of Defense Melvin R. Laird publicly confirms that some Marine units had crossed into Laos during the operation.

15 March
Manpower
The percentage of high school graduates among volunteer enlistees stands at 5.4 percent, while it is 71.5 percent among draftees. There are 1,071 college graduates in the Corps enlisted ranks.

18 March
Operation Dewey Canyon
The 9th Marines completes the operation, which results in 1,617 enemy killed, as well as the largest haul of Communist arms in the war. Among the items captured or destroyed are two 122mm towed howitzers, 66 trucks, 14 bulldozers, and hundreds of thousands of rounds of ammunition of all types and calibers.

26 March
Commanders
Lieutenant General Herman Nickerson, Jr., becomes the commander of III MAF. President Nixon names Lieutenant General Cushman, the previous MAF commander, the deputy director of the Central Intelligence Agency.

30 March
Vietnam
III MAF engineers and naval construction forces complete building a new Liberty Bridge across the wide Thu Bon River.

April
Technology
VMO-2 in Vietnam begins operating the Bell AH-1G Cobra gunship, the first true attack helicopter in the Corps' inventory.

3 April
Vietnam
American dead in the Vietnam War (33,641) now exceed those in the Korean War (33,629).

7–20 April
Operation Muskogee Meadows
The 5th Marines conducts operations to deny the rice harvest to Communist forces in the vicinity of An Hoa. In the process, the regiment kills 162 enemy at a cost of 16 Marines dead and 121 wounded.

17 April
Technology
The Marine Corps receives its first 175mm self-propelled guns in Vietnam, to replace its 155mm self-propelled guns.

22 April
Commandants
The Senate approves legislation granting four-star rank to the Assistant Commandant of the Marine Corps, as long as the strength of the Corps exceeds 200,000 at the time of appointment. The House already had passed the measure.

Left: *"Vietnam Episode, I Corps Area," Robert Benney, Marine Corps Art Collection*

Opposite: *"Green Hell," Sgt Richard L. Yaco, USMC, Marine Corps Art Collection*

25 April
Training
American and Brazilian Marines conduct a combined amphibious landing at Vieques, the largest such maneuver involving the two countries since WWII.

27 April
Mishap
A grass fire near the ammunition dump at Da Nang ignites a store of unserviceable ammunition and spreads to other areas, destroying 38,000 tons of ground and air munitions and 20,000 drums of fuel, as well as closing the airbase for 18 hours. One Marine and a civilian are killed and dozens injured.

2 May
Operation Maine Crag
The 3rd Marines search and destroy operation south of Khe Sanh, begun on 15 March, results in 157 enemy killed. Marine losses are 21 dead and 134 wounded.

6 May
Vietnam
III MAF reaches its fourth anniversary. It commands the 1st and 3rd Marine Divisions, 1st MAW, Force Logistics Command, the Army's XXIV Corps headquarters, the Americal Division, the 101st Airborne Division, and the 1st Brigade of the 5th Infantry Division. It rivals the size of Tenth Army at Okinawa and is a field army in all but name only.

8 May
Operation Purple Martin
Begun on 23 February, this 4th Marines operation cleared the northwest area of Quang Tri Province, forcing an NVA regiment back into the DMZ. Marine losses are 79 dead and 268 wounded, while Communist dead amount to 252.

9–12 May
Arizona Territory
The 5th Marines conducts a search and clear operation using air and artillery that kills 230 enemy in the area northwest of An Hoa.

29 May
Operation Oklahoma Hills
The 7th Marines completes a search and clear operation south of Da Nang. The regiment killed 596 enemy in 60 days, at a cost of 53 Marine dead and 487 wounded.

2 June
Commandants
Assistant Commandant Lew Walt becomes the first in his billet to hold the rank of four-star general. It also marks the first time the Marine Corps has two four-star generals on active duty at the same time.

7–12 June
Arizona Territory
1/5 defeats several enemy night attacks and destroys an NVA battalion command group, inflicting over 300 dead.

8 June
Vietnam
President Nixon announces that he will withdraw 25,000 troops from Vietnam by the end of August. This will include the 9th Marines. American troops strength in country had reached 540,000 following the Tet Offensive.

15 June
Vietnam
The 1st Amphibian Tractor Battalion begins redeploying to Okinawa.

23 June
Operation Cameron Falls
The search and clear mission headed by the 9th Marines and concentrated in the area southeast of Khe Sanh results in 120 enemy killed. During the 24-day operation, Marines losses are 24 dead and 137 wounded.

30 June
Manpower
The strength of the Marine Corps on active duty is 25,698 officers and 284,073 enlisted. This is the highest manpower total for the Corps since 1945. Of these, over 82,000 are in Vietnam. The reenlistment rate reaches its lowest level since before the Vietnam War, with 12 percent of first-term volunteers and only one percent of draftees signing on for another contract.

1 July
Force Structure
MAG-49 is activated as part of 4th MAW.

9 July
Operation Utah Mesa
This joint Marine-Army operation, begun on 12 June and conducted southwest of Khe Sanh, comes to an end. Marine losses are 19 dead and 91 wounded, while the Army suffers 94 casualties. Reported enemy dead total 309. This is the last operation of the 9th Marines in Vietnam.

14 July
Vietnam
1/9 sails for Okinawa, marking the beginning of the departure of the 9th Marines as part of the initial drawdown of U.S. forces in country.

16 July
Space
An element of the 2nd Amphibian Tractor Battalion stands by at Cape Kennedy in Florida as a secondary recovery team in case of a failed launch of Apollo 11, the mission that would place the first men on the moon.
Operation Virginia Ridge
The 3rd Marines wraps up a search and clear mission north of the Rockpile. Since its inception on 1 May, the operation has resulted in 560 enemy killed, at a cost of 108 Marines dead, one missing, and 490 wounded.
Operation Herkimer Mountain
The 4th Marines complete this operation northeast of Khe Sanh, which they had initiated on 1 May. The regiment suffers 25 dead and 219 wounded while killing 137 enemy.

20 July
Camp Lejeune
A confrontation on the base between racial groups results in the death of one Marine.

24 July
Space
Elements of HMX-1 accompany President Nixon on his trip to greet the Apollo 11 astronauts, while the Marine detachment of *Forrestal* (CVA-59) provides security for the Mobile Quarantine Facility temporarily housing the Apollo crew.

31 July
Sergeants Major
Sergeant Major Joseph W. Dailey succeeds Sergeant Major Sweet as the fifth Sergeant Major of the Marine Corps.

1 August
Legal
As part of the implementation of the Military Justice Act of 1968, Brigadier General Duane L. Faw and Colonel Ralph K. Culver join seven Navy officers and three civilians on the new Navy Court of Military Review.

13 August
Vietnam
HMM-165 flies from Marble Mountain to *Valley Forge* (LPH-8), the first 1st MAW element to depart the country as part of the reduction in forces. The 1st LAAM Battalion also begins to leave Da Nang for 29 Palms, while the last elements of the 9th Marines board ship the next day for Okinawa.

18 August
Vietnam
HMM-362 departs. The last active-duty squadron flying the UH-34D, it will be redesignated HMH-362 and re-equip with the CH-53 upon arrival at its new station.

26 August
Vietnam
VMFA-334 relocates from Chu Lai to Iwakuni, Japan.

3 September
Vietnam
North Vietnamese leader Ho Chi Minh dies.

17 September
Vietnam
The United States announces a second troop withdrawal amounting to 40,500 personnel, of which 18,500 will be Marines.
Manpower
The October draft call will include 1,400 men destined for the Marine Corps, bringing its number of draftees for the year to 11,878.

18 September
Vietnam
USMACV decides that the Marine slice of the pending troop withdrawal will consist primarily of the 3rd Marine Division. Personnel transfers within III MAF would shift Marines with time left on their tour in country from this division to other units remaining behind.

21 September
Force Structure
Secretary of Defense Laird announces that the 5th Marine Division, with the exception of the 26th Marines in Vietnam, will be deactivated soon.

27 September
Operation Idaho Canyon
The 3rd Marines terminates a search and clear mission in the area southwest of Con Thien that has been going on since 17 July. At a cost of 95 dead and 450 wounded, the regiment killed 565 enemy.

Opposite: *Marine lieutenant, January 1968. (National Archives)*

Right: *2/5 Marines in gas masks in Hue. (National Archives)*

29 September
Manpower
The Marine Corps announces a cut of 20,300 in its active-duty strength.

1 October
Manpower
The Corps implements stricter reenlistment criteria, in particular with regard to disciplinary records.

10 October
Manpower
The Marine Corps reduces unaccompanied tours to units in Japan and Okinawa from 13 months to 12.

15 October
Force Structure
Nearly all units of the 5th Marine Division, with the exception of the division headquarters, are deactivated.

19 October
Vietnam
1/4 embarks on ship for transport to Okinawa. HMM-164 and HMH-462 depart the next day.

22 October
Vietnam
VMO-6 departs for Okinawa.

28 October
Force Structure
HMM-561 is deactivated at El Toro.

31 October
Force Structure
MAG-39 is deactivated in Vietnam.

1 November
Force Structure
With the 3rd Marine Division returning to Okinawa, 9th MAB is deactivated.

7 November
Vietnam
The last significant elements of the 3rd Marine Division sail for Okinawa. The 1st Marines terminates Operation Pipestone Canyon in the Dodge City and Go Noi Island areas south of Da Nang. Underway since 26 May, it resulted in 488 enemy dead at a cost of 54 Marines killed and 540 wounded.

Force Structure
I MEF is established on Okinawa to command all FMF units in Japan and Okinawa.

15 November
Vietnam
MAG-36 begins its transfer from Vietnam to Okinawa.

19 November
Manpower
At the request of President Nixon, Congress passes legislation basing the draft on a lottery system using birth dates. It goes into effect on 1 December

26 November
Force Structure
The headquarters of the 5th Marine Division is deactivated and is replaced by the 5th MAB, which will command remaining ground units at Camp Pendleton.

15 December
Vietnam
President Nixon announces a third round of troop withdrawals, to be completed by 15 April 1970.

17 December
Technology
Battleship *New Jersey* is decommissioned and placed into mothballs again.

31 December
Vietnam
The number of Marines in country is down to 54,559 (out of a total Marine strength of 301,675). Over the course of the year, 1st MAW provided 547,965 helicopter sorties and about 66,000 fixed-wing sorties. During these operations, the wing lost 44 helicopters, 34 fixed-wing aircraft, 92 Marines killed, 514 wounded, and 20 missing. Marine casualties during the year totaled 2,258 dead and 16,567 wounded.

1970

6 January
Que Son Valley
Fire Support Base Ross receives 250 rounds of mortar fire and a ground attack from a sapper unit. Marine units, primarily elements of 1/7, lose 13 dead and 63 wounded. Known enemy casualties are 39 killed.

8 January
Vietnam
III MAF establishes the Combined Unit Pacification Program (CUPP), a cousin to the Combined Action Program. Unlike CAP, Marine rifle squads deployed to villages under CUPP receive no special training and remain a part of their parent companies.

11 January
Vietnam
III MAF activates the Combined Action Force, a new headquarters to control the four Combined Action Groups of the CAP program. The CAP force mustered 42 Marine and two Navy officers, 2,050 enlisted Marines, and 126 corpsmen organized into 114 platoons.

18–25 January
Training
The 2nd Reconnaissance Battalion conducts Operation Snowfer in Camp Drum, New York, for environmental and cold weather training.

19 January
Training
Operation Springboard, a three-month exercise involving 110 ships and 260 aircraft from seven

Opposite: *Moving through the rubble of Hue. (National Archives)*

Right: *Echo Company, 2/7, during Operation Oklahoma Hills in April 1969. (National Archives)*

nations, begins in San Juan, Puerto Rico. It involves units from Brazil, Canada, Columbia, the Netherlands, United Kingdom, United States, and Venezuela.

19–23 January
Okinawa
The Okinawa Military Employees Labor Union's five-day strike is held without major confrontation. It does not seriously affect the continuation of essential Marine Corps activities.

24 January
Training
Recruit training increases from eight to nine weeks in length.

28 January
Vietnam
The third wave of withdrawal of U.S. forces begins. It will result in the permanent departure of 50,000 more personnel, including 12,900 Marines, by 7 April. The major Marine units involved are the 26th Marines, MAG-12, VMA-223 and 211, VMFA-542, and HMH-361.

31 January
Vietnam
Intelligence indicates that NVA traffic along the Ho Chi Minh Trail (the infiltration route from North Vietnam) increased during January to 10 times the level of September and October 1969.

1 February
Manpower
HQMC announces it is expanding its early-out program because of troop cutbacks in Vietnam. Only Vietnam veterans can apply for this program, which can release them from active duty as much as 14 months prior to original separation dates.

17 February
Vietnam
President Nixon declares that Vietnamization (the turning over of increasing responsibility for combat duties to South Vietnamese armed forces) is proceeding on schedule.

19 February
Iwo Jima
The United States and Japan hold combined ceremonies at Mt. Suribachi to commemorate the dead of both nations on the 25th anniversary of the battle. Major General William K. Jones, commanding general of the 3rd Marine Division, represents the Commandant of the Marine Corps.

23 February
Manpower
The Gates Commission recommends prompt pay increases for members of the armed services and other reforms to permit an end to the draft by 30 June 1971. The findings are referred to a White House study group for review.

24–27 February
Technology
The Marine Corps holds a Tactical Employment conference to begin establishing doctrine for the British-built Hawker Siddeley AV-8A Harrier, a revolutionary jet aircraft that could take of and land vertically.

9 March
Vietnam
In a reversal of roles, III MAF turns over operational control of American military forces in the I Corps Zone to the Army's XXIV Corps and becomes a subset of its former subordinate. This change in command took place because Marine redeployments from the area left Army forces in the majority there. III MAF still retained direct control of the 1st Marine Division and 1st MAW, maintaining the Marine air-ground team.
Commanders
Lieutenant General Keith B. McCutcheon assumes command of III MAF from Lieutenant General Nickerson.

13 March
Training
The Basic School is increased in length from 21 weeks to 26.

23 March
Civil Support
President Nixon authorizes the activation of Reserve units to assist the U.S. Postal Department in New York City during a strike. Units included are 2/25, 6th and 11th Communications Battalions, VMA-131, HMM-768, and Headquarters and Maintenance Squadron 49.

25 March
Civil Support
Three hundred Marine reservists are employed at the main post office, Brooklyn, New York. As of this date, 120 officers and 2,081 enlisted of the Marine Corps Reserve had been activated in the New York area. The situation is resolved the next day and the reservists are demobilized.

1 April
Reserve
Headquarters of the 4th Marine Division at Camp Pendleton assumes training responsibility for all Marine Corps Reserve ground forces. This training was formerly under the control of the director of the Marine Corps district in which the unit was located.

2 April
Vietnam
The number of Marines in country drops to 43,600.

10 April
Vietnam
Lieutenant Larry Parsons, a helicopter pilot believed killed in action near the border between Vietnam and Laos, is rescued after spending nearly 20 days in the Laotian jungle.

14 April
Training
The 11th MEB depart Okinawa enroute to Yang Po Ri, Korea, to participate in Exercise Golden Dragon, a combined USMC/KMC amphibious exercise.

20 April
Vietnam
President Nixon announces he will withdraw 150,000 more U.S. troops over the next year.

22 April
Caribbean
In response to a request by the Trinidad government, which is experiencing a military

mutiny, the United States dispatches 2,000 Marines to the area to stand by as a precautionary measure for the protection of U.S. citizens.

23 April
Caribbean
Lead elements of the Caribbean landing force, including BLT 3/2 and HMM-261, depart San Juan, Puerto Rico, for a position off the coast of Trinidad.

Opposite: *Helping hand, Dewey Canyon. (National Archives)*

Above: *Comforting a Vietnamese orphan. (National Archives)*

Right: *Final tribute. (National Archives)*

27 April
Vietnam
This is the first day in 1970 in which no Marines casualties are reported in Vietnam.

28 April
Caribbean
The Caribbean landing force depart the waters of Trinidad and resumes normal operations.

29 April
Cambodia
U.S. Army and ARVN units attack Communist base areas in Cambodia. Marine participation is limited to a handful of bombing missions and advisors with the VNMC.

30 April
Force Structure
The 26th Marines and 1/13 are deactivated at Camp Pendleton.
Civil Support
1/6, 3/6, and 3/8 deploy to Quonset Point, Rhode Island, to standby aid local authorities in handling a civil disturbance in New Haven. They remain there until 3 May, but are not employed.

1 May
Marine Band
The director of the Marine Band, Albert Schoepper, is promoted to the rank of colonel, the first Marine musician to attain this rank in the 172-year history of the band.

10 May
Civil Support
To counter possible civil disturbances in Washington, D.C., resulting from antiwar demonstrations, a Quantico-based battalion moves to the Anacostia Naval Air Station. The 6th Marines goes on six-hour alert for possible deployment to the area.

14 May
Training
The 3rd Marine Division begins a three-week operation, Exotic Dancer III, along the coastal areas of North Carolina. Over 60,00 troops from all branches of the armed forces are involved.

31 May
Peru
HMM-365 and a company of 1/2 are ordered to South America to conduct disaster relief operations after an earthquake. They proceed there on *Guam* (LPH-9). For 11 days Marines and sailors deliver food and medical supplies and evacuate the injured.

11 June
Vietnam
Communist forces begin a series of attacks, the largest since the Tet Offensive, against Marine Combined Action Program units and pacified villages in I Corps Zone. In some cases, the enemy kills numerous civilians in undefended villages.

18 June
Aviation
A Marine Corps KC-130 Hercules and its aircrew begin supporting the Navy's Blue Angels flight demonstration team.

24 June
Vietnam
The Senate repeals the Gulf of Tonkin Resolution by the vote of 81 to 10.

25 June
Force Structure
Marine Barracks Argentia, Newfoundland, is deactivated. Marines had manned this post continuously since January 1941.

30 June
Vietnam
The 1st Marine Division has had few major contacts in the first six months of the year. During the period it has killed 3,955 enemy at a cost of 283 Marines dead and 2,537 wounded.
Force Structure
VMFA-542 is deactivated at EL Toro, while the 3rd Anti-tank Battalion is deactivated at Camp Pendleton.
Manpower
The strength of the Marine Corps on active duty is 24,941 officers and 234,796 enlisted.

3 July
Vietnam
Vietnamese militia forces supported by Marine CAP units, helicopter gunships, and artillery defeat Communist attacks on several villages south of Quang Tri City. The allies lose 16 dead and six missing, while killing 135 enemy.

9 July
Vietnam
The fourth round of U.S. troop withdrawals begins. It will include 17,021 Marines, with the major units being the 7th Marines, 3/11, MAG-13, VMA(AW)-242, VMFA-122 and 314, HMM-161, and VMCJ-1.

15 July
Vietnam
Nearly 5,000 South Vietnamese troops begin a major sweep of NVA base camps west of Da Nang. Marine helicopters land the assault troops and their U.S. advisors. Elements of the 5th Marines begin Operation Barren Green to deny the corn harvest in the Arizona Territory to the enemy. The latter ends on 27 July, after Marine forces kill 18 enemy and destroy 10,000 pounds of grain.

16 July
Operation Pickens Forest
Remaining elements of the 7th Marines begin a search and clear operation southwest of Da Nang and soon uncover large food caches hidden by the enemy. The operation ends on 24 August and accounts for 99 enemy killed at a cost of four Marines dead and 51 wounded.

31 July
Force Structure
The 2nd Antitank Battalion is deactivated at Camp Lejeune.

8–13 August
Marksmanship
Marine shooters take 12 of 17 events during the 9th Annual Interservice Rifle Championships held at Quantico.

17 August
Training
Exercise High Descent is held at Camp Pendleton as a climax to two weeks of annual training for more than 19,000 reservists of 4th MAW and 4th Marine Division.

20 August
Manpower
A DOD study indicates that about 30 percent of U.S. service personnel have used marijuana or other illegal drugs.

22 August
Marksmanship
Marine individual and team shooters win 20 out of 24 matches in the National Rifle and Pistol Championships at Camp Perry, Ohio. For the first time in 14 years, the Marines win both the National Trophy Rifle and National Trophy Pistol matches.

27 August
Force Structure
3rd Force Reconnaissance Company is deactivated.

31 August
Operation Imperial Lake
Just after midnight, the 11th Marines opens the operation with one of the largest bombardments in its history: 13,488 rounds fired from 10 batteries for more than six hours on 53 selected targets in the Que Son Mountains. After an additional two

Opposite: *1/4 during Operation Scotland II. (National Archives)*

Above: *PFC Rex L. Brochet takes a break on patrol. (National Archives)*

Right: *A-4M Skyhawks of VMA-311. (National Archives)*

Left: *Marine mortarmen on a search and clear operation, June 1970. (National Archives)*

Opposite: *Mike Company, 3/3 near the DMZ in September 1969. (National Archives)*

hours of air strikes, elements of the 7th Marines move in to search for enemy forces and base camps. This operation will continue until the 1st Marine Division leaves Vietnam in 1971.

10 September
Technology
The Marine Corps Tactical Systems Support Activity is activated at Camp Pendleton. The unit will test, evaluate, and provide programming support for all the tactical systems and related equipment within the Marine Corps.

11 September
Jordan
Elements of the Sixth Fleet move into the eastern Mediterranean for possible evacuation of airline passengers in planes hijacked by Palestinian guerrillas and flown to Jordan.

13 September
Civil Support
President Nixon directs the military services to furnish 800 personnel (including 90 Marines) for Operation Grid Square, providing security for U.S. international passenger flights.

15 September
New York
A Navy-Marine Corps recruiting station in the Bronx was damaged by a bomb explosion for which the radical Weathermen group reportedly claimed responsibility.

18–21 September
Operation Catawba Falls
The 11th Marines begins the operation with 76 helicopters lifting 14 artillery pieces and 4.2-inch mortars and 10,000 shells onto a remote mountain top and turning it overnight into Fire Support Base Dagger. Four days of bombardment and bombing sorties are intended to deceive the enemy into preparing for a ground assault, while Marine ground forces redeploy unmolested near Da Nang.

19 September
Jordan
After the Jordanian government begins to suppress Palestinian armed groups in the country, the U.S. dispatches 8th MAB to the Mediterranean, where it will join up with BLT 2/2. 8th MAB arrives in the area on 2 October and remains until the end of the month. VMA-331 is also deployed on board *Independence* (CVA-62) during the crisis.

21 September
Vietnam
The Combined Action Force headquarters in Chu Lai is deactivated. The remaining CAP units, under 2nd Combined Action Group, now consist of 600 Marines and corpsmen and operate solely in Quang Nam Province.

1 October
Vietnam
The number of Marines in country has fallen to 29,600.

7 October
Chu Lai
The Marines turn over the base to the U.S. Army.
Manpower
The Department of the Navy tells a special House Armed Services Military subcommittee that more than 7,000 Marines and sailors will probably be discharged from the service in 1970 for drug violations.

12 October
Heritage
Retired Master Sergeant Paul Woyshner dies at the age of 75. Creator of many early recruiting posters, he coined the motto "Once a Marine, Always a Marine" for the Marine Corps League in 1917.

15 October
An Hoa
The Marines turn over An Hoa Combat Base to the South Vietnamese.

15–30 October
Training
Both U.S. and Philippine Marines conduct Exercise Fortress Light in the Philippines.

21 October
Philippines
SLF Alpha (primarily HMM-164) assists in disaster relief operations in the wake of Typhoon Joan.

30 October
Force Structure
The last of the Marine Corps amphibious artillery units is deactivated when the 4th Armored Amphibian Company furls its flag. Activated in 1952, the company was the only remaining one of its kind.

13 November
Force Structure
HMM-265 is deactivated at El Toro.

18 November
Mishap
A CH-46 helicopter crashes into a mountain near Da Nang, killing 15 Marines.

19 November
Training
The Marine Corps announces that it will resume its annual rifle squad competition at Quantico beginning in September 1971. The competition was discontinued in 1965 due to commitments in Vietnam.

20 November
Vietnam
A U.S. joint force (Army, Air Force, and Navy) conducts a heliborne raid at Son Tay, about 23 miles west of Hanoi, in an unsuccessful attempt to free American prisoners of war. The men had been moved a few weeks prior to the operation.

21 November
Force Structure
The Seventh Fleet's Special Landing Force Alpha is redesignated 31st Marine Amphibious Unit (MAU). Although the MAU (or MEU) designation has been used occasionally before, it now becomes the formal title for any Marine unit afloat built around a BLT and a helicopter squadron.

1 December
Force Structure
The 1st LAAM Battalion is deactivated.

15 December
Diego Garcia
The State Department announces that the United States will build a $19 million naval communications facility on the Indian Ocean island of Diego Garcia, a British possession.
Force Structure
MAG-33 is deactivated at El Toro.

22 December
Civil Support
The first military personnel are released from duty with Operation Grid Square.

24 December
Commanders
Lieutenant General Donn J. Robertson replaces Lieutenant General McCutcheon as commander of III MAF.

31 December
Operation Imperial Lake
In this ongoing campaign, the 1st Marine Division has lost 22 dead and 158 wounded while killing 196 enemy.
Manpower
The active-duty strength of the Marine Corps is 231,667, of which 25,394 Marines are in Vietnam. Marine casualties in Vietnam for the year total 535 killed and 4,278 wounded.

1971

4 January
Manpower
General Chapman announces that the Corps will not relax conduct and appearance standards but will adhere to its traditional rules: "We've decided that the Corps is going to be leaner, tougher, more ready, more disciplined and more professional than ever before."

6 January
Malaysia
After 100 inches of rain causes severe flooding, 31st MAU moves toward the Gulf of Thailand for possible disaster relief operations. It arrives on the 10th and remains in the area until the 25th.
Technology
The Marine Corps receives the first of its newest jets, the AV-8A Harrier.
Vietnam
Secretary of Defense Laird states that the U.S. program of Vietnamization is running ahead of schedule and that the combat mission of American troops would end by mid-summer.

Left: *An M60 team fires on a tree line in the Arizona territory. (National Archives)*

Opposite: *VMF(AW)-312 provides close air support in 1966. (National Archives)*

11 January
Operation Upsher Stream
1/1 and reconnaissance teams conduct search and destroy missions to deter rocket attacks on Da Nang. The operation lasts through 29 March, but results in minimal contact.

13 January
Vietnam
The sixth round of U.S. troop withdrawals begins. The number of Marines in Vietnam will be reduced by 12,198. The main units to depart will be the headquarters elements of both 1st Marine Division and 1st MAW, plus the 5th Marines, elements of the 11th Marines, VMFA-115, HMM-263, HMM-364, HML-167, and VMO-2.

19 January
Vietnam
While in night defense positions south of Hoi An, G Company 2/5 drives off a ground attack, killing 12 of the enemy.

20 January
Technology
The Navy announces that it will reduce the number of new amphibious assault ships of the LHA class from nine to five.

20–21 January
Vietnam
Company B, 1/1 loses 11 Marines wounded due to booby traps during Operation Upsher Stream. A CH-46 from HMM-463 on a medevac mission is hit by enemy ground fire and crashes, killing four Marines and a corpsman and wounding 16.
Cambodia
DOD reveals that Marine helicopters on *Iwo Jima* and *Cleveland* (LPD-7) in the Gulf of Siam are supporting South Vietnamese and Cambodian troops operating in Cambodia.

28 January
Manpower
President Nixon asks for a two-year extension of the draft and proposes a 50 percent pay raise for new recruits to achieve his goal of an all-volunteer military and an end to the draft by the mid-1970s.

30 January
Vietnam
South Vietnamese and U.S. Army forces begin Operation Lam Son 719 in Quang Tri Province.

2 February
Turkey
Ships of the Sixth Fleet set sail from Ismir, cutting short a scheduled visit, after anti-American demonstrations and incidents.

3 February
Manpower
The Marine Corps convenes a board to determine which lieutenant colonels, majors, and captains should be released from active duty to meet manpower reduction requirements.

7 February
Laos
In an expansion of Lam Son 719, South Vietnamese forces, supported by U.S. helicopters, fixed-wing aircraft, and artillery fire, enter Laotian territory to strike at Communist base camps. During the operation, VMA-311, VMA(AW)-225, and VMFA-115 fly 950 sorties into Laos. HMH-463, supported by the gunships of HML-367, flies 2,992 sorties during the operation and loses a CH-53 helicopter in Laos.

12 February
Vietnam
The 31st MAU takes station off the coast of North Vietnam, 50 miles east of Vinh. It remains there until 6 March to divert North Vietnamese troops during Lam Son 719.

16 February
Training
The Staff NCO Academy is officially opened at Quantico.

18 February
Vietnam
A CH-53D explodes in flight and crashes northeast of Phu Bai. All seven Marines on board are killed. Four AH-1J Sea Cobras arrive in Vietnam for combat evaluation and are assigned to HML-367.

27 February
Laos
VMA-311 Skyhawks destroy three NVA PT-76 amphibious tanks attacking a South Vietnamese firebase.

28 February
Force Structure
HMM-365 is deactivated at New River.

March
Vietnam
Marine aircraft fly 20,435 combat sorties during the month, nearly 1,200 by fixed-wing aircraft, including 160 into North Vietnam.

5 March
Manpower
Secretary of Defense Laird announces a major new program that will require every person entering the armed services to attend classes in race relations.

18 March
Manpower
Navy Secretary Chafee testifies before a Senate committee: "I would be less than candid were I to imply that we have the drug problem fully under control" in the Navy and Marine Corps. The secretary also indicated that racial tensions were growing within the two services.

30 March
Vietnam
The Marine Corps Reserve Civic Action Fund closes out. Marines and friends of the Corps had funneled $4,784,000 worth of help to the South Vietnamese people through this program.

7 April
Technology
The first Bell UH-1N twin-engine Huey is delivered to HMA-269 at New River.

8 April
Vietnam
Operation Lam Son 719 is terminated. Although the operation began in Quang Tri, the heaviest fighting occurred in Savannakhet Province, Laos. The operation had gone well until the planned withdrawal turned chaotic and many heavy weapons were abandoned.

Left: *Exiting a CH-53 on Charley Ridge. (National Archives)*

Opposite: *PFC Terry Perrigo reacts to enemy fire while on patrol. (National Archives)*

13 April
Vietnam
Defense Secretary Laird reaffirms that the U.S. ground combat role would end this summer, but that air and naval forces would remain indefinitely.
Force Structure
HMM-364 is deactivated at Santa Ana, California.

14 April
Vietnam
III MAF relocates to Okinawa. 3rd MAB is activated at Da Nang to command remaining Marine units in country. The MAB has 15,516 Marines and Navy personnel, concentrated mainly in the 1st Marines, 1/11, MAG-11, and MAG-16.
Force Structure
5th MAB is deactivated at Camp Pendleton and the 1st Marine Division assumes control of all ground forces there.

15 April
Vietnam
The CUPP program comes to an end after 18 months. During that time it had accounted for 578 enemy killed at a cost of 46 Marines dead.

16 April
Force Structure
Three AV-8A Harriers arrive at Beaufort and VMA-513 is activated to receive them, thus becoming the first Harrier squadron in the Corps.

23 April
Caribbean
A battalion landing team from Camp Lejuene rushes to sea ahead of schedule during Operation Exotic Dancer IV as part of a show of force designed to discourage Cuba from taking advantage of the political instability in Haiti following the death of president Francois Duvalier.

1 May
Civil Support
Marines from Quantico, Marine Barracks 8th and I, and Camp Lejeune deploy to Washington, D.C., to assist local authorities in controlling antiwar demonstrations. They remain there until 7 May.

7 May
Vietnam
3rd MAB ceases ground and fixed-wing combat operations.

11 May
Vietnam
The 2nd Combined Action Group is deactivated, bringing the CAP program to an end.

27 June
Vietnam
3rd MAB is deactivated as the last Marine units depart the country. There are 547 advisors and other Marines still serving in Vietnam, along with more than 240,000 other U.S. troops.

30 June
Manpower
The strength of the Marine Corps on active duty is 21,765 officers and 190,604 enlisted.
1 July
Force Structure
HMA-269 is commissioned at New River.

9 July
Manpower
The Secretary of the Navy grants exemption from disciplinary action and discharge under other than honorable conditions to those members of the Navy and Marine Corps who make voluntary disclosure of their illegal drug usage or possession.

9–10 July
Heritage
The first reunion of the WWII Navajo Code Talkers is held in Arizona.

15 July
Force Structure
MAG-56 is deactivated in southern California.

20 July
Manpower
The Cleveland Plain Dealer reports that the Marine Corps has the highest desertion rate of all the services, 59.6 men per 1,000.

6 August
Manpower
CMC's Advisory Committee for Minority Affairs holds its first meeting. Composed of 12 volunteer civilian leaders from across the country, its mission is to help ease racial tensions within the Corps and help recruit minority personnel.

7–12 August
Marksmanship
Marine shooters win 12 of 13 individual matches, the Interservice Rifle Team match, and the 1000-yard team match at the 10th Annual Interservice Rifle Championships.

11 August
Bases
The Secretary of the Navy issued a directive to Navy and Marine Corps base commanders instructing them to advise local government officials, community leaders, and private groups that failure to enforce open-housing laws would be a factor in any future decision to close bases.

13 August
Vietnam
The USMC Night Observation Gunship System detachment, flying two specially adapted OV-10s, completes the last of 207 missions conducted to test an integrated 20mm gun and an infrared target acquisition system.

26 August
Technology
The first production vehicle of the Corps' newest assault amphibian vehicle, the LVTP7, is delivered to the Corps. It hauls 25 troops and has a water-jet drive capable of pushing it through the ocean at 8.4 mph.

Left: *Marines rush to unload a CH-46 bringing in supplies. (National Archives)*

Opposite: *A Marine of India Company, 3/1, on patrol in 1969. (National Archives)*

28 August
Manpower
The Naval Training Center and the Marine Recruit Depot in San Diego announce they will begin testing new recruits for drug use.

19 September
Mishap
Two Marine recruits die within 12 hours of each other after apparently unrelated training exercises at Parris Island.

22 September
Manpower
The Marine Corps Human Relations Instructors School is inaugurated. Human relations training will be given to Marines of all ranks.

25–29 September
Okinawa
1st MAW aircraft provide disaster relief in the southern Ryukyus after the islands were hit by Typhoon Bess.

30 September
Force Structure
HMA-169, an attack helicopter squadron, is activated at Camp Pendleton.

9–22 October
Training
Exercise Deep Furrow, a joint and combined NATO exercise, includes amphibious landings in Turkey by Marines and forces from Great Britain and Italy.

11 October
Heritage
Marine Corps icon Lieutenant General Lewis B. "Chesty" Puller dies in Hampton, Virginia, at the age of 73.

3 November
Aviation
VMA-214 completes qualifications on board *Hancock* (CVA-19), the first time since the beginning of the Vietnam conflict that a Marine jet squadron has operated on board a carrier on the west coast.

10 November
Okinawa
The U.S. Senate approves a treaty to return Okinawa to Japan. After reversion, the U.S. would maintain military bases on Okinawa on the same basis as it now does on the Japanese home islands, in accordance with the U.S.-Japanese Mutual Security Treaty.

10 December
Indian Ocean
Elements of Seventh Fleet, including part of 31st MAU, depart Vietnamese waters, heading toward the Indian Ocean for possible rescue of American citizens as a result of the war between India and Pakistan. The ships will remain in the area through 7 January 1972.

14 December
Vietnam
VMA(AW)-224 deploys on board *Coral Sea* (CVA-43) on Yankee Station for potential aerial action against North Vietnam.

20 December
Mishap
Four Marines are killed when their helicopter crashes while on a flight from *Tripoli* (LPH-10) in the Bay of Bengal.

21 December
Aviation
The Marine Corps authorizes a Civilian Pilot Training program designed to attract more applicants and upgrade the quality of aviation students in the Platoon Leader Class commissioning program.

26 December
Vietnam
President Nixon orders a temporary resumption of bombing of North Vietnam as peace talks stall. VMA(AW)-224 participates in these aerial raids. There are 156,800 American troops in South Vietnam.

30 December
Force Structure
VMFA-334 is deactivated at El Toro.

31 December
Vietnam
Marine casualties during the year totaled 41 dead and 476 wounded.
Commandants
General Chapman retires and is replaced by General Robert E. Cushman, Jr., the 25th Commandant of the Marine Corps.

1972

1 January
Manpower
Reenlistment standards are raised to require a high school diploma or its equivalent.

5 January
Civil Support
Marine Air Control Squadron 7 is tasked to activate a radar site near Tucson, Arizona, in support of the Bureau of Custom's Operation Grasscatcher, an

Above: *EA-6 in a shelter at Da Nang. (National Archives)*

Left: *A 105mm howitzer at Khe Sanh. (National Archives)*

Opposite: *Khe Sanh Valley 1968. (National Archives)*

effort to detect and intercept illegal air traffic crossing the border with Mexico. Marines participate in the operation until 28 February.

12 January
Force Structure
After an 18-month hiatus, VMA-542 is reactivated at Beaufort and equipped with Harriers.

14 January
Manpower
DOD announces manpower cuts that will reduce military strength to its lowest level since 1951. Marine Corps strength will drop to 193,000.

7–27 January
Training
Elements of the 2nd Marine Division and 2nd MAW joined naval forces of the Atlantic Fleet in cold weather landing operations at Reid State Park on the coast of Maine in Exercise Snowy Beach.

8 February
Technology
VMA-513 conducts initial sea tests of the AV-8A Harrier on *Guam*.

10 March
Vietnam
The 101st Airborne Division, the last U.S. combat division in Vietnam, departs the country.

14 March
Vietnam
VMA(AW)-224 and *Coral Sea* depart Yankee Station.

23 March
Vietnam
The United States suspends the Paris peace talks following a long period of Communist intransigence.

30 March
Vietnam
North Vietnam launches its long-planned conventional assault on the South. Soon dubbed the Easter Offensive, it involves 14 divisions, 26 separate regiments, and hundreds of tanks and artillery pieces. It has three major prongs directed against Quang Tri

in the north, Pleiku in central South Vietnam, and the area around Saigon in the deep south. The campaign initially makes significant gains.

1 April
Vietnam
31st MAU and BLT Bravo (BLT 1/9) and their respective amphibious ready groups (ARGs) deploy off the coast of Vietnam to standby to evacuate American military advisors if necessary.
Force Structure
HMA-369 is activated at Futema, Okinawa.

2 April
Dong Ha
Captain John W. Ripley, a Marine advisor, blows up a bridge over the Cua Viet River in the face of intense enemy fire and a column of tanks. His actions stall a major Communist drive south on Route 1.

6 April
Vietnam
MAG-15 and more than two dozen F-4s of VMFA-115 and 232 deploy from Iwakuni to Da Nang to provide close air support to the South Vietnamese. A detachment of VMCJ-1 flying from Cubi Point also participates in aerial combat operations.

7 April
Vietnam
U.S. aircraft resume bombing operations against targets in North Vietnam.

8 April
Vietnam
The headquarters of the 9th MAB arrives in the Tonkin Gulf to command Marine amphibious forces in the waters off Vietnam.

11 April
Vietnam
33rd MAU is activated on board ARG Charlie with BLT 2/4 and HMM-165. BLT 2/9 is assigned to ARG Delta. When deployed with 31st MAU and BLT Bravo, this is the largest wartime deployment of Marine amphibious forces since the Korean War.

14 April
Vietnam
A dozen F-4s of VMFA-212 arrive in Da Nang from Kaneohe, Hawaii.

15 April
Vietnam
The United States conducts its first bombing missions against Hanoi and Haiphong in North Vietnam since 1968.

27 April
Vietnam
Peace talks resume in Paris between the United States, South Vietnam, and the Communists, but are suspended again on 4 May.

1 May
Vietnam
Quang Tri City falls to the NVA.
Force Structure
MAG-29 is activated as a helicopter group at New River.

8 May
Vietnam
American aircraft mine the main harbors of North Vietnam, including Haiphong.

12 May
Vietnam
HMM-164 lifts Vietnamese Marines for a raid behind NVA lines near Hue City.

13 May
Training
In the final stages of a NATO exercise, U.S., British, and Greek Marines conduct an amphibious landing in southern Greece.

15 May
Okinawa
The United States ends 27 years of American administration and transfers control of the Ryuku Islands back to Japan.

16–25 May
Training
Operation Exotic Dancer V, designed to test joint tactical doctrine, takes place in the Carolinas. Among the 50,000 personnel conducting amphibious and airborne operations are elements of II MAF, 2nd Marine Division, and 2nd MAW.

17 May
Vietnam
MAG-12 (Forward), 32 A-4s of VMA-211 and 311, and supporting units arrive at Bien Hoa Airbase near Saigon from Iwakuni.

Opposite: *Operation Meade River. (National Archives)*

Right: *HMM-265 CH-46. (National Archives)*

Below: *3/1 in Elephant Valley. (National Archives)*

June
Civil Support
Marine reserve units provide disaster relief following severe floods in Pennsylvania's Wyoming Valley as a result of Hurricane Agnes.

1 June
Manpower
Secretary of Defense Laird announces that the Marine Corps and Army would temporarily pay a $1,500 bonus for a four-year enlistment in a ground combat speciality. This is a test to aid in achieving the goal of an all-volunteer military.

15 June
Force Structure
VMA(AW)-225 is deactivated at El Toro.

16 June
Vietnam
The first Marine F-4s arrive at Nam Phong, Thailand, as part of a re-deployment of combat aircraft from South Vietnam. VMFA-115 flew the first Marine combat mission out of Nam Phong the next day.

20 June
Vietnam
VMA-533 and its A-6 Intruders begin arriving at Nam Phong from Iwakuni.

22 June
Vietnam
HMA-369, with seven AH-1J Cobras on board *Denver* (LPD-9), begins flying armed reconnaissance missions to interdict water-borne logistics craft along the coast of North Vietnam. These operations continue until 15 January 1973.

27 June
Vietnam
31st and 33rd MAUs conduct an amphibious feint off the coast north of the Cua Viet River to divert NVA forces resisting the South Vietnamese counteroffensive.

28 June
Vietnam
South Vietnamese forces begin a counteroffensive to drive back the NVA in the former I Corps Zone.

29 June
Vietnam
The U.S. Army's 196th Infantry Brigade, the last American ground combat force in country, departs Vietnam. Helicopters of 9th MAB lift two Vietnamese battalions into the rear of enemy lines south of Quang Tri City. Naval gunfire and Marine helicopters continue providing support to the South Vietnamese in the coming weeks.

30 June
Manpower
The strength of the Marine Corps on active duty is 19,843 officers and 178,395 enlisted.

8 July
Civil Support
2/6 is deployed to Homestead Air Force Base, Florida, for potential duty controlling disturbances during the Democratic Party national convention.

13 July
Vietnam
The Paris peace talks resume.

14 July
Vietnam
VMFA-333, embarked on *America* (CVA-66), begins flying combat missions when the carrier arrives off Vietnam.

22 July
Philippines
Elements of 9th MAB assist in flood relief operations. The effort lasts through 15 August.

24 July
Force Structure
The headquarters of 4th MAB is activated at

Above: *HMM-262 CH-46 in Que Son Mountains, December 1970. (National Archives)*

Right: *F Company, 2/7, trading fire with the enemy in Happy Valley. (National Archives)*

Right: *Bravo Company, 1/4, during Operation Scotland I in December 1969. (National Archives)*

Norfolk, Virginia, to provide a command element for any contingency force sized between a MAU and a MAF.

31 July
Manpower
Commandant Cushman orders an end to "voluntary segregation" by race in living quarters at Marine Corps installations and on board ships.

12 August
Vietnam
Captain Larry G. Richard, an exchange pilot with the Air Force's 58th Tactical Fighter Squadron, downs a MIG-21 northeast of Hanoi. He is the second Marine pilot to claim an aerial victory in the war.

19 August
Civil Support
2/6 is again assigned to civil disturbance duty, this time in conjunction with the upcoming Republican Party national convention.

26 August
Vietnam
An F-4J Phantom of VMFA-232 is shot down by a MIG 70 miles southwest of Hanoi.

28 August
Manpower
President Nixon announces that there will be no draft calls after 30 June 1973.

1 September
Force Structure
MAG-43 is merged into MAG-49.

11 September
Vietnam
A VMFA-333 F-4 Phantom from *America* engages two MIG-21s, destroying one and damaging the other. It was the first MIG kill during the Vietnam War by an all Marine Corps team (Major Lee Lasseter and Captain John Cummings), and only the third overall.

11–30 September
Training
For the first time Reserve Marines participate in a NATO training exercise, Strong Express in Norway. This also marks the first overseas deployment of the new LVTP-7 amphibian assault vehicle.

15 September
Force Structure
HML-268 is activated at New River.

16 September
Vietnam
South Vietnamese Marines recapture Quang Tri City, which had been occupied by the NVA for 138 days.
Aviation
DOD reports that Navy and Marine aviators recorded their lowest accident rate in history in 1971.

24 October
Vietnam
The United States halts bombing attacks north of the 20th parallel due to progress in peace talks.

1 November
Force Structure
VMA-542 is activated at Beaufort.

1 December
Vietnam
The USMACV announces that during the last week of November no Americans died in Vietnam, the first week without fatalities there since January 1965.

18 December
Vietnam
Following another stalemate in peace talks, the United States launches Operation Linebacker II, a heavy aerial bombardment of North Vietnam that dwarfs any prior aerial campaign against the North. The main targets are in Hanoi and Haiphong. The operation lasts until 29 December.

27 December
Heritage
The Commandant's House and Marine Barracks 8th and I are placed on the National Register of Historic Places.

31 December
Vietnam
American troop strength totals 24,200 personnel.
Force Structure
VMGR-216 (a fighter and attack squadron until 1962) is deactivated.

1973

4 January
Manpower
Due to the Supreme Court's recent upholding of a lower court decision, Secretary of Defense Laird orders an end to compulsory attendance at religious services at military academies and elsewhere in the armed services.

15 January
Vietnam
Citing progress made in the Paris negotiations, President Nixon suspends all bombing, mining, shelling, and other offensive actions throughout North Vietnam.

19 January
Civil Support
A Marine battalion from Camp Lejeune arrives at Naval Air Station Anacostia to provide assistance with riot control if needed during the upcoming presidential inaugural.

23 January
Vietnam
President Nixon announces that the United States has reached an agreement in Paris, "to end the war and bring peace with honor in Vietnam." Under terms of the accord, all U.S. prisoners of war will

be released and the remaining 23,700 American personnel in South Vietnam will be withdrawn within 60 days.

27 January
Manpower
Secretary of Defense Melvin Laird declares that peace in Vietnam allows DOD to begin a complete reliance on voluntary enlistment immediately.

Opposite, top: *Radioman on patrol. (National Archives)*

Opposite, bottom: *Manhandling a 105mm howitzer into position. (National Archives)*

Above: *A former prisoner of war, Marine Captain James V. DiBernardo comes home on 8 March 1973. (National Archives)*

Right: *Mortarmen of Hotel Company, 3/4, near Cam Lo. (National Archives)*

28 January
Vietnam
The cease fire goes into effect, with NVA forces still occupying enclaves in South Vietnam. Marine casualties during and after the Easter Offensive total 18 killed, 68 wounded, and 21 missing.

30 January
Vietnam
MAG-12 departs Bien Hoa for Iwakuni, Japan.

31 January
Sergeants Major
Sergeant Major Clinton A. Puckett succeeds Sergeant Major Dailey as the sixth Sergeant Major of the Marine Corps.

1 February
Manpower
The last four enlisted naval aviation pilots (NAPs) on active duty retire from the Marine Corps, bringing to an end a program that stretched back to 1923. The Defense Department announces a tightening of military disability standards to "cut substantially" the number of officers leaving the services with disabilities.

9 February
Force Structure
9th MAB is deactivated, except for its headquarters element, which remains in existence as a deployable command element within III MAF.

12 February
Vietnam
The first 116 American prisoners of war released by North Vietnam arrive at Clark Air Force Base in the Philippines. This group includes four of the 26 Marines held in captivity by Communist forces.

16 February
Vietnam
The Marine Corps ends its advisory program with the Vietnamese Marines and the last two advisors depart Quang Tri City.

22 February
Laos
Following implementation of a ceasefire between Communist and non-Communist forces in Laos, the United States declares that it will discontinue all acts of force in that country.

23 February
Vietnam
Operation End Sweep, the Navy/Marine Corps minesweeping of North Vietnamese harbors and coastal waterways, begins. HMM-164 and 165 and HMH-463 assist in the effort. The operation continues through 18 July.

25 February
Cambodia
MAG-15, still based in Nam Phong, Thailand, begins flying combat sorties in support of Cambodian forces fighting Communist forces.

4 March
Vietnam
The second group of American POWs leaves Hanoi under terms of the Paris accords.

14 March
Vietnam
Sub Unit One, a detachment of 1st ANGLICO that has been providing support to South Vietnamese forces, is the last Marine unit to depart Vietnam.

18 March
Vietnam
A CH-53D of HMH-463 crashes into the water approximately 25 kilometers southeast of Haiphong while towing minesweeping gear. All personnel are rescued.

29 March
Vietnam
USMACV shuts down, the departure of all U.S. forces from South Vietnam is complete, and North Vietnam releases the last group of American POWs.

29–31 March
Tunisia
Helicopters of HMH-362 participate in disaster relief operations near Tunis.

April
Nicaragua
The U.S. Embassy in Managua is destroyed in an earthquake. Six Marine guards aid in rescue efforts and secure the compound.

5 April
Italy
A bomb severely damages the living quarters of the 13 Marines who guard the U.S. Embassy in Rome. There are no injuries.

26 April
Manpower
DOD increases the combat arms enlistment bonus for the Army and Marine Corps from $1,500 to $2,500.

14 May
Manpower
The Supreme Court rules that female members of the armed services are entitled to the same dependency benefits for their husbands as servicemen have always received for their wives.

29 May
Vietnam
Air Force Colonel Theodore W. Guy files charges against five Army and three Marine enlisted men, accusing them of misconduct while they were prisoners of war. The charges against the Marines are subsequently dismissed by the Secretary of the Navy.

25 June
Vietnam
Rear Admiral James B. Stockdale, a former prisoner of war, files charges against two other former prisoners, a Navy captain and a Marine lieutenant colonel. Although the Secretary of the Navy later dismisses the charges, he issues letters of censure and both officers retire.

Opposite: *A 2/9 81mm mortar crew near Vandegrift Combat Base. (National Archives)*

Right: *"Valor at Hue," Tom Freeman, courtesy of U.S. Naval Institute and U.S. Naval Academy Museum*

26 June
China
Marines raise the American flag over the U.S. liaison office in Peking during its formal opening following the establishment of diplomatic relations between the United States and Communist China.

30 June
Manpower
The strength of the Marine Corps on active duty is 19,282 officers and 176,816 enlisted.

31 July
Cuba
2/8 departs Guantanamo Bay and is relieved by a reinforced rifle company, marking the first reductions in security force requirements at the naval base since the 1960s.
Force Structure
After a hiatus of 11 months, VMA-231 is reactivated at Cherry Point and equipped with Harriers.

14 August
Indochina
Congress decrees the cessation of all funding for military operations in Southeast Asia. Marine air operations launched from Nam Phong, Thailand, against Cambodia, come to an end. MAG-15 begins to withdraw from Thailand on 25 August.

September
Manpower
The first selectees of the Marine Corps Enlisted Commissioning Education Program begin their study in September, with male Marines attending The Citadel and women Marines at the University of Washington, Seattle.

10–21 September
Training
Australia, Canada, New Zealand, and the United States conduct RimPac-73, a combined naval exercise in the Hawaiian Islands.

25 September
Space
Marine Lieutenant Colonel Jack R. Lousma pilots the record breaking Skylab II mission, which had begun on 28 July and ends this date setting a mark with 59 days in space.

17 October
Middle East
Arab nations institute an oil embargo against countries supporting Israel as it battles Egypt and Syria following their surprise attack on 6 October. The United States bears the brunt of the embargo as it rushes arms to Israel.

25 October
Middle East
U.S. forces world wide are placed on heightened alert following a Soviet threat to send troops to the Middle East. Later in the day tensions are reduced as an Arab-Israeli ceasefire takes hold. The alert is cancelled a few days later. 4th MAB, composed of BLTs 2/6 and 3/6 and HMM-261 and 264, is deployed in the Mediterranean during this time.

9 November
Department of Defense
The armed services implement strict energy conservation measures in response to shortages arising from the Arab oil embargo.

14 November
Technology
The Marine Corps adopts the M203 grenade launcher, which is attached under an M-16. One man in each fire team will now carry this 40mm weapon and double as a rifleman and grenadier.

16 November
Space
A new Skylab III team, commanded by Marine Lieutenant Colonel Gerald P. Carr, blasts off from the Kennedy Space Center atop the Saturn 1B rocket, for a 56-day mission.

1 December
Technology
The Navy launches *Tarawa* (LHA-1), the first general purpose amphibious assault ship.

5 December
Manpower
The Marine Corps becomes the last of the services to change its regulations in order to allow women to command units made up mostly of men.

1974

11 February
Reserve
Citing recent court decisions, Commandant Cushman announces that the Corps will permit reservists to wear short-hair wigs while drilling on weekends. Cushman said the prohibition on wigs was dropped because it was "no longer legally tenable," but that the decision "was not prompted by a desire to liberalize the Marine Corps standards of appearance and personal conduct."

Opposite, top: *UH-1E door gunner. (National Archives)*

Opposite, bottom: *"Roost at Eversharp Charlie," Maj A. M. Leahy, USCMR, Marine Corps Art Collection*

Above: *"Marble Mountain Patrol," John Groth, Marine Corps Art Collection*

Left: *Inside a CH-53. (National Archives)*

Below: *A Marine escorts a Vietnamese pilot and his family after their landing on* Hancock *in April 1975. (National Archives)*

14 February
Technology
Quantico and Camp Butler, Okinawa, are the first Marine bases to receive an innovative rifle range system known as SARTS (Small Arms Remote Target System).

1 March
Technology
The CH-53E makes its initial flight. The three-engine helicopter boasts twice the lift of the CH-53D.
Manpower
The Marine Corps selects 13 women Marines to be assigned billets in the 2nd MAW, Cherry Point, and the 1st Marine Division, Camp Pendleton. Women can now fill rear-echelon billets within FMF.

26 March
Aviation
DOD officials report that more than 5,000 Navy, Marine, and Air Force aircraft were not operationally ready because of shortages in spare parts and overdue maintenance.

30 June
Vietnam
The Marine Security Guard unit at the Saigon embassy is reduced from 174 to 57.
Bases
The Naval Disciplinary Command, Portsmouth, New Hampshire, is deactivated. Marines serving long sentences are transferred to the Army Disciplinary Barracks, Fort Leavenworth, Kansas.
Manpower
The strength of the Marine Corps on active duty is 18,740 officers and 170,062 enlisted.

July
Australia
33rd MAU participates in the largest peacetime military maneuver ever staged in Australia.

Approximately 2,000 Marines joined elements of the U.S. Navy and Army, as well as forces from Australia, New Zealand, and Great Britain, for land, sea, and air exercises.

1 July
Manpower
The Marine Corps switches to a new aptitude test for recruits, the Armed Services Vocational Aptitude Battery.

22 July
Cyprus
Following a coup and a Turkish invasion of the island, British Royal Navy and U.S. Marine (HMM-262) helicopters evacuate more than 400 citizens of the United States, Britain, and other countries from the British base at Dhekelia in southern Cyprus to *Coronado* (LPD-11), which transported the evacuees to Beirut.

27 July
Mishap
A Marine AV-8A Harrier crashes and burns at an air show in Milwaukee. The pilot survives after ejecting.

13 August
Force Structure
VMA-513 arrives at Iwakuni with 16 AV-8A Harriers. This is the first deployment of a Harrier squadron to the western Pacific.

19 August
Cyprus
Despite the efforts of a 15-man Marine Security Guard detachment, U.S. ambassador Roger P. Davies is murdered during a riot at the embassy in Nicosia.

21–28 August
Philippines
31st MAU helicopters assist in a flood relief effort.

Above: *A Marine holds a Vietnamese child while guarding a refugee ship in March 1975. (National Archives)*

Right: *A squad leader calls in the coordinates for an air strike. (National Archives)*

1975

15 January
Manpower
The Supreme Court reverses an earlier decision by a lower court and by a 5-to-4 vote upholds a law that requires discharge of male officers who are twice passed over for promotion.

27 January
Cambodia
The Communist Khmer Rouge guerrillas surround the capital of Phnom Penh as government forces near collapse.

1 February
Manpower
The Marine Corps raises enlistment standards by placing greater emphasis on the general-technical score of the Armed Services Vocational Aptitude Battery. Sergeant Major Eleanor L. Judge reports to Headquarters Squadron of MCAS Cherry Point, becoming the first woman to be assigned to the top enlisted slot of a predominantly male unit.

23 February
Manpower
DOD announces that two-year enlistments will be eliminated by the end of the current fiscal year, making three-year terms the shortest available.

28 February
Cambodia
31st MAU (BLT 2/4 and HMH-462) deploys to the Gulf of Thailand for a potential non-combatant evacuation operation (NEO) as Communist forces gain the upper hand in Cambodia.

Above: *A recon Marine about to land in an LZ. (National Archives)*

Left: *Marines move away after setting a demolition charge in Quang Tri. (National Archives)*

Right: *An element of the 4th Marines sweeps an area just south of the DMZ in 1969. (National Archives)*

March

The Marine Corps resumes urinalysis testing under a DOD program designed to identify and rehabilitate drug abusers.

5 March
Cambodia

The United States suspends its airlift of military supplies into Cambodia due to intense rocket attacks on the airport. In the Gulf of Thailand 1,500 Americans stand by on a helicopter carrier to hold the airport while U.S. nationals are flown out.

10 March
Vietnam

NVA units launch a large-scale offensive in the Central Highlands of South Vietnam.

17 March
Vietnam

South Vietnam abandons the central highlands provinces of Kontum, Pleiku, and Darlac to the NVA.

Left: *CH-53. (National Archives)*

Below: *A helicopter gunner adjusts the gun mount on a CH-46. (National Archives)*

Opposite: *On* Mayaguez. *(National Archives)*

22 March
Vietnam
HMH-463 at Kaneohe Bay, Hawaii, receives orders to load on board *Hancock* (CVA-19) and prepare for departure to Southeast Asia.

25 March
Vietnam
Hue City falls to an NVA invasion force heading south.

27 March
Vietnam
As the situation deteriorates in South Vietnam, III MAF stands up the Amphibious Evacuation RVN Support Group (BLT 1/4 and HMM-165), which sails soon after from Okinawa.

29 March
Vietnam
The Marine Security Guard detachment at Da Nang assists in the seaborne evacuation of the consulate staff, American citizens, and Vietnamese refugees the day before the city falls to the NVA.

1 April
Cambodia
President Lon Nol flees Phnom Penh for Indonesia with relatives and officials.
Vietnam
The Marine Security Guard detachment and the consulate staff at Nha Trang are withdrawn by helicopter to Saigon.

2 April
Vietnam
Marine security forces are assigned to four civilian merchant ships on charter to the Military Sealift Command as part of the evacuation of South Vietnamese refugees. One ship holds 16,000 people.

4 April
Vietnam
The Amphibious Evacuation RVN Support Group begins assisting refugees fleeing Communist forces in the vicinity of Cam Ranh Bay.

7 April
Vietnam
33rd MAU (BLT 1/9 and HMM-165) is activated in the Philippines.

9 April
Vietnam
NVA units penetrated Saigon's outer defense perimeter 37 miles northeast of the city.

11 April
Cambodia
HMH-463 and *Hancock* arrive in Cambodian waters.

12 April
Cambodia
31st MAU, reinforced by HMH-463, executes Operation Eagle Pull, the heliborne evacuation of American citizens and other third-country nationals from Phnom Penh. BLT 2/4 provides security on the ground as the helicopters of HMH-462 and 463 pull out 287 people (including 84 Americans). There are no casualties, despite enemy fire directed at the landing zone.

17 April
Cambodia
Phnom Penh falls to Khmer Rouge forces, ending the civil war in that country.

19 April
Force Structure
9th MAB, recently activated and consisting of 31st, 33rd, and 35th MAUs, reorganizes in preparation for evacuation operations in Vietnam. MAG-39 is activated on board command ship *Blue Ridge* (LCC-19) to command the air units (HMH-462 and 463, HMM-165, HML-367, and HMA-369), while the BLTs (1/9, 3/9, and 2/4) are consolidated into RLT 4. MAG-39 remains in existence until 12 May.

20 April
Vietnam
Hancock arrives in South Vietnamese waters with HMH-463 on board.

24 April
Civil Support
Marine Barracks Guam participates in setting up and guarding a refugee camp on the island. The camps remain in operation until 30 October.

28 April
Civil Support
Camp Pendleton is designated as a refugee reception center. MAG-13 is assigned to begin building a tent city for some of the 130,000 Vietnamese fleeing Communism. The first of the refugees begins arriving the next day. The camp, holding a maximum of 18,000 people, processes a total of more than 50,000 before it closes on 31 October.

29 April
Vietnam
Prior to dawn, Communist troops launch a fierce rocket attack on Saigon, killing two U.S. Marines and destroying an American C-130 at Tan Son

Nhut Airfield. 9th MAB executes Operation Frequent Wind, the evacuation from Saigon of Americans, other third-country nationals, and some South Vietnamese officials and citizens. With a security force of more than 800 Marines protecting the landing zones and controlling the evacuees, 68 Marine and 10 Air Force helicopters airlift 6,968 people from Saigon in 17 hours. The last Marine helicopter lifted off the roof of the U.S. Embassy at 0753 on 30 April carrying Marine security guards. An AH-1J Cobra and CH-46 Sea Knight crash, with the loss of two Marines dead.

30 April
Vietnam
Saigon falls to the NVA and Vietnam is effectively reunited under Communist rule.

12 May
Cambodia
Communist gunboats seize the U.S. merchant ship SS *Mayaguez* in the Gulf of Thailand. President Ford warns of serious consequences unless the ship and her 40-man crew are released promptly.

14 May
Cambodia
Marines of Company D, 1/4, carried by escort destroyer *Harold E. Holt* (DE-1074), board and retake the deserted *Mayaguez*. Air Force helicopters land elements of BLT 2/9 on Koh Tang Island in the Gulf of Cambodia in an effort to recover the merchant crew, which is not there. The helicopters take heavy ground fire and several are destroyed or heavily damaged. Cambodian forces release the merchant crew and it links up with the *Mayaguez* by fishing boat.

15 May
Cambodia
Under cover of air and naval gunfire, nearly 200 Marines are extracted by helicopter from Koh Tang. Losses in the operation total 14 Marines, two corpsmen, and two airmen killed and 41 Marines, two corpsmen, and six airmen wounded. Another 23 airmen died in a related but accidental helicopter crash in Thailand.

21 May
Vietnam
Marine security forces complete their mission of

maintaining order on merchant ships crowded with thousands of Vietnamese refugees.

29 May
Sergeants Major
Sergeant Major Henry H. Black succeeds Sergeant Major Puckett and becomes the seventh Sergeant Major of the Marine Corps.

30 June
Commandants
General Cushman retires and is replaced by General Louis H. Wilson, Jr., the 26th Commandant of the Marine Corps.
Manpower
The strength of the Marine Corps on active duty is 18,591 officers and 177,360 enlisted.

October
Training
For the first time since WWI, Marines train in northern Germany, as part of NATO Exercise Autumn Forge.

10 November
Heritage
The US Marine Corps celebrates the 200th anniversary of its founding.

Opposite: *"Patrol Near the DMZ," Sgt Richard L. Yaco, USMC, Marine Corps Art Collection*

Above: *A crewman arms his CH-53 for the evacuation of Saigon. (National Archives)*

Right: *"Vandegrift Burning," Lt B. F. Long IV, USMCR, Marine Corps Art Collection*

A FORCE
IN
READINESS
1976–2002

A FORCE IN READINESS

1976–2002

The Marine Corps had celebrated its 200th birthday on 10 November 1975, but it entered its next hundred years facing a number of tough challenges. Some of them reflected the difficult period that the nation itself was experiencing. The use of illegal drugs reached significant levels in the general population and in the military. Racial discord had been growing since the late 1960s. General distrust of the government and the military was making it more difficult to recruit quality personnel, a situation exacerbated by Vietnam-era decisions by the government to draft a large number of individuals with marginal intelligence into the services. The manpower problem, to include the difficulty of training unqualified people, came to the fore in early 1976 when a recruit in San Diego died of head injuries sustained in a pugil stick bout. All this was occurring at a time when the armed forces were trying to adapt to relying solely on volunteers.

As the other services often sought compromises or ways to make military life less challenging, the Corps made a conscious choice to advertise its toughness and elan, even if that meant taking in fewer people than it needed. There was no change in grooming regulations, no softening of boot camp. The Marine Corps even launched a war on drugs, and found the weapon to achieve victory when urinalysis gained legal sanction in 1982. Marines were thus in position to reap the most benefit when the American public began to reassert its patriotism in the early 1980s. The quality of recruits and officer candidates soared, and the personnel problems of the 1970s became a distant nightmare.

Increased spending on the armed forces in the 1980s permitted the Corps to acquire new generations of weapons, replacing such old stalwarts as the M1911A1 pistol and the jeep. The Harrier, first acquired in 1971, was improved and the new version of the vertical takeoff and landing jet (the AV-8B) joined the equally new F/A-18 as the mainstay of Marine fixed-wing aviation. The Corps also began experimenting with tilt-rotor technology in the form of the V-22, which would revolutionize helicopter operations by flying faster and farther. The Navy chipped in by building a fleet of landing craft (the LCAC) that "flew" over the water on a cushion of air. The LCAC, the V-22, and a new advanced amphibian assault vehicle promised to dramatically enhance amphibious operations, though the latter two had not yet reached the fleet by the end of the century.

The Corps continued to innovate in areas beyond equipment. In 1978 it instituted a unit training program known as the combined arms exercise (CAX). The desert mountains and valleys of 29 Palms made a perfect place for all elements of the MAGTF to train in a demanding live-fire atmosphere. A year later, the Marines began pursuing the idea of maritime pre-positioning, which would place a brigade's worth of equipment and 30 days of supply on commercial vessels.

Pages 616-617: *A Marine of 3/6 at a halt during a 1989 patrol in Panama. (Defense Visual Information Center)*

Right: *Marine honor guard on* John F. Kennedy *(CV-67) in 1983. (Defense Visual Information Center)*

Three squadrons, stationed overseas, would allow brigades to fly to trouble spots and marry up in an amazingly short period of time with all they needed to fight. In 1985, MAUs began a challenging new pre-deployment training program that certified them as special operations capable. They thus could conduct a number of advanced missions, such as the boarding and seizure of ships at sea or short-notice amphibious raids.

There were no shortages of real-world operations to keep the Corps busy during the 1980s. The decade began with a debacle at Desert One in Iran in April 1980, followed by the truck bombing of the Marine headquarters in Lebanon in 1983. But Marines demonstrated their aggressiveness and agility in Grenada, just days after the Beirut bombing, as a MAU overran most of the island while airborne forces struggled with their limited mobility once they hit the ground. The Corps played a smaller but still useful role in air attacks against Libya in 1986, the Tanker War in the Persian Gulf starting in 1987, and the invasion of Panama in 1989.

The emphasis on maritime pre-positioning and the CAX produced a spectacular result in 1990 after Iraq rolled over oil-rich Kuwait in a single day. Within days, Marine brigades were heading to the Persian Gulf and soon after they were deployed and ready to defend Saudi Arabia. In the largest U.S. military operation since Vietnam, I MEF (composed of the 1st and 2nd Marine Divisions, 1st MAW, and the 1st and 2nd Force Service Support Groups) achieved far more than anyone expected. Assigned to create a diversion with a frontal attack on the strongest Iraqi defenses, the MEF broke through and liberated the Kuwaiti capital in four days.

The big war in the Persian Gulf gave way almost immediately to a long string of small wars and operations short of war. Marines helped rescue the Kurds in northern Iraq in 1991, provide disaster relief to Bangladesh the same year, feed the starving and protect U.N. forces in Somalia from 1991 through 1995, control refugees and then police Haiti from 1991 through 1994, and stem the genocidal activities of Serbian nationals in the former Yugoslavia from 1993 through 1999. Along the way there were numerous calls to evacuate Americans and other foreign nationals from troubled points around the globe. The Corps' high state of readiness and its expeditionary capability was just what the United States needed in a troubled world following the end of the Cold War. As a result, the Marines retained more of their structure than the other services that had focused much more on the vanished Soviet threat.

The threat of international terrorism grew throughout the last three decades of the 20th century and culminated in the deadly attack of 11 September 2001. The nation's response, as it has been for over 225 years, was to "send in the Marines." The Corps, as always, was ready and able to answer the call and carry its share of the burden of defending democracy.

A FORCE IN READINESS

1976–2002

1976

13 March
Mishap
A mentally deficient recruit dies from head injuries received in late 1975 during a pugil stick bout. As a result of the incident, Congress conducts investigations into Marine recruit training.

29 May
Technology
Helicopter assault ship *Tarawa* (LHA-1) the first ship of its class, is commissioned. In addition to carrying roughly 1,900 Marines and a squadron of helicopters, it has a well deck.

30 June
Manpower
The strength of the Marine Corps on active duty is 18,882 officers and 173,517 enlisted.

27 July
Lebanon
As fighting between factions threatens foreign nationals, the Marine Security Guard detachment in Beirut assists 32nd MAU in the evacuation of 160 American citizens and 148 other foreigners.

1 August
Force Structure
VMO-8 is deactivated at El Toro.

1 September
Uniform
Marines begin wearing the new camouflage utility uniform in place of the old sateen uniform.

7 November
Sports
The first annual Marine Corps Marathon is held in Washington, D.C.

1977

17 March
Mishap
A Navy landing craft carrying a liberty party of 34th MAU is struck by a Spanish freighter in Barcelona Harbor, drowning 24 Marines and 25 sailors.

31 March
Sergeants Major
SgtMaj John R. Massaro succeeds SgtMaj Black and becomes the eighth Sergeant Major of the Marine Corps.

Left: *The six Marine-piloted RH-53Ds on their way from* Nimitz *to the ill-fated rendezvous at Desert One in Iran in April 1980. (Defense Visual Information Center)*

Right: *LVTP-7 tracked landing vehicles of 32nd MAU splash ashore in Lebanon on 29 September 1982. (Marine Corps Historical Center)*

17 May
Heritage
The Marine Corps Historical Center opens at the Washington Navy Yard.

26 May
Manpower
The Basic School graduates its first class containing both males and females.

30 June
HQMC
The office of Director of Women Marines ceases to exist as female Marines are no longer categorized as a separate entity within the Corps.
Manpower
The strength of the Marine Corps on active duty is 18,650 officers and 176,057 enlisted.

1 September
Force Structure
HMM-265 is reactivated at Kaneohe Bay after a hiatus of seven years.

21 October
Mishap
A CH-53D helicopter crashes during an exercise on Mindoro Island in the Philippines, killing 23 Marines and one corpsman, and injuring 13.

17 November
Force Structure
BLT 1/4 arrives in California from Okinawa as part of the new unit deployment program (UDP), which rotates units from the States to the Far East for six-month deployments to maintain unit cohesion, enhance combat readiness, and share out the hardship of unaccompanied tours.

1978

9–11 April
Training
5th MAB conducts Palm Tree 5-78, the largest exercise held to date at 29 Palms. The live-fire air-ground operation involves nearly 6,000 Marines.

6 May
Heritage
The Marine Corps Aviation Museum opens at Brown Field on board the base at Quantico.

11 May
Manpower
Margaret A. Brewer becomes the first female brigadier general in the Marine Corps.

30 June
Manpower
The strength of the Marine Corps on active duty is 18,388 officers and 172,427 enlisted.

6 July
Force Structure
Force Troops at Camp Lejeune is redesignated as 2nd Force Service Support Group. Similar name changes are made for Force Troops in Okinawa and Camp Pendleton.

21 August
Training
More than 2,000 reserve Marines participate in the first Combined Arms Exercise (CAX) at 29 Palms. The CAX will become a staple of Marine training for the next few decades, with units rotating through the base for the challenging air-ground live-fire operation.

1 September
Force Structure
MAG-39 is reactivated at Camp Pendleton as part of 3rd MAW

20 October
Department of Defense
President Carter signs legislation that makes the Commandant a full member of the JCS.

1 December
Bases
Marine Corps Air Station Santa Ana is renamed MCAS Tustin.

16 December
Taiwan
With the announcement of normalization of U.S. relations with Communist China, a mob of thousands bombards the U.S. embassy in Taipei with bricks and stones. Marine guards drive them back with tear gas and nightsticks.

1979

14 February
Iran
Two weeks after the Ayatollah Khomeini replaces the U.S.-backed Shah of Iran, demonstrators attack the U.S. Embassy in Teheran. Several Marines are abducted and held for over a week.

30 June
Manpower
The strength of the Marine Corps on active duty is 18,229 officers and 167,021 enlisted.

June–July
Nicaragua
Members of the Marine guard at Managua help evacuate 1,423 civilians during fighting in the city as Sandinista forces overthrow the Somoza dictatorship.

1 July
Commandants
General Wilson retires and is replaced by General Robert H. Barrow, the 27th Commandant of the Marine Corps.

15 August
Sergeants Major
Sergeant Major Leland D. Crawford succeeds Sergeant Major Massaro and becomes the ninth Sergeant Major of the Marine Corps.

19 October
Mishap
Typhoon Tip ruptures a 5,000-gallon fuel bladder at Camp Fuji, Japan. The gasoline pours downhill into the Marine base camp where it ignites and causes the death of 13 Marines of 2/4.

30 October
El Salvador
About 200 armed leftists attack the U.S. Embassy in San Salvador. The Marine security detachment holds them at bay with tear gas and warning shots until local authorities restore order. Two Marines are wounded.

4 November
Iran
A mob overruns the U.S. Embassy in Teheran. 65 Americans, including 13 Marine guards, are taken

hostage. Two weeks later, four Marines and nine others are released.

20 November
Pakistan
In Islamabad, a mob burns the U.S. Embassy as seven Marines defend the building and its 137 civilian occupants with tear gas. One Marine is killed during the attack.

21 November
Pakistan
A mob surrounds the U.S. Consulate in Karachi. Among the Marine security guard detachment are two of the 10 female Marines in the MSG Battalion. The wave of violence against American diplomatic compounds during the year soon results in an end to the pilot program to place women in the MSG program.

December
Doctrine
The Secretary of Defense announces that the Marine Corps will establish a Maritime Prepositioning Force. The MPF will have three squadrons, each consisting of five cargo ships filled with all the equipment and supplies needed to outfit a MAB for 30 days of combat. The Corps immediately begins outfitting six existing ships as a Near Term Prepositioning Force until the MPF is ready.

1980

1 March
Force Structure
The Rapid Deployment Joint Task Force is established in Tampa, Florida. It is a headquarters designed to control highly responsive forces (primarily amphibious and airborne) committed to a short-notice contingency, with a focus on the Middle East. The first RDJTF commander is Marine Lieutenant General Paul X. Kelley.

24 April
Iran
In what becomes known as Operation Desert One, Marines pilot Navy helicopters in a failed attempt to rescue the hostages held in Tehran. Three Marines and five other servicemen die in an accident on a desert landing strip after the raid is called off.

3 June
Force Structure
HMM-365 is reactivated at New River after a hiatus of nine years.

30 June
Manpower
The strength of the Marine Corps on active duty is 18,198 officers and 170,271 enlisted.

Opposite: *A 22nd MAU Marine mans a .50-caliber machine gun in Lebanon. (Defense Visual Information Center)*

Right: *M-198 155mm howitzer in Beirut. (Defense Visual Information Center)*

MARINE SECURITY GUARD BATTALION

The Marine Corps' relationship with the diplomatic service extends well back into the early history of the nation. Perhaps the first instance of mutual support came in the oddest way, as the Continental Navy frigate *Boston* carried John Adams across the Atlantic in early 1778 to serve as a commissioner to the French government. When the Americans spied a British armed merchantman, they prepared to attack. Much to the dismay of the ship's captain, he discovered the diplomat armed with a musket and standing among the Marines poised for action.

For the next several decades, Marines participated in a number of actions on behalf of U.S. consuls, oftentimes protecting American lives and property in a troubled foreign land or avenging actions against the United States. The most famous of these expeditions, of course, was Lieutenant Presley O'Bannon's support of William Eaton in the seizure of Derna in 1805. The most unusual probably took place in 1903, when a captain and 19 Marines escorted an American consul to Abyssinia (modern-day Ethiopia). They brought back with them two lions, presents from the emperor to the president.

On a number of occasions ships' detachments went ashore with the express mission of providing local security to a legation. The most challenging of these assignments came in 1900, when the Marines of *Oregon* and *Newark* landed in China and moved overland to Peking during the onset of the Boxer Rebellion. They helped other foreign troops fight off the Chinese rebels for 55 days before an international relief force came to the rescue. For long periods in the first half of the 20th century, Marines were assigned to guard the embassies in Peking and Managua due to the chronic instability of those countries. The frequent use of the Corps around the world on missions short of war led to a special relationship with the diplomatic corps—in the *Small Wars Manual of 1940*, the Marines even referred to themselves as "State Department troops."

After World War II, the State Department decided that it was time to cast off its previous policy of relying on hired civilians (American or local) to provide embassy security. Strangely enough, it turned first to the Army for support in 1947. Before those negotiations could bear fruit, someone recalled a provision in the Foreign Service Act of 1946 that allowed the Secretary of the Navy to assign Marines or sailors to embassy duty. There was no similar legal basis for the Army to do so. The official State Department request came on 22 June 1948. The Navy Department willingly agreed and President Truman approved of the deal on 5 November. The two agencies signed a formal memorandum governing the program on 15 December.

The first 83 Marines began three weeks of training at the Foreign Service Institute in January 1949, and the first 15 graduates departed overseas (for Bangkok and Tangier) near the end of the month. By May, over 300 Marines were on duty around the world. By 1953 the number had risen to nearly 700. In July 1954, Commandant Shepherd decided that more rigorous screening and schooling were needed. The first four-week course, run by the Corps, began on 4 November that year. Since then, the training syllabus has grown in length and difficulty. A significant organizational change in the program came on 19 February

1967, when the Corps formed the Marine Security Guard (MSG) Battalion to oversee the training of new volunteers and the administration of the far-flung detachments.

Although foreign governments are supposed to ensure the external protection of embassies and MSG detachments are primarily designed to provide internal security, on many occasions Marines have been called on to risk their lives to safeguard their embassies, fellow Americans, and foreign employees. A number of Marines have been killed or wounded in a wide range of hostile incidents over the decades. The first MSG Marine to die in the line of duty was Sergeant James Marshall, killed as he fought back against Viet Cong sappers attacking the U.S. Embassy in Saigon during the January 1968 Tet Offensive. Two more embassy Marines died in Saigon as the North Vietnamese Army overran South Vietnam in the spring of 1975. Corporal Charles McMahon, Jr., and Lance Corporal Darwin D. Judge were, in fact, the last Marines to die in that long war. In August 1977, Marines discovered a fire in the embassy in Moscow, evacuated the occupants, then accompanied Soviet firemen back into the building to safeguard classified material. Nine Marines were held hostage by Iran for 444 days following the seizure of the embassy in Tehran in November 1979. A terrorist bomb attack on the U.S. Embassy in Beirut killed Corporal Robert V. McNaugh in April 1983, six months before the destruction of the Marine headquarters at the airport.

More than a thousand Marines stand watch today at well over 100 U.S. diplomatic posts. Their pride and professionalism are often the most visible symbol of America to many people around the globe. For those who detest the United States and the values it supports, those embassies and their Marines also remain a primary target for hate and violence. The Marine Security Guard Battalion, recently made a part of the new 4th Marine Brigade (Antiterroist), will continue to be in the front lines of U.S. interaction with the governments and peoples of the world.

The Marine Security Guard Detachment of the U.S. Embassy at Moscow's Red Square. (Marine Corps Historical Center)

July
Force Structure
The Marine Corps activates 7th MAB headquarters at 29 Palms as the first force dedicated to the MPF mission. When fleshed out with subordinate elements, it stands ready to deploy by air to any port to link up with an MPF squadron.

1981

January
Norway
The Norwegian and U.S. governments sign an agreement providing for the prepositioning of supplies and equipment to outfit a MAB. An equivalent of MPF, these stocks will be maintained in special caves and allow a MAB to carry out the Corps' mission of reinforcing the Norwegian armed forces in the event of a Soviet attack.

20 January
Iran
The 52 American hostages held by Iran for 444 days are freed.

1 March
Force Structure
HMH-464 is activated at New River to fly the new CH-53E Super Stallion helicopters, which can refuel in flight and lift twice the load of earlier models.

13 April
Aviation
Two Harrier squadrons (VMA-231 and 542) deploy on board ship together to test a concept for augmenting fixed-wing aviation in the fleet during a contingency.

26 May
Mishap
A Marine EA-6B Prowler electronic warfare plane crashes while making a night landing on *Nimitz* (CVN-68). The three Marine aircrewmen and 11 others are killed, 48 are injured, and 20 aircraft are destroyed or damaged.

30 June
Manpower
The strength of the Marine Corps on active duty is 18,363 officers and 172,257 enlisted.

December
Technology
10th Marines receives the first of the new M198 155mm howitzers.

1 December
Manpower
Commandant Barrow announces his own war on drugs. Increased use of urinalysis testing will play a major role in the plan to decrease use of illegal drugs in the Corps.
Force Structure
HMH-465 is activated at Tustin.

1982

24 June
Lebanon
Marines of the 32nd MAU land in Lebanon to help evacuate 580 U.S. citizens from the port city of Juniyah following Israel's 6 June invasion to destroy the Palestine Liberation Organization (PLO). The mission is accomplished that day and the Marines return to their ships. A cease fire

Opposite: *A Marine held hostage in Iran comes home. (Defense Visual Information Center)*

Right: *Marine with M-40A1 sniper rifle in Beirut. (Defense Visual Information Center)*

between the Israelis, Syrians, and PLO finally takes hold, with Israel occupying the southern half of Lebanon and surrounding the PLO-occupied districts of west Beirut.

30 June
Manpower
The strength of the Marine Corps on active duty is 18,975 officers and 173,405 enlisted.

25 August
Lebanon
At the request of the Lebanese government, 32nd MAU (BLT 2/8, HMM-261, and MSSG-32) goes ashore and assumes control of the port of Beirut. It is part of a multi-national force with the mission of peacefully evacuating PLO forces and other Palestinians. 32nd MAU completes the mission and re-embarks on 10 September.

29 September
Lebanon
In response to massacres of Palestinian refugees by militiamen, 32nd MAU lands as part of a multinational force comprised of American, French, Italian, and British troops. The Marines take up positions at the Beirut International Airport.

18 October
Technology
The High Mobility Multipurpose Wheeled Vehicle (HMMWV) is announced as the replacement for the venerable jeep. The Corps will take its first deliveries in late 1985.

22 October
Technology
Completed field tests of the Meal Ready to Eat (MRE) show that Marines prefer the new field food to the old C Rations, which will be replaced by MREs as stocks are depleted.

30 October
Lebanon
The 32nd MAU is relieved by the 24th MAU (BLT 3/8, HMM-263, and MSSG-24).

9 November
Technology
The Commandant announces the fielding of the M16A2 rifle, a vastly improved version of the original M16 design.
Training
Following a two-day exercise in northern Somalia, 31st MAU participates in Exercise Jade Tiger 83, a four-day operation with Omani forces at Wahibah Sands, Oman.

7 December
Department of Defense
President Reagan approves the replacement of the RDJTF with Central Command, a new unified headquarters that will be responsible for the Middle East, southwest Asia, and the Indian Ocean.

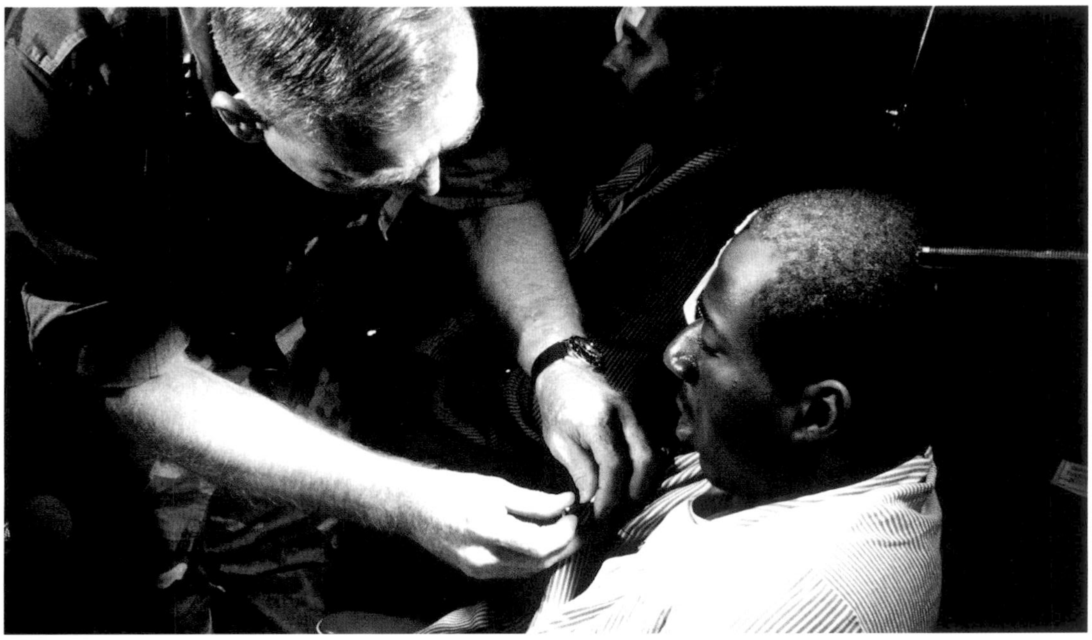

Left: *Commandant Kelley awards a Purple Heart following the Beirut bombing. (Defense Visual Information Center)*

Opposite: *Beirut bunker. (Marine Corps Historical Center)*

1983

7 January
Technology
VMFA-314 becomes the fist naval squadron to operate the McDonnell Douglas F/A-18 Hornet, which will eventually replace the F-4 and A-4 in the Corps.

February
Technology
The Kevlar helmet, shaped like the German WWII helmet, begins replacing the M1 steel helmet used by American forces since early in WWII.

2 February
Lebanon
Armed only with his .45-caliber pistol, Captain Charles B. Johnson steps in front of three Israeli tanks trying to pass through a U.S. checkpoint and stops them.

15 February
Lebanon
22nd MAU (BLT 2/6, HMM-264, and MSSG-22) relieves 24th MAU.

18 April
Lebanon
A car bomb placed by Islamic terrorists destroys the U.S. Embassy, killing 61, including 17 Americans (one of them a Marine guard).

26 April
Force Structure
HMM-266 is activated at New River.

30 May
Lebanon
24th MAU (BLT 1/8, HMM-162, and MSSG-24) replaces 22nd MAU.

28 June
Sergeants Major
Sergeant Major Robert E. Cleary succeeds Sergeant Major Crawford and becomes the 10th Sergeant Major of the Marine Corps.

30 June
Manpower
The strength of the Marine Corps on active duty is 19,983 officers and 174,106 enlisted.

1 July
Commandants
General Barrow retires and is replaced by General Paul X. Kelley, the 28th Commandant of the Marine Corps.

26 July
Force Structure
6th MAB is activated at Camp Lejeune as another headquarters dedicated to the MPF mission.

28 August
Lebanon
In one of many incidents since March, a Marine outpost comes under fire from opponents of the Lebanese government. For the first time, Marines return fire with small arms.

29 August
Lebanon
Marine positions at the Beirut Airport come under heavy bombardment. Casualties are two killed and 14 wounded. The Marines counter with their own artillery fire. This marks a major escalation in the fighting, with repeated exchanges of heavy fire thereafter.

8 September
Lebanon
In another escalation of the fighting, Marines call in naval gunfire from frigate *Bowen* (FF-1079) to silence a militia artillery battery in the Shouf Mountains above the airport.

12 September
Lebanon
31st MAU arrives off the coast from its normal station in the Pacific and Indian Oceans. It remains in the area until 1 October.

26 September
Lebanon
A cease fire goes into effect, but sniper incidents continue to inflict casualties on Marines, who return fire in kind.

21 October
Grenada
Following a Communist coup in this Caribbean nation, 22nd MAU is ordered to divert to the area to protect American citizens. It had just started its journey toward Lebanon.

23 October
Lebanon
A truck bomb destroys the building housing the headquarters of BLT 1/8. Marine casualties are 220 killed and 70 wounded, with 21 other American servicemen also dead. This is the highest one-day death toll in the Corps since WWII. A similar attack is made against the French position, killing

58. Elements of 2/6 begin deploying that day from Camp Lejeune to reinforce the BLT, while the Marine detachment of *New Jersey* comes ashore in the meantime.

25 October
Grenada
22nd MAU, Army Rangers, and elements of the 82nd Airborne Division invade the island to rescue over 1,000 Americans from factional fighting. Three Marine aviators die during the operation, which winds up on 2 November. Navy ships and Marine amphibian tractors and helicopters allow the MAU to secure a substantial potion of the island.

26 October
Technology
The Corps takes delivery of its first wheeled light armored vehicle, designated LAV-25.

6 November
Sports
Staff Sergeant Farley Simon becomes the first Marine to win the Marine Corps Marathon.

Left: *CH-46 on Grenada. (Defense Visual Information Center)*

Opposite: *A LAV-25 crosses the Bridge of the Americas in Panama. (Defense Visual Information Center)*

19 November
Lebanon
22nd MAU (BLT 2/8, HMM-261, and MSSG-22) relieves 24th MAU.

4 December
Lebanon
A heavy bombardment kills eight Marines and wounds two. This marks a resumption of heavy exchanges of fire.

14 December
Terrorism
A truck bomb hits the U.S. Embassy in Kuwait. Although dozens are killed and wounded, none are Americans. Marine security guards protect the damaged building.

1984

12 January
Technology
The Corps' first McDonnell Douglas AV-8B Harrier joins 2nd MAW at Cherry Point.

10–11 February
Lebanon
Following President Reagan's decision to withdraw most Marines from Lebanon, helicopters evacuate U.S. and foreign nationals from Beirut.

21–26 February
Lebanon
22nd MAU redeploys back to its ships.

24 March
Mishap
A CH-53 crash during Team Spirit 84 kills 18 U.S. and 11 Republic of Korea Marines.

4 April
Force Structure
The 2nd Light Armored Vehicle (LAV) Battalion is activated at Camp Lejeune.

2 May
Technology
Bell Aerospace Textron rolls out the first landing craft air-cushion (LCAC) in New Orleans. The Navy hover craft will bring new speed and range to amphibious operations.

30 June
Manpower
The strength of the Marine Corps on active duty is 20,366 officers and 175,848 enlisted.

14 July
Technology
Corporal Louis J. Hauge, Jr., the first ship designed specifically for the MPF, is launched in Maryland.

20 September
Lebanon
A suicide truck bomb explodes in front of the U.S. Embassy Annex in Beirut, killing 23 people and wounding numerous others, including four Marine guards.

28 September
Force Structure
HMM-364 is reactivated at Kaneohe Bay after a hiatus of 13 years.

30 November
Force Structure
HMH-466 is activated at Tustin.

1985

14 January
Technology
The 9mm Beretta 92SB-F replaces the M1911A1 .45-caliber pistol, which has been in service with U.S. armed forces for nearly 75 years.

6 May
Mishap
A CH-53D crashes in the Sea of Japan killing 17 Marines.

24 May
Training
A revised Marine Corps order increases the amount of combat-related training, to include marksmanship and defensive tactics, required of female Marines.

31 May
Force Structure
1st LAV Battalion is activated at Camp Pendleton.

14 June
Doctrine
Commandant Kelley directs a pilot program to train MAUs for some special operations. Following a lengthy training and evaluation program, 26th MAU is designated special operations capable and becomes the first MAU (SOC) in December.

19 June
El Salvador
Communist guerrillas fire on an outdoor café, killing 13 people, including four off-duty Marine embassy guards.

30 June
Manpower
The strength of the Marine Corps on active duty is 20,175 officers and 177,850 enlisted.

1 July
Force Structure
5th MAB headquarters is activated at Camp Pendleton.

13 September
Force Structure
HMM-166 is activated at Tustin.

15 October
Mishap
A CH-46 crashes off Camp Lejeune killing 14 Marines and a Navy chaplain.

27 November
Commanders
General George B. Crist takes the helm of Central Command, the first Marine ever to head a unified command.

1986

23–27 March
Libya
Freedom of navigation exercises in the Gulf of Sidra by three carrier battle groups result in the sinking of two Libyan missile boats. VMFA-314 and 323 and VMAQ-2 participate.

Left: *A Marine M-60 tank reinforces a Lebanese soldier manning a sentry booth. ("Beirut Watchers," Col Edward M. Condra III, USMC (Ret), Marine Corps Art Collection)*

27 March
Technology
The Corps takes delivery of its first Bell Textron AH-1W Super Cobra attack helicopter.

1 April
Force Structure
The three attack helicopter and three light helicopter squadrons begin the process of re-organizing into six light attack (HMLA) squadrons, each with Hueys and Cobras.

14 April
Libya
VMFA-314 and 323 participate in air strikes against Libyan targets following a Libyan-sponsored terrorist bombing of a night club in Germany frequented by Americans.

30 June
Manpower
The strength of the Marine Corps on active duty is 20,199 officers and 178,615 enlisted.

29 August
Mishap
A CH-46 crash during an exercise in Norway results in eight Marines dead and 13 injured.

11 September
Force Structure
The 3rd LAV Battalion is activated at 29 Palms.

22 September
Training
The Commandant directs that senior SNCOs replace officers in running the SNCO Academies at Quantico, Lejeune, and El Toro.

1987

10 April
Department of the Navy
James H. Webb, Jr., a Marine captain in Vietnam and noted author, becomes the 66th Secretary of the Navy.

16 April
Force Structure
Marine Corps Security Force Battalion, Atlantic, is activated at Norfolk as part of a restructuring of Marine detachments afloat and Marine barracks.

26 June
Sergeants Major
Sergeant Major David W. Sommers succeeds Sergeant Major Cleary and becomes the 11th Sergeant Major of the Marine Corps.

30 June
Manpower
The strength of the Marine Corps on active duty is 20,047 officers and 179,478 enlisted, the peak strength of the Corps since the Vietnam War.

1 July
Commandants
General Kelley retires and is replaced by General Alfred M. Gray, Jr., the 29th Commandant of the Marine Corps.

24 July
Persian Gulf
After an American-flagged oil tanker strikes a sea mine laid by Iran, elements of 24th MAU are dispatched to the gulf to assist Navy forces in securing the sea lanes for commercial shipping.

4 August
Technology
Amphibious assault ship *Wasp* (LHD-1) is launched at Pascagoula, Mississippi. It and its sister ships will replace the *Iwo Jima*–class helicopter carriers.

24 August
Legal
A court martial convicts Sergeant Clayton J. Lonetree of espionage and related charges involving his duties at embassies in Vienna and Moscow. He is the first Marine ever convicted of spying.

21 September
Persian Gulf
Marine helicopters assist in capturing *Iran Ajr*, an Iranian ship laying mines in the gulf.

8 October
Iran
With just 48 hours notice, Contingency MAGTF 1-88 is formed and sails on board *Okinawa* (LPH-3). Its mission is to relieve the detachment of 24th MAU on duty in the Persian Gulf. CM 1-88 remains on station until replaced by CM 2-88 on 20 February 1988.

9 October
Force Structure
Marine Barracks Portsmouth, New Hampshire, the second oldest post in the Corps, is deactivated after 174 years of service dating back to 1813.

6 December
Force Structure
Sea School, opened in 1923 at San Diego, is closed as part of the restructuring of Marine security forces.

Right: *A Marines sweeps the area outside the perimeter. ("Beirut Watch," Sgt Arturo Alejandre, USMC, Marine Corps Art Collection)*

1988

January
Manpower
Secretary of the Navy Webb decrees that Naval Academy midshipmen will now have to complete Officer Candidate School at Quantico in order to qualify for a Marine commission.

5 February
Force Structure
The titles of all MAGTFs are changed by replacing "amphibious" with "expeditionary" to reflect the wide range of capability they possess.

17 February
Terrorism
Lieutenant Colonel William R. Higgins, serving with a U.N. observer organization along the Israeli-Lebanon border, is abducted by terrorists. He is subsequently killed.

18 April
Persian Gulf
Marines of Contingency MAGTF 2-88 destroy the Iranian oil platform *Sassan* during U.S. strikes on sites used to launch attacks on ships in the Persian Gulf. A Marine Cobra helicopter and its two pilots are lost during the action.

May
Manpower
For the first time since the late 1970s, female Marines are authorized to become members of MSG detachments at American embassies.

23 May
Technology
Bell Textron rolls out the first V-22 Osprey, a revolutionary tilt-rotor aircraft that lands and takes off like a helicopter but flies like a prop-driven fixed-wing plane. It is designed to replace the aging CH-46 fleet.

30 June
Manpower
The strength of the Marine Corps on active duty is 20,079 officers and 177,271 enlisted.

9 September
Force Structure
VMGR-452 is activated as part of 4th MAW.

31 December
Force Structure
MAG-15 is deactivated at Iwakuni.

1989

7 January
Force Structure
HMA-775 is activated as part of 4th MAW at Camp Pendleton.

3 March
Force Structure
2/6 and 3/1 are placed in cadre status as part of a reduction of three infantry battalions and the addition of a fourth rifle company to the remaining 24 active-duty battalions.

17–20 March
Mishaps
The crash of a CH-46 and a CH-53D three days apart during Team Spirit in Korea result in the death of 17 Marines and one corpsman.

11 May
Panama
Following General Manuel Noriega's refusal to recognize the results of elections in his country, the United States deploys additional forces to U.S. bases there.

31 May
Mishaps
A CH-46 crashes during a night flight off *Denver* (LPD-9), killing 13 Marines and one corpsman.

30 June
Manpower
The strength of the Marine Corps on active duty is 20,099 officers and 176,857 enlisted.

11 July
Training
The Commandant establishes the Marine Corps Professional Reading Program for NCOs, SNCOs, and officers.

1 August
Training
The Marine Corps University is established to oversee a number of educational programs.

20 December
Panama
Four days after Panamanian security forces killed Marine Lieutenant Robert Paz at a roadblock, U.S. forces launch Operation Just Cause to overthrow the Noriega dictatorship, which has been implicated in illegal drug distribution. One company each of infantry and light armored infantry, a Fleet Antiterrorism Security Team (FAST) platoon, and the Marine Corps Security Force company participate in the operation, which is largely complete the first day. One Marine is killed.

1990

30 June
Manpower
The strength of the Marine Corps on active duty is 19,958 officers and 176,694 enlisted.

5 August
Liberia
Elements of 22nd MEU(SOC) fly into the U.S. Embassy compound in Monrovia and begin evacuating Americans and other foreign nationals as a civil war rages in the country. Operation Sharp Edge continues until 30 November and pulls out over 2,400 civilians.

7 August
Operation Desert Shield
Five days after Iraq invades Kuwait, President George W. Bush orders U.S. forces to the Persian Gulf to contain further Iraqi aggression against oil-producing states in the region.

Opposite: *A VMA-513 AV-8B Harrier loaded for bear during Operation Desert Shield. (Defense Visual Information Center)*

Right: *A CH-53E lands on* Raleigh *(LPD-1) in October 1990. (Marine Corps Historical Center)*

LIEUTENANT GENERAL FRANK E. PETERSON, JR.

From the time he saw B-29 bombers flying out of the airfield near his hometown of Topeka, Kansas, during World War II, Frank Peterson wanted to fly. From his father, who ran an electronics business, young Frank learned how to repair radios, work hard, and challenge life. After he graduated from high school in 1949, he wanted to enlist in the Navy and see the world, but his father wouldn't sign the papers for the 17-year-old. Frank instead went on to Washburn University. In early June 1950, just three weeks before the Korean War broke out, he joined the Navy. After boot camp, he went to electronics school. In April 1951, he won the opportunity to become a naval aviation cadet. In October 1952, he earned his wings and opted for a Marine commission.

After advanced flight training, Lieutenant Peterson went to Korea in April 1953 and was assigned to VMA-212. Truce negotiations were ongoing, but the fighting intensified as the Communists sought an advantage to use at the bargaining table. In the few short months remaining in the war, he flew 64 combat missions. The most harrowing came on 15 June. In response to a request for close air support, he led a division of Corsairs against a mortar position in mountainous terrain. Despite damage to his plane from heavy anti-aircraft fire, he pressed home the attack at low altitude and dropped the first bomb, marking the enemy position for the remaining aircraft. He then joined in subsequent bombing and strafing runs that wiped out the target. For his actions that day, he received the Distinguished Flying Cross. By the close of the campaign, he also had earned six Air Medals.

Following the war, Peterson spent a ground tour as an air liaison officer with the 1st Marine Division. Back in the States, he flew with VMF(N)-542 at El Toro and successfully converted to a regular commission. Other flying and school tours followed, including the chance to complete his college education at George Washington University. In June 1968, now a lieutenant colonel, he took command of VMFA-314 in Vietnam and led it through a year of hard fighting.

In August 1968, Peterson and his radar intercept officer took off in their F-4 Phantom from Chu Lai, on a mission to provide close air support for a reconnaissance unit in trouble up near the DMZ. On his second pass at the target, anti-aircraft fire struck the left engine and it burst into flames. The plane was streaking north at the time and was already into air space over North Vietnam. Unwilling to bail out and risk becoming a prisoner, the two men stuck with their burning aircraft. Peterson brought it around, but as they neared the DMZ again, the other engine caught fire. Finally, when the hydraulics and controls quit working, the pilot gave the order to punch out. Although he did not know it for some time, he was injured in the ejection, suffering a herniated disk and a hairline fracture of the hip socket. Two days later, he was back in the air. His squadron ultimately received the Marine Corps Aviation Association's Hanson Award as the outstanding fighter squadron of the year. He departed Vietnam in the summer of 1969 with another 300 combat missions in his logbooks.

Back at home, he found himself in a new and entirely different sort of battle, as the first Special Assistant to the Commandant for Minority Affairs. At a time of high racial tensions in the armed forces and the nation, it was a challenging and difficult assignment. Over the course of two years, he helped lead the effort to solve widespread problems in the Corps related to racism, drugs, and indiscipline. After a year at the National War College, he went back to the FMF and helped reinvigorate the post-Vietnam Corps. He served as a group commander in 2nd MAW, chief of staff of the 9th Marine Amphibious Brigade, assistant wing commander of 1st MAW, commanding general of 9th MAB, commanding general of 1st MAW, and finally deputy commander of FMFLANT. In October 1985, he became the Silver Hawk, the Corps' longest-serving active aviator. Two years later, he added the title Gray Eagle when he became the senior naval aviator. He retired from active duty in 1988 after two years as the commanding general of the Marine Corps Development and Education Command in Quantico and went on to a civilian career as a corporate executive.

LtGen Frank Peterson stands in front of a Corsair, similar to the ones he flew over Korea as a young Marine aviator. (Marine Corps Historical Center)

10 August
Operation Desert Shield
7th MEB (RLT 7, MAG-70, and BSSG-7) begins flying from the United States to Al Jubayl, Saudi Arabia, where it will link up with its MPF squadron.

17 August
Operation Desert Shield
The first elements of 4th MEB (RLT 2, MAG-40, and BSSG-4)) sail from Morehead City for the Persian Gulf.

19 August
Operation Desert Shield
RLT 4 and BLT 1/6 begin loading on ships in Okinawa for deployment to Saudi Arabia.

20 August
Operation Desert Shield
Lieutenant General Walter E. Boomer, commander of I MEF, arrives in Saudi Arabia. His headquarters will command all Marine forces in the operation, except for those afloat.
Liberia
Elements of 26th MEU begin relieving 22nd MEU in Operation Sharp Edge.

22 August
Operation Desert Shield
President Bush orders the mobilization of reserve forces to support the operation. More than 31,000 Marine reservists will ultimately be mobilized for service around the world.

25 August
Operation Desert Shield
1st MEB begins flying out of Hawaii to link up with its MPF ships at Al Jubayl.

2 September
Operation Desert Shield
7th MEB deactivates and is subsumed into I MEF. 1st MEB follows suit a few days later. The major subordinate elements of I MEF (3rd MAW, 1st Marine Division, and 1st FSSG) take control of their respective parts of the force.

7 September
Operation Desert Shield
13th MEU(SOC) arrives in the Persian Gulf and remains afloat under Navy command.

17 September
Operation Desert Shield
The last elements of 4th MEB arrive in the Persian Gulf and remain afloat under Navy command.

8 November
Operation Desert Shield
President Bush announces that the U.S. will double the size of its forces in the Persian Gulf. The additional Marine elements will include 2nd Marine Division, 5th MEB, 2nd MAW, and 2nd FSSG. 2nd MAW will be composited with 3rd MAW. 1st FSSG will provide general logistics support to the MEF, while 2nd FSSG becomes the Direct Support Command operating in the immediate rear of the ground combat forces.

Left: *A logistics vehicle proudly flies the U.S. flag during Operation Desert Storm. (Defense Visual Information Center)*

Right: *An AH-1 Cobra supports AAVP-7s carrying the 1st Combat Engineer Battalion on 26 February 1991. (Defense Visual Information Center)*

1 December
Operation Desert Shield
5th MEB (RLT 5, MAG-50, BSSG-5), with 11th MEU(SOC) embedded, sails from California.

18 December
Technology
The first Marine Corps M1A1 Abrams tank is rolled off the assembly line. 2nd Tank Battalion will be the first to receive the new tanks and will deploy to the Persian Gulf with them.

1991

1 January
Operation Desert Shield
The 24th Marines (less 1/24) deploys from the States to Al Jubayl to assume the rear area security mission for I MEF.

2 January
Somalia
Elements of 4th MEB on board *Guam* (LPH-9) and *Trenton* (LPD-14) sail from the Persian Gulf area with the mission of evacuating American personnel from the U.S. Embassy in Mogadishu as a result of a civil war.

5 January
Somalia
Operation Eastern Exit gets underway at 0147 when two CH-53Es and a security force launch 466 miles from Mogadishu. Two in-flight refuelings from KC-130s are required to reach the objective. The dangerous, long-range mission is dictated by Somali looters attempting to invade the embassy compound. A return flight evacuates the first 61 civilians. Another 220 civilians, including the Soviet embassy staff, are lifted out the next day when the ships arrive off the coast.

10 January
Operation Desert Shield
The U.S. Army's 1st Brigade of the 2nd Armored Division (known as the Tiger Brigade) is attached to I MEF.

11 January
Operation Desert Shield
All II MEF elements have reached the theater and joined I MEF. 5th MEB arrives in the Persian Gulf the next day and joins with 4th MEB, forming the largest amphibious task force since Inchon in 1950.

16 January
Operation Desert Storm
Following the expiration of a deadline for Iraq to withdraw its forces from Kuwait, coalition forces (including 3rd MAW) launch offensive air operations against Iraq.

20 January
Operation Desert Storm
I MEF begins conducting artillery raids against Iraqi forces in Kuwait.

Left: *M-1A1 Abrams tank with mine plow passes a burned-out Iraqi vehicle in Kuwait. (Defense Visual Information Center)*

Opposite: *F/A-18 Hornets over the desert. (Defense Visual Information Center)*

29 January
Operation Desert Storm
Iraqi forces launch three brigade-size night attacks across the Kuwaiti border. Two are repulsed. One captures the abandoned Saudi town of Al Khafji. eleven Marines die in these night battles, all in fratricide incidents.

1 February
Operation Desert Storm
Marine air, artillery, and observer teams assist Saudi and Qatari troops in retaking Al Khafji.

6 February
Operation Desert Storm
The Direct Support Command begins constructing a new forward logistics base. Dubbed Al Khanjar, the huge facility begins operations six days later.

23 February
Training
Reservists of 2nd MEB participate in Exercise Battle Griffin 91 and conduct the first full test of the Norway Airlanded MEB (NALMEB) concept—the prepositioned set of equipment and supplies created by a 1981 agreement.

24 February
Operation Desert Storm
The ground campaign begins before dawn, with 1st and 2nd Marine Divisions and the Tiger Brigade attacking toward Kuwait City through Iraqi obstacle belts. 5th MEB begins going ashore to become the I MEF reserve. Nearly all 3rd MAW sorties are in support of the MEF. I MEF strength, including attachments and 11,703 Marine reservists, is 84,515. Additional Marine forces afloat conduct deception operations to pin down Iraqi defenders on the coast.

28 February
Operation Desert Storm
President Bush declares a cease fire at 0800 Kuwaiti time. I MEF forces had reached Kuwait City, captured more than 22,000 prisoners, and destroyed hundreds of tanks, armored vehicles, and artillery pieces. Marine casualties for all of Desert Storm are 24 dead and 92 wounded. Five Marine aviators captured by the enemy are released soon after. Four Harriers and two Broncos were shot down, while five Hornets were damaged.

9 March
Operation Desert Storm
The first Marine units begin departing for the States. The last Marines will depart on 27 August.

15 April
Operation Provide Comfort
Following a failed revolt against Saddam Hussein's regime, two million Kurds are fleeing their homes in northern Iraq. A multinational relief operation

is underway, with 24th MEU(SOC) (BLT 2/8, HMM-264, and MSSG-24) moving inland to the Turkish town of Silopi. Within days, Marines move into northern Iraq to establish safe havens for returning refugees. Other Marine elements from around the world begin reinforcing the MEU, including Contingency MAGTF 1-91 from Okinawa. 24th MEU(SOC) remains part of Operation Provide Comfort until 19 July.

15 May
Bangladesh
Two weeks after a devastating cyclone strikes the country, 5th MEB (on its way home from Operation Desert Storm) arrives off the coast to support the international relief effort. 5th MEB participates in Operation Sea Angel through 28 May. It is replaced by Contingency MAGTF 2-91 from Okinawa, which remains through 7 June.

12 June
Philippines
Following the volcanic eruption of Mt. Pinatubo, Marines from III MEF and the barracks at Subic Bay begin assisting in relief work (dubbed Operation Fiery Vigil). The devastation results soon after in an early closure of damaged U.S. military facilities in the Philippines, including the naval base at Subic Bay, which had been home to Marines and sailors since 1898.

28 June
Sergeants Major
Sergeant Major Harold G. Overstreet succeeds Sergeant Major Sommers and becomes the 12th Sergeant Major of the Marine Corps.

30 June
Manpower
The strength of the Marine Corps on active duty is 19,753 officers and 174,287 enlisted.

1 July
Commandants
General Gray retires and is replaced by General Carl E. Mundy, Jr., the 30th Commandant of the Marine Corps.
Force Structure
VMFA(AW)-225 is reactivated at El Toro after a hiatus of 19 years.

August
Force Structure
As part of the post-Cold War drawdown, the Marine Corps begins deleting the fourth rifle companies from its infantry battalions.

6 September
Commanders
The Marine Corps adopts a formalized screening process to select lieutenant colonels and colonels for command billets.

22 November
Caribbean
Elements of II MEF begin deploying to Guantanamo Bay, Cuba, to assist in processing thousands of refugees from Haiti, where a military coup has created political turmoil. The operation continues through June 1993.

1992

February
Force Structure
The Marine Corps begins deactivating its six permanent MEB headquarters.

31 March
Force Structure
VMFA-333 and 531 are deactivated.

Left: *15th MEU Marine with an M249 squad automatic weapon (SAW) providing convoy security, December 1992. (Defense Visual Information Center)*

1 May
Civil Support
More than 1,500 Marines from Camp Pendleton deploy to Los Angeles to assist authorities in quelling riots following the acquittal of four policemen charged with beating a motorist.

30 June
Manpower
The strength of the Marine Corps on active duty is 19,132 officers and 165,397 enlisted.

20 July
Mishap
Three Marines and four civilians are killed when a V-22 crashes near Quantico. Test flights are suspended while the accident is investigated.

18 August
Somalia
President Bush orders U.S. military forces to assist in famine relief efforts by flying food from bases in Kenya into Somalia.

1 October
Force Structure
VMA-331 is deactivated. VMAQ-4 is reactivated as an active duty squadron at Cherry Point.

10 November
Force Structure
Marine Barracks Guam is disestablished following almost-continuous operation since 1899.

24 November
Force Structure
Marines depart Subic Bay following the transfer of the base to the Philippines.

9 December
Somalia
After the famine worsens due to continued instability, President Bush orders direct military intervention to permit effective relief operations. 15th MEU(SOC) begins landing to secure ports and airfields for additional forces for Operation Restore Hope. Marine Lieutenant General Robert B. Johnson and his I MEF headquarters assume command of the joint task force, which will grow to 30,000 troops, including the 7th Marines, MAG-16, and elements of 1st FSSG.

1993

19 July
Balkans
VMFA(AW)-533 begins supporting Operation Deny Flight, designed to limit Serbian aggression against ethnic minorities in Bosnia. Marine squadrons will serve almost continuously in this capacity for the next several years.

28 April
Manpower
Secretary of Defense Les Aspin promulgates new policy that opens more occupational specialties and billets to servicewomen, to include pilots and crew of combat aircraft.

30 April
Force Structure
MAG-32 is deactivated at Cherry Point.

4 May
Somalia
Lieutenant General Johnston passes command of Operation Restore Hope to Turkish General Cevik Bir, as the U.S. role in the effort shrinks. The last I MEF Marines depart Somalia.

20 May
Force Structure
VMO-2 is deactivated at Camp Pendleton as part of the phase-out of the OV-10.

24 June
Somalia
24th MEU(SOC) deploys to Mogadishu in support of U.N. forces facing increasing fighting with Somali warlords.

30 June
Manpower
The strength of the Marine Corps on active duty is 18,430 officers and 159,949 enlisted.

1 September
Manpower
The DOD Bottom Up Review approves a strength of 174,000 for the Corps, as opposed to the 159,000 once projected as part of the post–Cold War drawdown.

30 September
Force Structure
VMO-1 is deactivated at New River.

7 October
Somalia
Following the death of 14 American soldiers in Mogadishu a few days earlier, the United States sends additional forces, to include the 13th and 22nd MEU(SOC)s.

1994

25 March
Somalia
24th MEU(SOC) oversees the withdrawal of the last U.S. forces, except for a Marine security platoon at the embassy.

12 April
Operation Distant Runner
11th MEU(SOC) evacuates 230 civilians, including 142 Americans, who are escaping ethnic fighting in the African nation of Rwanda.

26 April
Force Structure
VMO-4, the last OV-10D Bronco squadron in the Marine Corps, is deactivated.

Right: *Manning a Mk-19 grenade launcher during a weapons sweep in Mogadishu. (Defense Visual Information Center)*

15–23 June
Training
U.S. Navy and Marine forces conduct their first-ever exercise with Russian Navy and naval infantry at Vladivostok.

30 June
Manpower
The strength of the Marine Corps on active duty is 17,823 officers and 156,335 enlisted.

21 July
Force Structure
The 9th Marines is deactivated on Okinawa.

20 September
Haiti
Special Purpose MAGTF Carib (built around the headquarters of the 2nd Marines, 2/2, and HMM-264) goes ashore at Cap Haitien as part of Operation Uphold Democracy. This is an unopposed intervention designed to restore the authority of the elected president of Haiti. The MAGTF will remain in Haiti for 12 days.

24 September
Haiti
A Marine lieutenant and a rifle squad engage Haitian military personnel at a police station, killing 10 and wounding one, at a cost of one sailor wounded.

1 October
Force Structure
HMH-366 is activated at Kaneohe Bay.

1995

1–3 March
Somalia
13th MEU(SOC), assisted by Italian Marines, provides security for the amphibious withdrawal of the last U.N. peacekeepers from the strife-torn country in Operation United Shield.

19 April
Terrorism
Two Marine recruiters are killed and four wounded in the truck bombing of the Alfred P. Murrah Federal Building in Oklahoma City, Oklahoma. There are also hundreds of civilian casualties.

24–25 May
Balkans
Marine aircraft participate in strikes on Serbian ammunition dumps in support of continuing NATO action in the troubled region.

8 June
Balkans
24th MEU(SOC) rescues Air Force Captain Scott O'Grady from Serb-controlled territory in Bosnia. His F-16C had been shot down by Serbian missiles six days earlier.

30 June
Sergeants Major
Sergeant Major Lewis G. Lee succeeds Sergeant Major Overstreet and becomes the 13th Sergeant Major of the Marine Corps.

Left: *Sgt C. Banks, Jr., of 2/2, distributes food in Cap Haitien, Haiti. (Defense Visual Information Center)*

Opposite: *Haiti. ("Getting Ready," Capt Charles Grow, USMC, Marine Corps Art Collection)*

1 July
Commandants
General Mundy retires and is replaced by General Charles C. Krulak, the 31st Commandant of the Marine Corps.

16 August
Manpower
In a change to the physical fitness test for female Marines, they are now required to run the same three-mile distance as their male counterparts.

29 August
Balkans
VMFA(AW)-533 at Aviano and VMFA-312 on board carrier *Theodore Roosevelt* (CVN-71) participate in the beginning of Operation Deliberate Force, an air offensive designed to force the Serbian government to end its brutal operations in Bosnia. The campaign continues through 21 December, when NATO forces are fully deployed in Bosnia to enforce peace.

26 September
Manpower
First Lieutenant Sarah Deal completes the training syllabus for the CH-53E and is assigned to HMH-466, thus becoming the first female Marine pilot.

30 September
Manpower
The strength of the Marine Corps on active duty is 17,831 officers and 156,808 enlisted.

1996

17 January
HQMC
The Commandant and other major elements of HQMC move into the Pentagon from the Navy Annex, where they have been located for more than five decades.

27 March
Manpower
Marine Major General Carol A. Mutter is the first female nominated for three-star rank in any of the services. She is promoted on 23 July.

April
Force Structure
The Chemical Biological Incident Response Force (CBIRF) is created to provide a Marine capability to deal with terrorist acts involving chemical or biological agents.

20 April
Liberia
Elements of 22nd MEU(SOC) fly into Monrovia and begin a weeks-long evacuation of thousands of Americans and other foreign nationals in the face of an ongoing civil war.

10 May
Mishap
A mid-air collision involving a CH-46E and an AH-1W over Camp Lejeune results in the death of 12 Marines, one sailor, and one soldier.

21 May
Central African Republic
Another element of 22nd MEU(SOC) flies into the country to evacuate Americans and assist the MSG detachment in protecting the embassy during an army mutiny.

14 June
Force Structure
VMFA-235 is deactivated at Miramar.

25 July
Manpower
As part of an increase of flag officers in the armed services, the Marine Corps is authorized an increase from 68 to 80 generals, giving it one more than it had during WWII.

30 July
Training
Commandant Krulak announces changes to recruit training. The most significant will be the Crucible, a 54-hour event near the end of the boot camp cycle that will challenge the mental and physical endurance of recruits and mark their transformation into Marines.

30 September
Manpower
The combined strength of the Marine Corps on active duty is 174,049 officers and enlisted.

30 December
Manpower
Female Marines begin reporting for the first time to Marine Combat Training, a post-boot camp program that provides infantry training to Marines destined to serve in non-infantry specialties.

1997

31 January
Force Structure
VMFA-451 is deactivated.

1–14 March
Doctrine
The recently activated Warfighting Lab conducts Hunter Warrior, an exercise at 29 Palms testing futuristic doctrine and technologies.

13–26 March
Albania
26th MEU(SOC) evacuates more than 900 Americans and other foreign nationals during chaotic conditions following the disintegration of the Communist government.

29 May
Sierra Leone
22nd MEU(SOC) begins evacuation of civilians escaping a civil war. Over the next five days, the MEU pulls out more than 2,500 people, including 450 Americans.

30 September
Manpower
The combined strength of the Marine Corps on active duty is 174,873 officers and enlisted.

1 October
Bases
The Marine Corps takes over Miramar from the Navy as a replacement for El Toro.

1998

31 January
Force Structure
The Marine Corps begins deactivating the last of its ships detachments.

3 February
Mishap
A Marine EA-6B on a training mission in Italy flies through a cable and sends a ski gondola crashing to the ground, killing 20 people.

6 June
Eritrea
KC-130s attached to 11th MEU(SOC) evacuate civilians following border clashes between Eritrea and Ethiopia.

7 August
Terrorism
Truck bombs explode at U.S. embassies in Nairobi, Kenya, and Dar es Salaam, Tanzania. More than 250 are killed, including one Marine security guard. FAST platoons deploy to secure the sites.

30 September
Manpower
The strength of the Marine Corps on active duty is 17,892 officers and 155,250 enlisted.

16 December
Iraq
31st MEU(SOC) and VMFA-312, on board *Enterprise* (CVN-65), participate in Operation Desert Fox, an air campaign launched in retaliation for Iraq's obstruction of a U.N. weapons inspection program. The operation lasts for four days.

1999

24 March
Balkans
NATO launches Operation Allied Force, an air campaign to force Serbian withdrawal from the ethnic Albanian province of Kosovo. Harriers of 24th MEU(SOC) participate.

30 April
Balkans
Elements of 26th MEU(SOC) go ashore in Albania to provide security and assistance to a camp housing refugees from Kosovo.

14 May
Technology
The Marine Corps takes delivery of its first production MV-22 Osprey.

20 May
Balkans
VMFA(AW)-332 and 533 begin flying in support of Operation Allied Force from bases in Hungary.

Opposite: *LAV in Operation Provide Comfort. (Defense Visual Information Center)*

Right: *Marine Hornet about to launch from* Enterprise. *(Defense Visual Information Center)*

10 June
Balkans
Operation Allied Force is suspended when the Serbian forces begin withdrawing from Kosovo. 26th MEU(SOC) begins deploying to the province to enforce the peace agreement. It remains ashore through 6 July.

28 June
Sergeants Major
Sergeant Major Alfred L. McMichael succeeds Sergeant Major Lee and becomes the 14th Sergeant Major of the Marine Corps.

1 July
Commandants
General Krulak retires and is replaced by General James L. Jones, Jr., the 32nd Commandant of the Marine Corps

2 July
Bases
The Marine Corps closes El Toro and Tustin as part of a reduction in military bases.

30 September
East Timor
31st MEU(SOC) helicopters support the deployment of Australian forces restoring peace in the region following post-election violence by armed gangs. 11th MEU(SOC) takes over on 26 October and remains on station through 7 December.

Manpower
The strength of the Marine Corps on active duty is 17,897 officers and 154,744 enlisted.

2000

12 January
Venezuela
Marines from II MEF deploy to provide humanitarian assistance following massive storms that devastated the northern area of the country. The Marines will remain on station till 12 March.

8 April
Mishap
A MV-22 Osprey crashes near Tuscon, Arizona, during a training exercise, killing 19 Marines.

30 September
Force Structure
HMH-366 is de-activated.
Manpower
The strength of the Marine Corps on active duty is 17,938 officers and 155,383 enlisted.

12 October
Terrorism
A boat bomb blasts a hole in the side of destroyer *Cole* (DDG-67), killing 17 sailors and injuring 39. The 13th MEU(SOC) and elements of 2nd FAST deploy to secure the ship in the harbor of Aden, Yemen.

Left: *Marines of Bravo Company, 1/8, wait inside a MV-22 Osprey for the start of a training mission. (Defense Visual Information Center)*

Right: *The Marine Corps Band in New York City's Desert Storm victory parade. (Defense Visual Information Center)*

11 December
Mishap
Four Marines are killed when their MV-22 Osprey crashes near Jacksonville, North Carolina. The second crash of the year leads to an indefinite suspension of MV-22 flights.

2001

17 August
Heritage
Fifty-nine years after they died in the raid on Makin Island in 1942, 13 members of the 2nd Marine Raider Battalion are buried in Arlington National Cemetery. Their remains had been recovered and eventually identified by teams from the DOD's POW-MIA office and the Central Identification Laboratory based in Hawaii.

11 September
Terrorism
Members of the Al Qaida terrorist organization hijack four jetliners, crashing one each into the Pentagon and the two towers of the World Trade Center in New York City. A fourth crashes in rural Pennsylvania. Marines in the Pentagon participate in rescue operations.

30 September
Manpower
The strength of the Marine Corps on active duty is 18,057 officers and 154,878 enlisted.

October
Department of Defense
General Peter Pace becomes the first Marine ever to serve as the Vice Chairman of the JCS.

7 October
Operation Enduring Freedom
U.S. forces begin an air and special operations campaign against Taliban and Al Qaida elements in Afghanistan. VMFA-251 and 314, on board carriers *Roosevelt* (CVN-71)and *Stennis* (CVN-74), and the Harriers of 15th MEU(SOC) participate in the aerial campaign.

29 October
Force Structure
4th MEB (Antiterrorism) is activated. It consists of existing forces: Marine Security Force Battalion and its two FAST companies, Marine Security Guard Battalion, CBIRF, and an interim antiterrorism battalion.

1 November
Operation Enduring Freedom
Task Force 58 is activated in Central Command to control the 15th and 26th MEU(SOC)s.

25 November
Operation Enduring Freedom
15th MEU(SOC) elements begin landing in Afghanistan more than 400 miles from the coast and take control of Forward Operating Base

Left: *MV-22 silhouetted against the morning sky as it lands on* Wasp. *(Defense Visual Information Center)*

(FOB) Rhino. Marine air and ground forces begin patrolling the region in search of Taliban and Al Qaida fighters.

28 November
Operation Enduring Freedom
A detachment from I MEF deploys to Kuwait to head up Combined Joint Task Force Consequence Management (CJTF-CM) with the mission of coordinating the response to any use of chemical or biological weapons in the region.

7 December
Operation Enduring Freedom
In the largest Marine fire fight of the campaign, a patrol kills seven enemy and destroys three vehicles while interdicting a road. Aircraft destroy several more occupied vehicles.

11 December
Operation Enduring Freedom
Elements of 26th MEU(SOC) secure the long-abandoned U.S. Embassy in Kabul, Afghanistan.

14 December
Operation Enduring Freedom
Elements of 15th and 26th MEU(SOC)s advance overland and take control of Kandahar Airfield. It soon becomes the primary detention facility for captured enemy personnel of key interest to the United States. Marine helicopters also support joint and coalition forces from this base.

23 December
Operation Enduring Freedom
Elements of 4th MEB (AT) assume responsibility for providing security to the U.S. Embassy in Kabul, Afghanistan.

24 December
Operation Enduring Freedom
15th MEU(SOC) begins re-deploying back to its ships. FOB Rhino is closed on 3 January 2002.

2002

4 January
Operation Enduring Freedom
Elements from II MEF (primarily 2nd FSSG) begin deploying to Guantanamo Bay, Cuba, to set up and operate a detention facility (soon known as Camp X-Ray) for Al Qaida and Taliban detainees. Four days later Marine Brigadier General Michael Lehnert assumes command of JTF- 160, newly established to run the camp. The first detainees begin arriving on 11 January.

Right: *Marines man an entry control point outside Kandahar, Afghanistan, in January 2002. (SSgt Michael D. Fay, USMCR)*

Below: *Weary Marines return from a nine-day patrol in Afghanistan. (SSgt Michael D. Fay, USMCR)*

9 January
Operation Enduring Freedom
A KC-130 of VMGR-352 crashes in Pakistan, resulting in the death of seven Marines.

17 January
Uniforms
The first of the new digital-pattern-camouflage utility uniforms are issued.

19 January
Operation Enduring Freedom
U.S. Army forces begin relieving Marine elements at Kandahar Airfield. 26th MEU(SOC) is back on board ships by 8 February. A CH-53E crashes, killing two Marines and injuring five.

1 February
Operation Enduring Freedom
Elements of the 3rd Marines deploy to Zamboanga on the island of Mindanao in the Philippines to support the Joint Special Operations Task Force providing assistance to Philippine forces fighting terrorists in that region.

13 February
Operation Enduring Freedom
Four CH-53E helicopters from 26th MEU(SOC) deploy more than 700 miles from the sea to Bagram Airfield to support Army operations. They remain ashore for a week.

26 February
Operation Enduring Freedom
TF 58 is de-activated.

4 March
Operation Enduring Freedom
Following a request from U.S. Army forces engaged in heavy fighting with Taliban and Al Qaida forces in the Shah I Khot Valley of

Afghanistan, five AH-1W Cobras and three CH-53E Super Stallions of 13th MEU(SOC) deploy to Bagram Airfield to support Operation Anaconda. Two days later, Harriers of 13th MEU(SOC) begin flying missions in the same operation. The aircraft continue their support through 25 March and fly hundreds of combat sorties.

29 May
Technology
MV-22 test aircraft resume flying following significant changes instituted in the wake of two major mishaps in 2000.

30 September
Manpower
The strength of the Marine Corps on active duty is 18,431 officers and 156,473 enlisted.

15 October
Operation Enduring Freedom
VMA-513 (-) deploys to Bagram Airfield in Afghanistan to support continuing operations against Taliban and Al Qaida remnants.

15 November
Operation Iraqi Freedom
The headquarters of I MEF Forward begins deploying to Kuwait to command Marine elements in the theater in support of efforts to force the Saddam Hussein regime of Iraq to give up its weapons of mass destruction. This campaign ultimately will be designated Operation Iraqi Freedom.

Above: *Marines set trip flares on a likely avenue of enemy approach outside their perimeter at Kandahar in January 2002. (SSgt Michael D. Fay, USMCR, Marine Corps Art Collection)*

Right: *Captain Susan Thompson, commander of a combat service support unit serving with the 5th Marines, reads her first mail from home during a chemical warfare drill in Kuwait prior to the start of Operation Iraqi Freedom. (Nuccio DiNuzzio, Chicago Tribune)*

Left: *Marine engineers bridged this waterway about ten miles east of downtown Baghdad in the final push to seize the Iraqi capital. (John Makely, Baltimore Sun)*

Operation Enduring Freedom
The command element of the 2nd Marine Division and detachments of II MEF are designated as headquarters of Combined Joint Task Force Horn of Africa (CJTF-HOA). It deploys on *USS Mount Whitney* (LCC-20) to take command of efforts to seek out and destroy terrorists operating in the vicinity of the Horn of Africa.

27 December
Force Structure
To simplify the future deployment of units to the Middle East, the Marine Corps orders all units serving in the Unit Deployment Program (UDP) in Japan and Okinawa to remain in place indefinitely.

2003

13 January
Commandants
General Michael W. Hagee becomes the 33rd Commandant of the Marine Corps. In a rare departure from custom, General Jones remains on active duty and transfers to become the Supreme Allied Commander, Europe (SACEUR) and Commander of U.S. European Command. He is the first Marine ever to hold this dual billet and the first former Commandant ever reassigned as a theater commander.

14 January
Manpower
The Marine Corps begins calling numerous Reserve units and individuals to active duty.

Right: *Marines lay down a base of fire for an assault across a field outside of the town of Aziziyah on 2 April during Operation Iraqi Freedom. (John Makely, Baltimore Sun)*

Left: *During the big sandstorm in the latter days of March, Marines work to free a bogged-down AAV as they move through south-central Iraq. (John Makely, Baltimore Sun)*

Below: *After a stiff firefight near the end of a week of war, Lance Corporal Marcco Ware carries a wounded Iraqi soldier back to receive medical care. (John Makely, Baltimore Sun)*

By April 2003, just over 50% of all Marines in the Ready Reserve will have been mobilized in support of Operations Enduring Freedom and Iraqi Freedom.

15 January
Operation Iraqi Freedom
The 2nd Marine Expeditionary Brigade (roughly 7,000 Marines and attached Navy personnel) departs North Carolina for the Middle East embarked in Amphibious Task Force East.

17 January
Operation Iraqi Freedom
The 1st Marines and reinforcing elements of I MEF (roughly 6,000 Marines and attached

Navy personnel) depart southern California for the Middle East embarked in Amphibious Task Force West. Ships of the Maritime Prepositioning Force begin to offload equipment and supplies in Kuwait.

21 January
Operation Iraqi Freedom
The remaining elements of I MEF and some reinforcing elements of II MEF begin flowing into Kuwait by air to marry up with material from the MPF squadrons.

22 January
Mishap
Four Marine Corps aviators of HMLA-775 die when their two AH-1W Cobra helicopters collide during night operations in Texas in support of Joint Task Force 6, which provides military assistance to counter-drug efforts along the southern border.

11 February
Operation Northern Watch
VMAQ-1 deploys overseas to support coalition air operations enforcing the no-fly zone in northern Iraq.

12 February
Operation Iraqi Freedom
The 15th MEU(SOC) (2/1 and HMM-161) goes ashore in Kuwait to reinforce I MEF.

16 February
Operation Iraqi Freedom
2nd MEB begins to go ashore in Kuwait to reinforce I MEF. Its aviation elements transfer to 3rd MAW control and the ground elements are re-designated as Task Force Tarawa.

24 February
Operation Iraqi Freedom
Amphibious Task Force West begins offloading its Marine units in Kuwait to reinforce I MEF.

17 March
Operation Iraqi Freedom
President George Bush issues an ultimatum to Saddam Hussein requiring him to leave the country with his sons in 48 hours. I MEF forces in place to enforce the ultimatum consist of the 1st Marine Division, Task Force Tarawa, 3rd MAW, 1st FSSG, the MEF Engineer Group, and the United Kingdom's 7th Armoured Division—a total of more than 80,000 personnel. The 1st Marine Division is organized with RCT 1 (3/1, 1/4, 2/23, and 2nd LAR Battalion), RCT 5 (1/5, 2/5, 3/5, 2nd Tank Battalion, and 1st LAR Battalion), RCT 7 (1/7, 3/7, 3/4, 1st Tank Battalion, and 3rd LAR Battalion), 11th Marines (1/11, 2/11, 3/11, 5/11, and the MLRS launchers of the U.S. Army's 3-27 Field Artillery Battalion), 1st Reconnaissance Battalion, 2nd and 3rd Assault Amphibian Battalions, 1st and 2nd Combat Engineer Battalions, and supporting elements. Task Force Tarawa includes the 2nd Marines (1/2, 2/2, and 2/8), 1/10, and supporting detachments. 3rd MAW includes MAG-11 (VMGR-352, VMAQ-1 and 2,

VMFA-232 and 251, and VMF(AW)-121, 225, and 533), MAG-13 (VMA-211, 214, 223, 311, and 542), MAG-16 (HMM- 163 and HMH-462 and 465), MAG-29 (HMM-162 and 365, HMH-464, and HMLA-269), and MAG-39 (HMM-268 and 364, and HMLA-169 and 267). The MEF Engineer Group is composed of the 22nd and 30th Naval Construction Regiments. The 7th Armoured Division consists of 7th Armoured Brigade, 16th

Above: *Marines kick in the gate of a Baath Party compound as they commence a search for loyalists of the Saddam Hussein regime in the town of Qalat Sukar. (Cpl Jeff Sisto, USMC)*

Left: *The 1st Marine Division's mechanized thrust follows the signs pointing toward the ultimate objective. (John Makely, Baltimore Sun)*

Air Assault Brigade, and 3d Commando Brigade (40 and 42 Commando Groups). The 15th MEU(SOC) is under tactical control of 3d Commando Brigade. In addition, VMFA-115 is on *USS Harry S Truman* (CVN-75), VMFA-323 is on *USS Constellation* (CV-64), and VMFA-312 is on *USS Theodore Roosevelt* (CVN-71), all participating in coalition air operations. The 24th MEU(SOC) (2/2 and HMM-263) is deployed in the Persian Gulf. Along with the U.S. Army's V Corps, I MEF is subordinate to the Combined Forces Land Component Command (built around the U.S. Army's Third Army headquarters). This is the first use by U.S.forces in a major campaign of the CFLCC concept, which mirrors the joint forces air component command (JFACC) used in previous operations.

20 March
Operation Iraqi Freedom
After the expiration of the 48-hour ultimatum, coalition forces launch Operation Iraqi Freedom. I MEF is responsible for liberating the eastern half of Iraq and securing the right flank of the U.S. Army's V Corps while the latter force advances to Baghdad in a zone west of the Euphrates River. The Iraqi forces in the southern half of I MEF's zone include two corps composed of two armored divisions, one mechanized division, and three infantry divisions—70,000 troops armed with 700 tanks and 500 artillery pieces. 3rd MAW conducts close air support for the MEF and deep strikes for the JFACC.

21 March
Operation Iraqi Freedom
The 1st Marine Division seizes control of the Rumaila oil fields, one of its key objectives for the campaign. Although Iraqi forces have set seven wells on fire, the early capture of this region prevents the mass destruction of oil wells experienced in Kuwait during the Gulf War. 3d Commando Brigade and 15th MEU seize the Al Faw Peninsula and the port of Umm Qasr, Iraq's primary sea link. The remainder of 7th Armoured Division drives on Basra, the second largest city in Iraq.

Opposite, top: *A gunner from BLT 2/2 mans his squad automatic weapon (SAW) in the fight for Al Kut. (Cpl Jeff Sisto, USMC)*

Opposite, bottom: *M1A1 tanks of Charlie Company, 1st Tank Battalion, take firing positions in an Iraqi field on 1 April as the division drives north toward Baghdad. (Sgt Paul Anstine III, USMC)*

23 March
Operation Iraqi Freedom
Task Force Tarawa begins operations to secure the city of An Nasiriyah and its key bridges over the Euphrates River. In some of the fiercest fighting of the war, Iraqi forces (including many irregulars) use feigned surrenders, human shields, and suicide bombers to deny Marines free movement in the city of a half million people. Fighting continues for two weeks.

24 March
Operation Iraqi Freedom
Marine Major General Henry P. Osman deploys to Salahuddin, Iraq, to head the newly established Military Coordination and Liaison Command (MCLC). Its mission is to establish links between Turkey and Iraqi Kurdish forces allied with the coalition in northern Iraq.

28 March
Operation Iraqi Freedom
The 24th MEU(SOC) begins to go ashore in Kuwait to reinforce I MEF operations in southern Iraq. 15th MEU(SOC) joins TF Tarawa in operations at Nasiriyah.

1 April
Operation Iraqi Freedom
Marines launch a diversionary attack near Nasiriyah to assist special operations forces rescuing one of eight American soldiers held prisoner by Iraqi forces.

2 April
Operation Iraqi Freedom
Elements of the 1st Marine Division cross the Tigris River 80 miles southeast of Baghdad at Numaniyah and complete the destruction of the Baghdad Division of Iraq's Republican Guard around Kut.

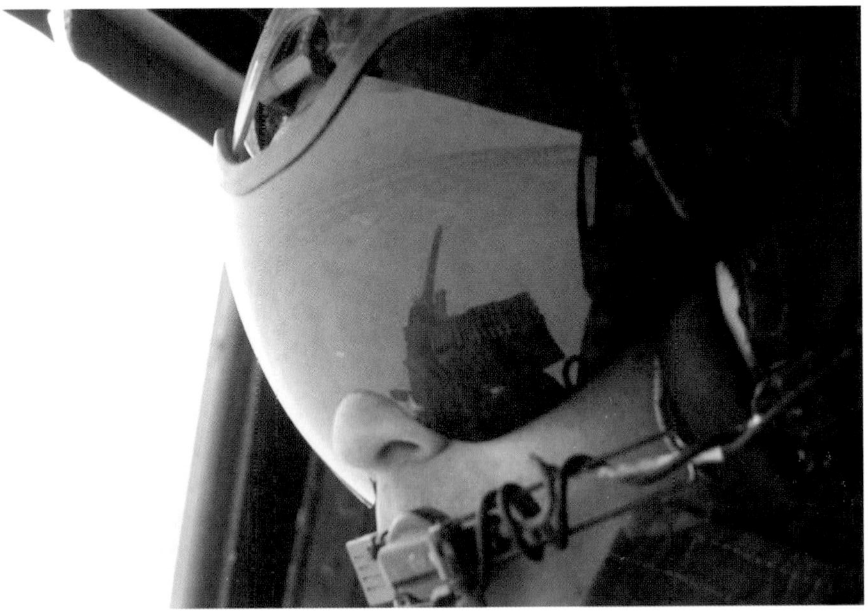

Above: *Cobras provide overwatch as Marine ground forces drive north in Iraq. (Sgt Joseph Chenelly, USMC)*

Left: *A crew chief keeps close watch as his UH-1N Huey flies a patrol over the Iraqi desert. (Sgt Joseph Chenelly, USMC)*

Left: *At a forward arming and refueling point inside Iraq, Corporal Alvin Hicks prepares an AH-1W Cobra gunship for another mission. (LCpl C. H. Fitzgerald, USMC)*

3 April
Operation Enduring Freedom
Marine Harriers participate in a major attack on a Taliban camp north of Spin Boldak, Afghanistan.

4 April
Operation Iraqi Freedom
The 1st Marine Division battles its way through the Al Nida Division of the Republican Guard and into the southeastern outskirts of Baghdad while the U.S. Army's 3rd Infantry Division consolidates its hold on Saddam International Airport in the western suburbs of the Iraqi capital.

7 April
Operation Iraqi Freedom
The 1st Marine Division crosses the Diyala River in eastern Baghdad using bridges built under fire by engineers. British forces attached to I MEF finish securing the city of Basra. Elements of the U.S. Army 3rd Infantry Division reach the western bank of the Tigris River in central Baghdad.

9 April
Operation Iraqi Freedom
Iraqi resistance in Baghdad collapses and U.S. forces occupy the remainder of the capital. Marines assist Iraqi civilians in toppling a large statue of Saddam Hussein in Firdaus Square, bringing a symbolic end to the regime. Corporal Edward Chin of 1st Tank Battalion alternately places American and Iraqi flags on the face of the statue before attaching a chain from a tank retriever to pull down the bronze edifice.

Right: *A M198 155mm howitzer fires a mission north of Umm Qasr, Iraq. (Maj K. A. Hoard, USMC)*

Left: *A SMAW gunner advances on the outskirts of Kut along with fellow Marine infantrymen. (Robert Nickelsberg, Time)*

Below: *Corporal Edward Chin of 1st Tank Battalion briefly places a U.S. flag over the face of a statue of Saddam Hussein as he helps Iraqi civilians tear down the symbol of repression. (Robert Nickelsberg, Time)*

13 April
Operation Iraqi Freedom
Following a dash from Baghdad, Task Force Tripoli (consisting primarily of 1st, 2nd, and 3rd LAR Battalions) takes control of Tikrit, Saddam Hussein's hometown and the last significant city held by the regime. Along the way, the Marines find the seven remaining American POWs.

15 April
Operation Iraqi Freedom
Elements of 26th MEU(SOC) (1/8, HMM-264, and a detachment of VMA-223) begin to flow into northern Iraq to control Mosul, a large city liberated days earlier by Kurdish forces.

20 April
Operation Iraqi Freedom
I MEF begins re-deploying its forces in central and northern Iraq into its zone of responsibility covering the southern third of Iraq. Its mission now is security, humanitarian assistance, and reconstruction. I MEF casualties through this point in the operation are 66 killed in action or dead from other causes and 246 wounded.

22 April
Operation Iraqi Freedom
The 24th MEU(SOC) begins deploying back toward its ships. It will be the first Marine unit to depart Iraq.

28 April
Sergeants Major
The Commandant appoints Sergeant Major John L. Estrada as the 15th Sergeant Major of the Marine Corps effective 26 June 2003. Sergeant Major Estrada is currently deployed with 3rd MAW in Operation Iraqi Freedom.

1 May
Operation Iraqi Freedom
The 26th MEU(SOC) departs Mosul and returns to its ships in the Mediterranean.

This book is an expanded update of the official Marine Corps chronology. As always, the staff of the Marine Corps History and Museums Division provided access to their invaluable materials. Jack Dyer, curator of art and a former combat artist, gave his sage advice in selecting illustrations. Reference historians Dan Crawford, Bob Aquilina, and Lena Kaljot made available their extensive files. Evy Englander, the librarian, never failed to find a book needed to fill in a missing link. In addition, Gail Munro (curator of the Navy Art Collection), Jim Zobel (archivist of the MacArthur Memorial), Paul Culp (curator of the Thomason Collection at Sam Houston State University Library), and Jim Ginther (archivist at the Gray Research Center), were of great assistance in mining material from their respective collections.

Colonel Jon T. Hoffman, USMCR, has spent his entire career as an infantry officer and military historian. During his 17 years of active duty, he has commanded two companies in an infantry battalion, taught history at the U.S. Naval Academy, and served as the deputy director of the History and Museums Division. He has published dozens of articles and two books. His first book, *Once a Legend: 'Red Mike' Edson of the Marine Raiders,* received the Marine Corps Heritage Foundation's 1994 Greene Award. His most recent volume, *Chesty: The Story of Lieutenant General Lewis B. Puller, USMC,* earned the 2002 Greene Award and was on *The New York Times* bestseller list. In 1998 he was honored as a *Marine Corps Gazette* Distinguished Author.

INDEX

Page numbers in *italics* indicate illustrations.

Adams, President John, 26–27, 624
Adams, LCpl John T., 565
Afghanistan, 649–651
Africa, 85, 530, 532, 534, 539
Aircraft
Bell AH-1 Cobra, 577, 592, 599, 632, *639*, 645; **Bell HTL**, *449*, 456, 468; **Bell Textron V-22 Osprey**, 634, 642, 647–*650*; **Bell UH-1 Huey**, 592; **Boeing CH-46 Seaknight**, *529*, 542, 551, 555, 563, *630*–632, 634–635, 645; **Boeing O2B-1**, 169, 217, 219, 224; **Brewster F2A Buffalo**, 264, 268; **Chance Vought F4U Corsair**, 265, 289, 301, *308*, 312, *326*, 329, 347, *375*, *454*, 489, *637*; **Chance Vought F-8 Crusader**, *505*, 517, 530, 535; **Chance Vought SB2U-3 Vindicator**, 267; **Consolidated OY-1 Grasshopper**, *399*; **Convair R3Y-2 Flying LST**, 508; **Curtiss F6C-3 Hawk**, 214; **Curtiss F7C-1 Sea Hawk**, *236*; **Curtiss SB2C Helldivers**, *346–347*, 414; **de Havilland DH-4**, 153, 168–169, 186, 190, 216–217, 219; **Douglas A-4 Skyhawk**, *510*, 523, 531, *587*; **Douglas AD Skyraider**, 475; **Douglas F4D1 Skyray**, 531; **Douglas SBD-2 Dauntless**, 275; **Douglas D-558 Skystreak**, 434; **Douglas F3D-2 Skyknight**, 488; **Fairchild R4Q Packets**, 498; **Fokker TA-2**, *225*, *231*; **Grumman A6 Intruder**, 557, 599; **Grumman EA-6 Prowler**, *596*, 626, 647; **Grumman F4F Wildcat**, *261*, 263–265, *269*, *274*–275, 288–289, *303*, 312, 436; **Grumman F6F Hellcat**, 265; **Grumman F7F Tigercat**, 477; **Grumman F9F Panther**, 467, 489; **Hawker Siddeley AV-8A Harrier**, 584, 590, 593, 597, 609; **Lockheed GV-1 Hercules**, 531, 535; **Lockheed KC-130 Hercules**, 557, 568, 571, 586, 639, 647, 651; **Lockheed TO-1 Shooting Star**, 449; **McDonnell Douglas AV-8B Harrier**, 630, 634–*635*; **McDonnell Douglas F/A-18 Hornet**, 628, *640*; **McDonnell Douglas F-4 Phantom**, 529, 599; **McDonnell FH-1 Phantom**, 435; **North American B-25 (PBJ-1) Mitchell**, 401–403; **North American FJ-4 Fury**, *513*, 525; **North American OV-10 Bronco**, 571, 594, 643; **Piasecki HRP-1 Flying Banana**, 428–429, 435, 441, 446; **Pitcairn OP-1 Autogyro**, 232, 428; **Sikorsky CH-37**, 516; **Sikorsky CH-53 Sea Stallion**, 558, 592, 608, 626, 630–631 *635*, 645, 651; **Sikorsky HO3S-1**, 428–429, 435, 438, 455; **Sikorsky HRS-1**, 429, *447*, 485, *509*; **Sikorsky HUS-1**, 516; **Sikorsky UH-34 Seahorse**, *529*; **Vought O2U Corsair**, 221, *231*
Alabama CSS, 93–94, 97, (BB-8), 132
Alaska, 102, 118
Albania, 646
Albany (sloop), 79, (CL-23), 151, 155, 208
Alcatraz Penitentiary, 420
Aleutian Islands, 278, 303
Alfred, *12*, 13, 18, 21
Alliance, 24–26, 109, 115
American Revolution, 10, 16, 25
Anderson, Col Norman, 532
Andre, Lt Jon W., 486
Anthony, Pvt William, 121
Apamama Atoll, 325, 327
Argentina, 57, 79, 117
Argus (brig), 36, 40, 47
Arundel Island, 317
Atlanta (cruiser), 114, 120, 140
Augusta (CA-31), 235, 242, 364
Axtell, Maj George C., Jr., 393

Badoeng Strait (CVE-116), 454, 467
Bahamas, 13–*16*, *20*–21, 25, 39–40, 251
Bairoko (CVE-115), 483, 485
Baker, Capt Doyle D., 566
Balkans, 642, 644–645, 647–648
Baltimore (C-3), 118–119, 122, 126–127
Bangladesh, 641
Barbary Wars, 29, 34, 38, 41, 52
Barber, Capt William E., 462
Barnett, MajGen George, 147, 155, 162, 165, 174, 179, 186–187, 199, 204, 258
Barnwell, SSgt Barbara O., 498
Barrett, MajGen Charles D., 317, 319
Barrow, Gen Robert, 464, 622, 626, 628
Barry, Sgt John, 20
Bataan (CVL-29), 467, 469, 485
Batraville, Benoit, 201, 204
Basilone, GySgt John, 292–293
Bauber, SgtMaj Francis D., 525, 537
Bauer, LtCol Harold W., 265, 290–291
Belleau Wood, France, 135, 176, 180, 182–183
Bennington (CV-20), 374, 377, 391, 398
Benson, PFC Kenneth R., 462–463
Bestwick, SgtMaj Wilbur, 516, 525
Betio Island, *314*, *317*, 325–326, 328, 330–331
Biddle, MajGen William P., 133, 147, 150, 162
Bikini Atoll, 345, 417, 422–424, 428
Binns, LCpl Ricardo, 565
Black, SgtMaj Henry H., 615, 620
Blanc Mont, France, 177, 187–189
Bladensburg, Maryland, 33, 48–50
Block Island (CVE-106), 379, 388, 395, 399, 405
Bodnar, Sgt John P., 360
Bolt, Maj John F., 497
Bonhomme Richard, *23*–24
Boomer, LtGen Walter E., 638
Borneo, 270, 399
Boston (frigate), 19, 31, (cruiser), 114, 118, 126
Bougainville Island, 302–303, *309*, *312*–314, 316–321, 323–329, 332–336, 349, 352–353, *375*, 380
Bowser, MajGen Alpha M., 532
Boxer (LPH-4), 521–522, 526
Boxer Rebellion, 129, 132–134, 624
Boyce, Capt Abraham, 17
Boyden, Lt Hayne D., 218–219
Boyington, Maj Gregory, 289, 317, 332, 334–335
Branch, Lt Frederick C., 343, 413
Brazil, 209
Breckinridge, BGen James C., 238
Brewer, BGen Margaret A., 621
Brewster, Lt Everett S., 187
Brice, LtGen William O., 510
Brooklyn (screw sloop), 94–95, *120*, (ACR-3), 141, 143, 182
Broome, Capt John L., 92
Brown, Cpl Charles, *107*
Brown, Capt James R., *263*
Brown, John, 90–91
Brown, Capt Leslie E., 457
Brown, Lt Walter V., 208
Brown, Lt William P., 394
Brunner, Sgt Frederick J., 360
Buckner, LtGen Simon B., 323, 398
Bull Run, Virginia, 88, 104–105
Bunker Hill (CV-17), 374, 378, 390, 395
Burrows, LtCol William W., 27–28, 30, 32, 34–35
Bush, President George W., 635, 638, 640, 642
Bush, Lt William, 43
Butler, BGen Smedley, 135, 146–149, 151, 154–155, *165*–166, 216–*217*
Button, Cpl William R., 201–202

Caco Revolt, 190, 198, 202, 204
Cafferate, PFC Hector A., Jr., 462–463
California, 61, 66–72
Cambodia, 585, 591, 604, 606, 610–614
Campbell, BGen Harold D., 370
Canada, 12, 17, 22, 42–43, 47
Cape Gloucester, 203, 235
Cape Gloucester (CVE-109), 390, 396, 399–400
Capodanno, Lt Vincent R., Jr., 572–573
Capolino, John J., *107*, *133*, *205*
Caribbean Sea, 21, 25, 27, 30–31, 54, 93, 118, 144, 210–211, 231, 241, 248, 251, 504, 528–529, 536, 584–585, 593
Carl MajGen Marion E., 265, 284, 434–437
Carlson, BGen Evans F., 282–283, *295*
Carlson, Lt Evans, *295*
Carmick, Maj Daniel, 28–30
Carr, LtCol Gerald P., 607
Cates, Gen Clifton B., *274*, 435, 439, 442, 448, 453, *455*, 480, 482
Central African Republic, 645
Central Command, 627, 631
Ceylon, 518
Chafee, John H., 576, 592
Chapman, Gen Leonard F., Jr., 567, 590, 596
Chapultepec Castle, 86
Chaumont, 210
Chenoweth, Col H. Avery, *52*, *175*, *334*, *447*, *451*, *481*
Chesapeake (frigate), 29, 38, 43
Chica, Sgt Robert J., 575
Chicago (cruiser), 114, 118
Chile, 47, 118
China, 61, 80–82, 84, 99, 102, 119, 126, 128–129, 132–136, 150–151, 154–155 209–211, 226, 233, 262, 267, 404–405, 410–414, 416, 418–427, 430–432, 434–435, 438–440, 442–446, 465
Chingwangtao, China, 215, 410, 426–427
Choiseul Island, 313, 318, 320–321
Chosin Reservoir, 235, 461–468, 491
Civil War, 33, 85, 88–101
Cleary, SgtMaj Robert E., 628, 632
Clymer, John, *50*, *60*, *109*
Coco River, Nicaragua, 222, 225
Coleman, Capt Jerry, 485
Colombia, 106–107, 120
Combined Action Program (CAP), 547, 582, 586, 588, 593
Commandant's House, 33, 49
Condra, Col Edward M., III, *632*
Congo, 528, 531
Congress (frigate), 51, 67, 74–75, 89
Conlon, Ned, *505*, *569*
Constellation (frigate), 27, 30, 34, 43, 58
Constitution (frigate), 28–*30*, *39*, 42–43, 52, 80, 109
Corporal Louis J. Hauge, Jr., 630
Corregidor Island, *266*, 268, 271, 273–274, 435
Cox, GySgt J. F., 142
Craig, BGen Edward A., 452
Cram, LtCol Jack R., 403
Crawford, SgtMaj Leland D., 622, 628
Crawley, Lt Lawrence N., 395
Crist, Gen George B., 631
Croizat, LtCol Victor J., 505
Cuba, 54–55, *120*–125, 144, 150–151, *162*–*163*, 170, 174, 190, 519, 522, 525, 528, 530, 532, 538–539
Cukela, GySgt Louis, 183
Culebra Island, 162, 211–*212*, 237, *239*, 243, 255
Cumberland (frigate), 66, (sloop), 88–89, *92*
Cummings, Capt John, 601
Cunningham, LtCol Alfred, , 151–154, 170, 178–179, 198, *205*, 322
Cunningham, Maj Walter, 575
Cushman Gen Robert E., 561, 577, 596, 601, 615
Cushman, BGen Thomas J., 452
Cyane (corvette), 53, 61, 67, 75, 78–80
Cyprus, 609

Daigh, Lt Haolrd D., 474
Dailey, SgtMaj Joseph W., 580, 604
Dale (sloop), 71, 74–75, 78, 89
Daly, GySgt Dan, 133–135, 166
Da Nang, Vietnam, *527*, *531*, 538, 544
Daniels, Josephus, 166, 171, 174, 186, 204
Darnall, Lt Grover C., 218
Davidson, J. O., *23*, *92*, *98*
Davis, Capt Oliver R., 493
Deal, Lt Sarah, 645
DeBlanc, Lt Jefferson J., 265, 300
Decatur, Comm Stephen, *34*–35, 52
DeLalio, Maj Armond H., 428

DeLong, Capt Philip C., 474
Dellamano, Lt Albert F., 396
Denver (C-14), 154, 211, 214–215, (CL-16) 222, 224, (LPD-9), 599, 635
Derna, Tripoli, 36, 38, 40–41
de Weldon, Felix, 481, 506–508
Dewey, Adm George, 122, 127, *137*
Diamond, MGySgt Leland, *301*
Dickson, Col Donald L., *11, 16, 37, 208, 279–280, 285, 291*
Dillard, Lt Joseph V., 394
Doctrine, 223, 442, 511, 624, 646
Dodson, Sgt James S., 555
Dominican Republic, *516, 522–526*, 535, 545–546
Donahue, Maj Archie, 392
Donahue, MTSgt Victor P., *327–328, 332*
Dorroh, Maj Jefferson D., 393
Douglas-Mansfield Act, 487
Dowdell, Sgt Frank E., 217
Doyen, BGen Charles A., 147, 182
Draper, William, *280, 355, 375*
Drewry's Bluff, Virginia, 92, 100
Dulinsky, MSgt Barbara J., 560
Dyer, Capt Jack T., Jr., *528*

Eaton, William, 36, 38, 40–41
Ebon Atoll, 345
Eby, Kerr, *280, 291, 324–325*
Eckes, LCpl Walter, 555
Edson, Capt Alvin, 70, 74
Edson, MajGen Merritt A., 222–225, 252, 282, 432, 506–507
Edson's Ridge, *285*–286, 292
Egypt, 109, 543
Eisenhower, President Dwight D., 493, 495, 497, 504, 507–508, 510, 530
El Salvador, 622, 631
Eldridge, Lt William W., 393
Ellice Islands, 316, 341, 343
Elliott, MajGen George F., 125, 128, 141–142, 145, 147
Elrod, Capt Henry T., 265
Emirau Island, 344, 346, 348
Eniwetok Atoll, 339–341, 343, *345–347*
Enterprise (sloop), 10, 30, 34–35, 38, 47, 54, (CV-6), 263, 284, (CVN-65), 647
Eritrea, 647
Essex (frigate), 34, 42, 44, 47, *50*, (steam bark), 116, (CV-9), 376–378, 387, 523
Ethiopia, 141
Evans, Lt Francis T., 170
Evans, Lt Jesse G., *308*
Exercises
Antietam Maneuvers, 212; **Battle Griffin**, 640; **Combined Arms Exercise (CAX)**, 622; **Desert Rock**, 485, *487*, 494; **Fleet Problem**, 237, 243; **FLEX**, 237, 241, 242, 243, 248; **Hunter Warrior**, 646; **LEX Baker One**, 483; **Louisiana Maneuvers**, 262; **Palm Tree**, 621; **Team Spirit**, 630, 634

Falklands, 57
Farragut, Adm David G., 92–94, 96–97
Farrell, Lt William, 397
Fessler, WO Dramus F., 493
Fiji Islands, 60, 81, 83
Fitzgerald, Pvt John, 125
Flagg, James M., *201, 249*
Fleming, Capt Richard E., 278
Florida, 24, 39, 42–43, 53, 55, 58–61, 88–89, 93
Folmar, Capt Jesse G., 489
Forney, LtCol James, 108
Forrestal, James V., 432–434, 438–439, 442, 444
Forsterer, Sgt Bruno A., 127
Fort Fisher, 95, 98–100
Fort Montagu, *13–16*
Fort Nassau, 14–15
Fort Sumter, 85, 88, 96, 100
Fort Ticonderoga, 10
Foss, BGen Joseph J., 265, 288–289, 294, 296, 299, 334
France, 19–20, 24, 97, 109, 117, 174–180, 182–183, 186–190, 335, 360, 364
Franklin, 12, *16*, (CV-13), 379, 388
Freeman, LtCol William H., 59
Fremont, John C., 66, 68–*70*
Fullam, Lt William, 117
Fuller, MajGen Ben H., 227, 233, 239

Gale, LtCol Anthony, 53–54
Galer, Maj Robert E., 265, *284*
Galveston (C-17), 143, 208, 214–215
Gamble, LtCol John M., 44–45
Garcia, PFC Fernando L., 522
Gavutu Island, 274–276, 279
Geiger, Gen Roy M., 175, 178, *230*, 285, 322–324, 362, *375*, 399, 416, 424, 428, 432, 510
Gendarmerie d'Haiti, 166, 202, 204
Gettysburg, Pennsylvania, 208
Ghormley, VAdm Robert L., 278, 291
Gibney, Richard M., *320, 324*
Gibraltar, 38
Gilbert, OSgt Aaron, 92
Gilbert Islands, 61, 266, 281, 316, 325–328, 332, 337
Gilbert Islands (CVE-107), 386, 392, 396–397, 399
Gillespie, Maj Archibald, 66, 68–*71*
Gillis, Maj Alexander J., 489, 497
Glenn, LtCol John H., Jr., *493*, 497, 517, 523, 536, 539
Goettge, LtCol Frank, 280
Graham, Pvt Annie E., 447
Gray, Gen Alfred M., Jr., 541, 633, 641
Great Britain, 23–24, 26, 191
Grenada, 629–*630*
Greene, Lt Israel, 90–91, 104
Greene, Gen Wallace M., Jr., 541, 550, 560, 567
Greenland, 114
Greenwich, 44, 47
Groth, John, *439, 458–459, 516, 607*
Grow, Capt Charles, *644*
Guadalcanal, 203, 235, 265, *271, 273–274*, 276–281, 283–303, 308, 322–323, 436
Guadeloupe, 27
Guam Island, 123, 127, *136*, 205, 230, 263, 266, 323, *331*, 343, 351, 353, 355–357, 360–*364*, 420, 642
Guam (LPH-9), 586. 597, 639
Guantanamo Bay, Cuba, *117, 119*, 123–127, 170, *250*, 254, 271, 404, 424, 525, 530, 538, 541–542, 550, 554, 558, 567, 606, 641, 651
Guardia Nacional Dominica, 171
Guardia Nacional (Nicaragua), 216, 230, 282
Guss, Capt William F., 480

Haiti, 116, 135, 162, 164–166, 190, 198–202, 204, 208, 234, 236, 322, 540–541, 593, 641, 644
Hamilton, John, *280, 291, 295, 354, 392*
Hamilton, Lt William, 17
Hammond, SSgt Robert J., 575
Hancock (frigate), 12, 19, (AP-3), 163–164, (CVA-19), 612–613
Hanneken, BGen Herman H., 201–203, 226
Hansen, Maj Herman A., Jr., 392
Hanson, Lt Robert M, 336–337
Harbord, MajGen James G., 182–183
Harding, President Warren, 205, 208
Harper's Ferry, Virginia, 84, 90–91
Harris, MajGen Field, 425
Harris, Col John, 84, 90, 97, 100, 104
Hart, MajGen Franklin A., 480
Hartford, 94, 96, 98, 102, 142
Hatfield, Capt Gilbert D., 218–219
Hawaii, 47, 108, 114, 117–118, 142, 213, 231, 243, 255
Hawkins, Lt William D., 328
Headquarters Marine Corps, 33, 136, 140, 150, 180–181, 198–199, 201, 204, 237, 241, 248, 300, 423, 482, 517, 531–532, 576, 645
Henderson (AP-1), 167, 211
Henderson, BGen Archibald, 33, *52*–54, 58–61, 83–84, 86–87
Henderson Field, 203, 265, 281, 284–286, 288–294, 297, 301
Henderson, Maj Lofton, 281
Heywood, MajGen Charles, 94, 98, 108, *114*–115, 117, 122, 140–141
Higgins, Andrew, 248, 274
Higgins, LtCol William R., 634
High Mobility Multipurpose Wheeled Vehicle (HMMWV), 627
Hochmuth, MajGen Bruno A., 566
Hoffman, Rep. Clare, 433
Hogaboom Board, 512–513
Hoglind, MSgt Han C., 492
Holcomb, Gen Thomas, 241, 250, 253–254, 270, 283, 310, 333–334
Holmes, Corpsman Billie D., 565
Honduras, 140, 145, 211–213, 535
Hook, Battle for the, 490–492
Hoover, President Herbert, 230, 232
Hopkins, Comm Esek, *12*–15
Hornby, Lester G., *179, 190*
Hornet (sloop), 43, 52, (CV-8), 273
Horvath, Robert T. *288, 403*
Howard, GySgt Jimmie E., 564–565
Howard, Col Samuel, *266*, 274
Hue City, Vietnam, 568–569, *581, 583*
Huff, SgtMaj Edgar R., 343, 552–553
Hunt, Capt Leroy P., 189
Huntington, LtCol Robert W., *119*, 122–124
Hulbert, Pvt Henry L., 127

Iceland, 250, *254*, 260, 262, 271, 275
Inchon, Korea, 106, 458–460, 639
Indonesia, 516–518
Iran, *620*, 622–623, 625–*627*, 633–634
Iraq, 635, 639–641, 647
Israel, 441, 443, 447, 627
Italy, 605, 647
Ivory Coast, 61
Iwo Jima, 293, 343, 370, *376, 378–379*, 381–392, 403, 507, 571, 583
Iwo Jima (LPH-2), 529, 591

Jackson, President Andrew, 51, 57–58
Jamaica, 145
Japan, 79, 96, 102–103, 117, 404–405, 411–417, 421–422, 528
Jefferson, President Thomas, 32, 34
Jensen, Lt Alvin J., 316
John Adams (frigate), 34, 36, (sloop), 60, 81
Johnson Capt Charles B., 628
Johnson, SgtMaj Gilbert H., 343
Johnson, Capt Henry, 20
Johnson, Louis A., 444–445, 448, 451, 458
Johnson, President Lyndon B., 541, 543, 546, 550, 565–565, 570, 575
Johnson, Capt Melvin C., 252–253
Johnson, Opha M., 187
Johnston Atoll, 248, 255–256, 266
Johnston, LtGen Robert B., 642–643
Joint Chiefs of Staff (JCS), 270, 276, 344, 365, 433, 438–439, 446, 448, 450, 452, 457, 487, 622, 649
Jones, Gen James L., Jr., 648
Jones, Capt John Paul, 23–26, 143
Jones, Lt Wilbur J., 309
Jones, MajGen William K., 583
Jordan, 588
Judge, SgtMaj Eleanor L., 610

Kearsarge, *65*, 97, 118, (battleship), 132
Keck, Capt L. K., 536
Keeley, Lt Edward C., 395
Kelley, Gen Paul X., 623, 628, 631, 633
Kelly, Pvt James J., 187, 189
Kennedy, President John F, 321, 531, 533–534, 537–539, 541
Kevlar helmet, 628
Khe Sanh, Vietnam, *505*, 557, 559–561, 566–571, 574, *596*
King, Adm Ernest, 267, 270, 272, 345, 350, 370, 395
Kirkpatrick, Capt Floyd C., 393
Klingman, Lt Robert R., 395
Korea, *103*, 106–*109*, 116, 119–120, 142, *414, 417–427, 429–435, 438*–499, 504, 568, 575
Korean Marine Corps (KMC), 470, 474, 476, 478, 497, 523, 527, 540, 556
Krulak, Gen Charles C., 645–646, 648
Kuwait, 630, 635, 639–640
Kwajalein Atoll, 281, 283, 338–339, 343, 426

Lake Champlain, 10, 17, *47*
Landing ships, craft, vehicles
Alligator, 254; **AAV**, 331; **Higgins Boat**, 248, 257, *276–277*, *312*; **LCAC**, 630; **LCI**, *333*; **LCM**, 274, *527*; **LCVP**, 257, *309, 350, 391*; **LST**, 349, *442*; **LSU**, *464*; **LVT**, 325, 330–331, *351, 391, 404, 531*, 594, 601. *621, 639*
Larsen, MajGen Henry L., 269, 362
Lasseter, Maj Lee, 601
Lebanon, 141, *518*–521, 620–*621, 623*, 625–630, *632*–634
Lee, 11–15
Lee, SgtMaj Lewis G., 644, 648
Lee, Gen Robert E., 84, 90–91, 99
Lee, Col William A., 227–229, 232
Lejeune, MajGen John A., 116, 141, 143, 163, *165*, 173, 183, 186, 188, 204–205, 210, 214, 226
Lentz, Capt Anne A., 299, 310
Lexington (brig), 13, 17, 20, (sloop), 57, (CV-2), 230, 273
Liberia, 61, 635, 638, 645
Libya, 631–632
Livingston, Capt Richard, 220
Lonetree, Sgt Clayton J., 633
Louisiana, 24, 92–93
Lousma, LtCol Jack R., 606
Lovell, Sgt Tom, *60, 279*
Lowe, Cpl Robert E., 400
Lyle, LCdr Alexander G., 179

MacArthur, Gen Douglas, 261, 267, 272, 345, 365, 401, 404, 451–452, 455, 461, 473
Machias (PG-5), 137, 140, 164
Mackie, Cpl John, 92
Mackin, Pvt Elton E., 176–177
Madagascar, 78
Madison, President James, 42, 52
Maguire, Sgt James, 152
Maine, *120*–121, *154*
Makin Atoll. 266, 281–283, 325–326
Malaysia, 590
Mameluke sword, 37, 55–*56*, 84
Marblehead (C-11), 119, 122–123
Mariana Islands, 344, 351, 362, 377, 405
Marietta (PG-15), 127, 137, 140, 144–145
Marine Band, 30–31, 33–34, 39, 121, 585
Marine Barracks
8th and I, 31–34, 42, 49, 56, 83–84, 104–105, 117, 136, 416; **Guam**, 642; **Newport**, 121; **Pensacola**, 121; **Port Royal**, 118–119, 126; **Portsmouth**, 47, 51, 633; **Puerto Rico**, 126
Marine Corps bases and stations
Beaufort, 527; **Bridgeport**, 540; **Camp Elliott**, 259–260; **Camp H. M. Smith**, 511; **Camp Kearney**, 259; **Camp Lejeune**, 101, 257, 298, 529; **Camp Matthews**, 258–259, 543; **Camp Pendleton**, 259, 272, 543; **Cherry Point**, 261, 275; Corvallis, 347; **Eagle Mountain Lake**, 287, *311*, 422; **Edenton**, 279, 313, 522; **El Centro**, 278, 313; **El Toro**, 301, 646, 648; **Ewa**, 255; **Futema**, 518, 526; **Iwakuni**, 518; **Kearney Mesa**, 301, 316; **Miami**, 178–179, 200, 485, 510, 519; **Miramar**, 259–260, 316, 646; **Mojave**, 290; **Montford Point**, 281, 285, 318, 329, 342–343, 447, 552–553; **New River**, 256–257; **Parris Island**, 118, 166, 174, 186, 254, 271, 426, 514–515, 595; **Quantico**, 171–173, 199, 208, *214*; **San Diego**, 167, 174, 198, 205, 210, 259–259, 438, 595; **Santa Ana**, 622; **Santa Barbara**, 280; **Tustin**, 622, 648; **Yuma**, 522; **29 Palms**, 512, 516
Marine Corps commands
2nd Advance Base Force, 200, 205; **III Amphibious Corps (IIIAC)**, 323, 347, 353, 355–356, 361–362, 364, 370–371, 390–391, 395, 399–401, 404–405, 410, 414, 421; **V Amphibious Corps (VAC)**, 316–317, 320, 345–347, 353–354, 358, 362, 364, 383, 386, 389, 405, 415–417; **1st FSSG**, 638, 642; **2nd FSSG**, 621, 638; **2nd Joint Training Force**, 262; **1st Marine Amphibious Corps**, 290, 294, 309, 317–319, 321, 323–324, 329, 345–347; **1st Marine Aviation Force**, 153, 179, 186, 190–191, 198–200, 322; **I MEF/MAF**, 523, 581, 638–640, 642–643; **II MEF/MAF**, 598, 639, 641, 651; **III MEF/MAF**, 525, 545–549, 551, 553, 556–557, 559–561, 566–567, 575, 577–578, 580, 582, 584, 593, 604, 612, 641; **VII MEF**, 541; **Advance Base Force**, *159*, 155, 170–172, 174–175; **Air Solomons (AirSols)**, 300, 309, 313–314, 320, 325, 333, 335, 338, 340, 344, 351; **Amphibious Force Atlantic Fleet**, 260, 284; **BSSG-4**, 638; **BSSG-5**, 639; **BSSG-7**, 639; **Department of the Pacific**, 205, 528; **East Coast Expeditionary Force**, 208–212, 214, 239; **Fleet Marine Force (FMF)**, 233, 236, 239–242, 256, 395; **FMF Atlantic**, 418, 426, 528, 637; **FMF Pacific**, 323, 345–346, 350, 364, 366, 370, 400–401, 404, 411, 418, 452–453, 510–511; **FMF Western Pacific**, 431, 434, 438, 442–444; **Force Troops**, 473, 529, 621; **Tactical Air Force (TAF)**, 376, 390.

392–395, 397–398, 400; **Task Force 58**, 650–651; **West Coast Expeditionary Force**, 200, 225, 233
Marine Corps divisions
1st, 235, 255–256, 260, 276–279, 298, 318, 329, 332, 337–338, 347–348, 365–366, 373, 390, *392*–395, 397–400, 412, 419, 421–*422*, 427, 429, 432–433, 435, *442*, 444, 446–447, 452–453, 455–461, 464, 466–476, 478–479, 481–484, 486–488, 490, 492–498, 508–509, 511, 523, 529, 538, 541, 550–551, 557, 571, 577–578, 584, 586, 588, 590–591, 593, 608, 638, 640; **2nd**, 223, 255–256, 260, 252, 299, 317, 325–326, 330–331, 344–345, 349–361, 390, 392, 396, 405, 413, 415, 417, 421–424, 426–427, 448, 453, 476, 504, 509, 534, 538–539, 597–598, 638, 640; **3rd**, 287, 321, 332, 336, 345, 355–357, 360–361, 363, 383, 335, 387–389, 415, 482, 484–485, 489, 495, 497–498, 505, 509, 523, 527, 530, *535*, 541, 545–547, 557, 559–560, 566, 576, 578, 580–581, 583, 586; **4th**, 283, 315, 317, 338–339, 344, 349–361, *379*, 332–383, *385*, 387–388, 412, 414, 538, 584; **5th**, 293, 335, 337, 341, *378*, 331–383, 389, 405, 413–415, 417, 550, 554, 558, 580–582; **6th**, 364, 390–392, 395, *396*–399, 401, *404*, *410*–412, 418–419
Marine Corps aircraft wings
1st, 260, 267, 281, 285, 322, 366, 374, 401, 405, 410, 423, 431, 434, 452–453, 456–458, 460, 470–475, 478, 483, 488, 491–492, 494, 496, 498, 512, 527–528, 541, 546, 555, 561, 558–569, 571, 575, 578, 580, 582, 584, 591, 595, 637; **2nd**, 261–262, 270, 315, 320, 353, 367, 374, 376, 400, 416–417, 437, 509, 511, 553, 58, 597–598, 608, 630, 637–638; **3rd**, 296, 349, 415, 482, 435, 510–511, 523, 529, 535, 622, 638–640; **4th**, 284, 315, 332, 339, 341, 373, 404–405, 418, 538, 634; **9th**, 346, 418
Marine Corps brigades
1st, 133, 162, 166, 198–199, 236, 240, 249, 251, 254–255, 250, 262, 271–272, 345, 354–357, 360–361, 363–364, *412*, 416–417, 419, 424, 427, 431–432, 437, 444, 446, *451*, 452–458, 512, 527, 541, 638; **2nd**, 198, 212, 216, 221, 230, 232, 241, 243, 250, 255, 257, 269–270, 302, 528, 640; **3rd**, 149, 156, 216, 226, 272, 275, 324, 419, 421, 425, 427, 433, 475–476, 482, 537–538, 546, 593; **4th**, 174, 178–179, 182–183, 186–192, *198*, 200, 511, 545, 600, 607, 625, 638–639, 650; **5th**, 187 *198*, 200, 205, 222, 258, 532, 539, 582, 593, 621, 631, 638–641; **6th**, 628; **7th**, 626, 628; **8th**, 526, 588; **9th**, 527, *531–532*, 544–545, 550, 556, 581, 598, 600, 604, 613–614, 637; **11th**, 540, 584; **16th**, 532; **1st Provisional Marine Air-Ground Task Force**, 510, 512
MEU/MAUs
8th, 528–529, 533; **11th**, 639, 643, 647–648; **13th**, 638, 643–644; **15th**, 642, 649–651; **22nd**, *523*, 628–630, 638, 643, 645–646; **24th**, *529*, 627–628, 633, 641, 643–644, 647; **26th**, 631, 638, 646–648, 650–651; **31st**, 589–590, 592, 595, 597–599, 609–610, 613, 627, 629, 647–648; **32nd**, 620–*621*, 626–627; **33rd**, 598–599, 608, 613; **34th**, 536, 620; **35th**, 613; **Contingency MAGTF**, 633–634, 641; **Special Purpose MAGTF Carib**, 644
Marine Corps RLTs/regiments
1st, 128, 130–133, 136, 144, 151, 163, 166, 190, 209, 211, 235, 256, *274*, 277, 298, 332–333, 347, 365–368, 390, 394, 398, 410–411, 420, 423, 432, 434, 454, 458–460, 464, 472, 474, 476, 479, 488, 494–495, 512, 520, 541, 550, 559, 564, 568, 570, 575, 581, 593; **2nd**, 131, 133, 136, 151, 163, 166, 236, 255, 276, 279, 295–296, 299, 325, 327, 331, 421, 438, 443, 453, 513, 518, 638, 644; **3rd**, 131, 209, 243, 278, 286, 321, 326, 333, 383, 386, 415–416, 434, 444–447, 475–476, 482–483, 516–518, 523, 540, 545, 562, 567, 571, 575, 578–580; **4th**, 162, 164, 166–167, 170, 204, 209, 212, 215–216, 231, 235, *240*–243, *249*, 258, 263, 267–268, 271, 273–274, 282, 338, 344–346, 364, 390, 392–393, 396, 398, 401, 404–405, 412, 415–416, 418–419, 421, 424, 441, 448, 482, 489, 505, 509–510, 519, 546, 550, 567, 575, 578–579, *611*, 613, 638; **5th**, 164, 174–178, 189, 211, 216, 230, 236, 277, 281, 294, 298, 333, *336*, 339–340, 344, 365–367, 369, 371–372, *391*, 394–395, 397, 410, 431, 447, 452, 454, 456–461, 464–466, 471, *478*–479, 494–495, 520, 525, 527, 535, 554, 556, 561, 563, 574–575, 577–578, 586, 591, 639; **6th**, 135, 174–175, 178–179, 189, 216, 226, 236, 243, 258, 260, 299, 352, 422, 425, 448, 456, 517, 521, 558, 586; **7th**, 174, 198, 203, 255, 272, 287, 332, 334–336, 365–369, 398, 423, 426–427, 445, 455–457, 459–462, 464–466, 470, 472, 474, 476, 478, 489–491, 496, 548, 554, 558, 570, 574–575, 578, 586–588, 638, 642; **8th**, 174, 186, 201, 250, 267, 296, 325, 327, 331, 356–357, 361, 372, *391*, 396–399, 405, 421, 438, 445, 523, 558; **9th**, 175, 178, 186, 270, 287, 321, 324, 332, 384, 387–388, 390, 392, 415, 434, 443–444, 446, 448, 482, 484, 509, 523, 525, 527, 532, 547–548, 555, 562, 566, 571, 576–577, 580, 644; **10th**, 178, 210–211, 255, 354, 405, 421, 558, 626; **11th**, 178, 187, 216–217, 221, 224, 226, 256, 392, 419, 427, 487, 495, 550, 587–588, 591; **12th**, 285, 287, 416, 482, 484; **13th**, 149, 183, 187, 335, 554; **14th**, 308, 315, 338, 538; **15th**, 198, 209, 365; **16th**, 204, 337, 349; **19th**, 287; **20th**, 308, 315, 364; **21st**, 279, 287, 321, 324, 329, 332, 334, 383–384, 388, 415, 440, 447; **22nd**, 320, 339, 340–*341*, 345, 364, 392, 395–396; **23rd**, 279, 287, 315, 338, 382, 538; **24th**, 302, 315, 338, 385, 538, 639; **25th**, 303, 315, 338–339, 538; **26th**, 335, 388, 411, 418, *505*, 550, 556, 561, 570, 580, 583, 585; **27th**, 335, 382, 554,568, 574; **28th**, 339, 382–383, 385, 558; **29th**, 348, 365, 392, 396; **1st Advance Base**, 130; **VAC Artillery**, 371, 388; **1st Force Service**, 522; **2nd Force Service**, 553; **3rd Force Service**, 551, 553; **2nd Infantry Training**, 511, 521; **1st Parachute**, 302, 328, 334, 338, 341; **1st Raider**, 301, 312–313, 316, 337, 338; **2nd Raider**, 336–337
Marine Corps aircraft groups
1st Aviation, 209, 212, 214; **1st Marine Aircraft**, 248–249, 260–261; **2nd Marine Aircraft**, 248, 255, 261; **11**, 261, 263, 271, 294, 365, 417, 497, 499, 521, 547, 550, 593; **12**, 271, 296, 302, 316, 320, 346, 348, 374–376, 378, 387, 388, 411, 418, 458, 466, 468, 478, 485–486, 494–495, 497, 523, 527, 546, 550, 583, 598, 604; **13**, 271, 273, 414, 472, 510, 521, 525, 556, 586, 613; **14**, 271, 291, 302, 315, 377, 379, 389–390, 396, 398, 417, 539; **15**, 271, 341, 389, 597, 604, 606, 634; **16**, 483, 494, 498, 518, 523, 525, 546, 549, 555, 593, 642; **20**, 533; **21**, 261, 271, 325, 360; **22**, 271, 275, 340–341, 396, 405, 411, 413–414; **23**, 271, 281, 291, 297, 317, 349; **24**, 271–272, 275, 299, 316, 373, 378, 390, 392–393, 400, 418, 431, 444, 518, 539; **25**, 275, 284–285, 353, 410, 416, 420, 431, 450, 511; **26**, 486, 516–517, 519, 526, 534, 539; **29**, 598; **30**, 528; **31**, 300, 319, 339, 401, 405, 410, 419, 421–422, 431, 535, 539; **32**, 300, 334, 373, 378–379, 383, 389, 391, 393, 400, 411, 431, 485, 539, 643; **33**, 300, 374, 392, 417, 452–453, 458–459, 470–471, 483, 486–487, 494, 509, 520, 590; **34**, 300, 372; **35**, 302, 347, 368, 519; **36**, 486, 520, 548–550, 582; **39**, 570, 581, 613, 622; **40**, 638; **41**, 298, 373, 411, 538; **42**, 298, 373, 411, 544; **43**, 298, 375, 390, 400, 538, 601; **44**, 298, 373; **45**, 338, 365, 369, 372–373, 414; **46**, 341, 373, 418, 538; **48**, 360, 372, 399; **49**, 579, 601; **50**, 639; **51**, 302, 364, 372, 405; **52**, 344, 372; **56**, 594; **61**, 313, 346, 354, 401; **62**, 400; **70**, 638; **71**, 274, 297, 303; **91**, 352, 372; **92**, 361, 372, 388; **93**, 346; **94**, 357, 372, 382; **Aircraft One**, 233, 236, 242, 248, 322; **Aircraft Two**, 233, 236, 242, 248
Marine Corps BLTs/battalions
1st, 58, 122, 126; **2nd**, 59, 128; **3rd**, 128; **4th**, 133; **6th**, 128; **1/1**, 432, 434, 461, 464–465, 467, 474, 522–523, 548, *557*, 568, 591; **2/1**, 332–333, *337*, 432, 434, 464–465, *488*, 538, 549, 553, 555; **3/1**, 333, *421*, 461, 465, 491, 518, 550–551, 554, *594*, *599*, 634; **1/2**, 499, 524, 532, 558, 586; **2/2**, 513, 516, 519, 520, 529, 532, 540, 588, 644; **3/2**, 277, 290, 488, 513, 519, 524, 528, 585; **1/3**, 324, 411, 415, 420, 518, 533, *535*, 544–545, 548, 555, 557, 561–562; **2/3**, 325, 534, 541, 544, 546, 550, 560–562, 566, 571; **3/3**, 325, 513, 520, 546, 548–549, 555, 560, *588*; **1/4**, 164–165, 414, 556, 559–561, 581, *587*, *601*, 612, 614, 621; **2/4**, 164–165, 415, 548, 550–551, 554–555, 558, 570, 598, 610, 613; **3/4**, 268, 270, 404, 415, 417, 424, 432, 434, 493, 498, 504, 511, 539, *540*, 545, 547, 555–556, 561, *603*; **4/4**, 273, 493, 498; **1/5**, 176223, 236, 271, 344, 431, 486, 493, 526, 551, 554, 569, 572–573, 579; **2/5**, 179, 215, 236, 276, 286, 290, 398, 465, *474*, 484, 486, 494, *499*, 516, 528, 554, 566, 568, *581*; **3/5**, 290, 334–335, 367, 444, 450, 458, *484*, 554–555, *570*, 572–573; **1/6**, 180, 236, 252, 325–326, 450, 453, 478, 517, 519, 585, 638; **2/6**, 189, *217*, 325–326, 472, 495, 499, 521, 524, 528, 530, 534, 600–601, 607, 628–629, 634; **3/6**, 211–212, 326, 355, 450, 456–457, 484, 516, 520–521, 528, 532–533, 542, 545, 551, 585, 607, *619*; **1/7**, 233, 235, 290, 292, 294–295, 410, 463, 465–466, 486–488, 548, 572, 582; **2/7**, 203, 233, 290, 294–295, 366, 405, *434*, 462, 479, 484, *488*, 547, 549, 550, 556, *571*, *583*, *600*; **3/7**, 294, 405, 410, 457, 487, 520, 547, 551, 566; 1/8, 372, 377, 476, 482, 504, 519–521, *523*, 533, 544, 558, 628–629, *648*; **2/8**, 493, 504, 520–521, 536, 550, 553, 567, 606, 627, 630, 641; **3/8**, 482, 521, 524, 528, 585, 627; **1/9**, 326, 329, 525, 546, 560, 562, 568, 570, 579, 597, 613; **2/9**, 525, 547, 550, *560*–561, 598, *605*, 614; **3/9**, 324, *531*, 533, 537, 544, 546, 548, 555, 558, 561–562, 613; **1/10**, 237, 296; **2/10**, 237, 260, 267; **1/11**, 272, 423, 431, 593; **3/11**, 426, 586; **4/11**, 426; **1/12**, 541; **2/12**, 532; **3/12**, 541, 555; **1/13**, 557, 585; **2/13**, 568; **1/21**, 329; **2/21**, 324, 414–415, 417; **1/22**, 537; **2/22**, 345, 533; **3/22**, 340, 345; **2/25**, 584; **1/26**, *528*, 556–557, 561; **2/26**, 548, 556, 561, 567–568, 574; **3/26**, 557, 566–567; **1/27**, 293, 554; **1/28**, 381; **3/28**, *384*; **1/29**, 412–413, 418; **3/29**, *404*; **2nd Airdrome**, 316; **1st Amphibian Tractor**, 467–468, 579; **2nd Amphibian Tractor**, 579; **3rd AAA**, 420; **12th AAA**, 370; **2nd Antitank**, 587; **3rd Antitank**, 518, 586; **1st Armored Amphibian**, 400; **1st Defense**, 248–249, 255–257, 262; **2nd Defense**, 249, 263, 267, 316, 327; **3rd Defense**, 248–249, 254–255, 262, 275, 279, 321, 352; **4th Defense**, 249, 255, 263, 267–268, 273, 279, 315; **5th Defense**, 255, 260, 341; **6th Defense**, 248, 255–256, 262; **7th Defense**, 255–256, 261, 270, 273, 275, 316, 341, 344; **8th Defense**, 273–274; **9th Defense**, 270–271, 309, 312–315, 317, 336, 356; **10th Defense**, 275, 314, 317, 340–341, 365; **11th Defense**, 278, 300, 314–315, 317; **12th Defense**, 279, 348; **13th Defense**, 290; **14th Defense**, 299, 356; **16th Defense**, 296; **51st Defense**, 281, 341–343, 365, 398, 412–413, 417; **52nd Defense**, 329, 343, 366, 394, 418, 420; **3rd Engineer**, 509; **6th Engineer**, 395; **1st LAAM**, 527, 544, 580, 590; **2nd LAAM**, 576; **5th LAAM**, 576; **1st LAV**, 631; **2nd LAV**, 630; **3rd LAV**, 632; **1st Machine Gun**, 174, 178; **5th Machine Gun**, 187; **6th Machine Gun**, 178, *197*; **1st Parachute**, 223, 257, 276–277, 279, 286, 302, 326–327, 336; **2nd Parachute**, 256, 299, 302, 320–321, 334, 336; **3rd Parachute**, 287, 302, 328, 332, 338, 380; **4th Parachute**, 302; **1st Pioneer**, 427, 431; **5th Pioneer**, 389; **1st Raider**, 223, 271, 274, 276–277, 279, 286, 290, 312–313; **2nd Raider**, 271, 275, 281, 283, *295*–298, 321, 324, 326; **3rd Raider**, 287, 300–301, 321, 324, 327; **4th Raider**, 294, 301, 308–309, 313; **1st Recon**, 524, 564; **2nd Recon**, 582; **3rd Recon**, 546; **3rd Recruit**, 443, 511; **1st Samoan**, 261; **1st Separate**, 271; **2nd Separate**, 271; **15th Separate**, 200–201; **12th Service**, 432; **1st Tank**, 336, 347, 427, 495; **2nd Tank**, 327–328, *524*, 639; **4th Tank**, 339; **VAC/FMF Amphibious Recon**, 354, 389–392; **Marine Corps Security Force**, 632, 635, 650; **Marine Security Guard**, 559, 623–625, 634, 645, 650
Marine Corps squadrons
1st, 205, 209; **3rd**, 204, 209; **4th**, 205; **111** (VMF), 260, 264, 412, 440; **112** (VMF), 271, 294, 300, 374, 392, 398, 405, 422; **113** (VMF), 298, 396, 405, 431; **114** (VMF), 309, 367, 531, 540; **115** (VMF), 289, 309, 348, 374, 383, 388, 411, 426–427, 483, 489, 494, (VMFA), 591, 597, 599; **121** (VMF), 260, 264, 288, 290, *422*, (VMA), *475*, 480, 495; **122** (VMF), 271, 368, 435, 517, 527, 528–529; **123** (VMF), 286, 312, 315, 377, 398, 405; **124** (VMF), 286, 301, 303, 315, 376, 387, 417, 422; **131** (VMFA), 204, (VMSB), 260, 262, 296, (VMTB), 308, 397, 405, 413, (VMF), 519, (VMA), 584; **132** (VMSB), 260, 294, 370; **133** (VMSB), 303, 373, 378, 400, (VMTB), 371, 396, 413, 422, (VMF), 519; **134** (VMTB), 303, 419, (VMF), 519; **141** (VMSB), 271, (VMTB), 394, 422; **142** (VMSB), 271, 296, 373, 383, 405, 421, (VMF), 421; **143** (VMSB), 286, 302, (VMTB), 303, 315, 392, 418; **144** (VMSB), 286, 315, (VMTB), 370, 401, 415, 422; **151** (VMJ), 260, 350, (VMO), 287, (VMSB), 287; **152** (VMR), 410, 450, 469, 536, (HMR), 511; **153** (VMJ), 271, 350, (VMR), 410, 430, 432, 443, 535, (HMR), 511; **154** (VMD), 287, 405; **155** (VMO), 290, 303, (VMF), 379, 411; **161** (HMR), 429, 440–441, 470, 478–480, 482–486, 488, 492–493, 511, (HMM), 586; **162** (HMR), 477, 483, 498, 516–518, 532–533, (HMM), 539–544, 628; **163** (HMR), 481, 498, 518, (HMM), 538–539, 544, 546–547, 551; **164** (HMM), 542, 551, 561, 581, 589, 598, 604; **166** (HMM), 631; **165** (HMM), 547, 568, 580, 598, 604, 612–613; **167** (HML), 569, 591; **169** (HMA), 595; **211** (VMF), 260, 263–264, 267, 273, 294, 374, 411, 432, 443, 446, (VMA), 487, 583, 598; **212** (VMF), 271, 273, 290–291, 318, 328, 377, 398, 459, 466–467, 469, (VMA), 486, 495, 521, 636, (VMFA), 598; **213** (VMF), 278, 309, 376, 387, 419; **214** (VMF), 278, 316, 317, 332, *367*, 388, 453–454, 467, 469–471, 475–476, 480, (VMA), *513*, 521, 595; **215** (VMF), 287, 318, 328, 336, 413; **216** (VMF), 298, 329, 332, 360, 379, 388, 418, 451, (VMGR), 602; **217** (VMF), 309, 360, 379, 388, 418; **218** (VMF), 309, 374, 411, 430, 444, 449; **221** (VMF), 261, 267–268, 270, 278, 303, 318, 374, 390, 395, 405, 436; **222** (VMF), 271, 332, 377, 398, 449, 499; **223** (VMF), 265, 274, 281, 284, 332, 377, 398, 436, (VMA), 516, 583; **224** (VMF), 274, 285, 339, 391, 405, 499, (VMA(AW)), 595–597; **225** (VMF), 298, 360–361, 486, (VMA), 513, 523–524, 528, 531, 546, (VMA(AW)), 591, 599, (VMFA(AW)), 641; **231** (VMSB), 198, 260, 267, 285, 340, 418, (VMF), 440, (VMA), 606, 626; **232** (VMSB), 260, 281, 284, (VMTB), 308, 315, 372, 393, 413, (VMF), 440, (VMFA), 214, 597, 601; **233** (VMSB), 274, (VMTB), 388, 405, 418, 424; **234** (VMSB), 274, 315, (VMTB), 395, 418, 422, (VMA), 519; **235** (VMSB), 298, 373, (VMF), 425, 458, (VMF(AW)), *505*, (VMFA), 646; **236** (VMSB), 298, 360, 373, 383, (VMF), 427; **241** (VMSB), 271, 278, 360, 373, 378–379, 400; **242** (VMSB), 271, 287, (VMTB), 309, 387, 414, (VMA), 529, 533, (VMA(AW)), 557, 561, 586; **243** (VMSB), 278, 373, 383,

405; **244** (VMSB), 287, 315, 373; **245** (VMSB), 309, 413; **251** (VMO), 263, 279, 377, (VMF), 379, 397, 422, (VMA), 474, 497, (VMFA), 649; **252** (VMJ), 260, 350 (VMR), 393, (VMGR), 226, 544, (HMR), 511; **253** (VMJ), 272, 350 (VMR), 385, 387, 393, 431, 451, 476, 498, 535, 536; **254** (VMD), 287, 389; **261** (HMR), 473, 482, 510, 517, 528–529, 534, (HMM), 537, 540, 546, 585, 607, 627, 630; **262** (HMR), 478, 482, 510, 517, 519, 524, 532–533, (HMM), *600*, 609; **263** (HMR), 486, (HMM), 536, 561, 591, 627; **264** (HMR), 524, 530–531, 535, (HMM), 545, 607, 628, 641, 644; **265** (HMM), 538, 544, 589, *599*, 621; **266** (HMM), 628; **267** (HML), 557; **268** (HML), 601; **269** (HMA), 592–593; **311** (VMF), 297, 391, 405, 467, 469–471, 480, 485, (VMA), 554, *587*, 591–592, 598; **312** (VMF), 308, 392, 395, 459, 470–471, 474, 480, 517, 527, (VMA), 483, 485, 489, 496, (VMF (AW)), *590*, (VMFA), 645, 647; **313** (VMF), 318, 374, 397; **314** (VMF), 318, 396, 405, 431, 482, 499, 537, (VMFA), 540, 550, 586, 628, 631–632, 636, 649; **321** (VMF), 300, 332, 372, 416, 422; **322** (VMF), 309, 392, 449, 477; **323** (VMF), 314, 392, 395, 454, 467, 469–471, 475, 479, (VMA), 487, 495–497, (VMFA), 631–632; **324** (VMF), 318, 411, (VMA), 484, 504; **331** (VMSB), 298, 328, 332, 341, 413, (VMA), 485, 528–529, 588, 642; **332** (VMSB), 309, (VMTB), 385, 413, (VMA), 485, 496, 537, (VMFA(AW)), 647; **333** (VMSB), 314, 412, (VMA), 485, (VMFA), 600–601, 641; **334** (VMSB), 314, 369, (VMA), 486, (VMFA), 580, 596; **341** (VMSB), 300, 373, 383, 405, (VMA), 519; **342** (VMSB), 309, 369; **343** (VMSB), 314, 414, 421, (VMA), 532; **344** (VMSB), 334, 369; **351** (VMO), 300, (VMF), 390, 413, 422; **352** (VMJ), 303, 350, (VMR), 450, 469, 531, 535, (HMR), 511, (VMGR), 651; **353** (VMJ), 301, 350, (VMR), 385, 387, 393, 417, 486, (VMGR), 539; **361** (HMR), 483, (HMM), 540–541, 563, (HMH), 583; **362** (HMR), 523, 534, (HMM), 536–538, 580, 605; **363** (HMR), 486, (HMM), *555*, 559; **364** (HMR), 534, (HMM), 541, 542–543, 591, 593, 631; **365** (HMM), 540, 543–544, 586, 592, 623; **366** (HMH), 644, 648; **367** (HML), 556, 591–592, 613; **369** (HMA), 597, 599, 613; **413** (VMB), 300, 401–402, 414, (VMF), 519; **422** (VMF), 298, 337, 396, 405, 419; **423** (VMB), 317, 401–402, 414; **433** (VMB), 317, 402, 414; **441** (VMF) 290, 391, 393, 405, 422, 480; **443** (VMB), 317, 401–402, 414; **451** (VMF), 339, 378, 391, 395, 405, 422, 472, 535, (VMFA), 646; **452** (VMF), 339, 379, 388, 449, (VMGR), 634; **453** (VMB), 353, 383, (VMTB), 399; **454** (VMSB), 341, (VMTB), 341, 416; **461** (VMF), 344, 450, (HMR), 516, 528; **462** (VMF), 347, 405, (HMR), 517, (HMH), 581, 610, 613; **463** (VMB), 355, 384, (VMTB), 400, 418, (HMR), 520, (HMH), 550, 558, 591, 604–605, 613; **464** (VMSB), 347, (VMTB), 397, 418, (HMH), 626; **465** (HMH), 626; **466** (HMH), 631, 645; **471** (VMF), 349, 405; **472** (VMF), 350, 369, 385, 415; **473** (VMB), 357, 388, (VMTB), 400, 418; **474** (VMSB), 346; **481** (VMF), 346, 369, 400, 405; **482** (VMF), 346, 369; **483** (VMB), 364, 388; **484** (VMSB), 346, 405; **511** (VMF), 334, 379, 405, 418, 519; **512** (VMF), 339, 386, 420; **513** (VMF), 339, 398, (VMF(N)), 453, 470–471, 476–477, 484, 486, 492–493 (VMFA), 540, 546–547, (VMA), 593, 597, 609, *635*; **514** (VMF), 340, 415; **521** (VMF), 346, 405; **522** (VMF), 346, 405; **523** (VMF), 348, 411; **524** (VMF), 349, 411; **531** (VMF(N)), 297, 317, 324, (VMFA), 540, 542, 544–545–546, 641; **532** (VMF(N)), 302, 339, 347, 431; **533** (VMF(N)), 318, 395, 396, 411, 426, (VMA), 599, (VMFA(AW)), 642, 645, 647; **534** (VMF(N)), 318, 360, 431, (VMF), 519; **541** (VMF(N)), 339, 367, 368, 374–376, 378, 411, 419; **542** (VMF(N)), 344, 372, 391, 405, 459, 471–472, 636, (VMFA), 583, 586, (VMA), 597, 602, 626; **543** (VMF(N)), 347, 392, 405, 419, 474, 547; **544** (VMF(N)), 348, 419; **561** (HMM), 581; **611** (VMB), 318, 390, 402–404, 414 (VMA), 519; **612** (VMB), 318, 392, 400, 402–403, 418; **613** (VMB), 318, 402, 413; **614** (VMB), 318, 415; **621** (VMB), 346, 379, 415; **622** (VMB), 349, (VMTB), 396, 417; **623** (VMB), 349, (VMTB), 382, 418; **624** (VMB), 352, 418, (VMTB), 382, 418; **711** (VML), 274, 303; **761** (HMR), *519*; **768** (HMR), 519, (HMM), 584; **773** (HMR), 520; **774** (HMR), 520; **775** (HMA), 634; **776** (HMR), 523; **911** (VMF), 353, 418; **912** (VMF), 354, 418; **913** (VMF), 355, 417; **914** (VMF), 362, 417; **921** (VMF), 363, 369; **922** (VMF), 363, 369; **923** (VMF), 365, 369; **924** (VMF), 346, 369; **931** (VMSB), 347, 417; **932** (VMSB), 349, 417; **933** (VMSB), 352, 392; **934** (VMSB), 357, 411; **941** (VMSB), 355, 369; **942** (VMSB), 364, 369; **943** (VMSB), 353, (VMTB), 373; **944** (VMSB), 346, 369; **952** (VMJ), 308, 350, 431, (VMR), 385, 387, 393; **953** (VMJ), 338, 350, 431; **954** (VMD), 367, 389, 417; **1st Barrage Balloon**, 262, 268, 298, 328; **2nd Barrage Balloon**, 262, 274, 315; **3rd Barrage Balloon**, 273, 286, 303, 328; **4th Barrage Balloon**, 275, 300; **5th Barrage Balloon**, 278, 290, 328; **6th Barrage Balloon**, 296, 298, 328; **1st Marine Aviation**, 174–175, 178–179; **1st Marine Aeronautic**, 174–175, 178; **HMX-1**, 428, 435, 438–439, 446, 452, 456, 460, 510, 580; **VB-4M**, 233, 242; **VB-6M**, 240, 242; **VF-1M**, 209, 214, 216; **VF-2M**, 227; **VF-3M**, 214, 216–217; **VF-4M**, 242; **VF-5M**, 227; **VF-6M**, 225, 227; **VF-8M**, 214, 230; **VF-9M**, 227, 242; **VF-10M**, 217, 225, 227, 233; **VJ-6M**, 225, 242; **VJ-7M**, 226, 242; **VMAQ-2**, 631; **VMAQ-4**, 642; **VMB-1**, 242, 260; **VMB-2**, 242, 260; **VMC-1**, 489; **VMCJ-1**, 545, 586, 597; **VMD-1**, 273, 287; **VMD-2**, 273, 287; **VMF-1**, 242, 260; **VMF-2**, 242, 260; **VMJ-1**, 242, 260, 483; **VMJ-2**, 242, 260; **VMO-1**, 251, 260, 320, 357, 643; **VMO-2**, 321, 390, 405, 551, 577, 591, 643; **VMO-3**, 328, 366, 390, 447, 556; **VMO-4**, 332, 384, 411, 643; **VMO-5**, 339, 384, 417, 557; **VMO-6**, 373, 390, 411, 426, 429, 452, 454–455, 478, 581; **VMO-7**, 376, 395, 397, 413; **VMO-8**, 376, 414, 620; **VMS-1**, 242, 260; **VMS-2**, 242, 260; **VMS-3**, 242, 260, 349; **VO-1M**, 209, 212, 217; **VO-4M**, 214, 216–217; **VO-6M**, 224–225, 231; **VO-7M**, 217, *226*, 232, 242; **VO-8M**, 217, *219*, 227, 233, 237, 242; **VO-9M**, 236, 242; **VO-10M**, 226–227; **VS-14M**, 230–*231*, 237; **VS-15M**, 230, 237; **ZKO-1M**, 227

Marine Corps units
1st Base Depot, 279; **8th Field Depot**, 383, 389; **1st Joint Assault Signal Co.**, 320; **1st Ammunition Co.**, 318; **8th Ammunition Co.**, 434; **1st Amphib Recon Co.**, 517; **2nd Amphib Recon Co.**, 517, 519; **4th Armored Amphibian Co.**, 589; **1st ANGLICO**, 604; **1st Depot Co.**, 301; **5th Depot Co.**, 553; **49th Depot Co.**, 434; **1st Force Recon Co.**, 517, 525, 529, 534; **2nd Force Recon Co.**, 519; **3rd Force Recon Co.**, 587; **2nd Parachute Co.**, 256; **1st Radio Co.**, 535; **6th Truck Co.**, 518; **VAC Recon Co.**, 325, 327, 338–339; **Advisory Team 1**, 541–543; **Chemical Biological Incident Response Force (CBIRF)**, 645, 650; **Fleet Antiterrorism Security Team (FAST)**, 635, 648, 650; **Horse Marines**, *216*, 235, *237*, *240–241*; **MSSG-22**, 628, 630; **MSSG-24**, 627–628, 641; **MSSG-32**, 627

Marine Corps schools
Advance Base School, 150, 152; **FMF Training Center**, 273; **Marine Combat Training**, 646; **Marine Corps Institute**, 33, 204; **Marine Corps Schools**, 173, 181, 238, 428, 450, 480, 542; **Marine Corps University**, 635; **Marine Officers School**, 146, 159; **Officer Candidate School**, 474, 634; **Officers' Training Camp**, 174; **Overseas Depot**, *161*, 182; **Platoon Leaders Class**, 240, 433, 596; **Sea School**, 633; **School of Application**, 117–118, 141; **Staff NCO Academy**, 592, 632; **The Basic School (TBS)**, 222, 514, 584, 621; **Training Center FMF**, 275; **Troop Training Unit Pacific**, 316

Marine Corps Association, 150, 155
Marine Corps Gazette, 238
Marine Corps League, 242, 457, 460, 589
Marine Corps Marathon, 620, 629
Marine Corps Museum, 529, 621
Marine Corps Reading Program, 635
Marine Corps Reserve, 170, 213–214, 226, 236–237, 243, 254, 419, 421, 427, 438, 440, 442, 453–454, 456, 460, 476, 487, 510, 538, 584, 592, 601, 638
Marine Corps Rifle Board, 252–253
Marine Corps seal, 504
Marine Corps War Memorial, 223, 481, 506–508, 533
Marine Corps Women's Reserve, 296, *298*–300, 302, 309–311, 374, 423, 440, 443
Maritime Prepositioning Force (MPF), 623, 626, 628, 630
Marontate, Lt William T., 265
Marshall, Gen George C., 270, 411, 416, 458
Marshall Islands, 338–341, 345, 347, 402
Marshall, Sgt James, 625
Marston, Capt Ward, 71
Martin, John, 13
Martinique, 16, 27, 251
Massaro, SgtMaj John R., 620, 622
Masters, Pvt Alfred, 275
Matanikau River, 203, *272*, 280, 285, 290, 292, 294–296
Mayaguez, 614
McBarron, H. Charles, *12–13*, *17*, *22*
McCawley, Col Charles G., 108, 117
McCutcheon, LtGen Keith B., 584, 590
McDonough, Rep Gordon L., 456, 460
McDougal, Cpl William, 82
McGill, Lt William, 378
McGinty, Lt Selva E., 393
McHugh, SgtMaj Thomas J., 537, 547
McIlvain, Lt W. M., 166
McKeon, SSgt Matthew C., 511–512
McMahon, Cpl Charles, Jr., 625
McMichael, Sgt Maj Alred L., 648
McNally, Sgt Michael J., 127
McNamara, Robert, 551
McNaugh, Cpl Robert V., 625
Meade, Col Robert L., 132–133
Meals Ready to Eat (MRE), 627
Mediterranean Sea, 56, 438, 440–441, 443, 445, 447, 450, 472, 476, 478, 482, 484, 488, 493, 495, 499, 504, 517, 519, 524, 532
Megee, BGen Vernon A., 447
Meuse-Argonne, France, 177, 180, 190
Mexican War, 33, *65–75*
Mexico, 66, 70–75, 78, 93, 106, 108, 155, 162–163, 165–167, 511, 557
Midway Atoll, 142, 248, 254–255, 262, 265, 267–268, 270, 275, 278
Miller, Cpl John, *298*
Miller, LtCol Samuel, 48, 50, 53–54, 59
Miller, LtCol Thomas H., 529
Mills, Lt Billy, 543
Mississippi (steamer), 74–*75*, *78*, 80, 84, 93, (BB-23), 163
Mississippi River, 20–*21*, 93, 96
Mitchell, MajGen Ralph J., 325, 344, 351, 371
Monroe, President James, 54
Morocco, 143, 513, 516, 527
Moscow, Soviet Union, 236, 625, 633
Moses, Col Franklin J., 150
Moskoff, Sgt Nicholas B., 198
Mount Suribachi, *376*, 381–383, 506
Mullan, Capt Robert, 16
Munda Field, 297–298, 309, 312–315, 320
Mundy, Gen Carl E., Jr., 641, 645
Muth, Sgt Lawrence, 204
Mutter, LtGen Carol A., 645
Myers, Capt John T., 128, 132

Nashville (PG-7), 128, 141, (CL-43), 375
National Matches, 205, 510, 587
National Security Act of 1947, 223, 433–434, 444–446, 448
Navajo code talkers, *355*, 593
Navy yards and bases
Boston, 55, 107; **Brooklyn**, 57, 93, 102–103, 106–107; **Mare Island**, 119, 210; **New York**, 83, 134; **Norfolk**, 43, 108; **North Island**, *211*–212, 258; **Pearl Harbor**, 263, 265; **Pensacola**, 88, 93, 165; **Philadelphia**, 97, 106; **Port Royal**, 146, 166; **Portsmouth**, 102; **Washington**, 34, 85, 88, *98–99*, 108, 217, 293, 464
Neary, Col Donna, *11*, *27*, *31*, *166*
Neilson, Lt Alexander, 17
Neville, MajGen Wendell C., *165*, 183, 186, 226–227
New Britain Island, 318, *327*–329, 332–340, 344, 347–348
New Caledonia, 272, 290, 298–299
New Georgia, 297–298, 302, 308–309, 312–316, 320
New Guinea, 272, 279, 347, 350
New Hebrides, 272–273, 275, 279, 294, 298, 316, 320, 325
New Jersey (BB-16), 167, (BB-62), 574, 582, 629
New Orleans, 20, 24, 29, 38, 51. 92
New Providence Island, 13–*16*, *20*–21, 26, 40
New York, 13, 18, 51, 57, 93, 96, 118, 121
New Zealand, 278–279
Nicaragua, 79–80, 119–121, 127, 146–148, 151, 154–155, 203, *207*, 208, *214–215*, 216–217, 220–222, 224–228, *230*, 232, 235, 605, 622, 624
Nicholas, Maj Samuel, 12–16, 18, 25–*27*
Nickerson, LtGen Herman, Jr., 577, 584
Nimitz, Adm Chester, 268, 273, 356, 438, 507
Nixon, President Richard M., 519, 576, 579–580, 582–584, 588, 591, 596, 601
Norman, Lt Harvey G., 190
Normandy, France, 350
North Carolina, 88, 92, 97–100
Northern Ireland, 278, 363, 413
Norway, 109, 542, 551, 626
Nukuhiva Island, 44–45, 47

O'Bannon, Lt Presley N., 36–37, 40–41
O'Brien, Lt George H., Jr., 491
Ocotal, Nicaragua, 217–219, *221*, 230–232
O'Grady, Capt Scott, 644
O'Kefe, Lt Jeremiah J., 393
Okinawa (LPH-3), 633
Okinawa Island, 78–81, 323, 343, 376, 385, 389–400, 403–*404*, 410, 420, 523, 534, 538, 583, 595, 598
Operations
Allen Brook, 570–571; **Allied Force**, 647–648; **Badger Hunt**, 566; **Beacon Hill**, 560; **Beaver Cage**, 561; **Buffalo**, 562; **Cameron Falls**, 579; **Catawba Falls**, 588; **Clam-Up**, 482; **Colorado**, 556; **Dagger Thrust**, 549; **Deckhouse**, 554, 556, *558*–559; **Deliberate Force**, 645; **Deny Flight**, 642; **Desert Fox**, 647; **Desert Shield**, 635, 638–*639*; **Desert Storm**, 35, 639–640, *649*; **Dewey Canyon**, 576–577, *585*; **DeSoto**, 558; **Distant Runner**, 643; **Double Eagle**, 550; **Eagle Pull**, 613; **Eastern Exit**, 639; **End Sweep**, 604; **Enduring Freedom**, 649–651; **Essex**, 566; **Fiery Vigil**, 641; **Foster**, 566; **Frequent Wind**, 614; **Golden Fleece**, 548; **Grid Square**, 588, 590; **Harvest Moon**, 549; **Hastings**, 555; **Henderson Hall**, 575; **Herkimer Mountain**, 579; **Hot Springs**, 554; **Idaho Canyon**, 580; **Imperial Lake**, 587, 590; **Jack Stay**, 551, *556*; **Just Cause**, 635; **Kentucky**, 576; **Killer**, 471, 474; **Kingfisher**, 562; **Lancaster**, 566–567, 575; **Linebacker**, 602; **Macon**, 555; **Maine Crag**, 578; **Mameluke Thrust**, 571; **MARLEX**, 486, 488; **Maui Peak**, 575; **Meade River**, 575, *599*; **Muletrain**, 482; **Muskogee Meadows**, 577; **Napoleon/Saline**, 575; **New Castle**, 560; **Niagara**, 567; **Oklahoma Hills**,

578, *583*; **Osceola**, 567; **Packard**, 428, 440, 446; **Pickens Forest**, 587; **Piranha**, 548; **Plumbbob**, 516; **Pipestone Canyon**, 581; **Prairie**, 558, 558–560; **Pronto**, 484; **Provide Comfort**, 640, *647*; **Purple Martin**, 578; **Restore Hope**, 642–643; **Ripper**, 472; **Ripple**, 488; **Rolling Thunder**, 561–563, 566; **Scotland**, 577, *587*; **Sea Angel**, 641; **Sharp Edge**, 635, 638; **Shufly**, 536, 538–544; **Starlite**, 548; **Stone**, 559; **Strangle**, 475; **Sussex Bay**, 574; **Swift**, 563; **Tally Ho**, 555; **Taylor Common**, 577; **Texas**, 551; **Thor**, 574; **Torch**, 296; **Union**, 560–561; **United Shield**, 644; **Uphold Democracy**, 644 **Upshur Stream**, 591; **Utah**, 550; **Utah Mesa**, 579; **Virginia**, *557*; **Virginia Ridge**, 579; **Watchtower**, 276–277, 279; **Windmill I**, 429
Ortiz, Maj Peter J., 335, 360
Overstreet, SgtMaj, 641, 642
Oviatt, Sgt Miles, 94–95

Pace, Gen Peter, 649
Page, Capt Arthur H., 227
Paige, Col Mitchell, *301*
Pakistan, 623
Palau (CVE-122), 428, 439–440
Palmyra Atoll, 248, *255*, 257, 273
Panama, 82, 85, 107, 114–115, 136–137, 140–143, 145, 211, 268, *619*, *630*, 634–635
Paraguay, 84
Parker, Capt Alton N., 226
Parsons, Lt Larry, 584
Pate, Gen Randolph Mc., 511–513, 519, 525
Paz, Lt Robert, 635
Peking (Peiping), China, 129, 132–133, *141*, 143, 151, 208, 212, *216*, *233*, 235, 242–243, 263, 282, 410–412, 423, 427, 442, 606, 624
Peleliu Island, 203, *235*, 323, *342*–343, 365–373, *411*, 430
Pendleton, Col Joseph H., 154–155, 167, 170
Penobscot Bay, 23–24
Pepper, LtGen Robert M., 532
Peralte, Charlemagne, 190, 201–202
Perry, Comm Matthew C., 70, 74–*75*, *78–81*
Peru, 57, 107, 586
Peters, SgtMaj Bertha L., 531
Peterson, LtGen Frank E., Jr., 636–637
Philadelphia (frigate), 34–35, 41, (C-4), 126–127, (CL-41), 364
Philippines, 122, 127–128, 130, 134, 136–*141*, 212–213, 261, 263, 266–268, 270–271, 273–274, 371–372, 374–379, 382–383, 387–390, 392–393, 396, 398, 402, 426, 516, 589, 609, 641–642
Pless, Capt Stephen W., 562
Polk, President James, 68, 85
Porter, Capt David D., 138
Porter, Adm David D., 44, 47, 55
Portsmouth (sloop), 67, 73–74, 82, 98, 108, *114*
Potomac (frigate), 57, 66, 93
Powhatan (steamer), 80–81, 107
Prairie (cruiser), 141, 151, 152, *165*, 167
President (frigate), 36, 39, 5
Price, MajGen Charles F. B., 274
Princeton (CV-37), 518, (LPH-5), 523, 536, 543, *555–556*
Providence (sloop), 16–17, 21–23
Pruitt, Cpl John H., 187, 189
Puckett, SgtMaj Clinton A., 604, 615
Puerto Rico, *54–55*, 122, 126
Puller LtGen Lewis B., 228–229, 232, 234–235, 290, 292, 338, 454–*455*, 471, 553, 595
Puller, Lt Lewis, B., Jr., 235
Purvis, Pvt Hugh, *107*
Pusan Perimeter, *412*, 454–458

Quasi War, 26–27, 31
Quick, SgtMaj John H., 123, 125, 138
Quilali, Nicaragua, 220–221
Quinn, Pvt Luke, 91

Rabaul, New Britain, 270, 297, 316, 332–338, 340, 401–402, 437
Rainbow (RS-7), 150–151, 154–155
Raleigh (frigate), 20, 22, (C-8), 126, (LPD-1), *635*
Randolph (frigate), 20–*21*
Ranger (sloop), 11, 21–23, (steamer), 140
Rapid Deployment Joint Task Force, 623, 627
Rattletrap, 20–21
Reagan, President Ronald, 627, 630
Reid, Col George C., 128
Remey, Capt William B., 109
Rendova Island, 309, 314
Reprisal (brig), 13, 16, 19
Reserve Officer Training Corps (ROTC), 430, 436
Reynolds, Maj John G., 87, 104–105
Rhea, LtCol Robert Y., 216
Rhode Island, 21–*22*
Richal, Lt Merton A., 221
Richard, Capt Larry G., 601
Rickenbacker, Eddie, 289, 299
Ridgway, LtGen Matthew B., 468–469, 473
Riley, BGen William E., 447
Ripley, Capt John W., 597
Risler, Sgt Jack R., 360
Robertson, LtGen Donn J., 590
Robinson, Cpl Robert G., 190
Roebling, Donald, 254, 330
Roi-Namur Island, 338–339, *344–345*, *348–349*, *352–353*
Roles and Missions, 117, 146, 411, 415, 420, 424, 427, 430, 432–433, 438–439, 444–446, 448, 450–451, 456, 460, 474
Roosevelt, Maj James, 281
Roosevelt, President Franklin D., 243, 249, 254, 256–258, 260–261, 275, 282, 298, 342, 392
Roosevelt, President Theodore, 146, 539
Rosenthal, Joe, *376*, 383
Ross, LtCol Richard P., Jr., *394*
Rowell, Maj Ross, 219
Royal Marines, 76, 464–465, 524
Rudder, Lt Earl, 441
Rupertus, MajGen William H., *282*
Rushman, Lt John W., 394
Russell, MajGen John H., Jr., 208, 233, 236, 238, 241
Russell Islands, 300–301, 317
Russia, 143, 182, 644
Rust, Lt Edward, *336*

Saipan Island, 223, 283, 343–344, 350–*356*, 358, *362–363*, 371, 373
Samar, Philippines, 136–140, 421
Samoa, 61, 116, 127, 142, 256, 261, 269–270, 272–275, 286, 292, 302, 319, 324
Sampson, Adm William P., 122, 124
San Clemente Island, 241–242
Sanderson, BGen Lawson, 405
Sandino, Augusto, 218, 227
Santo Domingo, 28, 30, 140, 142–143, *161*, 163, *166*–167, 170–171, 198, 200, 204–*205*, 212
Sapotillal Ridge, Nicaragua, 217, 220–221
Saratoga (sloop), 26, (ACR-2), 151, (CV-3), 230–*231*, 268
Schilt, Lt Christian F., 221
Sellers, Maj Thomas M., 497
Seminole Wars, 33, 58–61
Seoul, Korea, 459–460, 469, 472
Seringapatam, 44–45, 47
Shanghai, China, 80–81, 84, 102, 150–151, 154–155, 212–216, *223*, *230–232*, 235, *241–243*, *249*, 251, 263, *282*, 444–446
Shaw, Col Robert, 494
Shepherd, Gen Lemuel C., Jr., 181, 425–426, 428, 482, 506–507, 511, 624
Short landing field, 527, 536
Shoup, Gen David M., 525, 528, 532, 541
Sicily (CVE-118), 453–454, 467, 479, 488–489
Simon, SSgt Farley, 629
Singapore, 271
Skinner, Lt Sherrod E., Jr., 490
Slavery suppression, 53, 56, 61, 66, 78, 80, 83–84
Small Wars Manual, 223, 624
Smith, Gen Holland M., 260, 284, 290, 316, 345, *347*, 350–354, 359, 370, *375*, 382, 386
Smith, Maj John L., *265*, *282*, 284–285
Smith Gen O. P., 417, 425, 456, 465, 471–472
Smith, Willard, 94–95
Soissons, France, 176, 180, 183, 186
Solomon Islands, 276, 279, 300, 303
Somalia, 627, 639, 642–644
Sommers, SgtMaj David W., 632, *641*
Spain, 517
Spanish-American War, 33, *118*, 121–126
St. Mary's (sloop), 66, 82, 85, 99, 10
St. Mihiel, France, 176, 180, 187
Stallings, Laurence, 192
Steele, John, *503*, *521*, *566*
Stein, Cpl Tony, 380–381
Steward, Pvt Edward, 41
Stiff, Col Houston, *569*
Stillwell, Gen Joseph, 399
Stimson, Henry, 216
Stivers, Don, *90*
Stout, Pvt Robert, 25
Stratton, Maj William T., 492
Streeter, Col Ruth C., 300, 310–311
Stuart, Lt J. E. B., 90–91, 105, 193
Suez, 513
Sumatra, 57, 60
Sweden, 464
Sweet, SgtMaj Herbert J., 547, 580
Swett, Lt James E., 265, *301*, 303

Taiwan, 521, 527, 622
Talbot, Lt Ralph, 190
Tanambogo Island, 276–277, 279
Tarawa (LHA-1), 607, 620
Tarawa Atoll, 223, 283, *312*, 317–*318*, *320*, *324*–328, 330–331
Tasimboko Raid, 286
Task Force Drysdale, 464–465
Taylor, Lt Caleb W., 190
Taylor, Lt Walter W., 363
Tentative Manual for Landing Operations, 237–240
Terrett, Capt George, 87, 101, 104
Terrorism, 630, 634, 644, 647–649
Tet Offensive, 568, 571, 625
Thailand, 537–538
Thetis Bay (CVHA-1), *508*, 512, 541
Thomas, Lt Earl A., 217
Thomas, Gen Gerald C., 180–181, 276
Thomason, Col John W., *176*, *183*, 192–193, *205*, *214*, *224*, *226*, *261*
Thompson, Cpl Jerrald, 565
Thompson, Col John, 206–207
Thompson, Pvt George, 275
Tientsin, China, 119, 126, 129, 132–133, 208, 214, 216–*217*, 226, 243, 263, 405, 410–411, 431, 432, 434, 442
Tilton, Capt McLane, 99, *107*
Tinian Island, 223, 343–344, 351–352, 354, 356–361, *364*, 372, 377
Towle, Col Katherine A., 442, 464, 495
Trenton, New Jersey, 18
Trenton (screw steamer), 116, (LPD-14), 639
Trevett, Capt John, 15
Trinidad, 120
Tripoli, 34–36, 38, 40–41
Tripoli (LPH-10), 595
Troiani, Don, *101*
Truk Island, 414
Truman, President Harry S., 223, 343, 392, 397, 401, 415, 424, 426–427, 432–433, 439–441, 444, 446, 449, 451, 453, 456–458, 460, 470, 472, 476–477, 479, 487, 493
Tsingtao, China, *410*–411, 416, 420–421, 431, 434, 443–444, 446
Tulagi Island, 274, 276–277, 279
Tun Tavern, 16, 30
Tunisia, 605
Turkey, 533, 591
Turner, Col Thomas C., 230
Twiggs, Maj Levi, 86–87
Twining, Gen Merrill B., 276, *301*

Ulithi Atoll, 365, 367, 369, 372
Unit deployment program, 621
United States (frigate), 26–27, 42, 61
Uruguay, 81, 83, 103

V-12 Program, 309, 422
Valentine, Capt Herbert J., 397
Van Orden, Capt George, 165
Vandalia (sloop), 58–59, 83, 116
Vandegrift, Gen Alexander A., 180, *282*, 292, 298, 309, 317, 319, 323–324, 334, 388, 416, 420, 425, 430, 435
Vangunu Island, 309
Vaughn, OSgt Pinkerton, 93
Vella Gulf (CVE-111), 395, 398, 400
Vella Lavella Island, 314–315, 318, 334, 437
Venezuela, 118, 518–519
Veracruz, Mexico, 72–*74*, 87, 162–*165*
Verdun, France, 179, 182, *186*
Vieques Island, 237, 444, 450, 522
Vietnam, 401, 468, 478, 504–505, 508–511, 527–615
Vietnamese Marine Corps (VNMC), 508, 535, 585, 602, 604
Vinson, Rep. Carl, 445, 456
Virgin Islands, 55, 170–171
Virginia, 13, 22, 38, 43, 50, 88–92
Vogel, MajGen Clayton B., 262, 290, 309

Wachusett, 93, 99, 102, 114
Wade, Lt Robert, 394
Wainwright, LtGen Jonathan M., 272
Wake Island, 248, *256*–257, 262–263, 265–267, 401, 405, 416–417, 426
Walke, Lt H., *75*, *78*
Walker, Col John, *375*
Walker, LtGen Walton H., 452, 468
Waller, Col Littleton W. T., 128–129, 136–140, 144, 150, *165*
Walsh, Lt Kenneth A., 303, 316
Walt, Gen Lew, 546, 561, 578
Wanchek, TSgt Mary F., 430
War of 1812, 29, *39*, 42–51
Warfighting Laboratory, 646
Warren (sloop), 22–23, 56
Washington, D.C., 30, 32, 57, 83, 208
Wasp (sloop), 39, 42–*43*, 50–51, (CV-18), 379, 388, 528, (LHD-1), 633, *650*
Waterhouse, Col Charles, *14*, *17*, *19–23*, *29*, *33*, *35*, *41*, *43*, *45*, *47*, *49–50*, *52*, *54*, *56*, *58*, *65*, *67–68*, *70–72*, *92*, *99*, *114*, *120*, *122*, *129*, *135*, *139*, *188*, *220*, *229*, *240*, *421*, *481*, *503*
Watson, Lt James, 10
Watson, LtCol Samuel E., 74, 86
Weapons
Beretta 92SB-F pistol, 631; **Browning M1917A1 machine gun**, *267*, *341*; **Browning M1919A4 machine gun**, *349*, *438*; **Browning Automatic Rifle (BAR)**, 185, *334*; **Garand M1 rifle**, 252–253, 527; **HAWK missile**, 527; **Howtar**, *518*; **Johnson rifle**, 252–253; **LAV-25**, 629–*630*, *647*; **Lewis machine gun**, 184–185; **M1A1 Abrams tank**, 639; **M3 submachine gun**, 415; **M14 rifle**, 527, 559; **M16 rifle**, 559, 627; **M-26 Pershing tank**, 467; **M40A1 sniper rifle**, *627*; **M60 machine gun**, *549*, *563*; **M-60 tank**, *632*; **M79 grenade launcher**, *551*; **M-198 155mm howitzer**, *523*, 626; **M203 grenade launcher**, 607; **M249 squad automatic weapon**, *642*; **M1911A1 pistol**, 631; **Mk-19 grenade launcher**, 643; **Ontos**, 518, *524*, *532*, *574*; **Reising submachine gun**, 207; **Springfield M1903 rifle**, 156–157, 206, 252; **Thompson submachine gun**, 206–207, *340*
Webb, James H. Jr., 632, 634
Wellwood, Lt Robert, 396
Wersheimer, GySgt Harry B., 187
Westmoreland, LtGen William C., 542, 545, 567, 571
Wharton, LtCol Franklin, 35, 37, 53
Wilkes Expedition, 60–61
Williams, Maj Clifton C., Jr., 563
Williams, Lt Dion, *137*
Williams, Capt Ted S., 485, 493
Willing, Capt James, 20–*21*
Wilson, Gen Louis H., Jr., 615, 622
Witek, Pvt Frank P., 432
Witten, Pvt John, 41
Wodarczyk, Gunner Michael, 218–219
Woyshner, MSgt Paul, 589
Wren, Sgt Solomon, 35

Yaco, Sgt Richard L., *578*, *615*
Yohn, F. C., *113*, *190*
Yokosuka, Japan, 404–405, 410, 412, 414–417, 421
Young, OSgt Charles, 97
Yugoslavia, 438

Zaire, 646
Zeilin, BGen Jacob, 70, 76, 79, 96–97, 102, 108
Zinni, LtGen Anthony, *650*